For
Not to be taken
from the room.

reference

JOLIET JUNIOR COLLEGE
JOLIET, IL 60431

Guide to
Islamist
Movements

Volume 1

Guide to Islamist Movements

Volume 1

Edited by **Barry Rubin**

M.E.Sharpe
Armonk, New York
London, England

Copyright © 2010 by M.E. Sharpe, Inc.

All rights reserved. No part of this book may be reproduced in any form
without written permission from the publisher, M.E. Sharpe, Inc.,
80 Business Park Drive, Armonk, New York 10504.

Cover photos (left to right) provided by Getty and the following:
Bay Ismoyo/Stringer/AFP; Robert Nickelsberg; Salah Omar/Stringer/AFP.

Library of Congress Cataloging-in-Publication Data

Guide to Islamist movements / Barry Rubin, editor.
   2 v. p. cm.
 Includes bibliographical references and index.
 ISBN 978-0-7656-1747-7 (hardcover : alk. paper)
 1. Islam—Handbooks, manuals, etc. 2. Islamic fundamentalism—Handbooks, manuals, etc.
3. Political parties—Islamic countries—Handbooks, manuals, etc. 4. Islamic countries—
Handbooks, manuals, etc. I. Rubin, Barry M.

BP40.G85 2010
322′.1091767—dc22   2009010524

Printed in the United States of America

The paper used in this publication meets the minimum requirements of
American National Standard for Information Sciences
Permanence of Paper for Printed Library Materials,
ANSI Z 39.48-1984.

MV (c)   10   9   8   7   6   5   4   3   2   1

R
322.109
GUI
v.1

Contents

JOLIET JUNIOR COLLEGE
JOLIET, IL 60431

Maps

Maps

Preface

We wish to thank the authors for their contributions. We also wish to thank the staff members of the Global Research in International Affairs (GLORIA) Center for their work on this book, especially Yeru Aharoni, and also Anna Melman, Moshe Terdman, and Keren Ribo. In addition, we wish to thank Federico Petrelli and Sophie Sheldon for their translation assistance as well as Benjamin Gondro and Shauna Naghi.

The Arabic transliteration system used is geared to make comprehension as easy as possible for the English reader. Diacritical marks have been minimized. While attempting to be consistent, in chapters dealing with non-Arabic-speaking countries, local spellings were used, even if specific words are of Arabic-language origin. In addition, some Arabic names were kept as they appear when used by authors themselves for their own names and when citing authors and sources as they appear in English or French-language bibliographies.

An Introduction to Assessing Contemporary Islamism

Barry Rubin

Islamism has become the most important political ideology and most powerful movement for change in the world. Political Islam must be seen first and foremost as a revolutionary movement seeking to transform existing systems. Far from being something to be mystified about or seen in strict isolation, political Islam is parallel to many previous movements both from European and in Middle East history, including communism, fascism, nationalism, socialism, and liberalism.

The purpose of this book is to examine the Islamist movement in the many countries where it is present. It is intended as a factually oriented report and analysis discussing Islamism in five categories:

1. The groups along with their programs and degree of importance as well as their relationship to the politics and societies of the countries in which they function.
2. The movements' leaders, their orientations, ideas, and capabilities.
3. Those institutions involved in Islamist activities, whether independent or controlled by a specific political organization.
4. Ideologies that guide the movements in the choice of strategy and tactics.
5. Activities undertaken by the groups, whether violent or peaceful, and the events that affect their fortunes.

History of Islam and the Emergence of Islamism

The picture that emerges is intended to provide an understanding of how Islamism operates and has developed in all its variety, its chances for political victory, and details about the state of the movement throughout the world.

Islam has existed for almost 1,400 years, but the radical Islamist political philosophy is a modern creation. As proof that their interpretation of Islam is correct, Islamists can cite specific passages from the Koran, Muhammad's sayings, deeds of Islam's early years, and Islamic theologians of the Middle Ages, but their reading is highly selective and is often at variance with Islam as practiced over the centuries. Islamism, then, is a political creed, a response to very modern problems.

Shortly after it began in the early seventh century, the Islamic religion enjoyed remarkable military and political successes.

Consolidating its base of support in the cities of Medina and then Mecca, Islam spread further by its direct appeal and—even more significant—the fact that Muslim armies defeated both the Byzantine and Persian Empires, the latter in 637 C.E. Almost overnight, in historical terms, an extensive empire was created stretching from Afghanistan in the east, through the Fertile Crescent, Egypt and North Africa, and even all the way to Spain in the West.

To Muslims, this expansion seemed like a miracle, though aided by the fact that the political rivals it had defeated were already weak and demoralized. Nevertheless, success on the battlefield made Islam a mighty power in both religious and political terms—a factor that has lasted down to the present day. By various means of pressure and benefits—many of them economic—the great majority of the local non-Arab people were so thoroughly converted to the new religion that they would thereafter generally act as if they had never had any other previous identity.

How would the Muslim people be governed? As long as Islam's founding prophet, Muhammad, was alive, he was the clear leader, combining in himself both religious and political functions. After his death, he was followed by four caliphs who also held—at least nominally—these two functions. In retrospect, many Muslims view this era as a "golden age," the peak of their religion's piety as well as worldly success.

Most significantly for today, it is this time that Islamists idealize and to which they wish to return. Indeed, political Islamism claims legitimacy by arguing that it is this era of perceived high piety, close adherence to their religion's tenets, and Islam's political domination that is the proper model for living and governing current society. In comparison, the last 1,200 years of the actu-al functioning of the societies and polities in which Muslims live has been a deviation.

Was the golden age indeed so wonderful? In fact, three of the first four caliphs were assassinated, and the Muslim lands were repeatedly ripped by civil war—sometimes among factions with differing theological views. The most important and lasting split was between the Sunni and Shi'a, the result of a disagreement about who should be the next caliph. By 750 C.E.—a century after the spread of Islam—an Umayyad dynasty ruled from Damascus. Especially ironic was that this family had been among the leading opponents of Islam and of its founding prophet in the first place.

It should be added, though, that these facts are much better known among Western scholars than among Muslim believers. Historical inquiry and the critical examination of sources has been generally discouraged in Muslim lands, especially about Islam's early period. The myth of a political golden age when all were pious and everything went well for Muslims is deeply entrenched, furnishing ammunition for contemporary political Islamists who view this period as the basis for a modern-day utopia.

After the eighth century, a series of dynasties followed and the original unified caliphate was divided into sometimes warring states over the centuries. The caliph (religious leader) and the sultan (political ruler) were usually two titles held by a single person. However, in practice, it was the role of sultan that was primary.

In fact, then, the history of religion and politics in Muslim lands during the Middle Ages was roughly parallel to that in the West. Religious authorities had great power, but it was really the state and its kings or sultans that prevailed in the actual governing of the people. The same applies to law, with religious law nominally in command but with the law set by the state, nobles, and customs playing the more important role. Indeed, the intellectual and cultural peak of the Muslim states, during the Abbasid Caliphate in Baghdad of 1,000 years ago, was characterized by a libertine court in which poetry celebrated the joys of eroticism and wine.

What is different is the developments that followed in terms of the intellectual and technological spheres. In the Christian-dominated West, beginning around the 1400s, there was an age of invention, development, exploration, and colonization coupled with the Reformation, Renaissance, and Enlightenment. The political and worldly power of religious institutions declined, while secular thought pushed back the power of religion to restrict free inquiry.

By way of contrast, in the Muslim-ruled lands, conservative theologians prevailed. In the eleventh century, Ibn Salah al-Din al-Shahruzi issued a fatwa (religious edict) banning the study of logic as a "heresy delivering man into Satan's bosom." The advocates of such ideas favored the narrowest possible reading of Muslim texts as opposed to thinkers who tried to analyze them using the tools of comparison and logic. The former, victorious school preached, in the words of the contemporary Egyptian liberal thinker Tarek Heggy, who wrote in his article "Our Need for a 'Culture of Compromise,'" "a dogmatic adherence to the letter rather than the spirit of religion [which slammed] the doors shut in the face of rationality."

The rulers of the day preferred the conservative approach, which clamped down on dissent and defended the status quo against liberals who raised subversive questions. Consequently, the gates of *ijtihad*—letting qualified scholars debate the reinterpreta-tion of religious texts to fit new times and situations—were closed. Creative thinking or critical inquiry regarding the meaning of the Koran and later religious texts was forbidden. Only rulings already made and narrowly adhered to would be acceptable.

The greatest irony is that it had been Europeans who heeded the rationalist Islamic scholars of the Middle Ages in their revival of classical Greek thought. Thus, these Muslim scholars helped pave the way for Europe's great cultural and scientific progress while being forgotten by their own people. In the West, rationalists defeated dogmatists. The backward Middle Ages had given way to the Renaissance and Reformation. Had the same side won in Europe as in the Middle East, Heggy noted, Europe today would be at a far lower stage of development and enlightenment.

Yet even this does not tell the whole story. In practice, politics and society were highly conservative but also evinced a strong pragmatic streak. Traditional Islam as it was practiced for 1,000 years preferred that Muslims live under a Muslim ruler. Such a ruler, however, would be acceptable as long as he could be considered reasonably pious and he did not interfere with religious practice.

It was further accepted that Muslim clerics should steer clear of politics. Religious observance was strong, but not generally compelled in any detail or with a great degree of strictness. It was forbidden to accuse other Muslims—except in the most extreme and rare circumstances—of being heretical. Existing customs, including pre-Islamic ones or local traditional interpretations, were accepted.

The fact that traditional Islam as actually practiced was and is distinct from Islamism is a point of the greatest importance, the key factor explaining why most Muslims have not accepted Islamism as their political doctrine. At the same time, though, many Islamist arguments meet with more approval, because they can claim to be consistent with widely accepted principles—which explains why Islamism is as popular as it has been among Muslims. For example, mainstream Muslim clerics would once have laughed at any notion that suicide terrorist attacks were religiously proper, but now, because of the pressure and persuasion of Islamist groups, they are increasingly accepted as conforming to Islam.

There is, of course, then, a material basis for Islamism in historic Islam, but at the same time, modern Islamism contains profoundly original and deviant aspects as well. Conservative-traditionalist Islam might have governed social behavior and given legitimacy to rulers in many cases, but it essentially was removed from political governance. On one hand, then, the ideas of Islamism can be shown to be contrary to the way Islam was practiced for 1,000 years. On the other hand, however, the Islamists can also cite sources in their favor just as critics can point out contradictions.

The key point is that Islamism—whatever its roots—is very much a modern ideology. It is one that aims for primarily political rather than theological change, compelled by a vision of the ideal society and seeking to seize control of whole countries, and in some cases even the whole world.

As an alternative source of political and cultural identity, it tries to subsume both nationalism and class. Regarding the former, Muslims have long seen themselves as a community (*umma*) of believers. Islamism says that this should be the primary identity of its members, the "nation" to which they adhere that transcends existing national boundaries. Of course, in practice, Islamists by necessity and often predisposition orga-

nize and see themselves as functioning within state lines, though there have been many efforts to transcend this situation.

As for class and socialist/communist approaches, Islamists have presented Muslims as an oppressed group, the new proletariat, the mechanism of global revolutionary change. There are parallels here, though distorted ones, to Vladimir Lenin's view of imperialism, which later leftists read as meaning that the key divisions in the world were now among nations rather than among classes within states. In the Islamist concept, imperialism means that Muslims are oppressed by both external attack and internal backwardness resulting from foreign machinations.

In its diversity, Islamism might be described as a universe of discourse. There are other forms political Islam might take than radical Islamism, including Islamic democratic movements akin to European Christian Democratic ones or even a liberal brand of Islam that encourages progressive social change. The first category, however, is almost nonexistent outside of Turkey, while the second is restricted to extremely small groups of intellectuals, disproportionately found among Muslim minority communities in the West. The most popular variant outside of radical Islamism could be described as political Islamic lobbying, as in post–Saddam Hussein Iraq or in Saudi Arabia, in which groups do not seek total state power so much as they try to use political or social power to bring about a more "Islamic" society.

Nevertheless, from the time of the 1979 Iranian Revolution onward—and even more so in recent years—political Islam has been dominated by radical Islamists, who have even had tremendous influence in pulling conservative-traditionalist Muslims in their direction.

Modern Islamists have approached a problem quite parallel, despite its many differences in detail, to the roots of radical movements in the West and elsewhere. The goal is to seize control over history, to consciously and systematically shape the future. This is, on the one hand, a response to perceptions that the pace of development is too slow and, on the other hand, a protest against the direction of change.

The supposed goal in both cases was to ensure that "the people" lived better in an ideal society whose rules were set by the laws of life. Of course, Islamism, communism, and fascism defined all their guideposts in different ways but covered the same basic terrain. Moreover, in practice, the struggles waged often did not improve things but rather made things worse, both through the process of fighting (violence, destruction) and with the results of failed policies being implemented by successful revolutionaries.

What twentieth-century radical Islamists have done in the public sphere has been, in effect, the equivalent of what Marxist and fascist ideologues and politicians accomplished in the West. An ideology was created that directed groups of professional revolutionaries, gained support among at least a large sector of the public it addressed, and inspired political violence.

Another way to make this point is that revolutionary Islamism has been the adaptation—though the practitioners are themselves unaware of this point—of Marxism-Leninism to Muslim societies. Gone, of course, is the ferocious secularism of Communist movements, but most of the strategic and tactical elements are there. These include the concept of a guiding ideology, a vanguard party (or at least group), the view of imperialism as the main enemy, the legitimacy of violence, the designation of a revolutionary motive force (all proper Muslims), the idea of national liberation, and the ultimate dictatorship of those rightly guided by the correct ideology who will control all key institutions.

The proposed solution is something old in theory, but very new in practice: the rule of the society by Islamic law and spirit. Yet what this means in practice is very much a matter of debate. Some points are relatively obvious—the judicial rule of Shari'a—but others (the running of an economy, for example) have no simple answer. There can also certainly be a political Islam without Islamism, seeking a society more influenced by Islam without being totally ruled by an interpretation of it. Nevertheless, the vast majority of the individuals and groups advocating a political Islam are Islamists, and the problem they are faced with is how to gain power to implement their vision.

In this context, terrorism is only one tactic among many potential alternatives. For many groups, however, it has seemed to be the indispensable way of mobilizing support and seizing power. Each radical Islamist group has to choose how to attain power in a specific country. Different factions, organizations, and thinkers have put forward many strategies based on their individual views and conditions in the country where they operate. These tactics can include terrorism, insurgency, mass organizing, building a society within a society, elections, and other things. Another key issue is whether the priority is to attack a government within one's country or to try to win support by striking against foreign non-Muslims. Strategies and tactics also change over time. The common goal, however, is to get into power and presumably—or at least in theory—never to yield it again.

Defining Islamism

What then is Islamism? In content, it is an interpretation of Islam directed at achieving a political goal. Radical Islamism has been the overwhelmingly most powerful such standpoint, though of course not the only possible one. This is a revolutionary political ideology, parallel to such systematic programs as communism and fascism, liberal democracy and nationalism.

The main concepts of Islamism, though varying in detail, are found below:

First, Islam provides all the elements needed by both society and polity. As a result, it should be the commanding source of ideas and laws. This notion is embodied in a common Islamist slogan, "Islam is the answer." Ultimately, humans have no right to choose their systems or laws, because God has done so for them. Their job is merely to adhere to God's will.

Second, only a proper Islam is suitable as the governing doctrine, which means a strict view based on how the founders and early disciples of Islam would have interpreted it. Of course, not all Islamists agree on precisely what is proper Islam, and most Muslims do not agree with any of the Islamists about the definition of their religion. In addition, some Islamists are Shi'a while others are Sunni, which constitutes a divide in its own right. Still, despite all these issues, there is a great deal of overlap among Islamists.

Third, all the states where Muslims live— at least those where radical Islamists do not hold power—and their societies must be thoroughly purged and transformed. This concept challenges all existing standard traditional Islam, implying for example that the great majority of existing clerics are not practicing or teaching Islam properly. "Islamic Thought in the Last 100 Years Is Largely Un-Islamic," ran a revealing headline in the Iranian Islamist newspaper *Kayhan International* in May 1985. Most professing Muslims do not like the idea of having their behavior called hypocritical or improper. To say so seems heretical to them, and they are right to feel that way based on traditional Muslim doctrine. After all, Muslims had thought themselves properly religious for centuries without ever acting as the Islamists prescribed. The great clerics of the past had preached cooperation with the authorities or passivity until the messiah returned to put the world right. However, this problem could be played down by Islamists who could merely say that their societies are misgoverned and unjust, that the fault lies with impious rulers or anti-Muslim foreigners, and that the problem can be fixed once Islam is properly practiced in a future utopian Islamist state.

Fourth, Islamists have also revived the concept of jihad as a high-priority duty. The great majority of Muslims accept the idea that jihad means a struggle against non-Muslims to increase the area under the rule of Islam but have treated it as an archaic concept, something not suitable for today. In contrast, Islamists use jihad to mobilize revolutionary forces.

Last, the question remains as to whom to wage jihad against. If nominally Muslim rulers and officials are, in fact, in a state of apostasy, and since apostasy from Islam is punishable by death, it is justified to kill such people. If, however, the true culprits are foreign non-Muslims (the United States, the West, Israel, a Christian-Jewish conspiracy), the uncomfortable problem of fighting fellow Muslims is pushed aside. Even in this conception, however, those in power can be seen as instruments of these evil forces, what is called the "comprador" group in Marxist terminology.

It is interesting to note, however, that the

idea of the central problem being the victimization of Muslims by a Western-American-Zionist reign of imperialist oppression and aggression is not an Islamist innovation but a concept taken from the Arab nationalists who have dominated the political and intellectual scene there for a half century. Thus, this belief has already been constructed and reinforced into a powerful edifice. Viewing Arab nationalism as an inadequate response to the challenges faced by Arabs (or, in Islamist terms, Muslims) is a mere observation of the obvious.

The strictest form of mainstream Islam widely practiced—the Wahhabi version, which dominates in Saudi Arabia and Qatar—is not in itself Islamist, though its doctrine certainly parallels that school of thought. After all, Saudi Arabia is really a traditional state in Muslim terms, given that the religious and political authorities are quite separate though the religious ones have much influence and the political ones have strong Islamic credentials. Islamists do not see Saudi Arabia—which they view as too corrupt and subservient to the West even as they take its money—as their model. Indeed, Osama bin Ladin's original broader vision was as an Islamist revolutionary seeking to overthrow the Saudi regime.

Wahhabism, however, can be a portal to Islamism, because it trains people to believe that a stricter, less tolerant, form of Islam is normative. Moreover, Saudi Arabia is the source of massive funding funneled to radical Islamist groups and institutions, either out of genuine support or as protection money designed to deter the recipients from attacking Saudi Arabia itself.

In short, Islamism is a political ideology seeking to seize state power and transform existing societies. It says that the answer to the problems of countries where Muslims live is neither tradition nor nationalism nor liberal democratic pragmatism, but only rule by a regime based on a strictly interpreted version of Islam. It seeks the overturn of existing regimes, by violence or other means. It views all the problems of Muslim countries and societies as being created by the West and Israel or their local, superficially Muslim, collaborators. It rejects Western approaches to political or social issues but usually not Western technology. It demands the expulsion of Western political or cultural influences from their countries and societies and Israel's destruction. It argues that a victory achieving these goals is easy if Muslims are only united, willing to fight, and ready to sacrifice their lives.

Beyond this basic analysis and program, Islamism leaves many issues open. No single state, movement, or leader furnishes a model for all of its exponents. Islamists may view Iran or the Taliban regime in Afghanistan in a positive or negative light. They may disagree to the point of fighting among themselves. Sunni and Shi'a Islamists may champion the cause of their denomination and hate the other one or, at times, cooperate. Islamists may or may not favor a leading role for clerics or be led by self-taught figures whose level of theological knowledge is quite low.

Strategies and Tactics

Also left open and subject to change are questions of revolutionary strategy and tactics. On the tactical level, many Islamist movements have embraced armed struggle and terrorism, but this is by no means the only choice. Islamist groups can be involved in grassroots organizing and even elections, depending on the specific group and circumstances. Providing social services, at least to their own supporters, may or may not be important elements in building a popular base. As for strategy, some put the priority on overthrowing the local regime, as a stepping stone toward destroying Israel and defeating the West or—like bin Ladin—put the emphasis on attacking the West and Israel as a necessity for bringing down their own rulers. Groups may be jealously local, focusing on a single country, or internationalist.

Whatever their ideology, tactics, or priorities, it is by no means inevitable that Islamism will triumph, not only among Muslims in general, but even in any specific country. Since the 1979 Iranian Revolution—and with temporary exceptions in Sudan and Afghanistan—no Islamist regime has successfully seized power. The strength of existing rulers and the hostility or indifference of the majority of Muslims have prevented such an outcome. Yet Islamism has clearly become the main opposition force throughout the Arab world and in countries ranging from Nigeria to Indonesia. In the early twenty-first century, following the collapse of communism, it is also the leading alternative ideology to liberal democratic thought in the world.

Islamism, then, is a reaction to the dislocations of modern times, the influence of Western ideas, and the perceived failure of other political philosophies where Muslims live, especially in the Middle East, but also in such places as Indonesia, Malaysia, and Chechnya.

Modern Islamism can be traced to the founding of the Egyptian Muslim Brotherhood by Hasan al-Banna in 1928. It proposed to put Egypt under an Islamic regime based on Muslim law. The movement emphasized mass organizing but also had a secret armed group that carried out political assassinations. Banna himself was killed and his movement was suppressed by President Gamal Abdel Nasser's regime in the 1950s. By then, however, the Brotherhood had spread to other places—notably Jordan, Syria, and among the Palestinians.

The Muslim Brotherhood's most important ideologue, whose influence would spread very far, was Sayyid Qutb. Qutb, executed by Nasser's government in 1966, developed the idea that contemporary society in Muslim countries was comparable to the pre-Islamic era of *jahiliyya* (ignorance) and was hence illegitimate. Thus, it was possible for him to redefine jihad not so much as a struggle to spread Islam to non-Muslim lands but as one to revolutionize and purify countries already Muslim.

During this period, though—and especially in the 1950s and 1960s—Islam's political role was mainly as a conservative force used by monarchies to preserve traditional society and fight against radical, secularist Arab nationalist movements and regimes that were often allied with the Soviet Union. Islamic groups were sponsored by countries like Saudi Arabia and Jordan to counter revolutionary change.

This was the political Islam of conservative-traditional forces. It was mainstream Islam, because the religious leadership had for centuries made an accommodation with governments. As long as a country's rulers were at least publicly pious Muslims and Islam was not persecuted, the clerics accepted this division of power. Such a movement was the direct opposite of Islamism, which challenged the status quo and sought power for itself.

Radical Islamist movements, however, were gradually developing during the 1970s. For example, in Egypt, the government of President Anwar Sadat let the Muslim Brotherhood function again, seeking to use it as an ally against his leftist factional rivals. The group ran candidates for parliament indirectly and campaigned for imposing Shari'a as the basis for Egyptian law.

In Syria, the local Brotherhood organized against the government underground, with a measure of success until it was violently repressed in 1982.

However, the great impetus for the rapid growth of such groups was the victory of a radical Islamist revolution in Iran, which opened the first phase of Islamism as a major political force throughout the Middle East and beyond. Just as the Russian Revolution shaped the political left for decades thereafter, the 1979 upheaval in Iran had a similar effect on Islamist movements throughout the Middle East and beyond. Even when the groups had no loyalty or even liking for Tehran, the fact that the Iranians showed that a revolution of this sort could happen provided plentiful inspiration. Moreover, many of the Islamist groups held ideas parallel to the thinking of the Iranian revolution's leader, Ayatollah Ruhollah Khomeini.

If Qutb was the Islamist revolution's equivalent of Karl Marx for communism, Khomeini was the movement's Vladimir Lenin. According to Khomeini, there is a worldwide struggle between the forces of Islam and those of corrupt materialism, a struggle in which every Muslim must take sides. The Muslim masses must be mobilized to fight the West, and Western conceptions of freedom and social organization must be rejected. All existing regimes in Muslim-populated countries were illegitimate and should be overthrown.

The appeal of Iran's revolution also came at a time when the dominant force in the Arab world, Arab nationalism, was becoming increasingly discredited. The Arab nationalists had failed to drive out Western influence, destroy Israel, unite the Arab world, or provide rapid economic development and higher living standards. The atmosphere is well conveyed in Professor Hisham Sharabi's 1985 speech "Unity, Disunity and Fragmentation in the Arab World": "Today the Arab reality and the Arab dream appear separated by an unbridgeable gap. The hope that has animated the past generation's struggle . . . turned into cynicism and despair. . . . Power-holders throughout the Arab world seem to have found it fairly easy to get away with the contradiction between their verbal and actual behavior."

Into this moment of despair burst the Iranian Revolution's promise of a dramatic alternative offering total victory. This message's flavor and power is well represented in a 1987 sermon by Khomeini aired on Tehran Radio:

> [Islam] has answers for the needs of men from the beginning to the end . . . for daily [life], and for issues that might arise in the future and about which we know nothing now. . . . [It] satisfies all the material, spiritual, philosophical, and mystical needs of all humanity at all times until Judgment Day.

If Muhammad had stayed home and preached, said Khomeini, "we would have followed his example." Instead, he launched "an armed struggle and established a government. He then sent missionaries and representatives everywhere. . . . He brought the glad tidings that we are going to conquer the entire world and destroy everybody." Muslims today should imitate their prophet, "He set up a government, we should do the same. He participated in various wars, we should do the same. He defended Islam, we should also defend it." Muslims have a duty to fight to put this regime into authority everywhere in the world.

Khomeini was no mere impractical fanatic. He had outmaneuvered all rivals and proven himself a man of action, among the century's most successful politicians in mobilizing millions of people with his vision through demagoguery, ideology, and organization. In addition, he was blessed with a number of shrewd, capable lieutenants who immediately started building institutions to ensure that the revolutionary regime stayed in power. They proved relatively cautious— compared to their fiery rhetoric—about directly subverting their neighbors, because they realized that this could endanger the revolution's revival at home.

Khomeini's intention, however, was to convince Muslims to start a violent revolution. He regarded Iran as only the first step to creating a utopian Islamic empire that would bring, as he stated in his last testament, which he wrote in 1982 and was read to the assembly and then broadcast on national radio after his death in 1982: "absolute perfection and infinite glory and beauty." He urged Muslims: "Rise up! Grab what is yours by right through nails and teeth! Do not fear the propaganda of the superpowers and their sworn stooges. Drive out the criminal rulers! . . . March towards an Islamic government!" If only all Muslims cooperated in this jihad, they would be "the greatest power on earth."

If it is true that the relative backwardness of Muslim countries resulted from the shortcomings of local cultural or political traditions, these must be changed to be more like Western ones in order to achieve modernization. Not only would the road to development be long and hard, but it would also require the abandonment of many things held dear by Islamists. If, however, the essential problem was external, this meant that progress could only be attained by defeating Western "imperialism" and by reinforcing, rather than modifying or jettisoning, both tradition, the central role of religion, and a strict interpretation of Islam.

One of the shah's main crimes accord-

ing to Khomeini was linking progress to Westernization. In prerevolutionary Iran, as elsewhere in the Middle East, tradition was unfashionable, while things Western were seen as representing progress. Indifference to religion, Khomeini charged, was taken to be a symbol of civilization, while piety was a sign of backwardness to an elite that preferred to be tourists in Europe than pilgrims in Mecca.

To make matters worse from Khomeini's standpoint, this Western cultural invasion was also popular in many ways. People wanted cheaper, better-quality goods and liberating ideas. Assertions of defiance barely concealed a nagging conviction that Western ascendancy was inevitable and that one might as well join the winning side.

Khomeini thus had good reason to consider America, which was already the greatest power on earth, to be the most dangerous enemy of his ambitions. The United States, of course, had been a mainstay for the shah, whom he had overthrown. Yet Khomeini's problem was that Iranians liked or feared America so much that they did not want to fight against its influence. Even many of his top aides wanted to compromise with Washington, following an Iranian tradition of appeasing the strongest foreign power. They publicly denounced America, then secretly asked it for money, support, and favors.

The ayatollah feared that this U.S. leverage might temper his revolution by supporting moderate factions against militant ones—or that it might overthrow it altogether. Moreover, he knew that Washington would do everything in its power to prevent the spread of the Islamic revolution to Saudi Arabia and the other Gulf monarchies.

Thus, Khomeini and his most radical followers wanted a decisive break with the United States to eliminate its influence and show Iran's people that it could not defeat the Islamic revolution. Anti-Americanism would then be a useful device to rally the masses around the new regime. Yet he, and many other Islamists, also firmly believed that America was the satanic force preventing utopia on earth, deliberately keeping most of the world backward.

These are the reasons Iranian militants stormed the U.S. embassy in November 1979, kidnapped its staff, and held most of them hostage until January 1981. Khomeini called this a "second revolution," which would banish forever Iranian servility toward America. "For centuries," said Khomeini in a speech on February 11, 1986, Western propaganda "made all of us believe that it is impossible to resist." Now he rejected compromise, because he wanted to show that America could do nothing against Iran, that its strength was an illusion.

The revolutionary regime could be made safe only by cutting contacts with the United States, "the center for world imperialism," as Iran's ambassador to the UN called it (as cited by *Kayhan International*), which "can under no circumstances" be trusted, according to an article in *Iran Times*. The powerful speaker of parliament, Ali Akbar Hashemi Rafsanjani, boasted, "Today we don't make any decisions, great or small, under the influence of foreign powers [including] a blasphemous country like the Soviet Union or an imperialist aggressive country like America," as reported by the *New York Times* and the *Wall Street Journal*.

Thus, Iran's rulers saw the crisis in practical terms. The radicals used it to displace moderates in the regime and unite the country around themselves. At first, the imbroglio cost Iran almost nothing. It did not need the United States. Iran could still sell oil to others. Khomeini correctly calculated that Iran could thumb its nose at both the

United States and the USSR, knowing the superpower rivals would prevent each other from attacking him.

Khomeini, however, was not interested in merely being on the defensive. He thought the hostage crisis was an Iranian victory over America that would inspire a Muslim revolt against the West. Each day the hostages were held, Washington's credibility would fall among Iran's people and the Gulf Arabs. Iran was in no hurry to make a deal. Negotiations were slow, intermediaries made no progress, and the Western media counted off the number of days of "America held hostage."

Khomeini was militarily challenged, however, not by the United States but by his Muslim neighbors in Iraq. That country's dictator, Saddam Hussein, attacked Iran, because, on the one hand, he saw it as being weak. Having gone through so much disorder and having purged its own army, Iran might crumble before an Iraqi invasion. Moreover, since Tehran had expelled its American protector, thus totally isolating itself, Saddam reasoned, Iran could expect no help from anyone else.

On the other hand, Saddam was also prompted to attack Iran because its Islamism seemed so strong. Saddam had no intention of letting Iran foment a revolution to make itself master of the Gulf, much less overthrow his own government. Tehran was doing its best to foment an Iraqi Shi'a uprising, sponsoring an assassination attempt on Iraq's foreign minister and other terrorist acts. Iraq's already restive Shi'a majority might respond by rebelling against the ruling Sunni minority.

Even before Iran's revolution, Iraqi Shi'as had been organizing revolutionary cells. Shi'a underground groups ambushed government officials and bombed offices. Demonstrations broke out in the Shi'a holy cities at the annual processions marking Hussein's martyrdom 1,200 years earlier by the Sunni ruler Yazid, to whom Iranian propaganda was comparing Saddam. The crowds chanted, "Saddam, remove your hand! The people of Iraq do not want you!" A popular young Shi'a cleric, Bakr al-Sadr, was a prime candidate to be Iraq's Khomeini. The regime struck back with ferocious repression. About 600 clerics and activists were shot, including al-Sadr and his sister. Iraq also deported over 200,000 ethnic Persians who might conceivably be supportive of Iran.

While repressing the Shi'a opposition, Saddam also wooed Iraq's Shi'as by promoting more of them to top posts in the government, party, and army. As Ofra Bengio notes in her article "Baathi Iran in Search of Identity," Saddam reminded them in speech after speech that they were Iraqis by citizenship and Arabs by ethnicity. "God destined the Arabs to play a vanguard role in Islam," he ingeniously explained, so "any contradiction between a revolution which calls itself Islamic and the Arab revolution means that the revolution is not Islamic." Tehran's real inspiration was said to be Zionism, "Persianism," and the reactionary concepts of "the Khomeini gang."

On September 22, 1980, Saddam ordered his army to march into Iran, expecting a quick, easy victory to make him master of the Gulf and Arab world. Instead, it was the start of a bloody eight-year-long war that cost both countries dearly. The battle would seesaw for eight years, reducing the two prosperous states to near bankruptcy. The conflict would be a struggle for supremacy and survival between two dictators indifferent to casualties, and two systems—radical Arab nationalism and revolutionary Islamism—each determined to destroy the other. Iran encouraged its warriors to seek

martyrdom. "The path of jihad is the path to heaven," said Tehran International Radio in August 1985. Yet in the end neither side would win a clear victory.

Aside from Iran's revolution, the other event that most contributed to the new Islamism was the war in Afghanistan. Taking advantage of America's setback in Iran, the Soviet Union invaded Afghanistan in 1979 to back a Communist coup there. Afghans armed by the United States and foreign Muslim volunteers financed by Saudi Arabia fought a long guerrilla war against the Soviet army and its local allies.

One of the key advocates of using Afghanistan as a model for a worldwide Islamist revolution was Abdallah Azzam, a Palestinian educator who worked in Jordan and later played an important part in the building of the Arab Islamist forces fighting in Afghanistan, where he was killed. Azzam's most faithful disciple was a wealthy Saudi named Osama bin Ladin. Helped by the growing domestic crisis in the USSR that would soon lead to the collapse of the Communist regime in Moscow, the Islamist mujahidin (those who wage holy war) fighters overthrew the Communist regime in Kabul.

Now Islamists were intoxicated with their seeming victories. They claimed to have defeated both superpowers and overthrown a powerful regime in Iran. There was nothing, they argued, that Islamism could not achieve. Osama bin Ladin organized al-Qa'ida as a transnational revolutionary movement. Arab veterans of the Afghan war headed home with the goal of making more revolutions. Under the Taliban regime, Afghanistan became a safe haven and base for these Islamists.

In fact, though, while Islamism succeeded in building large movements and challenging the existing regimes, it totally failed to make any successful revolutions, except in Afghanistan, where the Taliban group eventually seized power in the confusion following the Soviet withdrawal, and briefly in Sudan. There were many reasons for this failure.

One reason is that Islamist Iran was no utopia. After all, if, as Khomeini claimed, all governments during 1,400 years of Islam had failed, why should his experiment be different? Human nature did not change so easily. In Khomeini's Iran, too, there were self-seeking leaders, bitter factionalism, and differences of opinion. Groups within the leadership constantly broke up into quarreling factions. While some Iranians benefited from the revolution, many fled the country. The new regime squandered resources and failed to produce jobs or development, though in this respect it was saved by a massive income from oil. Iran's performance was not so great as to encourage emulation.

Even Islamist Iran preferred to sell oil to the industrialized West for hard currency and preferred to buy its superior products. Many of the Revolution's leaders had Swiss bank accounts, and their taste for modern comforts was the butt of many jokes in Tehran. When a poor woman complained about the lack of soap powder, ran one popular anecdote, a pro-Khomeini cleric scolded her by saying, "The Prophet Muhammad's daughter didn't have that." "Yes," replied the woman, "but the Prophet Muhammad didn't ride around in a Mercedes limousine either."

Iran remained under Islamist rule, but by the 1990s, the majority of the population had turned against a government that remained in power by the same measures used by its hated Arab nationalist rivals. In the end, the experience of living under an Islamist regime was the most effective factor in convincing people to oppose Islamism. Among some clerics, even in Iran, this also exposed the threat that putting Islam into power could corrupt and discredit the religion itself.

However, there were many other factors in the failure of Islamism to achieve revolutionary victory. While a common Muslim identity was supposedly going to trump any other loyalty, conflicts among Persians and Arabs, Sunni and Shi'a Muslims, Iranians and Iraqis, and even adherents of different Islamist groups prevailed over the commonality of Islam. Egyptian or Lebanese Christians, non-Muslim Alawites and Druze, as well as Muslim Kurds and Berbers saw Islamism as a threat. Iran might claim to be a paragon of Islam, but this did not erase the hostility of most Arabs, who saw Iran as Persian in nationality, or most Sunni Muslims, who saw it as Shi'a in religion.

Still another set of factors concerned the cleverness of the regimes in fighting off the Islamist challenge. They used a wide variety of stratagems ranging from repression to co-optation, to using their own very significant Islamic assets. Pro-regime clerics criticized Islam while government officials portrayed themselves as the defenders of Islam—as well as Arab nationalism—against the nefarious forces of imperialism, Zionism, and liberal Arab reformers.

Radical Islamists assassinated Egyptian president Anwar Sadat in 1981 and waged a decade-long revolt but were soundly defeated. Revolts were also crushed in Algeria and Syria, with great loss of life. In Jordan, for example, Islamists were allowed to participate in electoral politics but were prevented from achieving beyond a limited quota. In Lebanon, Hizballah became a powerful force but could not even gain a monopoly within its own Shi'a community, much less overcome the Christian, Druze, and Sunni Muslim majority. Islamist groups were divided and often fought among themselves.

Yet perhaps the most significant single factor of all was that most Muslims did not accept Islamism as the legitimate—or at least preferable—interpretation of their religion. In theory, of course, all Muslims accepted Islam as the proper organizing principle for their lives and societies. Practice was altogether different. The great majority of traditionalist Muslims rejected Islamism's interpretation of their religion, while less-fervent Muslims were horrified by the idea of living in an extremist Muslim society. They might be culturally conservative and pious, yet from this standpoint, Islamism appeared to be a deviation from the Islam they had always known and practiced.

Even among Muslims, the Islamists remained largely on the defensive against this alluring onslaught of modernization and Westernization, with its movies, consumerism, love songs, fashions, delightful merchandise and luxuries, science, and education. Many of their compatriots were not so eager to boycott Western culture or ideas and an urgent desire for the West's respect infected even the most militant, anti-Western leaders. "The grandeur of the Islamic Revolution" was proven, Iranian speaker of parliament Ali Akbar Hashemi Rafsanjani said proudly, as cited by *Iran Times* in December 1985, because it impressed the West so much that Iran was now being compared to the USSR and France rather than to mere Third World states like Algeria or Vietnam. Yet this showed precisely the implicit view of many Muslims, and even Islamists, that the West was superior in some way.

Iran remained Islamist but, despite its strenuous efforts to obtain nuclear weapons, did not seem likely to realize its ambitions to spread the revolution abroad. Usually, Iranian policy was also more cautious than its ideology, concerned that foreign adven-turism might endanger the regime's survival at home. At any rate, the Arab and Muslim world had found new heroes after Khomeini's death, including the Arab nationalist Saddam Hussein and Osama bin Ladin. The Iranian revolution's influence had been powerful enough to spread Islamism, but it had also been limited enough not to bring it more victories.

Building on the philosophy of earlier Islamists, the experience of the Afghan war, and the success of Iran's revolution, a large number of radical Islamist movements developed wherever Muslims lived. There were significant movements in Asia, Africa, Europe, and the Middle East. Certainly, by the mid-1980s, the most significant opposition groups throughout the Arab world were Islamists. Everywhere, too, where the Muslim world came up against other groups—in Indonesia and the Philippines, Thailand and China, Chechnya and Nigeria, even France and Britain—Islamist groups became involved in conflict against the governments and other communities.

Islamist movements have employed a number of different tactics, strategies, and forms of organization in all these places, and these have created a number of important debates and distinctions. Within political Islam, aside from the Islamists are two other groups: a large Islamic one representing conservative, traditionalist Muslims (who usually, though not always, form the majority of clerics as well as laity) seeking to preserve these societies as they have been in the recent past; and a far smaller group that represents liberal Muslim reformers. Islamic forces try to influence society to be more pious, to maintain conservative ways, and to resist Western cultural influence. They seek to preserve or expand Islam's role in society rather than taking over the society.

Islamic and Islamist approaches can be allies, and Islamic activists can be converted to Islamist ones. Certainly, Islamists have succeeded in introducing new ideas into mainstream traditional Islam, ranging from the validity of suicide bombing to the revival of jihad's importance. If Islamists seem likely to gain power, they will enjoy far more support from this Islamic sector.

As for the small number of liberals, there is the possibility that they could in the future form what might be called Islamic democratic parties similar to the Christian Democratic parties of Italy and other European countries. The ruling coalition in post-Saddam Iraq has elements of this approach as does the Justice and Development Party (AKP) in Turkey, but this approach is still rare. To succeed, the liberals must also appeal to the Islamic mainstream, but since their effort is to update tradition—precisely the outcome that the conservatives most fear—it is hard to do so. Indeed, the Islamists have more in common with the majority of Muslims than do the reformers. This is an important reality in considering the futures of all these movements.

Islamism and Terrorism

One of the most controversial aspects of Islamism is its use of terrorism, either in practice or as something strongly approved. This is by no means inevitable. A number of Islamist groups have not used political violence of this nature, though far fewer condemn it in principle. There is also some ideological propensity for that approach, because Islamists regard themselves as having a monopoly of truth and view their opponents as enemies of God and demonize them. Yet, again, there are choices to be made. The jihadist groups connected with Osama bin Ladin's approach view an armed struggle based on terrorism as the only acceptable

strategy, while Muslim Brotherhood groups have often preferred political agitation, in part, because they consider that a revolutionary situation does not exist.

Some groups justify the use of terrorism against fellow Muslims, including al-Qa'ida, the Algerian Armed Islamic Group (GIA), and the Egyptian revolutionary groups of the 1980s and 1990s. Others reject this idea, however, and focus on rationalizing terrorism against non-Muslims: Westerners, Israelis, Jews, Christians, and Hindus.

A second set of issues revolves around what might be called Jihadism versus revolution. Some Islamists—and this was certainly the priority of the 1980s and 1990s—put the emphasis on overthrowing the regime ruling their country. However, the failure of these efforts sparked a shift among some elements to advocate making it a priority to attack the West in general and the United States in particular. This turn was influenced not only by the defeat of the domestic revolutionaries but also by the success in fighting the Soviets in Afghanistan and the view that groups battling against Israel—Hamas and Hizballah—enjoyed more relative popularity among Muslims than those struggling against the local regimes. The decision of the Algerian military to stage a coup rather than continue an electoral process certain to be won by the Islamic Salvation Front also brought doubts that the ballot box could bring Islamists to power.

Certainly, events of this period spread the doctrines of radical political Islam more extensively. Even conservative-traditionalist clerics accepted many of its premises. This shift was rationalized by a set of arguments grounded in the Islamist worldview. A central point is the idea that the power of the West makes it impossible to overthrow governments like those in Saudi Arabia and Egypt. Thus, without defeating, intimidating, as well as driving out Western influence and destroying Israel (the far enemy), the revolutionizing of Muslim societies by overthrowing their regimes (the near enemy) is impossible.

Moreover, it is claimed that the West and Israel, through a Christian-Jewish or imperialist-Zionist conspiracy, are attacking and trying to destroy the Muslims. Jihad, then, including the targeting of civilians, is portrayed as merely a matter of self-defense and is thus justified under classical Islamic practice.

The jihadist approach is also attractive for other reasons. The fact is that attacking and killing fellow Muslims while claiming that Islam as currently practiced is heretical has not enabled the Islamists to win the hearts and minds of fellow Muslims. Killing non-Muslims is simply more popular and less controversial. This was seen in the fact that Hizballah and Hamas (which could portray themselves as "national liberation" movements) became among the most successful Islamist groups, because they carried on terrorism against Israel. A large portion of Muslims—arguably a majority—will support such activities at least in terms of their opinions.

Exporting the struggle also reduces the incentive of Arab and other regimes to repress radical Islamists. These governments, too, may cheer on their efforts and even provide them with assistance. Thus, the war in Iraq—nominally against Western occupiers but often against Shi'a Muslims—became very popular among most Muslims. In various ways, Iran, Syria, and Saudi Arabia, as well as almost all the Arab media facilitated and endorsed the Islamist terrorist campaign there.

At the same time, though, some Islamists who favored making an internal revolution a priority criticized the jihadist approach.

They claimed that this shift was a sell-out, letting impious regimes off the hook. They also noted that once terrorism shifted against the West, Islamists lost former safe havens in Europe and elsewhere, as arrests were made and leaders were deported out of fear that they would foment terrorism in their host countries. The U.S.-led war on terrorism also cut into financial networks and operational capability.

As bin Ladin proved relatively unable to follow up on September 11, new experiences came into play, including both the prospect of electoral opportunities for Islamism and the Iraqi insurgency. All these factors shifted priorities and debate. The jihadists returned their focus home (as shown in al-Qa'ida's initiation of armed struggle within Saudi Arabia) and put many of their resources into the Iraqi insurgency. At the same time, though, Hizballah's good showing in Lebanese elections and Hamas's victory in Palestinian voting (as well as the electoral triumphs of Shi'a Islamists in Iraq and the Justice and Development Party (Adalet ve Kalkınma Partisi or AKP) in Turkey showed the opportunities in electoral politics.

A moderate political Islam also seemed more possible using democratic methods, though the existence of such a tendency was mainly visible in the writing of a few intellectuals and fewer clerics rather than any mass movements. Also clear was the existence of two competing Islamist groupings: al-Qa'ida and the Muslim Brotherhood offshoots. Another factor was the Sunni-Shi'a fracture, with some Sunni groups working with Iran while others explicitly attacked Shi'a counterparts.

A third set of issues concerns the relationship between Islamist groups and foreign governments. The possibility that Islamist groups may be used by one state against another adds an important dimension to Middle East politics, one which could have important repercussions in the future. Three such groups—Hamas and Islamic Jihad among Palestinians as well as Hizballah—receive backing from Iran and Syria, and also significant funding from the Saudis. A number of Islamist groups in the Arab countries bordering the Persian Gulf, and especially Iraq, have also received help from Iran. The insurgents in Iraq also obtain assistance from Syria. In the past, Libya has supplied money and help to Islamist groups in such diverse places as Sudan, the southern Philippines, and sub-Saharan Africa.

To what extent al-Qa'ida had contacts with and received help from Arab governments is highly controversial, but it does seem clear that Iran and Syria facilitated the escape of leading al-Qa'ida terrorists from Afghanistan and their safe passage to Lebanon and other countries. At times in the past, Syrian Muslim Brotherhood militants have been helped by Jordan, while it is possible that Syria returns the favor through its own covert efforts. An especially important example is Pakistan's use of radical Islamist groups against India—particularly those involved in trying to take over Kashmir and join it to Pakistan.

Islamic and Islamist groups tend to be strongest when religious and ethnonational identities join together. Aside from the examples analyzed above (as in Iraq, Syria, and among Palestinians), there are other such cases outside the Middle East. For example, Islam is the religion of the Uyghur people in northwest China, the Moros in the southern Philippines, and the Malays in Malaysia. As such it is a potent political weapon combining national and religious identities.

Islamist groups have also certainly become involved in a wide range of international conflicts. Even a short list includes:

the struggle for power in Indonesia; regional insurgencies against the Philippines, Russia, Thailand, China, and India; organizing terrorism in a wide variety of European states; communal conflicts in Nigeria, Sudan, and—to a lesser extent—Bosnia and Kosovo. Indeed, it is probably accurate to say that Islamist radical groups are at present not only the main global source of terrorism but also of instability and political violence generally. There has been significant Islamist political activity in more than 30 percent of the world's countries, including Australia, Asia, Europe, the Middle East, such African countries as Nigeria and Kenya, and North America.

Islamist Activity

Yet Islamist groups in all these places do far more than engage in terrorism. Their activities are as varied as, or even more than, those of other political organizations. Among them are:

Charitable activities: To build a base of support and service their constituencies, Islamist groups provide relief to the poor, money to support the families of those killed in warfare, and other services. For example, in Egypt, Islamist groups provided low-cost used textbooks to university students. In performing these kinds of activities, the groups not only gave benefits to their supporters—and thus strengthened the loyalty of existing ones while recruiting more—but also filled in areas where the government failed to provide for social welfare. The message was not only to suggest the groups' superiority to the regimes but also to create on a small scale an incipient Islamist state, intended to show how people would be better off living in that type of society. Funds raised for nominally charitable activities, however, are often diverted to finance terrorist operations.

Mosque efforts: A key asset of Islamist movements is the control of specific mosques and the backing of respected and popular preachers. Even in authoritarian states, the mosque and religious instruction were areas—often the sole ones—that the rulers could not completely control. Indeed, in many countries most mosques and religious schools came at least nominally under government ministries (for instance in the key areas of hiring and firing teachers or clerics). Preachers gave sermons that reflected Islamist ideas or even endorsed specific groups while religious teachers indoctrinated students.

Even in non-Islamist countries, the educational and religious sectors were often influenced or even controlled by Islamist or pro-Islamist government officials. In Kuwait, one such individual later emerged as bin Ladin's spokesman. In Saudi Arabia, a mother recounted how her sons were told by their teacher to celebrate the September 11 attacks. This teacher later became a leader in the armed insurgency against the government.

Seeking to take over professional associations: In countries like Egypt and Jordan, many such groups of lawyers, doctors, teachers, engineers, students, and others are led by Islamists. These influential people can be mobilized as activists in the movement and are in a good position to spread its message. The idea that Islamists recruit mainly among the poor and unemployed is, in proportional terms, mistaken.

Media activities: While radio, television, newspapers, and book publishing are usually closely controlled by governments,

Islamist groups have tried to create their own assets in the media wherever possible. There is substantial Islamist influence on satellite television networks, including al-Jazeera television.

Fund-raising efforts: Aside from charitable activities (see above), both in Muslim-populated countries and in the West, Islamist groups raise money directly to support armed struggle efforts. This is especially the case when the war is being waged against non-Muslims—as against Israel and in Iraq—and is thus more likely to enjoy governmental tolerance and public support. In Saudi Arabia, for example, telethons and public appeals have been organized to finance Hamas. Funds may also be raised as protection money, since those giving can fear they will themselves be attacked if they do not provide such support. In some cases, business enterprises may be set up as fronts or to finance groups. This is especially true of the Islamic banking sector, which promises to invest investors' money in a proper Islamic manner. In a number of cases, for example, in Egypt, such banks have turned out to be scams defrauding investors.

Youth activities: In addition to general work in education, Islamist groups often organize youth centers and activities including religious educational and physical education courses. These not only recruit youths but also let talent spotters pick out good candidates for suicide bombings or for joining underground military wings. Where possible, paramilitary training is also conducted and militias are formed.

Elections: Islamist groups can participate in elections. In some cases, they have a real possibility of winning, while in others, the governments, in effect, offer them a share of benefits and even some power while ensuring that they will always be limited to a certain quota of seats.

Evaluating Islamism and Its Significance

The evaluation of political Islam must be based on a political analysis, because it is a political movement. While rooted in theology, it has consciously and deliberately entered the world of worldly power. This also requires a comparison among alternatives such as nationalism and moderate pragmatism, as well as among varying forms of political Islam—including liberal and conservative-traditionalist forms of Islam as well as the many varieties of Islamism itself. Clearly, though, political Islam is a major feature of the contemporary world, and its study will be a matter of the utmost importance for many decades to come. These ideas and events may prove to be the principal political drama and crisis of this era in history.

Bibliography

Bengio, Ofra. "Baathi Iran in Search of Identity." *Orient* (December 1987).

Heggy, Tarek. "Our Need for a 'Culture of Compromise.'" *Al-Ahram,* September 29, 2002. Translation from www.heggy.org/culture_of_compromise.htm.

"Islamic Thought in the Last 100 Years Is Largely Un-Islamic." *Kayhan International,* May 19, 1985.

Khomeini, Ruhollah. Speech on Tehran Radio, November 10, 1987. Foreign Broadcast Information Service Daily Report (FBIS). November 12, 1987.

———. Speech of February 11, 1986. FBIS. February 12, 1986.

———. "Unity, Disunity and Fragmentation in the Arab World." Speech of November 15, 1985. FBIS. November 15, 1985. D-11.

Khorasani, Said Raja'i. *Iran Times,* January 24, 1983.

Rubin, Barry. "Dealing with Communalism." *Journal of Democracy* 17:1 (January 2006): 51–62.

Tehran International Radio. August 4, 1985. FBIS. August 7, 1985. I-4–5.

Global Jihad

Reuven Paz

In the past decade, al-Qa'ida has emerged as the leading element of the Jihadi-Salafi clash with the West. The Western world found it difficult not only to cope with worldwide terrorist operations or insurgencies but also to understand the motivations behind this phenomenon.

Many Islamic movements tend to portray their struggles as part of a larger clash between Muslim and Western religions and civilizations. Many Islamic and Islamist groups emphasize the struggle against Jews and Judaism as well, highlighting the Israeli-Palestinian conflict and the supposedly global scope of Jewish influence. In many Western societies, Islam in general has come to be identified with violence, terror, and fanaticism.

Terms such as "fundamentalist," "extremist," "Islamic," "Islamist," and "political Islam" are misused by many in the West. Many Arab regimes now feel threatened by any movement that is linked to Islam.

The "Islam versus the West" paradigm has grown partly because different Islamist groups have succeeded in gaining legitimacy and presenting their sociopolitical and cultural doctrines to much of the Arab and Muslim worlds as the only true commentary of Islam. A variety of social and nonpolitical Islamic movements and Sufi orders create an "Islamic atmosphere" throughout the region. At the next level are fundamentalist Islamist groups with sociopolitical aims, such as the Muslim Brotherhood in the Arab world, the Jama'at-i-Islam (Islamic Group) in India and Pakistan, or the Islamic Liberation Party (Hizb al-Tahrir al-Islami) in Central Asia. Such groups contribute to anti-Western sentiment and serve as greenhouses for the emergence of extremist groups. At the top of the pyramid stand the groups whose main message is jihad in the form of terrorism. Each level contributes to the one above it.

Therefore, it is important to distinguish between the terms "Islamic" and "Islamist." In general, Islamic movements are those that seek to do anything from injecting more religion into public affairs to gaining state power, to creating a single, unified Islamic state (*khilafa*) whose sole constitution is Islamic law (Shari'a). Since there is no distinction in Islam between religion and politics, these groups recruit support through political efforts alongside social-welfare and cultural activities, all of which they call *da'wa*.

In contrast, Islamists are a subset of Islamic groups which seek total power and the transformation of the existing societies to ones whose every detail is governed by their interpretation of Islamic law. As a result, Islamist groups view not only the non-Muslim world as the enemy, but also relatively less pious elements in their own countries.

Over the past decade, it seems that this kind of terrorism is still growing in scope. In fact, there is a real threat from two new developments: the radicalization of Muslim communities in the West, and the increasing hostility and alienation many younger Muslims feel toward the West, often based on sociopolitical secular grievances.

Since the emergence of al-Qa'ida, and only during the past 10 years, there has been an emergence of a global jihadi culture. This targets Arab and Muslim youth by using the Internet as a kind of "open university for jihad studies."

Four major elements have encouraged this phenomenon: first, the sense of facing a global conspiracy against Islam and the Islamic world; second, the sense of the impending apocalypse; third, the search for equal power with the enemy in every field of the clash; and finally, jihad as a doctrine of purported self-defense, hence justifying every doctrine or tactic. The apocalyptic element in particular seems to be shaping the whole culture of modern jihadists.

Jihadi Movements in Their Own Eyes

The best definition of the Islamist view has been written by Umar Mahmud Abu Umar "Abu Qatada," a Palestinian residing in London since 1993 and one of the main ideologues. In an article titled "The Comprehension of the Civilizational View and the Duty of Jihad," from his collection of "Articles Between Two Doctrines" (*Maqalat bayn Minhajayn*), he wrote:

> When we talk about the jihad movements in the Islamic world we mean those groups and organizations established in order to eliminate the evil [*taghutiyya*] heretic [*kafira*] regimes in the apostate countries [*bilad al-ridda*], and to revive the Islamic government that will gather the nation under the Islamic caliphate.
>
> But, the "true jihadist movements" differ from the variety of other Islamic groups that act in the various Muslim countries and seek political legitimacy of the "heretic" regimes. In such cases, the conflict between these last groups and the government is between a Muslim regime and its citizens, and not between a "heretic and apostate state and a group that seeks to eliminate and change it."

Another important definition, according to Abu Qatada, is that jihadi movements are those that have the proper ideology, including the view of a future world totally controlled by Islam. Since this idea is so important, Abu Qatada proposed a new term: the jihad movement of hope in the future.

The existing movements, he continued, have not yet reached this level. Moreover, those who focus on jihad in their homelands will not succeed. They must fight internationally as part of a united movement at the service of any appropriate commander who has the proper strategy and ideology.

The description or vision of Abu Qatada, written in 1994, is that of al-Qa'ida under Osama bin Ladin: various groups left their homelands and gathered in Afghanistan, where the prospects and hopes for establishing their vision of a true Islamic state were realized due to the Taliban regime; they gave their loyalty and confidence to a new commander, bin Ladin; and launched a global struggle against what they perceived as their definition of "Axis of Evil"—the United States and the Jews.

Muslim Radicalization in the West

New and larger bases of Islamist radicalism and terrorism seem to be developing in Muslim communities in Europe and North America. The notion is of global jihad as a religious duty, aimed at a perceived global conspiracy against Islam as a religion, culture, and way of life. Another cause is the emerging doctrine of the "nonterritorial Islamic state." This doctrine views Muslim communities as a kind of loose-knit Islamic state, though without the territorial and religious mission of reestablishing a caliphate. Islamic scholars in the United Kingdom have long provided the impetus for this view by emphasizing the cultural, economic, and political consolidation of these Muslim communities. Despite this pluralism, however, many of these groups went on carrying the fundamentalist banner of many of the Islamic movements in their homelands.

The interaction in the West between Muslim immigrants from various countries, cultures, and ideologies has greatly facilitated the growth of the caliphate doctrine. Such interaction has promoted both solidarity and a shared sense of a global threat to Islam and the Muslims. These factors have in turn led to the doctrine of global jihad and to the brotherhood felt by its adherents. This new doctrine resulted in establishment of multinational and multiorganizational terrorist cells among Muslim immigrants in the West.

Another emerging development among Islamist groups is the radicalism brought on by social ills and alienation—that is, terrorism motivated primarily by elements such as xenophobia (both by and against Muslims), growing unemployment, economic circumstances, difficulties in coping with Western modernization, the changing and dismantling of traditional values and family ties, and so forth.

For example, in an unsigned 1991 article appearing in its main journal *Filastin al-Muslima,* Hamas offered its best introduction to the global jihad doctrine: Muslims are being persecuted by the entire world and attacked by satanic powers which make their lives miserable and kill them. Since the existing life is so terrible and full of death, only martyrdom in battle is the true way to life.

This rhetoric would clearly appeal to those already afflicted by a sense of hopelessness or resentment. The implicit alienation in such statements becomes all the more striking when one considers that the September 11 hijackers lived in relative comfort in the United States for long periods of time before carrying out their operation, yet were apparently undeterred from their plans. The same applies to many of the volunteers for the jihadi insurgency in Iraq or to supporters of global jihad in many other places. Growing Islamist activity among Muslim immigrants, along with their shared notion of global struggle against the West, has encouraged a more rapid spread of radical doctrines among younger Muslim generations.

Furthermore, many of the people arrested in the West since the September 11 attacks—most on suspicion of links to al-Qa'ida—are generally more educated and familiar with Western culture. Yet instead of using this familiarity for personal benefits and for greater integration with Western culture, as their fathers did in the past, these "terrorists of alienation" hold on to their hostility and exploit the weaknesses of the societies in which they reside.

This process is not new in the Arab and Muslim worlds. Many university students and graduates tend to adopt radical Islamist positions and fight the regimes of their homelands. In many cases, they view themselves as social elites who must sacrifice themselves for the sake of their society. Their radical positions are also a result of various radical Islamist trends that developed in the 1960s and 1970s. During this period, under the influence of the Egyptian ideologue Sayyid Qutb, social justice became the key criterion by which Islamists began to judge their ruling elites and to accuse some of facilitating Western culture's conspiracy against Islam. Therefore, some of these radicals did not necessarily fit what was then the profile of the typical Islamist— that is, one whose commitment to religious observance is total.

Many of them blame personal failures on the secular cultures and ideologies that have influenced various modern Middle Eastern regimes; thus they look for salvation in a return to the glorious past of Islam. Since orthodox Islam is identified with Islamic establishments whose source of power is these regimes, many Muslims now support those who represent the opposite culture: the radical activists who oppose the national state and its interpretation of Islam.

The Globalization of the Islamist Struggle

The prospects for cooperation between various Islamist groups have improved during the period after 2000 for several reasons. Chief among them is the fall of the Soviet Union. Islamists perceived this collapse as a victory over "The Kingdom of Evil" and as a historic step toward the global triumph of Islam and Muslims. Twelve years earlier, the success of the Islamic revolution in Iran had been viewed in a similar fashion—it gave even the Sunni Islamic groups a revolutionary Islamic model, although they had many reservations about its content.

The United States has come to be seen as the sole leading force in this conspiracy. To Islamists, the United States represents the leading edge of the Western threat to the Islamic world, not so much through its military force or political colonialism but rather through its cultural influence.

Islamists also viewed the USSR's collapse as a consequence of their contribution to the Soviet defeat in Afghanistan, and many Arab volunteers in that war sought to continue the momentum of their victory in other places. Hence, Islamist involvement emerged in various religious-national conflicts around the world: Bosnia, Albania, Kosovo, Chechnya, Dagestan, Macedonia, Kashmir, and elsewhere.

The war in Iraq and the jihadi insurgency that has followed also serves as a wake-up call for other disputes within the Muslim world itself, primarily the Sunni-Shi'a one. Many observers have come to view this phenomenon of "Afghan Arabs," "Arab Chechens," or Arab volunteers in Iraq—what Islamists call Ansar—as a kind of "Islamist International," similar in many ways to the International Brigades of Socialist and Communist volunteers in the Spanish Civil War during the 1930s.

The center of the Islamist struggle has moved from the Arab world to the margins of the Middle East. From the Balkans to the Philippines, Malaysia, and East Timor, the globalization of Islamist movements eventually consolidated in Afghanistan, the meeting point between Arab and Asian Islamists.

The Ideology of Global Jihad

This ideology has developed through the consolidation of several existing doctrines. "The Islamic Salafist Fighting Movement" (al-Harakah al-Islamiyya al-Salafiyya al-Mujahida) was coined by one of its leading proponents, the Palestinian Abu Qatada. In one of his books, he promoted the idea that Islamists should fight in every place possible in countries around the world. One specific strategy granted legitimacy is the use of suicide terrorism. Islamic support and legitimation of this method became most apparent in April 2001, when a huge wave of hostility greeted Saudi grand mufti Shaykh Abd al-Aziz bin Abdallah Aal al-Shaykh's fatwa (religious edict) against it.

This same phenomenon was apparent in the contradictory Islamic rulings issued following the September 11 attacks in the United States. The subsequent American attack on Afghanistan and Iraq and the U.S. efforts to create a wide coalition of support in the Arab and Muslim worlds generated similar debates, much like the Gulf War had in 1991. These debates in turn fostered a measure of support and legitimacy within the Islamic establishments for Islamist terrorist groups and their means of struggle.

Secular regimes often demand that their religious establishment oppose Islamist terrorism, but many clerics tend to legitimize violence against Israel and the Western world. In some cases, these disputes reflect internal conflicts between the religious and political establishments, such as in Saudi Arabia, Egypt, and Pakistan.

Another important element in this trend of doctrinal consolidation was the recent adoption of the Palestinian cause by many Islamist groups that had failed to embrace it in the past. Many Palestinian Islamist scholars have been intensely involved in the development of the new ideology, including: Abdallah Azzam in Afghanistan, the spiritual father of the idea of al-Qa'ida; Shaykh Issam al-Burqawi Abu Muhammad al-Maqdisi in Jordan; the already mentioned Abu Qatada in London; and Fathi al-Shqaqi, who introduced to the Sunni Arab world the global aspirations of Islamic revolutionary Iran and the doctrines of Ayatollah Ruhollah Khomeini. They were joined by a number of Saudi-Wahhabi oppositionist scholars and Egyptian jihadi-oriented scholars. Thus, the new ideology took on the dimensions of a global terrorist struggle, justified by the perception that the jihad, like the Palestinian struggle, was an act of self-defense against a Western-Jewish global conspiracy.

The roots of global jihad lie in the collaboration of Egyptian and Palestinian Islamic jihad during the late 1970s and early 1980s; in the flow of Arab volunteers of different nationalities to Afghanistan during the 1980s; in the flow of volunteers from all over the Arab and Muslim world to Bosnia, Albania, Kosovo, and Chechnya during the 1990s, and to Iraq in the 2000s; in the massive terrorism against Israel over the past three decades; in the extensive massacres in Algeria during the 1990s; and in the growing support for Islamist doctrines during the 1990s, particularly among certain social, cultural, and welfare foundations, charity funds, and research institutes in the West, many of which served as fronts for other activities. Islamists have had the greatest ideological influence on those Muslims whose religious knowledge is poor. As a consequence of social pressures, such Muslims tend to emphasize social and political confrontation in their actions rather than religious rules or norms.

The simplistic understanding of jihad is perhaps best illustrated in the letter carried by the suicide hijackers of September 11. Copies of this letter—most likely written by the suspected leader of the operation, Muhammad Atta—were found among the remains of three of the planes that crashed into the World Trade Center, the Pentagon, and the field in Pennsylvania. The letter directed the hijackers to do the following on the morning of the operation:

> Tighten up your clothes [for] this is the medal of the righteous predecessors. . . . They used to tighten up their clothes before battle. . . . And do not forget to take some of the booty, even a cup . . . of water to gratify yourself and your companions [another norm of Muhammad].

In other words, throughout the operation, the hijackers were supposed to view themselves as if they had returned to the seventh century as Muhammad's companions (*sahaba*). The tone of the letter is one of men preparing themselves for battle in the manner of ancient warriors, not for a suicide operation against unarmed airplane passengers. The enemy in question is not an individual country—neither "the United States" nor "America" is named even once in the letter—but rather a "civilization of disbelievers" or, more often, an amorphous, faceless evil.

This basic understanding of Islam has become an initiation of sorts for adherents to global jihad. They tend to adopt norms of behavior that are simple to understand, and these norms in turn create a basis for unity among different groups and individuals, thus sidestepping the difficult terrain of ideological and theological interpretation. In past decades, Islamists in the Arab and Muslim worlds tended to split into numerous factions, generally on ideological grounds. Now, however, their tendency is to put ideological conflicts aside and cooperate on a far more practical basis—their duties within the wide framework of jihad.

Al-Qa'ida: The Doctrine of Brotherhood of Global Jihad

The most famous example of this trend is bin Ladin's group al-Qa'ida (literally, "the base"). This group developed from the infrastructure of the Afghan groups that fought against the Soviet Union in 1980–89, called Maktab al-Khidamat (The Office for Services). This office—established by Abdallah Azzam, a Palestinian who moved to Afghanistan from Jordan in 1980—gave the Afghan groups of mujahidin a religious, cultural, and social basis for their struggle. In April 1988, Azzam published an article in the magazine *al-Jihad*—the central organ of the Afghan groups, one that he founded and edited—entitled "The Solid Base" ("al-Qa'ida al-Sulba"), which laid the groundwork for the new group al-Qa'ida.

Toward the end of his article, Azzam prophesizes that America is trying to rule the world but that the solid base of true believers (*al-qai'da al-sulba*) would resist it at all costs. He wrote in similar terms in his 1984 book, calling for the control of a state as a solid base for spreading Islam, a fortress to protect the strugglers from all the impious Muslim regimes and societies. This description readily fits Afghanistan and parts of Iraq in recent years.

Azzam's implicit theme was the establishment of an Islamic army, using the Afghan struggle against the Soviets as a modern model and the fight of Muhammad and his companions as a classical one. The idea was to create a pioneering generation of fighters who would prepare themselves for a constant struggle against the West and its allies in the Muslim world. Azzam described the Afghan mujahidin as the sublime model of Islamic fighters who would lead the Muslim world toward a kind of eternal struggle against the evil powers of Western culture.

Another important element in the theory of al-Qa'ida was the sense of elitism that characterized this vanguard army. This elitism was spurred by two branches of Islam that had developed in Egypt and Saudi Arabia long before—*takfir* (excommunication) and radical Wahhabism. Many of the mujahidin in Afghanistan and later on in Iraq—especially those who came from other countries, either as exiles or on a voluntary basis—adopted the takfir principles of creating an isolated society of true Muslims waging jihad against the rest. They also seized upon the extreme brand of Wahhabism practiced in the 1930s by the Wahhabi Ikhwan zealots, who settled on the borders of the new Saudi Arabian kingdom and developed radical ideas that were counter to the rest of their society. According to Abdallah Azzam, the only way to consolidate all of these ideas was through protracted jihad. As Omar Abu Omar put it: "The only legitimate state that could represent the correct nature of Islam and rely on its essence, is the state that would be established through the armed struggle of jihad."

Azzam's "Solid Base" article is similar to others published in the late 1970s and early 1980s in two Islamic magazines—*al-Mukhtar al-Islami* (The Islamic Assortment) in Cairo and *al-Tali'ah al-Islamiyya* (The Islamic Vanguard) in London. The leading editors of these magazines were Fathi al-Shqaqi and Bashir Nafi (who used the name of Ahmad Sadiq), the cofounders of the Palestinian Islamic Jihad. While studying medicine in Egypt, they were in close contact with the founders of the Egyptian Islamic Jihad and the Egyptian Islamic Groups (al-Gama'at al-Islamiyya), as explained by Anwar Abd al-Hadi Abu Taha.

The union of the Islamic world, the Afghan base, and the Palestinian struggle took center stage in bin Ladin's famous interview on al-Jazeera television following the first American attack on Afghanistan in early October 2001. Yet the ideology of global jihad—a combination of jihad, takfir, and Wahhabism—had been developed many years prior to the creation of its global terrorist infrastructure.

Muslim Communities in the West: The Infrastructure of Global Jihad

Aside from these direct efforts to expand their influence, Islamists have found success in both the Muslim world and the West largely because of what we have described as the "Islamic atmosphere"—that is, the often indirect framework of support created by groups not connected to political violence or terrorism, some of whom even publicly condemn such methods. They serve as a greenhouse of sorts for such radical groups and the growth of views hostile toward the West or Western culture.

Furthermore, the social, political, cultural, economic, educational, and charitable infrastructure of some of these groups serves in part as the source of finance and support for Islamic projects whose by-products finance Islamist terrorist groups. Since many of their primary activities involve consolidating Muslim communities in the West, these groups often set the grounds—inadvertently or not—for massive fund-raising, political support, and even recruitment on the part of Islamist movements.

The Immigrant Experience

All of these elements have contributed to
the growth of support for jihad movements
among Muslim communities in the West
and to the increasing alienation felt by
many Muslims in Western societies. Hatred
of foreigners is not uncommon in Europe.
Further, many Muslim immigrants face poverty, unemployment, difficulty coping with
Western modernization and values, and disintegration of their own family values, all of
which have encouraged significant Islamist
social and political activity among them.
Islamist groups tend to view every symbol
and element of modern Western culture as
part of a conspiracy against Muslim culture.
A fatwa against Valentine's Day, issued in
February 2002 by the group al-Muhajiroun
in London, serves as a good example of the
difficulties of Muslim immigrants in coping
with Western culture.

The major conflicts of the 1990s—the
Gulf War, Iraq's campaign against its
Kurds, and conflicts in Bosnia, Albania,
Kosovo, Afghanistan, Algeria, Chechnya,
and Somalia—brought waves of Muslim
immigrants to Western Europe, seeking
refuge and work. Many immigrants entered
illegally and thus do not appear in official
statistics.

The increasing number of Muslim immigrants in Europe and the United States
was also a result of the political violence
that has occurred and has continued in
Muslim countries since the 1990s. In many
cases, these immigrants and asylum seekers
have supported or been actively involved in
violent activities and have thus been easily
affected by Islamist ideas once they arrived
in the West.

When Arab regimes started confronting Islamists forcefully, and as a result of
Islamist violence, many Islamist groups

experienced a significant decline in public
support in their homelands. For example,
the terrorist attack in Luxor on November
17, 1997—in which 59 tourists from various
countries were gunned down—shocked both
the Egyptian public and the Islamic establishment. Partly as a result of such changes, Islamist groups began to seek support
among Muslim communities in the West.

Social changes among Muslim communities in the West over the past two decades
have also contributed to the economic success of Islamist movements. They were
granted generous economic support in many
countries (primarily the United Kingdom,
Scandinavia, and Germany), as well as freedom of speech, organizational support, and
education. But the expectations that many
second- and third-generation Muslim immigrants had in the West often went unfulfilled, thus reinforcing their alienation.

More often than not, though, it was the
flood of financial support from the wealthier Muslim countries that allowed them
to become vocal advocates for their own
communities. Westerners' resentment of
foreigners in their midst, along with ongoing clashes of cultures and values (e.g.,
modernity versus tradition), encouraged the
formation of a wide range of Islamic infrastructures, many of which thrived under
Western democracy. These infrastructures
have served as a potent greenhouse for
Islamist movements.

Hotwiring the Apocalypse

The most important theme of the culture
of global jihad in the 2000s is the sense of
the coming apocalypse. Jihadi apocalyptic
discourse is one of the main innovations
that followed the September 11 attacks.
Waves of apocalyptic discourse are not new
in the modern Arab Islamic world. They

have accompanied almost every major war or disaster that has occurred in the Arab world in modern times. They also gave rise to more religious sentiments, and many people began to approach apocalyptic Arab Islamic literature, such as the famous book *Interpretation of Dreams* by the Arab scholar of medieval times, Ibn Sirrin. (Ibn Sirrin lived in the eighth century and is regarded as the greatest authority in Islamic history for the interpretation of dreams and visions, after Muhammad, the founder of Islam.)

Interpretation of visions—*tafsir* or *ta'wil al-ru'a*—is a legitimate science in Islam, and people tend during hard times, or "historical earthquakes," to consult such old literature or the living scholars who are known in this field. In modern times, there are only a few such persons who profess the interpretation of visions according to all the Islamic criteria and rules. Seeking answers in this manner results from feelings of crisis, insecurity, instability, or fear of the future. In addition, a sense of the Day of Judgment became widespread, and visions related to it spread among many Muslims.

The September 11 attacks were perceived in a totally different way. This was the first time in modern Islamic history in which the West was humiliated by such a sophisticated attack, and on its own soil. It was perceived in Islamic eyes as a turning point in the relations between the two parties and as a continuance of the Soviet defeat in Afghanistan in 1988–89 and the Soviet Union's final collapse in 1990. Muslims felt as if they were going to renew the spread of Islam in the seventh century and the defeat of the Crusaders in the twelfth century. The American response was viewed also in terms of a global war and conspiracy against Islam and Muslims in general, not just the "terrorists" among them.

Arab rulers have always sought to link their wars to the glory of Islamic history. One ruler who tried to do so was Saddam Hussein in 1980–88, 1991, and in 1998. Osama bin Ladin also did so in his declaration of war against Jews and Crusaders in February 1998. Such an atmosphere is an ideal breeding ground for apocalyptic discourse. Young supporters of global jihad sense that the turning point of history is in their favor. This became the essence of the culture of modern global jihad.

The War in Iraq—Apocalyptic Visions

The war in Iraq and the jihadi insurgency also serves as an important recruitment tool among wider circles of Arabs and Muslims. The Iraq War is also a source of apocalyptic visions for many Muslim youth, who express their views freely through the "virtual global jihad" of the Internet.

Many of these supporters view al-Qa'ida and the Taliban as "those who raise the black banners" (*ashab al-rayat al-sud*) that would come from the East on the eve of Islamic victory and proclaim the end of the world to pave the way for the appearance of the Mahdi, the Islamic messiah. In a March 9, 2003, Internet article, Usama Azzam based his conclusions on sacred Islamic sources as well as on the writings of contemporary scholars, mainly Abu Qatada—one of the leading scholars of global jihad in the Arab world and Europe—and his famous book *Ma'alim al-Tai'fa al-Mansura* (Characteristics of the Secured Community).

Azzam's main conclusion is that the end of the world is nigh, which means that Islam's total victory is almost at hand. The bringers of redemption would be al-Qai'da and the Taliban, who would assist the Mahdi in bringing Allah's rule on earth. The only alternatives to them were Arab and Muslim governments that were apostates, and the "Crusader West." Each individual could choose to be on the side of Allah or on the side of the devil.

An unsigned article published in February 2003 on what had been al-Qa'ida's main Web site—the Center for Islamic Studies and Research—attempted to disqualify these ideas. The article—"Allah Has Not Assigned Our Nation to Know the Person of the Mahdi Prior to His Appearance"—criticized those who were looking for the Mahdi to establish the Islamic State but in the meantime did nothing to promote its establishment. Those who believe in this Islamic principle "have fallen into a lot of exaggerations . . . and based their religion on false issues, until their religion turned feebler than the nest of a spider." Moreover, the anonymous author, who officially wrote on behalf of al-Qa'ida, attacked the theories of "the Black Banners that will appear from the East" as based on very weak hadith stories.

The expectations that bin Ladin will launch further attacks on American soil are enormous. Yet there is also the denial of such claims by bin Ladin and al-Qa'ida. This denial might be due to the Wahhabi nature of the Saudi element of the organization. Another reason could be the personality of bin Ladin, who has not yet made any attempt to create around him the image of an Islamic savior. The idea of al-Qa'ida is to establish solid solidarity of a new generation, front, or movement, that is not dependent upon individuals or miracles but on a united strategy and the hard work and the struggle of a community.

Many books speculating on the Mahdi, and precisely when he will emerge to deliver the Islamic community, have been published in the Sunni Arab world in the past several decades.

Jihadi Apocalyptic Discourse

In the four years that followed the September 11 attacks—with the ensuing collapse of the Taliban in Afghanistan, the declaration of a global war against jihadi terrorism, and the American occupation of Iraq on one hand and the jihadi Sunni insurgency there on the other—there was a major development in apocalyptic jihadi discourse. Jihadi scholars and sympathizers viewed the moment as a clear start of the process that would lead to the Day of Judgment. Numerous traditional Islamic terms came to be commonly used in jihadi forums during this time. Examples are: *dulab*—the circle of a century between each Mahdi; Mahdi; *mujadid al-zaman*—the person who renews the apocalyptic signs; al-Masih al-Dajjal—the false Messiah or Anti-Christ that will appear before the Day of Resurrection; *al-rayat al-sud*—the black flags that will come to fight from Khorasan in the East; Armageddon; *ru'iya*—visions; and *ahlam*—dreams.

Quite a few jihadists published their dreams and visions of the Salaf, the Prophet, historic events from early Islamic history, and other visions, asking for solutions, interpretations, and explanations that would prove that Osama bin Ladin, Abu Mus'ab al-Zarqawi, al-Qa'ida, modern jihad, the September 11 attacks, and other jihadi terrorist operations were all signs of the coming apocalypse. One Saudi scholar—Abu Bashir al-Najdi—became the "leader" of the interpreters of jihadi visions. There are several Islamist Web sites and sections in Islamist forums dedicated to dreams and visions to promote the sense of the apocalypse. Two of the more popular sites are the "Armageddon forum" and the Web site and forums of "Charms and Wars."

It is interesting that the spread of apocalyptic visions by jihadi-Salafists originates primarily from Saudi supporters of global jihad educated in a Wahhabi system. Wahhabis had always fought the spread of apocalyptic visions, fearing their deviant effect on the masses. Islamist millenarianism in Saudi Arabia around the year 1400 AH (1978) was one of the reasons for the seizure of the Ka'ba by Juhayman al-Utaybi and his group of followers, which caused trauma in the kingdom.

Yet the apocalyptic writings of al-Utaybi found a respected place in the largest "library" of jihadi-Salafism on the Web site of Abu Muhammad al-Maqdisi, www.tawhed.ws. The Utaybi affair is also used to legitimate the fight against the "apostate Saudi kingdom." Al-Maqdisi is one of the leading jihadi-Salafi scholars to attack the Saudi apostasy, and his book, *al-Kawashif al-Jaliyya fi Kufr al-Dawla al-Sa'udiyya* (The Clear Signs of the Apostasy of the Saudi State), is very popular among supporters of global jihad. (It has been downloaded from the Internet more than 53,000 times.) In his analysis of the Utaybi affair, al-Maqdisi forgave Utaybi and his group, and admitted to knowing them personally. He described them as "naïve and miserable people" who believed in the idea that "Muhammad bin Abdallah al-Qahtani was the Mahdi and Utaybi had just planned to declare his loyalty to him according to the Islamic doctrines."

One of the principal books that reflects these apocalyptic aspirations was written by the Saudi scholar Abu Jandal al-Azdi—also known as Faris bin Shawwal al-Zahrani—one of the leading younger scholars of al-Qa'ida in Saudi Arabia. A 606-page tome, it is titled *Bin Ladin—The Renovator of Times and Oppressor of the Americans*. The book places bin Ladin in line with the greatest Islamic scholars of history, such as Ibn Taymiyya, Muhammad bin Abd al-Wahhab,

or Hasan al-Banna—even though he is far from being a cleric or a scholar. Yet bin Ladin's ability to create such a tremendous turning point in Islamic history makes him a candidate for such a position in the eyes of the jihadi-Salafists.

Persistent posts about the connection between al-Qa'ida—and recently the Taliban as well—and the Islamic prophecies of the apocalypse can be seen in jihadi forums. The author of a March 6, 2006 post on www.alhesbah.org tried to prove, through detailed analysis of Islamic prophecies and traditions and the present confrontation between the mujahidin and the West, that signs of the apocalypse are being witnessed—that Osama's army is the army of the Mahdi. According to this post, this army will conquer Iraq, Syria, and the Palestinian territories—*bayt al-maqdis*—and will give authority to the Mahdi, then to Jesus/Issa, and from there the defeat of the enemy—al-Dajjal—is secured. No one on the forum opposed his analysis.

One of the enthusiastic supporters of the search for apocalyptic signs on a permanent basis is Saudi Shaykh Sulayman al-Alawan, another of the leading Saudi clerics to support global jihad. In an article titled "The Disputes over the Mahdi," also viewed as a fatwa, he encouraged the mujahidin to deal with the subject:

> Dealing with [the issue of] the Mahdi and the signs of the hour—a'lam al-sa'a—is one of the most important elements to encourage innovative effort of thinking—ijtihad—and to sail on the boat of salvation. . . . It is the best thing to do in order to spread religion, to prepare the soul for meeting Allah, and to promote the Divine Law.

The jihadi-Salafi encouragement, in addition to the sense of a historic moment and the great expectations created by al-Qa'ida, has brought about a greenhouse for apocalyptic views. The ongoing jihadi insurgencies in Iraq, Afghanistan, and Chechnya, as well as worldwide jihadi terrorism, have given rise to this sense.

Jihadi Perceptions of Weapons of Mass Destruction (WMD)

In recent years, al-Qa'ida and affiliated groups have issued a few pronouncements in which they threatened the use of WMD. The first direct reference appeared on December 26, 2002. Abu Shihab al-Kandahar, then moderator of the Islamist Internet forum www.al-mojahedoon.net, published a short article titled "Nuclear War Is the Solution for the Destruction of the United States."

The article could be viewed as a simple threat, exploiting a number of rumors from various sources. It might have also been deliberate disinformation regarding al-Qa'ida's possession of nuclear, biological, or chemical weapons. Alternatively, it could be propaganda aimed at encouraging Islamists. Regardless of its ultimate aim, al-Kandahar's article marked the first time that such a threat had been publicly issued by supporters of al-Qa'ida, or at least by a figure known to have been close to the propaganda apparatus of global jihad.

Thus far, the main modus operandi of al-Qa'ida has been suicide or martyrdom operations. Martyrdom attacks are not only a tactical tool of terrorism; they have also played a central role in the indoctrination of al-Qa'ida recruits. Over the past decade, the propaganda machinery of al-Qa'ida and global jihad has repeatedly asked the question posed in 2005, by the author of an article titled "Has the Global Crusader Alliance Learned the Lessons of the Mujahidin?" The author wrote: "We are really puzzled

to see [that] the Americans and their followers in the Western world think that they are able to confront people who wish to die more than they [the Americans] want to live." This idea of self-sacrifice that has since been reinforced by the phenomenon of suicide operations has spread across many parts of the world, along with the worldwide increase of general Muslim support for the suicide attacks against civilians in Israel. It is significant that this method, once controversial among Islamic clerics and scholars, enjoys growing support within religious and political communities alike. Thus far, in fact, it seems that radical Islam's focus has been not on mass killings, but primarily on self-sacrifice and on the proliferation of its attacks to different regions and places across the globe. The focus on personal martyrdom and suicide attacks among groups that adhere to the culture of global jihad—including al-Qa'ida, as well as groups with local and national aspirations, such as the Chechen Islamists and the Arab volunteers there, Kashmiri groups, the Kurdish Ansar al-Islam, or the Palestinian Hamas and Islamic Jihad (PIJ)—might explain why these groups have so far refrained from any large-scale use of WMD. Very rarely do clerics, scholars, or Islamist intellectuals who supply the ideological and doctrinal support for the culture of global jihad mention the issue of WMD.

Shaykh Nasir al-Fahd's Fatwa on WMD

On May 21, 2003, Saudi Shaykh Nasir bin Hamad al-Fahd published the first fatwa on the use of WMD. The author is among the younger leading clerics of the Saudi Islamist opposition that support the culture of global jihad and militant struggle against the West. Shaykh al-Fahd has published dozens of militant books and articles, some of which are viewed by the followers of global jihad as religious rulings that legitimate the fight against the United States.

Because of his preaching against the Saudi monarchy, Shaykh al-Fahd was arrested in June 2003 by the Saudi authorities and is still imprisoned without trial. He was forced, along with two of his colleagues, to renounce several of his rulings against the Saudi government. In January 2005, from prison, he rescinded his former renunciation through his supporters over Islamist Internet forums.

On September 21, 2002, al-Fahd published an article titled "The Divine Verses About the September Attack," in which he praised the execution of the September 11 attacks, especially for their technical sophistication and use of planes. One of his arguments was that the September 11 attacks were an air battle, or "dogfight" of sorts. "If the Americans are using F-15 or Tornado [and they are allowed], then if the mujahidin used Boeing or AirBus are they not allowed?"

Shaykh al-Fahd has repeatedly used such analogies with the West to provide Islamic legal justification for terrorist tactics in his other writings. When asked, for example, whether the use of WMD is allowed, his answer was straightforward: "Yes," it is allowed. "If the Muslims could defeat the infidels only by using these kinds of weapons, it is allowed to use them even if they kill them all, and destroy their crops and cattle."

Following the answer, Shaykh al-Fahd wrote a long and detailed memorandum on the relevant Islamic sources that he used as the basis for his ruling. First, he disqualified any terms of international law used by the West, since they are not part of the Islamic divine law. Second, he claimed that those countries that lead the campaign against the use of WMD—the United States and the United Kingdom—have already used WMD in the past against their enemies, not to mention that they, plus "the Jews," possess these weapons.

Third, he based his arguments on the saying of Muhammad in the hadith: "Allah has ordered you to do everything perfectly. Hence, if you kill, do it perfectly, and if you slaughter, do it perfectly. Everyone should sharpen his blade and ease his slaughter." He also relied on another saying of Muhammad: "If you are ordered to do something—do it according to your best ability." In al-Fahd's view, this principle is essential: Muslims should act according to their abilities. If there is no other way the mujahidin can defeat the enemy, then they should kill them, all of them, by every means possible. This principle is valid even if they have to kill women and children, or even other Muslims.

In al-Fahd's eyes, the principles of using WMD are divided into two categories. The first category concerns the general acceptance of their use in the case of jihad. The second category concerns the legitimacy of the use of WMD in a certain period against a certain enemy—an enemy that, in al-Fahd's eyes, clearly means the United States.

One controversial issue among Saudi scholars following the attacks against "infidels" has been the fact that innocent Muslims are also being killed by these attacks. Al-Fahd unambiguously believes, however, that if the killing of Muslims is necessary and there is no other choice, then it is permissible. In his view, which is based on previous rulings of Islamic scholars such as the fourteenth-century theologian Ibn Taymiyya, there are no limits at all to using WMD against the Western "infidels."

The Islamist Reaction to Shaykh al-Fahd

The strongest evidence of the relatively low regard for WMD within Islamist radical discourse lies in the military manuals distributed on the Internet by various global jihadi groups. Only a handful of references indicate planning for the use of such weapons.

In instances where the manuals refer to WMD, the emphasis is on the use of chemical weapons, which are easy to obtain and handle. Indeed, Islamist Web sites contain instructions on how to make homemade bombs using chemicals. Ultimately, the ability of Islamist terrorist groups to kill hundreds of people by conventional means might be more attractive to them.

Abu Mus'ab al-Suri and "The Call for Islamist Global Resistance"

In December 2004, a new attitude emerged in Islamist discourse. Mustafa Sit-Maryam—aka Umar Abd al-Hakim but better known as Abu Mus'ab al-Suri—a former leading trainer and scholar of al-Qa'ida, published two documents calling for an Islamist Global Resistance.

One way of waging a strong jihad without a strong mass base is to use weapons of mass destruction. Al-Suri talks at length about the importance of using WMD against the United States as the only way to fight it from a point of equality. He even criticizes Osama bin Ladin for not using WMD in the September 11 attacks and advocates such methods. Al-Suri asks North Korea and Iran to continue developing their nuclear projects. It is most unusual for a jihadi-Salafist scholar to hint at possible cooperation with countries such as Shi'a Iran or Stalinist North Korea, both of which are generally regarded as infi-

del regimes. However, al-Suri seems to advise that jihadi Sunni readers should cooperate with the devil to defeat the "bigger devil."

Al-Suri does not see much benefit from the guerrilla warfare waged against the United States by al-Qa'ida in Iraq. Hence: "The ultimate choice is the destruction of the United States by operations of strategic symmetry through weapons of mass destruction, namely nuclear, chemical, or biological means, if the mujahidin can achieve it with the help of those who possess them or through buying them." One other option, he says, is by "the production of basic nuclear bombs, known as 'dirty bombs.'"

Why are there so few references to WMD within the Islamist discourse of al-Qa'ida or related groups? Several assessments can be made.

WMD did receive some attention prior to October–November 2001, when Afghanistan, under the Taliban, served as a safe haven for al-Qa'ida and other Islamist groups. Until that time, al-Qa'ida maintained better relations with regimes and scientists involved in developing WMD such as Pakistan, Sudan, the Islamic republics of Central Asia, and perhaps with Iraq. After November 2001, however, most of the al-Qa'ida facilities in Afghanistan were destroyed or seized by the United States or Pakistan under President Pervez Musharraf, and Islamist forces were pushed into certain areas in eastern Afghanistan. It is possible that the culture of global jihad embraced "heroism" and the tactics of martyrdom operations as a result of these setbacks.

When al-Qa'ida had a base in Afghanistan, its attempt to acquire chemical, biological, radiological or nuclear (CBRN) facilities was handled in secret by a small group of operatives, the vast majority of whom did not possess the capabilities of dealing with CBRN, except for crude homemade bombs.

Due to the loss of their Afghan safe haven, and due to the difficulties of handling such weapons in occupied Iraq, only one arena remains where such weapons can be handled—namely, among Muslim communities in the West, especially in Europe.

In many Islamist writings, the term "WMD" refers to a broad array of social and moral diseases associated with the West, such as AIDS, cigarette smoking, and drug use. It is not presented as part of the Islamist struggle but rather as a term denoting the destructive diseases that will eventually ruin Western societies from the inside.

If the main source of assessment is the mind of the present generation of Islamists, modeled by al-Qa'ida, the threat of an immediate use of WMD is of low feasibility. Yet two other factors should be considered: First, there might be a new generation of Islamists not necessarily under the control of Saudi clerics or scholars which could possess fewer reservations about the acquisition and use of CBRN or WMD.

Second, a new generation of Islamist groups might be more willing to follow the fatwa of Shaykh al-Fahd or the book of Abu Mus'ab al-Suri and encourage the use of such weapons if and when the mujahidin find they have no other alternative.

The view of WMD use in a "Doomsday" scenario is an integral part of the apocalyptic aspirations of the "audience" of global jihad, but not necessarily of its clerics or scholars. These expectations slowly increase, which creates among the supporters of global jihad a sense of a coming "explosion" in Iraq, Europe, or the United States.

In addition, it can be cautiously said that the effect of religiously based debates among jihadi scholars or between scholars and Islamic institutions is weakening. Supporters of global jihad, especially those

that have access to the Internet, are more "thirsty" to watch video clips that document beheadings, bombings, or terrorism against their various "enemies" than to read innovative Islamic rulings. Hence, a sense of apocalyptic aspirations—either Islamist or of another type—linked to individual "candidates" for Mahdism, might increase.

So far it seems that leaders such as bin Ladin or Zawahiri do not encourage such a development. There is no sign that they perceive themselves as the future caliph or even that they might lead a caliphate. This is typical of radical Sunni leaders or scholars. However, al-Qa'ida is mutating, and on the margins of jihadi-Salafism there might emerge individuals or groups that could develop into someone who declares himself to be the Mahdi with a small group of followers and stages violent, spectacular actions in an attempt to prove it. Still, his chances to become an influential leader of the "mainstream" jihadi-Salafism are very low.

An important question to ask here is to what extent a sense of the apocalypse is driving jihadists to act now and not to "wait for the Mahdi to appear." One of the significant factors of this growing willingness might be the visual effect of horrors as reflected through the Internet. Bloody video clips, demonizing graffiti, and the total freedom of speech on this medium have a growing effect too.

Jihadi Use of the Internet—The Open University for Jihad

The main platform for developing and pushing the culture of global jihad forward has in recent years been the Internet. There are several reasons why jihadi movements, groups, clerics, and scholars turned the Internet into their main, and sometimes

only, vehicle for propaganda, indoctrination, publicity, and teaching of their messages. Besides the known advantages of this
medium of communication, several factors
should be noted: First, in most Arab and
Muslim countries opposition groups are
persecuted, rendering the Internet their
only vehicle for spreading their message.
Citizens and groups are prevented from
freely publishing books and newspapers or
from giving open lectures. They have no
access to the traditional means of Islamic
religious indoctrination, such as mosques,
Friday sermons, religious universities and
colleges, or religious ceremonies.

Second, the Internet is the best way to
reach the broadest possible audience. Every
jihadi event or message is instantly exposed
to the world, news agencies, and Muslim
countries whose populations do not read
Arabic.

One of the documents of indoctrination
published in 2003 and later recirculated
on most major jihadi forums by the Global
Islamic Media Front (GIMF, an organ of
al-Qa'ida and global jihad with growing
virtual activity) talks about the "university of global jihad." The author, nicknamed
Ahmad al-Wathiq bil-Allah, deputy director
of GIMF, presents al-Qa'ida as an "organization, state, and university" whose faculties
include propaganda, martyrdom, and the
technology of weapons development.

The article clearly summarizes the indoctrinating nature of global jihad and thus,
the center of gravity of this phenomenon—
the Muslim audience. An intensive reading
of these Web sites, and especially of the most
radical 15 to 25 jihadi forums and dozens
of message groups, reveals the highly serious approach and attitude of their participants, those who are targeted by this global
indoctrination. These jihadi Web sites have
gradually replaced the old *madrasa* of the

1980s–1990s as a tool for recruitment of
jihadists. The Internet, in fact, has become
one global madrasa.

Another recent publication by GIMF—
an analysis of the global strategy of al-
Qa'ida—is even more lucid. Under the title
"Al-Qaida's War Is Economic Not Military,"
Abu Mus'ab al-Najdi, the author, a Saudi
scholar and supporter of global jihad, ana-
lyzes the significant role that indoctrination
plays in the global movement, moving young
Muslims away from "oceans of pleasure and
lust" and listening to traitorous clerics who
have sold out to the regimes. Seeing photos
or videos of attacks have mobilized them to
participate in jihad. Bin Ladin, he explains,
is very influential and calls by him can, for
example, lead to attacks on oilfields in the
Gulf Arab states.

The long jihad that the West—and indeed
much of the rest of the world—is currently
facing uses the Internet to provide both
jihadists and the West with a wide spectrum
of diversified information. Western intelligence and security analysts can learn more
about the culture of jihad by reading the
lips of jihadi clerics, scholars, operatives,
commanders, leaders, and—above all—their
growing audience. Improving their ability
to do so—in the original language—must be
the West's priority.

Conclusion

The current trend among Islamist groups
is to move away from terrorism confined
to their individual countries and directed
against the "heretic" regimes that persecute
them, and to move toward operations that
are global in scope. This trend is rooted in
two organizationally distinct—yet ideologically connected—events of the 1990s. One
was the bombing of the World Trade Center
in 1993. The second was the participation

of Islamist volunteers in conflicts in Bosnia, Albania, Kosovo, Chechnya, Kashmir, and Dagestan throughout the 1990s. These two lines eventually merged through the establishment of an international Islamist front in Afghanistan. This union was also solidified by the oppression and violence that Islamists experienced under various Arab regimes, which created a camp of Islamist refugees who could no longer act in their homelands. In one sense, then, they were forced to pursue the new route of global terrorism. When they lost Afghanistan in December 2001, they moved to Iraq in 2003 and have started intensive indoctrination through the Internet since then in the rest of the Arab and Muslim world.

This global phenomenon has been exacerbated by a relatively old process, one that will actually accelerate in the coming years: the radicalization of Muslim, primarily Arab, immigrants in the West. This process is largely a consequence of the alienation that many second- and third-generation Muslim immigrants feel within Western societies, whether due to irreconcilable values, quashed expectations, or other factors. One result of this process has been the rapid development of an Islamic activist infrastructure within Western democracies, such that any number of organizations in Europe and the United States could serve as the logistical and financial backbone of Islamist terrorist groups.

This problem of social alienation among younger Muslims merits a study of its own. In short, though, any solution will require a better understanding in the West of the roots of Islamist violence as part of the culture of global jihad. The counterterrorism efforts of the United States and other Western countries—such as new legislation, better cooperation in the intelligence field, encouragement of counterterrorism efforts

by Arab and Muslim states, and extradition of arrested terrorists—are all important. Yet these measures do not address the fundamental causes of the problem and may even enhance the notion that the Islamist struggle is an ideological global clash between civilizations.

The September 11 attacks and the war against Islamist terrorism have paved the way for new ideological interpretations among jihadi scholars, clerics, and groups and produced new methods of dealing with the facts in light of Islamic constants. Islamist groups and Muslim intellectuals who determine this new vision publish fresh studies and dissertations. Formerly, the general vision and intellectual dissertations by Islamist groups were limited in scope to their regional problems. For example, the Islamist groups in Egypt and Algeria used to focus on ways of rebelling against the governing regimes and ways of responding to violators of Islam. In the Palestinian arena and Kashmir, the visions and related studies were focused on fighting occupation, exhorting Muslims to fight for this goal, and expounding the Shari'a principles that governed this activity. In contrast, the jihadi insurgency in Iraq and the recent renewal of the jihadi struggle in Afghanistan are producing a variety of wide-ranging doctrines, debates, and indoctrinating principles that are shared by a rapidly growing class of supporters of global jihad through the Internet.

Added to this is the sense of alienation that prevails in the ranks of many intellectuals in the Arab and Muslim worlds. All this could cause the Islamist movements to rearrange their action strategies in line with Islamic constants. They will deal with the facts, but without giving up their ideological fundamentals, abandoning the defense of oppressed Muslims, or giving up their sanctities regardless of the sacrifices that might be required. They might do so without reckless zeal in areas and situations where calm, sobriety, and wisdom are better qualities in working and making decisions. This is especially important when one remembers that the objective of the war on terrorism is viewed by the Islamists as aimed at destroying every Islamist activity and luring the Islamists into battles where they can be eliminated, prior to weakening Islamist groups everywhere and decisively destroying their capabilities.

An important consequence of the war on Islamist terrorism, primarily in Iraq, and a cornerstone in the jihadi strategy, is the shift of terrorist activity back to the Arab world and the Middle East. Despite the global nature of the Islamist phenomenon since the mid-1990s, Islamists' ideal remained the establishment of what they perceive as the true Islamic state in the heart of the Muslim world. The hardcore element of the global jihad movement is composed primarily of Arab Islamists, and the loss of the Afghan base brought them back to square one: their homeland. The U.S. occupation in Iraq added to the shift.

Regarding the American occupation of Iraq, Zawahiri wrote that only with the establishment of a proper Islamist state would the base for future progress be assured. Other key achievements would have to be the movement's proximity to the masses in order to "defend their honor" and "fend off injustice." He adds, "The people will not love us unless they feel that we love them . . . and are ready to defend them." But if the masses are not roused, the blame would lie with the movement's shortcomings in delivering its message and showing its readiness for sacrifice. No matter what the cost, the basic objective must be maintained.

One front in this effort, according to Zawahiri, is victory for Palestine, something the secular movements have failed to achieve. Any negotiations, compromise, or recognition of Israel in any form must be rejected. This issue is highly emotional and a rallying point.

Thus far, the phenomenon of the global jihad movement is unlikely to end soon. It is capable of making adjustments to its ranks, groups, and fronts, and moving its activity to other parts of the world—most likely back to the Middle East on one hand, and to Muslim communities in the West on the other. The global earthquake of the September 11 attacks and the global war on terrorism did not actually change the roots of Islamist rage, which feeds this phenomenon and its violent expressions and encourages Muslim publics to support if not Islamist terrorism at least the ideas that it represents.

Naturally, Western leaders in the fight against jihadi terrorism are interested in portraying the threat and image of al-Qa'ida and global jihad as in decline. They point to various successes, such as the thwarting of terrorist plots and other operations; the capturing and killing of several senior al-Qa'ida operatives; improved cooperation in the field of global counterterrorism; and a growing awareness among societies in many countries of the need for tighter security measures. Western leaders also tend to belittle the role of the jihadi insurgency in Iraq, Afghanistan, and Somalia in affecting Western security. Some underestimate and misjudge the adaptive capability and dynamism of global jihad, arguing that its targets are static and independent of developments in certain regions.

Since September 11, however, al-Qa'ida has managed to either initiate or inspire fatal terrorist attacks throughout the world. These attacks include several hundred suicide operations in Iraq, Afghanistan, the Sinai, Jordan, India, Indonesia, Kenya, Tunisia, Morocco, and Europe. Western counterterrorism successes notwithstanding, these attacks, as well as a multitude of foiled attempts, are clear evidence that al-Qa'ida and its affiliates, as well as more loosely affiliated local jihadi initiatives, are still capable of planning and executing major attacks. Moreover, the plot uncovered in summer 2006 in the United Kingdom involving attacks on international aviation shows that some of the planned operations are at least as sophisticated as, if not more than, the September 11 attacks. As a result of these ongoing threats, issues and terms such as immigration, "home-grown jihadists," "profiling," "red alerts," suicide bombings, charities, money-laundering, and "clash of civilizations and religions" have firmly penetrated Western life and the vocabulary of Western discourse.

Moreover, global jihad has clearly won the battle for the Internet. Al-Qa'ida and its affiliates dominate this medium as a means of indoctrination while the West and the Muslim world have so far failed to devise and effect a serious "counter-jihadi" response. On a daily basis, the entire Western media community is swimming in a sea of jihadi Web sites. The jihadi Web is swift, technologically advanced, highly adaptive to changing situations, and is consumed by the Western media as a serious source of information. The most significant role of the jihadi Internet is that of "Open University for Jihad Studies," the most effective means of jihadi indoctrination and inspiration.

Adding to these setbacks is the failure by the United States and its allies to apprehend the genuine leadership of al-Qa'ida, which as of 2009 not only remains at large but also manages to hotwire the apocalyptic senses of their followers by means of fre-

quent airing of audio and video cassettes. The distribution of these tapes has helped al-Qa'ida achieve the popularity of a rock band, revered by its supporters and held in awe by the Western media. Between July and mid-September 2006 alone, Ayman Zawahiri himself "posted" four tapes out of a total of 27 tapes posted since September 2001. This means of communication with both the supporters of global jihad and Western publics and governments gives al-Qa'ida, and especially its two leaders, a wealth of power, exercised with what seems to be a soaring level of self-confidence. A close examination and analysis of all the tapes released by Osama bin Ladin and Zawahiri since September 11 strongly suggests that their self-confidence developed tremendously during that period. Since 2003, these two al-Qa'ida leaders, especially Zawahiri, have portrayed themselves as respected scholars who talk to their "citizens" like pseudo prime ministers. An additional example of al-Qa'ida's domination of the media is the large number of tapes featuring Abu Mus'ab al-Zarqawi in the period of 2003 to mid-2006, as well as the thousands of video clips from Iraq, Chechnya, Afghanistan, and elsewhere documenting almost every terrorist operation. These releases indicate that the propaganda and indoctrination machinery of al-Qa'ida, which is initiated by a very small number of people, is well oiled and highly effective.

The vast body of assessments on the state of al-Qa'ida also features some experts who attempt to find the "golden path," claiming that several years after September 11, al-Qa'ida has mutated and is weaker as an organization or terrorist group but much stronger as a source of inspiration and ideology. Jihadists traveling to Iraq to blow themselves up, "home-grown immigrants" carrying out terrorist operations in Europe,

and activists in jihadi political subversion in
the Arab and Muslim world have not been
recruited by al-Qa'ida. They have "recruited" themselves to the service of global jihadi
ideology. The vast majority of them undergo
virtual mental, indoctrinating, and practical
training through the Internet, not in training camps in Afghanistan or madrasas in
Pakistan.

Furthermore, the ideological and doctrinal developments, which affect a growing number of youth, are not necessarily
inspired merely by religious interpretations
but are also influenced by sociopolitical
developments, taking place primarily within
the Arab world. On the other end—among
Western societies—there is a growing sense
that a clash with Muslim communities is
inevitable, which results in—among other
things—stronger support for harsher security measures, even at the price of certain
limitations on civil liberties.

Generally speaking, since September 11,
al-Qa'ida seems to have slowly expanded
as a source of support and appeal among
larger segments of Islamic—primarily
Arab—societies. Its organizational power,
meanwhile, has not declined significantly. However, its greatest success does not
appear to be its survival but, rather, the
development of the culture of global jihad as
an entity in and of itself. This entity is the
main framework of strategy and ideology; it
is independent of any persons or individuals
or specific terrorist operations. The community that evolved out of this culture emerged
within just 10 to 20 years. This community,
which is also global, is still a minority in the
larger Muslim world, but is able to gather
a growing number of supporters around
its strategy and ideology. The sense of the
apocalypse, on one hand, and oppression,
on the other, assists in promoting its targets
among these supporters, at least for now.

Bibliography

Al-Alawan, Sulayman bin Naser. *Al-naza'at fi al-Mahdi* (Debates About the Mahdi). January 23, 2003. www.al-alwan.org.

Al-Najdi, Abu Mus'ab. *Ma'rakat al-Qa'ida—Ma'rakah iqtisadiyya la askariyya* (The Battle of Al-Qaeda—Economic Battle not Military). October 3, 2005, www.al-farouq.com/vb/showthread.php?t=3383.

"Al Qaeda's Fatwa." Online News Hour, www.pbs.org/newshour/terrorism/international/fatwa_1998.html; and www.tawhed.ws/r?=733.

Al-Quds al-Arabi (London). February 23, 1998.

Al-Shu'aybi, Humud al-Uqla. *Fatwa on Recent Event*. www.sunnahonline.com/ilm/contemporary/0017.htm.

Al-Zahrani, Faris bin Shawwal. *Usama bin Ladin mujadid al-zaman wa-qahir al-Amri-kan* (Osama bin Ladin is the Renovator of Times and Defeater of the Americans). www.tawhed.ws/r?i=972.

Al-Zawahiri, Ayman. *Fursan tahta rayat al-nabi* (Knights Under the Prophet's Banner). London: *al-Sharq al-Awsat*, December 2–12, 2001, www.assharqalawsat.com/pcdaily/pcstatic/ny-attack/zawahri.html; FBIS Document No. FBIS-NES-2002–0108, date: 1/10/02.

"Ars al-Shahada" (The Wedding of Martyrdom). *Filastin al-Muslima*, Vol. 9 (September 1991).

Azzam, Abdallah. "Al-Qa'ida al-sulba" (The Solid Base). *Al-Jihad*, No. 41 (April 1988).

Azzam, Usama. *Hal Taliban wal-Qa'ida hum ashab al-rayat al-sud?* (Are Taliban and al-Qaeda the Owners of the Black Flags?). March 9, 2003, www.dawh.net/vb/showthread.threadid?php=12125.

The Center for Islamic Studies and Research. *Nahnu Umma lam yukallifna Allah bi-ma'rifat al-Mahdi qabla khurujihi* (We Are a Nation That Allah Did Not Inform About the Appearance of the Mahdi Before It Occurred). February 2003.

Edminster, Steve. "UNHCR, U.S. Government Gear Up to Double Refugee Admissions from the Middle East and South Asia." *Refugee Reports* 20:11 (December 1999). www.refugees.org/world/articles/unhcr_rr99_11.htm.

Emerson, Steve. *Jihad in America*. PBS documentary, November 29, 1994.

Ibn Sirrin, Muhammad. *Tafsir al-ahlam al-kabir* (The Great Exegesis of Dreams). Beirut: Dar al-Fikr, 1982.

Muntada al-malahim wal-fitan (Epic and Intriques Forum). http://alfetn.com/vb3/index.php.

Paz, Reuven. "The Saudi Fatwa Against Suicide Terrorism." *PeaceWatch* 323 (May 2, 2001). Washington, DC: The Washington Institute for Near East Policy.

Pinguet, Maurice. *Voluntary Death in Japan*. Cambridge: Polity Press, 1993.

"Al-Qaeda University for Jihad Studies." Al-Boraq Forum, March 14, 2006. http://alboraq.info/showthread.php?t=3219.

U.S. Committee for Refugees. *Asylum Cases Decided by Immigration Judges Approved or Denied, by Selected Country of Origin,* 1999. www.refugees.org/world/statistics/wrs00_table3.htm.

U.S. Committee for Refugees. *Country Report: United Kingdom,* 1999. www.refugees.org/world/countryrpt/europe/united_kingdom.htm.

SUB-SAHARAN AFRICA

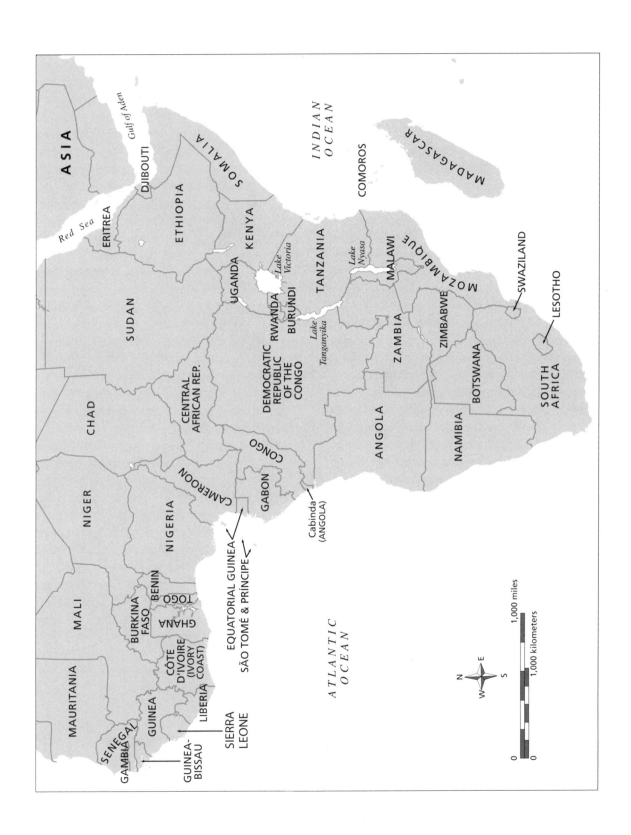

Africa

David McCormack

Islamism is challenging many polities and societies in sub-Saharan Africa. Terrorist groups such as al-Qa'ida and Hizballah have a strong presence in the region—primarily to finance, plan, and carry out attacks against Western targets both inside and outside Africa—while several local terror groups have emerged to wage jihad on sub-Saharan Africa itself. The 1998 bombings of U.S. embassies in Kenya and Tanzania, carried out by foreign terrorists with support from their local brethren, offer conspicuous evidence of this situation. Yet what might have a considerably greater effect in the long term on Africa and its relations with the world is the systematic imposition of a strict version of Islam there.

Indeed, far from advocating immediate, armed revolution, the vast majority of Islamists in sub-Saharan Africa—largely influenced by Wahhabism, Salafism, and Khomeiniism—have opted for a more gradual approach in attempting to bring society and state into conformity with their extremist interpretations of Islam. Where it takes root, Islamism contributes to the marginalization of women and non-Muslims, inhibits democratic government and the rule of law, discourages economic growth, violates accepted standards of

human rights, and leads to increased intercommunal violence.

This hardly reflects the history of Islam as a faith in sub-Saharan Africa, whose expansion there was a peaceful affair, initially facilitated by trade routes linking the region to the Arab world in a process of gradual diffusion. This had the effect of overlaying Islam on—rather than wholly eliminating—local belief systems and consequently played a much more limited role in organizing society and state than is advocated by Islamist movements today.

After more than a millennium of rejecting rigid interpretations of Islam in sub-Saharan Africa, why is Islamism gaining traction now? In part, the oppressive nature of African governments, combined with their inability to forge vibrant economies and stable social structures, attracted many to Islamism's promise of empowerment. When the tide of liberal democracy more recently swept across the region, Islamist forces were granted unprecedented freedom to implement their program.

Less often considered, however, is how Middle Eastern governments support Islamism's rise by using the Islamic message to advance their own interests. Sub-Saharan Africa provides an inviting target for this agenda. Its Muslim population of 250 million offers a massive base. Weak and corrupt states and economies make Islamist ideologies attractive to disenchanted populations, while porous borders and a steady flow of illicit arms contribute to an ideal operating environment for Islamists with militant appetites.

Although the actual sum is incalculable, at least tens of billions of dollars have been poured into the subcontinent from the Middle East in support of Islamism, with results that are hardly surprising. It is no coincidence that the Saudi state faith—Wahhabism—has become the most dynamic ideological strain of Islamism in sub-Saharan Africa, given that its Ministry of Islamic Affairs distributes so much money for activity in the region. As Eva Evers Rosander, scholar of Islamism in Africa, suggests, "In relations between African Muslims and foreigners from the Arab [oil] countries, those who have the financial means dictate the Islamic discourse."

The attribution of full responsibility to foreign influences would be overstated, however, as African Muslims have hardly been passive participants in the development of Islamism. Rather, as Rosander's counterpart, Roman Loimeier, points out, "On account of [the] vast differences in programs, styles, orientation, financial backing and claims of spiritual superiority in the Muslim 'North,' the Muslim movements of reform in Africa have always been able to 'play' with these rivalries and to balance 'Northern' influences in their own national and local strategies of development and political orientation."

Islamism is steadily advancing on virtually all sub-Saharan Muslim communities to one degree or another, evident in the proliferation of Islamist groups of all ideological stripes. Yet, while the tactical approaches among these groups are often varied, for the most part they pursue a common strategy that is clearly identifiable.

Given the traditional strength of African Islam's temperance, Islamists recognize that they must first raise African Muslims' awareness of global Islamic faith and culture as defined by the Islamists. Activity to promote social welfare—with significant assistance from international Islamist nongovernmental organizations (NGOs) such as the Muslim World League (MWL), the International Islamic Relief Organization (IIRO), and the World Assembly of Muslim Youth (WAMY)—is a primary tool employed to accomplish this objective. The short-term aim of such activity is the creation of distinct Islamized segments of society that can later be leveraged for Islamist purposes.

Once established, these Islamized populations are led toward acceptance of Islamism by measures intended to portray the status quo as antithetical to Muslim well-being. Islamist fringe elements attempt to foster a mood of defiance among Islamized populations against external influences by propagating a moralistic discourse that attacks those things deemed threatening to the health of Islam.

One of the most commonly used tactics is to petition that Muslims be permitted to be governed by Shari'a. The inevitable opposition that arises from non-Muslim quarters to this demand confirms to Muslims their sense of persecution, allowing increasingly radical rhetoric and action to become acceptable. By portraying themselves as defenders of legitimate Muslim rights, Islamists are thus able to wrest popular support from the moderate center.

Significantly, the different brands of Islamism operating in Africa have been willing to form short-term tactical alliances with one another, recognizing the imperative of Muslim unity for the immediate purpose of defeating external challenges. This often leads to the development of Islamist groups with indistinct doctrinal foundations. For example, it is not unusual to see Wahhabis working with Sufis, or to see Sunnis receiving Iranian patronage. Yet the common goal remains, as once expressed by the leader of Libya, Mu'amar Qadhafi, to "make Islam triumphant in Africa."

The growing influence of Islamism south of the Sahara is manifest, though it is by no means developing uniformly. Demographic, political, economic, and a host of other differences permit degrees of success that vary greatly from region to region, state to state, and even locality to locality. Yet similar patterns of Islamism's advance can be observed in virtually all of the subcontinent's Muslim communities. The following country studies display the general similarities and local adaptations in Islamism's transformation of sub-Saharan Africa.

Nigeria

Introduced by Arab traders in the eleventh century, Islam came to dominate the northern part of modern-day Nigeria—today home to 60 million Muslims who account for roughly half of the country's population—over the following centuries. Despite the religion's distinct influence on the region's cultural history, Nigerian Islam was by no means harsh or rigid, but rather permitted an environment in which Muslims of different doctrinal persuasions, Christians, and animists coexisted relatively peacefully for the better part of a thousand years.

As Britain began to disengage from West Africa in the 1950s following roughly a century of colonial rule, it was recognized that a functioning Nigerian state—one that incorporated both the predominantly Muslim north and the Christian and animist south—would have to be of a secular character. With independence in 1960, a penal code was established for northern Nigeria that excluded Shari'a from criminal proceedings, allowing its application only in matters of limited personal law for Muslims, as was traditionally practiced. Significantly, this jurisdiction was reinforced by subsequent constitutions adopted in the country.

The history of Islamism in Nigeria can largely be traced through the career of one man—Abu Bakr Gumi. Gumi began public life as deputy and spiritual adviser to Ahmadu Bello, dubbed the first prime minister of northern Nigeria. Gumi was trained in an austere legal tradition and was rabidly anti-Sufi (an indication of Islamism throughout sub-Saharan Africa), having lived several months in the Hijaz, where he became immersed in Wahhabi ideology. As scholar John Hunwick observed, Gumi would serve as "a conduit through which Saudi/Wahhabi ideas could flow and take root in Nigeria."

Gumi's Islamist program began in 1962, when he persuaded Bello to establish a pan-Nigerian Islamic organization—Jama'at Nasr al-Islam (JNI, Association for the Victory of Islam)—that can be considered the progenitor of today's Islamist associations in the country. A backlash by Sufis against Gumi's agenda, however, eventually led to their penetration of JNI and its disintegration into competing factions. Gumi's faction, established in 1978 and the most influential of them all, was the Jama'at Izalat al-Bida wa Iqamat al-Sunna (Society for the Eradication of Evil Innovation and the Establishment of the Sunna), better known as Yan Izala.

In addition to issuing religious edicts close to the views held by Wahhabism, Izala promotes social programs—including the establishment of an Islamic system of education—that help it gain broad-based Muslim support. As explained by Loimeier, "The new adherents of Yan Izala absorbed nothing of the old, 'un-Islamic' system of values, but categorically rejected it and instead accepted a new system of explanation."

Scholar M.A. Mohamed Salih explains that, with support from the Saudi Islamic Relief Association, Gumi and the Izala were able to promote their message on a wide scale, making effective use of mass media, through the establishment of radio programs on the Nigeria Broadcasting Corporation and of the Hausa-language newspaper *Gaskiya*. However, the noted Izala expert Muhammad Sani Umar observes that the movement was spread most effectively through two other means: the convening of thousands of preaching sessions across the country and the recording of Izala's sermons on audio-cassette for mass distribution.

Not wanting to lose ground in the face of Izala's magnetism, the traditionally dominant Sufi brotherhoods were forced to follow a similar path—adopting Islamist prescriptions to compete with Izala in being seen as "more Islamic" in a battle to be considered the legitimate defender of Muslim rights in the country. This had the effect of firmly entrenching Islamism in Nigerian Muslim life. Significantly, as Nigeria stumbled toward democracy and experienced expanding Christian missionary activity during the 1980s and 1990s, the imperative of Muslim unity began to erode traditional rivalries, leading even Gumi himself to famously declare in 1987 that "politics was more important than prayer"—a process that has continued apace ever since.

Although Gumi died in 1992, his legacy lives on. Today, Izala is led by Shaykh Muhammad Sani Yahaya Jingir, who main-tains popular support for the Islamist program through the funding of mosques, *madrasas* (religious schools), and hospitals, while advocating the continued application of Shari'a. This grassroots effort continues to attract a large following, especially in cities and towns and among the educated class.

Not surprisingly, numerous Islamist groups and movements have formed in the environment cultivated by Izala. The Nigerian Ikhwan (Muslim Brothers), for example, emerged in the early 1990s as a prominent player in Nigerian Islamism, recruiting heavily among university students and aiming "to bring about an Islamic revolution in Nigeria." The Ikhwan's estimated 10,000 members—led by Ibrahim al-Zakzaki, who was trained in, and reportedly received funding from, Iran—regularly hold rallies and demonstrations in support of Islamist issues.

In addition to these more loosely knit movements, several well-organized groups have been integral players in Nigerian Islamism, including both foreign and domestic agencies. The Supreme Council for Shari'a in Nigeria (SCSN), led by Ibrahim Datti Ahmad, has been at the forefront. Similarly, foreign-sponsored "charitable" organizations—such as the MWL, WAMY, and al-Muntada al-Islami—operate in Nigeria to draw Muslims to the Islamist cause.

Despite its spread from the 1960s onward, the extent of Islamism's grip on Nigeria became clear only with the country's liberation from military rule in 1999, which marked a rapid decline in the power of the central government. Free to implement their program at the state level, Islamists in northern Nigeria have embarked on a campaign to transform social and political life to conform to the dictates of their extremist interpretations of Islam. The Islamists' first action would be the implementation of a much more robust Shari'a, to include its application in criminal proceedings.

Ahmad Sani, Islamist governor of the state of Zamfara, began the political transformation on October 27, 1999, when he proclaimed that his state would henceforth be governed by Shari'a. A great admirer of Saudi Arabia, Sani modeled his legal system on that of the kingdom, stating, according to India's *Tribune* in October 1999, "It will be very, very good for people. We will have a society devoid of problems." His announcement, in fact, was made following solidarity visits from Saudi officials, and a number of judges were immediately sent to Saudi Arabia for training. Eleven other predominantly Muslim states in northern Nigeria would follow suit shortly thereafter. Those states are Bauchi, Borno, Gombe, Jigawa, Kaduna, Kano, Katsina, Kebbi, Niger, Sokoto, and Yobe.

The impact of Islamism since 1999 becomes apparent, as Sani indeed made good on his promise that Shari'a "is not limited to the laws. It is a comprehensive way of life." Public transportation has been segregated by gender and alcohol has been banned regardless of a citizen's faith. Corporal and capital punishment, including flogging and death by stoning, have been institutionalized. Furthermore, as in Saudi Arabia, a vigilante organization—the Joint Islamic Aid Group—was established to monitor compliance with the new laws. Additionally, Sani disclosed a plan—at an event organized by the Saudi embassy in Nigeria—to enforce the teaching and usage of Arabic in Zamfara and to begin paying Islamic preachers out of state funds.

Across northern Nigeria, Islamism has begun to erode accepted standards of human rights, primarily among the Muslim community. The Center for Religious Freedom has observed, in fact, that these violations contravene not only the Nigerian constitution but also the Universal Declaration of Human Rights, the African Charter on Human and People's Rights, and the International Covenant on Civil and Political Rights, to which Nigeria is party.

In one of the more conspicuous examples of Islamism's influence, beginning in late 2003 the governments of four northern states refused—at the insistence of Ibrahim Datti Ahmad and the SCSN—for nearly a year to take part in a countrywide immunization drive against polio, claiming that it was part of a Western plot to make Muslim women infertile. During this time, more than 400 new cases of polio were reported, accounting for almost 90 percent of new cases worldwide. As declared by the governor of Kano State, Ibrahim Shekarau, according to a February 2004 BBC report, "It is a lesser of two evils to sacrifice two, three, four, five, even 10 children [to polio] than allow hundreds of thousands or possibly millions of girl-children likely to be rendered infertile."

With such a perspective in tow, Shekarau stands alongside Sani—both of whom are allegedly members of Izala—as one of the two most prominent Islamist leaders in Nigeria today. A former activist in the Muslims' Student Society—a leading organization in rallying youths toward the Islamist cause that is influenced heavily by the writings of both Ayatollah Ruhollah Khomeini and Sayyid Qutb—Shekarau rose through the ranks of the Nigerian civil service to its highest office, during which time he became a leading figure in the push for Shari'a. In the 2003 elections, he managed to oust the governor of Kano, who had signed the state's Shari'a bill into law yet was considered much less committed to the Islamist cause than was Shekarau.

Mahmud Mustapha, a Nigerian pundit, describes the environment that has arisen in Kano under Shekarau:

> Shia . . . have been under threat of attack from blood thirsty Wahabis that have taken control of machinery of government. . . . Apart from allowing the Wahabis to continue to spew the venom of hatred against the Shias among the predominant Sunnis through calumny and fabrications, the government sponsored a systematic and sustained media campaign against Shia followers on its radio station which refers to suicide attacks by Iraqi Wahabi dissidents against Shias and their places of worship as Jihad.

Venom is quite often directed, in fact, at Nigeria's minority Shi'a population, which began to gain a following in the 1970s and that by some estimates composes as much as 5 percent of the total Muslim population (though that figure is likely high, because of the routine conflation of Shi'a with Sunnis who express solidarity with the Iranian revolutionary program, such as those of Zakzaki's Ikhwan).

Aside from intrareligious tensions resulting from Islamism's advance, its application across the northern region has created widespread interreligious tension that has led to violence on a massive scale. As estimated by the Center for Religious Freedom, as many as 10,000 people have been killed by such violence since 1999. Encouraging interfaith discord is, of course, a principle objective of the Islamists, knowing that it will convince more Muslims to rally around their rigid program.

For its part, the central government has tacitly accepted its own weakness and inability to rein in the Islamist tide and has raised only limited criticisms of the actions of the northern states, further emboldening Islamist ambitions.

The environment created by Islamism's progress in Nigeria has not gone unnoticed by global jihadists. In the wake of the September 11 attacks against the United States, a great outpouring of support for al-Qa'ida was on display in the northern region. Recognizing this atmosphere, in a May 2003 tape Osama bin Ladin named Nigeria as one of six states "most eligible for liberation."

In what could be considered a sign of the times, from December 2003 through January 2004, a group of some 200 militant Islamists calling themselves the "Taliban" waged a brief insurgency, intending to establish an independent Muslim state along Nigeria's border with the Niger Republic. Only after several weeks and after a number of murders by this group was the insurrection crushed by the Nigerian army.

Islamism is well advanced in Nigeria and has the very real potential to engulf the country in full-scale conflict. The Nigerian Nobel Prize winner in Literature, Wole Soyinka, captured the mood best, as quoted by *Nigeria's News* in February 2000: "The roof is already burning over our head . . . the prelude to war, civil war."

Kenya

Across the continent, Kenya—whose 3 million Muslims constitute roughly 10 percent of the population and reside primarily in the North-Eastern Province adjacent to the Somali border and in the Coast Province along the Indian Ocean seaboard—has been experiencing Islamism in a manner not unlike Nigeria but on a smaller scale.

Because of the Horn's geographic proximity to the Arabian Peninsula, Islam arrived early to Kenya (perhaps by the eighth century) principally through commercial exchanges, allowing it to maintain a close connection with the heart of the Muslim world. Still, the Islam that developed retained a distinctive nature that incorporated local religious practices and cultural (mostly Somali and Swahili) attributes, and moderate tendencies prevailed to the present age.

Upon emerging from colonialism in 1963, radical Islam in Kenya was contained by the muscular rule of the Kenya Africa National Union (KANU) party under the leadership of Jomo Kenyatta (1963–1978) and Daniel Arap Moi (1978–2002). At the same time, however, such quasi-dictatorial rule created a climate that convinced some Muslims to see the Islamist order as a desirable alternative. It was only with political liberalization—arising in the context of the first free elections held in 1992 and the first civilian transfer of power in 2002—that Islamists were finally given the freedom needed to advance their agenda.

The life of Shaykh Abdallah Salih al-Farsi features prominently in Islamism's early development there. A Zanzibari by birth who immigrated to Kenya in 1967, Farsi spent part of his spiritual life as a renowned scholar of a prominent East African Sufi order—a status that helped him gain appointment as chief *qadi* (Islamic jurist) of Kenya, a position he held from 1968 to 1980.

In the years that followed his selection, however, Farsi revealed himself as a fierce supporter of Wahhabi ideology, propagating versions of the Koran that he, himself, translated into Kiswahili, in addition to other literature from the Islamist intelligentsia. He also disseminated more than 50 original works that attacked "un-Islamic" religious practices, even becoming a vociferous critic of his former Sufi order. The com-

pilation of these ideas would reach a broad audience throughout East Africa.

The revolution in Iran was a watershed event in Islamism's advance on Kenya, as it was in many other parts of sub-Saharan Africa. In addition to awakening Kenyan Muslims—marginalized during the colonial period and after—to the global Islamic resurgence, it served as inspiration for those who sought radical transformation of their own society.

Hardly covert in its attempt to export its revolution to Kenya, Iran embarked on a campaign to facilitate the spread of Islamism in the country by publishing and distributing literature, convening public lectures, employing mass-media outlets, and inviting young Kenyans to study in Iran. In this, one of its most influential tools has been the monthly magazine *Sauti ya Umma*, printed in Kiswahili by the Foundation for Islamic Thought in Iran.

Libya has also figured prominently in Kenyan Islamism. By the early 1980s, Tripoli was sending Islamic teachers to Kenya and bringing Kenyan students to Libya for study. So strong was Qadhafi's support for unrest in Kenya that in 1987 Moi ordered the Libyan embassy closed and its staff expelled. Also, the hand of Riyadh has been evident through the work of its various NGOs—such as the Islamic Foundation that builds mosques and publishes a quarterly journal, *al-Islam*, in English and Kiswahili.

The Council of Imams and Preachers in Kenya (CIPK) can be considered the face of Kenyan Islamism, under the leadership of its long-time chairman, Shaykh Ali Shee, who in 1990 became head of the Jami'a Mosque, the country's largest Muslim holy site. He began advocating reducing the authority of the chief qadi, claiming the position was too closely tied to the government. In so doing, Shee directly challenged the authority of the established *ulama* (religious clerics), represented in the much larger Supreme Council of Kenyan Muslims (SUPKEM), which holds great sway over the qadi's appointment.

Recognizing the importance of Muslim unity to Islamism's success and hoping to undermine SUPKEM's influence, Shee—a Sunni of Yemeni descent—has called for greater cooperation between Sunni and Shi'a and for establishing stronger ties with Iran. This position led the committee that oversees Jami'a to force his resignation in 1996, but in so doing strengthened his credibility among Kenya's Muslims desiring a unifying force. Although he stepped down as CIPK's chairman in 2005, Shee's legacy lives on within the organization, which is currently led by Shaykh Muhammad Idris.

For its part, SUPKEM was established in 1973 with subsidies from the Islamic Foundation (as well as funding from Libya and Sudan, among other foreign countries) and the intention of unifying Kenya's Muslims. Its past loyalty to KANU, moreover, led the government to recognize it in 1979 as the only organization entitled to represent all Muslims in the country and to maintain links with foreign Islamic organizations. In the face of more recent attempts by other Islamist organizations to discredit it by claiming it was too closely tied to the interests of KANU, however, SUPKEM began to adopt an increasingly independent and Islamist line in the mid-1990s.

SUPKEM, whose leadership is elected every three years, seeks to coordinate the activities of approximately 150 registered Muslim associations through a tightly managed network of district councils set up across the country. Its work program covers the range of religious, political, and social matters. SUPKEM has, for instance, deeply involved itself in Islamic education by recruiting Arab scholars to teach in Kenya and by obtaining scholarships from Arab countries for Kenyan students to study abroad.

In competing over who has the best Islamist credentials, both CIPK and SUPKEM have done battle on numerous fronts. They have opposed the government's efforts to curtail terrorist activity, being vocal critics of measures such as the 2003 Suppression of Terrorism Bill. According to Kenya's *Nation*, they have condemned the investigation of madrasas suspected of harboring terrorists, represented in CIPK Secretary General Muhammad Dor's contention that the move was "influenced by the American government in its bid to suppress Islam." They have also criticized the government's closing of several Islamist charities on suspicion of supporting terrorism.

Kenyan Islamists found their most effective tool, however, to be Christian and secular opposition to the enshrining of qadi courts (Islamic courts) in the national constitution drafted in the years following the first civilian transfer of power in 2002. Such resistance provided Islamists the ammunition necessary to rally Kenyan Muslims to their program and quickly became one of the most divisive issues in Kenyan politics. Ali Shee even went so far as to threaten secession by Muslims in the North-Eastern and Coast Provinces if the courts were rejected.

Even efforts to find a resolution to the qadi courts dispute through democratic processes were portrayed by Islamists as attempts to suppress Islam. The suggestion that the issue become subject to a referendum, as favored by many among the opposition, was brusquely rejected by SUPKEM Secretary General Adan Wachu, who, according to a March 2004 report in *Ecumenical News International*, threatened that Muslims would fight for qadi courts "if it means going through fire or bloodshed."

This tension significantly subsided when, in 2005, the draft constitution was thoroughly defeated in a nationwide referendum widely seen as a confidence vote on the government rather than on the qadi courts. Still, the issue promises to flare up again, as the draft constitution continues to be reviewed with an eye toward making it amenable to a majority of the population.

Threats such as those from Wachu should not be considered idle, as political Islam in Kenya appears only one degree removed from violence. Kenya's porous borders, its proximity to the lawless and war-torn regions of Sudan and Somalia, and the increasingly radical Muslim population have made it inviting to Islamic militants. The 1998 bombing of the U.S. embassy in Nairobi and the 2002 attacks on Israeli targets in Mombassa demonstrate how Kenya is viewed as a soft target by Islamist terrorists, because of the large Western presence in the country.

CIPK itself has been closely tied to militant Islam—its support for which is evidenced by the group's organization of violent pro-Taliban rallies in late 2001. More specifically, according to Jordanian intelligence and statements by UN officials in the region, it is possible that CIPK helped al-Qa'ida set up operations in Kenya. Furthermore, an assessment by the French publication *Intelligence Online* suggests that "it appears improbable" the 2002 attacks in Mombassa "could have been planned without the help of elements gravitating around [CIPK]."

Although not nearly approaching the levels of the Nigerian situation, small signs of Islamism's potential to impinge on the rights of the individual—especially those who are Muslim—emerge. According to a March 2004 report in the *East African Standard*, SUPKEM, for instance, has expressed its

desire to disallow women from dressing in a manner that contravenes Islamic morals. Furthermore, in a possible sign of a larger-scale problem, in 2003 a madrasa was discovered in a Nairobi neighborhood where teenage boys were chained, tortured, and indoctrinated with violent anti-Christian ideas.

Education is an area of particular concern. Distrustful of the government's effort to expand secular education throughout the country, Kenyan Muslims began a program in the 1970s that saw the vast expansion of madrasas. The Islamic education offered, however, fails to equip students with the tools needed to succeed in the emerging modern order, exacerbating an education gap between Muslims and non-Muslims that polarizes society to the advantage of Islamism.

Not surprisingly, efforts to close this gap have been staunchly resisted by Islamists. For instance, according to a February 2004 report in Kenya's *Nation*, offers of funding for the improvement of these madrasas from the U.S. Agency for International Development were rejected in a campaign led by CIPK and the unregistered Islamic Party of Kenya (IPK), whose chairman suggested "an ulterior [anti-Muslim] motive behind the offer."

Thus far attempts by Islamists to organize politically have met with little success. As Kenya approached its first multiparty elections in 1992, Islamist politics began to coalesce around the IPK, led by radical Shaykh Khalid Balala since 1992. Having studied in Saudi Arabia for more than 10 years, Balala became Kenya's chief proponent of Wahhabi-style Islamism, arguing that Islam does not distinguish between religion and state and advocating for the strict application of Shari'a for the country's Muslims.

The fiery Balala—who, according to

Kenyan political observer Arye Oded, received financial backing from Arab and Iranian sources—gained widespread support from the Muslim community and drew many, especially youths, into the Islamist fold. One of the IPK's favorite activities over the past decade and a half has been the organization of mass demonstrations in support of the Islamist issue of the moment that have often led to rioting.

The IPK's influence has waned substantially since the height of its power in the mid-1990s. Nevertheless, it maintains a formidable, if unofficial, position in Muslim society through which it shapes Islamist discourse and policy in a manner similar to CIPK and SUPKEM. The IPK is led by its chairman, Shaykh Khalifa Muhammad—who doubles as organizing-secretary of CIPK—and Secretary General Abd al-Rahman Wandati, while Balala remains its spiritual leader.

By virtue of their strong numbers in the North-Eastern and Coast Provinces and the nature of the Kenyan electoral system, Muslims are of political importance disproportionate to their small numbers nationally. By bringing an increasing segment of this population into the fold, the Islamists have created a bloc significant enough to be courted heavily of late by KANU, which is today the main opposition party. For example, the party recently came out against the "harassment" of Muslims—demanding among other things the rejection of antiterrorist legislation.

Demonstrating the Islamists' restlessness, however, the *East African Standard* reported that CIPK declared in early 2006, "We are tired of being used as mere rubber stamps to propel others to power," and vowed to rally the country's Muslims around a single Muslim candidate in the 2007 presidential elections. Shortly thereafter, CIPK,

SUPKEM, and the IPK came together to announce their support for the bid of MP Najib Balala, who has Islamist sympathies, for that office.

That declaration offers a sign that Kenya's Islamist groups are increasingly willing to consolidate their efforts. If such unity is enhanced in the years ahead, one should expect Islamism to transform progressively the Kenyan political and social landscape.

South Africa

South Africa presents a third type of framework in which Islamists operate in sub-Saharan Africa, deftly exploiting limited opportunities that arise in a country whose 1.5 million Muslims account for only 2 percent of the total population.

Islam arrived comparatively late to South Africa. From the seventeenth through the nineteenth centuries, Muslim slaves, convicts, leaders disruptive of the colonial order in India and the Pacific islands, and later freed slaves from other parts of Africa were transplanted involuntarily into the country. Perhaps growing out of the Dutch colonial legacy that forbade open practice of the religion and because Muslims—almost all of whom were nonwhite—constituted a minority within an already marginalized segment of society, Islam in South Africa was highly decentralized and tended toward quietism for the better part of its history.

This began to change following the Afrikaner (Dutch colonist)–dominated Nationalist Party's consolidation of power in the 1950s, leading, however slowly, to the development of a debate within the Muslim community between those who favored continued separation from the political process and those demanding a confrontation with the apartheid regime's increasingly oppressive policies.

Abdallah Harun, appointed in 1956 as imam of the prominent al-Jami'a Mosque in Capetown, led the break, first organizing humanitarian relief for the oppressed black population and then proselytizing among them. Proclaiming Islam to be a total way of life, Harun saw little distinction between his religious and political commitments and began to mobilize his followers against the apartheid government.

Harun's sway was augmented considerably in 1960, when he became editor of the country's leading Muslim periodical, the *Muslim News*. Through this outlet, he set out to unify South African Muslims by focusing on global Islamist issues, often expounding a vitriolic anti-Israel message. In 1969 Harun was arrested on allegations of working as an agent of the outlawed Pan-African Congress and of sending its members abroad for military training and was murdered by authorities in prison.

By the early 1970s, the growing political awareness for which Harun was initially responsible, especially among the younger generation of Muslims, encouraged the establishment of the first Islamist-oriented organizations in South Africa. This trend was buttressed by the global Islamic resurgence of the same decade that significantly influenced the burgeoning Islamic-political discourse. As it did throughout much of the rest of the continent, Saudi Arabia actively supported the Islamist awakening in South Africa—for example, by funding an umbrella Islamist organization known as the Islamic Council of South Africa that was established in 1975. As elsewhere, the success of the Iranian Revolution provided inspiration to those who sought to impose Islamist ideologies adhered to by a minority within a minority within a minority.

The Muslim Youth Movement (MYM), founded in 1970, sought to challenge the traditionalist ulama—who dominated the Muslim Judicial Council that served a limited role in settling disputes between Muslims—for leadership of the community. In this vein, according to scholar Abdulkader Tayob, the MYM attempted to create the perception of a threat from powerful "un-Islamic" forces to the realization of an Islamic order. This effort was visible in its first leadership training manual, which contained a warning by Hasan al-Banna, founder of the Egyptian Muslim Brotherhood, from many decades earlier: "I would like to avow to you frankly that your message is yet unknown to many people, and that when they know of it and recognize its purpose, they will meet with the severest of opposition and the cruelest enmity."

The MYM was heavily influenced by Abul Ala Mawdudi, Qutb, and other Islamist philosophers. Consequently, it adopted a program based on that of the Muslim Brotherhood—with a focus on education and leadership training—and an organizational structure modeled after the Jama'at-i-Islami of South Asia.

In their early years, the MYM and other like-minded groups (most especially, the South African branch of the Muslim Students Association founded in 1974) remained absent from politics, choosing instead to focus on the Islamization of the Muslim community. Among other activities, the MYM hosted annual leadership training programs at which foreign scholars instructed youths in Islamist ideologies, in addition to less frequent orientation camps and weekly study circles that exposed them to the same. It also established Islamic centers throughout the country and set up its own press through which it inexpensively reproduced Islamist literature disseminated through a chain of bookshops financed by a loan from WAMY, explains Tayub.

By the early 1980s, however, greater political upheaval arising from the increasingly powerful antiapartheid movement led to a noticeable break from the past practice of eschewing politics. Recognizing that remaining on the sideline in this fight would leave them in a poor position to effect any change in the country, the MYM and its brethren began drawing closer to the secular opposition by promoting the idea that the Islamist program could be contextualized to agree with South African conditions, including support for democracy.

Far from attempting to transform society along revolutionary lines, then, the Islamist agenda would henceforth remain largely within the parameters of what could be digested by their newfound allies. The move would pay off, as this partnership has afforded Islamists significant influence within the African National Congress (ANC) that has governed South Africa since 1994.

Despite their tempered program, the Islamists have nevertheless pressed their campaign to alter South African society by identifying narrow targets of opportunity. Recognizing the impossibility of effecting the full implementation of Shari'a, for instance, Islamists set out to oust the apartheid regime to secure the legal recognition of limited aspects of Shari'a that could be applied to South Africa's Muslims in the areas of marriage, custody, and divorce. This push for the institutionalization of Muslim personal law (MPL) met with no opposition from the ANC, perhaps as a reward to proponents of MPL who had contributed to the antiapartheid struggle and undoubtedly to gain their support in future elections.

Toward this end, a government-sponsored MPL Board (later replaced by the Project Committee on MPL) was established in 1994 to determine the nature and scope of MPL. However, a stark ideological divide between its members has deadlocked the process, with pragmatists favoring bringing MPL into line with rights guaranteed by the South African constitution, and the more hard-line Islamists arguing that Shari'a is divine and cannot be modified by any man-made document.

Despite their limited capacity to transform South African society, Islamists have achieved measurably greater success on global Islamist issues, which are of little concern to the broader population that generally defers on these matters to what can be identified as an Islamist foreign policy. This has, importantly, been a unifying force among the disparate groups.

The brunt of this effort is focused on cultivating anti-U.S. and anti-Israel sentiment, as Islamists of all persuasions regularly join together to host demonstrations against the two and to meet with government officials to discuss related issues. That the Islamist line is often adopted by the ANC is evident. For instance, upon receiving a memorandum from a coalition of Islamist groups upset with Israel's efforts to combat terrorism in 2005, South Africa's deputy minister of foreign affairs, Aziz Pahad, told *Al-Jazeera Online*, "I can ensure [*sic*] you your government is totally committed to the just cause of the Palestinians and we will continue doing everything to ensure that the Palestinian cause is successful."

This influence even reaches the highest levels of the country's political establishment. Following the terrorist attacks of September 11, an Islamist backlash— manifest in large demonstrations opposing U.S.-led strikes against the Taliban and al-Qa'ida—to Nelson Mandela's determination that Osama bin Ladin's al-Qa'ida network should be "smashed" persuaded the former president to recant, later apologizing for views that were "one-sided and overstated," according to a January 2002 CNS News report.

The published reaction—quoted by Charlotte A. Quinn and Frederick Quinn in *Pride, Faith, and Fear: Islam in Sub-Saharan Africa*—of the Jami'at al-Ulama (JU, Council of Theologians) in KwaZulu-Natal (KZN) Province to the attacks provides perhaps the greatest insight into the position and objective of the Islamist foreign policy:

> It is indeed a great pity that ordinary civilians become victims of political deception and duplicity. They are the innocent pawns who pay the price of embargos, sanctions, murder, and pillage on behalf of their political masters. . . . We must guard against falling prey to internal conflict within the Umma, by debating the integrity of the Taliban, by questioning the legitimacy of their rule; this is not the time for Muslim discord and bickering.

JU is one of the more prominent Islamist organizations in South Africa and is strongly influenced by the Deobandi-inspired fundamentalist Tablighi Jama'at, which Ebrahim Moosa, the foremost scholar on Islamic affairs in South Africa, maintains is one of the fastest-growing religious movements in the country. JU's membership consists of "qualified" ulama that are well organized at the provincial level but more loosely knit nationally, with its strongest branches located in KZN and Gauteng.

Through its fatwa department, JU's ideology strictly promotes the line that Shi'a are apostates and it advocates segregation of the sexes. This creates friction with other Islamist and Muslim groups pressing for inclusiveness. Further, it proclaims that suicide bombers are "evil but this evil is opposed by a greater evil for which there is no adequate substitute, therefore, their act will be justified as lesser of the two evils in terms of Islamic law."

Currently led by Harun Abasoomar, JU (KZN) engages the community particularly effectively through its various agencies, which include judicial, social welfare, and public relations committees. To spread its message even further, JU operates the radio station Radio Islam—which, prior to a threat from the government to shut it down, had refused to allow women on the air—and issues an assortment of publications. According to the organization, however, education and the establishment of madrasas have been of "primary importance."

The Islamist penetration of education is an area of increasing concern to authorities. The country's large South Asian Muslim population has made South Africa a natural spot for the illegal relocation of students and teachers displaced by the closing of extremist madrasas in their home countries, especially Pakistan and Malaysia. Muslim officials in South Africa report a surge in construction of new madrasas to accommodate this influx, and government officials have expressed worries that international terror networks may be operating out of these.

One organization above all has served as the face of Islamism in South Africa. Qibla was established in 1977 by associates of the MYM and MSA who were disaffected by the lack of vigor with which Islamism was being applied. When the model presented itself two years later in Iran, the group began working to promote the aims of that revolution in South Africa under the banner "One solution, Islamic revolution," and is, according to South African terrorism expert

Anneli Botha, manipulated by Iranian intelligence. Unlike many other Islamist groups in the country, Qibla rejects adjusting the Islamist agenda to the country's status quo and thus remains an opponent of the ANC government.

The ultrasecretive Qibla is organized into small cells that seek to penetrate and gain sway over other Islamic groups. In the early 1990s, the fiery Ahmad Cassiem assumed leadership of Qibla and set out to unify the Islamist movement behind his outfit. In 1994 Qibla created the Islamic Unity Convention (IUC), which claims to serve as an umbrella organization for over 250 Islamic groups operating in South Africa. To spread its message, the IUC set up Radio 786 in 1995 to voice support for terrorist organizations and deny the Holocaust. Furthermore, the IUC is perhaps the greatest player in organizing rallies that support the spectrum of Islamist causes.

While the activities of these groups are largely nonviolent, they have demonstrated a willingness to try the alternative approach when conditions appear permissible. Around late 1996, Qibla's infiltration of the popular People Against Gangsterism and Drugs (PAGAD)—set up a year earlier as a community advocacy group to confront rampant criminal activity in the Western Cape—reached a level that allowed it to gain sway over the organization.

Under Qibla's control, the well-organized PAGAD—which has legal, education, and social welfare departments, among others—initially engaged the Muslim community primarily by convening anticrime rallies intended to create broad-based opposition to those things deemed un-Islamic. Covertly, however, PAGAD developed an underground structure of militant cells known as the G-Force. These units carried out hundreds

of acts of violence over the following years, including some against the United States and other Western targets. Although the arrest of many of its members and the turning of public opinion against PAGAD have brought these attacks to a halt, it is reasonable to believe the organization will resume its violent campaign if it again senses an amenable climate.

International terrorists have also made use of South Africa, albeit largely for fund-raising and money laundering rather than training and recruiting. The country, in fact, has been an integral part of the route in al-Qa'ida's trade of African gemstones used to finance its global activities. As acknowledged by South African intelligence minister Ronnie Kasrils in the *Armed Forces Journal* in February 2006, "The activities of suspected international terrorists have been an area of focus of the South African Intelligence Services for some time."

Islamism in South Africa is weak relative to its position in many other sub-Saharan countries, primarily because of the small Muslim population available to be leveraged to achieve its objectives. Yet, when able to unify on issues of little concern to the broader population, the Islamists have demonstrated a remarkable ability to influence the position of the government and the direction of society, although the prospect for increased cooperation on issues beyond foreign affairs remains unclear.

Conclusions and Indications for the Future

The motivation for, and aim of, Islamism's advance on sub-Saharan Africa remains as once described by the movement's most prominent theoretician, Sayyid Qutb, quoted by scholars A.H. Abdel Salam and Alex de Waal:

> When Islam entered the central parts of Africa, it clothed naked human beings, civilized them, brought them out of the deep recesses of isolation. . . . It brought them out of the narrow circles of tribe and clan into the vast circle of the Islamic community.

As observed in the three countries examined in this chapter, Islamism is by no means uniformly achieving its goal. Yet it unvaryingly maximizes the opportunities presented through a general pattern that first works toward the Islamization of society, then co-opts this awakened population by creating a perception of the existence of threats to the Islamic order.

Not only has Islamism become a permanent feature of the region's landscape, but the future also appears favorable for its continued expansion. The weakness of African governments inhibits them from addressing conditions that draw Muslims to the movement, and foreign states have demonstrated little willingness to curtail the export of extremist ideologies to Africa.

The likely result will be the further transformation of a moderate and integrated Muslim population into one that is ever more radical and isolated from its non-Muslim neighbors. Along the way, Islamism's rise will entail an erosion of individual rights and present a challenge to the authority of African governments. It will lead to intrafaith conflict between moderates and extremists while generating progressively unmanageable intercommunal strife between Muslims and non-Muslims. Additionally, it will create an increasingly hospitable environment for the operation of Islamist terror networks. Let there be

no doubt: Islamism is on the march in sub-Saharan Africa.

BIBLIOGRAPHY

Abdel Salam, A.H., and Alex de Waal, "On the Failure and Persistence of Jihad." In *Islamism and Its Enemies in the Horn of Africa*, ed. Alex de Waal, 21–70. Bloomington: Indiana University Press, 2004.

Botha, Anneli. "PAGAD: A Case Study of Radical Islam in South Africa." *Terrorism Monitor* 3:15 (July 28, 2005).

Brenner, Louis, ed. *Muslim Identity and Social Change in Sub-Saharan Africa.* Bloomington: Indiana University Press, 1993.

Brown, Karima. "SA Fears al-Qaeda Men Hiding in Local Schools." *Independent Online* (October 4, 2004). www.iol.co.za/index.php?set_id=1&click_id=13&art_id=vn20041004100210304C720798.

Burns, Jim. "Mandela Changes View of Bin Laden." *CNSNews.com* (January 2, 2002). www.cnsnews.com/ViewForeignBureaus.asp?Page=\ForeignBureaus\archive\200201\FOR20020102f.html.

Center for Religious Freedom, ed. *The Talibanization of Nigeria: Radical Islam, Extremist Sharia Law, and Religious Freedom.* Washington, DC: Freedom House, 2002.

Constantin, Francois. "Muslims & Politics: The Attempts to Create Muslim National Organizations in Tanzania, Uganda & Kenya." In *Religion and Politics in East Africa*, ed. Holger Bernt Hansen and Michael Twaddle, 19–31. Athens: Ohio University Press, 1995.

De Waal, Alex, ed. *Islamism and Its Enemies in the Horn of Africa.* Bloomington: Indiana University Press, 2004.

Drogin, Bob, and Greg Miller. "Tape Urges All Muslims to Defend Iraq." *Los Angeles Times*, February 12, 2003.

Hill, Geoffrey. "'Madrassas' a Concern in South Africa." *Washington Times*, October 17, 2003.

Hunwick, John. "Sub-Saharan Africa and the Wider World of Islam." In *African Islam and Islam in Africa: Encounters Between Sufis and Islamists*, ed. Eva Evers Rosander and David Westerlund, 39. Athens: Ohio University Press, 1997.

Loimeier, Roman. "Patterns and Peculiarities of Islamic Reform in Africa." *Journal of Religion in Africa* 33:3 (2003).

Marshall, Paul. "Radical Islam's Move on Africa." *Washington Post*, October 16, 2003.

Mayoyo, Patrick. "Support from US Is Suspect, Say Muslims." *Nation* (Kenya), February 25, 2004.

McGreal, Chris. "Mood Ugly as Nigeria's Mullahs Lay Down Laws." *Tribune* (India), October 27, 1999.

Miles, William F.S. "*Shari'a* as De-Africanization: Evidence from Hausaland." *Africa Today* 50:1 (Spring/Summer 2003): 60.

"Minister's Remarks on Dress Queried." *East African Standard*, March 11, 2004.

Moosa, Ebrahim. "Worlds 'Apart': The Tabligh Jamat Under Apartheid 1963–1993." *Journal of Islamic Studies* 17 (1997): 28–48.

"Muslims to Demonstrate Over Kadhi Courts." *East African Standard*, April 24, 2003.

"Muslims to Go for the Presidency." *East African Standard*, January 22, 2006.

Mustapha, Mahmud. "Kano Shias Under Wahabi Threat." *Gamji.com*, undated. www.gamji .com/article5000/NEWS5105.htm.

Nzwili, Fredrick. "Kenyan Christians Angered by Place of Islamic Courts in Constitution." *Ecumenical News International*, March 18, 2004.

Oded, Arye. *Islam & Politics in Kenya*. Boulder, CO: Lynne Rienner, 2000.

Ostien, Philip, Jamila M. Nasir, and Franz Kogelmann, eds. *Comparative Perspectives on Shari'ah in Nigeria*. Abuja, Nigeria: Spectrum Books Limited, 2005.

Ottoway, David B. "U.S. Eyes Money Trails of Saudi-Backed Charities." *Washington Post*, August 19, 2004.

"Polio Boycott Is 'Unforgivable.'" *BBC News Online*, February 26, 2004. http://news.bbc .co.uk/2/hi/africa/3488806.stm.

Quinn, Charlotte A., and Frederick Quinn. *Pride, Faith, and Fear: Islam in Sub-Saharan Africa*. Oxford, UK: Oxford University Press, 2003.

Rosander, Eva Evers, and David Westerlund, eds. *African Islam and Islam in Africa: Encounters Between Sufis and Islamists*. Athens: Ohio University Press, 1997.

Salih, Mohamed M.A. "Islamic N.G.O.s in Africa." In *Islamism and its Enemies in the Horn of Africa*, ed. Alex de Waal, 146–81. Bloomington: Indiana University Press, 2004.

Shillinger, Kurt. "Al-Qaeda in Southern Africa: The Emergence of a New Front on the War on Terrorism." *Armed Forces Journal*, February 1, 2006. www.armedforcesjournal .com/2006/02/183653/.

Tape, Nurah. "S Africans Decry Threats to al-Aqsa." *Al-Jazeera Online* (May 25, 2005). http:// english.aljazeera.net/NR/exeres/D15F2C2B-38CA-48B1–800A-3AA1288375FD.htm.

Tayob, Abdulkader. *Islamic Resurgence in South Africa: The Muslim Youth Movement*. Cape Town, SA: UCT Press Ltd., 1995.

"This is the Prelude to War—Soyinka." *The News* (Nigeria), February 29, 2000.

Umar, Muhammad Sani. "From Sufism to Anti-Sufism in Nigeria." In *Muslim Identity and Social Change in Sub-Saharan Africa*, ed. Louis Brenner, 155–78. Bloomington: Indiana University Press, 1993.

"Wahhabi Networks in Mombasa." *Intelligence Online*, December 18, 2002. www .intelligenceonline.com/archives/p_som_ archives.asp?num=442&year=2008.

Somalia

Moshe Terdman

Somalia has a long and intimate history with Islam. However, the country's social structure and organization—including the low level of urbanization, the coexistence of pastoral production systems in a large part of the country and agriculture in the interriverine area, and a system of clanship—have shaped a form of Islam distinct from that of other countries in the Horn of Africa.

Religious Sufi orders (*turuk*) have played a significant role in Somali Islam. Sufi orders appeared in Somali towns during the fifteenth century and rapidly became a revitalizing force. Three Sufi orders have been prominent in Somalia: the Qadiriyya, the Idrisiyya, and the Salihiyya. The Rifa'iyya, an offshoot of the Qadiriyya, was represented mainly among Arabs resident in Mogadishu.

Although Islam has been prevalent in Somalia since the ninth century and 99 percent of the population is Muslim, there is a major difference in social practices within the country. The Islamic ideal is a society organized for the implementation of Muslim precepts in which there is no distinction between the secular and the religious spheres. Among Somalis this ideal has been approximated less fully in the north than among some groups in the settled regions of the south, where religious leaders were at one time an integral part of the social and political structure. Among nomads, the exigencies of pastoral life gave greater weight to the warrior's role, and religious leaders were expected to remain detached from political matters. This phenomenon explains the existence of a democratic regime in Somaliland, in which the religious scholars do not have a say and which fights radical Islam successfully.

In Somalia it had been difficult to adapt Islam to the social, economic, and political changes that began with the expansion of colonial rule in the late nineteenth century. One response was to stress a return to orthodox Muslim traditions and to oppose Westernization totally. The Sufi orders were at the forefront of this movement, personified in Somalia by Muhammad Abdallah Hasan in the early 1900s. Generally, the leaders of the Sufi orders opposed the spread of Western education. Another response was to reform Islam by reinterpreting it. Hence, reformers attempted to prove that Muslim scriptures contain all elements needed for dealing with modernization. Islamic socialism, identified particularly with the Egyptian nationalist Gamal Abdel Nasser, belongs to this school of thought. His ideas appealed to a number of Somalis, especially those who had studied in Cairo in the 1950s and 1960s.

The 1961 constitution guaranteed freedom of religion but also declared the newly independent Somalia to be an Islamist state. The first two postindependence governments paid lip service to the principles of Islamic socialism but made relatively few changes. Yet the coup of October 21, 1969, installed a radical regime committed to profound change. This regime preached scientific socialism, which it claimed was based on the altruistic values that inspired genuine Islam. According to the regime, religious leaders were to leave secular affairs to the regime, which strove for goals that conformed to Islamic principles. Soon after, the government arrested several protesting religious leaders and accused them of disseminating counterrevolutionary propaganda and of conniving with reactionary elements in the Arabian Peninsula. The authorities also dismissed several members of religious tribunals for corruption and incompetence.

The campaign for scientific socialism intensified in 1972. On the occasion of Idd al-Adha, the Somali president defined scientific socialism as half practical work and half ideological belief. He declared that work and belief were compatible with Islam because the Koran condemned exploitation and money lending and urged compassion, unity, and cooperation among Muslims. He stressed the distinction between religion as an ideological instrument for the manipulation of power and as a moral force. Religion, according to President Siyyad Barre, was an integral part of the Somali worldview, but it belonged in the private sphere, whereas scientific socialism dealt with material concerns such as poverty. Thus, religious leaders should exercise their moral influence but refrain from interfering in political or economic matters.

In early January 1975, evoking the message of equality, justice, and social progress contained in the Koran, Siyyad Barre announced a new family law that gave women the right to an inheritance on an equal basis with men. Some Somalis believed the law was proof that the regime wanted to undermine the basic structure of Islamic society. In Mogadishu, 23 religious leaders protested in their mosques. They were arrested and charged with acting at the instigation of a foreign power and with violating state security; 10 were executed. Most religious leaders, however, kept silent, though some religious people who were already concerned by the growth of Somali cooperation with communist countries thought that the military regime would eventually lead Somali society toward atheism.

Nevertheless, the most crucial factor in the rise of Islamism in Somalia was not to be found in the political debates, though they did play an important role in triggering a new Islamic consciousness. Rather, it was because Somalia did not remain the isolated country it had been. In February 1974, Somalia became a member of the Arab League, mostly to get increased international aid and diplomatic support against Ethiopia. Through grants and scholarships, this decision helped to increase the number of students trained in foreign religious institutions, not only in the still-quiet Sudan but also at al-Azhar in Egypt and in Saudi Arabia, where new Islamist trends were developing. This dynamic was not reversed by Somalia's alignment with the West after the Somali army was defeated in the Ogaden War of 1977–78. On the contrary, Islamism was invigorated during this period. The Iranian Revolution in

1979 and its effect on the Arab countries fostered the development of political Islam throughout the region. In the 1980s, this alignment was strengthened by the United Arab Emirates becoming an important trading partner, though to a lesser extent than Saudi Arabia or Italy. Flights connected the two countries twice a week, and the movement of people from Somalia to the Gulf States increased.

The Rise of Islamism

Somali Islamism can be traced to a common source, Wahdat al-Shabab al-Islami (Islamic Youth Unity, known in Somali as Waxda) and Jama'at Ahl al-Islami (also known as al-Ahli Group). Waxda was established in August 1969 in Hargeysa, the capital of the former British colony of Somaliland. It was an Islamic institution whose teachings referred to Sayyid Qutb, Abul Ala Mawdudi, Abu al-Hasan al-Nadawi, and other Islamist thinkers. When the secularist trend became prominent in the regime, the group went underground and started publishing leaflets against the "socialist" regime. In 1978, in the aftermath of the defeat in Ogaden, dozens of members were arrested and jailed in southern Somalia. After the national Somali army destroyed most of Hargeysa and Burao in 1988, Waxda started up again in the refugee camps in Ethiopia. The group supported the Somali National Movement (SNM), which was leading the struggle against the regime in Somaliland. After 1991, when Somaliland declared its independence again, this group became deeply involved with educational institutions, maintaining close links with Kuwait.

The other group, Jama'at Ahl al-Islami, was founded by Shaykh Muhammad Mu'alim after he received his religious degrees from al-Azhar. This important figure of Somali Islam was Qadiri and initiated *tafsir* (commentary on the Koran) at the Abd al-Qadir mosque in Mogadishu with modern references and a wish to address contemporary issues. After the religious scholars became openly critical of the regime in 1975, many followers were arrested, and Ahli disbanded completely. Some members who escaped to Saudi Arabia set up a new group under the leadership of Shaykh Muhammad Ahmad Garyare that became known as Jam'at Islah. This group was the first and only one to be acquainted with the Muslim Brotherhood.

With time, other groups, more radical in their approach, arose in Mogadishu. Takfir wal-Hijra already had a few followers. By 1980 a new group of former religious students of Saudi institutions established a group called Salafism, characterized by a strong adhesion to Wahhabism. This growth of Islamist groups, especially in Mogadishu, but in other urban centers too, meant that an Islamist trend was growing among the urban youths.

Nevertheless, Islamism was too weak then to appear as an alternative to the regime. Its organizations were not strong enough and could not effectively appeal to large sections of the population, especially the rural communities and nomads who had a very different understanding of Islam and politics. As the framework for political activities became increasingly clan based, Islamic militants had little to offer. Moreover, although political Islam was not marginal in the 1980s, it could not get support from large portions of the youth and urban populations. The reasons are linked not only to the social fabric of Somali society (clanship) but to other factors as well. For example, its leading figures were considered too young, lacking the moral authority of clan elders. Furthermore, their propaganda was seen as too alien to Somali society.

With the government's collapse in 1991, Islamists experienced unprecedented freedom. An array of Islamic associations suddenly emerged, each representing a discrete religious doctrine. Their common denominator was the desire for an "authentic" form of Islamic governance in Somalia. To a certain extent, the differences between Somalia's Islamist groups were doctrinal: Traditionalists resisted the encroachment of what they considered to be alien reformist strands of Islamic thought. Among the reformists, there was friction between modernist thinkers affiliated with the Muslim Brotherhood and conservative groups inspired by Salafism. Moreover, conventional Salafists disapproved of those from their ranks who embraced political and military action.

Such distinctions, however, are only part of the picture. As the French scholar Roland Marchal has observed, many Somali Islamist groups share the same intellectual reference points, including Muhammad ibn Abd al-Wahhab, Hasan al-Banna, and Sayyid Qutb. Therefore, there are no clear-cut doctrinal or ideological boundaries between them, and sympathizers may shift from one group to another. The reason there are so many of these groups is because of the numerous differences among them on issues such as ablution, age of marriage, and so forth. Rituals more than ideology have been the bone of contention. Even more important in distinguishing one group from another has been the character of the leadership and the dominant clan affiliation of the members. In this respect, the behavior of the Islamist groups has differed little from that of the more "secular" and overtly political factions competing to fill the power vacuum left by the disintegration of the state: They have cooperated little, entering into opportunistic and short-lived alliances; they have quar-

reled and split, often along clan lines; and members have moved with relative freedom from one group to another.

Islamic Associations and Organizations

As elsewhere in the Muslim world, there have been three main currents prevalent in Somali Islamic activism since 1991: political, missionary, and Salafi-jihadi. The behavior of Somali Islamist groups is characterized by competition and disaccord. They are neither uniformly anti-Western nor hostile to Somalia's neighbors, and only a tiny minority has been associated with terrorist violence.

Three main groups are affiliated with the political Islamism category: Harakat al-Islah, Ahl al-Sunna wal-Jama'a, and Majma Ulimadda Islaamka ee Soomaaliya. Harakat al-Islah (The Reform Movement) originated in 1978 as a loose network of affiliated underground groups, borrowing its vision from the Muslim Brotherhood. Today, it publicly professes its commitment to the basic tenets of democracy and cultural pluralism. Its stated commitment to this philosophy of inclusion is enshrined in the organization's social makeup and mode of action. The organization's forward-looking views on religion and politics and attempts to reconcile the tenets of Islam with the modern notion of democracy are apparent in its internal structure. Members of its "High Council" are elected by Majlis al-Shura for five years and limited to a maximum of two terms. Al-Islah's democratic credentials, however, have so far failed to translate into broad public support. In effect, it remains a relatively small organization dominated by a highly educated urban elite whose professional, middle-class status and extensive expatriate experiences are alien to most Somalis.

With the overthrow of the Barre dictatorship, al-Islah has come out of the shadows and has operated exclusively for the promotion of social and humanitarian activities. Al-Islah members play prominent roles in the state's educational apparatuses. Its current leadership comprises Ali Shaykh (the president of Mogadishu University), who serves as the chairman; Abdirahman Baadiyo, the vice chairman; and Ibrahim Dusuqi, who is the secretary general. Al-Islah has nothing to do with radical Islam. On the contrary, its leaders condemn violence and *takfir* (the practice of proclaiming fellow Muslims to be heretics) as un-Islamic and counterproductive. They have long called for building a shared future that transcends the extremism and bigotry embodied in the Salafi-jihadi groups.

Ahl al-Sunna wal-Jama'a (ASWJ) is another modern political Islamist group, comprising traditional Somali Sufi leaders, created in 1991 as an offshoot of Majma Ulimadda Islaamka ee Soomaaliya to counter the influence of the most radical Islamist trends. The movement brings together politically motivated shaykhs whose primary goal is to unify the Sufi community under one leadership capable of consolidating the powers of the three main Sufi orders into one front. Its sole mission is the rejuvenation of the "traditionalist" interpretation of Islam and the delegitimization of the beliefs and political views of the radical Islamist movements. The organization remained little known until 2002, when it reinvented itself as a modern political umbrella group under which politically motivated shaykhs from the Sufi orders could join to espouse a traditionalist interpretation of Islam. Its most important activity is to preach a message of peace and delegitimize the beliefs and political platform of any radical movement. On this basis, the group's leadership began to

play an active role at the Somali peace talks in Kenya, where it campaigned against the inclusion of radical Islamist groups.

The third political Islamist group is Majma Ulimadda Islaamka ee Soomaaliya. It represents an assembly of Islamic scholars who follow the Shafi'i school of law and whose main goal is the establishment of a Somali government that will rule in accordance with the Shafi'i school of law's interpretation of Shari'a. In the early 1990s, it became involved in a variety of peace initiatives. Since then, it has concentrated more and more on performing basic social functions, such as religious education and engagement and marriage services. Although it has remained detached from politics, its commitment to the realization of Shari'a is manifest in its support for the Islamic Courts Union. The organization has been led by Shaykh Ahmad Abdi Dhi'isow since the death of its founding chairman, Shaykh Muhammad Ma'alim Hasan in 2001. He heads an executive committee of 11 members, many of them clerics who served in government mosques under the previous regime. The group's total membership is estimated to be between 200 and 300 and comprises religious leaders from most clans and regions of Somalia.

There are differences of view among the three political Islamist groups concerning the nature of the state, but a general consensus seems to have developed among them about the need to apply a certain interpretation of Islam within a modern framework of government.

Missionary Islamists largely avoid engaging in political activism—even if their brand of activism has some political objectives and implications. This current is represented by Salafiyya Jadida and the most structured movement in Somalia, Jama'at al-Tabligh.

Not much is known about the Salafiyya

Jadida movement. However, it is best exemplified by Shaykh Ali Wajis, a prominent Salafi ideologue who has gone from supporting and briefly leading the Salafi-jihadi group al-Itihaad al-Islaami to opposing its violent dogmatic theology. Wajis's qualified repudiation of the jihadi ideology and his reexamination of its theoretical position in light of a rational reassessment of the Islamic rules of warfare and the prevailing realities on the ground exemplify the fractures rocking the jihadi and Islamist movements. It is also an encouraging sign of the debate occurring within the new Salafi and Salafi-jihadi circles concerning the need for a contextualized understanding of the issues of jihad and political violence.

The Tabligh movement, launched in India in 1926 by Jama'at al-Da'wa wal-Tabligh (the Group for Preaching and Propagation) as an apolitical, quietist movement, constitutes the largest group of religious proselytizers in Somalia. It owns the largest mosques and centers of instruction. Tablighi missionaries' aggressive and dedicated peaceful and apolitical preaching tactics are part of the reason for the great increase in the number of Tablighi sympathizers and supporters. This notable success in recruitment and significant growth in membership left the movement wide open to infiltration and manipulation by radical groups. Out of the 500 to 700 foreign shaykhs present in Somalia, many are from the Arab world, but they also come from Afghanistan, Pakistan, Chechnya, and other regions. Given the size and heterogeneity of the movement, its infiltration by jihadi elements should come as no surprise.

The Salafi-jihadi current represents the third type of Islamist activity. Unlike the political and missionary currents, Salafi-jihadi activists are committed to violence, because they are involved in what they consider to be the defense of dar al-Islam (The Muslim world) and the community of believers against infidel enemies. In Somalia, this form of Islamist activism has very few sympathizers, although it is actively involved in trying to recruit or infiltrate missionary organizations such as Salafiyya Jadida and the Tabligh movement. Its fortunes have ebbed and flowed over the years.

This current was represented by al-Itihaad al-Islaami (AIAI). In fact, AIAI did not start out as a jihadi organization, and its gradual embrace of extremism and militancy proved divisive and ultimately self-destructive. From its formation in the early 1980s to its peak in 1992, the movement's failure to attain its objective of a pan-Somali, Salafi emirate resulted in its steady and involuntary decline. By 2005 it had essentially ceased to exist. A few "alumni" of the organization, however, went on to establish a new and ruthless jihadi network with links to al-Qa'ida and no clear political aims.

The background for the establishment of AIAI was the steady growth of the Salafiyya during the 1970s. One of the most successful Wahhabi centers emerged at Eel Hindi, a suburb of Mogadishu. The group, al-Jama'a al-Islamiyya, considered itself a Salafi society concentrating on "purification of the faith." Several of the group's clerics became renowned for the instruction in *tafsir* they offered after evening prayers, and their mosques were often full. Its most prominent imams were Shaykh Dahir Indhabuur, Shaykh Abdallah Ali Hashi, and Shaykh Abd al-Qadir Ga'amey—all of whom later became prominent as leaders of al-Itihaad. During the early 1980s, the leadership of al-Jama'a developed a relationship with Wahdat al-Shabab al-Islamiyya, a northern Somali Islamist group popular among secondary school teachers and students in Hargeysa and Burao. Although essentially Wahhabi in its outlook and teachings, al-Wahdat also drew inspiration from the Muslim Brotherhood—especially in its emphasis on education and the promotion of a public social role for women. Among the leaders was a Muslim cleric from the northern town of Burao, educated in Saudi Arabia, Shaykh Ali Warsame, who went on to become a key figure in al-Itihaad.

The merger of the two organizations at some point between 1982 and 1984 brought with it the new name of al-Itihaad al-Islaami (AIAI). In practice, however, the organizations retained their identities, and toward the end of the 1980s, al-Wahdat reemerged as a distinctly northern entity with only a few members—Warsame among them—retaining their AIAI affiliation. In Mogadishu, AIAI soon began to attract attention both for its growing popularity and for its radical new message. The movement's visibility grew as its membership expanded to include faculty and students at secondary schools, colleges, and the Somali National University.

AIAI's assertion that Islam could not be separated from politics offered a bold challenge to the regime at a time when Barre's "revolution" had run out of steam. It also challenged Somalia's Sufi orders, ridiculing their emphasis on spirituality and disparaging some of their traditional practices as un-Islamic. In return, Sufi leaders denounced AIAI adherents as "innovators" and labeled the movement *"al-Saruriyyin"*—an epithet referring to the disciples of Shaykh Muhammad Zayn al-Abidin Sarur, a Saudi religious dissident expelled from the kingdom for his radical teachings. Toward the end of the 1980s, tensions between the Salafists and the Sufis began to overflow from the mosques into the streets. Clashes between youths from the two groups were common and occasionally cost lives.

Following the collapse of the Barre regime, northeastern Somalia had fallen under control of the Somali Salvation Democratic Front (SSDF). The seat of the SSDF administration was the port town of Bosasso. With the tacit blessing of the SSDF chairman, General Muhammad Abshir Musa, AIAI took control of strategic facilities across the northeast, including the Bosasso port and hospital. They also established a large base near Qaw, some twenty kilometers west of Bosasso. Modeled on training facilities in Afghanistan, it was known as Nasr al-Din and rapidly became the hub of AIAI activity in the region. By mid-1991, an estimated 1,000 AIAI militia members were based in the region. AIAI derived part of its revenue from Bosasso port charges but got much more from foreign donors, including the Saudi charities the Muslim World League (MWL) and the International Islamic Relief Organization (IIRO). On the morning of June 19, 1992, al-Itihaad's forces in Garoowe sealed the roads leading to and from the town and seized control of a former military compound on the outskirts, where the SSDF leadership was in session. At the same time, they attacked three locations throughout the northeast, including Bosasso. With the leadership of the SSDF and the key strategic towns of the regions in their hands, they declared a new Islamic administration for the northeast. AIAI's Islamic emirate was short lived. SSDF forces, supported by hastily assembled militias from local clans, responded quickly and effectively. Hundreds of AIAI militia and their leaders were killed, and the movement was routed. By June 26, 1992, over 600 AIAI militia members had been killed, and no jihadi fighters remained in SSDF-controlled areas of the northeast.

Following this failed attempt to create an Islamic emirate, a second attempt was conducted, this time in the Gedo region, near the Ethiopian border. The AIAI first established a presence in Luuq, the principal town of Gedo region, in August 1992. Over the next few years, it emerged as the preeminent military and political force in Gedo, largely thanks to the order and discipline it represented in the otherwise lawless and chaotic environment. The new administration banned the carrying of weapons by private citizens, guaranteed a measure of security, and persuaded a number of international NGOs and donors to carry out activities. However, the Islamists' efficiency did not translate into popularity. Edicts such as those calling for strict implementation of Shari'a law and the banning of *khat* (a narcotic plant native of East Africa and the Arabian Peninsula) were unpopular.

Just as AIAI's influence in northeastern Somalia had brought the movement into conflict with the SSDF, its presence in Gedo antagonized the Somali National Front (SNF), a politico-military faction anchored in the Marehaan clan. The SNF found an ally in the Ethiopian government, which had long sought to eliminate AIAI presence in the Somali-inhabited "Fifth Region" of Ethiopia. In communications with Ethiopia, the SNF alleged that AIAI camps near Luuq and Armo were training Islamist guerillas from Somalia, Ethiopia, Eritrea, Kenya, and Uganda in a variety of activities that included the use of small arms, guerilla warfare, mines and explosives, espionage, and logistics. According to the SNF, the camps were financed in part by an Islamic NGO based in Dublin, Mercy International Relief Agency (MIRA).

The most virulent strain of AIAI militancy emerged in Ethiopia, where the movement's armed struggle against Ethiopian control over Somali-inhabited territories in the east culminated in a series of terrorist attacks in Addis Ababa and Dire Dawa. In

1990, or even earlier, al-Itihaad al-Islaami ee Soomaaliya Galbeed (the Islamic Union of Western Somalia) began to agitate for the liberation of the Ogaden. It envisioned the reunification of all Somali territories within a single polity. Yet its objectives included an Islamic political order based on a narrow interpretation of the Koran and the Sunna (tradition). The organization described itself as a front for *da'wa* (the call to Islam) and jihad and cast its struggle in terms of the liberation of Muslims from a Christian oppressor. The organization continued to develop its military wing, building a fleet of gun-mounted four-wheel-drive vehicles and maintaining training facilities at various facilities in the Ogaden. AIAI fighters made their presence known throughout the region by steadily escalating guerilla actions. As a result, Ethiopian forces stepped up ground and air attacks on AIAI along the Somali borders in late 1993 and early 1994. In December 1994, Ethiopian military pressure appeared to be paying off when al-Itihaad agreed to meet with the Ethiopian regime's representatives for peace talks, which broke down in March 1995. The breakdown of the peace talks signaled the resumption of hostilities between the two sides.

The collapse of the talks heralded a new phase in al-Itihaad's campaign against Ethiopian rule. In May 1995, a grenade attack at a busy outdoor market in Dire Dawa, Ethiopia's second-largest city, claimed 15 lives. Eight men, all alleged members of AIAI, were subsequently convicted by an Ethiopian court. Less than a year later, bomb blasts at two hotels in Addis Ababa and Dire Dawa left 7 dead and 23 injured. An AIAI spokesman in Mogadishu subsequently claimed responsibility on behalf of the organization. In July 1996 Ethiopian Minister for Transport and Communications Abd al-Majid Husayn, an ethnic Somali, was shot when arriving at his office, though he survived. Once again, the AIAI spokesman in Mogadishu claimed responsibility. Ethiopia resolved to eliminate AIAI. Thus, on August 9, 1996, it launched the first of two raids on AIAI bases across the border in Somalia at Luuq and Buulo Haawa. The strike was limited and targeted but failed to find and destroy the AIAI leadership, which had gone into hiding. In January 1997 Ethiopian forces returned. Many of the Islamists were killed or injured, the training camps were dismantled, and AIAI's short-lived terrorist activities in Ethiopia came to an end. Officially, at least, AIAI, both in Ethiopia and in Somalia, ceased to exist. In 2001 the United States named AIAI as a group linked to international terrorism.

The dissolution of AIAI did not mean its total disappearance. Its leaders returned to their communities as respected Salafi clerics and have continued to inspire followers with their beliefs. Many other members stepped into visible public roles as religious leaders, judges, elders, and businessmen. Only a few, such as Hasan Dahir Aweys and Hasan Turki, have continued to be associated with militancy.

Since 2003, evidence has emerged of a new, ruthless independent Somali jihadi network, called al-Shabab, whose most visible figure has been a young militia leader known as Adan Hashi Farah Ayro. Based in Mogadishu, its core membership probably numbers in the tens. Since August 2003, Ayro's group was linked to the murders of four foreign aid workers and over a dozen Somalis believed to be working with Western counterterrorism networks. Ayro himself was in some respects a product of AIAI. He was the protégé of its former vice chairman and military commander, Hasan Dahir Aweys, and was reportedly trained in Afghanistan. In July 2005 Ayro was appointed commander of the Ifka Halane court militia in Mogadishu.

In Mogadishu, these new jihadists appear to be an alarming new player on the Somali stage. Ayro's appointment as Ifka Halane militia commander established a disturbing link between jihadi Islamists and the Islamic Courts Union (ICU). Signs of support for Ayro's militia from the businessmen reinforced the perception that the jihadists are no longer as isolated as they once were and may be set to assert themselves even more boldly. The new face of Somali jihadism resembles less the AIAI of the 1990s than the many other local radical groups worldwide inspired by al-Qa'ida. Its adoption of fluid organizational structures and unconventional and terrorist tactics has proved to pose a greater menace to regional and wider international security than the old AIAI.

The Islamic Courts Union

All the above-mentioned currents have merged in the form of the Islamic Courts Union. Mogadishu's first Islamic court was established in the Madina district by former members of AIAI in 1993. In 1994 Ali Dheere, a shaykh with alleged links to AIAI, presided over the establishment of Islamic courts in north Mogadishu and introduced draconian sentences, including amputations. Dheere was a member of the Abgaal subclan of the Hawiye, and his courts only had jurisdiction among the Abgaal, the most populous subclan in north Mogadishu. Public opposition soon put an end to the draconian sentences. Nevertheless, the Islamic courts had effected a dramatic improvement in security, and Abgaal political leaders began to fear its influence, militia, and conservative Islamic agenda. In February 1998 they secured the dissolution of the courts. The effectiveness of the Abgaal Islamic courts did not escape notice, and other communities began to emulate them. In 1996 the Xawaadle clan of Beledweyne established an Islamic court, and a number of clan-based Shari'a courts were opened in Mogadishu. In 1998 Hasan Dahir Aweys was a central figure in the establishment of an Islamic court in western Mogadishu known as Ifka Halane and another in Marka, the principal town in Lower Shabelle region. In the absence of a police force, each court maintained its own militia, usually paid for by contributions from the clan's businessmen. In comparison with the various clan and factional forces in the anarchic Mogadishu, the court militia acquired a reputation for discipline and good conduct.

In early 2000, a group of court leaders took the initiative to form the "Shari'a Implementation Council" to unify the efforts of the various courts in Mogadishu and consolidate resources and power. Its assembly of 63 members elected as its chairman Shaykh Ali Dheere, and Hasan Dahir Aweys was appointed secretary general. The council's primary functions included prisoner exchanges and occasional joint militia operations. Although they represented only some of the clans in the area, the collective leverage of the courts was formidable: Their influence extended throughout much of Mogadishu and the Lower Shabelle region; their militia numbered in the thousands; and they physically controlled many major courts and prisons. Few people shared the courts' puritanical religious views, but they were popular for their ability to provide security.

In 2004 a new umbrella organization was established for Mogadishu's Shari'a courts: the Supreme Council of Islamic Courts of Somalia. The council members elected as its chairman Shaykh Sharif Shaykh Ahmed,

a cleric previously associated with the traditionalist Sufi association Ahl al-Sunna wal-Jama'a (ASWJ), which had played a leading role in the establishment of the judicial system in Middle Shabelle. Several other members represented the traditionalist Shafi'i organization, Majma. Under the leadership of the new council, and in collaboration with the voluntary "neighborhood watch" committee, the Shari'a court system in Mogadishu experienced unprecedented expansion.

The courts came into conflict with the secular warlords, who controlled most of Mogadishu. In reaction to the ever-growing power of the ICU, a group of Mogadishu warlords formed the Alliance for the Restoration of Peace and Counter-Terrorism (ARPCT) in February 2006. In May 2006 the clashes between the two groups escalated into street fighting in the capital. This fighting ended on June 5, 2006, when the ICU took over Mogadishu.

The ICU consisted of three groups, each with its own goal and objective. At the head of the moderate group stood Shaykh Sharif Shaykh Ahmad. In general, its main goals are to bring back security and unite the country. Shaykh Hasan Dahir Aweys heads the Salafi-jihadi element, which wants to establish a Taliban-like regime in Somalia. The third group consists of the remnants of the Greater Somalia advocates. Greater Somalia comprises Somalia and Somali-inhabited regions in Ethiopia and Kenya.

On October 5, 2006, the "Supreme Islamic Court of Banadir" was created with the aim of organizing the courts into a more coherent organization, with the most senior judges forming this high court. This court dealt with wide issues as well as with foreign relations and commanded the ICU military forces as a whole. Shaykh Sharif Shaykh Ahmad was its chairman. A consultative Shura Council chaired by Shaykh Hasan Dahir Aweys approved the decisions made by the Supreme Islamic Court and was therefore called the "real power" in the ICU. This was not entirely true, however, because the Shura could not act unilaterally either. Below the Supreme Council and Shura Council were the regional courts spread throughout Somalia, which governed over the day-to-day issues of justice and law. These courts had enormous independence, so the laws and regulations in ICU territory could vary widely from town to town, based on the particular moderation or radicalism of the specific court.

Another body affiliated with the ICU was Hizb al-Shabab, also known as al-Shabab, which was mentioned earlier in connection with the jihadi elements active in Mogadishu following the dissolution of AIAI. It was a radical and independent organization under the ICU umbrella. It was integrated quite tightly with the ICU armed forces, acting as a sort of "special forces" for the ICU. The Shabab abducted journalists, harassed overly hip youngsters, and even murdered wounded Juba Valley Alliance soldiers in a Bu'aale hospital. The Shabab was headed by Adan Hashi Ayro.

The analysts' attempts to explain the ICU's success in defeating the warlords and taking control of Mogadishu (and a short time later, most of southern Somalia) have focused on the weariness of Somalia's population with chronic conflict and its weakening effects and on disaffection with the warlords who were responsible for the distress. Yet, above all, the ICU's ability to move so effectively with singleness of purpose resulted from the eruption of Somali nationalism throughout the first half of 2006. Thus, the immediate cause for the ICU's power surge was the revelation in early 2006 that the ARPCT had been receiving funds to arm itself from the United States through the CIA, working with the Ethiopian secret services. This revelation, and especially the implication of Ethiopia, Somalia's traditional adversary, in the affair, set off a nationalist reaction, which was exploited to the full by the ICU.

Following its taking control of Mogadishu, internal divisions emerged between moderates and radicals within the ICU over whether to negotiate with the Transitional Federal Government (TFG) on a national unity government or to form a separate government based on Islamic law. Another bone of contention between the two factions was their attitudes toward foreign influences. The hardliners wanted to curb foreign influences, while the moderates did not.

At first, it seemed like the moderates had gained the upper hand. At that time, the ICU wanted to solidify its rule while reassuring the West that it was not its intention to impose an extremist, Taliban-like government on Somalia. To further prove the point that the group's aim was to bring back security to chaotic Mogadishu and the rest of Somalia, on July 3, 2006, the ICU announced new guidelines on travel to Mogadishu, saying it wanted to boost traveler safety. On July 15, 2006, it opened Mogadishu's international airport, which had been closed for the previous 11 years. On August 15, 2006, the ICU captured Haradhere, some 500 kilometers northeast of Mogadishu, which had become a safe haven for pirates who had forced shipping firms and international organizations to pay large ransoms for the release of vessels and crews. On August 25, 2006, the Islamic Courts reopened historical Mogadishu seaport, which was formerly one of the busiest in East Africa but had been shut down for 10 years.

However, with time the situation reversed and the more radical elements prevailed over the moderates. Thus, already at the beginning of its rule, the radical elements within the ICU were shutting cinema halls and barring residents from watching the World Cup Soccer games. Furthermore, the ICU's militias had beaten members of the Mogadishu Stars, a musical band, with electric cables after they performed at a wedding ceremony, because the wedding included the mixing of men and women as well as the playing of music, which was regarded as un-Islamic. All these radical measures culminated on November 17, 2006, with a ban on the use, sale, and transportation of khat, while the Islamic Court of Kismayo banned the sale of cigarettes. This was a controversial move, as khat was the main source of income for many war widows and orphans and a huge export-import business in the whole Horn of Africa region.

These and much more repressive measures that were enacted against the population, which contrasted with the moderate Islam that had dominated Somali culture for centuries, led the Somalis to demonstrate against the regime. The ICU, which in the beginning was regarded as bearing the banner of Somali nationalism, was now regarded as preaching radical Islamism, alien to most Somali citizens, who belonged to Sufi orders.

The ICU seemed unstoppable in its quest to unite the country under strict Islamic laws and to destroy its rival, Somalia's internationally recognized but weak secular interim government, the TFG, headquartered in the town of Baidoa. The Islamists said that their aim was to restore law and order in Somalia. However, the Islamists were perceived as linked directly to al-Qa'ida, through people such as Shaykh Hasan Dahir Aweys and others. Thus, even before the taking of Mogadishu by the ICU, the U.S. government was funding the ARPCT because of concerns that the ICU was linked to al-Qa'ida

and was sheltering three al-Qa'ida leaders involved in the 1998 U.S. embassy bombings in Kenya and Tanzania. Later, following the taking of Mogadishu, the Ethiopian government decided to support the exiled warlords in order to oppose what in their view was a critical threat posed by the ICU to their administration of the Ogaden region. It was spurred primarily by the ICU's expansion and troop deployment up to the Ethiopian border. By mid-June 2006, Ethiopia began vocally referring to the ICU as "al-Qa'ida allies" and "terrorists." The TFG also adopted this American and Ethiopian perception of the Islamists as sheltering al-Qa'ida members. From the beginning, then, the rise to power of the ICU in Somalia was regarded as another victory for al-Qa'ida. The United States, Ethiopia, and the TFG were determined to fight the ICU and al-Qa'ida until victory was achieved. The United States regarded this war against the ICU as part of its global "war on terror" policy. Hence, a local conflict between the warlords and the TFG on the one side and the ICU on the other evolved into a global conflict between the United States and al-Qa'ida, in which the United States won a partial victory.

Thus, the war in Somalia was in essence an armed conflict in which the Ethiopian and the TFG forces fought against the ICU and affiliated militias over control of the country. The war officially began on December 21, 2006, when the ICU's leader, Hasan Dahir Aweys, declared Somalia to be in a state of war and called on all Somalis to take part in the jihad against Ethiopia. Three days after that, Ethiopia stated that it would actively fight against the ICU. The ICU was engaged in fighting against the forces of the Somali TFG and the autonomous regional governments of Puntland and Somaliland, all of which were backed by Ethiopian troops. The outbreak of heavy fighting began on

December 20, with the Battle of Baidoa. This was after the one-week deadline the ICU imposed on Ethiopia for withdrawing from Somalia lapsed. Ethiopia, however, refused to withdraw from its positions around the TFG interim capital in Baidoa, and thus, to leave the TFG to the mercy of the ICU. On December 29, after several successful battles, TFG and Ethiopian troops entered Mogadishu following the evacuation of the TFG one day earlier. On January 12, 2007, the Ethiopian army-backed TFG forces captured Ras Kamboni, the last remaining stronghold of the ICU in southern Somalia, after five days of heavy fighting. Thus, it completed the defeat of the ICU.

Insurgency and Conciliation

Following the victory of the Ethiopian-backed TFG forces over the ICU, chaos returned to rule Somalia, especially Mogadishu, as all attempts to disarm the various Somali clans failed and were met with resistance. Indeed, since February 2007, Mogadishu has been witness to a great deal of violence, consisting of mortar and rocket attacks on TFG and Ethiopian installations and Mogadishu's airport and seaport; machine-gun attacks on police stations and checkpoints; targeted assassinations of public officials, military and security personnel, nongovernmental activists, and their relatives; unexplained homicides; intraclan gunfights; car hijackings; and the erection of roadblocks by local militias to extol tolls from motorists. The fighting has escalated since the end of March 2007, when the insurgents introduced new warfare tactics that are more and more reminiscent of Iraqi scenes of war, such as the downing of planes, the burning of TFG and Ethiopian soldiers and the mutilation of their bodies, open artillery duels instead of hit-and-run

mobile mortar assaults, the use of roadside bombs and other improvised explosive devices, and suicide-bombing operations. This fierce fighting caused hundreds to be killed, thousands to be wounded, and more than 200,000 to flee Mogadishu. This conflict symbolized the transition of the insurgency against the TFG, Ethiopian occupiers, and the African Union Mission in Somalia (AMISOM) Ugandan peacekeepers from one that was merely inspired by Iraqi-style tactics to one that emulated them.

The most prominent groups among the insurgents have been the Islamist ones. At first, the Popular Resistance Movement in the Land of the Two Migrations (PRM) was the most prominent group among the insurgents. It was established on January 19, 2007, exactly the same day that the AMISOM mission was formally defined and approved by the African Union at the sixty-ninth meeting of the Peace and Security Council. It repeatedly warned African Union peacekeepers to avoid coming to Somalia and threatened to shoot down airplanes using the Mogadishu International Airport and to carry out suicide attacks against them. On March 24, 2007, the PRM created a "comprehensive plan to isolate the enemy that has come to Mogadishu," called Operation Suffocate the Enemy. The plan included operational instructions for 29 "Squads of the Resistance" to be concentrated in Mogadishu.

The place of the PRM, which may have ceased to exist, is now held by the Youth Mujahidin Movement (Harakat Shabab al-Mujahidin), which announced its establishment on March 26, 2007. It presented itself as an Islamist Salafi movement, which achieves its goals by Islamic legal means, including propagation (*da'wa*) and jihad. Among the operations against the TFG, the

Ethiopians, and the Ugandan peacekeepers for which they claimed responsibility are the suicide bombing at an Ethiopian army base, the detonation of roadside bombs on Ethiopian army vehicles, the shooting down of an Ethiopian plane, the shooting down of a Belarusian cargo plane near Mogadishu Airport, artillery shelling of the army airport in Mogadishu while the Ugandan peacekeepers arrived, and more. It seems like this movement is an offshoot of the military arm of the ICU, which was also called Shabab and was under the command of Aden Hashi Ayro, who is still alive and in hiding somewhere in Somalia. Therefore, it is possible that some of its members might have been members of the former Shabab. More important, it seems like the leading role among the Islamist insurgent groups is now reserved for the Youth Mujahidin Movement, while the PRM has disappeared completely from the scene.

Yet, despite the prominent role of the Islamist groups within the Mogadishu insurgency, the leading role is still reserved for the Hawiye clan leaders, those who declared war on Ethiopian troops and called on all Somalis to join them following attempts to disarm them, and who were also responsible for brokering cease-fires with the Ethiopians and the Ugandan peacekeepers.

Thus, the attempts of the Ethiopian and TFG forces to forcibly disarm the Hawiye clan members while giving key security posts to members of President Abdallah Yusuf's clan, the Darod, have alarmed the Hawiye clan. Much more important than that, it seems as though these moves have caused the Hawiye subclans to unite their forces in opposition to Ethiopia and the TFG. Since a large segment of the Islamists was always based on the Hawiye, they seem now to adhere to their clan identity and affiliation while still maintaining their

Islamist teachings and giving the insurgency a taste of Iraqi-style insurgency.

This national reconciliation conference was announced by President Abdallah Yusuf on March 1, 2007, to be held in Mogadishu to reconcile differences among Somalis and to move Somalia toward a stable, democratic future. According to the announcement, the conference would bring together 3,000 participants from throughout the country and the diaspora for two months of meetings and discussions. The basis of the talks would be "reconciliation among clans," which ruled out the participation of any representatives of the Islamists. Of course, this announcement was met with immediate rejection from the opposition. Most important, major elements of the Hawiye clan held a meeting and issued a statement urging the TFG to hold an open reconciliation conference that would include the ICU as a political entity. The statement also requested that the international community affect the withdrawal of Ethiopian forces from Somalia and organize a "real national reconciliation meeting" based on political representation in a "neutral place." The ICU also responded to the TFG's reconciliation project, with its moderate wing—based in Yemen—expressing willingness to negotiate, but only as political equals. On March 1, 2007, the ICU issued an official statement, in which it called for a reconciliation process that would include all sectors of Somali society in the political process, especially intellectuals, experts, traditional elders, members of civil society, and civil servants.

Conclusions and Indications for the Future

Politically, Somalia has now returned roughly to where it was when the TFG was formed in October 2004. The government is weak, unpopular, and faction ridden, and the power vacuum in southern Somalia is rapidly being filled by the same faction leaders and warlords the ICU overthrew less than a year ago. Many Mogadishu residents resent the ICU's defeat, feel threatened by the TFG, and are dismayed by the presence of Ethiopian troops in Mogadishu. Ethiopia's military victory has dismantled only the most visible part of the ICU: the regional administrative authority in south-central Somalia, which essentially served as a political platform for Hawiye clan interests. Other elements, including the militant Shabab leadership, remain largely intact and have dispersed throughout the country, threatening to wage a prolonged war. The grassroots network of mosques, schools, and private enterprises that has underpinned the spread of Salafi teachings and their extremist variants remains in place and continues to expand, thanks to generous contributions from Islamic charities and the private sector. Whether the Islamists, including their more extreme jihadi element, can stage a comeback depends largely on whether the TFG can restore stability and win public support across southern Somalia.

Yet it should be recalled that despite the important role played by the Islamists in the insurgency and despite the six-month rule of the ICU over most of southern Somalia and the security and order it brought with it, Islamist extremism has failed to take a broader hold in Somalia because of Somali resistance—not foreign counterterrorism efforts. The vast majority of Somalis desire a government—democratic, broadly based, and responsive—that reflects the Islamic faith as they have practiced it for centuries: with tolerance, moderation, and respect for variation in religious observance. Somalis in general show little interest in jihadi Islamism; most are deeply opposed. Somali militant movements have failed to gain broad popular support, encountering instead widespread hostility.

Thus, the situation in Somalia is unpredictable and precarious. The potential for violence remains high because of clan rivalries, resentment of the government's Ethiopian backers, and the risk of a relapse into the previous warlord-controlled anarchy. With the Ethiopians still present in Somalia and the Ethiopian-backed TFG refusing to have anything to do with the ICU's moderate leaders, the moderates within the ICU, even those who still wish to negotiate with the TFG, will be radicalized too. This radicalization process, which might happen very fast, is the real threat for Somalia. If it can be prevented, then a national reconciliation can prevail and, as a consequence, law and order can be established. If not, the destiny of Somalia might relapse into chaos again.

BIBLIOGRAPHY

Boukhars, Anouar. "Understanding Somali Islamism." *Terrorism Monitor* 4:10 (May 18, 2006): 3–6. http://jamestown.org/terrorism/news/article.php?articleid=2369999.

Crisis Group Report. "Counter-Terrorism in Somalia: Losing Hearts and Minds?" *Africa Report* 95 (July 11, 2005). http://somali-jna.org/downloads/ICG percent20Report percent2095 percent20Counter_terrorism_in_somalia.pdf.

Crisis Group Report. "Somalia: Countering Terrorism in a Failed State." *Africa Report* 45 (May 23, 2002). www.somali-jna.org/downloads/ICG percent20Countering percent20Terrorism.pdf.

Crisis Group Report. "Somalia's Islamists." *Africa Report* 100 (December 12, 2005). http://merln.ndu.edu/archive/icg/terrorism-somalia.pdf.

Lewis, I.M. *A Modern History of the Somali: Nation*

and State in the Horn of Africa. Athens: Ohio University Press, 2002.

Marchal, Roland. "Islamic Political Dynamics in the Somali Civil War." In *Islamism and Its Enemies in the Horn of Africa*, ed. Alex de Waal, 114–45. Bloomington: Indiana University Press, 2004.

Menkhaus, Ken. "Political Islam in Somalia." *Middle East Policy* 9:1 (2002): 109–23.

Middle East Media Research Institute (MEMRI). "Somali Journalist: Shabab al-Mujahideen Has 'Pledged Allegiance to a Man Hiding in a Cave.'" *Threat Monitor, Special Dispatch*, 2223 (February 2, 2009). www.memrijttm.org/content/en/report.htm?report=3014&param=AJT.

Nzwili, Fredrick. "Leadership Profile: Somalia's Islamic Courts Union." *Terrorism Focus* 3:23 (June 13, 2006): 5–6. http://jamestown.org/terrorism/news/article.php?articleid=2370028.

Rabasa, Angel. *Radical Islam in East Africa*, Arlington: Rand Corporation, 2009.

Shank, Michael. "Understanding Political Islam in Somalia." *Contemporary Islam* 1:1 (June 2007): 89–103.

Terdman, Moshe. "The Mogadishu Insurgency." *Islam in Africa Newsletter* 2:2 (April 2007): 3–8. www.e-prism.org/.

———. "Somalia Following the Defeat of the Union of Islamic Courts—Al-Qaeda's Next Front?" *Islam in Africa Newsletter* 1:2 (January 2007): 9–23. www.e-prism.org/.

Sudan

Harvey Glickman and Emma Rodman

Islamism in Sudan reflects both modern and older cultural-historical movements. While similar to Islamist movements in the wider Middle East, it is distinguished by the sophisticated leadership of its ideological and strategic engineer, Hasan al-Turabi; by a period of official empowerment and support among elites in Khartoum as well as among acolytes outside the capital; and by violent implementation campaigns during the 1980s and 1990s. Islamism's proponents, including Sudan's leaders, have not only called for a return to Shari'a as well as for an Islamic constitution; they have also mounted a thorough program of social engineering ("the Comprehensive Call to God"), which, for a brief period in the early 1990s, threatened to proselytize non-Muslims and forcibly impose an Islamist orthodoxy on Sudan's population. Such an agenda also supposes an active, sometimes violent, homogenization of the community of Muslims. Its engine is a reinterpreted, rerooted Islam, relevant to the technology of modernity but resistant to the perceived cultural pollution of liberalism and secularism.

The brief Islamist rule by the Mahdist movement in the late nineteenth century offers a precedent for strict Islamic government in Sudan. Yet there are three problems here. First, in Sudan even a unified national identity remains contested as well. Second, the population of the country is not unanimously Islamic. Third, the character of historical Islam in Sudan, as well the population itself, is pluralistic. At the same time, Khartoum's Islamist program reflects a political agenda more than a religious revival.

Historical Islam, the nominal religion of most of the country, provides perhaps a logical platform for a thrust toward Islamist militancy and Islamic nationalism, but at the grassroots it provides a weak and divided foundation for constructing such a regime. The Islamist agenda has waxed and waned through several decades, imposed by force at times and in different regions. The two main bases are the Arab-centered version in the capital, Khartoum, and in the Nile Valley—and a variant version in the west of the country. The southern part of Sudan, where the Muslim population is proportionately smallest, has, after years of warfare, won a constitutional barrier to Islamism being imposed there.

The logic of the still-contested appeal of the National Islamic Front (NIF)—renamed the National Congress Party (NCP) and now in charge of the government—is a product of four factors: a legitimate, indigenous development of Islam and Islamic law; the rise of a wily and charismatic Islamist leader, Hasan al-Turabi; a mixing of derived and locally developed Islamist ideas; and the political utility of this doctrine for the ruling, Arabized elites.

Present Circumstances

In comparison to neighboring territories, Islam was late in coming to Sudan. Nearly 900 years elapsed between the death of Muhammad and the official acceptance of Islam by the Sudanese ruling elite. The area of present-day Sudan is home to African, Christian, Nubian, Egyptian, Arab, and Islamic religious and cultural traditions. Yet Sudan was the first Islamist state in the world, under the Mahdi (Redeemer) between 1885 and 1899. Sudan was also the first modern Sunni state in the late twentieth century to adopt explicitly rigorous Islamic government and laws, with the seizure of power by the National Islamic Front in 1989.

Violence and warfare have characterized Sudan in the 1955–72 and 1983–2005 periods. Waxing and waning throughout Sudan's half century of postindependence history, with but a decade of respite, Africa's longest-running internal conflict reflected deep differences, largely between the northern and southern parts of Sudan and their populations over issues of power sharing, wealth, identity, and Islamization. More recently, Sudan's proclivity toward civil strife and ideological battles with the West converged in Darfur, a region encompassing three provinces in the far west of Sudan along the Chadian border. The fighting there is rooted in a lack of power and access in Khartoum, a failed Islamist project, and

economic underdevelopment and exploitation. On April 23, 2006, as reported by Reuters, Osama bin Ladin, long-linked to the NIF government and once a Khartoum resident, called on "the mujahidin and their supporters in Sudan . . . to wage a long-term war against the Crusaders in western Sudan." For Khartoum, jihad is a powerfully evocative term that mobilizes domestic and international support.

Sudan is at the boundary between the Arab-Islamic world and the African world of various and mixed traditions. Estimates for Sudan's population range from 36 to 41 million people, of which about 15 million claim Arab descent, living along the Nile River in north-central Sudan and in or around Khartoum. Aside from Khartoum—whose residents are diverse, the whole of the north is generally characterized as Muslim, and the south as the home of Christianity and traditional African beliefs. In Sudan as a whole, Sunni Muslims account for between 60 and 70 percent of the population. Islam in Sudan, however, according to Francis Deng, "tends to be associated with Arabism as a composite concept of race, ethnicity and culture," allowing for a complex schism of ostensibly Muslim Sudanese into ethnic, geographical, and sectarian groups.

Sudan's heterogeneity and pluralism—with over a hundred languages, it cannot objectively be called anything else—compete with its Muslim majority and heritage for the national soul. Khartoum is not only the population center but also the country's political heart. Educated urban elites from the military academies and universities formed the overwhelming majority of those pressing for, and eventually designing, the country. The Graduates General Conference, which demanded self-determination in 1942, sprang from university-schooled Arab Muslims. The educated Arab elites dominate the political life of the country in disproportion to their numbers. Ethnically—and to some extent religiously—distinct groups, such as the Nuba, the Fur, the Beja, and the Dinka, have historically been in inequitable relationships with the Arabized elite. The bias toward Arab Muslim leadership under colonial rulers, Khartoum's location as the seat of Ottoman and British administrations, along with the educational and economic opportunities available in the capital, all contributed to Arab-Muslim political hegemony.

Crisis of Identity in Independent Sudan

The political history of Sudan after independence can be divided into two period types: parliamentary "democracy" and military dictatorship, which alternated in three cycles, culminating in the 1989 coup/takeover by military allies of the National Islamic Front. Afflicting both periods, however, has been the lack of agreement on Sudanese nationhood, reflected by years of civil strife in the southern and western provinces and in the continued inability to write an acceptable, durable constitution. The first parliamentary period lasted two years before the advent of the first dictatorship, that of General Ibrahim Abboud. His ouster, in 1964, preceded an incompetent parliamentarianism. In 1968 two claimant coalition governments functioned simultaneously in different buildings, unable to form a coalition.

Attempts at power grabs alternated between the two main parties: the Umma and the Democratic Unionist Party (DUP), which was the political wing of the Khatmiyya Brotherhood. These two parties also represented two possible paths for Sudan. The Umma platform called for a strong Sudanese and Islamic state; the DUP favored close ties and eventual integration with Egypt in a pan-Arab alliance. Smaller parties, including the Islamic Charter Front, Communist Party, and trade and professional unions, completed the mix of interests wrangling over power. In 1969 Colonel Gaafar Nimeiri seized power in the second military coup; his reign lasted until 1985.

In the third parliamentary period, government continued to be juggled between the two parties, which were based more on family history and religious affiliations than on political platforms. Their influence waned under the pressures of increasing urbanization and economic downturns. Marxism and Islamism were emerging in the urban centers of Khartoum and Omdurman, paralleling the growth.

In Sudan, the Muslim Brotherhood emerged in 1949 as the Islamic Charter Front (ICF), in part from student groups organizing in the universities. Its members were urban and highly educated. Unlike the Brotherhood in Egypt, the Sudanese branch drew on elite support and lacked membership from the lower classes or rural poor. In 1964 the dean of the law school at the University of Khartoum, Hasan al-Turabi, was elected secretary general of the ICF. Turabi had recently returned from studies at the University of London and the Sorbonne in Paris, where he had been active in Muslim student organizing. The U.S. September 11 Commission Report labeled him "Sudan's longtime hard-line ideological leader." By mixing the historical Islamism of Shari'a along with some adaptive philosophical interpretations, he related doctrinal Islam to a contemporary political agenda. He has focused on drafting for Sudan an Islamic constitution and on instituting Shari'a. He has also generated a program, the Comprehensive Call of the 1990s, toward social transformation and the imposed practice of social virtues. Although deprived of official authority for long periods, he has nevertheless driven the politics of the country for more than 40 years.

Sudan confronted two kinds of political Islam. There was the Islam of the old sects and families that reflected accommodation with tradition as well as elements of modernization. It evinced broad social concerns and remained intermittently interested in something like a comprehensive Islamic government. In parallel was the Islam of Turabi and the National Islamic Front, radically Islamist and seeking a government strictly by Islamic law. Turabi has been the force behind the National Islamic Front, the Islamic Charter Front, the Muslim Brotherhood, and other incarnations of Islamism in the country. Turabi and the National Islamic Front interweave with the third period of dictatorship, of President Umar Bashir. Since 1989, the country has shifted profoundly toward Islamic government, seeking to suppress Muslim and other elements of the pluralistic traditions of Sudan.

The Roots of Modern Islamism

Shari'a gained a strong foothold in a unified Sudanese legal system with the rise of the Mahdiyya, the indigenous, messianic Islamic state that ousted the Ottomans in 1885. The Islam of the Mahdiyya was puritanical and harsh. Shari'a was enforced in its more extreme forms. Women who left their homes unaccompanied, who were unveiled, or who spoke in loud voices were flogged. Visits to the tombs of Sufi saints were banned, and variant and local forms of Islamic practice were rejected. The

Mahdiyya was the product of both localized Sudanese traditions—the Mahdist myth of deliverance—and imports from outside the country, specifically the African jihadists in Nigeria and elsewhere in West Africa, especially in the early nineteenth century, distinguished scholars whose views rested on a tradition of authoritarian, unchallengeable authority. It also reflects the Wahhabist movement of the Hijaz, exemplified in Saudi Arabia, which sought to establish a purified Islam and railed against Sufi idolatrism and other localized innovations.

Shari'a and the question of Sudan's legal code continued to haunt the country after independence. Wrangling over a constitution contributed to the overthrow of parliamentary civilian government in 1958. General Abboud's military government failed to write a constitution, choosing instead to emphasize the national identity issue via Islamization and by suppressing political and cultural differences in the south. The Sudan African National Union, formed in 1963, grew increasingly active in the refugee camps and among guerrilla groups in opposition. As noted by Øystein Rolandsen, "It was only after the military coup led by General Abboud in 1958 . . . that occasional skirmishes escalated into a full-fledged civil war. The escalation was mainly caused by Abboud's program of Islamization, which led to increased repression in the south." Islamization, in the form of the penetration of Islamist philanthropy and nongovernmental organizations, along with the threat of introducing universal Shari'a, combined to inflame north-south tensions and guaranteed a stalemate over writing a national constitution.

Ironically, Shari'a served, after Abboud, as both a rallying point for national unity and a source of deeper division. Despite the country's heterogeneity, the possibility of

Islam as a national identity was persuasive to many Arab Muslim leaders in the north. After another brief parliamentary interlude, the Sudanese Free Officers Movement took power in a second military coup, declaring Colonel Gaafar Nimeiri prime minister in 1969. Influenced by leftist trends in the Arab world, Nimeiri—who admired Egypt's Gamal Abdel Nasser and his Arab socialism ideology—raised the banner of Arab socialism and outlawed all political parties. In an attempt to consolidate his socialist position, Nimeiri published a provisional constitution in August 1971, describing Sudan as a "socialist democracy." His newly acquired political ideology attracted rewards from the Soviet Union. Between 1969 and 1971, the USSR supplied Sudan with arms and advanced military equipment for the struggle against the "Anya Nya" rebels in the south.

After a coup attempt against him by more orthodox Marxists in the Sudanese Communist Party, Nimeiri cooled toward socialism. By the late 1970s, he reached out to other political elements, including Hasan al-Turabi's Muslim Brotherhood and Sadiq al-Mahdi's Umma Party. Nimeiri's later embrace of the Islamist movement in Sudan was the cornerstone of his 1977 policy of national reconciliation. To cement this new alliance, he appointed Turabi chairman of a new committee for the "return of the laws to compatibility with the sharia," notes Gabriel Warburg. This enabled him to exchange military aid from the Soviet Union for donations from Saudi Arabia.

In southern Sudan, which had been granted some autonomy under the 1972 Addis Ababa peace agreement (ending the first era of civil war in the country), local politicians began to campaign for extending their authority. Nimeiri struck back by suspending the Southern Regional Assembly in 1981. Two years later he redivided the south into the three former provinces of Bahr al-Ghazal, al-Istiwai, and Ahali al-Nil. Additionally, in a move doubtless influenced by Turabi's position as attorney general, Nimeiri introduced Shari'a in September 1983 as the national law of Sudan, including the controversial *hudud* corporal punishments, a move applauded by the Muslim Brotherhood. Nimeiri, having shifted dramatically from socialist to Islamist, insisted that military officers swear allegiance to him as the imam of the Sudanese *umma* (nation). The implementation of Shari'a was equally dramatic: Thousands of bottles of alcohol were dumped into the Nile, and public corporal punishments ensued. People in the south and moderate northern Muslims staggered under the wave of amputations and floggings. Reportedly, even Turabi fainted upon witnessing a public amputation. Shari'a, however, had become the premier law of 1980s Sudan. It remained in place after Nimeiri's removal in 1985.

Equally important as the effect of Islamism and Shari'a inside Sudan has been their influence on Sudan's international image. Turabi and the Islamic Charter Front (later the Muslim Brotherhood and the National Islamic Front, and now the National Congress Party) received a great deal of aid from pro-Islamist Saudi banks and charities. Pro-Islamist relief agencies—such as Da'wa al-Islamiyya, secretive and suspected of connections to jihadism as well as to more benign charitable associations—moved in. Relations between Sudan and neighboring Arab states were ambivalent but strengthening in the 1970s and early 1980s. Turabi cultivated connections with maverick Islamic states, such as Libya, where he spent three years in exile during the Nimeiri years. Turabi and the Sudanese Islamists continued to press for an Islamic constitution. In Sudan, this encounter between a burgeoning pan-Arab trend and previous indigenous trends meshed—revolving around the application of Shari'a law and a growingly open Arab racism against "blacks" in the east—and ran parallel to ideological changes in Sudan's past, ranging from the Funj Kingdom through the Mahdi era, and into Nimeiri's "socialist" period.

The Islamic State: Sudan After the National Salvation Revolution

On June 30, 1989, a third parliamentary period in Sudan's history abruptly ended in a coup. Colonel Umar Bashir established the Revolutionary Command Council (RCC) for National Salvation. He commenced governing the country in adherence to Islamist principles, committed to retaining Nimeiri's Shari'a laws. In a bit of tactical jujitsu, the RCC imprisoned the major leaders of the National Islamic Front, including Turabi, to safeguard the legitimacy of the NIF by distancing it from the coup and to gain international acceptability, especially from Egypt, by avoiding the taint of hard-line Islamism. The RCC regime achieved immediate recognition by Egypt and the United States. After a few months in jail, Turabi popped up in the new government.

Under the NIF, Sudan attracted Islamist groups, many with terrorist pedigrees, including Osama bin Ladin and his al-Qa'ida network. Into the 1990s, Sudan cultivated its dual status as problematic global pariah and magnet for Islamic and Arab organizations unwelcome in other states. When Iraq invaded Kuwait on August 2, 1990, the Organization of the Islamic Conference (OIC), as well as the Arab League, urged Iraq's immediate withdrawal. Bashir denounced the invasion. However, after

Turabi emerged to side with Iraq, Sudan abstained from the ultimate vote in the OIC. Reflecting the tide of evidence placing Sudan in the midst of Islamist destabilization efforts in Egypt, Yemen, and Saudi Arabia, in 1993 the U.S. State Department placed Sudan on the list of state sponsors of terrorism. The United States, already alienated by Sudanese statements of support for Iraq, had protested to the Sudanese government when anti-American demonstrators threw rocks and burned American flags at the U.S. embassy in Khartoum. American disapproval mounted as reports of terrorist support and FBI investigations pointed to Khartoum.

State-Sponsored Terror

Sudan's isolation grew in the 1990s, parallel to the implication of Sudan's state apparatus in assisting terrorist networks in its international neighborhood. Much material and consultative assistance flowed to Sudan from Iran. In 1994 Turabi disingenuously claimed that there were no Iranian military personnel in Sudan, "not one Iranian businessman or even tourist," as quoted by the *Islamic Republic News Agency Report* in December 1994. Turabi was personally committed to the relationship as an example of ideological and political rapprochement between Sunni and Shi'a Islamist organizations, one of the goals of his Popular Arab and Islamic Conference (PAIC), envisioned as a rival to the older pan-Islamic, pan-Arab organizations. In November 1989, after a visit to Tehran by Ali Usman Taha—then second vice president of Sudan—the presidents of Iran and Sudan met there. President Bashir sought material support for his radical direction. Iran's president Ali Akbar Hashemi Rafsanjani promised a major road-building project and agreed to cooperate on security and intelligence matters.

Turabi diligently built working relationships with the Iranian mullahs and facilitated, with bin Ladin, a training alliance between the Iranian-sponsored Lebanese Hizballah and bin Ladin's Sudan-based al-Qa'ida, as noted by J. Millard Burr and Robert O. Collins in their *Revolutionary Sudan: Hassan al-Turabi and the Islamist State, 1989–2000*. Furthermore, Shaul Shay writes in *The Red Sea Terror Triangle: Sudan, Somalia, Yemen and Islamic Terror* that in September 1991, while visiting Sudan to provide assistance, an Iranian military delegation prepared a military cooperation pact between the two countries. In late 1991 President Rafsanjani traveled to Khartoum, where he proclaimed the north-south civil war a "jihad" that should be pursued with all vigor. To underscore his point, he presented Sudan with a gift of $300 million in Chinese arms. In a pattern similar to its relationship with Hizballah in Lebanon, Iran assisted with arms, commercial development, and jihadi training in camps established around Khartoum—camps actually run by al-Qa'ida with help from the Sudanese security services. Iranian advisers died in battle in 1992, participating in the jihad in Kordofan, opposed by the Sudan People's Liberation Army (SPLA) forces, during the period of the renewed civil war. The Sudanese government also opened Port Sudan to Iranian use; Iranian warships were occasionally spotted in the Red Sea en route to Sudan, write Burr and Collins.

In March 1990 the Sudan government had officially welcomed all "Arab brothers," who could henceforth enter Sudan without a visa, thus commencing a mass migration of Islamist militants and peripatetic terrorists. This prefigured a rise in Arab racism in the burgeoning Darfur conflict. Many Afghan-Arab fighters, unwelcome in their home countries at the end of the Afghan-Soviet war—often traveling through Iran—wound up in Sudan. At the Khartoum airport, according to Collins, mujahidin were welcomed with grants of Sudanese passports; influential people received diplomatic passports. Operatives departed Sudan for Bosnia, Eritrea, Somalia, Libya, and other Arab countries in a widening effort to help Islamic militants.

The long, interrupted, and renewed civil war, especially in the 1990s, invited intervention by Sudan's neighbors. Southern resistance groups, especially the largest and most renowned, John Garang's Sudan People's Liberation Movement and Army (SPLM/A) drew help from Ethiopia and Uganda. Sudan reciprocated in those countries by funding antigovernment guerrilla movements. Eritrea, Ethiopia, Egypt, Libya, Chad, and Uganda all have accused the Sudanese government of providing material support to armed insurrectionists. Uganda, for example, charged the NIF government with funding the Lord's Resistance Army, a cult militia that regularly kidnapped child soldiers. Uganda retaliated by supporting the SPLA. Sudan channeled resources to Islamists struggling in other countries, such as Somalia and Yemen.

Membership in the International Islamist Club

Al-Turabi's Islamist project went beyond pan-Islamic unity. The object was to bring together various extremist Islamic organizations to discuss theory, strategy, and insurrectionary tactics. To this end, with President Bashir's blessing, Turabi organized a meeting of militant and terrorist groups in the Popular Arab and Islamic Congress (PAIC), a direct competitor to the Organization of

Islamic Conference and the Arab League. Delegates representing over forty states attended the first PAIC General Assembly, in Khartoum, April 25–28, 1991. Turabi presided and was elected secretary general. In attendance were Yasir Arafat and representatives of Hamas, as well as bin Ladin, members of the Filipino Abu Sayyaf movement, Imad Mughniya of Hizballah, Tunisian leader Rashid al-Ghannushi, Anwar Haddam of the Algerian group Islamic Salvation Front (FIS), and Ayatollah Mahdi Karrubi, head of the Iranian Society of Combatant Clergy. The group spanned a wide range of the geographic, sectarian, and ideological groups within the now global Islamist movement. As Turabi noted in an address in Madrid in August 1994, he envisioned the PAIC as a means to assemble "Muslims from all over the world," overcoming "internal divisions, Shia, Sunni, differences in jurisprudence or spiritual orders." Both the first and second general assemblies offered Turabi and his cohorts opportunities to attack the West, expatiate on Islamist principles, and expand the PAIC as an Islamist intellectual clearinghouse. Turabi envisioned Islamism playing as historic a role as liberalism in the West, providing the materials of a global revival. In London in 1992, at a time when he was publishing and recording sermons and lectures widely distributed in the Arab world, al-Turabi paused to enunciate a grand strategy for Islamists:

> The historical test for Muslims has always been to recover after every setback, seeking through the renewal of faith (*iman*), the renewal of thought (*ijtihad*) and the resurgence of action (jihad) to salvage religion from temporal containment and ensure its progressive development, relevance and continuity in history.

Turabi's vision of Sudan as the philosophical and logistical heartbeat of the global Islamist movement also encompassed jihad and violence. The 1993 bombing of the World Trade Center in New York in some part involved Sudanese nationals, some working in Sudanese diplomatic offices in the United States and linked to the NIF regime itself, according to a prepared statement before the U.S. Senate Judiciary Committee Subcommittee on Terrorism in 1998. Al-Qa'ida's bombings of the U.S. embassies in Nairobi and Dar es Salaam in 1998 led to American retaliation, the bombing of a site purportedly involved in manufacturing chemicals for explosives in Khartoum, after bin Ladin departed Sudan for Afghanistan. The June 25, 1995, assassination attempt against Egyptian President Husni Mubarak in Addis Ababa, Ethiopia, has been traced to Khartoum. Sudan's failure to meet UN demands for the extradition of suspects from that country led to the imposition of UN sanctions.

Facing Problems at Home

In a limited sense, the Islamist project in Sudan has instigated some mobilization of opinion and action toward a vague international goal. The threat of militant Islamism has also stiffened governments in neighboring states against ties with Sudan. Libya has blown hot and cold on spillover actions from Darfur, which had an impact on the politics of Chad. Sudan's ideological hard line has invited economic repercussions, by way of international sanctions, the loss of humanitarian and military donors, and escalating war costs. Internally, as well, by most measures, domestic Islamist policies have failed. The implacable commitment to Islamism of the regime's early years led to a turn to Islamic solutions for economic and social problems unconnected to needs and realities on the ground. Ideology trumped workability. While the NIF regime faced the conditions of a "failed state" when it took over in 1989, the regime's tenure has resulted in little improvement in basic infrastructure, economic conditions, and human development.

Economic Stagnation and Failure

In the 1980s, the country's economic crisis deepened; traditional investors divested, but Islamic banks and businesses expanded with assistance from tax incentives, access to hard currency, and political connections to the powerful Muslim Brotherhood. Nimeiri's regime, increasingly Islamist in orientation, encouraged the Islamic economic institutions with large-scale exemptions from private-sector regulations. The Faisal Islamic Bank, for example, reaped spectacular results, as a result of exemption from most banking regulations and from profits and capital gains taxes, write Adbel Salam Sidahmed and Alsir Sidahmed. Several Islamic banks were owned or linked to the Saudi royal family, which supported the "neo-Wahhabi" Islamists of the Muslim Brotherhood inside Sudan. These banks served to funnel money through unregulated channels into terrorist networks. Saudi and Sudanese links to the Islamic banks in Khartoum led several families of 9/11 victims to file a lawsuit seeking damages for the Sudanese government's involvement in financing al-Qa'ida, according to an August 2002 *CBS News Report*.

As early as September 1990, divergent Sudanese policies evinced concern about continued Saudi support. Sudanese support for Iraq during the first Gulf War led Minister of Finance Abd al-Rahim Hamdi

to worry that Saudi Arabia would restrict Khartoum's banks and force the closing of those with Saudi royal ties, note Burr and Collins. Nevertheless, the NIF regime continued to support Islamic banking practices and restrictions. Bashir's announcement that Shari'a would continue to govern the country involved expanding Islamic economic practices, including state collection of *zakat*—the charitable contribution enjoined on every Muslim—and the banning of usury and the collection of interest. Quasi-governmental organizations, such as the Diwan al-Zakat and the Islamic Pious Endowments Organization, were established to regulate the expanding Islamic orientations of the financial sector, write Alex De Waal and A.H. Abdel Salam.

Economic problems, however, continued to plague the NIF regime, especially connected to increasing entanglements in terrorism. In 1995 the UN instituted minimal sanctions against Sudan for its refusal to hand over suspects in the investigation of the failed Mubarak assassination. The United States instituted economic restrictions in 1997 and commenced assistance to the exiled opposition group of Sudanese, the National Democratic Alliance (NDA), which was operating out of Eritrea, Ethiopia, and Uganda. Then Secretary of State Madeleine Albright met with representatives of the NDA and of John Garang's Sudan People's Liberation Movement in Kampala in December 1997. The Saudi government, too, grew reluctant to provide assistance, as it became clear that Sudan was supporting insurgent elements inside Saudi Arabia, including bin Ladin, whose Saudi citizenship had been revoked in 1993 and who was implicated in the bombing of the Khobar Towers there in 1996. Even Iran cooled its ardor for the

NIF regime, responding to a 1997 request for military material with a modest offer of a team of mechanics.

While the regime was facing a problem of willing donors, it also faced a surge of expenditures. The war in the south was costing over $1 million a day. The regime had inherited a crippling international debt. Sudan had been declared ineligible in 1986 for additional International Monetary Fund (IMF) lending, because of account arrears to the Fund. In 1993, the IMF took the drastic step of suspending Sudan's voting rights. In 2000 Sudan's accumulated debt stood at $20 billion, including $1.6 billion to the IMF.

Among the remaining sources of funding available to the regime was the international network of Islamic charities that had provided support for the civil war, as well as for famine relief and social services. In 1993 Sudan received a large payment from the massive Iranian Foundation for the Oppressed. Sudan had already received large sums from Saudi charities, as well as from humanitarian charities in the United States and Western Europe. Yet "Islamic economics" failed to provide the stability and revenue stream required by the international donor community. By 1994 Sudan had adopted the standard liberal economic reforms and austerity measures prescribed by the IMF and the World Bank in a desperate bid to return to eligibility for the international donor pool.

Petroleum, not Islamic economics, saved the Sudanese economy. By 2000 oil alone had caused Sudan to achieve a trade surplus for the first time in 20 years. In 2005 Sudan was producing an average of 363,000 barrels of crude oil per day at its Unity and Heglig fields in the south, according to the U.S. Energy Information Administration.

National Disunity and Civil War

Coming to power, the NIF government faced two major domestic political issues. First, it had inherited a country divided by civil war and heterogeneity—a continuing problem exacerbated by the NIF's rigorous ideological and religious stances. Second, the NIF lacked a popular mandate to govern, seizing power and discouraging both dissent and the possibility of countercoups. Southern rebel victories in the early 1990s and the expanding insurgency in Darfur, the east, and the Nuba Mountains undermined confidence in the regime. Reaction grew apace against the intransigent Islamist policies begun under Nimeiri and the NIF. Moderate and secularized Muslims in the north mounted stronger opposition to policies of Arabization or Islamization on pragmatic grounds. Finally, the sociocultural pluralism of the country blocked the formation of a unified Sudanese national identity, making law and government a patchwork of compromises at best and incitement to mutiny at worst. The second issue, legitimacy of authority, remained untethered to the fractured national identity and the continuing controversy over an acceptable constitution. Several military coup attempts failed. This web of unresolved issues contributed to the unification of all the opposition parties—the Umma, the Democratic Unionist Party (DUP), the trade unions, the Darfur rebels, and the southern rebel forces—against Khartoum.

The NIF regime tackled the first problem in a feckless fashion: The lack of a national identity putatively would be remedied by embarking on a program of Islamization, making Sudan a Muslim country and suppressing the Christian and animist obstacles to Shari'a. The government initiated Comprehensive Call (*da'wa*) in southern

Sudan between 1992 and 1996, replete with extensive funding from Islamic charities. The project sought to unify education, proselytization, humanitarian development, economic assistance, and counterinsurgency efforts by forcibly establishing camps for black Africans, where they would be instructed in the Koran and in subservience to Khartoum. Apostasy became a criminal offense; Shari'a continued to be enforced as the law of Sudan.

The NIF articulation of a national Islamic character had been flawed by an inability to separate Islam from Arab descent. A malignant racism has characterized relationships with fundamentalist Muslims in the Beja Mountains and in Darfur. In 1999, when Turabi was sidelined by Bashir, the Sudanese Islamist movement split mainly along ethnic lines. Most of the westerners supported Turabi, although not without recriminations and bitterness, while the central Arabs supported Bashir. Turabi's fall in 2000—Bashir suspended parliament and declared a state of emergency to remove him—seems to reflect a subtle shift in Sudanese politics, although belied by few immediate substantive policy changes, as Bashir's government has continued to rely on the backing of the Muslim Brotherhood and the NIF/National Congress Party, as explain Gerard Prunier and Rachel Gisselquist in "The Sudan: A Successfully Failed State."

The division caused by the civil wars (in the south and in the east) was addressed solely as a military, rather than a political or cultural, matter. The NIF poured money into the wars, hoping for a swift military solution. The government conscripted the jihadist Popular Defense Front (PDF), forcing northern Muslims to wage a bloody and indecisive war against the southern rebels—largely non-Muslim, and including minority Christians, who invited aid and succor from Christian missionary charities and Christian politicians in the West, especially in Britain and the United States. The government contributed to the religious war label by enlisting support for its campaign in Islamist terms to muster assistance, domestically and internationally. In 1989, al-Turabi characterized the war in the south as a jihad; in 1992, six progovernment ulama (Islamic scholars) in Kordofan issued a *fatwa* in support of jihad in the Nuba Mountains. But with jihad came a "scorched earth"—even genocidal—military strategy. A 1991 *Africa Watch* report on the Nubian people in Eastern Kordofan Province described widespread killings, disappearances, attacks on the educated and leadership class, and forcible efforts to Islamize the Nubians—tantamount to ethnic cleansing. President Bashir reinforced the Islamist rhetoric on Sudanese Independence Day in 1995, when he called for a mass public jihad against all unbelievers in Sudan.

Exacerbating the second issue of severely limited domestic legitimacy, Khartoum embarked on an equally ambitious program of elimination of dissenters and opponents of the regime. The notorious "Ghost Houses" of Khartoum appeared; stories of disappearances and torture were rampant throughout the city. Reports of violent repression against opponents were met with the blithe pronouncement by Turabi, quoted by de Waal and Abdel Salam, that "Islam does not permit such things." Many prominent politicians were jailed, exiled, or fled. In 1992 the government invaded the headquarters of the DUP and the Umma in Khartoum North; tortured Sid Ahmad al-Husayn, the most senior member of the DUP; and arrested the Khatmiyya leader Shaykh Muhammad al-Hadiyya, according to a June 2006 report in the *Sudan Tribune*. Egypt, Eritrea, Western Europe, Canada, and the United

States attracted large numbers of a growing Sudanese expatriate community. Contacts increased among the leaders of exiled organizations and the Sudanese rebel movements operating inside the country. The 13 major parties, including the SPLM, formed an umbrella opposition-in-exile group called the National Democratic Alliance in 1989 and helped augment international opposition to the NIF regime, although the political, religious, and ethnic factions inside and outside Sudan have little in common even today, besides their intense dislike of the NIF regime. However, they constitute a large slice of the numerical population and potential political influence inside Sudan. To counter them, the NIF regime continues to oscillate between brute force and tactical conciliation.

Reconciliation and Defiance

In January 2005, the Khartoum government of NIF/NCP and the main Sudan People's Liberation Army\Movement southern factions signed a comprehensive peace agreement (CPA) in Nairobi, Kenya, to end the decades-long civil war. The CPA spells out the terms of the peace settlement in detail, including power sharing, wealth (including oil revenues) division, security arrangements, and the disarmament and integration of southern militia units into the national army. In addition, the CPA allows the south to hold a referendum, after six years, on the question of independence. Under the integrated Government of National Unity (GoNU), an interim national constitution and declaration of principles was signed on July 5, 2005, preliminary to drafting a permanent constitution.

With the help of African Union mediators and international support, the GoNU and one major Darfurian rebel faction at Abuja signed a peace agreement on May 5, 2006. Since the signing of the CPA, some senior Sudanese officials have recognized that lasting peace in other parts of the country must be based on a similarly comprehensive power- and wealth-sharing model. The Minni Minawi faction of the Sudan Liberation Army/Movement (SLA/M) signed the peace accords, but three other rebel splinter factions remained unconvinced that their demands were fully addressed. A joint statement from Asmara, Eritrea, on June 7, 2006, as cited by Burr and Collins, asserted that the Abuja peace was brought about by international "intimidation"—that it merely reproduces "old divisive and partial solutions that cannot bring peace to Darfur or Sudan." The three outlying rebel factions signed a cooperation agreement in Asmara, Eritrea, in late June 2006 and founded the National Redemption Front, pledging to continue their struggle against Khartoum in Darfur and elsewhere in Sudan.

Continuing International Pressure

Obviously, the NIF regime faces obstacles to acceptance in the international community. The International Monetary Fund has issued positive interim reports about Sudan's debt repayment scheme. The continued flow of oil revenues ensures a new era for Sudan's credit rating. Sudan has made concerted efforts to repair relations with Egypt and Libya, as well as with other Arab nations. In both the south and in Darfur, African mediators have succeeded in crafting peace agreements, serving to improve Sudanese relationships within Africa. Perhaps most remarkably, Sudan has emerged as a strategic U.S. ally in the war on terrorism, providing key information about global Islamist networks and detaining suspects within its borders, as an April 2005 *Los Angeles Times* report notes. At the same time, while the regime accepted an African Union peace-keeping monitoring group in Darfur, an actual end to fighting and the emplacement of international or UN peacekeeping troops elude international efforts—indeed, such efforts are resisted by Sudanese authorities as a return to colonialism.

Despite this mix of developments, Sudan's international legitimacy remains tarnished by the Darfur crisis, where ongoing accusations of, at minimum, extensive human rights violations and, at maximum, genocide, have deterred diplomatic progress in greater measure. Amidst three years of public international discussion and debate, UN officials have issued several statements and brought forth Security Council resolutions on the situation. Resolution 1590 of the Security Council, dated March 24, 2005, authorized 10,000 troops for a UN Mission in Sudan (UNMIS) to monitor peace arrangements in the south and to implement the CPA. The UN has pushed for a similar force to regulate the 2006 Darfur peace agreement. Sanctions and travel restrictions have been placed on Sudanese leaders deemed to be supporting the violence in accordance with UN Security Council Resolution 1672. The Security Council has referred the situation in Darfur to the International Criminal Court for investigation into possible "crimes against humanity." The Sudanese government agreed only to a UN study mission in mid-2006.

Walking the Tightrope

The fate of Islamism in Sudan hangs in the balance for the Government of National Unity between an effort toward renewed international (especially economic and commercial) acceptance and the residue of the sometimes bloody campaign to create a unified national and Islamic identity. Bashir's modified isolation of Turabi suggested a shift toward greater pragmatism. Nevertheless, despite divisions among its adherents, Islamism remains influential in official circles, particularly in the security services and in the military. An Islamist posture appears central to the president's grip on the country. An increase in cooperation with the United States in the realm of anti-terrorism ruffles the feathers of militants in Khartoum. Bashir's June 2006 pronouncement, as quoted by Reuters, that he will not allow "colonizing forces" to "internationalize" the Darfur conflict represents a gesture of appeasement.

Salah Gosh, the head of Sudanese national security and intelligence, revealed death pledges from members of the security services and the Popular Defense Forces, asserting, as quoted by Reuters: "[I]f the choice is between re-colonization of Sudan and incursion into its soil by foreign troops, then interior of earth is better than its surface." Concurrently, Gosh cultivates a close relationship with U.S. intelligence services. Gosh made an unpublicized flight in April 2005 to Washington, D.C., aboard a CIA jet to attend high-level meetings with intelligence staff, described in the State Department, according to an April 2005 *Los Angeles Times* report, as providing "specific information that is . . . important, functional and current"; Gosh acknowledges that Sudan's partnership with the U.S. intelligence community is strong. Sudan cooperates with the United States in an effort to shed sanctions and to be dropped from the U.S. State Department's list of state sponsors of terrorism. While the 2005 *Report on Terrorism* still designates Sudan as active, it also stresses Sudan's "cooperative commitment against known and suspected international terrorist elements" and its ability to produce "desired results" against them.

Regime stability remains a challenge in Sudan as long as the Government of National Unity (formed by the Coalition Peace Agreement) barely functions as a unit. Vice president and representative southerner Salva Kiir (successor to his SPLM chief, the late John Garang), claimed that the coalition was not consulted concerning the rejection of UN troops. At a rally in the southern city of Juba on June 30, 2006, Kiir announced, as quoted in the *Sudan Tribune*, "The position of the SPLM is obvious and has no problem with the deployment of international forces in Darfur." In the past, Kiir favored secession for the south. His regional popularity renders ignoring him a problem for Bashir and the present National Congress government.

Internationally, Bashir's rejection of a transition from African Union to UN peacekeepers leaves the global community with few options for dealing with the Darfur crisis. Furthermore, it is unclear whether an expanded peacekeeping force could operate effectively in Darfur, because there is little peace to keep. The Darfurian National Redemption Front of rebel factions diminishes hopes that a series of weakly observed cease-fires provide any form of security there.

Where does this leave Islamism in Sudan? An enforced and effectively administered settlement with the south jeopardizes the campaign of militants in the north, especially in Khartoum, to impose Islamist governance over the whole country. As a consequence of the CPA, Shari'a no longer applies to the southerners. Islamism did not lose its national voice as its devotees diminished in national politics. Still, Islamism as officially promoted jihad has lost steam, as has its most powerful promoter, Turabi. He now shares influence with other actors, most less philosophical, some more simplistically militant, and some less ideological and more pragmatic. In some respects, the present position of Islamism in Sudan, as ideology and political program, resembles that in Pakistan.

BIBLIOGRAPHY

Abduh, Muhammad. *The Theology of Unity.* Trans. Ishaq Masa'ad and Kenneth Cragg. London: Allen and Unwin, 1966.

Adams, William. *Nubia: Corridor to Africa.* Princeton, NJ: Princeton University Press, 1977.

African Development Bank. "Selected Statistics on African Countries." *African Development Bank* 25 (2006).

Ahmed, Abd al-Salam Sid. "Tehran-Khartoum: A New Axis or a Warning Shot?" *Middle East International Magazine* (London) (February 7, 1992): 36–49.

Al-Banna, Hasan. "Al-Ikhwan al-Muslimun fi ashar sanawat" (Speech to the Fifth Conference of the Society of Muslim Brothers). *Al-Nadhir* 35 (1939): 22.

Al-Turabi, Hasan. "Islam as a Pan-National Movement and Nation States: An Islamic Doctrine on Human Association." Text of Address, London: Royal Society of Arts. April 27, 1992. Reprinted. London: The Sudan Foundation, 1992.

———. "Islamic Fundamentalism in the Sunna and Shi'a World." Address in Madrid, Spain. August 2, 1994.

"Bin Laden Call for Jihad Clouds UN Darfur Mission." Reuters, April 24, 2006.

Burr, J. Millard, and Robert O. Collins. *Revolutionary Sudan: Hassan al-Turabi and the Islamist State, 1989–2000.* Boston: Brill, 2003.

Carney, Timothy. "The Sudan: Political Islam and Terrorism." In *Battling Terrorism in the Horn of Africa*, ed. Robert Rotberg, 119–40. Washington, DC: Brookings Institution, 2005.

"Chad Army Battles Rebels." *The Guardian,* July 3, 2006.

Central Intelligence Agency (CIA). "Sudan." In *The World Fact Book.* Central Intelligence Agency, 2006.

Comprehensive Peace in Sudan Act. December 23, 2004, Public Law 108-497, 108th Congress of the United States. U.S. GPO: 2004.

Country Analysis Briefs: Sudan. U.S. Energy Information Administration, March 2006.

"The Darfur Crisis." FPRI e-notes, Foreign Policy Research Institute, Philadelphia, July 18, 2006, revised archive edition. www.fpri .org.

"Darfur Hold Out Leaders Urge International Community to Make a Difference." *Sudan Tribune,* June 15, 2006.

Davis, Joyce. "Hassan al-Turabi, Popular Arab and Islamic Conference, Sudan." In *Between Jihad and Salaam: Profiles in Islam*, 1–28. New York: St. Martin's Press, 1997.

De Bono, Andrea. "Letter to the British Consul General in Khartoum." In *The Europeans in Sudan: 1834–1878*, trans. and ed. Paul Santi and Richard Hill, 72. Oxford, UK: Clarendon Press, 1980.

De Waal, Alex, and A.H. Abdel Salam. "Islamism, State Power and Jihad in Sudan." In *Islamism and Its Enemies in the Horn of Africa*, ed. Alex de Waal, 71–113. Bloomington: Indiana University Press, 2004.

De Waal, Alex, and Julie Flint. *Darfur: A Short History of a Long War.* New York: Palgrave Macmillan, 2005.

Deng, Francis. "The Sudan." *Brookings Review* 12:1 (1994).

———. *War of Visions: Conflict of Identities in the Sudan.* Washington, DC: Brookings Institution, 1995.

Duncan, J.S.R. *The Sudan: A Record of Achievement: 1898–1947.* Edinburgh: William Blackwood and Sons, 1952.

Emerson, Steve. *Foreign Terrorists in America: Five Years After the World Trade Center Bombing.* Prepared Statement before the U.S. Senate Judiciary Committee, Subcommittee on Terrorism, Technology and Government Information. Federal News Service: February 24, 1998.

"Eritrea Proxy Wars on Ethiopia." *Sudan Tribune,* June 26, 2006.

Esposito, John, and John Voll. "Hasan al-Turabi: The Mahdi-Lawyer." In *Makers of Contemporary Islam*, 118–49. New York: Oxford University Press, 2001.

———. "Sudan, The Mahdi and the Military." In *Islam and Democracy*, ed. John Esposito and John Voll, 78–101. New York: Oxford University Press, 1996.

Fluehr-Lobban, Carolyn, and Hatim Babiker Hillawi. "Circulars of the Shari'a Courts in the Sudan, 1902–1979." *Journal of African Law* 27:2 (Autumn 1989): 79.

"Funding Terror: Investigating the Role of Saudi Banks." *In These Times*, December 20, 2002.

Garang, John. *John Garang Speaks*, ed. Mansour Khalid. New York: Routledge, 1997.

Gardner, George, and Sami Hanna. *Arab Socialism: A Documentary Survey.* Salt Lake City: University of Utah Press, 1969.

Glickman, Harvey. "Islamism in Sudan's Civil War." *Orbis* 44:2 (Spring 2000): 273–79.

Holt, P.M. *A Modern History of the Sudan, from the Funj Sultanate to the Present Day.* London: Weidenfeld and Nicolson, 1961.

———. *The Sudan of the Three Niles: The Funj Chronicle of the Three Niles.* Boston: Brill, 1999.

Johnson, Douglas H., with James Currey. *The Root Causes of Sudan's Civil Wars.* Bloomington: Indiana University Press, 2003.

Kapteijns, Lidwien. *Mahdist Faith and Sudanic Tradition: The History of the Masalit Sultanate 1870–1930.* Boston: Routledge, 1985.

Khomeini, Ruhullah. "Islamic Government." In *Islam in Transition: Muslim Perspectives*, ed. John Donohue and John Esposito. New York: Oxford University Press, 2006.

Lesch, Ann. "Osama bin Laden's Business in Sudan." *Current History* 100:655 (May 2002): 203–10.

Lia, Brynjar. *The Society of the Muslim Brothers in Egypt: The Rise of an Islamic Mass Movement 1928–1942.* Reading, UK: Garnet, 1998.

Maddy-Weitzman, Bruce, and Meir Litvak. "Islamism and the State in North Africa." In *Revolutionaries and Reformers: Contemporary Islamist Movements in the Middle East*, ed. Barry Rubin, 69–90. Albany: State University of New York Press, 2003.

Mahmoud, Muhammad. "Sufism and Islamism in the Sudan." In *African Islam and Islam in Africa: Encounters Between Sufis and Islamists*, ed. David Westerlund and Eva Evers Rosander, 162–92. Athens: Ohio University Press, 1997.

Mughniyyah, Muhammad Jawad. *The Five Schools of Islamic Law*. Qum, Iran: Ansariyan Publications, 2003.

The National Commission on Terrorist Attacks upon the United States. *The Complete 9/11 Commission Report*. Washington, DC: U.S. Government Printing Office, 2004.

"9/11 Families Sue Saudis, Sudan." *CBS News*, August 16, 2002.

O'Ballance, Edgar. *The Secret War in the Sudan: 1955–1972*. Hamden, CT: Archon Books, 1977.

———. *Sudan, Civil War and Terrorism: 1956–99*. New York: St. Martin's Press, 2000.

O'Fahey, R.S., and J.L. Spaulding. *Kingdoms of the Sudan*. London: Methuen, 1974.

"Official Pariah Sudan Valuable to America's War on Terrorism." *Los Angeles Times,* April 29, 2005.

Pakistan's Sharia Law Criticized," *BBC News Online*, June 3, 2003. http://news.bbc .co.uk/2/hi/south–asia/2958316.htm.

"Profile: Salva Kiir." *BBC News Online.* August 2, 2005. http://news.bbc.co.uk/2/hi/africa/3488806.stm.

Prunier, Gerard, and Rachel Gisselquist. "The Sudan: A Successfully Failed State." In *State Failure and State Weakness in a Time of Terror*, ed. Robert Rotberg, 101–28. Washington, DC: Brookings Institution, 2003.

Qutb, Sayyid. "Social Justice in Islam." In *Islam in Transition: Muslim Perspectives*, ed. John Donohue and John Esposito, 103–8. New York: Oxford University Press, 2004.

Reeves, Eric. "Khartoum's Central Role in the Assassination Attempt on Egyptian President Hosni Mubarak." Sudanreeves. org, October 3, 2001. www.sudanreeves.org/Sections-article385-p1.html.

Rolandsen, Øystein. *Guerrilla Government: Political Changes in the Southern Sudan During the 1990s*. Oslo: Nordiska Afrikainstitutet, 2005.

Salama, A.M. Said. *Arab Socialism*. New York: Barnes and Noble, 1972.

Shay, Shaul. *The Red Sea Terror Triangle: Sudan, Somalia, Yemen and Islamic Terror.* New Brunswick, NJ: Transaction Publishers, 2005.

Sidahmed, Abdel Salam and Alsir Sidahmed. *Sudan*. New York: Routledge, 2005.

"Sudan's Bashir Takes Tough Line on UN Troops." Reuters, June 20, 2006.

"Sudan's Security Chief Rejects UN Force, Calls for Martrydom." *Sudan Tribune,* June 20, 2006.

"Sudan Stops Support to Ugandan Rebels: President." *Chinese People's Daily,* August 21, 2001.

"UN Peacekeepers Divide Sudanese Government Partners." *Sudan Tribune,* July 2, 2006.

UN Security Council Resolution 1672. March 29, 2005.

United Nations. *Sudan Situation Report*, July 2, 2006.

U.S. Department of State. *Country Reports on Terrorism 2005*. Washington, DC: U.S. Department of State, April 2006.

"U.S. Calls Killings in Sudan Genocide." *Washington Post,* September 10, 2004.

U.S. Department of State. *Patterns of Global Terrorism*. Washington, DC: U.S. Department of State, 1993.

U.S. Energy Information Administration. "Sudan: Country Analysis Brief." U.S. Energy Information Administration, 2009.

U.S. Library of Congress. *Sudan Country Profile*. Library of Congress, Federal Research Division, December 2004.

Voll, John. "Islam, Islamization and Urbanization in Sudan: Contradictions and Complementaries." In *Population, Poverty and Politics in Middle Eastern Cities*, ed. Michael Bonine, 285–303. Gainesville: University Press of Florida, 1997.

———. "Sufi Brotherhoods: Transcultural/Transstate Networks in the Muslim World." In *Interactions: Trans-regional Perspectives on World History*, ed. Jerry Bentley, Renate Bridenthal, and Anand Yang, 30–47. Honolulu: University of Hawaii Press, 2005.

Wai, Dunstan. "Pax Brittanica and the Southern Sudan: The View from the Theatre." *African Affairs* 79:316 (July 1980): 375–95.

Warburg, Gabriel. *Islam, Sectarianism and Politics in the Sudan Since the Mahdiyya*. Madison: University of Wisconsin Press, 2003.

———. "The *Shari'a* in Sudan: Implementation and Repercussions." In *Sudan: State and Society in Crisis*, ed. John Voll, 90–107. Washington, DC: Middle East Institute, 1991.

Woodward, Peter. "Sudan: Islamic Radicals in Power." In *Political Islam: Revolution, Radicalism or Reform?* ed. John Esposito, 95–114. Boulder, CO: Lynne Rienner, 1997.

ASIA

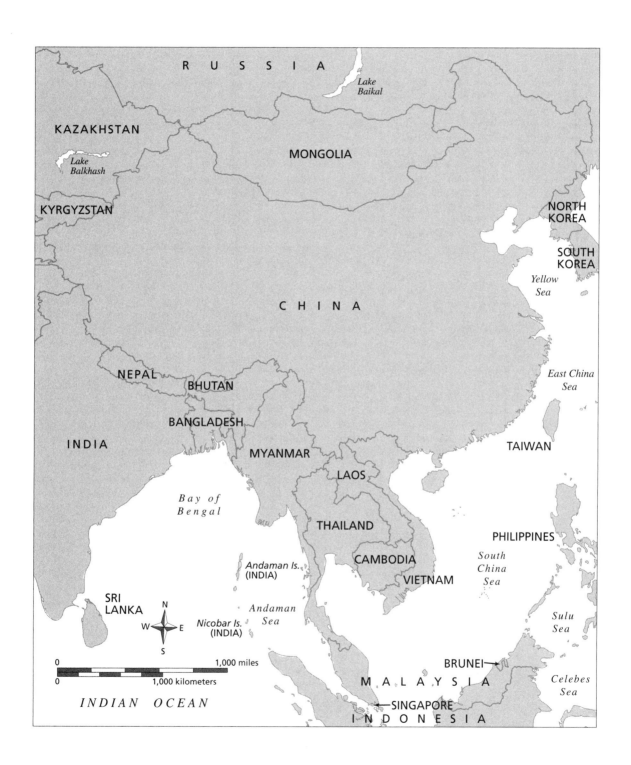

R U S S I A

Lake Baikal

KAZAKHSTAN

Lake Balkhash

MONGOLIA

KYRGYZSTAN

NORTH KOREA

SOUTH KOREA

Yellow Sea

C H I N A

NEPAL

BHUTAN

BANGLADESH

East China Sea

INDIA

MYANMAR

TAIWAN

LAOS

Bay of Bengal

THAILAND

Andaman Is. (INDIA)

PHILIPPINES

CAMBODIA

South China Sea

VIETNAM

SRI LANKA

N

W E

S

Andaman Sea

Nicobar Is. (INDIA)

Sulu Sea

0   1,000 miles

0   1,000 kilometers

BRUNEI

M A L A Y S I A

Celebes Sea

INDIAN OCEAN

SINGAPORE

I N D O N E S I A

Bangladesh

Maneeza Hossain

Bangladesh is experiencing the possibility of an irreversible transformation. Slowly but surely, proponents of a monolithic understanding of Islam have been implementing various facets of a program of cultural "purification" by means that vary from the peaceful to the violent. Social forces that have supported a more open conception of society, culture, and politics have not reacted to the emergent threat with any coherent program.

Questions that ensue are therefore: Does this impetus for transformation and the lack of response reflect a changing cultural mood in Bangladesh or does it result from extrinsic political factors? More important, can Bangladesh survive as a pluralistic, tolerant society?

The goal of the Islamists posits a fictionalized "society of the Prophet" as a model of emulation to the detriment of the experiences and traditions of Bengali culture, creating a conflict where none existed between the components of a cultural reality. The apogee of Bengali culture was a synthesis of Islamic values and cultural input with local traditions and practices. Islam has always been an integral part of Bengali culture, while Bengali culture has been the backbone of the moral, intellec-

tual, literary, and civil life of the Muslims of Bengal.

Background: Islam's Place in Bengali Society

With a population of over 145 million, Bangladesh is home to the third-largest Muslim community in the world. Having gained independence in 1971, Bangladesh (formerly East Pakistan and prior to that East Bengal) has witnessed a tumultuous political history, including the assassination of two presidents who were also the founders of the major political parties that dominate politics to this day. Shaykh Mujibur Rahman, charismatic leader of the Awami League (AL), whose daughter Sheikh Hasina is the current opposition leader, was killed in 1975. Ziaur Rahman, founder of the Bangladesh National Party (BNP), the main partner in the ruling coalition led by Rahman's widow, Khaleda Zia, was killed in 1981.

After almost a decade of military dictatorship, the restoration of the democratic process in 1991 brought a new era of political invigoration to Bangladesh. However, the political system was prone to corruption. Successive elections relied heavily on patron-

JOLIET JUNIOR COLLEC-
JOLIET, IL 60431

age and cronyism, leading to a growing disenchantment with the democratic process and the two main political formations. This gave Jamaate Islam, the prominent Islamist party, an opportunity to stand out with a platform seeking the implementation of a long-term program toward the fundamental transformation of Bangladeshi society and eventual creation of a Shari'a-based state (a state based on Islamic law).

The status of Islam in Bengali identity is deeply rooted. The important function of Islam in Bengali life prompted even secularist ideologues, such as Mujibur Rahman, to seek to accommodate it. Yet, while Islam has a long history in Bangladesh, it is important to underline that Islamism in Bangladesh is a recent phenomenon. "Islamism" for our purposes is defined as a movement that considers that Islam as a religion has a primary function in politics. Islamists do not limit themselves to Islamic values in politics, but seek to implement what they consider to be an Islamic vision of the political state. These notions were not dominant even under British rule, in the context of the Pakistan movement. Muslim leaders under British control conceived of an Indian-Muslim nation but did not constrain themselves with a rigid constant formula presumed to embody the essence of Islam.

The idea of Pakistan as an "Islamic state" understood "Islamic" as cultural and social, not ideological or political. The "Islamic state" was then the state of the Muslims, whether they chose a socialist, capitalist, or another political formula of state. The dominant perception of the role of Islam in society was that of a shared heritage common to all, which did not affect political outlook. In retrospect, the minority view promoted by Abdul Ala Mawdudi Ala Mawdidi fusing Islam and politics was a core precursor of the Islamist movements of today. However, it is important to underline that in then–East Bengal and East Pakistan, Mawdudi's conception was at the margins of the political and cultural spectrums.

Against the background of rising Bengali nationalism in East Pakistan in the 1960s, many Bengali ideological supporters of Mawdudi backed the notion of a unified Pakistan and therefore stood against the aspirations for independence and self-rule of fellow Bengalis. This position was taken despite the nonreligious character of the Pakistani state. It should be noted that the Pakistani leadership, while not religious or Islamist, did use Islamic rhetoric to mobilize support against the nascent Bengali independent movement. Many of the atrocities committed by the West Pakistani recruits in the Pakistani army were driven by the conviction that the enemy being fought was not "Muslim." The potential for harm, even genocide through Islamic rhetoric, was demonstrated in the killings and rapes of up to one million East Pakistanis.

With the triumph of Bangladesh and the assertion of Bengali nationalism, the growth of Islamism in Bangladesh was checked, with the role of the many Islamists who opposed the emergence of the nation becoming part and parcel of the political discourse. These Islamists were denounced as *razakar* (traitors). The fading of memory as time has passed has given these groups a new lease on life. Their reemergence, while shy in many respects, is taking on complex forms. It is useful to classify the various activities in which Islamist formations engage into four categories:

1. open political activism, above-surface action often in the form of organized political parties engaged in elections;

2. underground political militancy of a more intransigent ideological outlook rejecting the current order and often engaged in violent actions;

3. social and cultural work in the form of civil society organizations and nongovernmental formations (NGOs) providing services in direct or indirect coordination with the aforementioned political parties;

4. economic initiatives and enterprises that espouse the ideological foundations of Islamism but operate independently of any stated political purpose.

The collective effect of this intricate web of structures is to imbue Bangladesh with an intensified "Islamic" character that serves the Islamist purpose. An Islamic bank, a rural orphanage, a band of armed militants, and a student association affiliated with a political party represented in government might not have direct links among themselves, but they reflect an ideological agenda that seeks the transformation of Bangladesh.

The following survey is illustrative rather than exhaustive. It provides a spotlight into the various areas of activism and action that Islamist thought and practice have established in Bangladesh. It is not an Islamist conspiracy. There is no central command directing the new Islamist reality in Bangladesh. There is, however, awareness among leading Islamists of some evolving patterns and a desire to intensify and capitalize on them.

Open Political Activists: Jamaate Islam and the Lesser Islamists

Islamist political activism in Bangladesh has been dominated by Jamaate Islam (alternatively Jamaate Islami, or JI), the flagship Islamist organization. It is headed by Mawlana Motiur Rahman Nizami, former minister of industries in the BNP-led government (2001–2006). The Jamaate Islam presents itself as "the vanguard of the Islamic Movement in Bangladesh" and explicitly aims to establish an Islamic social order in Bangladesh.

History

The Jamaate Islam has its roots in the mother organization of the same name, founded in prepartition India by Syed Ab'ul Ala Mawdudi in 1941. "Mawlana" Mawdudi moved to Pakistan from India after Pakistan gained independence. However, Jamaate had opposed the creation of a separate state for the Muslims of India. While persisting in his anti-Pakistan ideology, Mawdudi wrote in one of his books, "If we have ever uttered a single word in the favor of creation of Pakistan, it must be proved with references." That is why Jamaate Islam also did not support the Muslim League, the largest Muslim party, in the key elections of 1946.

After the creation of Pakistan, Jamaate Islam was divided into separate Indian and Pakistani organizations. Jamaate Islam Bangladesh originates from the Jamaate wing in former East Pakistan.

Critics of Jamaate often accuse its core leaders of having opposed the independence of Bangladesh during the liberation war in 1971. They formed paramilitary structures like Razakars, al-Badr, and Peace Committees. The party is accused of actively aiding the Pakistani army throughout the war. It is alleged that its ex-chief, Golam Azam, and most of its top leaders, such as Motiur Rahman Nizami, Ali Ahsan Mujahid, Muhammad Kamaruzzaman, and Delwar Hossain Sayeedi, helped the Pakistani army in the war against India in 1971. These accusations lost potency with time, with Nizami becoming the minister of industry and Mujahid the minister of social welfare in the BNP-led cabinet in 2001. The Jamaate denies these allegations. However, they do not deny that they were opposed to the creation of Bangladesh as a nation-state. They argued that, instead, they actively campaigned for greater autonomy in East Pakistan.

For this stance, and for allegations of collusion with the Pakistani army, the Jamaate was initially banned and members were arrested and often killed in revenge attacks. Though the Jamaate members' role was forgiven publicly by Shaykh Mujibur Rahman, Jamaate's political activities were banned and the citizenship of Golam Azam, the leader of Jamaate, was revoked. Jamaate was allowed to carry out political activities again in 1977, when Ziaur Rahman reintroduced a multiparty system and formed the Bangladesh Nationalist Party. He also allowed Golam Azam to return to Bangladesh from Great Britain. Azam came back and retook the position as the leader of Jamaate.

After the end of military rule in 1990, protests began against Golam Azam and Jamaate by groups that saw him as an Islamist. As a result of these protests, his citizenship was challenged by the state. Yet the supreme court of Bangladesh gave Azam Bangladeshi citizenship, because the panel of judges agreed that he was a Bangladeshi by birth.

Modus Operandi

Even if Jamaate Islam of Bangladesh had never had organizational connections with other national Islamist movements, its grassroots mobilization and political action methods resemble them. The model is one that capitalizes on the inefficiency of government, corruption, and lack of political vision in the mainstream, providing alternatives in practice, morality, and ideology. In the case of Bangladesh, as in other cases, this Islamist formation has behaved not as a conventional political party, which monitors the government's performance and points out deficiencies, but rather as the kernel of a completely alternative system.

Jamaate strives to espouse a polished version of Islamism, presumably consistent with democratic practices and civil liberties. Occasionally, though, notably in the treatment of minorities, this behavior is more akin to a facade. In October 2003, for example, as reported by Human Rights Watch, a Jamaate leader in Jessore, Mawlana Aminur Rahman, led a mob attack in which Muhammad Shah Alam, local leader of Ahmadiyya, a religion Islamist groups consider heretical, was killed.

While open Islamist activism is dominated by the Jamaate, Islamism also manifests itself through smaller formations. These "lesser" parties often offer a stricter, more radical version of the Islamist ideology espoused by the Jamaate, positioning the latter as a result closer to the center of the political spectrum.

One such party is the Islamic Oike Joyte (IOJ). This small Islamist party formed part of the BNP-led coalition government between 2001 and 2006. Its two top leaders, Mawlana Azizul Haq and Mawlana Fazlul Haq Amini, were both arrested in connection with the lynching of a policeman in violence that followed a ruling by the Bangladesh High Court banning the use of fatwas (religious edicts). In addition, the IOJ leaders allegedly threatened the two judges who banned the issuance of fatwas.

Another, more recent, formation is Islamic Shasantantrik Andolan, the Islamic

Constitution Movement led by Mawlana Fazlul Karim, an influential Sufi leader. Notwithstanding the presumed implications of the "Constitutional" label affixed to it or the Sufi background of its leadership, this movement has demonstrated overt intolerance. On November 18, 2006, one of its top leaders declared that the country was being made un-Islamic by reserving three seats for women in each local council.

Intolerance, in this case of the Ahmadiyya community, is also the openly declared purpose of another formation, the International Khatme Nabuwat Movement (IKNM). The goal of this formation is to ban the Ahmadiyya religious movement as un-Islamic. Outside of the party politics, IKNM is probably best known for announcing the dates of their planned attacks on minority groups in Bangladesh. In the fourth quarter of 2004, the government took a more active stance against this vigilante formation that had spearheaded anti-Ahmadiyya agitation, stopping two planned marches on the Ahmadiyya headquarters in Dhaka by an effective combination of political pressure and police deployments. Under government direction, police in Ahmadiyya communities also became more active in protecting Ahmadiyya members.

However, in other cases, according to the U.S. State Department's *International Religious Freedom Report* for 2005, police did not stop extremist demonstrators from placing provocative signboards at Ahmadi mosques. Ahmadiyya mosques have been attacked. Ahmadiyya families have been ostracized and occasionally subjected to violence. Promoters of cultural radicalization have succeeded in inserting intolerance and calls to violent actions into the normal public discourse in Bangladesh. Even English-language dailies, including *British Broadcasting Corporation* (*BBC*) *News*

(January 9, 2004), have published the dates and locations of the intended attacks on Ahmadiyya mosques, against a background of seeming apathy on the part of the government and beyond.

While the government has occasionally shown its willingness to curb the aggressiveness of militant Islamists, in their ongoing rivalry, neither of the two main political parties has been immune to courting Islamist formations. For enhancing their activities and credibility, Islamist parties have been playing down their ideology to gain voter support. According to Aataai Gazi Mahbub, writing for *OhmyNews*, the Islamic Constitution Movement (ICM), along with other groups such as the Bangladesh Tarikat Federation (BTF), Islamic Kelaphat Majlish (IKM), and Islamic Unity Front led by Mawlana Meshbahur Rahaman, has been discussing joining any political coalition. Reuters reports that they have been increasingly active in the prepoll agitation with their demands.

Underground Political Activists: Jamatul Mujahideen Bangladesh and Others

Jamatul Mujahideen Bangladesh (JMB) is the most notorious of the violent jihadist organizations operating in Bangladesh. Mawlana Abdur Rahman is the chief of the JMB, which was formed in 1998. JMB claims to be an outgrowth of Jamatul Mujahideen, though there are also reports that it is a youth front of the outlawed militant group Harkat ul-Jihad. The JMB follows the ideals of the Taliban militia and propagates a movement based on a strict Salafist interpretation of Islamist activism. The JMB openly rejects the prevailing political system in Bangladesh and aims to "build a society based on the Islamic model laid out in Holy Quran and Hadith," as described by Hiranmay Karlekar. Karlekar explains in his book *Bangladesh: The Next Afghanistan?* that the JMB is opposed to democracy as a form of governance. Its position was spelled out in leaflets written in Bengali and Arabic, which were found at various bombing sites following its massive terrorist campaign on August 17, 2005, as reported by the *Los Angeles Times* (December 7, 2005):

> In a Muslim country there can be no laws other than the laws of Allah. . . . The Qu'ran or hadith do not recognize any democratic or socialist system that is enacted by infidels and non-believers. . . . [We] reject the constitution that conflicts with Allah's laws and call upon all to abandon the so-called election process and run the affairs of state according to the laws of Allah and the traditions of the Prophet.

In August 2005 the group launched more than 300 small bomb attacks simultaneously in 50 cities and towns across Bangladesh, including in the capital, Dhaka. The attacks were shocking, despite an otherwise "rich" history of terrorism. Other notable episodes include a February 13, 2003, mishap, during which JMB militants inadvertently triggered seven bomb explosions at one of its hideouts. These bombs had been prepared to explode in northern Bangladeshi towns during International Mother Language Day. In addition, on January 12, 2005, the JMB claimed responsibility for bomb blasts at two separate cultural events in the Sherpur and Jamalpur districts, which injured 25 and 10, respectively. In yet another bombing, on January 15, 2005, two were killed and over 70 people were injured at performances in Bogra and Natore.

With its open recourse to terrorism and

its proclamations to work for the establishment of a Shari'a state in Bangladesh, the JMB was banned by Prime Minister Khaleda Zia's government in February 2005. It therefore espouses a radical Islamist ideology that considers violence as a means toward achieving its goals. The JMB has international connections, at least within South Asia, with Jamatul Mujahideen (based in India) and Jamatul Mujahideen Pakistan. However, its statements reveal a Salafist jihadist doctrine that is common across international radical Islamist organizations.

Beyond ideology, international links have also been alleged at the financial level. The JMB is claimed to have received financial assistance from individual donors in various Middle Eastern countries. Reports have also alleged that funding for the JMB has come from international NGOs based in Kuwait, Saudi Arabia, Qatar, and the United Arab Emirates. These claims, however, remain unproven.

What is certain is that the JMB is but one star, albeit the most notorious, in a jihadist constellation in Bangladesh. Other organizations include Jama'atul Jihad, Ahle Hadith Andolan Bangladesh (AHAB), Ahle Hadith Jubo Shangha, Jagrata Muslim Janata Bangladesh (JMJB), Harkat ul-Jihad al-Islami (HUJI), Hizbut Tawhid, Tawhidi Janata, Islami Jubo Shangha, Islami Shangha, al-Falah A'am Unnayan Shanstha, and Shahadat-e al-Hiqma. Mostly tracing their origins to the obscure al-Mujahideen network of the 1990s, these formations surface periodically, often in conjunction with gun battles or other violent confrontations. The same group of militants sometimes goes by many different names, with the intention to confuse.

It is thus believed that Jagrata Muslim Janata Bangladesh (JMJB) was part of the

JMB. However, it publicly began calling itself the JMJB following an August 15, 2003, gunfight between its cadres and the police at its secret training camp in the village of Khetlal in the Joypurhat district. The JMJB has nonetheless accumulated a record of its own. Newspaper reports suggest that taxes have been levied on villagers by the JMJB and women have been ordered to wear *hijabs* (head scarves). Those who defy these decrees are subjected to physical abuse or their property is damaged. Both the JMB and the JMJB have terrorized people in western and southwestern Bangladesh. The two organizations identify antisocial elements by their own definition and mete out vigilante justice. They kill their victims in gruesome ways and often mutilate their bodies.

The JMJB has also threatened numerous journalists, with more than 55 receiving death threats between September and December 2005. In addition, several captured members of the group have claimed that their targets include traditional Bangladeshi cultural organizations and NGOs such as Building Resources Across Communities (BRAC, formerly the Bangladesh Rural Advancement Committee), Proshika, and the Grameen Bank.

Militant jihadism has also reached the frontiers of Bangladesh, as exemplified by Harkat ul-Jihad, an outlawed militant group engaged in terrorist activities in parts of Chittagong district (in association with several Rohingya Muslim militant organizations from Burma).

Apolitical Activism? The Tablighi Jamaat and Social Movements

The Tablighi Jamaat, an Islamic revival movement, was founded in India by Mawlana Ilyas. It advocates strict adherence to Islamic values and religious practices. One of the movement's main objectives has been to rid local Islam of perceived "Hindu influence." As this author has written in "The Rise of the Islamic Tide in Bangladesh," the Tablighi Jamaat is a self-described "apolitical" Islamic movement and prominent missionary group that encourages the Islamization of politics in Bangladesh by seizing on growing political, economic, and social discontent to radicalize the disaffected. The movement has become particularly strong in Bangladesh. After the annual pilgrimage to Mecca, the world's second-largest Islamic pilgrimage takes place in Tongi, a town only two miles outside the Bangladeshi capital, Dhaka. As reported in the Dhaka newspaper, *New Nation*, up to 4 million Muslims travel to a three-day Biswa Ijtema, or Islamic prayer meeting. Preachers and their congregation travel in large groups from different areas of the region to hear speeches delivered in Arabic, Urdu, and Bengali.

Tablighi Jamaat should be a serious concern for South Asian stability. As Alex Alexiev asserts in "Tablighi Jamaat: Jihad's Stealthy Legions," the movement's sister organization in Pakistan encourages "Wahabi brethren to go on missions with them" and share their knowledge with one another. This collaboration ensures a stream of support and income from wealthy Saudi Arabian sources. In 1992 the group spawned a Bangladeshi branch of the Pakistan-based Harkat ul-Jihad al-Islami. Its leader, Fazlur Rahman, a powerful cleric from the port city of Chittagong, was one of the signatories of Osama bin Ladin's 1998 declaration of "Jihad Against Jews and Crusaders."

The Islamist parties have not developed in isolation. Oil-rich Middle Eastern countries have funded both public and private Islamic activities, including NGOs, *madrasas* (religious schools), Koran societies, and orphanages. The increasing price of oil has translated into greater resources for Islamists, usually channeled through Islamic development organizations and banks like al-Arafah Islami Bank and al-Haramain Islamic Foundation, as reported in the July 4, 2004, *Bangladesh Observer.* Many Islamists run financial institutions, schools, hospitals, and industries backed by foreign funding. The most prominent NGOs with an international Islamist dimension in the Bangladeshi context include:

1. Al-Haramain Islamic Foundation: An Islamic social welfare institution, initially known to organize orphanages in the region and was banned in Bangladesh in 2002. However, it soon disseminated its activities under a new name, the Qatar Charitable Society.
2. Islamic Relief Organization: One of the hundreds of NGOs, such as the Ishra Islamic Foundation and al-Maghrib Eye Hospital, that are registered with the social welfare department. Their activities have significantly increased since the Jamaate Islam leader became head of the Social Welfare Ministry.
3. Rabitat al-Alam al–Islam: Also known as the Muslim World League, it is a Mecca-based international organization operating several hospitals in the southeastern region of Bangladesh (Chittagong and Cox's Bazaar). The organization, led by Dr. Abd al-Mohsin al-Turki as its secretary general, has been active in promoting Islamic charity work. As written on the Jamaate Islam Web site, the organization has had frequent exchanges with the leading officials of the Jamaate party in Bangladesh.

4. Revival of Islamic Heritage Society: A Kuwait-based organization believed to fund militants who attacked the premises of the largest local NGOs, the Grameen Bank, and BRAC.

Building Blocks: Islamic Banking and Beyond

In the banking sector, the Jamaate-influenced Islamic Bank has been outperforming other banking institutions. This has effectively created a parallel economy that fosters Islamist businesses while remaining out of the mainstream control of the state. In what may be an ominous sign of further Islamization of the banking system, the largest state bank was recently purchased by Saudi interests.

Public medical care in Bangladesh is full of gaps, but the Jamaate-sponsored Ibn Sina Hospital provides state-of-the-art health services that until recently were unheard of in the country. In the health sector, as well as education and banking, Jamaate institutions are viewed as models of performance, efficiency, and integrity. In addition to providing necessary services for the population at large, these Jamaate institutions are excellent venues for employment for young professionals associated with the Jamaate movement.

Where the state has failed in providing the expected services in education, banking, health, and social welfare, the Jamaate has stepped in with exemplary—albeit highly ideological—institutions. The result is the creation of an effective state-within-the-state, one that does not rely on conventional measures to assert its influence.

The Jamaate's 12 seats in the 2001–2006 parliament were often dismissed by those who did not see the growing influence of Jamaate institutions all over Bangladesh.

The criterion used here does not take into account that the Jamaate seeks power through transforming society, not by gaining parliamentary seats. All indicators point to this transformation as taking place.

Conclusions and Indications for the Future

Islamism in Bangladesh is a complex phenomenon with components that have local antecedents as well as newly introduced international dimensions. Proponents of liberal democratic values have often noted the innate compatibility of the notions they advocate with Bangladeshi culture. The current situation is indeed the test of this proposition.

According to this view, promoters of radical political views have succeeded in initiating a cultural transformation by various means, including an effective "bait and switch" approach. It is against a backdrop of political corruption and bureaucratic inefficiency that promoters of radical formulations present themselves, often credibly, as a countermodel of efficiency and integrity. The cultural dimension is therefore not their primary offering. It does, however, follow. Presented as the "true" form of the religion to a pious society, the transformation progresses forward often as a by-product of the political dimension. The implications of this phenomenon in Bangladesh are also considerable in the Bangladeshi diaspora. Cultural radicalization paves the way for political formulations that often espouse violence as the means for change. Europe has already experienced the effects of a radicalization that originated overseas.

It is essential to note that the future of cultural radicalization is conditional to the success of its promoters in positing a clash of cultures in Bangladesh.

BIBLIOGRAPHY

Alexiev, Alex. "Tablighi Jamaat: Jihad's Stealthy Legions." *Middle East Quarterly* 7:1 (Winter 2005). www.meforum.org/article/686.
"Ameer of Jamaate Spends Busy Days in Saudi Arabia." Jamaate Islam Web site. 2006. www.jamaat-e-islami.org/main-1.htm.
"Bangladesh Bans Islam Sect Books." *British Broadcasting Corporation (BBC) News*, January 9, 2004. http://news.bbc.co.uk/1/hi/world/south_asia/3382931.stm.
Bureau of Democracy, Human Rights, and Labor, U.S. Department of State. *Bangladesh. International Religious Freedom Report 2005*. 2006. www.state.gov/g/drl/rls/irf/2005/51616.htm.
"Dangerous Ties." *Los Angeles Times*, December 7, 2005.
Hossain, Maneeza. "Rise of the Islamic Tide in Bangladesh." *Current Trends in Islamist Ideology*. Hudson Institute, February 2006.
Human Rights Watch: Bangladesh Overview. 2006. http://hrw.org/reports/2005/bangladesh0605/2.htm.
Karlekar, Hiranmay. *Bangladesh: The Next Afghanistan?* New Delhi: Sage Publications, 2005.
Mahbub, Aataai Gazi. "Islamists Seek to Capitalize on Strife in Bangladesh: Religious Parties Trying to Cash in on Political Deadlock." *OhmyNews*, November 22, 2006. http://english.ohmynews.com/.
"The Nexus Between Al-Haramain and Global Terrorism Is Cracked Now by Saudi Action." *Bangladesh Observer* (Dhaka), July 4, 2004.
"Three-day Biswa Ijtema Begins." *New Nation* (Dhaka), December 4, 2004. http://nation.ittefaq.com/artman/exec/view.cgi/25/14314/printer.

China

Dru C. Gladney

Muslims in China struggle over the answer to two fundamental questions regarding their religious and national identity. These questions, once thought resolved, reemerged with critical relevance in the aftermath of September 11 and the war over terrorism that has affected China's Muslims more directly than any of its other peoples.

Since the end of the nineteenth century, China has been engaged in an unremitting project of nationalization and secularization that includes, among other things, emancipation from its imperial past, engagement with Western political institutions, and the establishment of its sovereignty over its territory. One recent challenge to this nationalist project, with roots in the early twentieth century, is that of a widespread separatism movement among one Muslim group known as the Uyghurs. That the largest Muslim group in China, known as the Hui, have not participated in or been sympathetic to such a movement speaks volumes regarding the diversity of Islamic identity and practice in China. China's government has suggested that Uyghur militants have killed and are threatening to kill other Chinese citizens in the name of radical Islam, drawing direct parallels to current events in nearby Chechnya.

One of the defining moments of secularization for China's Muslims involved the redefinition of their very identity. In China, the people now known as the Hui have from the beginning been what Jonathan Lipman calls in the title of his Hui history, familiar strangers. Not only do they have an entirely different culture than that of China, but despite over 1,300 years of intermarriage and integration, they are still regarded as a separate race. In China, "Race . . . would create nationhood," according to Frank Dikötter's thesis, and it had much to do with Han Chinese representations of Hui otherness. Even their name, "Hui," can mean "to return" in Chinese, as if they were never at home in China and destined to leave. Descended from Persian, Arab, Mongolian, and Turkish Muslim merchants, soldiers, and officials who settled in China from the seventh to fourteenth century and intermarried with Han women, largely living in isolated communities, the only thing that some, but not all, had in common was a belief in Islam. Until the 1950s in China, Islam was simply known as the "Hui religion" (*Hui jiao*)—believers in Islam were Hui jiao believers. Until then, any person who was a believer in Islam was a "Hui religion disciple" (*Huijiao tu*).

The term "Hui" narrowed in the late nineteenth and early twentieth century from a generic term including all Muslims, no matter what their ethnolinguistic background, to denote mostly Chinese-speaking Muslims who were caught up in the nationalist movements of twentieth-century China. Jamal al-Din Bai Shouyi, the famous Hui Marxist historian, was the first to argue persuasively that "Islam" should be glossed in Chinese as *Yisilan jiao* (Islam), not the Hui religion (Hui jiao). In a chapter entitled "The Huihui People and the Huihui Religion," Bai argued that even though Hui are descendants of Muslims and have inherited certain Muslim cultural traditions such as pork abstention, they do not all necessarily believe in Islam. "Muslim" is different from "Hui person" (*Hui min*), and one should not use the term *Hui jiao* (Hui religion) but "Islam" (*yisilan jiao*). He argued that the Hui believed not in their own religion but in the world religion of Islam, and are therefore Muslims in faith. In ethnicity they are the Hui people, not Hui religion disciples. In Marxist terms, he identified the process of the indigenization of a world religion, in this case Islam, to a local context, which for the communities now known as the Hui had been occurring for 1,200 years. Muslim groups were identified by Chinese linguists according to what was seen to be their own language and derived their ethnonym from their language family; in this way the Uyghur, Kazakh, Tajik, Uzbek, Kyrgyz, and Tatar groups were identified. In this, the Chinese were heavily influenced by the 1920s Soviet identification of these peoples in Soviet Central Asia.

Walker Connor quotes the following statement by Stalin in 1923 that revealed his early intention of passing on their nationality policy to China: "We must here, in Russia, in our federation, solve the national problem in a correct, *a model way*, in order to set an example to the East, which represents the heavy reserves of our revolution" (emphasis in original). Bai Shouyi went on to identify the Muslim peoples not distinguished by language or locality as a catchall residual group known as Hui min, not Hui jiao. Thus, the official category of the Hui was legitimated, and one might even say invented, so far as the legal definition of who was considered Hui is concerned.

For China's Muslims, the two questions raised above strike at the heart of their ethnoreligious identity: Should they die for the nation, or should they support terror in the name of religion and heed the call of jihadi Islam? With the sequence of events before and after the turn of the century in Xinjiang, as well as deteriorating violence in nearby Chechnya and Uzbekistan, not to mention the ongoing presence of Osama bin Ladin in neighboring Afghanistan/Pakistan (most likely in the mountainous areas bordering China), these questions are increasingly demanding responses.

As part of China's continuing efforts to maintain national unity and police separatist movements at home and abroad, on December 14, 2003, for the first time in its history, China's Ministry of Public Security released a list of four organizations and 11 individuals that it deemed to be terrorist. This list included the Eastern Turkistan Islamic Movement (ETIM), which was identified as an international terrorist organization by the United Nations in 2002 after Chinese and U.S. prompting, as well as the Eastern Turkistan Liberation Organization (ETLO), the World Uyghur Youth Congress (WUYC), and the Eastern Turkistan Information Center (ETIC).

The 11 identified "Eastern Turkistan" terrorists, according to a report in *Xinhua*, include: Hasan Mahsum, Muhanmetemin Hazret, Dolqun Isa, Abu Dujayli Kalakash,

Abu al-Qadir Yapuquan, Abudumijit Abduhammatkelim, Abdallah Kariaji, Abu Limit Turxun, Huadaberdi Haxerbik, Yasin Muhammad, and Atahan Abuduhani. Interestingly, Hasan Mahsum, the reputed leader of ETIM, appeared on the list, though he had been reportedly killed in a Pakistani raid on an al-Qa'ida camp in Waziristan on October 2, 2003, according to Radio Free Asia. On November 10, 2003, the author had actually met Dolqun Isa, a young Uyghur living in Munich, who was also included on the list as one of 11 identified international terrorists and the elected president of the World Uyghur Youth Congress (also listed as one of four terrorist organizations). During that meeting he claimed that he had nothing to do with terrorism, that such violence was contrary to his devout faith in Islam, and he presented a printed antiterrorism brochure of the East Turkistan (Uyghuristan) National Congress that was entitled: "Help the Uyghurs to Fight Terrorism."

These rather conflicting reports raise important questions about Muslims, Islam, the institutional links between the state and the status of religion, and Muslim identity politics in the People's Republic since September 11, 2001. Do all Muslims support Uyghur separatism? What are the roots of Uyghur separatism? Why do the Hui not support an independent Islamic state? How do these differences illustrate the "unity and diversity" of Islam in China today? How have Islamist movements appealed to both Hui and Uyghurs, and why have they not been adapted by many?

China's Muslims are now facing their second millennium under Chinese rule. Many of the challenges they confront remain the same as they have for the last 1,200 years of continuous interaction with Chinese society, but many others are new as a result of China's transformed and increasingly glo-

balized society, and especially the watershed events of the September 11 terrorist attacks and subsequent events. Muslims in China live as minority communities amid a sea of people who, in their view, are largely pork-eating, polytheist, secularist, and "heathen" (*kafir*). Nevertheless, many of their small and isolated communities have survived in rather inhospitable circumstances for over a millennium.

Though small in population percentage (about 2 percent in China, 1 percent in Japan, and less than 1 percent in Korea), the Muslim populations of East Asia are nevertheless large in comparison with those of other Muslim states. In fact, there are more Muslims living in China today than there are in Malaysia, and more than in every Middle Eastern Muslim nation except Iran, Turkey, and Egypt (and about the same number as in Iraq). Indeed, China's primary objection to NATO involvement in Kosovo centered on its fear that this might encourage the aiding and abetting of separatists, a potential problem in light of the fact that independence groups in Xinjiang, Tibet, and even Taiwan remain a major Chinese concern. As Muslims in Asia, Chinese Muslims are part of the largest Islamic population in the world.

Islam in China Today

According to the reasonably accurate 2000 national census of China, the total Muslim population is 20.3 million, including, by group: Hui (9,816,805); Uyghur (8,399,393); Kazakh (1,250,458); Dongxiang (513,805); Kyrgyz (160,823); Salar (104,503); Tajik (41,028); Uzbek (14,502); Bonan (16,505); and Tatar (4,890). (These statistics are further analyzed by Yang Shengmin and Ding Hong.) The Hui speak mainly Sino-Tibetan languages; Turkic-language speakers include those of the Uyghur, Kazakh, Kyrgyz, Uzbek, Salar, and Tatar groups; combined Turkic-Mongolian speakers include those of the Dongxiang and Bonan groups, concentrated in Gansu's mountainous Hexi corridor; and the Tajiks speak a variety of Indo-Persian dialects. It is important to note, however, that the Chinese census registered people by nationality, not religious affiliation, so the actual number of Muslims is still unknown, and all population figures are clearly influenced by politics in their use and interpretation. Nevertheless, there are few Han converts to Islam, and perhaps even fewer members of the 10 nationalities listed above who would dare to say they are not Muslim, at least in front of their parents. As the author has argued elsewhere, Muslim identity in China can best be described as ethnoreligious, in that history, ethnicity, and state nationality policy have left an indelible mark on contemporary Muslim identity. It is almost impossible to discuss Islam in China without reference to ethnic and national identity.

Archeological discoveries of large collections of Islamic artifacts and epigraphy on the southeastern coast suggest that the earliest Muslim communities in China were descended from Arab, Persian, Central Asian, and Mongolian Muslim merchants, militia, and officials who settled first along China's southeastern coast from the seventh through the tenth centuries. Later, larger migrations to the north from Central Asia under the Mongol-Yuan dynasty in the thirteenth and fourteenth centuries added to these Muslim populations through gradual intermarriage with the local Chinese populations and the raising of their children as Muslims. Practicing Sunni, Hanafi Islam and residing in independent, small communities clustered around a central mosque, these communities were characterized by

relatively isolated, independent Islamic villages and urban enclaves that related with each other via trading networks and later came to be known as the *"Gedimu"* (from the Arabic, *qadim,* for ancient) or traditionalist Hui Muslims. Nevertheless, these scattered Islamic settlements shared a common feeling of belonging to the wider Islamic community (*umma*), which was validated by origin myths and folktales and continually reinforced by traveling Muslim teachers known locally as *Ahong.*

Hui Muslims and Islamic Acculturation to Chinese Society

Islam in China has been propagated over the last 1,300 years primarily among the people now known as Hui, but many of the issues confronting them are also relevant to the Turkic and Indo-European Muslims on China's inner Asian frontier. Though Hui speak a number of non-Chinese languages, most Hui are closer to Han Chinese than to other Muslim nationalities in terms of demographic proximity and cultural accommodation. The attempt to adapt many of their Muslim practices to the Han way of life has led to criticisms among some Muslim reformers. In the wake of modern Islamic reform movements that have swept across China, a wide spectrum of Islamic belief and practice can now be found among those Muslims in China referred to as the Hui.

The Hui have been labeled "Chinese-speaking Muslims," "Chinese Muslims," and most recently, as "Sino-Muslims," as both Lipman and the author explain. However, this terminology is misleading, because by law all Muslims living in China are "Chinese" by citizenship, and there are large Hui communities whose members primarily speak the non-Chinese languages dominant in the areas where they live. To paraphrase Aihwa Ong, in this case citizenship, like religious membership, has been rather inflexible in China since the end of the last dynasty. (Uyghurs waiting for an independent Uyghuristan find Chinese citizenship the least flexible, especially when threatened with extradition while in the diaspora, while Hui have rarely challenged Chinese citizenship. Similarly, membership in the Muslim community in China is legislated by birth, in the sense that once born a Hui, always a Hui, regardless of belief or even membership in the Communist Party.)

This is the case, for example, with the Tibetan, Mongolian, Thai (*Dai zu*), and Hainan Muslims of China, who are also classified by the state as Hui. These "Hui" Muslims speak Tibetan, Mongolian, or Thai as their first language, with Han Chinese the national language that they learn in school, along with the Arabic and Persian that some of them also learn at the mosque. Interestingly, since Tajik is not an official language in China, the Tajik schoolchildren of Xinjiang (who speak a Darian branch language, distantly related to old Persian and quite different from the Tajik languages spoken in Tajikistan) study in either Turkic Uyghur or Han Chinese. (Tajik is the only official nationality still lacking a script, and speakers must learn in either Uyghur or Han Chinese in their own Tajik Autonomous Country of Tashkurgan, according to an interview with the Tashkurgan County chairman on August 25, 2001. Yang Shengmin has indicated that Uyghur cadres opposed granting a separate written language to the Tajiks; however, political concerns over links to Iran and Tajikistan through the promulgation of a Persian script are clearly an important factor.) The Tajiks are the only Shi'a Muslims in China. They adhere to Isma'ili Shi'ism and are quite distinct from the majority Sunni Tajiks in neighboring Tajikistan.

Nevertheless, it is true that compared to the other Muslim nationalities in China, most Hui are closer to the Han Chinese in terms of demographic proximity and cultural accommodation, adapting many of their Islamic practices to Han ways of life. However, this type of cultural accommodation can also be the target of sharp criticism from some Muslim reformers. In the past, this was not as great a problem for the Turkic, Mongolian, and Tajik groups, as they were traditionally more isolated from the Han and their identities not as threatened, though this has begun to change in the last 40 years. As a result of the state-sponsored nationality identification campaigns launched in the 1950s, these groups began to think of themselves more as ethnic nationalities, as something more than just "Muslims." The Hui are unique among the 55 identified nationalities in China in that they are the sole nationality for whom religion (Islam) is the only unifying category of identity, even though many members of the Hui nationality may not actively practice Islam. Indeed, in Shengmin's ethnography of China, the Hui are included with the Han in the section dedicated to "Han language nationalities" (*Hanyu Minzu*).

The Nationalist's Guomindang (GMD) "nationality" policy identified five peoples of China, dominated by the Han. They included Uyghurs under the general rubric of "Hui Muslims," which referred to all Muslim groups in China at that time. The Communists continued this policy and eventually recognized 56 nationalities. Uyghurs and eight other Muslim groups were split off from the general category "Hui" (which henceforth was used only with reference to Muslims who primarily spoke Chinese or did not have a separate language of their own). As a policy of ethnic control, this owed much to practices that the Soviet state had applied earlier in Central Asia. It proved to be an effective means by which the Chinese Communists could integrate the religion into China.

The institution most responsible for regulating and monitoring Islamic practices in China is the China Islamic Affairs Association (Zhongguo Yisilanjiao Xiehui). This association was founded in 1956 at the same time China formed the "Three Self Organization" responsible for monitoring all Christian (Catholic and Protestant) activities. The China Islamic Affairs Association makes the final recommendations to the government regarding the establishment of new mosques, the formation of Islamic schools, and general policy regarding the legality of certain Islamic practices (such as outlawing head scarves in public schools). It also plays an increasingly important role in China's Middle Eastern international affairs, as well as supports particularly Islamic schools among the Hui.

In the Northwest, in addition to allowing from two to four students (khalifat) to train privately in each mosque, the government approved and funded several Islamic Schools (yixueyuan) throughout the region. In 1988 the state provided funding to establish a large Islamic seminary and mosque complex outside the West Gate of Yinchuan near Luo village. Similarly, in Urumqi, the Islamic college was established in 1985, and other regional and provincial governments have followed suit. This indicates a "regionalization" of state-sponsored Islamic education, which until the 1980s had been officially concentrated at the China Islamic Affairs Commission in Beijing, located near the Oxen Street Mosque in the Xuanwu District

in southwest Beijing, Graham Fuller and Lipman explain.

The increased promotion of exchange with foreign Muslim countries is exposing more urban Hui to international aspects of their Islamic heritage. Though in the past coverage of the Palestinian-Israeli conflict was rather minimal, increased coverage of the first Gulf War raised Muslim awareness of political and religious conflicts in the Middle East. Widespread coverage of the wars in Iraq and Afghanistan on China's border have exposed Muslims in China like never before to the many tensions in the region. Among urban Hui, Islamic knowledge tends to be higher than in rural areas, perhaps because of increased educational levels and more media exposure. Unlike the vast majority of Hui in rural areas, many urban Hui interviewed keep up on international affairs, and they often read the magazine published by the China Islamic Affairs Association, *Zhongguo Musilin* (China's Muslims). Few were aware of and interested in the sectarian disputes in the earlier Iran/Iraq conflict, but most knew of Shi'ism, and most were keenly interested in the developments in the U.S.-led war in Iraq.

Institutions engaged in managing China's Muslims, and the Muslims themselves, have all been strongly affected by Middle Eastern affairs since the 1990s. The People's Republic of China (PRC), as one of five permanent voting members of the UN Security Council and as a significant exporter of military hardware to the Middle East, has become a recognized player in Middle Eastern affairs. With a temporary but precipitous decline in trade with many Western nations after the Tiananmen massacre in June 1989, the importance of China's Middle Eastern trading partners (most of them Muslim, because China did not recognize Israel until 1992), rose considerably. This may account for China's establishment of diplomatic relations with Saudi Arabia in August 1990, with the first direct Sino-Saudi exchanges taking place since 1949. (Saudi Arabia canceled its long-standing diplomatic relationship with Taiwan and withdrew its ambassador, despite a lucrative trade history.) In the face of a long-term friendship with Iraq, China went along with most of the UN resolutions in the first Gulf War against Iraq. Although it abstained from Resolution 678 on supporting the ground war and did not endorse the U.S.-led coalition war against Saddam Hussein in 2003, China continues to enjoy a fairly "Teflon" reputation in the Middle East as an untarnished source of low-grade weaponry and cheap reliable labor, as both Lillian Harris and Yitzhak Shichor explain. In the words of the late Hajji Shi Kunbing, former lead imam of the famous Oxen Street Mosque in Beijing, whom the author interviewed during Ramadan in 1985, "With so much now at stake in the Middle East, the government cannot risk antagonizing its Muslim minorities."

Interestingly, although China's government did not endorse the U.S.-led coalition war against Iraq and only voiced "strong concern" about the possible collateral injury of civilians, urging a peaceful resolution, its Muslim population was ahead of the government in publicly condemning the U.S.-led war. In a statement issued on March 23, 2003, by Chen Guangyan, vice president of the China Islamic Association, and quoted by the *South China Morning Post*, he said the following:

> We strongly condemn the United States and its allies for attacking Iraq and not turning to diplomacy to resolve this conflict. . . . We side with the war protesters in the United States and elsewhere around the world. We strongly urge the United States to stop its campaign and to return to the negotiating tables to resolve this issue. War is wrong.

The next day, Hajji Muhammad Nusr Ma Liangji, lead imam of the Great Mosque in Xi'an that boasts 70,000 members, made the following statement, quoted in the same article in the *South China Morning Post:*

> Though we don't go to the Middle East that often, we are all part of the same brotherhood. . . . Mr Bush's invasion of Iraq is an incursion of Iraq's sovereignty. Islam is a religion of peace and the United States shouldn't do this. No one in the world agrees with this and we in the Muslim community in China absolutely object to this.

The author visited the headquarters of the China Islamic Association in the Niujie district of Beijing shortly after these statements were made. Hajji Yu Zhengui, president of the China Islamic Association, confirmed that Muslims across China were deeply angered by the U.S.-led war and had been asking the government for permission to engage in a public street protest. There were rumors of small Muslim protests in Changzhi (Shanxi), Tianjin, Nanjing, Beijing, and Shandong. The Chinese did give permission for some limited protests by foreigners and students in late March and early April, but perhaps out of fear that a Muslim protest might get out of hand, possibly disturbing social stability, or even worse, disrupting the improving Sino-U.S. relationship, Muslims were never allowed to protest the war on Iraq. These examples illustrate the increasing international role of institutions engaged in managing China's Muslims and their Islamic expression.

Hui Islamic Orders and Chinese Culture

Sufism began to have a substantial effect in China proper in the late seventeenth century, arriving mainly along the Central Asian trade routes with saintly shaykhs, both Chinese and foreign, who brought new teachings from the pilgrimage cities. These charismatic teachers and tradesmen established widespread networks and brotherhood associations, including most prominently the Naqshabandiyya, Qadiriyya, and Kubrawiyya. Islamic preachers in China, including Ma Laichi, Ma Mingxin, Qi Jingyi, and Ma Qixi, spent most of their time trying to convert other traditionalist Gedimu Muslims to their religious order, leading to disputes that would have a great influence on twentieth-century Islam in China. Nevertheless, Islam in China for the most part has grown biologically through birth and intermarriage. Historical records do not yield evidence of large conversions of non-Muslims to Islam in China, except through birth, adoption, and intermarriage. The later mode of Sufi Islam was perhaps popular among traditionalist Gedimu, as it offered immediate experiential access to God without formal mosque training in Arabic or Islamic theology, in addition to providing patron-client protection of Hui adherents during the declining social order of the late Qing dynasty.

The hierarchical organization of Sufi networks helped in the mobilization of large numbers of Hui during the economic and political crises of the seventeenth through nineteenth centuries, assisting widespread Muslim-led rebellions and resistance movements against late Ming and Qing imperial rule in Yunnan, Shaanxi, Gansu, and Xinjiang. In the late nineteenth and early twentieth century, Wahhabi-inspired reform movements, known as the Yihewani, rose to popularity under Nationalist and warlord sponsorship. They were noted for their critical stance toward traditionalist Gedimu Islam, which they viewed as being overly acculturated to non-Muslim Chinese practices and to forms of popular Sufism such as saint and tomb veneration.

Beyond such internal Muslim critiques, the Chinese state also launched its own criticisms of certain Islamic orders among the Hui. The stakes in such debates were often economic as well as ideological. For example, during the land reform campaigns of the 1950s, the state appropriated mosque and *waqf* (Islamic endowment) holdings from traditional Muslim religious institutions. These measures met with great resistance from the Sufi *menhuan* (saintly lineage) that had accumulated a great deal because of their hierarchical centralized leadership. As the author has suggested elsewhere, the earlier movements of Islamic peoples and ideas into China can be divided into the initial diaspora mode of traditionalist Gedimu Islam and the later mode of interconnected alliances of Sufi patron-client networks. A third mode, or to use Joseph Fletcher's terms, the tide of Islam in China, was caught up in the very nationalist conflicts that gave rise to World War I.

The Third Mode: Scripturalist Concerns and Modernist Reforms

An important new Islamic modality swept China's Muslims, perhaps as a response to increasingly popular nationalism and secularization, in the late nineteenth and early twentieth century. Nationalist reformers sought to modernize China and overthrow the imperial regime. Among Muslims, there was a period of increased interaction between China and the outside world, as many Muslims began traveling to the Middle East. China was exposed to many new foreign ideas and, in the face of Japanese and Western imperialist encroachment, sought a Chinese approach to governance. Intellectual and organizational activity by Chinese Muslims during this period was intense. Increased contact with the Middle East led Chinese Muslims to reevaluate their traditional notions of Islam. The Protestant missionary Claude Pickens recorded that from 1923 to 1934 there were 834 known Hui Muslims who made the Hajj, or pilgrimage, to Mecca. In 1937, according to one observer, over 170 Hui pilgrims boarded a steamer in Shanghai bound for Mecca. By 1939 at least 33 Hui Muslims had studied at Cairo's prestigious al-Azhar University. While these numbers are small compared with pilgrims on the Hajj from other Asian Muslim areas, the influence and prestige attached to these returning Hui Hajji were profound, particularly in isolated communities. "In this respect," Fletcher once observed, "the more secluded and remote a Muslim community was from the main centers of Islamic cultural life in the Middle East, the more susceptible it was to those centers' most recent trends."

As a result of political events and the influence of foreign Muslim ideas, numerous new Hui organizations emerged. In 1912, one year after Sun Yat-sen was inaugurated as provisional president of the Chinese Republic in Nanjing, the Chinese Muslim Federation was also formed in that city. This was followed by the establishment of other Hui Muslim associations: the Chinese Muslim Mutual Progress Association (Beijing, 1912), the Chinese Muslim Educational Association (Shanghai, 1925), the Chinese Muslim Association (1925), the Chinese Muslim Young Students Association (Nanjing, 1931), the Society for the Promotion of Education Among Muslims (Nanjing, 1931), and the Chinese Muslim General Association (Jinan, 1934).

The Muslim periodical press flourished as never before. Although it was reported that circulation was low, over 100 known Muslim periodicals were produced before the outbreak of the Sino-Japanese War in 1937. Thirty journals were published between 1911 and 1937 in Beijing alone, prompting one author to suggest that while Chinese Islam's traditional religious center was still Linxia (Hezhou), its cultural center had shifted to Beijing. This took place when many Hui intellectuals traveled to Japan, the Middle East, and the West. Caught up in the nationalist fervor of the first half of the century, they published magazines and founded organizations, questioning their identity as never before in a process that one Hui historian, Ma Shouqian, has termed "The New Awakening of the Hui at the end of the 19th and beginning of the 20th centuries." As many of these Hui Hajji returned from their pilgrimages to the Middle East, they initiated several reforms, engaging themselves once again in the contested space between Islamic ideals and Chinese culture.

The Rise of the Secularist/ Modernist Islam in China: The Yihewani

Influenced by Wahhabi ideals in the Arabian peninsula, returning Hui reformers introduced the Yihewani (Chinese for the Ikhwan al-Muslimin) to China—a religio-political movement that sometimes supported China's nationalist concerns and at other times supported its warlord politics. While the Ikhwan Muslim Brotherhood elsewhere in the Islamic world has been depicted as antimodernist and recidivist, this is not true of the movement in China. In fact, the Yihewani in China eventually diverged so far from its Ikhwan Muslim Brotherhood beginnings that it is misleading to even refer to the Yihewani in China as "Ikhwan" or as a single movement or order. It has now become merely another type of Islamic practice, an alternative to "Gedimu" traditional Islam and Sufism in China.

The beginnings of the Yihewani movement in China can be traced to Ma Wanfu (1849–1934), who returned from the Hajj in 1892 to teach in the Hezhou area. The initial reformers were primarily concerned with religious scripturalist orthodoxy—so much so that they are still known as the "venerate the scriptures faction" (zunjing pai). Though the reformers were concerned with larger goals than merely "correcting" what they regarded as unorthodox practice, such as previous reforms in China, it is at the practical and ritual level that they initiated their critique. They proscribed the veneration of saints and their tombs and shrines and sought to stem the growing influence of well-known individual Ahong and Sufi menhuan leaders. Stressing orthodox practice through advocating a purified, "non-Chinese" Islam, they criticized such cultural accretions as the wearing of a white mourning dress (dai xiao) and the decoration of mosques with Chinese or Arabic texts. At one point, Ma Wanfu even proposed the exclusive use of Arabic and Persian in all education instead of Chinese.

Following strict Wahhabi practice, Yihewani mosques are distinguished by their almost complete lack of adornment on the inside, with white walls and no inscriptions, as well as a preference for Arabian-style mosque architecture. This contrasts sharply with other more Chinese-style mosques in China, typical of the "old"

Gedimu, whose architecture resembles Confucian temples in their sweeping roofs and symmetrical courtyards (with the Xi'an Huajue Great Mosque as the best example). The Yihewani also rejected the adornment of their mosques with Arabic, and especially Chinese, Koranic texts and banners, whereas this is the most striking iconographic marker of Sufi mosques and worship centers in the Northwest, whose walls and tombs are often layered with Arabic and Chinese texts on silk and cloth banners in the distinctive Hui-style art that fluidly combines Arabic and Chinese calligraphy.

The Yihewani flourished in Northwestern China under the patronage of several Muslim warlords during the Nationalist period, most notably Ma Bufang. In a modernist approach, arguing that the Yihewani supported education, a rationalized, less mystical religious expression, and a strong Chinese nation, Ma Bufang supported the expansion of the Yihewani throughout Northwestern China. He must have been also aware that wherever the Yihewani went, the hierarchical authority of the Sufi shaykhs and the solidarity of their menhuan were contested, thus protecting Ma from other organized religious institutions that might orchestrate an effective resistance to his expansion. This could not have been lost on the early Communists either, who traveled through Ma Bufang's territory and the Northwest on their Long March, which ended in Yan'an, near Ningxia, a heavily populated Muslim area dominated at that time by Ma Hongkui, a cousin of Ma Bufang's, who also supported the Yihewani.

After the founding of the People's Republic, the state quickly suppressed all Sufi menhuan as feudalistic and gave tacit support to the Yihewani. Though Ma Bufang and Ma Hongkui both fled with the Nationalists to Taiwan, their policy of opposing Sufi organizations was left behind with the Communists. The China Islamic Association, established in 1955, was heavily dominated by the Yihewani and supported the 1957–58 public criticisms and show trials of Naqshabandi Shaykh Ma Zhenwu specifically, and Sufism in general, as feudalist and exploitative of the masses. After the purges of the Cultural Revolution, in which eventually all Islamic orders were affected, the Yihewani was the first to receive renewed state patronage. Most of the large mosques that were rebuilt with state funds throughout China, as compensation for damages and destruction caused by the Red Guards during the now-repudiated Cultural Revolution, were Yihewani mosques, though all orders were equally criticized during the radical period.

While no Chinese official will admit that the Yihewani receive special treatment, this is cause for some resentment among Muslims. The great South Gate Mosque in Yinchuan city, the capital of the Ningxia Hui Autonomous Region, was one of the first mosques rebuilt in Ningxia with state funds—it just happened to be staffed by Yihewani imams, though the state claimed it was a "nonsectarian" mosque. After the state spent over 50,000 yuan to rebuild the mosque in 1982, the local Muslims, most of whom were Gedimu and Khufiyya, refused to attend. The building sat almost empty for the first few years, and the state attempted to recoup its losses over the large Arab-styled architectural structure by turning it into a tourist attraction and selling tickets at the entrance. This, of course, only confirmed its lack of religious legitimacy among many local Hui Muslims, especially the Gedimu and Sufis. In 1985 a visiting Kuwaiti delegation became aware of the situation and instead of donating money to the South Gate Mosque as originally planned, they gave $10,000 (about 30,000 yuan) toward refurbishing the much smaller traditional Central Mosque, a Gedimu mosque popular among the locals.

The Yihewani continue to be a powerful Islamic group throughout China. Like the Gedimu, the Yihewani emphasize leadership through training and education rather than inheritance and succession. The Yihewani differ from the Gedimu primarily in ritual matters and their stress on reform through Chinese education and modernism. Unlike the Gedimu, they do not chant the scriptures collectively, do not visit tombs, do not celebrate the death days of their ancestors, and do not gather for Islamic festivals in remembrance of saints. Because of their emphasis on nationalist concerns, education, modernization, and decentralized leadership, the movement has attracted more urban intellectual Muslims.

The Yihewani's nationalistic ideals, and their cooptation by the earlier Nationalists and later Communists, led many of the more religious Yihewani to become disillusioned with the order. It was seen by many to no longer be a fundamentalist agent of reform but rather an institutionalized organ of the state for systematizing and monitoring Islamic practice. Though still influential politically, it has lost its dynamic appeal to many of the most conservative Muslims in China. For the vast majority of urban Hui Muslims, and even many rural Muslims in the small towns of the northern plains, however, it is merely the mosque that they belong to by virtue of birth or marriage, and few could distinguish between Yihewani and Gedimu, let alone between the myriad orders of Sufis. One Hui worker in Hangzhou once said that the basic difference between the Gedimu (he used the term *laojiao*, "old teachings") and in this case the Yihewani (*xinjiao*, "new teachings") was that the Yihewani did not eat crab and the Gedimu did.

The isolation of the early Gedimu communities was mitigated somewhat during the collectivization campaigns in the 1950s, when Han and Hui villages were often administered as clusters by a single commune. They have also been brought closer together through national telecommunications and transportation networks established by the state, including such umbrella organizations as the China Islamic Association, established in 1955, which seeks to coordinate religious affairs among all Muslim groups. With the complete dismantling of the commune in China, however, these homogeneous Hui communities are once again becoming more segregated. While these disparate communities among the Gedimu were generally linked only by trade and a sense of a common religious heritage—an attachment to the basic Islamic beliefs as handed down to them by their ancestors—it was the entrée of the Sufi brotherhoods into China that eventually began to link many of these isolated communities together through extensive socioreligious networks.

While the total population of the various Islamic associations in China has not been published, one Muslim Chinese scholar, Yang Huaizhong, estimates that of the 2,132 mosques in Ningxia Hui Autonomous Region in 1990, 560 belonged to the Yihewani, 560 to the Khufiyya, 464 to the Jahriyya, 415 to the traditional Gedimu, and 133 to Qadiriyya religious worship sites (some of which include mosques). The most comprehensive estimate given so far for Hui membership in Islamic orders throughout China is by the Hui historian Ma Tong. Out of an estimated total in 1988 of 6,781,500 Hui Muslims, Ma Tong recorded that 58.2 percent were Gedimu, 21 percent Yihewani, 10.9 percent Jahriyya, 7.2 percent Khufiyya, 1.4 percent Qadiriyya, and .7 percent Kubrawiyya.

The Rise of the Salafiyya: A Fourth Mode of Fundamentalist Islam?

The extent of the rise in popularity of the Salafiyya in Northwestern China is difficult to assess, because there are no published figures of its membership or number of mosques and few discussions of the movement in the voluminous literature on Islam in China. However, many Muslims formerly associated with the Yihewani or Gedimu said they had either recently joined the Salafiyya or were considering doing so. Perhaps discontent with the official patronage of the Yihewani by the political warlords and official organs of power in China, the Salafiyya originally arose out of the Yihewani in the mid-1930s and quickly spread throughout the Northwest. Since the reforms of the early 1980s, when religious expression was again officially allowed in China, the Salafiyya have flourished perhaps more than any other Islamic movement among the Hui. One Chinese scholar, Da Yingyu, calls them "the faction that is most faithful to the original teaching of Islam."

Unlike the Yihewani leadership in China, the Salafiyya stressed a nonpoliticized return to Wahhabi scripturalist ideals. Arguing that the Yihewani had been corrupted by Chinese cultural accretions, such as the loss of its original founder's ideal to pursue pure Islamic education in Arabic and Persian, as well as being co-opted by the state, the Salafiyya represent one of the most recent versions of reform movements in China. While their scripturalist debates with the Yihewani did not lead to a "battle for the Koran" in China, the struggle for legitimacy of both Yihewani and Salafiyya took place in a discourse of Koranic textualism.

Like previous Islamic reform movements, the Salafiyya were transmitted (and translated) to China through the agency of a returned Hajji from the Islamic heartlands who began spreading his "new teaching" in China's own Muslim heartland, Hezhou. In 1934 a small group of Hui members of the Yihewani left Hezhou on the Hajj, led by Ma Debao, from the heavily Muslim-populated Guanghe County's Bai (White) village, along with Ma Yinu, Ma Zhenliu, and Ma Ling, the four "Ma's." ("Ma" is the most common surname among Hui Muslims in China, tracing its origins to the Ming dynasty, when many Muslims were required to take on Chinese surnames. "Ma" most closely resembled the first syllable of "Muhammad." It is also the Chinese character for "horse," and since many Hui were engaged as caravaneers, it was a natural choice for a surname.) While on the pilgrimage, Ma Debao came under the influence of a Salafist named in the Chinese sources as Huzhandi, who is reported to be from the Soviet Union. It is not known if this Huzhandi was a direct disciple of Muhammad Abduh, the founder of the Salafiyya and a disciple of al-Afghani, but many Salafiyya Hui believe this to be the case. Many of China's Muslims were educated at al-Azhar in Egypt, where Muhammad Abduh himself was schooled, so it is not unlikely that there would have been some connections. In addition to bringing back to China his new interpretations of the Koran and other original sources, he brought two Salafi manuals, listed in Chinese sources as the *Buerhenu Satuier* (the "Glorious Explanation") and the *Xianyoushe Islamu* (the "Army of Islam").

Upon his return to China, he was further trained under a visiting foreign Salafiyya teacher, Jialei Buhali, reportedly an Arab from Bukhara, according to Da. Under their teaching, Ma Debao began to suspect that Islam in China had been too influenced by Confucian, Buddhist, and Daoist ideas. He

wished to return to a more purified, Arabian Islam, free from Chinese cultural and syncretic adaptations. Ma Debao was confronted with a similar challenge as the founder of his order, only from a different direction. As Ira Lapidus notes, "For Abduh the central problem was not political but religious: how, when Muslims were adopting Western ways and Western values, could they maintain the vitality of Islam in the modern world?" For Hui Muslims in 1930s China, caught between the fall of the last Chinese dynasty, the imperial aggrandizements of the Western colonial powers, and the civil war between Nationalists and Communists, their concerns were certainly political and religious. However, for Ma Debao and his followers, it was thought that only through a fundamentalist return to the precepts of the Koran and the teachings of Muhammad would the Muslims be able to survive this stormy period and help renew their nation, as opposed to the Yihewani, whom he saw as seeking the patronage of one political faction over another.

Since Ma Debao and his followers were critical of the Yihewani for moving away from their earlier Wahhabi ideals, they held several open debates with famous Yihewani scholars, particularly disputing the authority of the four schools of jurisprudence. In 1937 the Salafiyya in China formally split from the Yihewani. Since the Yihewani were under the patronage at that time of the Nationalist warlord Ma Bufang, the Salafiyya were severely restricted in their movements, persecuted as "heterodox" (*xie jiao*) and followers of "foreign teachings" (*wai dao*), unable to propagate their order except in secret. It was only after the founding of the People's Republic in 1949 that they began to again come out into the open. By 1950, of the 12 Yihewani mosques in Hezhou's Bafang Muslim district, there were

2, the New Fifth Mosque and the Qi Mosque, that belonged to the Salafiyya, along with seven imams. This period of open propagation was short-lived, however, as in 1958 the state initiated a series of radical Religious Reform Campaigns, which regarded almost all religious practices as feudal, forcing the Salafiyya once again to go underground.

Public approval did not come until 20 years later under the economic and social reforms of Deng Xiaoping, who in 1978 once again allowed more open religious expression. It was not until 1982, however, that most Muslims in the Northwest began to rebuild their mosques and practice Islam openly. According to the Linxia Hui Autonomous Prefectural Basic Situation Committee, the central mosque for the Salafiyya in Hezhou became the Qianhezhe Mosque in the Bafang district. The Salafiyya also claim to have mosques and followers throughout the Northwest, including in Qinghai, Ningxia, and Xinjiang, particularly in such market and urban centers as Linxia, Lanzhou, Weixian, Wuwei, Tianshui, Zhangjiachuan, Pingliang, Yinchuan, and Xian.

Because of its suppressed and rather secretive beginnings, the Salafiyya became known by various names. Since Ma Debao was from Bai (White) Village, outside of Hezhou, and the movement gained quick acceptance there, it became known as the Bai, or White, Teaching. Since the Salafiyya emphasize that "*salaf*" in Arabic means "ancestral" or "the previous generations," they say that their order reveres the first three generations of Islam. They signify their adherence to these first three generations by raising their hands three times, with palms extended upward, during *namaz*. Among outsiders, therefore, they have been derided as the "teaching of the three salutations" (*Santaijiao*), as most Muslims in China raise their hands only once during

prayer, as Shulin Qiu explains. Instead, they prefer to be known as either the Salafiyya, or in Chinese, the Shengxun pai (Faction of the Prophet's Teaching).

Following the Yihewani, the Salafiyya promote a scripturalist Islam that is rationalist and antiexperiential. Like the late Rashid Rida (1865–1935), their fellow Salafi leader in Syria, they emphasize opposition to Sufism and cultural syncretism, rather than modernism, as Lapidus writes. Perhaps as a result of the drift of the Yihewani toward secularism and nationalism, the Salafiyya in China put more stress on scripturalism and orthodox practice. Again publicly repudiating other Islamic expression in China at the level of practice, they emphasize divine unity and criticize the Sufis and Gedimu alike for their patronage of tombs, saints, and the miraculous. They also will not receive alms during readings but offer to use the money to buy scriptures instead. They regard the burning of incense during worship, still practiced by the Gedimu and Yihewani, as the syncretistic influence of Buddhism and Daoism. They also reject the commemoration ceremonies on the fourth, seventh, fortieth, one-year and three-year memorial death days as frequently practiced by Gedimu, Sufis, and some Yihewani. They also oppose the collection of fees for performing engagement and marriage ceremonies, as is common among the Yihewani. Like the Yihewani, the inside of their mosques are unadorned with Islamic insignia or scripture, while the outside may have one Arabic verse, in contrast to the Chinese frequently seen on the outside of Gedimu and even some Yihewani mosques, and the ornate Arabic and Chinese banners throughout Sufi mosques and tombs.

Like their founder, Muhammad Abduh, the Salafiyya see renewal as a result of educational, legal, and spiritual reform. Yet, for them, these reforms are all based on the Koran, whereas the Yihewani allow for secular and even Marxist educational training. Both Dale F. Eickelman and Lapidus argue that just as the discrediting of the Sufis and urban Muslim intellectuals by the French in Morocco helped to promote the cause of the Salafiyya, so the domination of the intellectual elite among the Yihewani and other Islamic orders by the Communist Party in China might have contributed to the Salafiyya movement's call for a purified, nonaccommodationist, and largely nonpolitical Islam. The further discrediting of the Communist Party in most of the world, if not eventually in China, may also give credence to the Salafiyya's cause. The Salafiyya are one of the few Islamic movements in China that can claim both a resistance to Chinese cultural assimilation and a refusal to collaborate with the state. This may account for their dramatic rise in popularity since 1980 and may augur for their place at the forefront of a new tide of Islamic reform in China. It is one of the few Islamic movements to coalesce and flourish after the founding of the People's Republic, when China's diplomatic relations with Middle Eastern Muslim relations took several critical twists and unexpected turns.

Islam and Chinese Nationalism

In the twentieth century, many Muslims supported the earliest Communist call for economic equality, autonomy, freedom of religion, and recognized nationality status and were active in the early establishment of the PRC. However, many of them later became disenchanted by growing critiques of religious practice during several periods in the PRC beginning in 1957. During the Cultural Revolution (1966–76), Muslims became the focus for both antireligious and antiethnic nationalist critiques, leading to widespread persecutions, mosque closings, and at least one large massacre of 1,000 Hui following a 1975 uprising in Yunnan Province. Since Deng Xiaoping's post-1978 reforms, Muslims have sought to take advantage of liberalized economic and religious policies while keeping a watchful eye on the ever-swinging pendulum of Chinese politics. There are now more mosques open in China than there were before 1949, and Muslims are allowed to go on the hajj to Mecca, as well as engage in cross-border trade with coreligionists in Central Asia, the Middle East, and increasingly, Southeast Asia.

With the dramatic increase in the number of Muslims traveling back and forth to the Middle East came new waves of Islamic reformist thought, including criticism of local Muslim practices in China. Through similar channels, other Chinese Muslims have also been exposed to various types of new, often politically radical, Islamic ideologies. These developments have fueled Islamic factional struggles that have continued to further China's Muslims' internal divisions. For example, in February 1994 four Naqshabandi Sufi leaders were sentenced to long-term imprisonment for their support of internal factional disputes in the southern Ningxia Region that had led to at least 60 deaths on both sides and the intervention of the People's Liberation Army.

Increasing Muslim political activism on a national scale and rapid state responses to such developments indicate the growing importance Beijing attaches to Muslim-related issues. In 1986, Uyghurs in Xinjiang marched through the streets of Urumqi protesting against a wide range of issues, including the environmental degradation of the Zungharian plain, nuclear testing in the Taklamakan district, increased Han immigration to Xinjiang, and ethnic insults at Xinjiang University. Muslims throughout China protested the publication of a Chinese book, *Sexual Customs,* in May 1989, and a children's book in October 1993 that portrayed Muslims, particularly their restriction against pork, in a derogatory fashion. In each case, the government responded quickly, meeting most of the Muslims' demands, condemning the publications and arresting the authors, and closing down the printing houses.

These developments have influenced all Muslim nationalities in China. However, they have found their most overtly political expressions among those Hui who are most faced with the task of accommodating new Islamic movements within Chinese culture. By comparison, among the Uyghurs, a more recent integration into Chinese society as a result of Mongolian and Manchu expansion into Central Asia has forced them to reach different degrees of social and political accommodations that have challenged their identity. In terms of integration, the Uyghurs as a people are perhaps the least integrated into Chinese society, while the Hui are, because of several historical and social factors, at the other end of the spectrum.

Increased Muslim activism in China might be thought of as "nationalistic," but it is also a nationalism that may often transcend the boundaries of the contemporary nation-state, via mass communications, increased travel, and more recently, the Internet. Earlier Islamic movements in China were precipitated by China's opening to the outside world. No matter what conservative leaders in the government might wish, China's Muslim politics have reached a new stage of openness. If China wants to further participate in the international political sphere of the nation-states, this is unavoidable. With the opening to the West in recent years, travel to and from the Islamic heartlands has dramatically increased in China.

Uyghurs, Muslims, and Chinese Citizenship

In 1997 bombs exploded in a city park in Beijing on May 13 (killing one) and on two buses on March 7 (killing two), as well as on February 25 in the Northwest border city of Urumqi, the capital of Xinjiang Uyghur Autonomous Region (killing nine). Though sporadically reported since the early 1980s, such incidents have been increasingly common since 1997 and are documented in several scathing reports on Chinese government policy in the region by Amnesty International (1999, 2002, 2003).

Most Uyghurs firmly believe that their ancestors were the indigenous people of the Tarim basin, which did not become officially known in Chinese as Xinjiang (New Dominion) until 1884. It was not until 1760 that the Manchu Qing dynasty exerted full and formal control over the region. This administration lasted for a century before it fell to the Yakub Beg rebellion (1864–77) and expanding Russian influence, as Hodong Kim explains. With the resumption of Manchu Qing rule in the region, the area became known for the first time as Xinjiang, the "new borderland" in 1884, writes James A. Millward. The end of the Qing dynasty in 1912 and the rise of Great Game rivalries between China, Russia, and Britain saw the region torn by competing loyalties and marked by two short-lived and drastically different attempts at independence: the establishment of an East Turkestan Republic in Kashgar in 1933 and another in Yining in 1944, led largely by secular nationalist Uyghurs influenced by Soviet-style bolshevism, as explained in books by Linda Benson and David D. Wang.

As Andrew Forbes has noted, these rebellions and attempts at self-rule did little to bridge competing political, religious, and regional differences among the Turkic peoples who had only became known as the Uyghurs in 1921 under the Nationalist governor, Sheng Shicai. He was catering to Soviet nationality "divide-and-rule" strategies of recognizing groups such as Uyghur, Uzbek, and Kazakh as separate Turkic nationalities. Furthermore, Justin Rudelson's research suggests, there remains persistent regional diversity along three, and perhaps four, macroregions of Uyghuristan: the northwestern Zungaria plateau, the southern Tarim basin, the southwestern Pamir region, and the eastern Kumul-Turpan-Hami corridor.

Uyghur Identity and the Challenge to Chinese Sovereignty

The "*minzu*" policy under the Chinese Nationalists identified five peoples of China, with the Han in the majority. The recognition of the Uyghurs as an official Chinese nationality (minzu) under a Soviet-influenced policy of nationality recognition contributed to a widespread acceptance of the idea of a continuity with the ancient Uyghur kingdom and their eventual concept of "Uyghur" as a *bona fide* nationality. This policy was continued under the Communists, who eventually recognized 56 nationalities, with the Han occupying a 91 percent majority in 1990. The "peaceful liberation" of Xinjiang by the Chinese Communists in 1949, and its subsequent establishment as the Xinjiang Uyghur Autonomous Region on October 1, 1955, perpetuated the Nationalist policy of recognizing the Uyghurs as a minority nationality under Chinese rule, as Burhan Shahidi explains.

However, the designation of the Uyghurs as a "nationality" masks tremendous regional and linguistic diversity. It also includes groups such as the Loplyk and Dolans that have very little in common with the oasis-based Turkic Muslims who had come to be known as the Uyghurs. At the same time, contemporary Uyghur separatists look back to the brief periods of independent self-rule under Yakub Beg and the Eastern Turkestan Republics, in addition to the earlier glories of the Uyghur kingdoms in Turpan and Karabalghasan, as evidence of their rightful claims to the region.

Today a number of Uyghur separatist organizations exist, based mainly in foreign cities such as Istanbul, Ankara, Almaty, Munich, Amsterdam, Melbourne, and Washington, D.C. They may differ in their political goals and strategies for the region, but they all share a common vision of a Uyghur claim on the region that has been disrupted by Chinese and Soviet intervention. The independence of the former Soviet Central Asian Republics in 1991 has done much to encourage these Uyghur organizations in their hopes for an independent "Turkestan," despite the fact the new, mainly Muslim Central Asian governments all signed protocols with China in the spring of 1996 that they would not harbor or support separatist groups.

Within the region, though many portray the Uyghurs as united around separatist or Islamist causes, Uyghurs continue to be divided from within by religious conflicts—in this case competing Sufi and non-Sufi factions—territorial loyalties (whether they be oases or places of origin), linguistic discrepancies, commoner-elite alienation, and competing political loyalties. These divided loyalties were evidenced by the attack in May 1996 on the imam of the Idgah mosque in Kashgar by other Uyghurs, as well as by the assassination of at least six Uyghur officials in September 2001.

It is also important to note that Islam is only one of several unifying markers for Uyghur identity. For example, to the Hui Muslim Chinese, the Uyghurs distinguish themselves as the legitimate autochthonous minority, since both share a belief in Sunni Islam. In contrast to the nomadic Muslim peoples (Kazakh or Kyrgyz), Uyghurs might stress their attachment to the land and oases of origin. In opposition to the Han Chinese, the Uyghurs will generally emphasize their long history in the region. It is this contested understanding of history that continues to influence much of the current debate over separatist and Chinese claims to the region. The multiple emphases in defining their identity have also served to mitigate the appeal that Islamic fundamentalist groups (often glossed as Wahhabiyya in the region) such as the Taliban in Afghanistan has had among the Uyghurs.

Alleged incursions of Taliban fighters through the Wakhan corridor into China where Xinjiang shares a narrow border with Afghanistan led to the area being swamped with Chinese security forces and large military exercises, beginning at least one month before the September 11 attacks. These military exercises suggested growing government concern about these border areas much earlier than September 11. Under U.S. and Chinese pressure, Pakistan returned one Uyghur activist, apprehended among hundreds of Taliban detainees, to China, which follows a pattern of repatriations of suspected Uyghur separatists from Kazakhstan, Kyrgyzstan, and Uzbekistan. During the war in Afghanistan, U.S. forces arrested as many as 22 Uyghurs fighting with the Taliban; they have been incarcerated in Guantánamo Bay, Cuba, as reported by the Agence France-Presse. Amnesty International has claimed

that Chinese government roundups of so-called terrorists and separatists have led to hurried public trials and immediate, summary executions of possibly thousands of locals. Troop movements to the area, related to the nationwide campaign against crime known as "Strike Hard," launched in 1998, which includes the call to erect a "great wall of steel" against separatists in Xinjiang, were reportedly the largest since the suppression of the large Akto insurrection in April 1990. (This was the first major uprising in Xinjiang. It took place in the Southern Tarim region near Baren township and initiated a series of unrelated and sporadic protests that took place in that region.) In September 2005, the BBC reported that at the 50th-year anniversary celebrations of the establishment of the Xinjiang Uyghur Autonomous Region in October 2005, Party Secretary Wang Lequan, promoted in 2004 to membership in the Politburo for his effective suppression of Uyghur separatism in the region, stated that the threat had not subsided and that there would an escalation of the Strike Hard campaign.

International campaigns for Uyghur rights and possible independence have become increasingly vocal and well organized, especially on the Internet. Repeated public appeals have been made to Abdulahat Abdurixit, the Uyghur People's Government chairman of Xinjiang in Urumqi. Notably, the elected chair of the Unrepresented Nations and People's Organization (UNPO), based in the Hague, is a Uyghur, Erkin Alptekin, son of the separatist leader Isa Yusuf Alptekin, who is buried in Istanbul, where there is a park dedicated to his memory. In spring 2004, Erkin Alptekin was elected by several international Uyghur organizations as the head of a newly formed World Uyghur Congress. The growing influence of "cyber-separatism" and international popularization of the Uyghur cause concerns Chinese authorities, who hope to convince the world that the Uyghurs do pose a real domestic and international terrorist threat.

China's Uyghur separatists are small in number, poorly equipped, loosely linked, and vastly outgunned by the People's Liberation Army and People's Police. It is also important to note that though sometimes disgruntled about some rights abuses and mistreatment issues, China's nine other official Muslim minorities do not in general support Uyghur separatism, as Nicolas Becquelin argues. There is continued enmity between Uyghurs and Hui (often known as "Dungan" in Xinjiang and Central Asia; see Ildíko Bellér-Hann). Few Hui support an independent Xinjiang, and 1 million Kazakhs in Xinjiang would have very little say in an independent "Uyghuristan." Local support for separatist activities, particularly in Xinjiang and other border regions, is ambivalent and ambiguous at best, given the economic disparity between these regions and their foreign neighbors, including Tadjikistan, Kyrgyzstan, Pakistan, and especially Afghanistan. There are strong memories in the region of mass starvation and widespread destruction during the Sino-Japanese War and the civil war in the first half of the century, including intra-Muslim and Muslim-Chinese bloody conflicts, not to mention the chaotic horrors of the Cultural Revolution.

Many local activists are not calling for complete separatism or independence but generally express concerns over environmental degradation, nuclear testing, religious freedom, overtaxation, and imposed limits on childbearing. Many ethnic leaders are simply calling for "real" autonomy according to Chinese law for the five autonomous regions that are each led by first party secretaries who are all Han Chinese controlled by Beijing. Freedom of religion, protected by China's constitution, does not seem to be a key issue, as mosques are full in the region and pilgrimages to Mecca are often allowed for Uyghurs and other Muslims (though some visitors to the region report an increase in restrictions against mosque attendance by youths, students, and government officials). In addition, Islamic extremism does not as yet appear to have widespread appeal, especially among urban, educated Uyghurs. However, the government has consistently rounded up any Uyghur suspected of being "too" religious—as Fuller and Lipman report—especially those identified as Sufis or the so-called Wahhabis (a euphemism in the region for strict Muslim, not an organized Islamic school). Also, in contrast to most strict Wahhabi practices, it is clear that Uyghur Islam continues to celebrate the mystical, enjoying tomb veneration and saint patronage, as well as Uyghur cultural practices such as raucous singing and dancing, as described by Bellér-Hann. The periodic roundups, detentions, and public condemnations of terrorism and separatism have not erased the problem but have forced it underground, or at least out of the public's eye, and have increased the possibility of alienating Uyghur Muslims even further from mainstream Chinese society.

BIBLIOGRAPHY

Amnesty International. *People's Republic of China: China's Anti-Terrorism Legislation and Repression in the Xinjiang Uighur Autonomous Region.* London: Amnesty International, March 2002. http://web.amnesty.org/library/index/ENGASA170472002.

———. *People's Republic of China. Gross Violations of Human Rights in the Xinjiang Uighur Autonomous Region.* London: Amnesty International, April 1999.

———. "Uyghurs Held in Guantánamo Bay." *Urgent Action Bulletin* 356/03 (December 4, 2003). AMR 51/147/2003.

Anderson, Benedict. *Imagined Communities: Reflections on the Origin and Spread of Nationalism.* London: Verso Press, 1983; 2nd ed., 1991.

Bai, Shouyi. "Huihui minzu de xingcheng" (The Nature of the Hui Nationality). *Guangming Ribao,* February 17, 1951.

Barfield, Thomas. *The Perilous Frontier: Nomadic Empires and China.* Cambridge, UK: Basil Blackwell, 1989.

Becquelin, Nicolas. "Xinjiang in the Nineties." *The China Journal* 44 (2001): 1–25.

Bellér-Hann, Ildíko. "Making the Oil Fragrant: Dealings with the Supernatural Among the Uyghurs in Xinjiang." *Asian Ethnicity* 2:1 (2001): 9–23.

———. "Temperamental Neighbors: Uighur-Han Relations in Xinjiang, Northwest China." In *Imagined Difference: Hatred and the Construction of Identity,* ed. G. Schlee, 57–82. Munster, Hamburg, London: LIT Verlag, 2001.

Benite, Zvi Ben-Dor. *The Dao of Muhammad: A Cultural History of Muslims in Late Imperial China.* Cambridge, MA: Harvard University Asia Center, 2005.

Benson, Linda. *The Ili Rebellion: The Moslem Challenge to Chinese Authority in Xinjiang, 1944–1949.* Armonk, NY: M.E. Sharpe, 1990.

Black, Cyril E., et al. *The Modernization of Inner Asia.* Armonk, NY: M.E. Sharpe, 1991.

Bovingdon, Gardner. "The Not-So-Silent Majority: Uyghur Resistance to Han Rule in Xinjiang." *Modern China* 28:1 (2002): 39–78.

Cheng, Allen T. "A Surprise Move by the Mainland's Islamic Community." *South China Morning Post,* March 25, 2003.

"China Releases List of International Terrorists." *Xinhua.* Received by NewsEDGE/LAN, December 14, 2003.

"China Warns of Xinjiang 'Danger.'" September 29, 2005. http://newsvote.bbc.co.uk/mpapps/pagetools/print/news.bbc.co.uk/2/hi/asia-pacific/4292466.stm.

Connor, Walker. *The National Question in Marxist-Leninist Theory and Strategy.* Princeton, NJ: Princeton University Press, 1984.

Da, Yingyu. "Zhongguo Yisilanjiao Sailaifeiye pai shulue" (A Brief Narration of China's Islamic Salafiyya Order). In *Zhongguo*

Yisilanjiao yanjiu wenji (Compendium of Chinese Islamic Research), ed. Chinese Islamic Research Committee. Yinchuan: Ningxia People's Publishing Society, 1988.

Duara, Prasenjit. *Sovereignty and Authenticity: Manchukuo and the East Asian Modern.* New York: Rowman and Littlefield, 2003.

Fletcher, Joseph. *Studies on Chinese and Islamic Inner Asia,* ed. Beatrice Forbes Manz. Hampshire, UK: Variorum Press, 1995.

Forbes, Andrew D.W. *Warlords and Muslims in Chinese Central Asia.* Cambridge, UK: Cambridge University Press, 1986.

Franke, Herbert, and Denis Twitchett. *Cambridge History of China: Volume 6. Alien Regimes and Border States (907–1368).* Cambridge, UK: Cambridge University Press, 1994.

Fuller, Graham E., and Jonathan N. Lipman. "Islam in Xinjiang." In *Xinjiang: China's Muslim Borderland,* ed. Frederick S. Starr, 320–52. Armonk, NY: M.E. Sharpe, 2004.

Gladney, Dru C. *Dislocating China: Muslims, Minorities, and Other Subaltern Subjects.* Chicago: University of Chicago Press, 2004.

———. *Muslim Chinese: Ethnic Nationalism in the People's Republic.* Cambridge, MA: Harvard University Press, 1996.

Harris, Lillian. *China Considers the Middle East.* London: I.B. Tauris, 1993.

"Help the Uyghurs to Fight Terrorism." Munich: East Turkistan (Uyghuristan) National Congress, collected November 11, 2003.

Hopkirk, Peter. *The Great Game: The Struggle for Empire in Central Asia.* New York and Tokyo: Kodansha International, 1994.

Kim, Hodong. *Holy War in China: The Muslim Rebellion and State in Chinese Central Asia, 1866–1877.* Stanford, CA: Stanford University Press, 2003.

Lapidus, Ira M. *A History of Islamic Societies.* Cambridge, UK: Cambridge University Press, 1988.

Linxia Hui Autonomous Prefectural Basic Situation Committee. *Linxia Huizu zizhizhou gaikuang* (Linxia Hui Autonomous Prefectural Basic Situation). Lanzhou: Gansu Nationalities Publishing Society, 1986.

Ma, Dazheng. *The State Takes Precedence: Research and Analysis on the Xinjiang Stability Problem.* Urumqi, PRC: Xinjiang People's Publishing House, 2003.

Millward, James A. *Beyond the Pass: Economy,*

Ethnicity, and Empire in Qing Central Asia, 1759–1865. Stanford, CA: Stanford University Press, 1998.

Ong, Aihwa. *Flexible Citizenship: The Cultural Logic of Transnationality.* Durham, NC: Duke University Press, 1999.

Qiu, Shulin, ed. *Zhongguo Huizu dacidian* (Great Encyclopedia of China's Hui Nationality). Yinchuan, China: Jiangsu Ancient Relics Publishers, 1992.

Rossabi, Morris. *China and Inner Asia from 1368 to the Present Day.* London: Thames and Hudson, 1981.

Rudelson, Justin Jon. *Oasis Identities: Uyghur Nationalism Along China's Silk Road.* New York: Columbia University Press, 1998.

"Separatist Leader Killed in Waziristan." Radio Free Asia, December 15, 2003. www.rfa.org/service/index.html?service=uyg.

Shahidi, Burhan. *Xinjiang: Wushi nian* (Xinjiang: Fifty Years). Beijing: Wenshi Ziliao Chubanshe, 1984.

Shichor, Yitzhak. *East Wind over Arabia: Origins and Implications of the Sino-Saudi Missile Deal.* Berkeley: University of California Press, 1989.

Sinor, Denis, ed. *The Cambridge History of Early Inner Asia.* Cambridge, UK: Cambridge University Press, 1990.

Stern, Jessica. *Terror in the Name of God: Why Religious Militants Kill.* New York: Ecco/Harper Collins, 2003.

"U.S. Keeps Uighurs at Guantanamo After Found Innocent: Rights Group." Agence France-Press, August 1, 2005.

Wang, David D. *Under the Soviet Shadow: The Yining Incident: Ethnic Conflicts and International Rivalry in Xinjiang, 1944–1949.* Hong Kong: The Chinese University Press, 1999.

Yang, Shengmin, and Ding Hong, eds. *Zhongguo minzu zhi* (An Ethnography of China). Beijing: Central Nationalities Publishing House, 2002.

Malaysia

Joseph Chinyong Liow

The centrality of Islam in modern Malaysian politics can be traced to the advent of the administration of Prime Minister Mahathir Muhammad in 1978 or farther back to developments immediately following the May 1969 race riots, which revealed the flaws of the country's secular, pluralistic approach. Consequently, the 1970s saw Muslim society evolve along two tracks: the first along the United Malays National Organization (UMNO)–orchestrated and Islamic Party of Malaysia (PAS)–supported lines of economic restructuring and affirmative action, and the second along a path of Islamization capitalizing on the global Islamic revival and taking the form of nongovernmental activist pressure groups such as Angkatan Belia Islam Malaysia (Malaysian Islamic Youth Movement, ABIM) as well as other less politically oriented organizations such as Jama'at Tabligh and Darul Arqam. The pertinent role that these organizations played attests to the social origins of Islamism in Malaysia, commonly known in Malaysian academic parlance as *dakwa*.

The Social Origins of Islamism

According to the Malaysian Department of Statistics, Malays constituted a majority of 50.4 percent of the Malaysian population in 2004, while the percentage of Chinese and Indians stood at 23.7 percent and 11 percent, respectively. Islam assumes further significance by virtue of the fact that according to the constitution, one of the chief criteria for the definition of "Malay" was that a person must be Muslim. Such is the intimate relationship between ethnicity and religion that to convert to Islam, a person is deemed to have *masuk melayu* (to become Malay). Beyond this, the role of Islam as a core foundation of Malay identity has taken on further credence because the two other pillars on which this identity is constructed, namely language and royalty, no longer carry the same weight. The Malay language remains of consequence politically, but this is precisely what led the state to engender an education policy based on its primacy in the national curriculum. As a result, simply put, knowledge of the Malay language was no longer the exclusive prerogative of the Malay people. Similarly, royalty in Malaysia today has a highly problematic relationship with the Malay ruling elite, where it is seen by the latter as a competitor to their legitimacy. Moreover, the royals have also further undermined their own legitimacy in the public eye as a result of a number of controversial episodes and scandals over the past few years.

The May 13, 1969, incident in Malaysia, which saw the outbreak of race riots after the worst electoral performance by the UMNO-led Alliance coalition party in the preceding general elections, was the precursor of several far-reaching affirmative action policies that essentially cemented the primacy of the Malay community in Malaysia's social-political constellation. One such policy was the allocation of large numbers of government scholarships to Malay-Muslim students to pursue university education abroad.

The effect of this policy of sending Malay-Muslim students overseas during the height of the worldwide resurgence of Islamic identity and consciousness cannot be overemphasized. This sojourn offered them the opportunity to acquaint themselves and interact with various Muslim students through activities on university campuses in Europe, North America, and Australia, as well as in the Middle East and North Africa at the height of the global Islamic resurgence. It was also during this period that they engaged in various activities organized by well-structured, well-endowed social networks and Islamic charities that had been underwriting much of the civil society activism associated with this Islamic resurgence.

The experience abroad had a dual effect on the students. On the one hand, they were exposed firsthand to the "decadence" wrought by Westernization and modernization that was so heavily criticized by various Islamic groups during this period. On the other hand, they were also exposed to various new streams of Islamic scholarship and translations of major works that allowed them access to a wider pool of knowledge about their faith. These students brought these values and perspectives back home to Malaysia upon completion of their education, and these quickly shaped how they viewed their own society back home, perceiving Westernization to be rampant and Islam practiced in ways that did not adhere to strict and purist interpretations. This transplanted movement found institutional expression locally through the formation of numerous Islamic student associations and societies (*persatuan Islam*) on campuses throughout the country, as well as the formation of nongovernmental organizations (NGOs) such as ABIM and Jama'at Tabligh.

Imported back to Malaysian soil from abroad, these ideas and activities had a profound effect on traditional Malaysian society, whose practice of Islam was steeped in the folk and syncretic traditions of the religion that had for a long time characterized its various forms in Southeast Asia. This social movement would soon find politicized expression in the UMNO-PAS Islamization "race" that has come to define the contours of Islamism in Malaysia.

Genesis of Islamist Politics

PAS has long been the primary Malay-based opposition in Malaysian politics. As a political party, PAS was ironically born within UMNO itself, when members of the Religious Bureau of UMNO called into question the commitment of the party's leadership to Islam and Muslim interests and broke away in 1951. Regardless of the party's overtly religious character and motivation, however, its track record in Malaysian politics is certainly more checkered. Through the 1950s and 1960s, the party, under the leadership of the Muslim-socialist intellectual Dr. Burhanuddin al-Helmy, lined up as an Islamic-socialist party. After the May 1969 race riots, PAS, under Muhammad Asri

Muda, moved further to the right of the ideological spectrum. Against the backdrop of heightened communitarian consciousness, it transformed into a Malay-nationalist party that contested UMNO's claim to the leadership of the Malay community.

Subsequently, the period from 1974 to 1977 saw PAS join UMNO in a coalition that was an ill-fated attempt at conciliation. Yet membership in this coalition set in motion the political events that eventually led to the loss—in the 1978 elections—of its power base in Kelantan for the first time since independence. As a result, the internal coup in the party at its 1982 *muktamar* (convention) purged the party of its old-guard nationalists—led by Asri Muda—and brought into power *ulama* (religious clerics) led by Yusuf Rawa and a core group comprising Fadzil Noor, Nakhaie Ahmad, Abdul Hadi Awang, and Muhammad Sabu, who were bent on returning Islam to the party's political agenda.

The reorientation of PAS in 1982 cannot be attributed solely to the failure of Asri Muda's strategy of allying the party with UMNO. The early 1980s witnessed key global events in the Muslim world that shaped this reorientation not only in PAS but in UMNO as well. This included the Afghan mujahidin, or struggle; the Iranian Revolution; the introduction of an Islamic government in Pakistan; intensification of Islamism in the political realm in Egypt, Tunisia, and Turkey; and the generally heightened Islamic consciousness of the Malay-Muslim population as calls toward Islam as "the solution" gained greater currency across the country.

It would be wrong to suggest that it was only in the 1980s that Islam emerged as a factor in Malay politics, because UMNO had from very early on been regularly pressured by opposition forces to prove its Islamic credentials and responded with the creation of institutions such as the Islamic Welfare Organization (Persatuan Kebajikan Islam Malaysia, PERKIM). Nevertheless, it was in the 1980s that the logic of Islamic governance became more sharply defined and Islamic influence expanded.

Mahathir Muhammad, who had taken over from the ailing Hussein Onn as Malaysia's fourth prime minister in July 1981, was quick to anticipate the challenges posed to the ruling administration by international and domestic developments, and his response was swift. The Mahathir administration sought to seize the initiative by harnessing and mobilizing Islam to justify its developmental policies. It did so by orchestrating an Islamization process that found expression in the host of Islamic-oriented institutions that flowed from this policy. This stood in marked contrast at the time to developments elsewhere in the Muslim world, where regimes experiencing similar pressures from Islamist opposition forces, such as in Egypt and Turkey, chose to discredit, rather than take over, the Islamist agenda.

Key elements of Mahathir's Islamization program included the creation of a religious bureaucracy under the auspices of the state, Islamic courts, Islamic banking and financial systems, and Islamic education—including a tertiary institution, the International Islamic University, which is fast becoming one of the most prestigious centers of Muslim higher education in the region, if not in the entire Muslim world.

An important initiative under the Mahathir administration was the creation of several research institutes that contributed to articulating and developing the government's Islamization project. The Malaysian Institute for Islamic Understanding (IKIM) and the Institute for Islamic Thought and Civilization (ISTAC) played a crucial role.

Also of importance, in the case of former Deputy Prime Minister Anwar Ibrahim, was the Institute Kajian Dasar (Institute of Policy Studies, IKD), which, among other things, served to generate many of Anwar's ideas on modernist/progressive Islam, which he employed to great success during his tenure as deputy prime minister. Of particular significance was the creation of state religious committees, which were granted powers to police and monitor the content and expression of Islam. Further, at the government level, an Islamic department, the Jabatan Kemajuan Islam Malaysia (JAKIM, or Department for the Advancement of Islam), was established under the auspices of the prime minister's office, with its own minister and secretariat. State religious departments enjoy powers of appointment for imams and mosque committees and perpetuate incumbent rule through the selection of UMNO supporters to these posts. Conversely, known opposition activists have been removed, as was the case with the imam of the Damansara Utama Mujahidin Mosque. Sermons, too, are prepared by the state religious departments and distributed to all the mosques in the state.

This shift in government policy was further mirrored in the foreign policy of the Mahathir administration, when Malaysia began taking an active interest in Arab-Muslim affairs and positioned itself as the international spokesman of the Muslim world. Perhaps the most significant component of the Mahathir government's Islamization strategy was the successful co-option of Anwar Ibrahim. Then an active leader of the youth movement ABIM, Anwar was courted both by UMNO and PAS. However, it was Mahathir who ultimately masterminded the co-option of Anwar; in him the ruling regime found not only a popular leader with strong Islamist credentials but, more important, a key ideologue who could convincingly articulate a comprehensive Islamization program that mapped out the trajectory of political Islam in Malaysia.

Needless to say, several consequences flowed from the Mahathir administration's Islamization strategy. Malaysia has become the model of an "Islamic state" par excellence in the eyes of the West. However, the Mahathir administration narrowed the political space in Malaysia, which, given the pluralistic contours and patterns of Malaysian society, threatened to curtail democratic discourse and alienate Malaysia's large non-Muslim population.

Islamism as Discourse

In reaction to the changes in PAS after the 1982 Muktamar, the corresponding UMNO General Assembly in 1982 saw Mahathir announce that UMNO would be embarking on a new strategy focused on "the struggle to change the attitude of the Malays in line with the requirements of Islam in this modern age." This logic subsequently underpinned his introduction of a policy of *penerapan nilai-nilai Islam* (inculcation of Islamic values). The longstanding objective of improving the lot of the Malay community was repackaged as an objective sanctioned by, and to be pursued in reference to, Islam. Mahathir's vision of Islam, however, was one couched in developmentalist language, and his claim to "authenticity" was based on his argument that there is no tension between modernization and religion in "true Islam." For instance, in a speech at the International Islamic Symposium in March 1986, he noted that it was only by accepting the pursuit of knowledge and advancement of technology that Muslims could "sincerely try to regain the essence of Islam that so inspired the early Muslims so that not only did they manage to spread the teachings far and wide but they brought greatness to Islam in the fields of human endeavour."

For Mahathir, Islam sat comfortably with modernity and material progress. Following this train of thought, PAS was correspondingly caricatured as the mirror opposite—obscurantist in ideology, backward in outlook, and fundamentally opposed to progress. In other words, PAS exemplified all that Mahathir saw wrong with Islam today. Yet, insofar as PAS was concerned, Islam provided a trenchant counternarrative to modernization as defined by the government, which to its mind created myriad social problems for the Muslim community. The Islamization strategy of the Mahathir administration was criticized and delegitimized as nothing more than a manipulation of religion.

A major feature of the heavily contested discursive terrain of Muslim politics has been the debate over Malaysia's characterization as an Islamic state, as well as the conceptual and practical blueprints that both UMNO and PAS put forth for Malaysia as an Islamic state. While Mahathir had on previous occasions during his long tenure described Malaysia as an "Islamic country," his pronouncement on September 29, 2001, that Malaysia "was already an Islamic state" marked a fundamental watershed that sparked an intense national debate and further demonstrated the centrality of Islam in the Malaysian political orbit.

At first glance, Mahathir's declaration does appear to have fulfilled a key political objective—to preempt PAS and seize the initiative for UMNO. The claim that Malaysia was already an Islamic state, however, needs to be viewed in context. First, this "Islamic state" that Mahathir implied Malaysia already was had been mainly a construction of his own administration and a logi-

cal outgrowth of his Islamization program over the previous two decades. In tandem with the general inconsistent tendencies of UMNO Islamization, in hindsight it does not appear to have survived its progenitor's retirement and has since been supplanted by Abdallah Badawi's more palatable but equally complex concept of *Islam hadhari* (civilizational Islam), which articulated ten broad principles of Islamic governance for Malaysia related to development, ethics, education, and pluralism.

Second, Mahathir's logic, as many Islamic scholars were quick to point out, was fundamentally flawed. While Mahathir maintained that Malaysia could be an Islamic state without the implementation of Islamic law, this contention goes against the grain of most theories of the Islamic state. For all its vagaries, there is general consensus that Shari'a is the definitive characteristic of an Islamic state. To that effect, the Islamists could contend, rightly so in accordance to Islamic political philosophy, that Mahathir's pronouncement was groundless and exemplified the mobilization of religion for political ends. Finally, as with much of the problem with the ongoing discourse of Islamization in Malaysia, Mahathir's statement threatened to push Malaysia further down the road of Islamization and alienate Malaysia's substantial non-Muslim minorities.

Under pressure from reformists within the party, PAS's Islamic State Document was released on November 12, 2003, and was presented as the high point of the party's struggle to entrench its position in its core electoral base of the Malay-Muslim community by emphasizing its Islamic credentials. The document attempted to reconcile the need for Shari'a in Malaysia, with provisions for greater democracy under the auspices of an Islamic state. At the same time, it attempted to allay non-Muslim fears that an Islamic state in Malaysia would be a theocracy by assuring them of religious and cultural freedoms and the option to live under Islamic criminal laws or the current secular constitutional system. Beneath the rhetoric, however, was a realization that the document was urgently required to counter the religious standing that Abdullah Badawi had brought to UMNO.

This debate, which continues, speaks to the inflation of Islamist discourse by both parties and underscores an increasingly tense rivalry over the form and content of Islam in the Malaysian political sphere. Unlike previous UMNO-led administrations that roundly rejected the notion of the Islamic state, UMNO under Mahathir appropriated PAS discourse on it. Both UMNO and PAS employ the language of religion to serve their political objectives of discrediting and undermining each other.

To be sure, beyond the Islamic state, this process has generated concepts more palatable to Malaysia's pluralistic society and more amenable to democracy and reform. In 1996 then Deputy Prime Minister Anwar Ibrahim sought to capitalize on the overall heightened Muslim consciousness as well as his own personal popularity by manufacturing a new, catchy organizing principle for a pluralistic society based on Islamic precepts of democracy, good governance, inclusiveness, and civil relations between ethnic groups. This proposed to restructure fundamentally Malaysia's hitherto communally oriented national consciousness. The catchphrase *masyarakat madani* (civil society) was contrived to define such a society; the concept was presented as a polity where Allah had endowed rights to individuals that were to be recognized; respected; and insofar as the state was concerned, protected and where democratic principles were to be enshrined.

As Anwar himself explained at the Sixth Malaysia-Singapore Forum in December 1996, "Only the fostering of a genuine civil society or *masyarakat madani,* a critical component to the establishment of democracy, can assure the path of sustained growth including economic, social, and political." The concept of masyarakat madani, as Anwar imagined it, was anchored by the notion of *Keadilan Sosial,* or social justice. Through the efforts of his *Institut Kajian Dasar,* masyarakat madani, Keadilan Sosial, and Anwar's attendant call for intercivilizational dialogue—which underpinned his 1996 compendium of speeches titled *Asian Renaissance*—soon became the focus of trendy intellectualism as road shows, seminars, and conferences were held throughout the country to promote the concept and reach out across ethnic and class schisms.

Skeptics viewed masyarakat madani merely as a manifestation of Anwar's ambition and his own brand of leadership in preparation for his eventual succession to the leadership. Anwar was slated to be Mahathir's successor and was building on his reputation as an activist and modernist Muslim leader, which he had garnered during his ABIM days and which later saw him emerge as a popular Muslim intellectual, chancellor of the International Islamic University, and personification of all that was progressive and modern about the government's Islamization program. Even so, this initiative did contain certain ideas that sought to transcend the communal structure of society and politics in Malaysia. Concepts such as democracy and human rights, long rejected (when articulated in relation to Western understanding of such ideas) by the Malaysian establishment under Mahathir, stood then at the forefront of discourse on the future of the Malaysian polity. Masyarakat madani, however, appeared to have died a premature death with Anwar's removal from office. Later, however, under Abdullah Badawi's administration, which used the term *Islam hadhari*, masyarakat madani appears to have been revived.

Islam hadhari was an adaptation of the thought of Ibn Khaldun, a fourteenth-century Muslim historian and sociologist, adapted to the Malay community's struggle for independence and development. Briefly, Islam hadhari emphasized the enhancement of "the quality of life" through acquisition of knowledge; development of the individual and the nation; and establishment of a dynamic economic, trading, and financial system. To Abdullah's mind, such a balanced development would produce an *umma* (community) of knowledgeable, pious people with noble values such as honesty and trustworthiness, able to take on challenges of modernization without compromising religious belief. Islam hadhari, as later explained in a 60-page document drafted by JAKIM and published by the government, further emphasized the central role of knowledge in Islam, along with hard work, honesty, good administration and efficiency, as well as an appeal to Muslims to be tolerant and outward looking. Committees have since been established to spread the message throughout Malaysia, and UMNO imams have been instructed to preach it during Friday sermons.

Consequences of the Rise of Islamism

Not surprisingly, the government-sanctioned policies that have amounted to the bureaucratization of Islam brought a backlash from non-Muslim communities suspicious of government attempts to impose Islamic values on them. Legislation over the issue of religious proselytizing clearly illustrated this partiality. While the constitution ensures the right of every person to "profess and practice his religion," only Muslims are allowed to propagate their belief. Beyond that, the Malaysian government has itself actively engaged in dakwa, or proselytizing to non-Muslims. This has included the expansion of Islamic programs over public radio and television, more stringent legislation controlling the building of non-Muslim religious buildings, and the curtailment of land plots for non-Muslim burial sites. Indeed, the essence of popular concern—particularly from the non-Muslim population—is not so much with the introduction of Islamic institutions and practices but the hegemony of Islam in public life in Malaysia.

UMNO-run state governments have also advanced and implemented Islamic policies that fulfill the UMNO's politically driven Islamist agenda. At the same time, though, there is a constant rivalry between PAS representatives seeking popular support and members of the UMNO leadership, who have sought to tone down their zeal. An instance of federal-state tension that sparked much interest and controversy was the arrest under the Selangor Islamic Criminal Enactment of 1995 of three Malay women for participating in a beauty contest in June 1997. Afterward, comments by the prime minister and deputy prime minister calling for caution against extremism among state religious officials were publicly rebuffed by the then mufti of Selangor. This incident was symptomatic of the increasing assertiveness of Islamic identity among the Malay populace and the political pressures this has created, spawning not only a more assertive cultural expression of Islamic consciousness—manifested most vividly in the popularity of Islamic dress—but also in legislation that has impinged on the cultural space of the non-Muslim community. This has included local policies that, among other things, prohibit non-halal foods in certain school cafeterias, ban signboards associated with alcohol in certain states, and deny permits to celebrate Chinese cultural festivals in some schools.

Other concerns revolved around the move by elements within UMNO to formulate a Faith Protection Bill (known as the *Aqida,* or Faith Act) in November 2000, legislating against apostasy and similar to a bill passed in June 2000 in the UMNO-controlled state of Perlis. This followed earlier attempts by then PAS deputy president Abdul Hadi Awang to obtain parliamentary passage of a bill making apostasy an offense punishable by death. While the UMNO motion was less severe, it was nevertheless indicative of the extent to which the party was prepared to go in defending its Islamic credentials.

Debates have also surfaced over revelations that students in Christian mission schools have been forced to recite Islamic prayers in Penang, as well as increased incidences of Islamist-style checks on non-Muslims' activities in Perak and the closing down of entertainment establishments in Selangor by state authorities. Other instances of state-sanctioned Islamization policies include the requirement for the consent of Muslim neighbors before the application or renewal of dog licenses in Johore Bahru; the ban on the sale of pork in open-air markets in Kajang; the removal of liquor and beer advertisements in Selangor; and the moral policing by the Ipoh Municipality and Kuala Lumpur City Council, which resulted in the arrest of couples for holding hands in public. In September 2002, a seminar organized by the Selangor state government entitled "Understanding Malaysia as an Islamic State" saw a proposal by UMNO state officials for constitutional amendments to declare the Koran and Sunna sources of federal law.

Negotiating Islam

To be certain, there have been alternative voices from within the Malay-Muslim community that have attempted to provide their own interpretation of Islamism. These have taken the form of civil society movements and dakwa associations looking to expand democracy. While there are numerous active Islamic NGOs operating in Malaysia, two of the most important mainstream organizations at the forefront of this effort have been ABIM and SIS (Sisters in Islam).

ABIM has stood out as one of the most influential and well-organized Muslim civil society groups that has had an influence on Malay-Muslim politics. Formed in 1971 under the leadership of Anwar Ibrahim, ABIM successfully mobilized modernist Malay-Muslim students as a pressure group during the Razak and Hussein Onn administrations. It demonstrated its power and influence most profoundly in December 1974, when it orchestrated a mass student uprising against the government's rural development policies, resulting in the arrest and detention of numerous ABIM leaders under the Internal Security Act. Such was the influence of ABIM in the 1970s that the government amended the Societies Act, the Misuse of Religion Act, and the Universities and University Colleges Act to proscribe Muslim civil society activity.

ABIM's key ideological contribution to Islamization was the introduction of a universalist interpretation of Islam in the 1970s that accommodated Malaysia's pluralistic society. ABIM, for example, was a staunch critic of the government's affirmative action NEP (National Economic Policy) on Islamic grounds, and after the movement's retreat from activist pressure politics, when Anwar was co-opted into the UMNO, the mantle of Malay-Muslim opposition to the NEP was passed on to PAS.

While ABIM in its current permutation no longer resembles the highly politicized student movement of the 1970s, the legacy of its activism continues to shape the process of Islamization in Malaysia. Many ABIM members who had agitated for the introduction of Shari'a in Malaysia and had challenged the deep-seated aspects of Malay culture that did not resonate with Islam internalized these values and expressed them when they went on in the 1980s and 1990s to assume positions in Malaysian bureaucracy and government offices, forming the backbone of the bureaucratization of Islam in the Mahathir and Abdullah administrations.

Another important group that has in recent times played a critical role is Sisters in Islam, which is among the most vocal advocacy groups. Established in 1988, SIS has challenged male-dominated Islamist orthodoxy on matters such as Shari'a, women's rights, apostasy laws, domestic violence and polygamy, public participation, and the hegemonic discourse on Islam propounded by ulama from either UMNO or PAS camps. Its efforts to use Islamic discourse and provide alternative visions, in the hope of expanding the democratic space for Malaysian Muslims, have been rebuffed and at times condemned by the religious establishment. Its leaders and activists have been heavily criticized as lacking the level of Islamic knowledge and educational background required for them to be challenging ulama. More traditional religious leaders have attacked their activities as deviationist attempts to reinterpret scripture.

Religious Extremism and Militancy in Malaysia

As early as the 1970s, religiously based radical groups had already started surfacing in Muslim-majority Malaysia. The Penang-based Crypto cult movement, formed in 1977, claimed that the Malaysian government was not giving Islam its proper due and aimed to set up a theocratic order by means of violent jihad (holy war). It was only in 1992 that the Malaysian government took action to clamp down on the movement.

Another group whose interpretation of Islam threatened the incumbent regime was the Koperasi Angkatan Revolusi Islam Malaysia (KARIM, or Malaysian Islamic Revolutionary Front). Formed in 1974 in Kuala Lumpur, KARIM preached the overthrow of the government through violence. It was later banned and its leaders detained under the Internal Security Act. In 1980 riots in Kedah by farmers demonstrating against the government's move to introduce a forced-savings scheme were traced to a militant organization called Pertubuhan Angkatan Sabillullah, which, according to the government, had numbered among its associates members of the Muslim opposition party PAS.

Later, in 1988, elements from within the Malaysian government moved again to incriminate PAS by linking it to Muslim militancy. This time, young members of PAS were accused by their UMNO adversaries of concealing weapons in the PAS seminary Muassasah Darul Ulum in Kedah. Though a subsequent crackdown by security forces yielded nothing, several PAS members were later rounded up under "Ops Kenari," a security crackdown on opposition politicians under the pretext of security "threats," in response to UMNO's further complaint that they were attempting to disrupt a UMNO rally in Semarak. During this crackdown, weapons were apparently discovered in the possession of PAS members. Nevertheless, attempts to censure the party failed because of insufficient evidence to implicate PAS of involvement in militancy. It was in November 1985, however, that the Malaysian government recorded its first violent encounter with militant Islam, when security forces clashed with PAS stalwart Ibrahim Mahmud and his supporters in Kedah.

Ibrahim Mahmud, or "Ibrahim Libya," as he was popularly called, was a member of the Islamic opposition PAS and had held senior positions in the party organization at both district and state levels. Trained at the University of Tripoli and al-Azhar, Ibrahim was a popular religious teacher stationed at a *madrasa* in Kampung Memali in Baling, Kedah. In his capacity as religious teacher and PAS leader, Ibrahim was accused by the Malaysian government of exploiting Islam by spreading radical teaching in the states of Kedah, Penang, and Perak that incited Muslims to conduct jihad against the state. The government responded by calling Ibrahim Mahmud a "deviant" Muslim and limiting his activities. This showdown reached its climax when government security forces stormed the compound of Ibrahim Mahmud's residence while he was conducting religious lessons. After apparent armed resistance from Mahmud's supporters, the event ended with 18 deaths and 160 arrests, according to a December 1985 article in the *Far Eastern Economic Review.*

Another manifestation of militant Islam was the Maunah (Brotherhood of Inner Power) movement that managed to pull off an arms heist from two Malaysian Armed Forces military camps in Perak in June 2000. According to police reports, the membership of al-Maunah, a cult led by former army corporal Muhammad Amin Razali, numbered several hundred and claimed to be an NGO involved in martial arts. Among its supporters were civil servants, security service personnel, and even some UMNO members.

Malaysian security forces launched a high-profile operation against the Maunah camp in Sauk, Perak, in July 2000. During the standoff, 19 members were captured, but only after four hostages were taken and two non-Muslims among them executed. Members of al-Maunah apprehended in the raid were charged with treason and plotting to overthrow the government in order to create an Islamic state. While the organization was consequently disbanded and outlawed, what remains most alarming about the episode was the ease with which the militants breached security and gained access to a large cache of weapons.

In June 2001 the specter of militant Islam reared its head again in Malaysia when nine members of another organization that claimed to champion the creation of a purist Muslim society in Malaysia via jihad were arrested in a failed bank robbery bid. Known as the Jihad Gang, this group of militants was connected to a range of crimes over a period of two years, including the bombing of a church, an Indian temple, and a video store, as well as an attack on a police station, the murder of a local politician, attempted murder in shooting two ethnic Indians, and armed robbery. Police investigations subsequently revealed that all nine members were Malaysians educated in the Middle East and Pakistan and had fought in Afghanistan during the 1980s and later in Ambon (Indonesia) during the religious riots there. It was during investigations into the activities of the Jihad Gang that information on another jihadi organization surfaced.

Several months after the uncovering of the Jihad Gang, Deputy Home Minister Datuk Zainal Abidin Zin informed the parliament that the government had detained a further 10 Islamist activists on the grounds that they were members of an underground militant group called Kumpulan Militan Malaysia (KMM). The KMM was uncovered when a Malaysian was arrested for an attempted bombing of a shopping mall in Jakarta, Indonesia, in August 2001. It was alleged that the KMM was formed on October 12, 1995, by Zainon Ismail, and had its roots in Halaqah Pakindo, a clandestine movement formed in 1986 as an alumni association for Malaysian graduates from religious institutions in Pakistan, India, and Indonesia. The government later disclosed that eight of the 10 KMM detainees were PAS members, including Nik Adli Abdul Aziz, the son of Kelantan Mentri Besar Datuk Nik Aziz Nik Mat. Nik Adli was allegedly elected leader at a meeting of 12 senior members in Kampung Seri Aman, Puchong, in early 1999. Yet the government later contended that real leadership came from Abu Bakar Ba'asyir and Riduan Isamuddin, better known as Hambali. According to government investigations and Nik Adli's own admission, the 34-year-old teacher had made frequent trips to Afghanistan. This admission formed the basis of government allegations that Nik Aziz was active in the mujahidin in Afghanistan during the Afghan-Soviet war and upon his return maintained connections with militants in the region.

What differentiated the KMM from other militant organizations uncovered in Malaysia was the alleged regional scope of its operations. Though KMM was established in Malaysia, the government has suggested that the organization enjoys close links with the Jemaah Islamiyah in Indonesia. Malaysian government sources have also revealed that the KMM is, in fact, led by Abu Bakar Ba'asyir and Hambali, while Nik Azli is merely a "nominal leader." KMM was suspected to have participated in religiously inspired riots in Maluku and Ambon and of having supplied arms to radical Muslims in the case of the latter. Upon their arrests, as reported in the *Asian Wall Street Journal* in January 2002, the leaders were reportedly found to have had in their possession "documents on guerrilla warfare and map reading, along with studies of militant groups in the Philippines, Chechnya, Afghanistan and Indonesia." Concomitantly, the Malaysian security forces launched a nationwide operation to capture remaining KMM members. At the end of 2006, more than 70 were detained without trial under the Internal Security Act for allegedly trying to overthrow the government through violent means in the name of jihad.

The Future of Islam in Malaysia

There is no doubt that the UMNO-PAS Islamization "race" is the most telling expression of Islamism as it takes shape in Malaysia. During the 22-year-long administration of Mahathir Muhammad, Islam moved from the fringe to the political mainstream, with the Islamist opposition PAS attaining a level of maturation and sophistication sufficient to pose a fundamental challenge to Mahathir's UMNO-led government, questioning the UMNO's Islamic credentials as a centerpiece of its strategy.

The process of Islamization itself continues to gain new impetus and momentum. There is no denying that Islam has advanced as a major influence on the lives of Muslims in Malaysia over the last 30 years. While the Islamization of Malaysian politics can be plausibly traced to former prime minister

Mahathir's calibrated policies, the globalization of Islam generated by sociopolitical and cultural forces has meant that Islamization in Malaysia can no longer be confined to the realms of UMNO-PAS politics. Nor can it be controlled by the political actors whose preference has been to harness its power and ride its waves in order to enhance their appeal and legitimacy among the Malay-Muslim electorate rather than to curtail it.

BIBLIOGRAPHY

Abu Bakar, Mohammad. "Islamic Revivalism and the Political Process in Malaysia." *Asian Survey* 21:10 (October 1981).

"Asian Militants with Alleged Al Qaeda Ties Are Accused of Plotting Against Embassies." *Asian Wall Street Journal,* January 2, 2002.

Bakar, Osman. "Islam and Political Legitimacy in Malaysia." In *Islam and Political Legitimacy,* ed. Shahram Akbarzadeh and Abdullah Saeed, 127–49. London: Routledge, 2003.

"The Battle for Memali." *Far Eastern Economic Review,* December 5, 1985.

Department of Statistics Malaysia. *Key Statistics.* Kuala Lumpur, Malaysia: Department of Statistics Malaysia, 2005.

Funston, John. *Malay Politics in Malaysia: A Study of the United Malays National Organisation and Party Islam.* Kuala Lumpur: Heinemann Books Asia, 1980.

Jomo, K.S., and Ahmad Shabery Cheek. "Malaysia's Islamic Movements." In *Fragmented Vision: Culture and Politics in Contemporary Malaysia,* ed. Joel Kahn and Francis Loh Kok Wah, 79–106. Sydney: Allen and Unwin, 1992.

Liow, Joseph Chinyong. "Exigency or Expediency? Contextualising Political Islam and the PAS Challenge in Malaysian Politics." *Third World Quarterly* 25:2 (March 2004).

———. "Political Islam in Malaysia: Problematising Discourse and Practice in the UMNO-PAS 'Islamisation Race.'" *Commonwealth and Comparative Politics* 42:2 (July 2004).

Muhammad, Mahathir. Speech at the 33rd Annual UMNO General Assembly, Hilton Hotel, Kuala Lumpur, September 10, 1982.

Mutalib, Hussin. *Islam in Malaysia: From Revivalism to Islamic State.* Singapore: Singapore University Press, 1993.

Muzaffar, Chandra. *Islamic Resurgence in Malaysia.* Petaling Jaya: Penerbit Fajar Bakti, 1987.

Nagata, Judith. *The Reflowering of Malaysian Islam: Modern Religious Radicals and Their Roots.* Vancouver: University of British Columbia Press, 1984.

Nair, Shanti. *Islam in Malaysia's Foreign Policy.* London: Routledge, 1997.

Noor, Farish. *Islam Embedded: The Historical Development of the Pan-Malaysian Islamic Party (PAS) 1951–2003.* Kuala Lumpur: Malaysian Sociological Research Institute, 2004.

Shamsul, A.B. "Identity Construction, Nation Formation, and Islamic Revivalism in Malaysia." In *Islam in an Era of Nation-States: Politics and Religious Renewal in Muslim Southeast Asia,* ed. Robert W. Hefner and Patricia Horvatich, 207–27. Honolulu: University of Hawaii Press, 1997.

Thailand

Tiffany Kay Hacker and Linda Michaud-Emin

About 4.6 percent of Thailand's population is Muslim, including such diverse groups as Hui (better known as Yunnanese or Haw) from China, Cham from Cambodia, Bengalis from South Asia, and Southeast Asian Muslims from Indonesia and the Philippines. The majority, however, originate from the historical Patani Sultanate (which fell in the late eighteenth century) along the country's southern border with Malaysia. This group is ethnically Malay and speaks a dialect similar to that used across the frontier in Malaysia. Some 85 percent of all Muslims in Thailand reside in the three southernmost provinces of Pattani, Yala, and Narathiwat. This is also the area where an Islamist insurgency has developed.

About two-thirds of all the mosques in Thailand are located in the five southernmost provinces, almost all of which are Sunni. While the Thai government provides financing for mosques, schools, and clerics, foreign financial assistance has become steadily more important. Most Muslims attend Islamic private schools, which are actually government funded. In the south, though, many Malay Muslims prefer to send their children to these traditional *pondok* schools to receive an exclusively Islamic education. After violent uprisings in 2004, the Thai government encouraged pondoks to register in order to receive government funding. After registering, the schools are still permitted to retain their status as pondok schools.

The origins of Islamism in Thailand are very much entwined with the history of a separate Muslim state in the south, ethnic nationalism, the presence of an Islamist-oriented Malaysia next door, and controversies over Muslim political power within the country. During the 1930s, Malay Muslims were underrepresented in the country's parliament, while hoping for autonomy or even independence. A Communist insurgency in the Thai-Malaysia border region led the government to declare a state of emergency there in 1948. This led to incidents of clashes between the army or police and local people. This was followed by the development of underground separatist movements such as the Barisan Nasional Pembebasan Patani (BNPP, or Patani National Liberation Front) in the early 1960s and the Patani United Liberation Organization (PULO), which, as noted by Syed Serajul Islam, claimed to be an *"invisible government* whose tactic was to work by ambush"* for an independent Islamic state, in 1968.

The Thai government tried to discourage Malay-Muslim separatism through concessions. Malay Muslim names were again permitted, and the role of the state counselor for Islamic Affairs was enhanced. During the 1980s, the Thai government continued its effort to ease friction by supporting cultural rights for Muslim Malays as well as economic development in the south. The Southern Border Provinces Administrative Center (SBPAC), established in 1981, simultaneously worked as a counterinsurgency coordinator and as a liaison between Muslim leaders and Bangkok. It also put an emphasis on removing corrupt officials who were antagonizing local people. Another important institution was the Joint Civilian Police Military (CPM) Task Force 43, which coordinated the Border Patrol Police, armed forces, Thahaan Phran (civilian mercenaries known as Rangers), intelligence agencies, and provincial governors. This campaign was not a narrow military one but one that built good connections with southern communities, developed welfare and educational programs, and worked with the Malaysian government to enhance border security. Many of the separatist movement's cadres quit the struggle.

The election of Thaksin Shinawatra as prime minister in 2001 brought a change. He dismantled the SBPAC and CPM, returning authority to the police. Demonstrations in 2004 led to clashes, and martial law was declared in the south. The 2006 military coup, however, led to a return to a softer-line policy, including amnesty for former rebels and the reestablishment of the SBPAC and CPM. Despite this shift, however, violence remained at very high levels.

Understanding Islam and Violence in Southern Thailand

The violence in southern Thailand has claimed the lives of about 2,000 to 2,500 people—over 1,200 deaths occurred in 2004–2005 alone. From 2002 on, markets, schools, monasteries, military posts, and individual travelers or workers on the job have been attacked. The insurgents themselves have remained mysterious, with no public claims of responsibility or political manifestos being issued.

For example, on January 4, 2004, 18 schools in the southernmost provinces were set aflame, while a reported 50 armed men stole about 300 weapons from an army storehouse. The Thai government enforced martial law, and insurgents killed police, teachers, and Buddhist monks, for instance, during the ransacking of Promprasit temple, as Imtiyaz Yusuf and Lars Peter Schmidt write. On April 28, 2004, military posts and police checkpoints were attacked in Yala, Songkhla, and Pattani. The conflict culminated at the Krue Se Mosque, where 32 Malay Muslim militants were shot dead when they resisted the military's attempts to capture them, according to Raymond Scupin. Since a mosque was attacked, even though this was the result of the insurgents' decision to fight there, many Malay Muslims were antagonized and implied that it was a massacre.

On October 25, 2004, a crowd of nearly 1,000 people gathered around the Tak Bai police station to protest what they believed to be the wrongful incarceration of six local security volunteers by the police. The protest was believed to have been instigated. Six protesters were killed in clashes with police, and as many as 78 died afterward when they suffocated in overcrowded army trucks after being arrested.

Small-scale attacks occur regularly, and the government's Emergency Decree allows police to arrest and detain suspects for 30 days. Nevertheless, less is known about the leadership, ideology, and organization of the Thai insurgency than about any other Islamist movement in the world.

Economic Factors in the Islamist Uprising

Historically, separatist violence in the southern provinces has occurred during periods of economic hardship, including a depression in the rubber industry, food shortages, and disease epidemics. The area's location also makes it a center of arms trafficking and drug dealing, which can help finance insurgents. The areas of southern Thailand with the highest living standards—Songkhla and Satun—have far less insurgent violence than Narathiwat, Pattani, and Yala, the poorer provinces.

Cultural Factors in the Islamist Uprising

Since the 1930s, the Thai state has tried to create a single national identity through assimilationist policies in the south as in other parts of the country. The emergence of Muslim insurgency movements has peaked during periods when such cultural centralization was most pervasive. During such a period in the late 1940s, Haji Sulong, leader of the Patani People's Movement and president of the Islamic Council, was arrested for high treason by the Thai government, according to Pierre LeRoux. Around the same time, a group of people claiming to represent half of Yala, Pattani, and Narathiwat signed a petition to the UN asking for secession from Thailand. GAMPAR (Movement for Great Malay Patani), one of the first armed resistance movements in the south, was also created then. Militant groups used the historic Muslim sultanate of Patani and the ethnic connection with Malaysia as alternative identity models to win them legitimacy and support.

At the same time, though, Thai Muslims in the south did gain many cultural rights, including the public use of their languages, the right to choose traditional Islamic schools, government bank services in accordance with Islamic banking principles, state financial assistance to schools and to building mosques, and special state loans for pilgrimage to Mecca.

Political Factors in the Islamist Uprising

As Islamist violence increased, so did Muslim political power. In the period after 2000, 14 MPs as well as senators, members in the provincial legislatures in the southern provinces, and mayors were Muslims. The head of the military and the chairman of the parliament from 1996 to 2001 were Muslims, as Wattana Sugunnasil notes. While these numbers declined somewhat in the 2005 elections, this was attributed to a few Muslim MPs and officials publicly criticizing the violence. Still, while the Muslim population in the south may compose 80 percent of the population there, they make up only about 12 percent of the local bureaucracy, as cited by the Lowry Institute.

Islamist Insurgent Groups

Some Islamist separatists prefer a federation with Malaysia; others want to unite the five southern provinces into a Patani Dar-al-Islam, an Islamist sultanate.

Gabungan Melayu Patani Raya (GAMPAR)

The Gabungan Melayu Patani Raya (Union of Malay for a Great Patani), also known as GAMPAR, was founded in 1948 by Tengku Mahyiddin, the youngest son of the last sultan of Patani. Its goal was a political union with Malaya, now Malaysia. GAMPAR was the predecessor of the Barisan Revolusi Nasional (BRN).

Barisan Revolusi Nasional

During the late 1950s, Field Marshall Sarit Thanarat staged a coup in Thailand and ruled as dictator until his death in 1963. He put the Muslim pondoks under the Ministry of Interior in an unpopular move that led to a strike by hundreds of pondoks. This step also marked the beginning of the armed movement in which the BRN (National Revolutionary Front) played an important role. It has a strong relationship to the pondoks, as Amporn Marddent explains, where religious teachers can indoctrinate students with Islamist ideas. This was especially true of the Thamma Witthaya, which waged an armed campaign against the Thai government and played an important role in the BRN's development.

Formed in 1963 by Haji Abdul Karim Hassan, a teacher, the BRN was influenced by both pan-Arab nationalism and Malaysia's independence. At times its goals were contradictory. It spoke of both an independent socialist Islamic state in the south and of joining the Malaysian federation. The headquarters of the BRN are believed to be in Malaysia, and its base of support is largely built through the pondoks.

The BRN suffered from factionalism and ideological differences, leading to the movement's division into three groups in the mid-1980s: the BRN Coordinate Group, an urban-based group dealing with sabotage; the BRN Ulama, a faction backed by clerics; and the BRN Coordinate Group, known as BRN-C, which has been the most active. The latter group recruits mainly through the Pemuda student group, established in 1992. Several teachers connected with BRN-C and Pemuda were arrested in 2006 for pos-

session of weapons as well as bomb-making materials and instructional videos. The Thai government also reported that a number of BRN-C members train in Indonesia.

Barisan Nasional Pembebasan Patani (BNPP)

Founded in Kelantan—the easternmost state of Malaysia, which borders Thailand—in 1959 by Tengku Abdul Jalal, the BNPP movement's objective was the establishment of an Islamist state in the five southern provinces. They tried to attain their goal by attacking symbols of Thai central authority such as civil servants, schoolteachers, and police as well as non-Muslim residents, including both Buddhists and ethnic Chinese. The group was largely inactive between 1990 and 2002, when it changed its name to the Barisan Islam Pembebasan Pattani (BIPP), which puts more emphasis on the Islamic character of the group. The political branch of this group even participates in Malaysian state-level politics.

Pattani United Liberation Organization

The Pattani United Liberation Organization (PULO) was founded in 1968. Despite the group's Salafi background and the fact that most of the early members were Muslim-Pattani pilgrims on the hajj in Mecca, the PULO always claimed to be a "secular" organization whose goal was to create an independent state, though not necessarily an Islamist one. The original name for the armed branch of the PULO was the Patani United Liberation Army, or the PULA, which at its peak is thought to have consisted of 300 members. The PULO split in 1992 into two factions. The first was the PULO

Leadership Council, with its military wing known as the Caddan Army and headed by Dr. A-rong Muleng, while the second group was known as the PULO Army Command Council, or the MPTP, headed by Hayihadi Mindosali and Hajji Sama-ae Thanam. The second group was involved in terrorist activities; the name of its army was Abudaban.

In 1995 the PULO split again, with the offshoot called the New PULO. Both factions were largely unable to coordinate their activities, though they did form a tactical alliance in 1997. Both the old and new PULO have lost significant influence in the region. Its problems included a rejection by some members of its turn toward terrorism; the arrests of some leaders and flight to Europe of others; and the defection of more than 900 militants in both factions who joined the government-sponsored rehabilitation program, as Angel Rabasa explains, which gave them land, education, and other opportunities. Although the organization has attempted a revival, it has no operational control over the insurgency.

Barisan Kemerdekaan Pattani (BERSATU)

The BERSATU (United Front for the Independence of Pattani) is an umbrella organization for insurgent groups, including the BIPP, BRN Congress, BNP, and the New PULO. It never developed very far, however, and has reportedly met only twice.

Gerakan Mujahideen Islam Pattani (GMIP)

Despite internal factionalism, the GMIP has been kept going by a group of veterans from the Afghan war. The GMIP can be labeled a separatist organization, according to Joseph Liow, although its members have

been involved in an array of criminal activities such as extortion, kidnapping, murder, and terrorism and are reportedly responsible for much of the insurgency violence in the region.

The Mujahideen Pattani Movement (BNP)

Established in 1985, the goal of the BNP was to unite several of the separatist organizations, much as BERSATU had intended. Many of its leaders came from the BIPP, and it has not achieved much in Thailand; its political activity is largely restricted to Malaysia.

Jihadi Battle or Internal Struggle?

Despite the fear that Muslim-Thai militants may increasingly use the language of jihadi extremism, the separatist insurgency remains local and is still largely unrelated to "global jihad" witnessed elsewhere in the world. However, external actors have been playing at least an indirect role. Parts of Malaysia where Islamists are strong, for example the state of Kelantan, are believed to offer Thai Muslim militants a safe haven and logistical support. Libya has also provided support to Thai separatist groups in the past. There is speculation, but not evidence, that Jema'a Islamiyya, a group from Indonesia that is affiliated with al-Qa'ida, provides support. The same has also been said of the MORO Islamic Liberation Front of the Philippines and the Free Aceh Movement (GAM) of Indonesia.

Many analysts are further concerned by the hundreds of students who study Islam abroad in such places as Egypt, Pakistan, and Indonesia who are funded by the Thai government or other nations such as Saudi

Arabia. In some cases, these students are believed to have become militant activists.

BIBLIOGRAPHY

"Ambassadors to Go on PR Offensive: Diplomats to OIC, Asean Told to Detail Govt's Actions." *The Nation,* August 22, 2005.

Bonura, Carlo J., Jr. *Political Theory on Location: Formations of Muslim Political Community in Southern Thailand.* Ann Arbor, MI: UMI Dissertation Services, 2003.

Central Intelligence Agency (CIA). *The 2008 World Factbook.* www.cia.gov/cia/publications/factbook/geos/in.html.

Croissant, Aurel. "Unrest in South Thailand: Contours, Causes, and Consequences Since 2001." *Strategic Insights* 4:2 (February 2005).

"Deep South Insurgency: Seven Arrested in Pre-dawn Offensive." *The Nation,* August 19, 2005.

Islam, Syed Serajul. "The Islamic Independence Movements in Pattani of Thailand and Mindanao of the Philippines." *Asian Survey* 38:5 (May 1998): 441–56.

Jory, Patrick. "From '*Melayu Patani*' to 'Thai Muslim': The Specter of Ethnic Identity in Southern Thailand." Asia Research Institute (ARI), Working Paper Series No. 84, February 2007.

LeRoux, Pierre. "To Be or Not to Be . . . The Cultural Identity of the Jawi (Thailand)." *Asian Folklore Studies* 57 (1998): 223–55.

Liow, Joseph. "The Security Situation in Southern Thailand: Toward an Understanding of Domestic and International Dimensions." *Studies in Conflict & Terrorism* 27 (2004): 537.

Marddent, Amporn. "Buddhist Perceptions of Muslims in the Thai South." Paper presented at the Association for Asian Studies Annual Meeting in Boston, March 22–25, 2007.

McCargo, Duncan, ed. *Rethinking Thailand's Southern Violence.* Singapore: National University of Singapore Press, 2007.

Rabasa, Angel. *Indonesia's Transformation and the Stability of Southeast Asia.* Santa Monica, CA: Rand, 2001.

Reynolds, Craig, ed. "National Identity and Its Defenders: Thailand, 1939–1989." Clayton, Australia: Monash Papers on Southeast Asia No. 25 (1991).

———, ed. *National Identity and Its Defenders: Thailand Today.* Chiang Mai, Thailand: Silkworm Books, 2002.

Satha-Anand, Chaiwat. *Islam and Violence: A Case Study of Violent Events in the Four Southern Provinces of Thailand, 1976–1981.* USF Monographs in Religion and Public Policy No. 2. Tampa, FL: Department of Religious Studies, University of South Florida, 1986.

Scupin, Raymond. "Muslim Intellectuals in Thailand: Exercises in Reform and Moderation." In *Dynamics and Dimensions of Inter-Religious Contacts in Southeast Asia: Examining Buddhist-Muslim Relations in Thailand,* ed. Omar Farouk. Singapore: Marshall Cavendish, 2006.

Sugunnasil, Wattana. "Islam, Radicalism, and Violence in Southern Thailand: *Berjihad di Patani* and the 28 April 2004 Attacks." *Critical Asian Studies* 38:1 (March 2006): 119–44.

Suhrke, Astri. "Irredentism Contained: The Thai-Muslim Case." *Comparative Politics* 7:2 (January 1975): 187–203.

———. "The Thai Muslims: Some Aspects of Minority Integration." *Pacific Affairs* 43:4 (Winter 1970–71): 531–47.

"Tak Bai Residents Asked to Put Aside Pain, Work to Revive District." *Bangkok Post,* August 15, 2005.

Thailand Human Development Report 2007, Annex 1, Human Achievement Index. www.undp.or.th/NHDR2007/index.html.

U.S. Pacific Command (CINCPAC) Virtual Information Center. *Primer: Muslim Separatism in Southern Thailand* (July 23, 2002): 9–10. www.globalsecurity.org.

Yusuf, Imtiyaz. "Faces of Islam in Southern Thailand." *East-West Center Washington Working Papers* 2 (March 2007): 6–51.

Yusuf, Imtiyaz, and Lars Peter Schmidt. *Understanding Conflict and Approaching Peace in Southern Thailand,* 2nd ed. Bangkok: Konrad-Adenauer-Stiftung, 2006.

AUSTRALIA AND THE PACIFIC

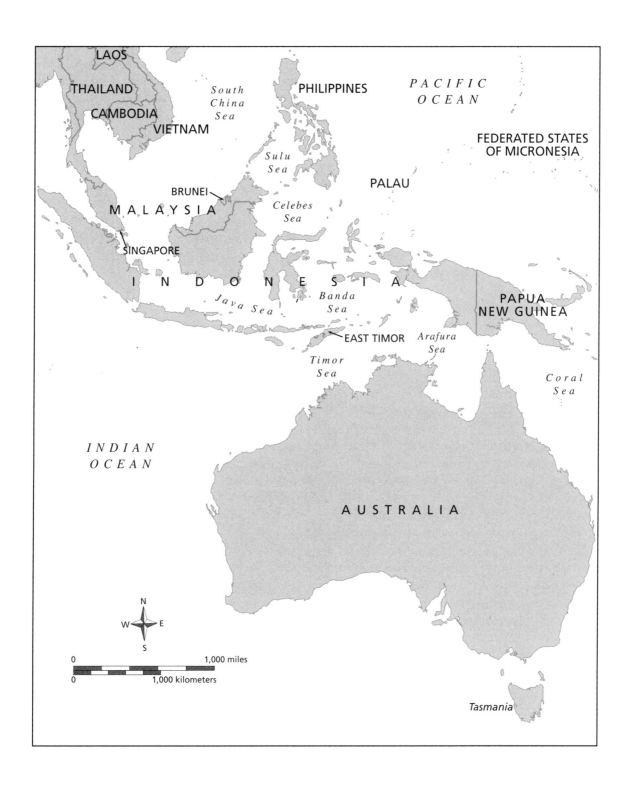

Australia

Leanne Piggott

In a February 2006 speech about Australian citizenship, Peter Costello, a senior federal politician, identified the key principles underpinning Australian culture and values as being respect for "the rights and liberty of others" and "the rule of [Australian] law." Those who do not embrace these principles, Costello argued, "threaten the rights and liberties of others." As a case in point, he quoted the Muslim cleric Abdul Nacer Benbrika, who had stated in an August 2005 interview on ABC TV that the obligation to obey Australian law was a "big problem" for Australian Muslims. "There are two laws," Benbrika explained. "There is an Australian law [and] there is an Islamic law." Three months later, Benbrika was arrested together with 18 other Muslim Australians on charges related to membership in a terrorist organization and the planning of an imminent terrorist attack.

Costello's speech was made within the context of a wider debate in Australia about multiculturalism, national security, and the view of the government that immigrants should embrace basic Australian values to achieve community harmony, social cohesion, and stability. The prime minister at the time, John Howard, called on Muslim leaders to address intolerance and extrem-

ism among a minority in the Islamic community who are "utterly antagonistic to our kind of society." The debate reached fever pitch in October 2006, when a Ramadan sermon of Taj al-Din Ahmad Abdallah al-Hilali, the then mufti of Australia, made media headlines. In the sermon al-Hilali described women as Satan's soldiers, wielding the weapons of seduction, and likening women who do not stay at home and wear the veil to uncovered meat left out for cats to snatch. On previous occasions, as cited by an October 2006 report in *The Australian*, al-Hilali had argued in favor of "a social and legal structure consistent with 7th-century Arabia" and preached from the writings of Sayyid Qutb, the ideologue of the Muslim Brotherhood, of which he was a former member.

While some Muslims were outraged by al-Hilali's comments, others claimed they had been taken out of context, meant only for "his specific audience," and that the mufti was the latest victim of serial "Muslim bashing" in Australia by politicians and the media who misrepresent Islam as resistant to modernity and multiculturalism. Muslim leaders in Australia regularly complain that government spokespeople and the media victimize their community by wrongly attributing to all Muslim Australians the extremist and separatist views of a small minority.

However, implicit in this complaint is an acknowledgment that there are some Muslim Australians who, as Abdallah Saeed reports:

> insist that Australian values, culture and society are foreign to Islam and therefore unacceptable to them. They think that the more Muslims are integrated into Australian society, the less "Muslim" they are. Their interpretation of Islam emphasises maintaining a distinction between Islam and anything perceived to have originated outside of Islam.

Or, put more succinctly, "You cannot be a good Muslim and a good Australian." Some go further, believing that it is their duty to establish an Islamic state and implement Islamic law wherever they are, even in a minority context. However, only a small fraction of Muslim Australians share such Islamist beliefs, and there is "little demand" for Shari'a to be introduced in Australia.

Political Islamism in the Australian Muslim Context

Muslims first visited Australia in the mid-seventeenth century, when fishermen from the Indonesian island of Macassar spent the early months of each year in beach camps along the northern coast of Australia. The next group of Muslims to arrive were the Afghan camel drivers who accompanied the British colonialists in the 1860s. They were followed over the course of the next century by very limited numbers of Muslims from Indonesia, Malaysia, and the Balkans. Relatively larger numbers of Muslims began to immigrate to Australia from the

1970s on, following the abolition of the White Australian Policy in 1966. They came mainly from Lebanon, Turkey, Afghanistan, Pakistan, and the former Yugoslavia. By the time of the 2006 Census, there were 340,392 Muslims in Australia. (Although less than 2 percent of the total population, this was an increase of around 21 percent on the previous 2001 Census). More than a third of Australian Muslims were born in Australia, the remainder having originated from more than 70 countries, the largest numbers coming from Lebanon and Turkey, and more recently from South Asia (excluding India).

Because of their diverse national, social, and cultural backgrounds, Muslims in Australia are fragmented along national and sectarian lines, as is evident in their city associations, schools, and mosques. Most Muslims in the state of New South Wales are Arab, while most Muslims in the state of Victoria are of Turkish or Albanian ethnicity. While Turks dominate the Islamic bodies in Melbourne's western suburb of Broadmeadows, for example, in Sydney the Lebanese dominate the Sunni Imam Ali mosque at Lakemba and the Shi'a al-Zahra mosque in Arncliffe. The majority of Muslims in Australia are Sunni, with a smaller number of Shi'a having come from Iran, Lebanon, and Afghanistan. An even smaller number are Alawis and Isma'ilis. New South Wales has the largest Muslim population, followed by Victoria and then Western Australia. There are over 100 mosques and at least 21 Muslim primary and secondary schools in the country. The largest mosques are in Sydney (Lakemba and Auburn) and in Melbourne (Preston). Perth has the oldest continuous mosque, founded in 1904 by immigrants from Afghanistan and (modern) Pakistan.

Political Islamism has been a part of the Muslim landscape in Australia for many decades, largely as a result of the propagation of Salafi Islam by shaykhs and institutions funded by Saudi Arabia. Salafism is an "approach to Islam" that seeks, in response to "the modern Muslim predicament," to return to, or rectify, what its adherents see as the purest form of Islam, that practiced by Muhammad and his companions (the *salaf*). While the Salafi movement includes such diverse figures as Osama bin Ladin and the mufti of Saudi Arabia, Salafists are united by a common religious creed (*aqida*) centered on the concept of *tawhid* (the oneness of God). The three main tenets of the Salafi creed are: the one God is the sole creator and sovereign of the universe; God is supreme and entirely unique, and as God is the supreme legislator, humans are obligated to follow the Shari'a in its entirety (hence the rejection of secularism and separation of church and state); and God alone has the right to be worshipped.

It is estimated that since the 1970s, the Saudi government and its royal family and private citizens have provided more than $75 million to Australia for building mosques and schools, including the largest mosques— Sydney's Lakemba mosque and Melbourne's Preston mosque—and some of the country's best-known Islamic schools, including Al-Faisal College, Malek Fahd School, and King Abdul Aziz College in Sydney; King Khalid College in Melbourne; and the Australian Islamic College in Perth.

Jihadi-Salafism took root in Australia during the early to mid-1990s with the import of ideas from the successful mujahidin campaign against the former USSR in Afghanistan. Jihadi-Salafists are Salafi factions that support the use of violence to promote their anti-Western, literalist version of Islam, including those who seek to establish an Islamic state or caliphate.

Reflecting divisions within the Muslim mainstream in Australia, Islamist groups have been closely associated with particular ethnic and sectarian subgroups. However, on occasion, Asian groups such as Jama'a Islamiyya, and Arab groups such as Ahl al-Sunna wal-Jama'a, have found common ground in shared beliefs and experiences that enable them to bridge previously existing ethnic and cultural divisions. These groups have attracted adherents who consider themselves to be members of an *umma* (Muslim community) that transcends national and cultural boundaries and who therefore identify less with a particular subgroup. This trend is stronger among second- and third-generation Muslim Australians and among an increasing number of converts.

Below is an overview of seven political Islamist groups in Australia.

Jama'a Islamiyya

Jama'a Islamiyya (JI) has its origins in the oldest of the Indonesian Islamist movements, Dar al-Islam. According to an official JI statement released in October 2003, the organization was founded as a breakaway group in 1993 by the Indonesian religious scholar Abdallah Sungkar and within 10 years had become a transnational movement and the most lethal terrorist organization in Southeast Asia. Inspired by the writings of Sayyid Qutb and the Egyptian group Jama'a Islamiyya, JI views itself as part of the global jihadi-Salafist network, modeling its mission of jihad on ideologues such as Abdallah Azzam, Ibn Taymiyya, and Abu Qatada. JI's strongest operational links have been with al-Qa'ida, but it has also engaged in joint operations and training with the Filipino separatist group the Moro Islamic Liberation Front (MILF).

JI's ideology and aims are set out in its official text, *Pedoman Umum Perjuangan al-Jama'a al-Islamiyya* (General Struggle Guidelines of Jama'a Islamiyya). Its central pillar is to create a *dawla Islamiyya nusantara* (archipelagic Islamic state), a "genuinely Islamic space" within which Shari'a (Islamic religious law) would be comprehensively implemented and where, as quoted by Fealey and Hooker, "[y]oung Muslims could behave strictly according to the teachings of the pious ancestors." The Nusantara would first encompass Malaysia, Singapore, Indonesia, the Philippines, Brunei, and southern Thailand. This realm would then provide a base for the restoration of a global Islamic state under a caliph. On occasion, JI's leaders have also advocated that Australia (or at least the north of Australia) be incorporated into the Nusantara.

When initially established, JI's structure consisted of horizontal command networks based around four *mantiqis* (territorial organizations): "Mantiqi 1," responsible for Malaysia (where Sungkar lived in exile until the fall of Suharto in 1998) and Singapore; "Mantiqi 2," responsible for most of Indonesia (JI's heartland and main area of operations); "Mantiqi 3," responsible for the southern Philippines, the Malaysian state of Sabah, and the Indonesian provinces of East Kalimantan and North and Central Sulawesi; and "Mantiqi 4," responsible for Australia and West Papua. All members swore loyalty to the *amir jama'a* (commander or leader). Sungkar was the leader until his death in 1999, when he was replaced by his close companion Abu Bakar Ba'asyir.

Established in 1993, Mantiqi 4 was the smallest of the JI divisions, and it remained the least developed and operationally capable of JI's four territorial groups. It was headed by an Indonesian immigrant to Australia, Abd al-Rahim Ayub, and found support within the Indonesian community based around the mosque in Dee Why,

a northern beach suburb of Sydney, as well as at Lakemba, the focal point of Sydney's Lebanese Muslim community. Abd al-Rahim was joined for the task by his twin brother, Abd al-Rahman Ayub, who arrived in Australia seeking refugee status. Abd al-Rahman had trained with al-Qa'ida in Afghanistan and fought with the MILF in the southern Philippines. Together, the Ayub brothers became the face of JI in Australia.

From his base in Sydney, Abd al-Rahim lived by the General Struggle Guidelines in recruiting members, instructing them in the Koran and Islamic law, collecting donations to send to the leadership in Malaysia, and conducting physical training to be ready for jihad. At its height, the membership of the Australian *jama'a* reached about 30 formal members and about 100 informal supporters and raised funds of up to around $14,000 per month.

Members of Mantiqi 4 also hosted Sungkar and Ba'asyir during their 11 annual visits to Australia during the 1990s. The two clerics were popular among immigrant Indonesian Muslims, who thronged to hear them speak. They explained JI's ideology and aims plainly and simply: that the struggle for Islam is a "life or death mission," and that it is as necessary to wage it in Australia as in any other part of the globe. The reasons for this were provided by Ba'asyir in a speech given in Sydney in 1993, cited by Sally Neighbour:

> It is abasement for a Muslim to live in a non-believing nation, it is forbidden. . . . And if we do not live in an Islamic state then we must do all we can to bring one about. . . . The Islamic faithful in Australia must [therefore] endeavor to bring about an Islamic state in Australia, even if it is 100 years from

now . . . and may God bless the struggle of our brethren in Australia who have demonstrated such loyalty, despite being surrounded by non-believers.

The JI leaders also found support among the Sydney-based Islamic Youth Movement (IYM). The IYM's magazine and Web site, *Nida'ul Islam* (The Call of Islam) published articles by and interviews with Sungkar and Ba'asyir. In the February-March 1997 edition, Sungkar was introduced as "a part of a group devoted to the establishment of the Law of Allah upon this earth" and set out the main guidelines of JI's methodology:

To realize an Islamic Community by the materialization of three strengths: a. Quwwatul Aqidah (Faith's strength) b. Quwwatul Ukhuwwah (Brotherhood's strength) c. Quwwatul Musallah (Military strength). These three elements of strength are essential in order to establish Dawlah Islamiyya (Islamic State) by means of Jihad. These amongst others form points which are deemed vital by Jama'ah Islamiyya, whereas other Jama'ahs ignore and generally disregard these strengths.

In 1999, following a "turf" dispute between the Ayub brothers and the leadership of the Dee Why mosque, Abd al-Rahim moved JI Australia's operations to Perth, where he took a job as teacher in the al-Hidayah Islamic School. He instructed the members of the jama'a who remained in Sydney to boycott the Dee Why mosque and to attend the Haldon Street prayer room in Lakemba, known for the Salafi teachings of Shaykh Omran and Shaykh Zoud. Omran is the leader of the Ahlus Sunnah wal Jemaah Association of Australia (ASWJA) and was an associate of both Sungkar and Ba'asyir

(whom he first met in 1988 at the Preston mosque in Melbourne) and friend and confidant of the Ayub brothers. Through these relationships, JI and ASWJA forged close operational ties.

It was also in 1999, on the orders of the head of Mantiqi 1, Riduan Isamuddin—also known as Hambali—that Mantiqi 4 transitioned to a terrorist recruitment cell for attacks within Australia. (Hambali had worked closely with al-Qa'ida, having fought with the mujahidin in Afghanistan in the 1980s. He was arrested in 2003.) Australia came to be viewed by JI as a legitimate target for jihadi terrorism as a direct result of the role played by Australia in supporting predominantly Catholic East Timor's independence from Indonesia and leading a UN military mission when the Indonesian army and its local militias launched a campaign against the East Timorese. During 1999–2000, Australia played a leading role in the International Force East Timor (INTERFET) and in the succeeding UN Transitional Administration East Timor (UNTAET). This Australian role was viewed by JI (and other militant Islamist groups) as a hostile act. Australia was also seen more generally by JI as part of the West, closely allied to the United States and therefore an enemy of Islam.

To carry out Hambali's directive, Abd al-Rahim conducted jihad classes among local sympathizers. He also ran training camps in the bush land outside Perth and in secluded spots in New South Wales and Victoria, where Mantiqi 4 members were joined by the IYM and members of Ahl al-Sunna wal-Jama'a. Paintball war games and weapons training camps were included in the curriculum and were conducted by Asman Hashim, a Malaysian jihadist who had trained in bomb making with al-Qa'ida and who had fought with Abd al-Rahman in the southern Philippines. As reported by Australia's ABC

TV, members of these groups also raised significant funds for the MILF, up to $1 million for the purchase of vehicles and to support an MILF arms factory,.

Among Mantiqi 4's jihadi recruits were Jack Roche and Joseph "Jihad Jack" Thomas, both converts to Islam. The choice of converts to assist with terrorist operations in Australia was deliberate. It was felt that "white Muslims," to use bin Ladin's term, might have more success in carrying out surveillance and other preparatory tasks without attracting the attention of Australian security services. In 2000 Hambali arranged for both men to go to bin Ladin's Camp Faruq in Afghanistan to train in explosives and to continue their instruction in jihadi-Salafism. Here they met with a number of al-Qa'ida operatives, including Khalid Shaykh Muhammad, the mastermind of the September 11, 2001, attacks.

Roche returned to Australia with money and instructions to carry out a terrorist attack on the Israeli embassy in Canberra and to assassinate the Jewish mining magnate Joe Gutnick. At the time when he began surveillance of his targets, Roche wrote to his son expressing his fervor for the Islamist cause and his commitment to jihad, describing it—as cited by Western Australia's district court's Web site—as the

> greater sacrifice worthy of the highest reward from Allah. . . . As Muslims we are obligated to perform jihad to uphold the laws of Allah. As we see today, the disbelievers are now out of control and believe that their ways based on inequality, arrogance, et cetera, are right. I hate them for that and need to learn more about how to combat them.

However, Roche's conspiracy was aborted in August 2000 when Ba'asyir intervened on behalf of Abd al-Rahim who had been angered by Roche's refusal to hand over al-Qa'ida money to Mantiqi 4 and for taking direct orders from Hambali. In the meantime, the Internal Security Department of Singapore had alerted the Australian Security Intelligence Organization (ASIO) and the Australian Federal Police (AFP) to the existence of JI cells in Australia. Roche, too, had second thoughts when other Muslim converts he tried to recruit were critical of his terrorist plans. He was eventually arrested after the Bali bombings in October 2002, when he was charged with participating in a plan to destroy internationally protected persons and property. In June 2004, Roche was convicted and sentenced to nine years in jail.

Having fought with the Taliban against the Northern Alliance, Jack Thomas returned to Australia in 2002 after the Taliban regime collapsed. Back home, Thomas was eventually arrested in November 2004 on charges of traveling on a false passport and receiving funds and a plane ticket from al-Qa'ida. Although he was found guilty at his February 2006 trial, Thomas's appeal was upheld in August the same year by the Victorian Court of Criminal Appeal, which remitted the matter to the Victorian Supreme Court for a retrial. In the meantime, Thomas became the first person to be issued with a control order under the 2005 Australian Anti-Terrorism Act. Control orders impose restrictions on the movements and contacts of persons who are alleged by the police to pose a security risk to the community. Thomas challenged the constitutionality of the control order legislation in the High Court, but in August 2007, a majority of the High Court upheld the validity of the legislation. In October 2008, a Supreme Court jury found Thomas guilty of possessing a falsified passport, but he was acquitted of the other charges.

Another Australian jihadist who trained with Thomas in al-Qa'ida camps in Afghanistan (and earlier with the Pakistan-based terrorist group, Laskhar-e-Tayyiba) was David Hicks. Like Thomas, Hicks fought with the Taliban against the Northern Alliance but also with al-Qa'ida forces against the United States and its allies in Afghanistan, where he was captured by the Americans in December 2001 and incarcerated in Guantanamo Bay. At his arraignment before a military commission in March 2007, Hicks pleaded guilty to the charge of providing material support for terrorism and was sentenced to seven years imprisonment. All but nine months of his sentence were subsequently suspended for reasons that included the five years for which he had already been incarcerated. In May 2007 Hicks was returned to Australia, where he was detained in Yatala Labour Prison to serve the remainder of his sentence.

Meanwhile, Mantiqi 4 had been rendered nonoperational when Abd al-Rahman Ayub returned to Indonesia in early 2002 (after having his application for refugee status rejected), followed by Abd al-Rahim soon after the October 2002 Bali bombings. The two brothers have maintained a low profile but remain persons of interest to Indonesian intelligence. Interestingly, in October 2006, Abd al-Rahim's estranged, Australian-born sons, Muhammad and Abdallah Ayub, were arrested and later released in Yemen in relation to an alleged al-Qa'ida plot to smuggle small arms to Islamists in Somalia. According to their father, the boys are "eager to create a Muslim caliphate by any means," an ideology that Abd al-Rahim now claims he has disavowed.

Although the history of JI's active cell in Australia was a relatively short one, it highlights the effective collaboration between al-Qa'ida's core organization, its regional affiliates (in this case, JI) and their local recruits (including Roche and Thomas). According to the assessment of the Australian security services, small pockets of sympathy for JI's ideology and Islamist platform remain among the Australian Muslim community, particularly those from Southeast Asia. Intelligence analysts have also confirmed that JI members across Southeast Asia remain "intent on carrying out their goal of toppling regional governments and establishing an Islamic caliphate stretching across Southeast Asia and into Australia," and that there remain JI sympathizers or followers in Australia willing to provide money and other forms of support for those who actively pursue these goals. However, it is important to note that while the 2005–2006 annual report of Australia's intelligence organization noted that "Australia continues to be a target for Jemaah Islamiyah activities," the group was not mentioned in the 2006–2007 report, reflecting the fact that no JI-attributed terrorist attack had occurred in Indonesia or elsewhere since 2005. The 2007-2008 ASIO report again identified JI as a "diminished" but "resilient" threat, having "not abandoned its violent Islamist goals."

Lashkar-e-Toiba

Another transnational Islamist group that has supporters in Australia is the Pakistan-based Lashkar-e-Toiba (LeT, The Army of the Pure), believed still to be led by Hafiz Muhammad Saeed, one of the organization's original founders. LeT was established in 1989, in opposition to the Soviet presence in Afghanistan. During its early years fighting there, the organization formed a close affiliation with al-Qa'ida, with which it shares a jihadi-Salafi ideology. Following the withdrawal of the Soviets from Afghanistan, LeT transferred its efforts in the early 1990s to the insurgency in Indian-held Kashmir, with the aim of liberating Muslims in Jammu and Kashmir and making the region an Islamic state by incorporating it into Pakistan.

From the local Kashmir conflict, LeT developed into an international terrorist organization, advocating action within and against countries with non-Islamic governments and maintaining links with jihadists in the Philippines, the Middle East, and Chechnya. As cited by Martin Chulov, its ideology espouses the belief that to be in "a near-perpetual state of war against non-Islamic regimes was the best way to meet the obligations spelled out for Muslims in the Koran and to help realize the Islamic dream." In its efforts to be "an emphatic promoter of militant jihad," LeT has carried out attacks inside India, targeting Indian civilians, politicians, and the security forces, and has attacked police stations, airports, border outposts, and public transport. It also provides training camps for transnational jihadists inside Pakistan. This latter role became particularly important following the destruction of al-Qa'ida's training facilities in Afghanistan in 2001.

It has been an offense in Australia since March 2002 to fund or resource the LeT, but in December 2003, the LeT was proscribed under the 2003 Criminal Code Amendment (Hamas and Lashkar-e-Tayyiba) Bill, thus making it an offense to also train with, recruit for, belong to, or otherwise support the LeT. This was on the grounds that the government had received advice that the organization had links inside Australia and therefore posed a threat to Australia and Australian interests. The advice had been provided by the French government following its investigation into the activities of a French national and convert to Islam, Willie Brigitte (also known as Abderrahman), who

had arrived in Australia in April 2003 with the alleged intention of supporting a LeT cell to carry out a terrorist attack. Brigitte had been under investigation in France for his involvement in a radical jihadi group in Paris with links to al-Qa'ida.

The cell that Brigitte had come to assist was headed by Fahim Khalid Lodhi, a Sydney architect who had emigrated from Pakistan in 1998. Lodhi had spent time at a LeT camp in Pakistan in 2001–2002 and upon his return to Australia, was "committed to jihad" with a "clear mission from the LeT commanders" to act upon his convictions. He was instructed to "lay low" until another LeT operative was sent to assist him in the task. While waiting for Brigitte to arrive, Lodhi made one more trip to Pakistan and took with him a young medical student of Pakistani descent, Izhar ul-Haque, whom he had hoped to recruit to his Sydney cell. According to Chulov, ul-Haque later reported that while in Lahore, Lodhi told him that jihad was a good thing, and that it "was wrong to live among infidels and not resist their ways. . . . The secular lifestyles of the West were an affront to Muslims around the world and a corrupting force for the society the prophet envisaged. He should join him as a Muslim Braveheart in a righteous fight."

Brigitte was in Australia for six months before he was detained by Australian authorities, who had been contacted by France's Direction de la Surveillance du Territoire (DST) and warned that Brigitte was "possibly dangerous." Brigitte was deported in December 2003, after which Lodhi and ul-Haque were investigated by ASIO. The investigation led to the arrest of both men in April 2004 on terrorism-related offenses, including an alleged plan to blow up Sydney's electricity grid as well as several defense sites. Lodhi was found to be in possession of numerous DVDs and CDs of jihadi doctrine and terrorism training, a "terror manual" with recipes for explosives and poisons, lists of chemical prices, maps of the national electricity grid, and aerial photos of three Sydney defense sites. Meanwhile, back in France, ABC TV reported that Brigitte had testified that while he was in Sydney, he had been involved in a LeT group formed around Lodhi, which "was preparing a large-scale terrorist act in Australia."

In June 2006, Lodhi was found guilty of intending to "advance violent giant jihad" in Australia and the following month was sentenced to a maximum term of 20 years, with a 15-year nonparole period. Lodhi became the first person to be convicted of planning a terrorist act on Australian soil under the antiterrorism laws enacted by the federal government in 2005. Ul-Haque stood trial in October 2007, but all charges against him were dropped the following month, when the judge determined that the ASIO officers involved in his case had acted unlawfully by intimidating and illegally detaining ul-Haque during their investigation.

According to a 2005 report by the South Asia Analysis Group, the LeT is believed to have only a small following in Australia, primarily among the Pakistani Muslim community. Regardless of the group's size, the events concerning Brigitte and Lohdi reveal that if a foreign terrorist is willing to travel to Australia to mount a terrorist attack, only a small number of local sympathizers are required in order to provide the essential support structure. The ease with which Brigitte assimilated into the Sydney "Islamic scene," including marrying an Australian convert, further highlights the interlinked nature of the global and Australian Islamist networks. The organization at the center of the nexus is Shaykh Muhammad Omran's Ahlus Sunnah wal Jamaah Association of

Australia. Lodhi, ul-Haque, and Brigitte had all frequented the organization's Sydney prayer room located on Haldon Street in Lakemba.

Ahlus Sunnah wal Jamaah Association of Australia

The Ahlus Sunnah wal Jamaah Association of Australia (ASWJA) was established in 1985 by the Jordanian-born cleric, Shaykh Muhammad Omran, known by his followers as Abu Ayan. He had been sponsored to come to Australia by the Medina University in Saudi Arabia, from where he had graduated the previous year. Before finally settling in Melbourne in July 2000, Omran lived and preached his Salafi brand of Islam in other capital cities, including Perth and Sydney, where he also established ASWJA prayer centers.

Ahlus Sunnah Wal Jemaah (ASWJ, Adherents of the Prophetic Tradition and the Community) is the generic term used to refer to the Sunni branch of Islam. However, those who adopt it as an organizational name, such as in Australia, Canada, and the United Kingdom, do so as adherents of the Salafi movement. According to a September 2005 issue of ASWJA's *Mecca News*, it claims to be a "call to the true and authentic Islam," as passed down through the *salaf al-salihin* (pious companions), "not turning to anything else whether it be in matters of belief or matters of action which are subject to Islamic rulings." Secular values are thus rejected, as are efforts to reform Shari'a "to make it compatible with so-called Western values." In the words of one Salafi shaykh quoted in the same *Mecca News*, "a reinterpreted Islam is no Islam":

> Reinterpretation of Islam . . . is a misnomer for distorting the religion and

replacing it with something else that has the same name. . . . When we insist on keeping Islam in its pristine purity, and when we invite people to accept it as such, we are in fact conveying to them the message which will lead them to salvation . . . it is true that there is much in Islam which is not compatible with Western values. But who said that it is only those Western values that suit our modern times?

Thus ASWJA calls on Muslims to resist assimilation into Australian culture and promotes instead the extension of its Salafi interpretation of Islamic law to mainstream Australian society, including the view that women and men are inherently unequal in status, rights, and obligations. The organization is supported in its efforts to propagate Salafi doctrine through what Omran has described as "an open flow of funds between Saudi Arabia and Australia." In an August 2004 report in *The Australian*, Omran is quoted as saying, "Years ago I could just write a letter to one of my friends in Saudi Arabia and the money would come easily." In 1997, according to a *Gulf News* article, Omran's associate, Shaykh Samir Mohtadi, also received significant funds from the United Arab Emirates to build a hall for the Muslim community in Melbourne; and as reported by *The Age*, in 2004 Saudi sources contributed to the $2.6 million raised by ASWJA to purchase a mosque in Belmore, Sydney.

"Offensive jihad" also plays a role in the ASWJA ideology. Over the years, articles calling Muslims to jihad have appeared on the Web site of the Islamic Information and Support Centre of Australia (IISCA), the Victorian branch of ASWJA. One example is "Jihad for Muhammad's Sake," which explained that

Jihad is an act of worship, it is one of the supreme forms of devotion to Allah. . . . Jihad is necessary not only for the spread of Islam, but in the way that Allah selects the best and the purest of heart among humanity. . . . They say that Jihad is only for defence. This lie must be exposed.

Omran spoke openly about armed jihad in the years before the September 11, 2001, terrorist attacks. In more recent years he has made contradictory statements, asserting, as reported in the September 2003 edition of the *Bulletin*, that armed jihad would be "inappropriate" in Australia but also that "if someone has to do it, it has to be from outside." Concerning Australian interests overseas, ASWJA's Web site presents an unambiguous line: "Today we say to America and its Allies—You are not the first to have fought Islam. Actually there are many before you. However, what was the result? Allah destroyed everyone that stood against the path of Islam." When asked on an SBS TV program if it is the duty of a good Muslim to fight for jihad in Iraq against Australian and other coalition forces, Omran replied: "I would say yes."

Omran is well connected to overseas Islamist organizations and considers himself a longtime friend of a number of convicted al-Qa'ida terrorists, including Abu Qatada and Abu Dahdah. (In 2005, Abu Qatada was jailed for life in Spain for his role in the terrorist attacks perpetrated there in 2003. Abu Dahdah is accused of being an international courier and go-between for al-Qa'ida, having met Muhammad Atta, the ringleader of the September 11 attacks.) In 1994 Omran hosted a visit by Abu Qatada to Melbourne, providing him with a platform to preach at the Preston and Brunswick mosques. According to Chulov, during his speeches Abu Qatada "spoke out against Arab governments for not being Islamic enough, for not adhering to pure Sharia law." He stressed that it was the duty of all Muslims to ensure that they did not sit idly by in a secular country. "It was every Muslim's destiny to rise up to defend his faith from non-believers." As one listener recalled, "He was radicalized and politicized. We had never heard this stuff before. His impact was enormous and that is where it all began." Indeed, Abu Qatada's 1994 sermons have been given the "honor" of birthing "radical Islam" in Australia.

Following Abu Qatada's visit, Omran, too, began to introduce a militant edge to his sermons in which, according to Chulov, he "legitimized jihad as a righteous way to safeguard the integrity of Islam whenever it was deemed to be under threat." It was not long before he became "a lightning rod for the disaffected youths of mainstream Islam, who flocked to him seeking purpose in their lives." Indeed, Omran has come to be regarded, in the words of Neighbour, as the mentor "of radical Islamists in Australia," having attracted those who consider the teachings of Shaykh al-Hilali of Sydney and Shaykh Fehmi Naji al-Imam, the Imam of Melbourne's Preston mosque, to be "too moderate."

The Sydney branch of the ASWJA located in the Haldon Street prayer room is led by the Lebanese-born Shaykh Abd al-Salam Muhammad Zoud. Sourcing his teaching on the works of Ibn Taymiyya and Abdallah Azzam, Zoud champions the need for an Islamic state where secular law is replaced by Shari'a law, and, if necessary, violence is to be used to shake off the influences of a secular world and create a modern Islamic "utopia" in the model of Islam's early days. He explained in a post on the IISCA's Web site:

The Messenger of Allah said: "A group of my umma will continue to fight in truth, manifest till the last day. . . ." And so the caliphate will return once again by the will of Allah, and in accordance with the way of the prophet. Therefore it is incumbent upon all Muslims to strive with all that they have been given towards its revival. Fortunate is he, who works hard towards its establishment and believes in it. Brothers and sisters in Islam—Sticking together as one nation is one of the requirements of the Islamic Sharia, and one of its obligatory requirements based on what Allah has said. . . . Indeed the Islamic Message has great objectives that include: Spreading Islam to all mankind; Making the religion of Islam prevail over and above all other religions; Jihad—in order for the name of Allah to be the highest, and so the words of the disbelievers are the lowest.

In his sermons and writings, Zoud takes a tough line against any diversion from the "pure" teachings of the Koran, condemning any Muslim who comes up with any ideas, words, or exercises of judgment that go against the consensus of the umma. Chulov explains that his followers are known to keep within a "tight-knit brotherhood," with "little interest in moderate Islam, or other elements of [the wider] society, except those prepared to come to terms with their hardline ways of life."

LeT operative Willie Brigitte also frequented ASWJA's Haldon Street prayer room when he was in Australia in 2003. Shaykh Zoud had presided over his marriage to Australian convert Melanie Brown. Following Brigitte's arrest in France on terrorism charges, Zoud continued to proclaim his innocence, stating, according to a March

2004 article in the *Sydney Morning Herald,* "He's not a terrorist in my eyes." Zoud was identified by a French judge in the Brigitte case as "the chief recruiter for a terrorist network operating in Australia."

Another ASWJA imam is Shaykh Feiz Muhammad, a founder of the Global Islamic Youth Center at Liverpool in Sydney's southwest. A protégé of Omran, Feiz is also known for his fiery orations accusing Jews of global conspiracies, referring to the "so-called war on terrorism" as "nothing but a war on Islam and the Muslims to ensure the Zionist—those pigs—the Zionist-American domination in every corner of this earth." In his sermon entitled "The Enemy's Plot," which is widely available on the Internet and quoted by Neighbour, Feiz warns Muslims not to take non-Muslims as friends or advisers

> for they will spare no efforts to corrupt you. They desire to harm you severely. Hatred has appeared from their mouths. However, what their hearts conceal is far greater, far worse. . . . These people are evil, they are cunning, they work in a subtle way! . . . They [Christians and Jews] have poisoned you, induced in you poison, and this war, this type of attack takes place by means of school curriculums, general education, TV, internet, vaccinations, fashion, publications media, theories, philosophies. . . . The attack is within your very home, your very lifestyle, the way you walk, the way you sit, the way you eat, the way you drink, the way you live. Look and reflect! . . . When they succeed in this plot, what's gonna happen? It's gonna be easy for them to assault us—to brutally shed our blood, to rape our children and women, to destroy our mosques! They are determined to wipe the name

of Islam from the face of this earth. Brothers and sisters—what are you living for? What are you doing here? . . . Go to Iraq today and see your brothers and sisters—see them, see what is happening there—it's gonna happen to you one day! Don't think because you're in Australia, you're comfortable. . . . [We] are too comfortable with cultivation. We're too scared to go to jihad. What are you living for?

One of Feiz's enthusiastic supporters was JI's Jack Roche. Neighbour recounts that after listening to one of the shaykh's sermons in 1999, Roche told a friend that "at long last we've met someone who has something to say about Islam. You get sick of all the rhetoric, of listening to all the bullshit." It was at this time that JI was recruiting for jihadists, and Roche had become convinced that "the greatest way to die was for jihad as you then become a martyr." He told the same friend that "he had no problems in carrying out jihad against anyone, including Australians."

The call to jihad by ASWJA's shaykhs had resonance among other followers, such as the Egyptian-born immigrant Mamduh Habib, who traveled to Afghanistan in March 2000 "to live an Islamic life in the Bin Ladin camp." During this first trip, which lasted two months, Habib trained at an LeT camp. When he returned to Afghanistan in July 2001, he is believed to have trained with al-Qa'ida in a camp near Kabul. On his way back to Australia in the wake of the September 11 terrorist attacks, Habib was arrested by the Pakistani police. He was sent first to Egypt and then to Guantanamo Bay, from where he was released in February 2005. Back in Australia, Habib remains a person of interest to the national security services.

While Omran and Zoud have not been formally accused of planning or perpetrating terrorist actions within Australia, they have been accused of inciting hatred and separatism. The contents of the ASWJA's Melbourne and Sydney bookshops provide testament to this. Most damning is Mustapha Kara-Ali, a young Muslim leader and member of former Prime Minister Howard's Muslim Community Reference Group, who is among those who have accused Shaykhs Omran and Zoud of propagating the same teachings as the former Taliban regime and Osama bin Ladin. As reported in *The Australian* in June 2006, Kara-Ali charged that "Omran's conspiratorial pussyfooting over the issue of terrorism is producing more bin Ladins in the suburbs, and it's turning more of Australia's youth towards the path of destruction and terror." He added that "Omran's organisation has a 'hidden agenda' to 'further recruit' more Australian Muslims and 'disenfranchised youth' into his radical sect." A spokesman for the shaykh denied the claims.

However, Kara-Ali's accusations seem to hold some weight when considering the list of Muslim Australians who have been arrested in the past few years on terrorism-related charges and who at some point previously had been followers of, or associated in some way with, Omran's ASWJA. These include Jack Roche, Jack Thomas, Bilal Khazal, Willie Brigitte, Saleh Jamal, Fahim Khalid Lodhi, Izhar ul-Haque, and most recently, the 22 men arrested and charged at the end of 2005 and early 2006 as part of Operation Pendennis.

Mindful of the number of yet unexplained connections that Shaykh Muhammad Omran has had with supporters and sympathizers of terrorism abroad and here in Australia, he and his increasing number of followers remain of interest to the Australian authorities. This growing influence is evidenced by his organization's increasing, Australia-wide membership, which now has, according to the organization's Web site, seven centers across the country—four in Sydney (including the al-Azhar mosque in Belmore), the two largest mosques in Melbourne, and one in Perth. According to the ABC's *Four Corners*, the ASWJA has taken over the mosque at Dee Why, once the home of the members of JI's Mantiqi 4.

According to a June 2004 article in *The Age*, Omran boasts that he leads "the most influential Islamic organization in Australia," with 12 nationalities represented on its council and "followers, believers, worldwide, not (just) Australia-wide." He is referred to publicly as "the unofficial mufti in radical realms," and his teachings receive popular support beyond the immediate circle of ASWJA members, evidenced by the significant number of participants who attend its annual "Da'wa Conference." Omran, too, is a regular guest and speaker at "mainstream" Muslim community events and seminars held by Muslim university groups, while the ASWJA Web site is hosted on many other Australian Muslim community group Web sites and on the Islamic directories at various Australian universities.

According to Mustapha Kara-Ali, there now exists within the Australian Muslim community "shades" of political Islamism—he calls it Wahhabism—for which there are "circles of security and protection." At the inner core of these concentric circles "are the Omrans of this world," while at the "outermost rings" are the "deceived youth at university campuses or down the street. How wide are those rings, the outermost rings? I think they encompass at least 30 percent of the community." As Lapkin documents, university Muslim student groups have indeed come to provide an important platform for the propagation of Islamist teachings, influential among those considered to be the future leaders of the Australian Muslim community.

Islamic Youth Movement (IYM)

Perhaps the most notorious Australian Islamist group is the Sydney-based Islamic Youth Movement (IYM), founded and led by Lebanese immigrant Bilal Khazal. Group members considered Shaykh Omran to be their religious mentor and attended Shaykh Zoud's Lakemba prayer room.

In 1995, Khazal and Omran co-founded IYM's magazine (and accompanying Web site), *Nida'ul Islam*. Its stated purpose is "striving towards a section of the society which understands Islam to be its true reality, and which realizes that Jihad is the only path to establish the Islamic State, and which therefore acts accordingly" and to give "the youth generation the attention it requires, since it forms the fuel for the Islamic movement in general and the Jihad stream in specific."

With articles such as "Sovereignty Is Only for Allah" and "Jihad Defined," the magazine has provided a forum for the teachings of radical clerics and jihadi ideologues such as Sayyid Qutb, Syed Abu Ala Mawdudi, and Abdallah Azzam and has run interviews with JI's Sungkar and Ba'asyir, the "blind shaykh" Umar Abd al-Rahman, al-Qa'ida's Osama bin Ladin and Abu Qatada, Ansar al-Islam leader Fatih Krekar, and MILF leader Hashim Salamat. According to Neighbour, bin Ladin's interview, obtained just after his 1996 "Declaration of Jihad," expounded on the "necessity for armed struggle . . . in order to repel the greater Kufr (infidels)" and decreed that "terrorizing the American occupiers is a religious and logical obligation." In the February–

March 1997 issue, an article entitled "The True Understanding of Islam" argued the case that those who define "Islam" as having been derived from the root word *salam*, which means peace, are what Sayyid Qutb calls "apologists":

> If we are indoctrinated with the concept that Islam means peace then what inclination would we have to shed blood for its cause? If the very religion which we follow literally meant peace, how could we fight and kill its enemies to make it supreme? . . . There is only one way to make Allah's word supreme and that is to fight his enemies to lower their words and raise His own. . . . May Allah bless and reward the Mujahidin and make us to be of them.

The publication also featured regular updates on battles and terror strikes around the Middle East, praise of the Taliban regime, articles for university students on how to develop an "Islamic state of mind" in order "to participate in the reconstruction of the Islamic State," and advice for parents on how to deal with the "negative and destructive effects" of what children are "taught in the Kufr school and the base media." Articles have also been submitted by Australian Muslim leaders such as Keysar Trad, who provided an analysis of the "egoist nature of Western society."

IYM first came to the attention of ASIO in the early 1990s, when it was discovered that some of the group's members had trained in camps in Afghanistan. In 1993 in Lebanon, Khazal was convicted in absentia on terrorism charges; and in Spain, during the prosecution against al-Qa'ida, he was identified as an acquaintance of Abu Dahdah and as a member of "the Islamic Youth Movement . . . their principal activity [being] recruitment of Mujahadeen in Australia," as reported by an October 2003 SBS *Insight* program. In Sydney, Khazal was stabbed and shot at in battles between rival Muslim groups, and according to a June 2003 *Four Corners* program, he was the main focus of the CIA's 2002 report on al-Qa'ida's presence in Australia. In 2004 Khazal was arrested by Australian authorities for compiling a terrorist instruction manual and posting it on the Internet. The text was entitled "Provision in the Rules of Jihad—Short Wise Rules and Organisational Structures That Concern Every Fighter and Mujahid Fighting Against the Infidels" and included sections on attaining martyrdom and the reasons and targets for assassination and stages in the process.

Nida'ul Islam ran articles protesting Khazal's innocence, but in 2006, a New South Wales Supreme Court judge deemed certain documents relating to the case to be so "significant in terms of national security sensitivity" that Khazal's legal team were denied access. Based on the materials seen by the judge, *The Australian* reported that he stated that it "is all too easy to dismiss the risk of a terrorist attack in Australia as unlikely. The reality is that, in the present political and ideological climate, Australia may face real prospects of being subject to a serious terrorist attack or attacks within the confines of its shores."

Eleven months earlier, the New South Wales and Victorian police arrested 19 men who they believed were planning such an attack. The group's leader, Abdul Nacer Benbrika, had been a former teacher at Omran's Brunswick mosque and had been in the audience in 1994 to hear Abu Qatada give his fiery sermons calling Australian Muslims to jihad. Members of the Sydney cell prayed at the ASWJA Haldon Street prayer room of Shaykh Zoud.

The Abdul Nacer Benbrika Cells

The Algerian-born Benbrika had first come to public attention in Australia when he declared in an August 2005 television interview with *The 7.30 Report* that Islam "doesn't tolerate other religion. It doesn't tolerate. The only one law which needs to spread—it can be here or anywhere else—has to be Islam." Concerning Osama bin Ladin, Benbrika declared: "He is a great man. Osama bin Ladin was a great man before September 11, which they said he did it, until now nobody knows who did it." He went on to defend Muslims fighting against coalition forces in Iraq and Afghanistan, stating that "according to my religion, jihad is a part of my religion and what you have to understand is that anyone who fights for the sake of Allah, when he dies, the first drop of blood that comes from him out all his sin will be forgiven." The following day, Ameer Ali, the then president of the Australian Federation of Islamic Councils, put out a press release, posted on the organization's Web site, condemning Benbrika's comments, saying that such extremist views were against the teachings of Islam and calling on the media to not provide him with the publicity he was seeking.

By this time, Benbrika was already a subject of "concern" to ASIO. Months of surveillance that had begun in 2004 had identified him as the leader of a radical Islamic group that had cells in both Melbourne and Sydney, members of which had traveled to Pakistan and Afghanistan in 2001, training with al-Qa'ida and the LeT. Back in Australia, the group had participated in Islamist training camps run by the IYM and JI's Asman Hashim. Sydney cell members Khalid Sharrouf and Abd al-Rakib Hasan had also provided support for LeT operative Willie Brigitte during the time he spent in

Australia in 2003, allegedly planning a terrorist attack.

According to a November 2005 report in *The Australian*, Benbrika's Melbourne cell members were

> hardened street boys armed with attitude and the Koran, who saw in Benbrika a father figure and a way to reclaim their lost souls. His group was small but tight-knit and [had] spread its tentacles into Sydney where Benbrika's radical name preceded him and gained him more followers.

Before their arrests in November 2005, the Melbourne and Sydney cell members had been under surveillance for 16 months, in an operation code-named "Operation Pendennis." In their recorded conversations, group members discussed their intention to conduct a terrorist attack against major landmarks in both cities, including the Stock Exchange and Flinders Street Station in Melbourne, while one group member, Abdallah Mehri, expressed his willingness to become a "suicide bomber." They were recorded discussing bomb making, including the acquisition of the necessary chemicals as well as firearms.

When members of the group began to purchase significant quantities of solvent and bleach, key ingredients in bomb making, the police decided to move. The November 8, 2005, raid on the homes of Benbrika and three of his followers uncovered hundreds of liters of chemicals, laboratory equipment, 165 detonators, 132 digital timers, batteries, firearms, and ammunition. Nine men were arrested in Melbourne and eight in Sydney. Two days later, another Melbourne man was arrested; on December 22, 2005, another Sydney man was arrested; and three more Melbourne men on March 31, 2006,

were caught, bringing the total arrested as a part of Operation Pendennis to 22. All were charged with terrorism offenses, while Benbrika was also charged with directing the activities of a terrorist organization. Two of the Melbourne men were also charged with supporting al-Qa'ida in its efforts to carry out a terrorist operation. The trials began in February 2008.

Three months before Benbrika's arrest, when asked by a reporter on *The 7.30 Report* if he represented any kind of threat to Australia, he replied, "I am not involved in anything here. I am teaching my brothers here the Koran and the Sunna, and I am trying my best to keep myself, my family, my kids and the Muslims close to this religion." Yet despite Benbrika's claim, the evidence presented at trial revealed that Operation Pendennis had foiled his group's plan to carry out terrorist attacks on targets within Australia. In September 2008, a jury found Benbrika guilty of intentionally directing the activities of a terrorist organization and of being a member of a terrorist organization. Six of his followers were found guilty of belonging to a terrorist organization plotting to wage "violent jihad." Four other followers of Benbrika were found to be not guilty of all charges. The jury was not able to reach a verdict on charges against one of the men, requiring his retrial. In February 2009, Benbrika was sentenced to 15 years jail with a nonparole period of 12 years. His six followers received minimum jail terms of between 4½ and 7½ years.

Federation of Australian Muslim Students and Youth

The Federation of Australian Muslim Students and Youth (FAMSY) is an umbrella organization for Muslim youth associations with branches throughout most states of

Australia. Its Web site reports that FAMSY was established in 1978 to provide a support structure for students and youth Australia-wide. (Other sites give 1968 as the organization's starting date. The organization operated under different names until 1991, when FAMSY was adopted.) According to one FAMSY Web site iteration, its aims are to "provide educational programs for members and supporters based on the correct understanding of the Quran and Sunna and to culture them, using a structured Tarbiyya Program, to accept Islam as a complete way of life including but not limited to strong moral and ethical values." An earlier Web site had added that

> FAMSY seeks to remind the Muslim people (umma) of their position, duties, and responsibilities as the representatives of Islam to the world. This in turn necessitates that Muslims organize themselves into an organized group (jammaa) whose final objective is the establishment of Islam in all parts of the world.

While FAMSY does not identify its agenda to be that of political Islam, its credentials are evident from its close affiliation with the World Assembly of Muslim Youth (WAMY), which established an Australia and South Pacific branch in 2002, receiving $170,000 from the head office in Saudi Arabia to sponsor "camps and activities for young Muslims, religious classes, buying books and for sponsoring Muslim-related projects across the country," as reported in *The Australian* in August 2004. WAMY is an arm of the Saudi government's Muslim World League (MWL), an organization established with the aim of propagating Wahhabi Islam around the world. (The WML has been named on a number of occasions in relation

to one of its charities, the Islamic Relief Organization, which has been accused by the U.S. Department of Treasury of sponsoring terrorism.)

WAMY sponsors FAMSY's Lakemba bookstore, which offers a wide range of English Islamic books while its Web site also promotes Salafi literature, such as programs by the Council on American-Islamic Relations (CAIR), an organization that likewise enjoys Saudi Wahhabi patronage.

Through its camps, seminars, and annual conferences, FAMSY propagates the teachings of Salafi scholars generally and the Muslim Brotherhood in particular, the motto of the latter being: "Allah is our goal; the Messenger is our model; the Koran is our constitution; jihad is our means; and martyrdom in the way of Allah is our aspiration." Its international speakers have included CAIR's executive director, Nihad Awwad, and Abd al-Rahim Ghouse, reported to have had business dealings with Shaykh Yassin al-Qadi, an alleged al-Qa'ida financier. Members of the Muslim Brotherhood who have come to Australia to speak at FAMSY functions include Kamal Hilwabi, a former senior member of the Egyptian branch of the Brotherhood; Ahmad Elkadi, founder of the Brotherhood in the United States; Tariq al-Suwaydan, a leading member of the Kuwaiti branch; and Anas al-Tikriti, former president of the Muslim Association of Britain (MAB), which has associations with the Muslim Brotherhood, and the son of Usama al-Tikriti, the leader of the Iraqi branch of the Brotherhood.

Another organization that has increasing support on university campuses and beyond is Hizb al-Tahrir. While this organization is banned in nearly every Arab country, Germany, and Russia, it has not been proscribed in Australia.

Hizb al-Tahrir

Hizb al-Tahrir (HT, Liberation Party) is an international movement founded in Jerusalem in 1953 by the Palestinian Islamist Taqi al-Din al-Nabhani. Today it has followers across the Middle East, Western Europe, Central Asia, and Southeast Asia, with branches in some 40 countries, and political party representation in many of these, including Lebanon and Yemen. However, in other Arab states and throughout Europe, HT has been accused of violent activities, including terrorism, and has thus been proscribed.

As Fealy explains, central to HT's ideology is the revival of the Islamic caliphate as the blueprint for reshaping Muslim society and the state. "The group argues that few Muslims currently live as God commanded because they're dominated politically, culturally, and economically by non-believers. Only under a caliphate can Muslims be free of subjugation and live as God prescribed." Thus HT's Web site declares its ambition to install the Islamic way of life and convey the Islamic da'wa to the world, that it is dedicated to bringing "back the Islamic guidance for mankind and to lead the Umma into a struggle with Kufr, its systems and its thoughts so that Islam encapsulates the world." As reported by *The Guardian* in 1994, HT's ideology condemns democracy as "deceptive, dangerous and unworkable. The party considers it is *haram* [forbidden] to establish or participate in parties which call for capitalism, socialism, secularism, nationalism or any religion other than Islam."

As for the role of jihad in the ideology of HT, Jalaluddin Patel, former head of HT in Britain explained it as follows:

We say that the work required for establishing the Khilafah state does not involve in any of its stages the concept of material struggle or Jihad. . . . However there is a difference between establishing a Khilafah state and defending one's land. It is the duty of Muslims to defend their lands from invasion. . . . Therefore the defensive Jihad requires no authority to sanction it. . . . [Whereas] in an offensive situation, where there is an Islamic state that possesses the appropriate political and military capabilities, it is the only authority that can sanction and undertake offensive Jihad.

HT branches are directed globally by a *qiyada* (central leadership), headed by the Jordanian Ata Abu Rishta. This leadership sets the international agenda and strategy, which is in turn interpreted and implemented by the regional branches.

The Australian branch of HT—Hizb al-Tahrir Australia (HTA)—has its headquarters in Sydney. Its membership, which is believed to number some 200, is led by Wassim Doureihi, who is assisted in the task by his brothers, Ashraf and Soadad. Information about HTA is provided via its Web site, pamphlets, and public lectures. It also holds weekly meetings for members only, during which they discuss, as one journalist put it, "how to unite all Muslims under a giant pan-Islamic state, or caliphate, under strict Sharia law." In an address cited by *The 7.30 Report* concerning the objectives of HTA, Soadad Doureihi explained: "We must ensure that the acceptable—the 'acceptable' Western—version of Islam does not prevail and it is not carried by our Muslims, our scholars, our community leaders."

Consistent with the international platform of HT, Australian branch members preach nonassimilation and the rejection of the values of the *kufr* generally and

Australian values in particular. "The push-ing to integration," Wassim Doureihi told an audience in April 2006, "is to get us to think and believe and feel in a certain way that Islam will not condone." Soadad clari-fied his brother's point, cited by the *Sydney Morning Herald*:

> [We] must be aware of the plot of the kafir, the plot of the Western society to enforce on [us] a palatable Islam. . . . Secularism is a clear assault on the fun-damental belief of a Muslim. Democracy is a clear assault on the fundamental belief of a Muslim also . . . Islam can never coexist one under the other or one within the other. When the [Islamic] state is established, when people can see the mercy of Islam, they will embrace Islam in droves.

Not surprisingly, HTA has taken a firm position in response to statements made by Australian government officials concern-ing the need for all members of Australian society, Muslims included, to embrace core Australian values—democracy, secularism, the rule of law, and loyalty to Australia being among them. Indeed, the 2005 speech by Peter Costello noted at the outset of this chapter has been used in subsequent HTA presentations to condemn the "Western creed" and to promote instead Islamic val-ues considered to be incompatible with the values Costello had articulated. In a 2006 presentation entitled "The Values Debate: Should Muslims Subscribe to Australian Values?" one of the speakers proclaimed that when Muslims look to Islam, its values and its sources:

> We find major issues with values like democracy and an over-riding com-mitment to a nation-state . . . Islam

rejects secularism and its organization of human life on earth goes beyond mere moral advice and included principles and systems of social organization, econom-ics, politics and judicial review, amongst others. . . . The problems with [giving primacy to civil laws and the priority to universal human rights] from the Islamic perspective is clear, the secular value relegates Allah to the margins of public life and places human beings above him. This, to put it bluntly, is as blasphemous as it gets. . . . The rule, command, sovereignty is for Allah, he commands that we worship none but him. Democracy places sovereignty or the right to legislate with the people as a whole, this is its essence. . . . In Islam, we need to be very clear that sovereign-ty belongs to Allah alone. This, then, is the Islamic methodology of dealing with our matters and our affairs, public or private. . . . That is all we have to say in regards to secularism and democracy. As for an overriding loyalty to Australia then we have no more to say than that the overriding commitment of a Muslim is Allah and Allah alone.

The speaker concluded by reinforcing one of the key principles that lay at the heart of political Islam: "The Islamic ways and values stand head and shoulders above Western values and way of life. Thus, we have seen that Western values are not wor-thy of human subscription. Whether we look at the ideological foundations, their systems or their practical texts they have nothing to compare with the pristine values of Islam." Thus HTA's message for Australian Muslims, living in a non-Muslim majority country, is the need to defend against what a second speaker referred to as a "forced conversion":

If as a Muslim we aspire to lead humanity in a specific direction based upon
Islam, lifting mankind from the dust
of oppression by Islam, how can we
achieve this objective if we establish
our platform on something other than
Islam. The adoption of Australian values undermines in the strongest possible way the cause of Islam and the
Muslims. How can you feel for the
plight of Muslims if your loyalty is to
Australia? . . . How can you support the
work to implement the Sharia in Islamic
lands if you believe in secularism? How
can you work to establish the caliphate if
your cause is democracy? The adoption
of Australian values is clearly a direct
assault on your Islam. . . . Brothers and
sisters of Islam, it is time to reclaim our
rightful place on this earth. Further and
future generations will judge us on the
choices we make today. We would not be
Muslims today if our forefathers chose
to compromise their Islam yesterday,
so do not compromise your Islam today.
So what is the best course for Muslims
living in Australia? It is to loudly reject
these values and hold tightly onto your
religion so that you may pass it on to the
rest of Australian society.

HTA is not aligned with any other organizations in the Australian Muslim community and is described by some mainstream
Muslim leaders as a "provocative fringe
group." On occasion, the group has been
warned to stop distributing its recruitment
literature near local mosques, literature
that openly espouses strict Shari'a law,
including amputation of hands for theft as
well as capital punishment. However, HTA
representatives have on occasion shared the
speakers' platform at mainstream Muslim
community functions and are popular on

university campuses, where they are hosted
by Muslim student groups. Indeed, it is
primarily among university students and
graduates that HTA has found most of its
recruits. This has led one Muslim commentator, Irfan Yusuf, to surmise that for many
young Muslims, "HT is a temporary pit-stop
on their way to more refined and sophisticated Islamic thinking."

HTA came under the scrutiny of Australian
security services following the London
bombings in 2005, but the government
has remained satisfied that the Australian
group has not "planned, assisted in, or fostered any violent acts which are the current
legislation tests under the criminal code for
proscription." In the wake of the Operation
Pendennis arrests, ASIO has stated that
it continues to monitor the activities and
literature of HTA while other government
officials have noted that the group remains
"of concern," as elements of the organization have called for attacks against U.S.-
coalition (including Australian) forces in
Afghanistan and Iraq.

The Future of Political Islam in Australia

As yet there has been no poll conducted
among the Muslim communities in Australia
to determine the extent to which political Islam views are supported. However,
it would appear from the broad range of
sources surveyed here that Muslims who
profess to strive in an organized way, either
socially or politically, for the universaliza-
tion of Islam and Shari'a law, while not significant in numbers, do have a sympathetic
community base that reaches beyond "a tiny
fraction of practicing Muslims in Australia,"
as is claimed by official Muslim spokespeople and academics. Salafi Islam, in particular, is propagated on a regular basis in

mosques and prayer halls, and on university campuses around the country. The import of Saudi ideology and money has thus far proved successful in providing Australian Islamists with both the financial means and the "critical mass" of followers to produce recruits to engage effectively in this steadily growing global phenomenon.

While those who profess the legitimacy of violence as a tool for propagating their values might be relatively small in number, the arrest and, in some cases, conviction of Islamists in Australia for plotting terrorist acts has shown that the threat of jihadi-Salafism to Australia's national security is a very real one. The collaboration between local Islamist groups and global jihadi networks has served to strengthen the jihadi supporter network that took root in Australia in the mid-1990s.

BIBLIOGRAPHY

Abedin, Mahan. "Inside Hizb ut-Tahrir: An Interview with Jalaluddin Patel, Leader of Hizb ut-Tahrir in the UK." *Terrorism Monitor* 2:8 (2004). www.jamestown.org/terrorism/news/article.php?search=1&articleid=2368393.

"After the Bombs: Being Muslim in Australia." *Encounter.* ABC Radio National, August 7, 2005. www.abc.net.au/rn/relig/enc/stories/s1427935.htm.

Ahmed, Tanveer. "Islam Can Modernise." *The Australian,* October 30, 2006.

Allan, Lisa. "Terror Suspect's Lawyers Denied Papers." *The Australian,* October 26, 2006.

Al Qahtani, Mohammad. "Jihad for Muhammad's Sake." http://iisca.org/knowledge/jihad/jihad_for_allah.htm.

Al-Uthaymeen, Muhammad ibn Saalih. "A Reinterpreted Islam Is No Islam." *Mecca News,* September 2005.

Australian Security Intelligence Organisation. *Report to Parliament 2005–2006.* Canberra: Commonwealth of Australia, 2006.

———. *Report to Parliament 2006–2007.* Canberra: Commonwealth of Australia, 2007.

———. *Report to Parliament 2007–2008.* Canberra: Commonwealth of Australia, 2008.

Chulov, Martin. *Australian Jihad: The Battle Against Terrorism from Within and Without.* Sydney: Macmillan, 2006.

Costello, Peter. "Worth Promoting, Worth Defending—Australian Citizenship." *The Sydney Papers* 18:2 (2006): 77–83.

Department of Foreign Affairs. *Transnational Terrorism: Threat to Australia.* Canberra: Commonwealth of Australia, 2004.

Devine, Miranda. "Wolves in Sheep's Clothing on an Extremist Mission." *Sydney Morning Herald,* April 23, 2006.

El Gafi, Gabr. Interview on *Four Corners.* ABC TV, June 12, 2003. www.abc.net.au/4corners/content/2003/transcripts/s878332.htm.

FAMSY Web site: www.famsy.com/famsy/.

Fealy, G., and A. Borgu. *Local Jihad: Radical Islam and Terrorism in Indonesia.* Canberra: Australian Strategic Policy Institute, 2005.

Francis, C. "Arab in Australia Tries to Spread Word of Islam." *Gulf News,* November 17, 1997.

"General Struggle Guidelines of Jemaah Islamiyah." In *Voices of Islam in Southeast Asia: A Contemporary Sourcebook*, ed. G. Fealy and V. Hooker 364–70. Singapore: Institute of Southeast Asian Studies, 2006.

"Hizb ut-Tahrir." *The 7.30 Report.* ABC TV, August 22, 2005. www.abc.net.au/7.30/content/2005/s1443606.htm.

Hizb ut-Tahrir Web site: www.hizbuttahrir.org.uk.

Issa, H. "Family Breakdown: Causes and Cures." *Mecca News,* October 2005.

Kerbaj, R. "Radical Islamic Conference at Uni." *The Australian,* June 29, 2006.

———. "Sheik Hilali Praises Iraq Jihadists." *The Australian,* October 30, 2006.

Lapkin, S. "The Best and the Brightest: Hate and Extremism in Australian Universities." *The Review* (June 2006). www.aijac.org.au/review/2006/31–6/slapkin31–6.htm.

Lyons, J. "I Am Behind Every Muslim in This Country." *The Bulletin,* September 10, 2003.

Muhammad, Feiz. *The Enemy's Plot.* Audio available at www.kalamullah.com/Sheikh%20Feiz/Sheikh%20Feiz%20-%20The%20Enemy%27s%20Plot.mp3.

Neighbour, Sally. "The Australian Connections." *Four Corners*. ABC TV, June 12, 2003. www .abc.net.au/4corners/content/2003/ transcripts/ s878332.htm.

———. *In the Shadow of Swords: On the Trail of Terrorism from Afghanistan to Australia.* Sydney: Harper Perennial, 2005.

Peled, Naomi. "Jihad in the Suburbs." *The Review* 30:8 (2005). www.aijac.org.au/ review/2005/30-8/hatebooks30-8.html.

Petersen, F., and J. Clark. "Sheik Knows Little—Except bin Ladin Is Innocent." *Sydney Morning Herald,* March 23, 2004.

"Radical Time-Bomb Under British Islam—'Purify Every Inch.'" *Guardian,* February 7, 1994.

Raman, B. "Jihadi Terrorism in S.E.Asia." South Asia Analysis Group. 2005. www.saag.org/ common/uploaded_files/paper1566.html.

Saeed, Abdallah. *Muslim Australians: Their Beliefs*, *Practices and Institutions.* Canberra: Department of Immigration and Multicultural and Indigenous Affairs, 2004.

Schwartz, L. "Cleric in Struggle for Power." *The Age,* June 6, 2004.

Stewart, C. "The Day One Man Infected a Community with Hatred." *The Australian,* November 12, 2005.

Stewart, C., and T. Harris. "Extremist Cash Caution Pays Off." *The Australian*, August 28, 2004.

"Suspect Claims ASIO Surveillance Unjust." *The 7.30 Report.* ABC TV, August 4, 2005. www .abc.net.au/7.30/content/2005/s1430601.htm.

Sungkar, Abdullah, "Suharto's 'Detect, Defect and Destroy' Policy Towards the Islamic Movement." *Nida'ul Islam* 17 (February–March 1997): 4–7.

Walsh, K. "September 11 Is God's Work: Mufti." *Sydney Morning Herald,* February 29, 2004.

Wiktorowicz, Q. "Anatomy of the Salafi Movement." *Studies in Conflict and Terrorism* 29 (2006): 207–39.

"Willie Brigitte." *Four Corners.* ABC TV, February 9, 2004. www.abc.net.au/4corners/ content/2004/s1040952.htm.

Yasmeen, S. "'Dealing with Islam' in Australia: After the London Bombings." *The Sydney Papers* (Winter/Spring 2006): 38–39.

Yusuf, I. "Why Hizbut Tahrir (HT) Are No Security Threat in Australia." 2005. http:// planetirf.blogspot.com/2005/08/why-hizbut-tahrir-ht-are-no-security.html.

Zoud, A. "Jamaa'ah and Imaarah" (The Muslim Group and Leadership). http://iisca.org/ articles/document.jsp?id=32.

Indonesia

Greg Barton

A range of Islamist forces exists in Indonesia, from those successfully working within democracy to violent radical groups that remain powerful but so far largely unsuccessful in political terms.

Organizations competing for the allegiance of the country's 210 million Muslims include violent Islamist militias such as the Defenders of Islam Front (Front Pembela Islam, FPI) and, until its disbanding in October 2002, Laskar Jihad; underground jihadi networks such as Darul Islam and Jemaah Islamiyah (JI); and semiunderground social movements such as Hizb al-Tahrir.

There have always been groups that strive to see Indonesia become an Islamic state. Suppressed throughout the 1960s and 1970s, radical Islamism found new impetus in the wake of Iran's 1979 revolution. Although the works of Iran's Ali Shariati were translated and read widely, these groups were typically modeled on the Salafi activism of the Muslim Brotherhood, with some Saudi Wahhabi influence, rather than on the Iranian experience.

Nevertheless, while these groups retain the power to disrupt and distract and have a social base more extensive than is generally acknowledged, prospects of achieving a Sunni, Southeast Asian version of the Islamic Republic of Iran are so utterly remote as to not be worth serious consideration.

Radical Versus Moderate Islamism

Radical Islamists in Indonesia today do not face the convenient foil of an authoritarian secular regime against which to rally the support of a frustrated society, nor do they have a vast network of *ulama* (religious clerics) and mosque communities prepared to support revolution. Of special importance is that in Indonesia such ideology has always had to compete for support with a democratic Islamic alternative that has an equal claim on Islamic legitimacy. There is thus a struggle by these two sides to win over the majority.

A significant minority of traditionalist Muslims associated with the mass-based Nahdlatul Ulama (NU) have supported political parties such as the Partai Persatuan Pembangunan (PPP, the United Development Party) and Partai Bintang Reformasi (PBR, the Reform Star Party) that have a moderate Islamist platform.

The moderate Islamism of these parties is

a product of the social conservatism in much of Indonesian society but is particularly prevalent among the largely rural members of the NU. Whereas radical Islamists aspire to see society radically transformed, moderate Islamic forces are concerned with conserving a role for Islam in public life.

From its formation as an amalgam of several Islamic parties in 1973 by the Suharto regime through to the collapse of that regime in May 1998, the PPP was directed to function as an Islamic party but forbidden from using Islamic imagery or promoting Islamist ideas. The Suharto regime had earlier moved to block new incarnations of the Sukarno-era modernist Masyumi party, banned by Sukarno in 1960 because of its association with regional rebellions, fearing the Islamist ambitions of its key leaders. As Robert W. Hefner explains, after the 1971 elections, the regime disbanded Indonesia's nine opposition parties, including the NU, and replaced them with one Islamic party, the PPP, and one secular nationalist party, Partai Demokrasi Indonesia (PDI, the Indonesian Democracy Party). It is hardly surprising then that in the post-Suharto period, the PPP has relished the freedom to adopt, even if only nominally, an Islamist platform and to use Islamic symbols.

In the 1999 elections, the PPP achieved 10.7 percent of the national parliamentary vote. In the 2004 elections, this dropped to 8.2 percent, but the PBR, which had recently splintered from the PPP, achieved 2.4 percent, suggesting that total support for this stream of moderate Islamist politics was stable. As can be seen in Table 1, the total support for radical Islamist parties in these two elections was of a similar level with the Partai Keadilan Sejahtera (PKS, the Prosperous Justice Party), a direct successor to the Partai Keadilan (PK, the Justice Party), and the Partai Bulan Bintan

(PBB, the Crescent Moon and Star Party), respectively attracting 7.3 percent and 2.6 percent of the vote in the 2004 elections. In the same election, the two large Islamic mass-based parties with explicitly non-Islamist platforms—the traditionalist-orientated Partai Kebangkitan Bangsa (PKB, the National Awakening Party) and the modernist-orientated Partai Amanat Nasional (PAN)—achieved 10.6 percent and 6.4 percent respectively of the national vote.

In 1999 the two large nonreligious parties, often referred to as secular-nationalist parties, Golkar and Partai Demokrasi Indonesia Perjuangan (PDIP, the Indonesian Democracy Party of the Struggle, a successor to PDI), achieved 56.1 percent of the total national vote. In 2004 the (now four) large secular nationalist parties achieved 49.7 percent. This included the new Democratic Party (Partai Demokrat, PD) of Susilo Bambang Yudhoyono, who replaced Megawati Sukarnoputri as president. In 2004 PD and a plethora of small parties gained the support of voters who turned away from Megawati's PDIP. The non-Islamist Islamic parties (PKB and PAN) gained 19.7 percent of the national vote in 1999 and 17.0 percent in 2004, whereas the Islamist parties achieved 18.0 percent and 20.9 percent. The remaining vote went to the numerous small, non-Islamic (including several Christian) parties contesting the elections. This means that the total vote for all Islamic parties was 37.7 percent in 1999 and 38.7 percent in 2004. These more recent figures match the figures for the 1955 elections surprisingly closely.

The 1955 election was the only one conducted during the reign of President Sukarno (1949–65). As can be seen in Table 2, four large parties attracted almost 80 percent of the total vote, split almost equally between two large nonreligious parties and two large Islamic parties (38.7 percent and 39.3 percent respectively). Partai Komunis Indonesia (PKI, the Communist Party of Indonesia) and Partai Nasionalis Indonesia (PNI, the Nationalist Party of Indonesia) received 16.4 percent and 22.3 percent respectively, with the NU and Masyumi receiving 18.4 percent and 20.9 percent of the total national vote.

What these figures suggest is that despite a 44-year hiatus between free and fair elections in 1955 and 1999 and the enormous social and political changes over the life of this young nation, voting patterns scarcely changed at all when it came to choosing between Islamic and non-Islamic parties. What is not clear is whether the electoral appeal of Islamism has changed significantly. Whereas the Islamist/non-Islamist split in the Islamic party vote is clear in the 1999 and 2004 results, the proportion of 1955 voters for the NU and Masyumi who supported Islamism is unknown. At the time of these elections, the NU and Masyumi both had what would now be called pro- and anti-Islamist factions, but these were not clearly defined. Cultural and religious factors, together with key leaders' positions, suggest that support for radical Islamism was much stronger in Masyumi than it was in the NU, but there is no way to quantify this.

With around one in five Indonesian voters supporting Islamist parties in the free and fair elections held before and after the period of the Suharto regime, Islamism can be said to have enjoyed greater success in Indonesia than in most other open democracies in the Muslim world.

Islamic Modernism

It is impossible to understand both the enduring appeal of Islamism in Indonesia and its limits without first understanding the history of Islamic modernism. This is because virtually all radical Islamist groups and leaders in Indonesia have arisen out of modernist organizations or have in some other way been directly shaped by modernism. This is true also for radical Islamist political parties such as the PKS and PBB.

The Islamic modernist movement associated in the late nineteenth and early twentieth centuries with the Egyptian scholar Muhammad Abduh had enormous influence on the development of Islamic thought and social movements in Indonesia. Indeed, the Islamic modernist movement has been more influential there than in virtually any other country.

It seems likely that Islamic modernism came to Indonesia through two channels: students who had been at Al-Azhar University in Cairo, where Abduh (1849–1905) was teaching; and others studying in Mecca and Medina influenced by Abduh's disciple, Rashid Rida (1865–1935). After Abduh's death in 1905, Rida, via his magazine *al-Manar* (*The Lighthouse,* published 1898–1935), was a very strong source of influence on the development of modernist thought in Indonesia. Over the next century, Islamic modernism in Indonesia was caught between two poles: the progressive religious thought of Abduh and the politically orientated thought of Rida. As they were published, the writings of Pakistan's Mawdudi joined Rida's essays in shaping thinking about an Islamic state and a distinctly Islamic approach to modernity in Indonesia.

Islamic modernism first established itself within the newly emerging urban white-collar and petit bourgeois communities of Javanese cities such as Yogyakarta. It was there that in 1912 the Islamic scholar Ahmad Dahlan (1868–1923) founded the Muhammadiyah, a new mass-based Islamic

Table 1

Performance of Major Parties in the 1999 and 2004 Elections

Big Parties	Leader/Key Figure	Orientation	Notes	1999 % Votes	1999 Seats* 462+38	2004 % Votes	2004 Seats 550
Golkar	Wiranto/ Tandjung	Secular nationalist	Indonesia-wide	22.4	118 (21.5 %)	21.6	128 (23.3 %)
PDIP	Megawati	Secular nationalist	Java/Bali strength	33.7	151 (30.2 %)	18.5	109 (19.8 %)
Partai Demokrat	Susilo B. Yudhoyono	Secular nationalist	Indonesia-wide	—	—	7.5	57 (10.4 %)
PDS		Secular nationalist	Christian party	—	—	2.1	12 (2.2 %)
			Subtotal of large secular nationalist parties	56.1	269 (53.8 %)	49.7	306 (55.6 %)
PKB	A. Wahid	Pluralist Islam NU masses	Dependent on Wahid (Gus Dur)	12.6	51 (10.2 %)	10.6	52 (9.5 %)
PAN	Amien Rais	Pluralist Islam Muhammadiyya	Now arguably less liberal	7.1	34 (6.8 %)	6.4	52 (9.5 %)
			Subtotal of secular Islamic parties	19.7	85 (17.0 %)	17.0	104 (18.9 %)
PPP	Hamza Haz	Moderate Islamist	Radical Islamist element	10.7	58 (11.6 %)	8.2	58 (10.5 %)
PBR	Zainuddin MZ	Moderate Islamist	Breakaway from PPP	—	—	2.8	13 (2.4 %)
PBB	Yusril Mahendra	Radical Islamist	Yusril influential in cabinet 1999–2005	1.8	13 (2.6 %)	2.6	11 (2.0 %)
PKS	Hidayyat Nur Wahid	Radical Islamist	Renamed; previously PK	1.3	7 (1.4 %)	7.3	45 (8.2 %)
			Subtotal of Islamist parties	13.8/18**	78 (15.6 %)	20.9	127 (23.1 %)
			Total of all Islamic parties	37.7**	163 (32.6 %)	38.7	231 (42.0 %)
			Grand total of all major parties***	89.6	432 (86.4 %)	88.4	537 (97.6 %)

Source: Greg Barton, *Indonesia's Struggle: Jemaah Islamiyah and the Soul of Islam* (Sydney: UNSW Press, 2004), 72–73. Reproduced with permission of the University of New South Wales Press.

* Elected representatives, 462, and TNI appointees.

** Totals, including minor party organizations. See note below for further explanation.

*** Grand totals do not add to 100% because, for the sake of clarity, the many very small minor parties have been left out of the table.

Note: The subtotal for Islamist parties, 13.8%, is the sum of the votes gained in 1999 by the PBB, PK, and PPP (the major Islamist parties). However, in 1999, small parties captured a much larger share of the vote, when 48 parties competed in the election, than they garnered in 2004, when parties that achieved less than 2% of parliamentary seats in 1999 were excluded; hence, the PK was reinvented as the PKS. The subtotal for Islamist parties of 18% reflects the sum of the vote that was gained in 1999 by the PBB, PK, PPP, and 15 very small parties. This support appears to have been given to the PKS in 2004. This last point is important because it suggests that while no doubt many voters in 2004 supported the PKS owing to the party's clean, professional image, most did so because of its radical Islamist agenda. Some of the 2004 backers of the PKS had voted for smaller radical Islamist parties in 1999. In 2004 there was one other Islamist party, the Indonesian United Awakening of the Islamic Community Party (Partai Persatuan Nahdlatul Umma Indonesia, PPNUI), a new party, contesting the general elections; it achieved 0.78% of the votes but was not able to secure a parliamentary seat.

Table 2

Performance of Major Parties in the 1955 Elections Compared with Their Successor Parties in the 1999 and 2004 Elections

1955		1999		2004	
Party	Results (%)	Party	Results (%)	Party	Results (%)
NU traditionalist	18.4	PKB	12.6	PKB	10.6
		PPP	10.7	PPP	8.2
				PBR	2.4
Masyumi Modernist	20.9	PAN	7.1	PAN	6.4
		PK	1.4	PKS	7.3
		PBB	1.9	PBB	2.6
PNI nationalist	22.3	PDIP	33.8	PDIP	18.5
		Golkar	22.5	Golkar	21.6
				PD	7.5
PKI Communist	16.4	—	—	—	—

organization committed to philanthropy and reform of Islamic thought and society. However, few of the businessmen and clerks who made up the rapidly swelling ranks of the Muhammadiyah had either the intellectual training or inclination to build on the foundation laid by Abduh. Instead, they focused on practical projects such as building a network of modern "secular" schools, orphanages, health clinics, and hospitals. The major theological innovation was to turn away from the many traditional practices that sought to bridge the worlds of the living and the dead while at the same time stressing a common-sense rationality that embraced modernity, modern education, and urban culture.

A small number of Javanese ulama joined their colleague in the Muhammadiyah's modernist project. Most, however, did not. They were caught between admiration for the rapid and fruitful growth of the Muhammadiyah as a modern organization clearly achieving an immense amount of practical good and the concern that the Muhammadiyah's reform project would threaten the *pesantren* (residential *madrasa*) that formed the base of their social networks. It was not so much that they disagreed with the idea of modernizing per se but rather that they were concerned that the Muhammadiyah's opposition to "non-Islamic superstition" involved the rejection of even the most orthodox approaches to *tasawwuf,* or Sufism.

At the same time, they were appalled by the modernists' lack of regard for not just tasawwuf but classical Islamic scholarship in general. In 1926 a group of prominent ulama drew on their informal social networks linking individual ulama and their pesantren communities to launch a mass-based Islamic organization called Nahdlatul Ulama, the awakening of the ulama. Nahdlatul Ulama, or NU as it is typically known, followed certain aspects of the Muhammadiyah while at the same time consolidating and strengthening the pesantren networks to ensure a long-term future for the pesantren and for classical Islamic scholarship in Indonesia.

The Muhammadiyah and Nahdlatul Ulama have succeeded in becoming two of the largest religious organizations in the Muslim world. Today, it is estimated they have somewhere between 30 and 40 million supporters respectively. In the first decades of the century, traditionalists outnumbered modernists by a much greater extent than these numbers suggest. It is a measure of the Muhammadiyah's success in modern schooling and urban social networks that its membership came to rival that of the NU's populous rural base.

The Muhammadiyah is not, however, the only modernist organization in Indonesia. In 1915, three years after the formation of the Muhammadiyah, the Sudan-born scholar Ahmad Surkati established Jam'iyat al-Islah wal-Irshad (the Community for Reform and Guidance), better known simply as al-Irshad. Whereas the Muhammadiyah began as, and has remained, an essentially moderate movement seeking to balance modernism's Salafi reformism with Abduh's "neo-Mu'tazilis" rationalism, al-Irshad was from the outset a much more reactionary organization. Al-Irshad's membership was substantially rooted in Java's predominantly Hadrami ethnic Arab community. This gave it a solid foundation but also limited its growth and influence. Nevertheless, al-Irshad's madrasas in Jakarta, Surabaya, Surakarta/Solo, Tegal, and Malang exercised significant influence in Salafi pan-Islamist—later radical Islamist—circles.

Al-Irshad was joined eight years later, in 1923, by Persis (Persatuan Islam, the Islamic Union), another Salafi organization that grew to exert an influence out of all proportion to its modest membership base. The leader (although not the founder) of Persis was A. Hasan, an ethnic Tamil *alim* born in Singapore. Hasan established the influential conservative madrasa Pesantren Persis in Bangil, East Java, where future Laskar Jihad leader Ja'far Umar Talib spent two years as a student, according to Saiful Umam.

Both al-Irshad and Persis can be understood as Islamic modernist organizations

closer to the spirit of Rida than Abduh. They were also influenced by the iconoclastic reformism of the Arabian peninsula's Wahhabi movement, very much a rising force in the first few decades of the twentieth century.

When Abd al-Aziz bin Sa'ud took over the two holy cities of Medina and Mecca in 1924 and 1926 and his Wahhabi allies cleaned them of places of private prayer and objects of veneration, Salafi Muslims saw it as a triumph for a newly purified and empowered Islam. Traditionalist Muslims everywhere, however, lamented the desecration of numerous ancient tombs and sites of pilgrimage. Even in distant Indonesia, this loss was acutely felt. In fact, the conquest of Medina and the impending conquest of Mecca led directly to the meeting that gave rise to the NU. In 1925 ulama from across Java began discussing how they should respond to the desecration in the holy cities. A delegation of ulama was eventually dispatched in 1928 to beseech Abd al-Aziz's intervention, but it was all to no avail.

Nevertheless, the crisis provided the catalyst for Indonesia's traditionalist ulama to join together in a modern organization. The January 1926 meeting convened between 12 prominent ulama to plan the ineffectual Hijaz delegation, as it was known, gave birth to a new association of ulama: Nahdlatul Ulama, a social network that was to become one of the largest Islamic mass organizations in the world.

Influence of Wahhabism

In the early nineteenth century, well before the advent of Islamic modernism in Indonesia and the emergence of the Saudi kingdom, Wahhabi ideas transmitted by scholars returning from Arabia made a profound impact on Islamic thought and behavior in the ethnic Minangkabau region of West Sumatra. There, Wahhabi reformism contributed to the emergence of the militant Padri movement that opposed both local custom (*adat*), with its distinctive matrilineal elements, and Dutch colonial rule. However, while the Padri movement was confined to West Sumatra, the influence of Wahhabism in Indonesia after the conquest of Mecca and Medina a century later was much more pervasive.

The rise of Wahhabi Salafism in the heart of the Muslim world in the 1920s and 1930s was no less consequential for the Muhammadiyah and Indonesia's modernists. Ahmad Dahlan died in 1923. The much-admired teacher was only in his mid-fifties and left a void in the Muhammadiyah's intellectual leadership. Few of the organization's senior figures shared his background and scholarly expertise. Even fewer shared his understanding of, and commitment to, Abduh's progressive ideas. From this point forward, the small number of Muhammadiyah leaders who were qualified ulama became increasingly dominated by scholars returning from studies in Mecca or Medina who had studied with Wahhabi teachers.

In 1929 the Muhammadiyah established the Tarjih Council, a board of religious scholars tasked with providing definitive legal rulings for the organization's million members. With the significant exception of a five-year period under the leadership of progressive intellectual Amin Abdallah in the late 1990s, the Tarjih Council has been a bastion of conservative Salafi thinking. In its philanthropic initiatives, social activism, and organizational structure, the Muhammadiyah remained a modernist organization. Yet in its religious thought, it became a conservative movement shaped by Wahhabi Salafism.

This period also saw the Muhammadiyah, like the NU, drawn into the growing nationalist movement working toward independence. The combination of Wahhabi puritanism in religious thinking and anticolonial nationalism in political thinking naturally oriented the Muhammadiyah's leaders toward the newly emerging Islamist ideas of Pakistan's Abu al-Ala Mawdudi (1903–1979) and Egypt's Hasan al-Banna (1906–1949). In influential books published during the 1930s, Mawdudi developed ideas such as "theo-democracy" and laid the foundations for modern Islamism. In 1941 he founded Jama'at-i-Islami and gave the world a template for Islamist politics. In 1928 al-Banna and his friends founded the Muslim Brotherhood. The writings of Mawdudi and al-Banna and the growth of Jama'at-i-Islami and the Muslim Brotherhood exerted a powerful influence on the leaders of the Muhammadiyah, al-Irshad, and Persis.

Islamism in Independent Indonesia

Two days after Japan's surrender ended World War II—on August 15, 1945—Indonesian nationalists declared independence. The leaders of the Muhammadiyah, Persis, and al-Irshad assumed the vast majority of their members, and indeed all Indonesia's observant Muslims, favored an Islamic state. What happened next would be the first of a series of bitter disappointments and setbacks for Indonesia's Islamists.

Sukarno and the other nationalist leaders wanted a compromise that would allow leftist, secular non-Muslims (perhaps 10 to 20 percent of the population), nonobservant Muslims (possibly more than half the population), and Islamic political groups and communities to work together. A state philosophy was devised that would allow the new nation to be "theistic" without being sectarian. Known as Pancasila (the Sanskrit word means five precepts) and partly modeled on the Buddhist code of ethics of the same name, this statement spoke of belief in God, just and civilized humanity, the unity of Indonesia, deliberative democracy/government by the people, and social justice for all Indonesians. Moderate and progressive Islamic leaders, modernist and traditionalist alike, saw Pancasila as reflecting essential Islamic values while avoiding sectarian language. Islamists saw it as a sellout. Their outrage was compounded by a last-minute decision to dispense with a preamble containing a clause relating to the first precept.

The vital "seven words" of this preamble, known as the Jakarta Charter (*Piagam Jakarta*) added to "Belief in God" the words: "with the obligation for adherents of Islam to carry out Islamic law." They had been formulated as a way of making Pancasila more palatable to Islamists. It had been agreed that the Jakarta Charter was to accompany the constitution when it was revealed on August 18, 1945, the day after the formal declaration of independence. Isa Anshary, an outspoken Masyumi Islamist, proclaimed the dropping of the Jakarta Charter "a magic trick . . . an embezzlement against the Muslim stance," as cited by Adam Schwartz. Sukarno and his colleagues sought to balance the removal of the seven words by adding to the first precept of Pancasila the words: "belief in the one and only God." This was sufficient for many in the NU but did not appease the Islamists in the Muhammadiyah and the other modernist groups.

Initially, the vast majority of modernist and traditionalist *santri* Muslims agreed to join forces in Masyumi, an Islamic party established in 1943 by the Japanese occupation administration to harness local support. (*Santri* is derived from an ancient Sanskrit word and is the root of the Javanese word for a residential madrasa, *pesantren-santri* being students of a *pesantren*. By extension, it has come to be used to refer to pious, orthopraxis Muslims, a usage popularized by Clifford Geertz in *The Religion of Java*.) Masyumi's leaders expected that they would achieve a plurality of votes in the election. The Islamists who dominated the leadership, including the respected nationalist Muhammad Natsir (1907–1993), believed that the democratic process would lead steadily toward an Islamic state. These aspirations faced a series of setbacks throughout the course of the 1950s, the effects of which reverberate through to the present.

Throughout the bitter revolutionary struggle against the Dutch, from August 1945 to the nationalist victory on December 27, 1949, the Muhammadiyah, the NU, and the other mainstream Islamic groups worked together in Masyumi. With such a broad coalition united in a single party, it looked as if Masyumi would dominate the elections. However, in 1952 the NU leaders announced that they were leaving Masyumi to become a separate political party. The traditionalist politicians appeared to have grown tired of being treated as "dumb country cousins" by modernist colleagues. It is likely that differing convictions about Islam and the modern state, however, also contributed to the split. One of the NU's most brilliant leaders, Wahid Hasyim, had worked closely with Sukarno on the Investigating Body for the Preparation of Indonesian Independence, supporting both the thinking behind Pancasila and the dropping of the Jakarta Charter.

Wahid Hasyim, the one-time minister for religious affairs and son of NU founder

Hasyim Asyari, was a charismatic leader
and was well known for his pluralist convictions and opposition to the Islamist aspirations of Muhammad Natsir and other
Masyumi leaders. Tragically killed in an
automobile accident in 1953, Wahid Hasyim
was not around to participate in the 1955
elections and the debate that followed. His
eldest child, Abdurrahman Wahid, then just
12 years old, had been traveling in the car
with his father that day. Left with a strong
sense of responsibility to fulfill his father's
mission, Abdurrahman went on to lead the
NU from 1984 to 1999, contributing to a
cultural shift in the organization that saw
youths encouraged to embrace progressive,
pluralist ideas and tolerant, open-minded
engagement with broader society.

The 1955 elections proved a watershed
in the development of Indonesian political
culture. For the modernists the results came
as a bitter surprise, for they had expected to
achieve a good outcome with a mandate for
implementing Islamic politics. Not only had
the Islamic parties Masyumi and Nahdlatul
Ulama failed to achieve a plurality of the
vote, it was clear that they could not agree
on Islam's role in the Indonesian state. At
the same time, the Communist Party had
achieved an unexpectedly high vote, further adding to the general anxiety felt by
Islamists.

Yet it was not just the election results that
disappointed the Islamists in Masyumi and
Nahdlatul Ulama. As soon as voting concluded for the parliament, a second round
was held to elect a constitutional assembly,
or Konstituante. The 514 members elected
to the constitutional assembly, from across
the political and religious spectrum, worked
reasonably well. The assembly was bogged
down by debate, however, over the Jakarta
Charter and role of Islam in the Indonesian
state.

Islamist Parties Under the Sukarno Regime

In mid-1959, Sukarno announced that he
was dissolving the constitutional assembly,
just nine months before the deadline for its
conclusion. Its failure to achieve consensus
regarding Islam's role gave Sukarno an
excuse not only to dissolve the assembly
but also to make a major shift to "guided
democracy" in which he wielded dictatorial
powers. Other contributing factors included
unstable parliamentary governments, economic problems, and a series of militant
separatist movements.

The most serious challenge came from
the Darul Islam movement in West Sumatra
and southern Sulawesi. This movement had
begun when the Islamist militia in those
areas had been denied a place in the armed
forces of postrevolutionary Indonesia and
had responded by violently resisting the
central government. Although the military
threat posed by a Darul Islam was effectively contained by 1960, its social networks
continue to the present day.

Initially, because of a political and social
response to local issues, the movement
increasingly acquired a radical Islamist
cast. In November 1957 an assassination
attempt was made on Sukarno, missing
the president but killing 11 and wounding
many, as John D. Legge writes in his biography of Sukarno. Darul Islam was blamed
for the attack. In 1958 another separatist
movement emerged in West Sumatra and
southern Sulawesi. Although Masyumi and
its leader Muhammad Natsir had no direct
links with the Darul Islam movement, they
were perceived to be sympathetic to this
rebellion and were also accused of involvement in the attempted assassination.

Sukarno banned Masyumi in 1960, and
Islamists did not again participate in an elec-

tion until 1999. However, after an alleged Communist-backed coup attempt on October 1, 1965, as many as 500,000 supposed Communist supporters were killed during the course of the next year. Modernists in Masyumi and Muhammadiyah, together with traditionalists in the NU, were responsible for much of the killing, spurred on by both malice and fear.

Islamist Parties Under the Suharto Regime

The Masyumi modernists had expected that the new right-wing, military-backed regime under the leadership of General Suharto would welcome them as natural allies. Instead, when in 1967 they established Parmusi as a direct successor to Masyumi, they were met with immediate suspicion and hostility. Suharto's men intervened, making it clear that they would not tolerate participation by Muhammad Natsir and other former senior Masyumi leaders. Natsir formed a social organization devoted to religious missionary work, Dewan Dakwah Islamiyah Indonesia (Indonesian Council for Islamic Missions).

It was only in the late 1980s that Suharto began to ease up on the Islamists. During the 1970s and 1980s, his regime had jailed hundreds of Islamist militants and outspoken critics. However, by the early 1990s, many had been rehabilitated and invited to work with figures close to the government. The turning point came in 1990 as Suharto sought to gain wider popular support for his regime and to win the support of Islamic leaders. In 1991 he traveled to Mecca and Medina on pilgrimage for the first time. This went a long way toward persuading his erstwhile critics that the 70-year-old leader was finally becoming serious about his Islamic faith. The previous year Suharto had given the green light for the establishment

of the Indonesian Association of Muslim Intellectuals (ICMI, Ikatan Cendekiawan Muslim Indonesia). As a sign of his support, he appointed his protege and long-serving minister of technology and research B.J. Habibie as chairman of ICMI when it was launched in December 1990.

Some very credible progressive Islamic thinkers such as Nurcholish Madjid and Dawam Rahardjo were involved in formulating the initial concept for the new organization. Nevertheless, many progressive Islamic intellectuals such as Abdurrahman Wahid and other religious and social leaders were concerned that ICMI represented a cynical bid by Suharto to rebuild his populist base using Islam. They feared that Suharto was unleashing forces that ultimately he would not be able to control. As it happened, while ICMI did result in the rehabilitation of many former critics, including both moderate and radical Islamists, the Islamists gained very little directly from involvement with ICMI.

Suharto spent the first half of the 1990s attempting to neutralize Abdurrahman Wahid's outspoken criticism of his attempts to woe the Islamists. By late 1996, Suharto had succeeded in getting Abdurrahman to seek a rapprochement with him and to refrain, at least for a while, from further public criticism. Yet by late 1997 Wahid was joined by Amien Rais in leading a broad popular movement calling for Suharto's resignation. Rais, chairman of the Muhammadiyah, had been expelled from ICMI early that year but became even more vocal in his critique of the Suharto regime, especially after the effects of the Asian economic crisis began to be felt in Indonesia in the second half of 1997. In the end, it was Amien Rais, Nurcholish Madjid, and Abdurrahman Wahid who led the public call for Suharto's resignation.

Islamist Parties Post-Suharto

Immediately after the resignation, preparations commenced for elections the following year. Several new political parties were formed, including a large number of small radical Islamist parties. Amien Rais, who had been expected to lead the moderate Islamist PPP, was instead persuaded to lead PAN, the new non-Islamist Muslim party. Abdurrahman Wahid, concerned that NU votes would automatically flow to PPP, formed PKB, a traditionalist counterpart to the mainly modernist-supported PAN. The most significant radical Islamist party, PK (later to become PKS), came to inherit the mantle of Masyumi. It was the product of religious instruction groups inspired by the Muslim Brotherhood, building social networks on secular university campuses. Nevertheless, it can be argued that Natsir's generation was responsible for the initial socializing of radical Salafi Islamism though groups such as Dewan Dakwah.

When Natsir started Dewan Dakwah, the organization was reasonably moderate, although clearly coming from a Salafi Islamist position and openly receiving support from the Saudi Arabia–based Muslim World League. Over the years, however, Dewan Dakwah grew steadily more reactionary. This extreme element established the Committee for Solidarity with the Islamic world (KISDI) in 1987.

Still, by 1987 it was clear that Islamist party politics held little appeal to the generations of Indonesian Muslims who had grown up since Masyumi. Lukman Harun, one of the initiators of KISDI, recognized that while young Muslims had little passion for reviving Masyumi, they were passionately concerned about the fate of the Palestinians. A decade later, KISDI gave rise to a new group with links to Dewan Dakwah, known as KOMPAK.

Whereas in the run-up to the 1955 elections, neither Masyumi nor the NU had decided within themselves on a clear position regarding the relationship between Islam and the state, in the 1999 and 2004 elections, the heirs to the tradition of the Islamic parties of the 1950s had split over Islamism. PPP and PK/PKS, together with PBB and a series of small parties, campaigned on an explicitly Islamist agenda. In the other camp, PAN and PKB adopted a secular nationalist ideology, explicitly rejecting Islamism while appealing to an observant Muslim base.

If PK/PKS was committed to the democratic process, the same cannot be said for some of the activities involving Dewan Dakwah. Many social commentators and religious leaders have been critical of the anti-Semitic, anti-Christian, and antiminority rhetoric of KISDI. Others, however, have argued that KISDI's rhetoric remains mere words and should not be regarded as truly threatening. Beginning in 1999, although it was only recognized years later, this rhetoric arguably formed a much more concrete threat than ever before. In late 1999, trainers from the terrorist group Jemaah Islamiyah traveled to Ambon in eastern Indonesia in the Maluku archipelago to set up training camps for mujahidin in anticipation of massive sectarian conflict. In 2000, when violence did indeed break out between Christian and Muslim communities, there were hundreds of local Muslims trained and equipped to fight. They were joined by thousands of mujahidin from Java who had come believing that their presence was required to defend against unprovoked attacks by Christians.

The reason that so many thousands of young Muslims believed this and were prepared for violent struggle was the result, in large measure, of their exposure to very effective propaganda videos produced by KOMPAK. The scene in Ambon in 2000 marked the point at which the sectarian propaganda of Dewan Dakwah and KISDI crossed the line dividing rhetorical hate speech from life-and-death violence. The fighting in Ambon and adjoining districts in Maluku was accompanied by similar violence in Sulawesi, the large island immediately west of the Maluku archipelago, in the port city of Poso in central Sulawesi. By the time the violence had largely ended in 2006, as many as 10,000 were dead and hundreds of thousands displaced, with consequent suffering.

In part, these events came out of the Suharto regime's collapse, resulting in a number of local groups feeling they could act violently without worrying about government intervention. They were also the result of a significant Muslim migration into those areas. That the population was split roughly evenly between Christian and Muslim communities contributed to a sense of threat. That thousands of mujahidin traveled to Ambon to fight resulted, in significant measure, from concerted efforts by KOMPAK to use propaganda campaigns to recruit and motivate.

Jemaah Islamiyah

At the time, scarcely anyone was aware of the existence of a well-organized network of several thousand jihadi terrorists across Indonesia and surrounding nations, now known as Jemaah Islamiyah (JI). It was only after the massive bomb attack in a district of Denpasar, Bali, popular with foreign tourists, claimed the lives of at least 202 people that JI became widely recognized. A team of local and international police were able to establish a link between the bomb-vehicle wreckage and the JI bombers. This led to the arrests of dozens—ultimately hundreds—of JI activists and to revelations about JI itself.

At the time of the violence in Maluku and Sulawesi in 2000 and 2001, the focus of attention was on Laskar Jihad rather than on JI and related groups such as Laskar Jundullah and KOMPAK. Laskar Jihad had emerged at the time of the violence as a jihadi militia led by a charismatic young Wahhabi scholar of Hadrami descent by the name of Ja'far Umar Talib. Disturbingly, the group appeared to have the support of some elements of the military, in keeping with a long-established pattern of the military clandestinely employing militia. The belligerent behavior of Laskar Jihad, which went as far as holding mass rallies in the large Merdeka square in front of the presidential palace, would have been unimaginable during the Suharto regime. During his administration from October 1999 to July 2001, President Wahid faced fierce opposition from both radical Islamists, who resented his pluralist stance and support of non-Islamic minorities, and military hardliners, who feared his reformist intentions.

Laskar Jihad, even with backing from renegade elements in the state apparatus, was ultimately to prove nowhere near as much a threat as JI was, despite very likely having killed more people. The former was a Wahhabi extremist militia, the latter a global jihadi terrorist network linked to al-Qa'ida. In keeping with Ja'far Umar Talib's loyalty to senior state ulama in Saudi Arabia such as Abd-al-Aziz bin Baz (1910–1999), who opposed jihadi violence directed against Muslim states, Laskar Jihad was a nationalist jihadi militia committed to upholding the Indonesian state.

The Defenders of Islam Front (FPI) was also a nationalist militia that adopted the rhetoric of jihad but, unlike Laskar Jihad, was more of a nuisance—smashing bars and nightclubs in "antivice" raids—than a perpetrator of bloody jihad. Like Laskar Jihad, FPI claimed to be acting in the defense of the Indonesian state. JI, however, does not recognize the legitimacy of either the Indonesian state or its government. It is committed to destabilizing and eventually toppling both, along with the governments of neighboring states, to create a "caliphate."

The arrests following the 2002 Bali bombing began to reveal more about the group. It was formed in 1993, having been directly inspired by the militant breakaway wing of the Muslim Brotherhood in Egypt of the same name. When Abdallah Sungkar and Abu Bakar Ba'asyir announced the formation of JI in 1993, they did so to formally break with Darul Islam. Sungkar and Ba'asyir got together in the late 1960s when they formed a radical *dakwa* radio station in the city of Solo in central Java. In 1971, in the village of the Ngruki on the outskirts of Solo, they established a madrasa named Pesantren al-Mukmin. This became the base of their activities, and Ba'asyir continues to live and teach at this institution.

Several years later they were drawn into open engagement with other radical Islamists through an elaborate sting operation concocted by Suharto's intelligence czar, Ali Murtopo. They allowed themselves to become identified with a group called Komando Jihad. Mortopo and his colleagues in military intelligence told their contacts that their help was needed to battle a reemergent Communist threat. When the radical Islamists were identified, the government changed its stance and arrested Sungkar and Ba'asyir in 1978. The two were released on appeal several years later. Hearing news that they would be rearrested in 1985, they fled to Malaysia, stopping in Jakarta and Lampung, South Sumatra,

along the way to establish small religious communities.

To a considerable extent, Ali Mortopo's sting operation had backfired, and Sungkar and Ba'asyir emerged from jail with greater charismatic authority. They used their authority in Darul Islam circles while based in Malaysia to recruit mujahidin to fight against the Soviets in Afghanistan. By 1996, these totaled several hundred Southeast Asians. The JI's links with al-Qa'ida were established in Camp Sadda, the mujahidin training center established by Afghan mujahidin leader and confidant of Osama bin-Ladin, Abd al-Rasul Sayyaf, and its sister center, Maktab al-Khidmat in Peshawar, run by Abdallah Azzam, through which the Southeast Asian recruits were processed before being sent to Camp Sadda. In 1996 training shifted to a section of the Moro Islamic Liberation Front's main training complex, Camp Abu Bakar, in Mindanao, a move made possible through relations developed in Afghanistan. Soon after Suharto resigned in May 1998, Abdallah Sungkar and Abu Bakar Ba'asyir returned home to Ngruki. Sungkar died shortly afterwards of natural causes, and the less charismatic Ba'asyir took his place in leading JI.

In 2000 Ba'asyir held a national congress to launch a new group called Majlis Mujahidin Indonesia (the Indonesian Mujahidin Council), intended to link underground jihadi groups with other radical Islamist groups and political parties. Many within JI disagreed with Ba'asyir's strategy, and a younger clique pushed ahead with a strategy of bombing spectaculars targeting foreign elements in Indonesia. JI carried out a series of attacks throughout 2000, including an assassination attempt on the Philippines' ambassador and a series of well-coordinated small bomb attacks at Christian churches on Christmas Eve. It was not until the Bali bombing of October 12, 2002, however, that the authorities became aware of the group's presence.

On August 5, 2003, JI launched another bombing attempt at the JW Marriott Hotel in Jakarta. The attack was only partially successful. A year later, on September 9, 2004, JI's Azahari Husin and Nur al-Din Muhammad Top launched another largely unsuccessful attack involving a vehicle bomb, this time in front of the gates of the Australian embassy. The suicide bombers involved appear to have been directly recruited from Darul Islam circles by Top and not to have any connection with mainstream JI. A year later, on October 1, 2005, JI used pedestrian suicide bombers in bomb attacks at beachside tourist cafes in Bali.

JI continues to be surprisingly resilient even though it would appear that its strength has declined from a peak of several thousand members down to about 1,000 militants. Even though more than 300 arrests have greatly disrupted the group's capacity for large-scale attacks, there seems little reason to doubt that JI represents an enduring threat. Recognizing the futility of staging bombing spectaculars, JI now appears to have gone to ground, awaiting more favorable circumstances. Even in Poso, where it had enjoyed considerable success in sustaining sectarian conflict through the first half of the decade, it now finds it difficult to operate. It is instructive to note, however, that one of the key JI trainers (a graduate of the full three-year course in Camp Sadda), who established the JI training camps in Ambon in 1999 and who continues to train radical Islamist groups in Jakarta, is the son of one of the men who, half a century ago, attempted the assassination of president Sukarno at

Cikini in 1957, as revealed to the author in a November 2007 interview.

Indications for the Future

The development of stable democratic politics in Indonesia arguably goes a long way toward moderating Islamic politics and containing radical Islamism. PKS, the party that achieved the highest number of votes in big cities such as Jakarta in the 2004 parliamentary elections, is finding it harder and harder to maintain its profile as a clean and honest political party free of the compromises that plague other parties. At the same time, there is reason to believe that the experience of being in government will cause it to moderate its views. According to internal documentation, the party is committed to moving beyond democracy and the Indonesian state to achieve a pan-Islamic theocracy. Some PKS leaders, however, are now backing away from this radical position.

Meanwhile, the party is facing stiff competition from Hizb al-Tahrir for the hearts and minds of Indonesia's newly pious Muslims. Hizb al-Tahrir was established in Indonesia around 1982 by visitors from Australia with links to London and Jordan. It appears to be enjoying considerable success. A large public rally for Hizb al-Tahrir in Jakarta on August 12, 2007, drew about 100,000 supporters.

Yet, so long as the Indonesian economy continues to grow and the Indonesian government remains stable and open, it seems likely that radical Islamism will fail to build the popular support needed to shift Indonesia off its course of sustaining an open, tolerant, plural, and moderate Islam at home in a secular state. Islamism in all its guises, however, will remain a significant presence in Indonesia's political, social, and religious landscape for the foreseeable future.

BIBLIOGRAPHY

Abuza, Zachary. *Political Islam and Violence in Indonesia*. London: Routledge, 2007.

Azra, Azyumardi. *The Origins of Islamic Reformism in Southeast Asia: Networks of Malay-Indonesian and Middle Eastern "Ulama" in the Seventeenth and Eighteenth Centuries*. Sydney: Allen & Unwin, 2004.

Barton, Greg. *Abdurrahman Wahid, Indonesian President, Muslim Democrat: A View from the Inside*. Sydney and Honolulu: UNSW Press and University of Hawaii Press, 2002.

———. *Indonesia's Struggle: Jemaah Islamiyah and the Soul of Islam*. Sydney: UNSW Press, 2004.

———. "Islam and Democratic Transition in Indonesia." In *Religious Organizations and Democratization: Case Studies from Contemporary Asia*, ed. Deborah A. Brown and Tun-jen Cheng, 221–41. Armonk, NY: M.E. Sharpe, 2006.

———. "Islam, Islamism and Politics in Post-Soeharto Indonesia." In *Islam and Politics in Indonesia*, ed. Damien Kingsbury. Melbourne: Monash University Press, 2004.

———. "The Origins of Islamic Liberalism in Indonesia and its Contribution to Democratisation." In *Democracy in Asia*, ed. Michelle Schmigelow. New York: St. Martin's Press, 1997.

Barton, Greg, and Greg Fealy, eds. *Nahdlatul Ulama, Traditional Islam and Modernity in Indonesia*. Clayton, Australia: Monash Asia Institute, 1996.

Bubalo, Anthony, and Greg Fealy. *Between the Global and the Local: Islamism, the Middle East, and Indonesia*. Analysis Paper No. 9. The Brookings Project on U.S. Policy Towards the Islamic World. Washington, DC: The Saban Center for Middle East Policy at the Brookings Institution, 2005.

Boland, B.J. *The Struggle of Islam in Modern Indonesia*. The Hague: Martinus Nijhoff, 1971.

Diederich, Mathias. "A Closer Look at Dakwah and Politics in Indonesia: The Partai Keadilan." *Archipel* 64 (2002): 101–15.

Dobbin, Christine. *Islamic Revivalism in a Changing Peasant Economy*. London: Curzon Press, 1983.

Effendy, Bachtiar. *Islam and the State in Indonesia*. Singapore: ISEAS, 2003.

Eliraz, Giora. *Islam in Indonesia: Modernism, Radicalism and the Middle East Dimension*. Brighton, UK: Sussex Academic Press, 2004.

Esposito, John, ed. *Political Islam: Revolution, Radicalism or Reform?* London: Lynne Rienner, 1997.

Fealy, Greg. "Hizbut Tahrir in Indonesia: Seeking a 'Total' Muslim Identity." In *Islam and Political Violence: Muslim Diaspora and Radicalism in the West*, ed. Shahram Akbarzadeh and Fethi Mansouri, 151–64. London and New York: I.B. Tauris, 2007.

———. "Militant Java-based Islamist Movements." In *A Handbook of Terrorism and Insurgency in Southeast Asia*, ed. Andrew Tan, 63–76. Cheltenham, UK: Edward Elgar, 2007.

Fealy, Greg, and Aldo Borgu. *Local Jihad: Radical Islam and Terrorism in Indonesia*. Canberra: Australian Strategic Policy Institute, 2005.

Federspiel, Howard M. *Islam and Ideology in the Emerging Indonesian State: The Persatuan Islam (Persis) 1923–1957*. Leiden, Netherlands: Brill, 2001.

Geertz, Clifford. *The Religion of Java*. New York: Free Press, 1960.

Hasan, Noorhaidi. *Laskar Jihad: Islam, Militancy, and the Quest for Identity in Post-New Order Indonesia*. Ithaca, NY: Cornell Southeast Asia Program, 2006.

Hefner, Robert W. *Civil Islam: Muslims and Democratization in Indonesia*. Princeton, NJ: Princeton University Press, 2000.

———. "Islam, State, and Civil Society: ICMI and the Struggle for the Indonesian Middle Class." *Indonesia* 56 (October 1993): 1–35.

———. "Islamization and Democratization in Indonesia." In *Islam in an Era of Nation States: Politics and Religious Revival in Muslim Southeast Asia*, ed. Robert W. Hefner and Patricia Horvatich, 75–127. Honolulu: University of Hawaii Press, 1997.

———. "Print Islam: Mass Media and Ideological Rivalries in Indonesian Islam." *Indonesia* 64 (October 1997): 77–103.

International Crisis Group. "Al-Qaeda in Southeast Asia: The Case of the 'Ngruki Network' in Indonesia." *Asia Briefing* 20 (August 8, 2002; corrected on January 10, 2003).

————. "'Deradicalisation' and Indonesian Prisons." *Asia Report* 142 (November 19, 2007).

————. "Impact of the Bali Bombings." *Asia Briefing* 23, 24 (October 2002).

————. "Indonesia: Jemaah Islamiyah's Current Status." *Asia Briefing* 63 (May 3, 2007).

————. "Indonesia: Tackling Radicalism in Poso." *Asia Briefing* 75 (January 22, 2008).

————. "Indonesia: Violence Erupts Again in Ambon." *Asia Briefing* 32 (May 17, 2004).

————. "Indonesia Backgrounder: How the Jemaah Islamiyah Terrorist Network Operates." *Asia Report* 43 (December 11, 2002).

————. "Indonesia Backgrounder: Jihad in Central Sulawesi." *Asia Report* 74 (February 3, 2004).

————."Indonesia Backgrounder: Why Salafism and Terrorism Mostly Don't Mix." *Asia Report* 83 (September 13, 2004).

————. "Jemaah Islamiyah in South East Asia: Damaged but Still Dangerous." *Asia Report* 63 (August 26, 2003).

————. "Recycling Militants in Indonesia: Dar ul Islam and the Australian Embassy Bombing." *Asia Report* 92 (February 22, 2005).

————. "Terrorism in Indonesia: Noordin's Networks." *Asia Report* 114 (May 5, 2006).

Jackson, Karl D. *Traditional Authority, Islam, and Rebellion: A Study of Indonesian Political Behavior.* Berkeley: University of California Press, 1980.

Jahroni, Jajang, et al. "Defending the Majesty of Islam: Indonesia's Front Pembela Islam (FPI) 1998–2003." *Studia Islamika* 11:2 (2004): 197–56.

Legge, John D. *Sukarno: A Political Biography.* Singapore: Achipelago Press, 2003.

Liddle, William R. "Media Dakwah Scripturalism: One Form of Islamic Political Thought and Action in New Order Indonesia." In *Intellectual Development in Indonesian Islam*, ed. Mark Woodward and James Rush, 71–107. Tempe: Center for Southeast Asian Studies, Arizona State University, 1996.

Mobini-Kesheh, Natalie. *The Hadrami Awakening: Community and Identity in the Netherlands East Indies 1900–1942.* Ithaca, NY: Cornell Southeast Asian Program, 1993.

Nakamura, Mitsuo. *The Crescent Arises over the Banyan Tree: A Study of the Muhammadiyah Movement in a Central Javanese Town.* Yogyakarta, Indonesia: Gadjah Mada University Press, 1983.

Noer, Deliar. *The Modernist Muslim Movement in Indonesia.* Kuala Lumpur: Oxford University Press, 1973.

Ramage, Douglas E. *Politics in Indonesia: Democracy, Islam and the Ideology of Tolerance.* London: Routledge, 1995.

Ressa, Maria. *Seeds of Terror: An Eyewitness Account of al-Qaeda's Newest Center of Operations in Southeast Asia.* New York: Free Press, 2003.

Salim, Agus. *Transnational Political Islam: The Rise of Hizb al-Tahrir in Indonesia.* MA Thesis, Monash University, 2007.

Salim, Arskal, and Azyumardi Azra, eds. *Shar'ia and Politics in Modern Indonesia.* Singapore: ISEAS, 2003.

Schwarz, Adam. *A Nation in Waiting: Indonesia's Search for Stability.* Singapore: Talisman Press, 2004.

Sirozi, Muhammad. "The Intellectual Roots of Islamic Radicalism in Indonesia." *The Muslim World* 95 (January 2005): 81–120.

Umam, Saiful. "Radical Muslims in Indonesia: The Case of Ja'far Umar Thalib and Laskar Jihad." *Explorations in Southeast Asian Studies* 6:1 (Spring 2006).

van Bruinessen, Martin. "Genealogies of Islamic Radicalism in Post-Suharto Indonesia." *South East Asia Research* 10:2 (2002): 117–24.

van Dijk, Cornelis. *Rebellion Under the Banner of Islam: The Darul Islam in Indonesia.* The Hague: M. Nijhoff, 1981.

Wilson, Ian Douglas. "The Changing Contours of Organised Violence in Post New Order Indonesia." Asia Research Centre Working Paper 118 (Murdoch University, April 2005).

The Philippines

S.P. Harish and Joseph Chinyong Liow

The southern Philippines has been the scene of a violent conflict waged by a group using Islamist rhetoric targeting local Christians as well as the national government. The question, however, is how important the Islamist factor is in shaping this issue. Numerous observers, such as Zachary Abuza and Peter Chalk, have characterized the conflict as one between Christians and Muslims. Nathan Gilbert Quimpo and others claim that religion has been the root cause of the strife for the last few decades. Greg Sheridan sees the strife as part of a global Islamic jihadi network.

Given the statements made by the radical groups, these conclusions are understandable. While the majority of the Moros, as the residents of the southern Philippines have traditionally been known, are Muslims, what is most interesting about the Philippines is the extent to which Islamist rhetoric has been used to mobilize forces in what is essentially a historical regional and ethnic conflict.

A Fragile Moro Identity

According to Rizal G. Buendia, before the Spanish arrived in the Philippines, Muslim communities in Sulu and Mindanao had already been flourishing for about 200 years. While we do not know the exact date of Islam's arrival in the Philippines, Carmen A. Abubaker explains that in addition to being spread by Muslim traders and later by missionaries, Islam also benefited from the arrival of political associations affiliated with the Islamic rulers of Sulu, Maguindanao, Lanao, Borneo, and the Moluccas.

It is important to note, as Barbara Watson Andaya and Yoneo Ishii state, that the Spanish, like the Portuguese, came to Southeast Asia with a mandate to spread Christianity in the region. When the Spanish landed, the Sulu and Maguindanao sultanates had very little influence in the central and northern Philippines. The spread of Christianity in these areas was thus met with little resistance. However, when the Spanish drive to evangelize the local population reached the southern areas, it was met with defiance. To the Spanish, the hostility of the Muslims in the Philippines reminded them of their confrontation with the North African Moors, hence their use of the term *moros* as a designation for Filipinos who resisted them. This resistance did not stop the Spanish from attempting to convert the Moros. They believed that once the Moros embraced Christianity, they would be loyal.

The Moro Wars, as they are known today, began in 1565. For two centuries, the Spanish and Moros fought each other with no clear winner. There was hardly religious unity among the Muslims, as Thomas M. McKenna argues. Instead, there was a deep factionalism along ethnolinguistic lines, involving the Badjao, Iranun, Jama-mapun, Kalagan, Kalibugan, Maguidanao, Maranao, Molbog, Palawani, Samal, Sangil, Tausug, and Yakan. Some of the Muslims also allied themselves with the Spanish to wage conflict against rival ethnic groups.

As far as the Moros were concerned, religion played a peripheral role in their conflict with the Spanish. It was only during the later part of the American occupation that the Moros increasingly began to assert a religious identity, and though this limited change, it did not eliminate their ethnolinguistic rivalries.

A Nascent Muslim Identity

The dynamics of the conflict changed in 1899 when the United States took over from the Spanish as the new colonizers of the Philippines. In the initial years of the U.S. occupation, there was a remarkable camaraderie between the Moros and the Americans, according to T.J.S. George, because the former saw the newcomers as an alternative to the establishment of a northern, Christian-dominated Filipino state. To combat the Filipino independence movement, which fought the United States between 1899 and 1901, the Americans signed the Bates Agreement in August 1899 with Sultan Jamalul Kiram II of Jolo, promising the security of the Moros in return for their support in fighting the Filipinos.

Once the Americans had subdued the Filipino opposition, however, they decided to assimilate the Moros into the larger Philippine state. In 1903 they established a Moro Province composed of the Zamboanga, Lanao, Cotabato, Davao, and Sulu districts, as explained by W.K. Che Man. The introduction of American models of administration was perceived by the Moros to be an erosion of their established local forms of governance. In particular, the antislavery law and the call to disarm the Moros met with some resistance from the local elites.

The administrative changes, though Western in nature, did not seek to convert the Moros to Christianity, as the Spanish had. Moro opposition was a response to centralization and a loss of traditional power. Just before World War I, the process of unification of the southern provinces into the Philippine state gained momentum. In 1913 the Department of Mindanao and Sulu replaced Moro Province. Increasingly, the administration of the Moro areas fell directly under Manila, sidelining many of the local elites in the process. In the 1920s the United States began to put in place a plan whereby the administration of the Philippines would be handed over to the Filipinos. This was a cause of great apprehension for the Moros, because they feared a return to Spanish-style Christian imposition.

Driven by these reservations, the Moros decided to petition the United States. Peter G. Gowing states that their initial appeals were for the governance of Sulu and Mindanao separately from the Philippine state. Nevertheless, the U.S. Congress approved the Tydings-McDuffie Act in 1934, giving the Filipinos full control over the affairs of the Philippine state. Moro leaders then drafted letters to the governor general and to U.S. president Franklin Roosevelt, expressing their concern over their religious freedom. The rejection of the petition led many Moros to assert their religious identity, and they began to persuade fellow Moros to accept being called Filipino-Muslims, writes Buendia.

Meanwhile, the centralization of administrative and legislative power in Manila continued during the period of the Philippine Commonwealth (1935–46). This inevitably led to the erosion of some customary forms of social structure in Sulu and Mindanao. For instance, the successor to Sultan Jamalul Kiram II was not recognized by the American administration. This period of American occupation contributed to the formation of a religious Muslim identity in the southern Philippines. There was a sense that a Filipino could only be considered to be Christian, and therefore, in order to distinguish themselves, the Moros had to include the appendage "Muslim" to their soon-to-be national identity.

As Samuel Tan argues, the religious identity formed during the American occupation was weak. Like the case of Moro resistance against the Spanish, religion was not the driving force in the Moros' confrontation with the Americans. Moro society was still divided along ethnolinguistic lines, and there was a deep sense of mistrust among the Muslims that stemmed from the primacy given to familial interests and allegiance to clans.

The creation of the Republic of the Philippines in 1946 led to the consolidation of power in Manila under the Filipinos. Similar to the situation in other countries in Southeast Asia, decolonization brought about the huge task of assimilating the Moros into the Filipino nation-state. The administrative integration took place during the 1950s. This resulted in Filipino Muslims being elected to both local and national levels of government, as described by Gowing. However, the Commission of Nation Integration (CNI) that was cre-

ated in 1957 to further integrate Filipino Muslims was not able to achieve its goals and was also mired in the misappropriation of funds, according to Che Man. Increasingly, Filipinos saw the term "Moros" as indicative of those who were "backward" and "stubborn."

Mohammed Ayoob asserts that the Muslims in the southern Philippines also shunned the rhetoric of Filipino nationalism and instead chose to associate themselves with the worldwide resurgence of Islam after World War II. According to Che Man, Sulu and Mindanao saw an influx of Islamic teachers from the Middle East, and prestigious universities such as al-Azhar offered scholarships to Filipino Muslims. The number of Islamic institutions in the southern provinces increased, and the local populace increasingly began identifying themselves as Bangsamoro. Meanwhile, the Philippine government, in an attempt to further assimilate Filipino Muslims, embarked on a policy of resettling other Filipinos in the southern provinces. The relocation attempt helped boost the economy of Sulu and Mindanao, but the economic inequalities between the Filipino Muslims and the Filipinos increased. However, Buendia asserts that for the most part, during the 20 years after independence, the legitimacy of the Filipino state was not questioned.

A Tenuous Bangsamoro Ethnic Identity

After President Ferdinand Marcos came to power in 1966, he initiated a series of efforts to improve relations with neighboring countries, including Malaysia, with whom relations had soured as a result of the Filipino claim over Sabah, as discussed by Lela Garner Noble. Manila long alleged that Sabah was once part of the Sulu sultanate and should now be part of the Philippine state. Its first formal claim was made in the early 1960s after Malaysia included Sabah as part of its federation. This resulted in a diplomatic spat between the two countries. Marcos was planning covert operations aimed at infiltrating Sabah. When the Moro recruits for this exercise mutinied, 28 of them were killed by the Philippine army. This incident, commonly referred to as the Jabidah Massacre, marked the beginning of the contemporary rebellion in the southern Philippines.

In reaction to the Jabidah episode, Udtog Matalam created a rebel group called the Muslim Independence Movement (MIM). While the group's name reflected the perception that the Jabidah incident was directed against Muslims, this particular slant was not viable. At the time, the nationalist sentiment of the Moros overruled their religious outlook. Very soon, the name of the organization was changed to the Mindanao Independence Movement. This change can be seen as an attempt to highlight the territorial rather than religious nature of the conflict. There was a struggle within the MIM over whether resistance against the Filipino government was shaped by religious or secular nationalist imperatives. Members such as Rashid Lucman leaned toward a religious rebellion, while younger leaders such as Nur Misuari were more secular in their ideological orientation. While the traditional religious elite was fighting on behalf of the Filipino Muslims, the secular leaders wanted the loyalty of the Bangsamoro people. Misuari went so far as to deride the Islamic religious elite, calling them adversaries of the Bangsamoros, according to George.

As Che Man explains, the disillusionment of the secular leaders of the MIM led them to create the Moro National Liberation Front (MNLF), with assistance from Malaysia. More than religious consciousness, it was

economic grievances that shaped MNLF ideology. According to one commander of the MNLF, as cited by Noble, the formation of the organization can be attributed to "the Corregidor Massacre, land grabbing, and the disappointment of the broad masses toward government failure to solve social, political and most of all, economic problems." In addition, the objective of the MNLF was not articulated as a defense of Muslims. Rather, it chose to identify with Moro ethnic identity. Nor has there been any evidence that the initial support provided by Malaysia to the MNLF was driven by religious coaffiliation. If anything, Malaysia's backing of the MNLF was driven by its perceived mistrust of the Marcos government.

The momentum of the resistance increased during the 1970s, when the MNLF was involved in a number of skirmishes with the Filipino government. According to Che Man, the dead and wounded in the Lanao provinces alone totaled 30,000 during the 1969 to 1976 period. Other provinces recorded many casualties. Cotabato witnessed 28,000 fatalities; Zambaoanga, 20,000; Basilan, 18,000; while Sulu and Tawi-Tawi registered 18,000 each. Malaysian and Libyan support for the MNLF was instrumental in sustaining the latter against the Philippine armed forces. Although Nur Misuari supported the secular agenda, he managed to play the religious card during his trips to Libya and to convince the Mu'amar Qadhafi government that Muslims in the southern Philippines were being oppressed by the central government. In return, Libya offered training and arms to the MNLF. It also used its influence in the Organization of the Islamic Conference (OIC) to put pressure on the Marcos government.

During the Fifth Islamic Conference of Foreign Ministers in Kuala Lumpur in 1974, Libya effectively lobbied for a resolution that acknowledged the MNLF as the sole representative of the people of the southern Philippines and encouraged the Marcos government to begin talks with them, Noble states. The internationalization of the conflict in the southern Philippines allowed the MNLF to gain formal recognition at the OIC during the Sixth Islamic Conference of Foreign Ministers in Jeddah in 1975. In short, the MNLF managed to ride the wave of Islamic consciousness and harness support from international Muslim organizations as an Islamist group in order to advance its nationalist objectives.

Under pressure from the OIC countries, Marcos launched a peace process with the MNLF in January 1975, according to Ivan Malloy. Libya kept a close watch over the proceedings, and in December 1976 both sides signed a peace accord, popularly known as the Tripoli Agreement. The accord retained the unity of the Filipino state while granting some autonomy to the southern provinces. While the central government kept control of defense and foreign affairs, the administration of education, finance, revenue, and security in thirteen provinces was conceded to local institutions, as Noble explains.

The euphoria soon subsided and both sides were divided over Article 16 of the Tripoli Agreement, which called for Manila to "take all necessary constitutional processes for the implementation of the entire Agreement." While the MNLF inferred this clause to be a decree from Marcos, the Philippine government wanted to hold a referendum. This impasse continued for many months, after which Marcos unilaterally decided to hold a referendum despite MNLF opposition. The MNLF did not want the plebiscite to be held, as it could mean an erosion of their legitimacy in those areas. This caused a lot of distrust and misgivings on both sides, and it was clear that neither side wanted to truly achieve peace.

Soon after, the MNLF decided to return to its old position of fighting for an independent state. By this time, Libyan support for the MNLF was waning, as Libya felt that the MNLF was unreasonable in its demands for independence. Libya made it apparent that it was no longer going to put pressure on the Philippines, and Marcos rejected the OIC as a mediator. In 1977 the MNLF resumed armed struggle, even as Nur Misuari exiled himself to the Middle East. While the OIC did attempt to revive the Tripoli Agreement, as of March 1980 the Marcos government considered the accord to be "lapsed" and also ignored the suggestion that the MNLF solely represented the Philippine Muslims, explains Noble.

Shortly after the collapse of the Tripoli Agreement, fissures began to appear in the MNLF ranks. According to the International Crisis Group's *Asia Report*, Hashim Salamat, who studied at al-Azhar University from 1959 to 1969, broke away from the MNLF. Hashim was more Islamic in orientation than Nur Misuari, and this led him to create another insurgent group, the Moro Islamic Liberation Front (MILF). According to Che Man, Dimas Pundato was another disgruntled leader who split with the MNLF; he created the MNLF-Reformist Group in March 1982. Attempts were made to unite the three factions under a common Islamic banner, but they ended in failure. In January 1983 the Muslim World Congress tried to bring the different blocs together, but all three leaders—Nur Misuari, Hashim Salamat, and Dimas Pundato—stayed away from the meeting.

A Divided Islamic Identity

The Moro Islamic Liberation Front (MILF) was officially formed in 1984 (although Hashim Salamat broke away from the MNLF as early as 1977). With its formation came an increasing focus on the religious nature of the conflict in the southern Philippines. The creation of an Islamic state was the ultimate objective of the MILF, and this ran directly counter to the nationalist agenda of the MNLF. To cement the religious nature of MILF leadership, Hashim Salamat ensured that clerics occupied key positions in the organization's hierarchy. In terms of political agenda, Hashim saw the 1976 peace deal between the Philippine government and the MNLF as having fallen short of his goal of a separate Islamic state. At the time, he had vowed to continue the resistance against the Philippine government.

Certainly, the creation of the MILF brought the religious cleavage in the conflict to the forefront. Yet, while the religious/secular divide between the MNLF and MILF is important, so are the different clan and class backgrounds of the two leaders. It is significant that Misuari is a nonelite Tausug; he studied at the University of Philippines and has a distinct leftist ideology. Hashim Salamat, conversely, had an elite Maguindanao background, as Mely Caballero-Anthony asserts.

In the last 20 years, the claim to represent the Moros has not been the exclusive domain of the MNLF and the MILF. According to Buendia, in 1991 Abdurajak Janjalani founded the Abu Sayyaf Group (ASG), or the Bearer of the Sword. Janjalani studied Islamic law in Saudi Arabia, received military training in Libya, and also fought in the war between Afghanistan and Russia. He pronounced that the mandate of the ASG was to protect Islam. After he was killed in battle in 1998, his brother, Khadafi Janjalani, became the head of the ASG. After the September 11 attacks, there were suspicions, cited by Rohan Gunaratna, that the ASG was colluding with al-Qa'ida. In

contrast, the MILF distanced itself from the ASG and, according to Buendia, labeled it a "group of bandits that has given Islam a bad name." Also significant is that, unlike the Maguindanao-led MILF, the ASG was composed of the Tausug and Sama groups.

In 1996 the MNLF signed a peace agreement with the Philippine government after four years of negotiations. However, peace was short lived when the MNLF again split in November 2001 to form a new group that called itself the Council of 15. With Misuari's power within the MNLF reduced to a symbolic status, the Council also managed to get official recognition from the Philippine government as the main representative of the Muslims in the southern Philippines. Yet a faction loyal to Nur Misuari broke away and formed the Misuari Breakaway Group in February 2005. This led to claims and counterclaims about who leads the "real" MNLF.

After Hashim Salamat's death in July 2003, factionalism within the MILF again threatened. His designated successor was Alim Abdulaziz Mimbantas, also a graduate of al-Azhar University, according to ICG Asia Report. However, Mimbantas was a Maranao and could not be seen as heading a Maguidanao-led group. Al-Haj Murad Ibrahim, however, was a Maguidanao and had considerable clout within the organization. After a brief power struggle with Mimbantas, Murad became the new MILF leader. In early 2006 rumors of yet another internal power struggle within the MILF surfaced, as reported by *Jane's Terrorism and Security Monitor.*

At the heart of the issue is which group represents the genuine interests of the Moros. The attempts so far can be seen as a quest to unite a disparate people under a common Moro umbrella. At times a nationalistic rhetoric was employed, and at others religion was used. The unity aspect is important, because the rebel organization that succeeds in this claim will be able to gain legitimacy to negotiate with the Philippine government. In the current period, the MILF has been engaged in peace talks since 1977, when Fidel Ramos initially brought them to the negotiating table.

The attacks of September 11 in the United States brought the issue of Islamism in the southern Philippines conflict to sharp focus. To the United States and the Armed Forces of the Philippines (AFP), there is little distinction between the ASG and the MILF because both of them largely espouse an Islamic agenda. Yet it is important to note that, as Chinyong Liow asserts, in contrast to the ASG, MILF has not echoed the Islamist agenda of regional terrorist organizations.

Basically, then, the conflict is based on a set of ethnic and regional issues, reinforced with the Muslim identity of the Moros. Some of those involved are Islamist, others use Islamism to promote their cause, and still others are relatively secular nationalists.

BIBLIOGRAPHY

Abinales, Patricio. *Making Mindanao: Cotabato and Davao in the Formation of the Philippine Nation-State.* Quezon City, Philippines: Ateneo de Manila University Press, 2000.

Abubakar, Carmen A. "The Advent and Growth of Islam in the Philippines." In *Islam in Southeast Asia: Political, Social and Strategic Challenges for the 21st Century*, ed. K.S. Nathan and Mohammad Hashim Kamali, 45–63. Singapore: Institute of Southeast Asian Studies, 2005.

Abuza, Zachary. *Militant Islam in Southeast Asia: Crucible of Terror.* Boulder, CO: Lynne Rienner, 2003.

Andaya, Barbara Watson, and Yoneo Ishii. "Religious Developments in Southeast Asia c. 1500–1800." In *The Cambridge History of Southeast Asia*, ed. Nicholas Tarling. Cambridge, UK: Cambridge University Press, 1999: 508–71.

Ayoob, Mohammed, ed. *The Politics of Islamic Reassertion.* London: Croom Helm, 1981.

Buendia, Rizal G. "The State-Moro Armed Conflict in the Philippines." *Asian Journal of Political Science* 13:1 (2005): 109–38.

Caballero-Anthony, Mely. "Revisiting the Bangsamoro Struggle: Contested Identities and Elusive Peace." *Asian Security* 3:2 (2007): 141–61.

Chalk, Peter. "Separatism and Southeast Asia: The Islamic Factor in Southern Thailand, Mindanao and Aceh." *Studies in Conflict and Terrorism* 24 (2001): 241–69.

Che Man, W.K. *Muslim Separatism: The Moros of Southern Philippines and the Malays of Southern Thailand.* Singapore: Oxford University Press, 1990.

George, T.J.S. *Revolt in Mindanao: The Rise of Islam in Philippine Politics.* Kuala Lumpur: Oxford University Press, 1980.

Gowing, Peter G. *Muslim Filipinos: Heritage and Horizon.* Quezon City, Philippines: New Day, 1979.

Gunaratna, Rohan. *Inside Al-Qaeda: Global Network of Terror.* London: C. Hurst, 2002.

Hall, D.G.E. *A History of Southeast Asia.* New York: St. Martin's Press, 1981.

Harish, S.P. "Towards Better Peace Processes: A Comparative Study of Attempts to Broker Peace with MNLF and Gam." Working Paper No. 77, Institute of Defence and Strategic Studies (2005).

ICG Asia Report. "Southern Philippines Backgrounder: Terrorism and the Peace Process." Singapore/Brussels: International Crisis Group, 2004.

Islam, Syed Serajul. "The Islamic Independence Movements in Patani of Thailand and Mindanao of the Philippines." *Asian Survey* 38:5 (1998): 441–56.

Liow, Joseph Chinyong. *Muslim Resistance in Southern Thailand and Southern Philippines: Religion, Ideology and Politics.* Washington, DC: East-West Center, 2006.

Majul, Cesar Adib. *Muslims in the Philippines.* Diliman, Quezon City: University of the Philippines Press, 1999.

————. "Theories of the Introduction and Expansion of Islam in Malaysia." *Silliman Journal* 11:4 (1964): 335–98.

McKenna, Thomas M. *Muslim Rulers and Rebels: Everyday Politics and Armed Separatism in the Southern Philippines.* Pasig City, Philippines: Anvil Publishing, 1998.

"MILF Internal Strains Arise." *Jane's Terrorism and Security Monitor,* March 24, 2006.

Molloy, Ivan. "The Decline of the Moro National Liberation Front." *Journal of Contemporary Asia* 18:1 (1988): 59–76.

Noble, Lela Garner. "The Moro National Liberation Front in the Philippines." *Pacific Affairs* 49:3 (1976): 405–24.

————. "Muslim Separatism in the Philippines, 1972–1981: The Making of a Stalemate." *Asian Survey* 21:11 (1981): 1097–1114.

Quimpo, Nathan Gilbert. "Options in the Pursuit of a Just, Comprehensible and Stable Peace in the Southern Philippines." *Asian Survey* 41:2 (2001): 271–89.

Ramos, Fidel V. *Break Not the Peace: The Story of the GRP-MNLF Peace Negotiations, 1992–1996.* Philippines: Friends of Steady Eddie, 1996.

Santos, Soliman M., Jr. *Peace Negotiations Between the Philippine Government and the Moro Islamic Liberation Front: Causes and Prescriptions.* Washington, DC: East-West Center, 2005.

Sheridan, Greg. "Jihad Archipelago." *National Interest* 78 (2004): 73–80.

Tan, Andrew. *Security Perspectives of the Malay Archipelago: Security Linkages in the Second Front in the War on Terrorism.* Cheltenham, UK: Edward Elgar, 2004.

Tan, Samuel. *Selected Essays on the Filipino Muslims.* Marawi City, Philippines: University Research Center, Mindanao State University, 1982.

CENTRAL ASIA

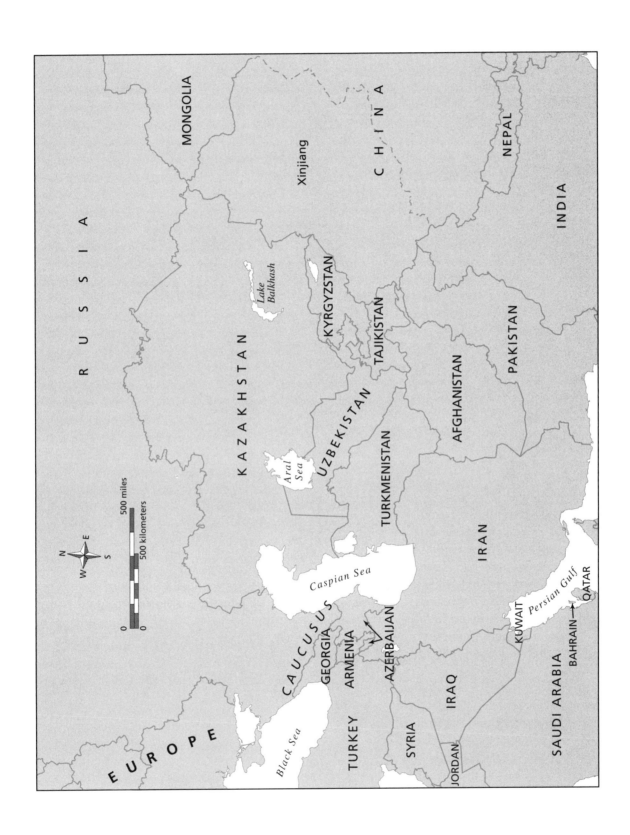

Central Asia

Zeyno Baran

There are five states in Central Asia: Kazakhstan, the largest, with a geographic area larger than that of Western Europe; Uzbekistan, the most populous, which contains over half the region's population; Tajikistan, which is still recovering from a devastating civil war in 1992–97; Kyrgyzstan; and Turkmenistan. Central Asia is located to the east of the Caspian Sea and to the immediate south of Russia. The region borders Afghanistan and Iran to the south and the Chinese province of Xinjiang to the east.

Historical Role of Islam

The historical role of Islam has been of considerable significance in Central Asia. First introduced to that region by the Arab incursions of the late seventh century, it was only in the ninth century that Islam emerged as the region's dominant faith. Enriched by the early influences of Zoroastrianism, Hinduism, Buddhism, and Shamanism, Central Asians came ultimately to accept the relatively liberal Hanafi School of Islamic thought. In comparison with the other three main Islamic schools (Shafi'i, Maliki, and Hanbali), the Hanafi School is the most accommodating of the pre-Islamic rituals and habits of the local population. Its adoption thus fostered social cohesion among the region's diverse populations. Central Asians also mostly follow the Matrudi school *aqida* (creed), which highlights the importance of belief rather than actions. In this setting, the *ulama* (senior clerics) served mainly as spiritual leaders—and did not adopt the political role played by their counterparts elsewhere in the Islamic world.

Early Islam in Central Asia

Soon after adopting Islam, Central Asians began making their own contributions to the religion, notably in the field of theology. The outstanding Islamic theologian Imam al-Bukhari was born in present-day Uzbekistan in 810 CE. Al-Bukhari collected and verified the authenticity of more than 600,000 *hadiths* (sayings and deeds of Muhammad) and recorded over 200,000 more. His collection, entitled "The Authentic Code," is regarded today by many Sunni Muslims as the most reliable Islamic source after the Koran itself. Such was his reputation that the great city of Bukhara was named in his honor. Today, Bukhari's tomb near Samarkand is an important place of pilgrimage.

In the fourteenth and fifteenth centuries,

Bukhara and Samarkand became major centers of Islamic scholarship and scientific learning. The "Uzbek Golden Age" was ushered in by the rule of Amir Timur (known to the West as Tamerlane) and his grandson, Ulugh Beg. Tamerlane was able to consolidate the various Central Asian kingdoms into a centralized and powerful state, with its capital in Samarkand. In the second part of the fourteenth century, he extended his reach outward, acquiring territory in Iran, the Caucasus, Syria, Iraq, Turkey, and northern India. Under the political and economic unity brought about by Tamerlane, the area covering most of contemporary Uzbekistan, Tajikistan, and Turkmenistan became one of the most important centers of Islamic civilization.

Nourished by an environment favorable both to scientific analysis and religious inquiry, the region produced many advances in both fields. In addition to his political accomplishments, Ulugh Beg also became a notable astronomer—whose discoveries were comparable to those of Copernicus. He plotted the positions of the moon, the planets, and over a thousand stars, and calculated the length of the year with almost perfect accuracy. As Robert Kaplan explains in *The Ends of the Earth*, these intellectual traditions were later carried on by other Islamic scholars, such as Abu Ali ibn Sina (known to Westerners as Avicenna), who is considered to be among the forefathers of modern medicine, and al-Khorezmi, who coined the terms "algebra" and "algorithm," and who is credited with helping to establish the Arabic numeral system and the use of decimal notation.

Sufism in Central Asia

The intellectual and cultural heights reached during this period were made possible in part by the richness and strength of Sufism. First appearing in Central Asia after 1258—following the Mongol conquest of Baghdad—Sufism rapidly accepted converts from a variety of religions while remaining tolerant of those who did not accept Islam. Bukhara became the principal center of the influential Naqshabandi Order—one of the oldest traditional Sufi orders still in existence.

Sufism spread much more rapidly than other Islamic traditions because of its openness and acceptance of other religions, as well as its emphasis on simplicity, piety, and purity. As Dr. Timothy Gianotti, a professor of religion at the University of Oregon, writes in "History, Theology and Orders," Sufism "preached with cultural sensitivity, promoted tolerance and inter-religious cooperation, and never abandoned the inner life and the spiritual core for the sake of solely political activism." Since its practices and traditions were spread predominately by merchants and traveling scholars, Sufism was able to gain a ready audience in both urban and rural areas.

For Sufis, the core value of Islam is righteousness (*al-ihsan*). Gianotti explains that this concept is understood to mean the "inner awareness or mental orientation that strives to place every moment of one's life in the presence of God; an awareness unobstructed by ego, vain imaginings, preoccupations with the past or the future and worldly distractions." Thus, for Sufis the goal of Islam is "to prepare the individual . . . for his or her ultimate encounter with the divine." This preparation takes the form of an intense personal struggle against human weakness. Only in striving for spiritual purity do Sufis wage jihad. The perversion of the term *jihad* to mean a struggle against non-Muslims is a recent one that would have been unknown to the Central Asian Muslims of the Golden Age.

With the gradual encroachment on the region of the Russian Empire and other powers, Sufi culture became much less prominent, although it was not eradicated. Despite the crushing of several Muslim uprisings against tsarist Russia during the nineteenth century, Islam survived in the Russian Empire and later in the USSR mainly because of the strength of Sufi networks, particularly that of the Naqshabandi Order.

Central Asian Islam Under the Soviet Union

Through the ruthless methods of the Red Army and the secret police, the Soviets suppressed organized religion throughout the regions it controlled—notably in Central Asia. Islamic networks became a particular target, because they were viewed as a potential challenge to Communist rule. In particular, the decade between 1920 and 1930 is remembered as the "cultural assault," in which the Soviets attempted to destroy the position of religion in daily life. New decrees banned Islamic education, public prayer, and other activities, and all *madrasas* and institutions of secondary and higher Islamic learning closed in the late 1920s (although the Naqshabandi Mir-i-Arab madrasa in Bukhara was reopened in 1946). Muslims were prevented from embarking on the hajj (one of the five pillars, or central duties, of Islam, it encompasses the pilgrimage to and acts of worship in Mecca, which should be completed at least once in a Muslim's lifetime), most mosques were closed, and the property of Islamic institutions was confiscated.

As a result of such repression, the size of the active Islamic community in Central Asia diminished substantially. For example, Charles Fairbanks explains that in Bukhara, the number of the ulama declined from 45,000 at the time of the Russian Revolution in 1917 to 8,000 by 1955. Sufis bore the brunt of this repression; Sufi Imam Shamil waged a successful military campaign against Russia in North Caucasus in the eighteenth century and became a very famous leader during the eighteenth and nineteenth centuries. Russian experience with Shamil in the North Caucasus led them to suppress all Sufi orders across the Soviet Union. Thus, one can speak of a resulting "loss of the collective memory of Sufism in Central Asia," as Alan Godlas asserts in "Sufism in Eurasia." Sufi leaders were arrested, and many were executed. Furthermore, the religious schools in which they transmitted knowledge were closed, and Sufi texts were banned. Muslim children were instead indoctrinated with anti-Islamic material as an integral part of Soviet educational policy. Information about Islam was thus transmitted only within the family, if at all.

However, these attempts to suppress Islam in Central Asia ultimately failed, because Muslims were able to practice their faith in a clandestine manner. Islamic movements thus became more resilient—and more politicized. The skills acquired during this period later became essential to the propagation of radicalism during the 1990s. They were used to great success by organizations such as Hizb al-Tahrir, a radical Islamist group that modernized and perfected this underground operating system.

Radicalization of the Islamic Revival

Gorbachev's perestroika reforms (literally "restructuring," specifically of the Soviet economic and government bureaucracies) marked the first major relaxation in decades in the religious lives of Soviet Muslims. This relaxation, implemented at a time when the Afghan mujahidin (fighters) were fighting Communists and the Soviet Union was experiencing internal pressures, resulted in the first signs of open disobedience to Soviet rule by Central Asian Muslims. In this period, First Secretary of the Uzbek Communist Party Sharof Rashidov even dared to demand a burial according to Islamic ritual. Mosques were restored and Islamic political parties openly emerged. An Islamic revival began to take place across Central Asia, as people returned to spiritual values following decades of Communist atheism.

However, this "Islamic revivalism" did not succeed in resurrecting the same spiritual and enlightened Islam of Central Asia's history. When the five Central Asian states achieved independence in 1991, there was little concrete understanding left of Islam. Nevertheless, there was a strong demand for mosques, especially in Uzbekistan, where only 89 existed at the close of the Soviet era. Within a year after independence, this number had risen to 5,000. Similarly, while there were only 119 religious institutes in 1990, after a decade the number had reached 2,000. However, as a result of the consequences of previous repression, there were insufficient numbers of native imams and Islamic scholars to meet the new demand for instruction about indigenous Islamic culture and traditions.

Foreign Islamist activists had begun smuggling literature into Soviet Central Asia via underground networks as early as the 1950s. In the 1970s, Muhammad Hindustani Rustamov, a highly respected theologian, noted that several members of the Uzbek clergy had begun gradually to adopt Wahhabi beliefs. This in part resulted from the assiduous efforts of the Muslim Brotherhood, which had been active in the country since the 1970s. The Brotherhood branch in Uzbekistan consisted of an ethnically diverse group of Muslim students from countries such as Jordan, Iraq, and Afghanistan. These students created the "Tashkent Group," which attempted to establish cells in universities. The goal was to recruit local members in the hope of someday establishing a caliphate. While at first they operated in a clandestine manner, these Islamists began to act more openly as the reforms of perestroika began to take hold. They were further emboldened by the Taliban takeover of Afghanistan in the 1990s.

Funded by the petrodollars of Wahhabist Saudi Arabia and other Gulf states, Islamist preachers flooded the region, filling the religious vacuum with their own radical religious interpretations. They gained control of mosques and religious institutes and worked actively to discredit those imams who practiced traditional Central Asian forms of Islam. These Islamists focused particularly on fighting and discrediting Sufism, viewing it (accurately) as a critical obstacle to their goals. Unfortunately, the vast majority of Central Asians were unaware of the existence (let alone of the significance) of differences between Islamic traditions; they accepted with eagerness any group that claimed to be teaching Islam. However, as the Uzbek saying goes, "When you open up the window for sun, dust comes in as well."

The Islamist radicals were able to succeed most of all because of the lack of effective oversight or regulation. Governments and their state religious authorities were simply incapable of preventing the growth of fundamentalist and extremist movements. Because of their limited financial resources, the newly independent states were unable to provide adequate educational, law enforcement, and judicial services. As in other Muslim societies, the mosque soon became the most important center in Central Asian communities, serving as a school, a place of worship, and a gathering point where social and political issues could be discussed and solutions formulated. With the state's legitimacy at a low point, state-sponsored mosques bore the burden of illegitimacy as well. "Independent" Islamic organizations and religious movements thus enjoyed greater credibility as they competed to fill the governmental and ideological vacuum throughout the region. The dearth of civil services became so severe that these organizations arrogated to themselves the responsibility of fighting crime and providing youth and family services in many cities and villages across Central Asia—thereby further increasing their popularity.

A second, albeit indirect, entryway for Islamist ideology into Central Asia came through Pakistani madrasas. As S.V.R. Nasr writes, in 1947 there were 137 madrasas in Pakistan, compared to about 20,000 today—with many of the newer schools propagating more extreme interpretations of Islam than existing institutions. Much of the growth of these institutions has been driven by financial contributions from Persian Gulf monarchies, particularly Wahhabist Saudi Arabia. These funding efforts began initially as a response to the ideological threat of Communism after the 1979 Soviet invasion of Afghanistan. The Iranian Revolution of the same year also created concern among the Sunni Islamists that Shi'a Iran might export its revolution, and hence a great deal of money poured into the region to spread their version of political Islam. As a result, the writings of Sayyid Qutb and other Islamist thinkers found their way into the libraries, schools, and consequently the

hearts and minds of many in the region. Many graduates of these newer madrasas became prominent in Islamist militant movements, including those in Central Asia.

Meanwhile, the militant Islamists who had defeated the Soviet army in Afghanistan desired to continue their campaign of violent jihad against any perceived enemy of Islam. As Samuel Huntington explained in *The Clash of Civilizations and the Remaking of World Order*:

> The [Afghan-Soviet war] left . . . a legacy of expert and experienced fighters' training camps and logistical facilities, elaborate trans-Islamic networks of personal and organizational relationships . . . and, most importantly, a heady sense of power and self-confidence over what had been achieved and a driving desire to move on to other victories.

While some of these fighters returned to their diverse home countries, many others remained to form the core of the Taliban movement that over the course of the 1990s came to dominate Afghanistan. The ranks of the Taliban fighters were further swelled by the graduates of the aforementioned Pakistani madrasas. Furthermore, the Taliban were funded and advised by the Pakistani intelligence services—which by then had been radicalized—as well as by Saudi Arabia. Having established control over most of Afghanistan by 1996, the Taliban—led by Mullah Muhammad Omar—proceeded to impose a strict version of Islam on the population, which included a ban on music and female education.

The Taliban also welcomed Osama bin Ladin and his followers in the al-Qa'ida movement after they had fled their previous haven in the Sudan as a result of U.S.

pressure. The Taliban gave al-Qa'ida free rein to set up terrorist training camps on Afghan territory. They also welcomed and encouraged other terrorist groups, such as the Islamic Movement of Uzbekistan (IMU), to do the same. Thus, Afghanistan became fertile ground for cross-pollination between different radical Islamist groups. Thanks to the region's porous borders, Central and South Asian activists—both the already radicalized and the soon to be radicalized—were able to draw from the knowledge and experience of this emerging terrorist nexus. Accordingly, it was but a small leap for militants training in Afghanistan to make Central Asia itself the focal point of the next jihadist struggle.

The Spread of Islamism

The focus of Islamic revival—and the prime target of radical groups—has been the Ferghana Valley, an area with a dense, highly religious population divided among Uzbekistan, Kyrgyzstan, and Tajikistan. At first, four Islamist groups were active in the region: Adolat (Justice), Baraka (Blessings), Tauba (Repentance), and Islam Lashkarlari (Warriors of Islam). These groups existed underground during the Soviet period but emerged during the perestroika era. Over time other groups also became active in the region, including Hizb al-Tahrir and its splinter groups Akramiyya and Hizb al-Nusrat, as well as Uzun Soqol (Long Beards), Tablighi Jama'at (TJ), Lashkar-i-Taiba, Hizballah, and the IMU. Since the post–September 11 Western campaign in Afghanistan, the IMU has apparently splintered into additional groups, such as the East Turkistan Islamic Movement (ETIM), the Islamic Movement of Central Asia (IMCA), and the Islamic Jihad Group (IJG).

From Ferghana, many of these Islamist groups targeted Uzbekistan, recognizing it as the Islamic heart of Central Asia. The most active groups, Adolat and Islam Lashkarlari, were founded and led by the underground Islamist cleric Tahir Yuldashev. Adbulmutal Zakrulaev explains that at first these groups consisted of only a few hundred members, but in the absence of decisive action by the government in Tashkent, they were able to garner more recruits through the effective use of propaganda. Throughout their drive to power, the radicals in Namangan called themselves *amirs* (leaders), arrested the local mayor, and built a mosque and a madrasa with Saudi financial support.

Aside from the Ferghana Valley, the other principal areas of Islamist operations have been Tajikistan and southern Kyrgyzstan. Islamist radical groups served as the key drivers of resistance to the Soviet occupation of Afghanistan in the 1980s. They soon reached out to their ethnic brethren in Tajikistan and southern Uzbekistan, often infiltrating Soviet army units composed of Central Asian troops. After independence, these "resistance" movements began operating in Tajikistan itself. Southern Kyrgyzstan is exposed to many of the same currents that prevail in neighboring Uzbekistan and Tajikistan. By contrast, northern Kyrgyzstan, Kazakhstan, and Turkmenistan have seen considerably lower levels of Islamic activity.

While their methods and strategies may differ, almost all of the groups listed above have as a shared goal the overthrow of the secular system and the establishment of an Islamic state. The key Islamist groups active in the region run across the political spectrum, ranging from militant and terrorist groups such as the IMU, to self-proclaimed nonviolent groups, such as Hizb al-Tahrir and Tablighi Jama'at.

Hizb al-Tahrir al-Islamiyya (The Islamic Party of Liberation)

Hizb al-Tahrir al-Islamiyya (HT) is the only group in Central Asia to have a truly coherent ideology. Neither Osama bin Ladin nor former Taliban leader Mullah Omar nor IMU leader Tahir Yuldashev has come up with a better ideological and theological framework that justifies their actions. Instead, these and other leaders drew inspiration from the comprehensive teachings of HT, which is currently the most popular Islamist movement in Central Asia.

HT was founded in 1952 by Shaykh Taqi al-Din al-Nabhani in Jordanian-ruled East Jerusalem. After al-Nabhani died in 1977, he was succeeded as amir by fellow Palestinian cleric Abu Yusuf Abd al-Qadim Zalloum. He led the organization for almost three decades, stepping down in March 2003 because of his deteriorating health; he died a month later. He was succeeded by Ata Ibnu Khalil Abu Rashta, who previously served as the party's official spokesman in Jordan. Abu Rashta, alias Abu Yasin, is a Palestinian who lives in Jordan. Under his leadership, HT activities have become more aggressive. During the fall of 2003, the governing body (*kiedat*) is believed to have instructed members to engage in acts of aggression toward the diplomatic representations and other buildings of those countries that supported the war in Iraq. Today it is active in over 40 countries, with its "nerve center" in London and official headquarters in Jordan.

The main goal of the movement is to reestablish the caliphate. Although it claims to be nonviolent, the group acknowledges that violence may eventually be necessary in order to overthrow the regimes standing in the way of a global Islamic state. It is virulently anti-Semitic and anti-American, promulgating an ideology that is fundamentally in opposition to democratic and capitalist systems and to Western concepts of freedom. While HT as an organization does not engage in terrorist activities, its individual members often have. Furthermore, it has become the vanguard of a radical Islamist movement that encourages terrorist acts.

HT is the only self-described political party seeking to unite the *umma* (the worldwide Islamic community)—a unity that it wants to bring about by emulating the steps by which Muhammad established the original caliphate. According to al-Nabhani, this work was performed in "clearly defined stages, each of which he used to perform specific clear actions" at the end of which a Shari'a-based Islamic government was established.

HT effectively combines Marxist-Leninist methodology and Western slogans with reactionary Islamic ideology to shape the internal debate within Islam. As an organization, HT also bears striking similarities to the early Bolshevik movement. Both have a utopian ultimate goal (whether "true Communism" or the caliphate), and both show an intense dislike for liberal democracy while seeking to establish a mythical "just society." Both also function with a secretive cell system. Moreover, while it insists on nonviolence, HT does justify the use of force, just as Lenin and the Bolsheviks did in 1917.

Its party leaflets, accessible via the Internet in various languages, provide the umma with timely and coherent explanations of current events—explanations that always fit within HT's ideological framework. The language of these leaflets is simple and direct. For instance, many repeat the call to Muslims to "kill Jews wherever you find them."

The tightly compartmentalized structure of HT ensures that little information is known about its financial structure. Its members take oaths of secrecy on the Koran, oaths that are generally not broken even under interrogation. The "need-to-know" basis on which information is transmitted in the party ensures that data obtained from all but the most senior members is of little importance. This is why until today neither Central Asian nor Western authorities have been able to deny the group access to its funding sources.

HT does not require significant sums of money to sustain its activities. Its ability to create a virtual Islamic community through the Internet has allowed the movement to reach the hearts and minds of many without investing in an elaborate communications network or in party offices. Interviews with arrested group members indicate that local entrepreneurs, party members, and other sympathizers tend to make individual donations to the HT's local organs, while wealthier businessmen and Islamic charities are most likely to direct their money to the leadership committee—which, in turn, sends money to the movement's various regional branches. The majority of HT funds are raised via private donations and taxation of party members for financial support. The latter is particularly significant, because in Central Asia each member is obliged to donate between 5 and 20 percent of monthly income to the party.

Unlike many Islamist movements that shun female participation in politics, women are thought to make up 10 percent of HT's membership.

Ideology

Born in 1909 in the city of Haifa in the Ottoman Empire, al-Nabhani was educated at the al-Azhar University and Dar al-Ulum University in Cairo, Egypt. He served as a judge in various courts in Lebanon and Palestine, and also taught at the Islamic University in Amman, Jordan. Over time al-Nabhani became convinced that Islam's decline resulted from the submission of the umma to rapacious colonial powers. Unlike many of his peers, who believed Islam's shortcomings could be remedied through nationalist or economic policy prescriptions, al-Nabhani asserted that Islam could only be revived if it was restored as a comprehensive guide for daily life. Although hesitant to label most of his Muslim contemporaries as *kafirs* (unbelievers), he believed that their lives were dominated by a mixture of Islamic, Western, socialist, nationalist, partisan, regional, and sectarian thoughts and emotions, leaving them detached from authentic Muslim life. In 1950 al-Nabhani published *The Treatise of the Arab*, explaining his vision of "establishing the Islamic state in Arab territories and afterwards in non-Arab Islamic territories." To achieve this goal, he established HT.

The Muslim Brotherhood largely shaped al-Nabhani's political and religious philosophy. Al-Nabhani was at first a member of the Brotherhood but soon found its ideology too moderate and too accommodating of the West. After articulating his views in the book *Khilafa*, he founded HT as a more radical alternative to the Brotherhood, winning the loyalty of its many radical members, who soon became the rank and file of the new organization.

Al-Nabhani viewed Western civilization and Islam as dichotomous entities with mutually exclusive ideological underpinnings, both of which competed to dominate Muslim societies. According to al-Nabhani, Western societies employed two antagonizing ideological systems during the Cold War—capitalism and socialism—in order to assert control over Muslims. Although the capitalist forces eventually prevailed, al-Nabhani maintained that had the Communists acknowledged God and embraced Islam, socialist forces would have triumphed. With the fall of Communism, HT identified Western capitalism (led by the United States) as the primary impediment to establishing a truly Islamic society.

Al-Nabhani believed that the West has consistently borne animosity to Islam ever since the Crusades. Indeed, he argued that the West was engaged in a "cultural crusade" against Islam. Following his teaching, HT today considers the propagation of democracy by the West to be tantamount to cultural invasion, and as a result, promotes grassroots projects that compete with U.S. democracy-promotion efforts. HT members believe the "war on terror" is a euphemism for war on Islam and is used to fool the world's 1.3 billion Muslims.

HT's main goal is to overthrow the existing governments of Muslim countries. Moreover, in the conduct of international relations, "HT would allow non-Muslim countries to stay outside the Caliphate but collect taxes from them, and this would put them under the protection of the Caliphate. But, if these non-Muslim countries would refuse to pay taxes, then the Caliphate would launch military attacks against them," as Igor Rotar asserts in "Central Asia: Hizb-Ut-Tahrir Wants Worldwide Sharia Law." Hence, like Wahhabism, HT's theology departs from the common Islamic creed (*aqida*)—notably in its opposition to existing authority. HT's Islamist ideology is based in Arab nationalism, and also resembles Wahhabism in its strong support for Shari'a.

The Three-Stage Plan

HT's plan for establishing a universal caliphate has three stages. First is the recruitment and propaganda stage, in which Islam is taught from an HT perspective. After several months of study, individuals are asked to join the party. They operate in small "cells" of no more than six or seven people. The cells, in turn, form a pyramid structure, with no communication between them so as to ensure maximum secrecy. Members of the cell communicate with each other only via pseudonym, and only the leader of the cell is connected to the next level of the hierarchy; thus, it is very difficult for intelligence operatives to penetrate the group.

At the second stage, HT members form new cells and engage in open propaganda to build tension between citizens and their governments. They promote an Islamic way of life that they claim will bring justice and order. At the same time, because the goal is to penetrate into government positions and military and police forces, members of HT are "ordered" to drink alcohol (ordinarily forbidden by Islam) and change their behavior in other ways in order to blend in. At this second stage, HT members must focus on methodology rather than belief, attempting above all to infiltrate and control key components of the government and military.

When the second stage is complete and the ground is ripe for the establishment of Islamic governments that will be ruled by Shari'a, the third and final stage begins. HT members will not participate in violence until this stage is reached. As HT does not yet appear to have reached the third stage, it is hard to prove the existence of this plan, much less that it will lead to acts of terror.

HT's vision is extremely aggressive, anti-Semitic, and anti-American, as evidenced by its declarations such as these:

> America . . . is the head of *kufr* [sinner/ nonbeliever] in her hostility towards us, and the states behind her are enemies to us. . . . America needs to be treated as

a state with whom we are in actual war.
. . . We are the target of the conspiracies of the *kufr* from the Christians of
the West and the Jews, who are doing
this in collaboration with our rulers,
[who are] the hypocrites and traitors.
. . . Nothing can save you except your
Islam. . . . What is the matter with you,
that when you are asked to march forth
in the Cause of Allah (jihad) you cling
heavily to the earth?

Presence in Central Asia

Central Asia is one of HT's principal battle-
grounds. The post-Communist situation,
in which the vast majority of the populace holds only limited knowledge of the
tenets of traditional Islam, benefits a radical
movement such as HT. Furthermore, poor
economic performance has further undermined public support for governments that
provide few opportunities for socioeconomic
improvement. HT's public relations campaign has already succeeded in diverting the
world community's attention away from its
activities in Uzbekistan. As a result of this
propaganda effort, Western observers are
concerned more with the prison conditions
of HT supporters than the possibility of a
successful HT takeover.

HT writings were first brought to
Uzbekistan in the late 1970s by Jordanians
and Palestinians studying at the region's
institutions of higher learning. The second wave of HT expansion began in 1992,
but it took off in earnest in 1995, when a
Jordanian brought HT's literature to the
Ferghana Valley and disseminated it among
the ethnic Uzbek population. While HT is
still most active in the Ferghana Valley, it
has successfully spread over the last decade
to the rest of Uzbekistan, as well as to
Kyrgyzstan, Tajikistan, and Kazakhstan.

The movement found many recruits after
the February 1999 attacks in Tashkent,
when bombings killed sixteen people and
wounded at least a hundred. especially after
the authorities accused HT of participating
in the explosions. (This charge was later
retracted.) In response to the government's
accusations, HT published its first leaflet
targeting the Uzbek government in April
1999. The group then began the regular
issuance of such leaflets, at times releasing
over 100,000 copies of each leaflet about
twice a month.

As a result of the repressive methods used
by the authorities in the subsequent crackdown after the bombings, many HT members left Uzbekistan and moved to more
open Central Asian states, thus becoming
excellent missionaries for the movement.
At first, many settled in the ethnic Uzbek
regions of Kyrgyzstan and Kazakhstan, but
the group's activities have since expanded.
Within the last couple of years, HT members
have been arrested in northern Kazakhstan,
the Bishkek area of Kyrgyzstan, and in
Tajikistan's capital of Dushanbe—areas that
are neither near the border with Uzbekistan
nor known for significant Uzbek minority
populations.

The precise number of HT members in
Central Asia today is difficult to estimate. In
general, like other Islamist movements, HT
has been less successful in recruiting the traditionally less religious nomadic peoples (for
instance, the Turkmen and the Kazakhs)
and more successful among the more settled Uzbek, Kyrgyz, and Tajik peoples. HT
is numerically strongest in Uzbekistan,
with estimates there ranging from 7,000 to
60,000 members. It is also rapidly growing
in other Central Asian republics. Yet sheer
numbers are not central to HT's strategy,
which is based on the penetration of political power centers as a method of obtaining

power. Arrest patterns indicate that support for HT is growing throughout the region, including among teachers, military officers, politicians (especially those whose relatives have been arrested), and other members of the elite. Given that HT aims to penetrate political power centers as a method of obtaining power, even several hundred recruits in the right positions can make a significant difference.

The pattern of HT activity does not vary significantly from country to country in Central Asia, whether in distribution of the group's literature or in approaches to recruitment. HT first begins recruitment by approaching individuals most likely to embrace radical Islam, communicating and establishing links with them, and disseminating propaganda literature translated into local languages. HT distributes party literature all across the region. Local HT branches can download materials from the group's principal Web site and disseminate them after translation into local languages. Leaflets are convenient propaganda tools for Central Asian target audiences, because they can be printed locally and distributed easily. This is especially true in regions where Internet access is limited or nonexistent.

The operation of HT's three-stage method can easily be seen in Central Asia. During the first stage (early 1993 to February 1999), the group primarily engaged in religious and socioeconomic propaganda activities to recruit new members. These new members were organized into self-reliant groups of three to seven people, called *halkas*. These and other members were ordered to bring all their family members, including females, into the organization. The second stage (February 1999 to April 2003) followed the terrorist attacks in Tashkent. HT began to fill its ranks with new members, using open

agitation and propaganda methods, such as the distribution of leaflets in public places (all over Central Asia) and the organization of mass picketing at buildings of government agencies (mainly in Uzbekistan and Kyrgyzstan). HT has now entered the third stage, during which it will attempt to overthrow governments. In Uzbekistan, two sets of terrorist attacks took place in spring and summer 2004. Among the arrested were men and women "inspired" by HT literature. Since the spring of 2004, HT's activity in Kyrgyzstan, Kazakhstan, and Tajikistan has also intensified. Following the March 2005 revolution in Kyrgyzstan, and the May 2005 Andjian uprising, and especially the Uzbek government's killing of hundreds in response, HT may be in a good position to further increase its influence if the government does not establish democratic order and address the people's needs.

Hizb al-Tahrir Splinter Groups

While in principle a centralized movement, HT is known to have undergone several splits, including within Central Asia. Known HT splinter groups include:

- Palestinian Islamic Jihad (PIJ; founded in 1958): Shaykh Asad Bayyud Tamimi, a former HT member, founded both PIJ and a second splinter group called the Islamic Jihad Organization (also known as the al-Aqsa Battalions), which was created in 1982. PIJ has no known presence in Central Asia.
- Al-Muhajiroun (1996): Omar Bakri Muhammad, a former HT member, founded this extremely radical organization. Bakri has claimed to be "the eyes of Osama bin Ladin," and reports indicate that communication

between the two men dates back at least as far as 1998. Bakri disbanded al-Muhajiroun on October 13, 2004, and fled London after the July 2005 bombings. Al-Muhajiroun's two successors, namely the Saved (or Savior) Sect, al-Ghuraba'a, were officially banned in 2006 for "glorifying terrorism." Members of all three are now functioning under another UK-based Islamist group, Ahl al-Sunna wal-Jama'a (ASWJ). Though al-Muhajiroun and its various offshoots have no known presence in Central Asia, they often refer to the Uzbek government's repressive policies to radicalize British Muslims.

- Akramiyya (1995): Formed in the Uzbekistani section of the Ferghana Valley, it is a group with a primarily local focus (discussed below).
- Hizb al-Nusrat (1999): The Party of Assistance.

Radicalization of HT

Since 2001 there has been a clear and consistent trend toward the radicalization of HT. In June 2001 an article in its publication *al-Waie* stated unequivocally that it was acceptable to carry out suicide attacks with explosive belts. Since the beginning of the wars in Afghanistan and especially Iraq, it has further radicalized its language, declaring holy war against Christians and those who support them. In March 2002 HT argued that suicide bombs in Israel were a legitimate tactic of war, given that the enemy has sophisticated weapons and hence can only be defeated through attacks on so-called "soft targets" such as women and children. Since then, HT leaflets and writings have continuously emphasized that in the context of a clash of civilizations, offensive jihad against both Americans and Jews is acceptable.

What is even more troubling is that HT has paid increased attention to weapons of mass destruction. The fact that no weapons of mass destruction were found in Iraq only strengthened the group's interest in such weapons. With its emphasis on the inevitability of the clash of civilizations, HT may further "inspire" some Muslims to take this next fearsome step. It is yet to be established whether HT has already formed a militant wing or whether it is simply "inspiring" members independently to join terrorist groups or engage in terrorist acts.

The Islamic Movement of Uzbekistan (IMU)

The beginning of the struggle between the Uzbekistani government and the Islamists can be traced back to 1991. That year, riots erupted after President Islam Karimov visited the Namangan region to confront the growing challenge posed by the Islamist group Adolat. At the time, protesters had made the first calls for a political role for Islam, advocating the establishment of an Islamic state and the introduction of Shari'a. Faced with a swiftly deteriorating situation, the government finally responded in the spring of 1992 by arresting 27 Adolat members and banning the group. This action prompted the previously mentioned Tahir Yuldashev—an underground Islamic cleric who operated out of the Otavalihon mosque in the Namangan region of Uzbekistan—along with his ally, Juma Khodjiev Namangani, and others to flee to Tajikistan and Afghanistan. Most of those who went to Afghanistan underwent radical indoctrination and military training with other Islamist groups, while the majority of those who went to Tajikistan joined the local Islamic movement, participating in the country's civil war, which began in May 1992.

While Yuldashev's radical message continued to spread through the network of mosques and madrasas in the Ferghana Valley, he was traveling to Saudi Arabia, Pakistan, and Afghanistan and became increasingly influenced by Wahhabism and Deobandism. The Deobandi are a Muslim religious revivalist movement that developed in India in response to the perceived threat to Islam from British colonialism. The name derives from Deoband, India, where the first Deobandi Islamic seminary was founded. Like the Wahhabis, the Deobandi consider certain Sufi-related practices, such as seeking intercession of saints, to be "an innovation" and thus non-Islamic. Also, like the Wahhabis, they give precedence to the jurisprudence of earlier Islamic scholars over later ones. Their concept of jihad is also more open to the Wahhabi interpretation than the Sufis' conception of jihad. The Taliban follow the teachings of the Deobandi school.

Yuldashev also expanded his political and financial links with other militant Islamists. With the help of al-Qa'ida, the Taliban, Harakat al-Ansar, and al-Jihad, in 1992, Yuldashev brought together Adolat, Baraka, Tauba, and Islam Lashkari under the unified title of the Islamic Movement of Uzbekistan (IMU). Namangani, who became the military commander of the IMU, was one of his main supporters, along with the Saudi-trained militant Abd al-Ahad, as Abduljabar Abduvakhitov writes.

By 1998 hundreds of Uzbek mujahidin had trained in and operated between Tajikistan and Uzbekistan, taking advantage of Tajikistan's civil war. The first instance of IMU violence appeared in August 1999, when Namangani and his associates abducted a group of Japanese geologists, government officials, and military personnel in southern Kyrgyzstan, thus expanding that movement's activity to a third country. The IMU was also believed to be involved in launching carefully orchestrated attacks against Uzbekistan from neighboring Kyrgyzstan and Tajikistan, most notably the 1999 Tashkent bombings. Soon thereafter, when Namangani declared his aim to seize the region by force, thousands of refugees fled the Ferghana Valley. Namangani then headed for Afghanistan, where, with the permission of the Taliban, he established an IMU training camp. Militants from all over the Ferghana Valley began to flock to the camp to receive instruction in terrorist tactics under the guidance of the Taliban. As Marina Pikulina explains in "Hizb ut-Tahrir Organization and Financing," in the only interview he apparently has ever given to date, Yuldashev declared, "The goal of IMU activities is the creation of an Islamic State. We declared a jihad in order to create a religious system and government. We want a model of Islam that is nothing like in Afghanistan, Iran, Pakistan, or Saudi Arabia."

From July to August 1999, as many as 800 IMU guerrillas, together with members of rogue groups from Tajikistan, invaded southern Kyrgyzstan with the declared goal of establishing an Islamist state as a base for invading Uzbekistan. They were finally repelled in October 1999 with air and other support from Uzbekistan and Kazakhstan. Five hundred members of the IMU staged an incursion into Kyrgyzstan and Uzbekistan in August 2000 and were again repelled with aid from neighboring states. Yet another invasion was expected in summer 2001 but was averted when Osama bin Ladin secured the help of the IMU in battling the Afghan Northern Alliance that summer. According to Jim Nichol, after September 11 the IMU joined forces with the Taliban and al-Qa'ida against U.S.-led forces in Afghanistan (Operation Enduring Freedom).

While the IMU's infrastructure and manpower were significantly weakened by Operation Enduring Freedom—notably the death of Namangani in Afghanistan—there are still many IMU fighters who have the capacity to fight. Some IMU fighters fled to South Waziristan (a federally adminis-tered tribal area in Pakistan's North-West Frontier Province along the border with Afghanistan), along with other jihadists who also escaped U.S. entrapment at Tora Bora. Yuldashev, his son-in-law and chief lieuten-ant Dilshod Hodzhiev (who is in charge of IMU finances), and Ulugbek Kholikov (alias Muhammad Ajub, who heads the IMU's military section) are believed to be among those who survived and are in hiding in Pakistan. On orders from bin Ladin, IMU militants have taken a leading role in South Waziristan, with Yuldashev in command of military activities. Yuldashev is also thought to be cooperating with other international terrorist organizations and illegal arms traf-fickers. He also possesses portable antiair-craft missile launchers, potentially for use against American targets in Afghanistan.

Post–Operation Enduring Freedom Activities

A number of events since Operation Enduring Freedom have confirmed the con-tinued viability of the IMU. As reported by the U.S. Department of State, in May 2003 Uzbek and Kyrgyz security services arrested several terrorists who had planted and detonated bombs in the Kyrgyz towns of Bishkek and Osh and who had attempted to bomb the U.S. embassy in Bishkek. Igor Rotar explains that one of those arrested, Azizbek Karimov—a former chief of the IMU's security service—testified that he

and his companions had been ordered to commit these acts by the IMU, which had also provided them with funds. Karimov was executed in August 2004.

On March 28, 2004, a series of attacks rocked Tashkent and Bukhara. During four straight days of explosions, bomb-ings, and assaults—which included the region's first-ever female suicide bomb-ings—47 people were killed. The obscure Islamic Jihad Group (IJG) of Uzbekistan (reportedly an alias of the IMU) claimed responsibility for the violence. Suspected terrorists testified at a trial in mid-2004 that a Najmiddin Jalolov was the leader of IJG, that they were trained by Arabs and others at camps in Kazakhstan and Pakistan, and that the IJG was linked to HT, the Taliban, Uighur extremists, and al-Qa'ida. During this trial, on July 30, 2004, there were explosions in Tashkent at the American and Israeli embassies and the Uzbek Prosecutor General's Office, killing seven. As Jim Nichol writes, the IMU and IJG claimed responsibility and stated that the bombings were aimed against the trial and the "apostate" governments. The U.S. Department of State reported that the IMU was also blamed for an explosion in Osh in November 2004, which killed one police officer and one terrorist. The scale and the level of preparation of these attacks indicated support from outside Uzbekistan.

Uzbekistan's chief prosecutor alleged that all 85 individuals (including 17 women) arrested had been trained as suicide bomb-ers. The authorities believe that these female suicide attackers were trained in Pakistan, possibly by an Uzbek woman. In the home of a suspect, authorities also found computer files detailing informa-tion on training locations in Pakistan and Kazakhstan that are administered by Arab instructors who were themselves previously trained by al-Qa'ida militants. The director of the Shanghai Cooperation Organization's antiterrorist center, Vyacheslav Kasymov, further stated that mobile phones found at the homes of suspects in Uzbekistan showed they had called phone numbers in Kazakhstan. Suspects reportedly testified that they had come to Uzbekistan via Iran and Azerbaijan to target police stations and prisons. They are also believed to have revealed plans to attack embassies and the offices of Western organizations.

The fact that the 2004 attacks were the first suicide killings in Central Asia was another ominous indicator of the progress of Islamism in the region. Based on what has been written, two of the female killers, the 19-year-old Dilnoza Holmuradova and her 22-year-old sister, Shahnoza Holmuradova, came from a relatively affluent family in Tashkent and were well educated. Dilnoza reportedly spoke five languages and had attended the police academy. The decisive factor in their transformation into extremists was the type of people with whom they were associating. According to news reports, they began studying Islam in 2002 and then gradually stopped wearing modern clothes, listening to music, and watching television, which are the usual signs of Islamist extremism. They left home in 2004 and soon after carried out their attacks

It is clear that these perpetrators had been influenced by locally active Wahhabists, who led them to become terrorists. In fact, many well-to-do Muslims turn radical after they meet an Islamist at some vulnerable point in their lives. In the future, more women may carry out terrorist attacks, because women attract less suspicion from the authorities. Especially for women in search of a stable identity, martyrdom often seems like the only option. Unfortunately,

prevailing conditions portend a wide pool of potential recruits for suicide killings in the years to come.

Since 2004 there have been persistent, if not fully confirmed, reports of Islamist militant sightings in remote regions of Uzbekistan, as Rotar reports. In late January 2006, a Tajik official blamed the IMU for a prison raid in northern Tajikistan that freed a prisoner with alleged IMU ties. It again was not possible to confirm the accuracy of this report. The IMU has also been blamed for an attack on Tajik and Kyrgyz guard posts in May 2006. During these attacks, several border guards were killed and weapons were stolen, as reported in the *Central Asia-Caucasus Analyst*. Finally, IMU leader Yuldashev is alleged to have given a speech in September 2006, on the fifth anniversary of the September 11 attacks, where he threatened that "Karimov [president of Uzbekistan], Rakhmonov [president of Tajikistan], and Bakiyev [president of Kyrgyzstan] had better remember . . . that they will be punished for the crimes they are committing," as reported by *Central Asia News*. Thus, it would appear that Yuldashev has declared war against the governments of Uzbekistan, Tajikistan, and Kyrgyzstan.

Hizb ut-Tahrir and the IMU

The U.S. State Department has designated the IMU as a terrorist organization, but it has not yet done so in the case of HT. While both the IMU and the HT want to unify Muslims throughout the world into a single Islamic caliphate, the IMU is clearly involved in terrorist acts, whereas HT is not. However, it is more appropriate to state that HT has not yet succeeded in its attempted terrorist acts. In 1974 HT tried to seize weaponry from the Egyptian military academy to overthrow the Egyptian government. HT was also accused of plotting violent coups in Tunisia (1992) and in Jordan (1993). It is only a matter of time before they eventually succeed.

HT and the IMU do not have a formal alliance, because it runs contrary to HT's interests to be directly associated with a terrorist group. The main difference between the two groups is one of focus: The IMU openly advocates and carries out militant operations, while HT concentrates mainly on the ideological battle. The two nonetheless admit to the closeness of their goals and both are propelled closer to the achievement of their ends by the weakness of Central Asian states. According to Tajikistan Deputy Interior Minister Abd al-Rahim Kaharov, many HT activists are simultaneously members of the IMU and vice versa, because "these structures share goals that are fairly similar and [the] propaganda of one structure [HT] is backed by the military order and weapons of the other [IMU]."

Akramiyya

Akramiyya is named after its leader, Akram Yuldashev, born in 1963 in Andijan, Uzbekistan. Yuldashev is believed to have been a member of HT for one year, during which he became profoundly influenced by the thought of HT founder al-Nabhani. He then founded Akramiyya in his native Andijan region in 1992. He was first arrested in 1993 for Islamist radicalism and was released later that year following an amnesty. Following the February 1999 bombings in Tashkent, he was rearrested and sentenced to over 10 years in prison.

In 1992 Yuldashev wrote a theological pamphlet in Uzbek titled "Yimonga Yul" (The Path to Faith). According to Uzbek scholar Bakhtiyar Babadjanov, Yuldashev wrote a supplement to this tract in March 2005, in which

he outlined a five-stage process for the establishment of Islamic leadership. Akramiyya shares HT's conspiratorial methodology and its multistage process for achieving the ultimate objective of reestablishing the caliphate. Accordingly, the aim of Akramiyya is to gather enough strength to exert influence on regional authorities, if not to control them directly. With this aim in mind, Akramiyya promotes a simplified version of Islam to maximize its potential support base. Its structure is communal and cult-like, and members have limited exposure to outsiders.

Akramiyya seems to have been rather successful in developing a following by delivering on socioeconomic promises that the Uzbek government has been unable to fulfill, such as jobs and money. Wealthier followers set up small businesses such as bakeries, cafeterias, or shoe factories in which they employ young males who are then required to attend study groups after work (other Islamic movements practice similar methods of recruiting followers). The owners of these businesses contribute about one-fifth of their profits to a fund, which in turn assists poorer members of the group. They thus become a self-sustaining and separate Islamic community. This is one of the most successful examples of the bottom-up approach of pro-Islamic social engineering.

In May 2005, Akramiyya sympathizers perpetrated an uprising in Andijan. The immediate pretext was the ongoing trial of 23 local businessmen arrested the previous year for their alleged association with Akramiyya. While the details are still somewhat unclear, it is known that armed men approached an Andijan police post on May 12, 2005, overpowering and killing a number of the officers and removing weapons from their storage depot. Reportedly, these men then carried out a similar attack on a military facility, absconding with a large amount of weaponry. Their last destination was the prison, where they freed the businessmen along with one-third of the total inmates. The assailants then attacked the National Security and Police Department building, although they were fought off. Subsequently, they commandeered the local governmental administrative building, in which they blockaded themselves after capturing hostages to use as human shields. When negotiating with the authorities, one of their key demands was the release of Yuldashev from prison. Meanwhile, a large crowd had gathered in the area either to support the hostage takers, or simply to watch what was happening. Subsequently, negotiations broke down, shots were fired, and the situation spiraled out of control, with several hundred civilians being killed and many more fleeing for Uzbekistan's border with Kyrgyzstan.

The precise turn of events remains unclear. A videotape containing clips of the uprising was released by the Uzbek government—after more than a year had passed—though with clear indications that it had been edited. It is almost certain that some of the assailants were Islamists, as there were clear shouts of *"Allahu Akbar"* (God is great) from the organizers of the uprising. As Martha Brill Olcott and Marina Barnett write, it is also clear that some of them received rudimentary military training, given their success in attacking the police post and military base. Nevertheless, it is unclear to what degree Islamism was mixed with a sense of frustration with the poverty and stagnant economy under Uzbek president Karimov and a sense of injustice over the imprisonment of the 23 businessmen, to which there had been a peaceful protest of hundreds of people on the day before the incident, as Radio Free Europe/Radio Liberty reported.

In a sense, the events of Andijan illustrate precisely the means by which Islamist ideology penetrates the region. As Rotar writes, the same 23 businessmen accused of being Akramiyya members—in a similar vein to the Akramiyya business and charity practices previously mentioned—had paid their workers substantially more than did other employers and had given thousands of dollars to Islamic charities. It is impossible to tell for certain if they were motivated by the desire to propagate an ideology or to improve people's lives. Furthermore, eyewitness accounts establish that many who gathered in the square during the uprising were employees of the businessmen and were promised a day's pay if they would attend. Simply too little is known to draw a clear conclusion. That said, three months after the incident, one of the leaders of the uprising threatened a "campaign of terror" against Karimov's regime. The danger and existence of Islamist ideology in and around Uzbekistan cannot be denied—especially given the comeback of the Taliban in Afghanistan and its strengthened position in Pakistan.

Tabligh Jama'at (TJ)

TJ was established in India in the 1920s by Mawlana Muhammad Ilyas as a direct response to Hindu proselytizing. The group claims to follow the *Sunna* (way of life) of Islam's founder. To TJ members this means wearing long beards, robes, and leather shoes. Members are also required to conduct *tabligh*, that is, to try on a regular basis to convert others to Islam, and they each devote a certain amount of time to *da'wa* (cause). Members can spend this time camping in small groups in order to preach "the Prophet's way" in mosques. In Central Asia they also preach in bazaars. Today,

TJ has offices and schools in Canada and the UK, though its main centers are on the Indian subcontinent. Its annual gatherings in India and Pakistan attract hundreds of thousands. TJ's annual summit in Raiwind is the largest Muslim gathering in the world after the hajj.

The group does not involve itself in politics (and has been criticized by radical Islamists for being apolitical), but over time TJ has become an international movement, active mostly in South and Central Asia. TJ has succeeded in introducing Islamic networks to Europe and the United States and often functions in parallel to the Wahhabi Muslim World League. In recent years, like many other Islamic movements, TJ has also become radicalized. Consequently, those who learn about Islam from TJ today are at risk of supporting or joining terrorist groups.

Al-Qa'ida or other terrorist groups are believed to have used TJ as their cover to travel and smuggle operatives across borders; because the group is apolitical, Tabligh's members can fairly easily travel between countries. Other terrorist groups may have used the movement as a recruitment pool, because its failure to discuss politics leaves room for others to provide a political message. In Central Asia TJ is most active in the Ferghana Valley, especially in Andijan. The authorities in Uzbekistan believe that TJ members in the country are influenced by HT's ideology and by the radicalism of the Islamic Movement of Central Asia.

The Islamic Movement of Central Asia

While many at first assumed that the American military presence in the Central Asian region would make the IMU's operations more difficult, thus pushing more

group members into the nonviolent camp, the opposite has happened. The setbacks of the Taliban have led to a growing desire among various militants to consolidate their efforts and move into Central Asia. As chairman of the Kyrgyz National Security Service (NSS), Kalyk Imankulov stated Central Asian governments believe that in 2002 or 2003, the region's Islamic radicals united in a framework of a new underground organization called the Islamic Movement of Central Asia (IMCA). This umbrella group brought together the IMU, Kyrgyz and Tajik radicals, and Uighur separatists from China—whose own East Turkistan Islamic Movement had recently broadened to include Afghans, Chechens, Kyrgyz, Uzbeks, and Kazakhs who share its new goal of forming an Islamic state in Central Asia.

Accordingly, the multiplicity of different organizations of which radicals claim to be a part (including the bewildering range of group names used to claim responsibility for terrorist attacks) is sometimes a ruse to make it seem as though there are more organizations than there actually are. Therefore, the same individuals often make up several "different" organizations. Ultimately, all of these militants share the same goals, obey the same regional leaders, and communicate via the same networks, even as they act under different names and use different tactics. Thus, while many more radical Islamist organizations have mushroomed in the region over the last several years, almost all of them can be considered, in one way or another, to be under the IMCA umbrella.

Kyrgyz authorities believe that the IMCA's immediate goal is the creation of a caliphate in Uzbekistan, Tajikistan, and the Kyrgyz Republic, while reserving expansion to Kazakhstan, Turkmenistan, and northwest China for a second stage. The headquarters of IMCA, which is led by the IMU's Yuldashev, are believed to be located in Afghanistan's northeastern Badakhshan province. This unified, militant Islamic force seeks to destabilize Central Asian governments by attacking American and Israeli targets. According to Tokon Mamytov, the deputy chairman of the Kyrgyz NSS, the main insurgent targets are the American embassies and military bases in Central Asia.

Meanwhile, since 2006, the Taliban has experienced a resurgence in Afghanistan while engaging in heavy fighting with NATO forces. They are believed to be basing themselves in the lawless tribal areas on the border between Afghanistan and Pakistan, where bin Ladin and Yuldashev are thought to be hiding as well. Islamist radicals can use these places to recruit, train, and build their strength, then travel freely over the porous borders. Thus the issue of safe havens in the Central Asian region for Islamists remains as much of a problem as it did before September 11. Until the governments of Central and Southern Asia gain greater control over their territory, these problems will likely remain.

Conclusion: The Paradox of Islamism in Central Asia

It is clear that the spread of Islamist ideology is and will remain one of the enduring problems of Central Asia. In many ways the governments of the area, and, in turn, the Western governments that wish to help them, are faced with a paradox. On the one hand, irresponsive and ineffective autocratic governments have alienated their populations, providing political space within which Islamism can grow and gain further adherents. On the other hand, attitudes of openness and tolerance, as prevailed during perestroika, have also provided space for Islamist infiltration. No matter what

form of government prevails, the Islamists often find a way to slip through the cracks. Meanwhile, to advance their cause, they continue to make use of the chaos, civil wars, and crisis of governance throughout the region, from the Taliban fighting in Afghanistan, to the fighting in the tribal areas of Pakistan, to the perceived failures of Central Asian governments to provide economic and social justice; they also persist in making the case to the inhabitants of the region that their only hope for stability is to have an international caliphate.

The cure lies in both better governance and effective encouragement of the more moderate teachings of Islam. Governments in the region must take on the difficult tasks of being both responsive to and responsible for their people's economic needs, and of keeping a close eye on where citizens meet their spiritual needs. They must work to ensure economic prosperity and attempt to revive the forms of Islam that made Central Asia a great religious and scientific center in centuries past. They also need to protect their people from Islamist networks. In the end the Central Asian states will probably lack the resources to accomplish these tasks on their own. The West would do well to help them—especially considering the results of the last Islamist political takeover in the region.

BIBLIOGRAPHY

Abduvakhitov, Abduljabar. "Uzbekistan: Center of Confrontation Between Traditional and Extremist Islam in Central Asia." Presentation at a Nixon Center conference, Washington, DC, July 16, 2003.
"Activation of Hizb ut-Tahrir and Islamic Movement of Uzbekistan Is Reported in Tajikistan." Ferghana.ru information agency and Interfax news agency, October 16, 2006.
Babadjanov, Bakhtiyar, and Muzaffar Kamilov. "Muhammadjan Hindustani (1892–1989) and the Beginning of the 'Great Schism'

Among the Muslims of Uzbekistan." In *Islam and Politics in Russia and Central Asia*, ed., Stephane Dudoignon and Komatsu Hisao. New York: Kegan Paul, 2001.

Baran, Zeyno. *Hizb ut-Tahrir: Islam's Political Insurgency*. Washington, DC: Nixon Center, December 2004.

Baran, Zeyno, S. Frederick Starr, and Svante E. Cornell. *Islamic Radicalism in Central Asia and the Caucasus: Implications for the EU*. Baltimore: Central Asia-Caucasus Institute Silk Road Studies Program, July 2006.

Brill Olcott, Martha, and Marina Barnett. "The Andijan Uprising, Akramiya, and Akram Yuldashev." Web commentary, Carnegie Endowment for International Peace, June 22, 2006.

Daly, John C.K. "The Andijan Disturbances and Their Implications." *Central-Asia Caucasus Analyst*, June 29, 2005.

Fairbanks, Charles. "Sufism in Eurasia." In *Understanding Sufism and Its Potential Role in U.S. Policy*, ed. Zeyno Baran, 13–14. Washington, DC: The Nixon Center, March 2004.

Gianotti, Timothy. "History, Theology and Orders." In *Understanding Sufism and Its Potential Role in U.S. Policy*, ed. Zeyno Baran, 1–2. Washington, DC: The Nixon Center, March 2004.

Godlas, Alan. "Sufism in Eurasia." In *Understanding Sufism and Its Potential Role in U.S. Policy*, ed. Zeyno Baran, 7–9. Washington, DC: The Nixon Center, March 2004.

Huntington, Samuel. *The Clash of Civilizations and the Remaking of World Order*. New York: Touchstone, 1997.

Institute for War and Peace Reporting. "Uzbekistan: Affluent Suicide Bombers." RCA No. 278, April 20, 2004. http://iwpr.net/?p=rca&s=f&o=176631&apc_state=henirca2004, accessed September 2009.

Kaplan, Robert D., *The Ends of the Earth*. New York: Random House, 1996.

Kimmage, Daniel. "Uzbekistan: Bloody Friday in the Ferghana Valley." Radio Free Europe/Radio Liberty, May 14, 2005.

"Leader of the Islamic Movement of Uzbekistan Tahir Yuldashev Threatens Presidents Karimov, Bakiyev, and Rakhmonov." *Central Asia News*, September 13, 2006.

Nasr, S.V.R. "The Rise of Sunni Militancy in Pakistan: The Changing Role of Islamism and the Ulama in Society and Politics." *Modern Asian Studies* 34:1 (February 2000): 139–80.

Nichol, Jim. "Central Asia: Regional Developments and Implications for US Interests." *Congressional Research Service Report IB93108*. Washington, DC: Library of Congress, September 28, 2005. www.crsdocuments.com.

Nichol, Jim. "Kyrgyzstan: Recent Developments and US Interests." *Congressional Research Service Report 97-690 F*. Washington, DC: Library of Congress, October 17, 2005. www.crsdocuments.com.

Pikulina, Marina L. "Hizb ut-Tahrir Organization and Financing." Paper distributed at a Nixon Center conference, Washington, DC, July 16, 2003.

Pylenko, Zoya. "IMU Accused of Attack on Tajik, Kyrgyz Border Posts." *Central Asia-Caucasus Analyst*, May 17, 2006.

Rotar, Igor. "Andijan Leader Threatens 'Campaign of Terror' Against Karimov Regime." *Eurasia Daily Monitor* 2:155 (August 9, 2005). www.jamestown.org/single/?no_cache=1&tx_ttnews%5Btt_news%5D=30761.

———. "Central Asia: Hizb-Ut-Tahrir Wants Worldwide Sharia Law." *Forum 18*, October 29, 2003.

———. "The Islamic Movement of Uzbekistan: A Resurgent IMU?" *Terrorism Monitor* 1:8 (December 18, 2003). www.jamestown.org/programs/gta/single/?tx_ttnews%5Btt_news%5D=26187&tx_ttnews%5BbackPid%5D=178&no_cache=1.

———. "Uzbekistan: What Is Known About Akramiya and the Uprising." *Forum 18 News Service*, June 16, 2005.

Saidazimova, Gulnoza. "Central Asia: Is Islamic Movement of Uzbekistan Really Back?" Radio Free Europe Radio Liberty, February 2, 2006.

United States Department of State. "Terrorism Group Profiles: Islamic Movement of Uzbekistan." *Country Reports on Terrorism 2004*. Washington, DC: U.S. Department of State, 2005.

Zakrulaev, Abdulmutal. "Movarounnahr." In *Battle of Ideas*. Tashkent: Unpublished, 2000.

Afghanistan

Antonio Giustozzi

A central key to understanding Islamism in Afghanistan is the historic differentiation between the roles of the intelligentsia and the clergy. Movements led by clerics are the continuation of a trend started at the time of the first Anglo-Afghan War (1838–42), when village clergy started mobilizing politically. This pattern continued through the second Anglo-Afghan War (1878–80), to the numerous revolts against King Abd al-Rahman (1880–96), the 1928–29 civil war, and the great anti-Soviet jihad of 1978–92. Both clerics and nonclerics in these movements agreed that Islam should play a bigger role in the state but disagreed about who should lead this process. Moreover, each of these two main groups split internally over doctrine, social differences, and personal rivalries. The fragmentation of Afghan society along ethnic, linguistic, tribal, and local community lines made the creation of large movements quite hard, even if this was the ambition of most of the Islamist factions. With the exception of the Shi'a groups and some Salafi groups in the east, all other protagonists of the Afghan Islamist scene always stated their intention to create nationwide movements, but all ended up mainly representing a relatively narrow section of Afghan society.

From the Origins to the Taliban

Islamism as an organized force emerged in Afghanistan in the 1960s. As shown by David B. Edwards, several separate movements were formed. Some were led by the clergy, which for the first time created structured groups rather than relying on informal connections. Two such associations were Khuddam al-Furqan (Servants of the Koran), led by Naqshabandi leader Sibgatullah Mojaddidi, and Jami'at-e-Ulama-e-Muhammadi (the Association of Muhammad's Scholars), led by Hafizji Sahib. Such groups disappeared once the "democratic experiment" of the 1960s ended.

Other groups among the intelligentsia and the students proved more resilient. Among them were Qiyam-i Islami (Uprising of Islam), Madrasa i-Qur'an (School of the Koran), and Jawanan e-Muslimin (Muslim Youth). The first group was led by General Mir Ahmad Shah Rizwani and was mainly based within the army; it tried and failed to organize a coup in 1976. The second group was based on the charismatic leadership of Mawlana Fayzani, a self-styled Sufi *pir* (holy man) who later allied with other Islamist

groups, but the group was rapidly marginalized after his arrest in 1973.

The third group, whose members were to
play a much bigger role in Afghan history,
was initially led by Ghulam Muhammad
Niazi and was composed mainly of theology teachers and students from the Kabul
University faculty of theology and other
faculties. The stated purpose of the group
was to stem the rising influence of the left in
Afghanistan, particularly within the university. Although the left remained the strongest
force in Afghanistan's higher education, the
Jawanan-e Muslimin rose to considerable
influence during the late 1960s and early
1970s. The 1973 coup, which established
a republic in Afghanistan, marked the end
of open activities for the Jawanan, as the
two main leftist groups—Parcham (Banner)
and Khalq (Masses)—initially supported
President Muhammad Daud Khan and were
given positions in his cabinet. That marked
the beginning of relentless state repression
against Islamists, a few of whom were killed.
The majority either went underground or
fled to Pakistan, where they received the
endorsement of that country's government
for planning an uprising against Daud and
the leftists, attempted in 1975 but ending in
utter failure.

The failed coup in 1975 marked the beginning of a series of acrimonious splits within
the Jawanan, the first occurring in 1976. It
is not easy to pin down the exact ideological
differences between different factions of the
Jawanan. Personal rivalries and different
conceptions of how the movement should
organize itself appear to have been key
issues. The leading figure in the Jawanan
at that time was Gulbuddin Hekmatyar,
who had joined as an engineering student,
though he never completed his studies. He
was not popular among the teachers in the
movement because he was younger and

had no background in Islamic studies. As
Hekmatyar was imposing his own view that
the newly created organization should be a
tightly disciplined party, which he proceeded
to call Hizb-i Islami (Islamic Party), Burhan
al-Din Rabbani, who was the leading surviving figure among the "professors," quit
the Jawanan to form his own movement.
Choosing the name Jami'at-i Islami (Islamic
Society), Rabbani marked his preference
for a looser, less disciplined organization.
Another point of contention concerned strategic choices, with Rabbani being inclined to
compromise and negotiate with Daud's government and Hekmatyar being resolutely
opposed. The majority of young activists
stayed with Hekmatyar, with a minority following Rabbani. For about a year, there was
an attempt to reunify the two wings of the
Jawanan. A compromise figure, Qazi Amin
Wadad, was selected to lead the party, but
the attempt at unity collapsed in 1977.

Hizb-i Islami and Jami'at would become
the most prominent actors in the 1978–92
jihad against the pro-Soviet regime and
the Soviet army, but more splits occurred
between 1979 and 1981. In 1979 Mawlawi
Muhammad Yunis Khalis, a respected religious figure from Nangarhar and a graduate in Islamic law, split from Hizb-i Islami
and formed a group still called Hizb-i Islami
but that resembled Rabbani's Jami'at in its
loose organization and reliance on clerical
networks to attract support. In 1981 Abd
al-Rab Rasul Sayyaf, another theology professor who had been in Rabbani's group but
was doctrinally closer to Wahhabi views,
formed his Ittehad-i Islami (Islamic Union)
organization as a result of yet another
failed reunification attempt of the Islamist
ranks. Sayyaf had little personal following, but by virtue of his fluent Arabic and
contacts in the Arab world, he had access
to much financial support from that quar-

ter. He used it to recruit commanders and fighters to his party.

Mawlawi Nabi Muhammadi, a teacher who had not formally been a member of the Islamist movement but who had distinguished himself as a fierce critic of the leftists, formed his own group in 1980 after yet another botched attempt to reunify Hizb and Jami'at under his leadership. The new group took the name of Harakat-e Enqelab-e Islami (Movement of the Islamic Revolution). Nabi Muhammadi had a strong following among the *ulama* (religious scholars), and Harakat was, in fact, the most clerical of the Afghan Islamist groups. With Nabi Muhammadi, the clerical trend within Afghan Islamism mentioned at the beginning of the chapter found an organizational outlet for the first time since the 1960s, although it would take some imagination to define Nabi's organization as a party. It was, in fact, a loose network with even less interaction between the leadership and the rank and file than Rabbani's Jami'at. Sigbatullah Mojaddidi also resurfaced in 1980 with a new group, called Jabh-e Nejat-i Milli (National Liberation Front), which recruited among his Naqshabandi followers. The agenda of the group, however, was not explicitly Islamist, and the party was mainly known for supporting the return of King Zahir Shah (who had been deposed in 1973) to power.

Among Afghanistan's Shi'as, who make up around 15 to 20 percent of the population and mostly belong to the Hazara ethnic group, at least one specifically Shi'a Islamist group appeared in the 1960s, Paiman-e Islami (Islamic Alliance), led by Mir Ali Ahmad Gauhar. The group later allied with Sunni Islamist groups to oppose the policies of President Daud and was essentially wiped out in the repression. Those who survived the repression once again split between Shi'as and Sunnis and played only a minor role in the following years.

Another group originated among the Shi'a minority in Kandahar under the leadership of Shaykh Mohseni, who, despite not being a follower of Iran's Ayatollah Ruhollah Khomeini, was leaning toward political Islamism in the 1970s. He formed a party called Harakat-e Islami in 1978, after the pro-Soviet left took power, and became involved in the jihad. Khomeinist groups had little currency until the early 1980s, when mullahs and ulama trained in Iran and influenced by the Iranian Revolution started returning to Afghanistan in significant numbers, following the liberation of most of Hazarajat from government forces. Different power centers in Iran sponsored their own Afghan protégés, resulting in a multitude of parties being set up in Afghan Hazarajat (the central highlands), which had been abandoned by the central government.

Even after the first attempts to merge some of the groups, eight separate Khomeinist organizations still existed and engaged, to differing degrees, in an intra-Hazara civil war. Initially, the confrontation pitted a unified clerical front known as Shura-ye Ettefaq against local notables and the secular intelligentsia. Once the nonclerical rivals had been defeated, the Khomeinists confronted the traditionalist clergy aligned along the positions of the other leading Iranian religious figure, Ayatollah Abu al-Qassim al-Khoie, and defeated them too. A third phase of this Hazara civil war within the larger Afghan war saw different Khomeinist factions fight each other, with inconclusive outcomes. Only in 1988, following Iranian mediation, did the Khomeinists stop their internecine fighting and merge as a unified party, Hizb-i Wahdat. Nonetheless, they remained factionally divided, with a more nationalist tendency led first by Abd al-Ali Mazari and then by Karim Khalili, and a more religious-extremist one sponsored by the Iranian Pasdaran and led by Muhammad Akbari. These two factions started fighting each other once again during the civil wars of the 1990s, as Akbari supported the Jami'at-led government in Kabul and Mazari and Khalili opposed it. When the Taliban occupied Hazarajat in 1998, Akbari signed a deal with them, while Mazari was killed and the Khalili faction continued its resistance in very difficult conditions.

During the 1978–92 jihad, the original tiny groups of activists spread throughout Afghanistan and created large networks of supporters. Although the initial core group of just over 1,000 activists mostly stayed with Hizb-i Islami, through the clerical networks of Harakat, Jami'at, and Khalis the different parties all established their own constituencies. In the early years of the jihad, Hizb-i Islami was certainly much stronger, because the party was the best organized and often was the first to appear in different regions. By 1983 the other parties were also well established. From 1983 to 1992, Hizb-i Islami gradually lost strength as a result of the attraction by both the equally well-funded Ittehad in the south, east, and southeast and by Jami'at-i Islami northeast of Kabul. Ittehad attracted those commanders who resented the tight discipline imposed by Hekmatyar, while Jami'at attracted mainly Tajik commanders in areas where Hizb-i Islami was dominated by Pashtuns. Harakat-e Enqelab also lost much ground to better-funded parties, such as Khalis's group and Jami'at.

After 1992 Harakat-e Enqelab largely disintegrated, while Khalis's group also virtually ceased to function as an organized entity. Hizb, Jami'at, and Ittehad, however, were all deeply involved in the civil wars of that period. While Hizb-i Islami was fighting against Jami'at, which controlled most of the ministries in Kabul, for most of the time Ittehad remained allied with Jami'at and was mostly engaged in fighting against the Khomeinists, who were now unified in Hizb-i Wahdat.

The clergy, which had been mainly active within the ranks of Harakat-e Enqelab, disappeared from the scene until 1994, when it resurfaced as a key supporter of the newly established Da Afghanistan da Talibano Islami Tahrik (The Afghan Islamic Movement of the Taliban). Initially portraying itself as aiming to bring back to power the deposed king, once the Taliban had captured Kabul in 1996, it turned toward establishing an Islamic state and emerged as the most radical of all Islamist groups in Afghanistan. Apart from much of what had been Harakat-e Enqelab, from whose ranks the Taliban originated, during its expansion throughout Afghanistan the Taliban absorbed most of Sayyaf's and Khalis's followers, including Khalis himself, big chunks of Hizb-i Islami and Jami'at (despite the attempt of their leaderships to oppose the rise of the Taliban), and even a considerable portion of Hizb-i Wahdat. After initially supporting the Taliban against old rival Hizb-i Islami, the Jami'atis were soon locked in a bitter confrontation with the Taliban, in alliance with portions of Hizb-i Wahdat and Ittehad.

By mid-2001, the Taliban controlled almost all of Afghanistan, with the exception of a portion of the northeast and isolated pockets in the northern and central regions. Their ability to mobilize active support among the Afghan population was always limited, however, and a large part of their fighting force was composed of foreigners, mainly Pakistani Pashtuns but also volunteers from several Arab and Islamic countries. Yet the anti-Taliban alliance led by the Jami'atis was facing great difficulties in mobilizing support, with the population tired from many years of war. Furthermore, the various Islamist factions were largely discredited for having failed to rule the country effectively after 1992.

Afghanistan's Islamists After 2001: The Moderates

During the final offensive against the Taliban regime at the end of 2001, the main role by far was played by Jami'at, especially among Islamist groups. Both the Khomeinists and Sayyaf, however, took part in the battle, the latter with very marginal forces. These groups were rewarded with positions in post-Taliban administrations. Once the Taliban was defeated, Hizb-i Islami tried to resurface, first as an active network of "old comrades" and then as an organized force.

Even before the first of the Hamid Karzai administration set foot in Kabul, Jami'at started splintering into rival factions. The tension within the party had long been simmering, but the need to present a united front against the Taliban prevented it from emerging. After 2001 the old leaders and the new generation that had risen up the ranks during the previous 20 years could no longer exist under the same roof. The group of military commanders and members of the intelligentsia who had gathered around the late commander Ahmad Shah Massoud succeeded in marginalizing Rabbani and his followers at the Bonn summit, leaving him without an official position, while the three main figures of the so-called Shura-i Nezar (Coordination Council) all got important jobs in the cabinet. The group included modernly educated Jami'atis, uneducated

commanders, and several former officers of the pro-Soviet regime, which diluted its Islamist identity. Together with their wish to keep their hands free in terms of potential alliances, this explains why they did not push too hard regarding the role of Shari'a in legislation, even if their most prominent spokesman, Yunis Qanuni, issued statements in its support from time to time.

The political parties that are derived from Shura-i Nezar—Afghanistan Newin (New Afghanistan) and Nehzat-i Milli (National Movement)—do not explicitly demand that Shari'a be the sole source of legislation nor particularly insist on expanding the role of Islam within it. It is therefore not clear whether from this point onward they can still be identified with Islamist positions. The ambiguity arises because in an attempt to conciliate the positions of the moderate Islamists with those of the secularists, the new Constitution—approved in 2004—confusingly recognizes a role for Shari'a whenever secular laws are silent. The two parties originating from Shura-i Nezar elected two dozen members of parliament (MPs) in 2005.

Rabbani and his circle, by contrast, maintained relations with the conservative clergy and remained somewhat more firmly within the Islamist galaxy, as Ron Synovitz explained on Radio Free Europe. Within what is left of Jami'at-i Islami, the positions concerning the role of Shari'a in legislation vary considerably. Rabbani himself has not been very vocal in support of it. Yet in remote areas with a strong clerical presence, such as several districts of Badakhshan and southern Takhar, the views of the Jami'atis in this regard hardly differ from those of the supposedly extremist Taliban. In urban areas such as Herat or Mazar-i Sharif, the followers of Jami'at usually have more moderate positions with regard to the interpretation of Shari'a. In general, however, as far as civil and penal law is concerned, it is difficult to find Jami'atis who, if challenged, do not totally endorse the application of the Shari'a. When Jami'atis come to the conclusion that the enforcement of the Shari'a is not a priority or is not the key political issue, they usually quit the party. As of early 2007, Jami'at's following was largely limited to Tajiks, mostly rural. However, it maintained some pockets of support among Pashtuns, mainly around Kandahar. During the 2005 parliamentary elections, the Jami'atis elected around 25 MPs (out of 249).

There is no doubt that Sayyaf remains a staunch supporter of Shari'a and of the most conservative interpretation of it. He continues to maintain strong connections with conservative Islamist circles in the Arab Gulf. In 2004 he renamed his party Dawat-i Islami but soon suffered the split of his deputy, Ahmad Shah Ahmadzai, to even more conservative positions. The latter refused to endorse Hamid Karzai's candidacy for the presidency in 2004, in contrast to Sayyaf, and ran against Karzai in the elections, gathering about 1 percent of the vote. Ahmadzai then formed his own party, which failed to win a single seat in the parliamentary elections. Sayyaf maintains some influence among pockets of conservative Pashtuns by virtue of his closeness to President Karzai and his considerable financial resources. Dawat elected at least eight MPs in 2005, including Sayyaf himself, although his election was marred by the discovery of massive fraud in his favor. He later failed to be elected as parliamentary speaker by a thin margin. Despite being more vocal in his support for conservative Islamist causes than his allies (he remains close to Rabbani), Sayyaf is also a shrewd tactician and a powerful speaker who on several occasions helped Karzai summon up support in the Loya Jirga and in the parliament. In this sense he can be described as a moderate, even if his personal views can be quite extreme on a number of issues.

The various Khomeinist groups that gathered in Hizb-i Wahdat in 1988 entered the post-Taliban period already divided between the supporters of Sayyid Muhammad Akbari, who had chosen to cooperate with the successful Taliban, and supporters of Karim Khalili and Muhammad Muhaqiq. Soon the split was formalized with the formation of two separate parties. Later, Khalili and Muhaqiq also parted ways over issues of leadership and their relationship with Karzai.

However, possibly the most important trend among the former Khomeinists is the evaporation of any consistently Islamist perspective. In part, this might be because of the minority character of Shi'ism in Afghanistan, which would make advocating legislation based on Shari'a counterproductive. However, there also seems to have been a genuine influence of reformist and post-Khomeinist ideas coming from Iran, as well as a rise of enthnonationalist sentiments among Hazaras, who represented the near totality of the supporters of the old Hizb-i Wahdat. Iran's loss of credibility as a source of political and ideological inspiration contributed decisively to this pattern, not least because of the mistreatment and racial abuse to which Afghan Hazaras were subjected in Iran as refugees or migrant workers. Explicit Islamist positions likely survive among elements of the Shi'a clergy but do not seem to feature on the agenda of any of the half dozen Shi'a groups on the Afghan political scene, despite the continuing dominance of the clergy in most of these organizations.

Hizb-i Islami was not part of the initial ruling coalition because of its near absence from the battlefield and its alignment with

Iran during the negotiations leading to the post-Taliban settlement. A number of former members of the party found their way to other groups, such as Jami'at, or made individual deals with the government. As a separate, organized force, Hizb-i Islami started reemerging in 2002, when a large meeting took place in Kabul, bringing together 200–300 leaders and members. Hekmatyar, who had already declared a jihad against foreign troops in Afghanistan, was absent, as were some of his closest military commanders. In any case, the attempt to form an official group based on the surviving Hizb-i Islami networks immediately faced attempts of disruption by the component of Jami'at most bitterly opposed to Hizb, that is Shura-i Nezar.

Thanks to its virtual control over the security services, the Shura-i Nezar network was able to launch a massive operation against the resurfacing Hizb and arrested hundreds of its supporters who were gathered in Kabul for the meeting. Although the security services claimed the discovery of a coup plot, according to International Security Assistance Forces (ISAF) officials the claim was unsubstantiated, and under international pressure they had to gradually release the prisoners. The obstacles created by Jami'at, in any case, significantly delayed the official launch of a legal Hizb-i Islami, which only took place in 2005 under the leadership of two midlevel leaders of the old party, Khalid Faruqi and Abd al-Hadi Arghandiwal. During interviews with members of the party, they presented their group as a peaceful alternative to the Taliban insurgency because of grassroots support for it in many areas inhabited by Pashtuns (chiefly the eastern region).

During the parliamentary elections of 2005, many former members of Hizb-i Islami were elected—as many as 42 according to one count. However, several of these had long ceased any association with Hekmatyar and Hizb-i Islami. It is estimated that about 30 to 35 of them maintained links with the party. As of fall 2006, about 15 had formally joined the new, legal Hizb-i Islami, with the rest wavering between different options. Faruqi's party was not the only claimant to the old Hizb-i Islami's inheritance. Several smaller groups also surfaced, such as Hizb-i Muttahed-i Islami (Islamic Unification Party), led by Wahidullah Sabawun, and Hizb-i Salah wa Wahdat (Peace and Unity Party), led by one founder of Hizb-i Islami, Abd al-Qadir Emami. Neither of these parties appears to have a significant influence, although Emami managed to get elected to parliament. Some key personalities of the party, such as Qazi Amin Wadad, who had been the leader in 1976–77, also abstained from involvement with any of the Hizb-i Islami derivatives and instead later cooperated with the National United Front (see below).

It is not clear what the agenda of the Faruqi-Arghandiwal group is, though it seems less a genuine splinter from Hekmatyar than a front for favoring negotiations with the outlawed (and militarily active) branch of the party and/or a means to infiltrate government institutions. As of May 2007, the Hizb-i Islami network centered around Faruqi's group also included a number of government officials, among them several provincial governors, two cabinet ministers, Karzai's chief of staff, and possibly the attorney general as well.

By contrast, Hizb-i Islami's military activities were relatively limited. Its main areas of military activity during 2006 were Kunar, Laghman, and Logar provinces (in that order), with smaller-scale activities going on in Kabul, Kapisa, Nangarhar, Paktya, Khost, and Paktika. On a more limited scale, some military activities had already started in 2002 and gradually grew afterward. This increased activity led to growing repression of Hizb-i Islami by the local security forces. Preemptive operations were also reported in the area of Jalalabad because of its high strategic importance, leading to the arrest of individuals accused of conspiring against the government. At least two commanders of Hizb-i Islami were arrested in February in unspecified locations of Nangarhar. NATO sources put the strength of Hizb-i Islami at 300 to 400 fighters in 2006, as cited by Anthony Cordesman, which looks low given the geographical spread of the party's activity. This should, however, be interpreted as an average for active fighters. A total figure of around 1,500 looks more realistic.

What all the groups examined so far have in common is their acceptance of elections as a way to select the political leadership, even if their interpretation of what elections should look like tends to vary and mostly does not go beyond some form of "limited democracy." With the exception of Sayyaf's Dawat, these groups also accept, to various degrees, the idea that women should be educated and should work. Within the Afghan context, therefore, all these groups could be described as relatively moderate. Several more radical groups are, however, also active in Afghanistan.

Afghanistan's Islamists After 2001: The Radicals

By far the most important radical Islamist group in Afghanistan is the so-called Taliban, which actually describes its adherents as the followers of the Islamic Emirate of Afghanistan, that is, the state overthrown by foreign intervention in 2001. Although military activities effectively never stopped, during the summer of 2002 a transition

occurred from the disorganized, sometimes desperate fight of remnants of the previous regime and associated foreign jihadi volunteers to a planned attempt to start a new insurgency. From then on, the level of violence continued to grow, although the yearly number of victims remained in the hundreds rather than the thousands until 2005, when for the first time it reached the 1,000 mark. Although it is difficult to come up with any meaningful estimate of how many Taliban insurgents there were in 2006–2007, clearly by then several thousand were active at any given time, and probably 15,000–20,000 individuals participated in the fighting on a full-time or part-time basis.

To a large extent, the leadership of the Taliban has stayed the same, confirming the claim that the insurgency was sponsored by the "Taliban state" gone underground. Mullah Muhammad Omar remained the unchallenged moral authority, although it is not clear to what extent he exercised effective leadership. The main development was the rise through the ranks of a number of former field commanders of the "Taliban's Emirate," who have now been incorporated in the leadership structures. This is clearly a consequence of the new situation faced by the Taliban, which for the first time is being forced to operate as a real insurgency movement.

The core elements of the Taliban's ideology remain the same, such as the strict scripturalist approach and the heavy influence of the Islamic revivalist school Deobandi, which is based on strict adherence to the Sunna and Shari'a. Its position toward the role of women in society (i.e., segregation), toward secular education, and toward elections has not changed either. Despite these elements of continuity, some changes have been noticeable in the Taliban's ideology, at least in part driven by tactical considerations. Its attitude toward new technologies is, for example, now very different from that of the past. Far from banning images and the filming of human beings, the Taliban now indulges in large-scale production of jihadi propaganda with videos featuring commanders and fighters in VCD and DVD format. Although until 2006 the Taliban was still "inviting" people to grow beards and avoid listening to music, since then it has dropped these demands in areas under its control.

Otherwise, the Taliban's behavior has often remained extreme. Executions not only of alleged government spies but also of state employees such as teachers and government officials were commonplace throughout 2002 to 2007 and were often carried out in a gruesome way. Nonetheless, despite having started their campaign of infiltrating Afghanistan from Pakistan in 2002, from 2003 the Taliban insurgents were able to obtain the support of several communities inside Afghanistan, first in Zabul (2003) and then in Uruzgan, Hilmand, Kandahar, and Ghazni. With its chief constituencies of madrasa boys, village mullahs, and illiterate villagers, the Taliban was not able to deploy sophisticated strategies and tactics. As a result, it usually fared badly in direct clashes with foreign troops and the Afghan National Army (ANA), although it did better against the poorly trained, undisciplined Afghan National Police (ANP).

However, thanks to the adoption of tactics from Iraq, such as roadside bombs and suicide attacks (from 2005), the Taliban was able to inflict significant casualties on its adversaries. According to official reports, from March 2006 to March 2007, the Taliban killed 200 ANA soldiers, up to 700 policemen, and 113 foreign combatants, as well as an undisclosed number of private militiamen and security guards for the loss

of up to 3,000 of its own. After some ill-fated attempts to confront the foreign contingents on open ground during 2006, in 2007 the Taliban focused efforts at expanding the geographical scope of its activities. In particular, it appeared to be investing large human and material resources on expansion toward western Afghanistan.

There is little question that the aim of the Taliban is to grab back power in Kabul. Although attempts to negotiate with the Kabul government have been going on for some time, it is not clear who among the Taliban has been involved. In 2003 some moderate elements of the former Taliban regime approached Kabul and eventually accepted a reconciliation offer. It is likely that later negotiations too only involved noncombatant elements of the old Taliban government or individual commanders. Sources close to the Taliban hint that serious negotiations could occur once the withdrawal of foreign troops starts, but there seems to be little room for the formation of a coalition government including both Taliban and pro-Western elements because the cultural and political distance between the two is huge.

A few smaller radical groups also exist on the Afghan scene. Small Salafi organizations have from time to time surfaced in Kunar and Nuristan provinces, which from the 1970s were gradually converted by Salafi preachers. The three main organizations among these are Jama'at al-Da'wa al-Salafiyya wal-Kitab (Society of the Salafi Movement and of the Book), the Bara bin Malik Front of Mullah Isma'il in Kunar, and the Dawlat-e Enqelabi-ye Islami (Islamic Revolutionary State) of Nuristan. The active followers of each of these organizations do not exceed the low hundreds, and their influence is very localized, usually to a district or two within the above-mentioned provinces.

Other radical organizations are essentially offshoots of the Taliban. Jaiysh al-Muslimin, for example, split in 2004 and was reabsorbed in 2005. For a while it appeared to have a significant following in Zabul and Hilmand, but lack of external support led to its collapse. A smaller group, Jaysh al-Mahdi, was also formed by a former Taliban supporter in 2002 and appears to remain militarily active, cooperating with international jihadi volunteers to organize cross-border infiltration.

Influence of Islamism Within Society

After the fall of the Taliban regime, it was widely believed that Islamist groups in Afghanistan attracted little support among the population. This was because of their less-than-impressive performance after 1992, when they indulged in internecine fighting and allowed whatever was left of the Afghan state to collapse. While this belief might have been true to some degree, the extent of Islamist groups' actual influence might have been underestimated. Unpopular in the cities, the Islamists maintained strong constituencies in most of the countryside, not least because of the coercive power of their militias. At least some of their electoral success has to be attributed to genuine support.

In most cases, it appears that Islamist MPs benefited from being the best-known candidates locally, which, together with superior financial resources and the support of armed militias, gave them an edge over rivals. Up to 116 MPs out of 249 were linked to Islamist groups in the parliament elected in 2005, including four former Taliban. In terms of ideological support, in the early post-Taliban years, the main constituency of the Islamists was the clergy. Afghanistan's clergy has traditionally been quite pluralist, with a strong presence of Sufi Tariqas (members of a particular school of Sufism), particularly the Naqshabandiyya and the Qadiriyya.

With some exceptions, during the jihad, these Tariqas stayed away from the Islamists (who were critical of them) and supported other parties and movements. However, the collapse of Afghanistan's educational system resulted in growing numbers of Afghan would-be mullahs being educated in Pakistan, where Deobandism was gradually becoming more and more dominant. Its anti-Sufi inclination resulted in the decline of influence of Sufi orders and, more broadly, of traditionalist mullahs in Afghanistan, as the new Pakistani-trained generation replaced the old. If the links forged between the clergy and Islamist groups during the anti-Soviet jihad are taken into account, it is not surprising that by the early years of the twenty-first century Afghanistan's clergy was closer to the Islamists and more politicized than it had ever been.

Although significant traditionalist tendencies still exist and are influential, particularly in some regions, the Deobandi stream is today probably the single-largest component of the clergy in Afghanistan. The only survey of the attitude of the clergy that has taken place in recent years, carried out by Cooperation for Peace and Unity (CPAU)—an Afghan research nongovernmental organization—for the International Peace Research Institute in Oslo (PRIO), indicates that while radical and extremist views are a minority, hostility toward the presence of foreign troops in the country is nearly universal, particularly among Pashtuns. According to Afghan officials and UN workers, the presence of mullahs preaching against foreign troops and in favor of armed struggle against them is reported not only in the regions directly affected by the insurgency but also throughout Afghanistan. Northeastern Afghanistan, a stronghold of anti-Taliban resistance until 2001, hosts a particularly conservative clergy, within whose ranks quite a few mullahs openly oppose the "occupiers." However, mullahs preaching against the foreign troops can be found even in Kabul.

While the mullahs' proclamations were initially paid little attention by a population too busy enjoying the reopening of the country after years of almost total isolation, the mood started changing in 2005–2006. Although gauging the direction of Afghan public opinion is not easy, press reports and conversations with Afghans and expatriates suggest that xenophobic and religious sentiments resurfaced following a combination of factors, ranging from the escalating violence in the south with its consequent loss of life to the perception that the Kabul government was paying much greater attention to the demands of foreign partners than to those of the Afghan population. Cases such as that of Abd al-Rahman, an Afghan convert to Christianity who was illegally shipped out of the country by President Karzai to avoid an embarrassing sentence for apostasy, contributed to widening the constituency of the conservative mullahs and their Islamist allies.

Although it is impossible to be sure of the degree of support enjoyed by the different groups, there are indications that Hizb-i Islami is currently the most popular of the "moderate" Islamist groups. The Jami'ati group lost much credibility because of its relatively long association with power (from 1992 until 1996 and from 2001 until Karzai started purging its members in 2005). This group also suffers from a tendency to disintegrate into local networks more concerned with immediate financial and status gains than with any ideological agenda. Rabbani's organizational model, based on loose networking and ideological eclecticism, is under strain due to the absence of a clearly identifiable threat to Jami'at, which could keep its members united. Despite being considered by many as bearing primary responsibility for the deadly fighting in Kabul from 1992 to 1996, Hekmatyar's party, based on strict discipline and ideological consistency, seems to navigate better the complex post-Taliban environment.

Foreign Support

During the 1978–92 jihad, all Afghan Islamist groups were dependent on external support to the tune of billions of dollars, of which probably less than half came from the United States. The rest was supplied by Arab supporters, both by governments such as that of Saudi Arabia and by private individuals. The different parties used the money in different ways. Some leaders, most notably Sayyaf and Rabbani, managed to save some of the cash and invest it, allegedly in Southeast Asia. After 2001 they started transferring part of their cash back to Afghanistan and invested it in the property sector, particularly in Kabul. Because of this they have been the target of accusations of corruption. But as a result of these dubious practices, they remain comparatively well funded, even if direct external support has either waned or has declined to a small fraction of what it used to be.

Hekmatyar, by contrast, seems to have invested all the cash received in support of the cause of jihad in the fighting, without accumulating sufficient reserves, or in any case, he burned his reserves in the early years of the civil war (1992–96) because he was trying to wrest control of Kabul in the absence of much external support. As a result, after 2001 Hekmatyar appeared decisively cash strapped, as he complained in public. By far the largest chunk of external support for jihadi forces after 2001 went to the Taliban, leaving just crumbs for Hizb-i Islami.

The role of Pakistan in supporting Islamist groups in Afghanistan is at the same time obvious and difficult to define. There is no question that support is delivered through Pakistani territory and that current or former Pakistani officials are assisting the Taliban with advice and training. What is not certain is whether the Pakistanis provide direct funding and supplies or simply channel whatever is sent by other sources. The Pakistanis are also known to support Hekmatyar politically and have been lobbying for his rehabilitation in Afghanistan but do not seem to provide much direct help to him. The extent of private support for the cause of the Taliban is, of course, unknown. Based on the 2006 level of Taliban activities, their annual expenditure seemed to be between $30 million and $40 million. However, the Taliban is also known to be raising revenue internally and might save its revenue for "rainy days," so that the actual level of external support might fall short or exceed that amount.

The Khomeinists have, of course, been receiving support from Iran, but in modest quantities during the jihad. During the years of the war against the Taliban, Iran emerged as a more important supplier not only for the Khomeinist groups but also for Jami'at. The extent of Iranian support after 2001 is, however, unclear. Allegations of the Iranian regime pumping money into charitable Shi'a organizations and social initiatives sponsored by the Khomeinist clergy are plentiful, but direct contributions to the coffers of Islamist organizations seem to take place on a more ad hoc basis, if at all. The Iranian embassy was very active in sponsoring the 2007 formation of the Jabh-e Muttahed-i Milli (National United Front), which includes several Islamist groups as well as secularist organizations and personalities. Cash is likely to have been used as an incentive for its formation. However, not even all the old Khomeinists joined the Front. In particular, Hazara-based groups stayed out, leaving Akbari as one of the few old leaders of Wahdat to join.

As widely reported in the press, with some exaggeration, the Iranians also appear to be busy establishing a network of contacts among old field commanders of the jihad and civil war periods, possibly even within the ranks of the Taliban, for future use in the event of American intervention against Iran. In terms of relations with Islamist leaderships, contacts are known to exist not only with the Khomeinists but also with various Jami'ati groups and presumably with Hizb-i Islami as well, given that Hekmatyar was residing in Iran until early 2002. Some observers believe that a particular component of the Taliban, that is the group led by Sayfullah Mansur in Paktya Province, might also entertain contacts with the Iranians and may receive help from them. Mansur's father had been one of the leaders of Harakat-e Enqelab but was forced to rely on Iranian support after he split from Nabi Muhammadi. From the summer of 2007, allegations of Iranian support for the mainstream Taliban began to surface.

During the anti-Taliban war, Russia also provided support to Jami'at-i Islami, but it is not clear whether this support continued after 2001. There is little evidence of any substantial transfer of funds, although at least some military supplies sent by Russia were handed over to the militias of Shura-i Nezar rather than to the Ministry of Defense.

Poised to Take Power Again?

Karzai's regime appears to be under siege from different Islamist forces. The Taliban insurgency has slowly been expanding beyond its traditional strongholds in southern Afghanistan, despite its failure to effectively challenge American and allied forces on the battlefield. The chances of the Taliban entering Kabul by force as long as foreign troops remain stationed in the country are nil, but the possibility of the Taliban forcing out some of the contingents deployed to Afghanistan should not be ruled out. Karzai's difficult predicament is going to be increasingly exploited by more moderate Islamists to extract concessions, namely a greater share of power at the central and regional levels. The various Jami'ati groups have been trying to use the National United Front as a way to gain more influence in Kabul, reminding Karzai that any moves against their strongholds in northern Afghanistan will lead to the government's destruction. At the same time, they have been urging him to invite his former allies back with substantial chunks of power.

In the absence of direct encouragement by a foreign supporter, the Jami'atis are unlikely to resort to violence, even if disappointed by Karzai. Moreover, their ranks are far from unified, with many local leaders courting Karzai's favor independently. The chances of Hizb-i Islami expanding its already growing role in government seem higher. It could use its strong presence in eastern Afghanistan, where it could decisively contribute to the prevention of an expansion of the insurgency, as a bargaining chip to ease off American suspicion. In exchange for more power and the rehabilitation of Hekmatyar, Hizb-i Islami could suspend military activities and work to contain other insurgent groups. As for

the longer-term perspectives of Islamism in Afghanistan, short of major international developments forcing an American withdrawal, any strengthening of Islamist influence will have to take place through power-sharing agreements. At the same time, in the event of American withdrawal, given that military power is largely concentrated in Islamist hands either directly or indirectly through their infiltration of the security agencies, Islamist groups would rapidly make a claim for state control. Since the divisions among the Islamists are as deep as ever, a new civil war would be the likely result.

BIBLIOGRAPHY

Coll, Steve. *Ghost Wars*. New York: Penguin, 2004.
Connell, Michael, and Alireza Nader. *Iranian Objectives in Afghanistan: Any Basis for Collaboration with the United States?* A Project Iran Workshop. Alexandria, VA: CNA Corporation, 2006. www.princeton.edu/~lisd/publications/finn_Iran_Afghanistan.pdf.
Cordesman, Anthony. *Winning in Afghanistan: The Challenges and the Response*. Washington, DC: Center for Strategic and International Studies, 2007.
Davis, Anthony. "Afghan Opposition Gains Coherence." *Jane's Terrorism & Security Monitor*, May 2003.
———. "Recent Violence Obscures Deeper Threats for Afghanistan." *Jane's Intelligence Review*, October 2002.
Dixit, Aabha. *Soldiers of Islam: Origins, Ideology and Strategy of the Taliban*. New Delhi: Institute for Defense Studies and Analysis. www.idsa-india.org/an-aug-2.html.
Dorronsoro, Gilles. *Pakistan and the Taliban: State Policy, Religious Networks and Political Connections*. Paris: CERI, October 2000. www.ceri-sciencespo.com/archive/oct000/artgd.pdf.
———. *Revolution Unending*. London: C. Hurst, 2005.
Edwards, David B. *Before Taliban: Genealogies of the Afghan Jihad*. Berkeley: University of California Press, 2002.

———. "The Evolution of Shi'i Political Dissent in Afghanistan." In *Shi'ism and Social Protest,* eds. Juan R.I. Cole and Nikki R. Keddie, 201–29. New Haven, CT: Yale University Press, 1986.

———. "Print Islam: Religion, Revolution, and the Media in Afghanistan." *Anthropological Quarterly* 68:3 (1995): 171–84.

———. "Summoning Muslims: Print, Politics, and Religious Ideology in Afghanistan." *Journal of Asian Studies* 52:3 (1993): 609–28.

Ghani, Ashraf. "Islam and Counter-Revolutionary Movements." In *Islam in Asia,* ed. John L. Esposito, 79–96. Oxford, UK: Oxford University Press, 1987.

Giustozzi, Antonio. *Koran, Kalashnikov and Laptop: The Neo-Taliban Insurgency in Afghanistan 2002–2007.* London: C. Hurst; New York: Columbia University Press, 2007.

———. "The Missing Ingredient: Non-Ideological Insurgency and State Collapse in Western Afghanistan, 1979–1992." *Working Paper* 11:2. London: Crisis States Research Centre, 2007.

Griffin, Michael. *Reaping the Whirlwind: The Taliban Movement in Afghanistan.* London: Pluto Press, 2001.

Human Rights Watch. "Lessons in Terror Attacks on Education in Afghanistan." *World Report 2006* 18:6 (2006).

Ibrahimi, Niamatullah. "At the Sources of Factionalism and Civil War in Hazarajat." *Working Paper* 2:41. London: Crisis States Research Centre, 2009.

———. "The Failure of a Clerical Proto-State: Hazarajat 1979–1984." *Working Paper* 6:2. London: Crisis States Research Centre, 2006.

"Increasing Afghan IED Threat Gives Forces Cause for Concern." *Jane's Intelligence Review,* August 2006.

International Crisis Group. "Countering Afghanistan's Insurgency: No Quick Fixes." *Asia Report* 123 (2006).

Johnson, Thomas H., and M. Chris Mason. "Understanding the Taliban and Insurgency in Afghanistan." *Orbis* (Winter 2007): 71–89.

Jones, Seth G. "Averting Failure in Afghanistan." *Survival* 1 (2006): 111–28.

Kemp, Robert. "Counterinsurgency in Eastern Afghanistan." In *Countering Insurgency and Promoting Democracy*, ed. Manolis Priniotakis. Washington, DC, Council for Emerging National Security Affairs Studies, 2007.

Maley, William. "Interpreting the Taliban." In *Fundamentalism Reborn?* ed. W. Maley, 1–28. London: C. Hurst, 1998.

Marsden, Peter. *The Taliban: War, Religion and the New Order in Afghanistan.* London: Oxford University Press, 1998.

Naylor, Sean D. "A Stronger Taliban Lies Low, Hoping the U.S. Will Leave Afghanistan." *Armed Forces Journal* 2 (2006). www.armedforcesjournal.com/2006/02/1404902/.

Olesen, Asta. *Islam and Politics in Afghanistan.* Surrey, UK: Curzon Press, 1995.

Rashid, Ahmed. *Taliban.* London: IB Tauris, 2000.

———. "The Taliban: Exporting Extremism." *Foreign Affairs* (November/December 1999): 22–35.

Roy, Olivier. *Afghanistan: From Holy War to Civil War.* Princeton, NJ: Darwin Press, 1995.

———. "Has Islamism a Future in Afghanistan?" In *Fundamentalism Reborn?* ed. W. Maley, 199–211. London: C. Hurst, 1998.

———. *Islam and Resistance in Afghanistan.* Cambridge, UK: Cambridge University Press, 1990.

———. "Islamic Radicalism in Afghanistan and Pakistan." *Writenet Paper* 06/2001. Geneva: UNHCR, 2002.

———. *Pakistan and the Taliban.* Paris: CERI, October 2000. www.ceri-sciencespo.com/archive/oct000/artor.pdf.

Rubin, Barnett R. *The Fragmentation of Afghanistan: State Formation and Collapse in the International System.* New Haven, CT: Yale University Press, 1995.

Shahzad, Syed Saleem. "Pakistan, the Taliban and Dadullah." *Briefing* 3. Bradford, UK: Pakistan Security Research Unit, 2007.

Smith, Ben. "Afghanistan Where Are We?" Defence Academy of the United Kingdom, Conflict Research Center, Central Asian Series, 05/30, June 2005.

Synovitz, Ron. "Division Between Islamists, Moderates Hampers Effort on New Constitution." Radio Free Europe/Radio Liberty, February 1, 2003.

Tahir, Muhammad. "Iranian Involvement in Afghanistan." *Terrorism Monitor* 5:1 (January 18, 2007). www.jamestown.org/programs/gta/single/?tx_ttnews[tt_news]=1004&tx_ttnews[backPid]=182&no_cache=1.

Trives, Sébastien. "Afghanistan: Réduire l'insurrection. Le cas du sud-est" (Afghanistan: Reduce the Insurgency. The Case of South-East). *Politique étrangère* 1 (2006): 105–18.

Wright, Joanna. "Taliban Insurgency Shows Signs of Enduring Strength." *Jane's Intelligence Review,* October 2006.

Yousaf, Mohammed, and Mark Adkin. *The Bear Trap.* London: L. Cooper, 1992.

The Caucasus

Zeyno Baran and Svante E. Cornell

In both the North and South Caucasus, the role and influence of radical Islam has risen significantly in recent years. In the North Caucasus, Chechnya has been the site of two ongoing wars in an effort to secure independence from Russia: The first took place from 1994 to 1996, while the second began in 1999 and is ongoing. In the South Caucasus, a slower growth of radicalism is also observable, though its political ambitions have been limited.

The most significant development regarding radical Islam in the Caucasus is the changing character of the insurgency in the North Caucasus. Over time, the rebel movement in Chechnya—which began as a nationalist insurgency—has gradually become more radicalized, and at this point it can be labeled as much Islamist as nationalist. Moreover, the movement has expanded beyond Chechnya and now aims to establish a caliphate spanning the entire North Caucasus. This ideology led the fighters to invade the neighboring province of Dagestan in 1999, which set off the second Chechen war.

The war in Chechnya has been brutal, with reports of massive civil rights abuses by Russian soldiers, and was exploited by Russian Prime Minister Vladimir Putin as a means of securing his election to the presidency in 2000. With Russia cracking down in Chechnya, the Islamists have scattered to the other five Russian North Caucasus republics, taking with them their violent campaign—some have made overt attempts to take over local centers of power. Chechnya is now only one of the theaters of the struggle, with Dagestan and Ingushetia considerably affected. Islamist ideology has, in turn, spread to parts of neighboring Azerbaijan and isolated areas of Georgia, though to a much lesser extent.

North Caucasus: The Russian Republics

As in Central Asia, the growing strength in the Caucasus of extremist Salafi ideology—often referred to as Wahhabism—over Sufism is relatively new and is the result primarily of outside influence, coupled with Russia's mismanagement of the region. Similar to other developments in Central Asia that began with perestroika (literally "restructuring," particularly of the Soviet economic and government bureaucracies), local Muslims were given the ability "to be Muslims again," and foreign (especially Saudi) missionaries were able to enter the North Caucasus area. Conditions also existed in the region that in many ways contributed to the growth of Islamism, such as severe poverty and deep disillusionment among Muslims with their collaborationist establishment leaders, who maintained control over both the political and religious structures of the republics. Moreover, 70 years of atheism had undermined knowledge of basic religious tenets among Muslims of the Soviet Union. As such, many of those who were actively looking for Islamic ideology were tempted to look abroad to the core areas of Islam and to the extremist groups originating in the Middle East, which claimed to know the true values of Islam.

What made the rather dramatic spread of Wahhabism possible was money—and lots of it. Saudi officials have indicated that they have spent over $80 billion assisting Islamic activities around the world since the mid-1970s, of which a considerable amount went to the North Caucasus. There are now over 160 Salafi mosques, countless madrasas, and many other radical Islamist institutions in the heart of a formerly moderate Muslim region. A large number of the Islamic publications and Islamic organizations in the region are extremist in nature—as much because of the financial poverty of the moderate groups as the wealth of the extremist ones. Indeed, homegrown Islamic associations, often of a conciliatory, moderate character, are virtually devoid of finances, while Salafi groups have seemingly endless pockets.

As a result of their proselytizing, the Salafis established a small but very powerful community comprising roughly 5 percent of the North Caucasian population. They eventually succeeded in spurring the radicalization of most of the Chechen resistance movement, turning many Chechen warlords into armed advocates of Wahhabism. As Alex Alexiev writes, as a result, in addition to attacking the Russians, the radicalized Chechen rebels also attacked Sufis, began destroying Sufi tombs, accused Sufi shaykhs of apostasy, and declared Sufis to be *kafirs,* or heretics.

Chechnya

The radicalization of elements of the Chechen resistance took place primarily after the first war in the republic, which was fought under the leadership of the secular nationalist leader Jokhar Dudayev. A former Soviet air force general and married to a Russian, Dudayev was as far from an Islamic extremist as could be. The first war had been a predominantly local affair, even failing to involve neighboring republics, though isolated mujahidin from across the Muslim world did make their way to Chechnya. Prominent among the Arab volunteers was the late Amir al-Khattab, a Saudi veteran of the wars in Afghanistan, Tajikistan, and Bosnia. Khattab made the Chechen cause his own while contributing greatly to changing the course of the conflict from a nationalist to a religious one. Persian Gulf organizations reportedly increased their presence in the region in 1995, when the Illinois-based Benevolence International Foundation is thought to have established links to the first Islamists in Chechnya. The group was originally devised to channel funds to the Afghan jihad, but later it was also heavily involved in Bosnia before it shifted its focus to Chechnya. (In 2002 the U.S. government identified it as a source of terrorist funding.)

Unlike in Central Asia, the Islamist movements of the North Caucasus have not developed into clear and visible organizations, instead remaining networks of individuals and subgroups that are known by various names. Foreign volunteers are, after their merger with Chechen guerrilla formations, organized in the form of small *jama'ats*, or societies. The principal radical figures are associated with entities that are known by a variety of names, including the Islamic International Peacekeeping Brigade, the Special Purpose Islamic Regiment (al-Jihad-Fisi-Sabililah), and the Riyadus-Salikhin (Garden of Martyrs) Reconnaissance and Sabotage Battalion of Chechen Martyrs. In Dagestan the most important group is Shari'a Jama'at, while in Kabardino-Balkaria it is Yarmukh. These labels are often secondary to informal personal and clan ties and loyalties to charismatic individuals. As Cerwyn Moore has noted, the notion of a coherent body of radicalized fighters within the Chechen resistance seems, at best, to be problematic. As a result, there is an amorphous character to these groups and the threat they pose, because they change their names, organizational structure, and membership with relative ease. This is a partial explanation for Russia's failure to stamp out these groups. Other reasons are lack of competence, in-fighting between government agencies, and not least the tendency of Russian governmental agencies to target secular or moderate Chechen groupings far more than radical ones, since the former enjoyed international recognition and therefore were seen to pose a greater danger to Russia's policy in the region. By contrast, as radical groups gradually came to dominate the resistance, Moscow enjoyed much greater tacit support or understanding from the West for its Chechnya policy. Only belatedly did Moscow work more effectively to stamp out the radicals, and the ensuing high death rates of leading Islamists in Chechnya has become a further factor impeding the development of clear-cut organizations.

The key native figure that came to lead the radicals was the notorious Chechen field commander, former computer engineer, and terrorist Shamil Basayev, who died on or around July 10, 2006. (Though it has been confirmed that he was killed in an explosion, it remains unclear if the explosion was an accident or the work of Russian soldiers. Most evidence points to an accidental death.) Alongside Basayev until his own death in 2002 was Khattab, who provided the chief linkage between the radicalized parts of the Chechen resistance and the international jihadist movement. Yet it should be noted that rather than establishing an organic link between Basayev and al-Qa'ida, the North Caucasus radicals have mainly sought to emulate the group's tactics and language. After Khattab's death, he was replaced by another Saudi known as Amir al-Walid. Walid was, in turn, killed in April 2004, leaving a vacuum in terms of contacts between the Chechen guerrillas and the Arab world. This also took place at the time of increasing focus on Iraq by militant Islamist groups, further contributing to pushing Chechen groups into the periphery of international jihadists.

Basayev and Khattab controlled areas of southeastern Chechnya in the 1996–99 interwar period, working incessantly to unite Dagestan and Chechnya into a joint Islamist state on the model of the imamate of Imam Shamil in the nineteenth century. Hence, Basayev organized and led the Islamic Majlis of Chechnya and Dagestan, an organization devised to be the nucleus of the joint state. From there, he staged an invasion of mountainous areas of Dagestan in September 1999, sparking the second Chechen war. Presently, following the death of Al-Walid in 2004, the leader of the foreign fighters in Chechnya is a less well-known figure known as Muhannad, a former disciple of Khattab's. He appears to have proven unable to rebuild the linkages to Middle Eastern beneficiaries that plummeted following Khattab's death.

In Chechnya itself, Moscow's policies have led to excessive reliance on one local power broker, the Kadyrov family, and its forces. Though Moscow at first sought to retain balancing forces against the Kadyrovs in order to be able to rein them in if necessary, the expansion of the Kadyrovtsi's power has been such that no faction in Chechnya, whether loyal to Moscow, separatist, or radical Islamist, could challenge it. Yet Kadyrov's power is based on fear, both among the fighters that join him and are loyal to his person, and among the general population. Kadyrov has clearly grown into an independent force, with strong tensions between him and the Russian military. His loyalty is a personal loyalty not to Russia but to Putin, and it remains unclear whether this loyalty is transferable on either end.

Kadyrov's exclusively personal loyalty to Putin generated concerns that changes in the power balance in Moscow could result in disturbances in the North Caucasus. Nevertheless, and perhaps mainly because of Putin's continued control over state affairs following his transition to the post of prime minister in spring 2008, Kadyrov's position has remained stable. Should Putin's power wane—a prospect that may appear unlikely at present but cannot be excluded—that could produce a new mode of government at the center that gradually rethinks its North Caucasus policy, implying new rules of the game to which Ramzan Kadyrov may not accede. Second, it is unclear what Kadyrov's demise—if, for example, he were assassinated as his father was—would imply. Whether a successor would emerge and whether this successor would be able to keep the Kadyrovtsi together as a coherent unit loyal

to the Kremlin is very much an open question. Hence, Moscow's Chechnya policy is hardly sustainable in the long term—this entirely aside from the fact that Moscow needs Kadyrov almost as much as Kadyrov needs Moscow's support; and that the possibility exists that Kadyrov could turn against Moscow at some point.

In the meantime, the Kadyrovtsi rule Chechnya with an iron hand, with crimes against the civilian population routinely committed. Disappearances of people, for example, remain a significant problem, generating widespread fear in Chechnya and providing a continued basis of recruitment for the resistance.

Dagestan

Dagestan is a key area in the development of radical Islam in the entire Caucasus, deeply interlinked with Chechnya but also with northern Azerbaijan. Dagestan is probably the most traditionally Islamic area in the Caucasus; this was true in Soviet times and remains the case today. Indeed, Dagestan was one of the first regions to convert to Islam; Derbent was a major outpost of the early Islamic armies in their struggle with the Khazar state in the North Caspian region. Whereas Azerbaijan later came under the influence of Shi'a Islam, Dagestan remained strongly Sunni, and governed by the stricter Shafi'i school of jurisprudence. By contrast, Chechnya and Ingushetia (a neighboring Caucasus republic, now also under Russian rule) were not converted to Islam until the seventeenth and eighteenth centuries, roughly the time of the conversion to Islam of the northwestern Caucasus. Hence pre-Islamic traditions and beliefs remain stronger in all of these republics than in Dagestan, where Islam took root early. This has also made Dagestan the most promising area for Islamist proselytism. Salafi movements first came to Dagestan in the late 1980s, and Dagestan in the 1990s gradually became a base for Islamists.

Following the Russian defeat in the first war in Chechnya in 1996, radical Islamist groups acquired an ever-stronger foothold in Dagestan as well, greatly influencing Chechnya's political development. Though only a small minority of the population of Dagestan was attracted to these radical ideologies, it was enough to ensure a trickle of fighters to Chechnya. These then returned to Dagestan and other home republics and began to spread the message in what turned out to be very fertile ground, given the rampant unemployment, corruption, and misrule in the region that Moscow has proven unable to reverse. The socioeconomic situation in the republic is best illustrated by the fact that over 80 percent of the republic's budget consists of direct subsidies from the Russian central government. Indeed, if the economic situation in the South Caucasus republics has gradually improved over the past few years, it has stagnated or deteriorated in the North Caucasus. A leaked Russian government report prepared by the president's special envoy to the region, Dmitry Kozak, assessed that the shadow economy constituted an estimated 44 percent of Dagestan's economy, as opposed to 17 percent in Russia as a whole, and that 50 to 70 percent of Dagestanis with some form of employment are thought to work in the shadow economy.

Several Dagestani villages (Chabanmakhi, Karamakhi, and Kadar) were seized and controlled in the aftermath of the Russian defeat in Chechnya by Salafi groups, which set up their local laws and denied Russian or Dagestani authorities control. Khattab seized on the opportunity by building links through marriage with these jama'ats and by

training young men in camps in Chechnya. Even though the Khattab-Basayev invasion failed and resulted in the debacle of the second Chechen war, Salafi radicals have continued to operate in Dagestan. Indeed, just as Moscow gradually managed to reduce the intensity of the war in Chechnya, the problem has grown worse in Dagestan. Since 2006, the number of armed confrontations between Russian forces and North Caucasian rebels is larger in Dagestan than in Chechnya.

The Dagestani rebels were led by Rappani Khalilov, an ethnic Lak who married into the same Dagestani family in Karamakhi as Khattab, until he was killed in September 2007. Khalilov was thought to be responsible for a major terrorist attack on a victory parade in the Dagestani city of Kaspiysk in May 2002. The group reorganized itself as the Shari'a Jama'at in early 2005. Presently, the frequency of military clashes between Islamist fighters and security forces in Dagestan equals or surpasses the number in Chechnya.

Other North Caucasus Republics

Since the onset of the second Chechen war, radicalism has spread in a significant manner to the remaining republics of the North Caucasus. The spread of Islamist radicalism has been exacerbated by Russian policies of extreme centralization, which have brought increased amounts of repression to the region since 2002. To that is added the dislocation of entrenched government elites and the appointment of politicians who are loyal to Moscow and who lack the strong grounding in the region required to lead the republics of the North Caucasus.

In the 1990s, an arrangement existed whereby the heads of the North Caucasian republics—typically representing the most powerful clan or alliance of clans in the respective republic—retained significant autonomy from Moscow. This meant that the local rulers took their power base in the opaque clan politics of the region; their loyalty to Moscow was not absolute. This impeded the central government's ability to implement policies in the region. But these forces also kept a certain level of stability in the region, as they respected local sensitivities and enjoyed some legitimacy among the local population. The logic of Putin's centralizing reforms may have been understandable: Yeltsin's Russia was weakly governed and Moscow could not implement its policies. But this policy backfired in the North Caucasus because Moscow moved to appoint its own representatives—many with a past in the security services—as the local power brokers, and these often lacked the support of the local networks of power and the people. As central appointees, these leaders are accountable only to Moscow and do not owe anything to the local elites; moreover, their appointment meant Moscow began using the very same repressive policies that had exacerbated the situation in Chechnya in neighboring republics.

The alienation of the North Caucasian population has progressively increased, and Russia's failure to resolve the socioeconomic situation in the North Caucasus in spite of its newly found oil wealth is making matters worse.

The emergence of the militant cells in the other republics of the region follows a general pattern: They are typically formed by a small number of individuals who have fought in Chechnya and received training by militants linked to Chechen radicalized formations. They are then sent back to their home republics, where they develop a greater following by recruiting young and disaffected members of society. These young, frustrated men are often without jobs or prospects either for creating a family or for self-realization. As a result, they are alienated from the political leadership of their republics, making them easy targets for the radical message of the Islamist jama'ats. In this way, the local militant groups have been able to grow and multiply, and militant cells now exist in the Caucasus republics of Ingushetia, Kabardino-Balkaria, and Karachai-Cherkessia. The Yarmuk group in Kabardino-Balkaria was the main group responsible for the carnage in the local capital Nalchik in October 2005.

While the Islamists still form a small minority of the population, the mismanagement of the region by federal and republican authorities demonstrably increases the number of people either willing or potentially willing to take up arms against the government. In particular, the Russian policy of assassinating moderate Chechen separatist leaders is gradually leaving the playing field in the hands of the radical groups. For example, the 2005 murder of Aslan Maskhadov, Chechnya's legitimate president, was followed by the murder of his successor, Abd al-Khalim Sadulaev, in June 2006. Sadulaev's successor in turn, Doku Umarov, Chechnya's rebel commander, appointed the now-deceased Shamil Basayev as vice president and a successor to Basayev, should he be killed as well. Whether by design or by accident, Moscow is ensuring that there are no moderate Chechen leaders left to negotiate with; though Umarov was earlier thought to sit on the fence in the confrontation between moderates and radicals, the power balance in the Chechen resistance has increasingly come to favor the radicals, something Umarov cannot ignore. Meanwhile, the radicals' control over the resistance in the North Caucasus becomes cemented.

The year 2006 saw a new spate of attacks on Russian forces. At the same time, the Moscow-supported prime minister of Chechnya, Ramzan Kadyrov, issued statements to the effect that his forces would chase militants into neighboring republics if he found it necessary. This policy, endorsed by Moscow, led to clashes with Ingushetian police, in which many were killed. Such a course of action may be a political ploy by Kadyrov to weaken his many political enemies in the region by sending forces loyal to them away from Chechnya into the neighboring republics. However, it may also strengthen the rebels' hand by stretching forces thin in Chechnya and by removing local government forces from some key rebel areas of operation.

During 2007 and 2008, Kadyrov was able to strengthen his relationship with Moscow and Russian president Vladimir Putin after his appointment as president of Chechnya. He led a violent crackdown inside Chechnya on suspected Islamists, some of whom "disappeared" without explanation.

Similar developments have made Ingushetia the perhaps least stable republic of the North Caucasus. Under the rule of FSB officer Murat Zyazikov, the republic saw a gradual increase in repression against all forms of opposition that was extreme even by Russian standards. As long as Putin remained president, Zyazikov's unquestioning loyalty was enough to keep him in power, in spite of a growing outcry among Russian experts and analysts, including those close to the Kremlin. As opposition to Zyazikov grew, a growing number of young men were attracted to the Islamist groups, including the violent resistance. By 2008, the violence in the republic had escalated to such a degree that Islamist militants openly challenged Interior Ministry forces in armed attacks. Only in November 2008 was

Zyazikov forced out of office and replaced by Yunusbek Yevkurov, a former officer of the Russian military intelligence (GRU). While Yevkurov appeared cognizant of the deep problems of the republic, it remains to be seen whether he can turn around the republic's downward slope.

South Caucasus: Azerbaijan

In the South Caucasus, Azerbaijan—being the region's only Muslim-majority country—has been the most affected state. Nevertheless, Georgia also experienced its share of Islamic extremism, given the weakness of state control over territory in the late 1990s and the existence of a Chechen community, including radical groups in the Pankisi gorge bordering Chechnya. This problem has gradually dissipated, especially with the new Georgian government in power since 2004, which has strengthened the state and asserted control over these regions.

In Azerbaijan, the vast majority of citizens remain committed to secularism, yet the public mood is gradually changing with an increasing number showing varying degrees of interest in Islam. It is widely known that both Saudi Arabia and Iran, as well as private groups from Dagestan, Kuwait, and Turkey, are actively trying to promote their brand of Islamist views in Azerbaijan by building new mosques and supplying local imams with radical Islamist literature. Radical movements sponsored by Iran and organizations in the Persian Gulf region have led to the growth of Salafi and radical Shi'a thought. Three areas of Azerbaijan have been particularly affected by Islamism. Azerbaijan's southern regions around Lenkaran are historically the most fervently Shi'a regions of the country and are also the areas where Iranian state-sponsored proselytism has been most active. A resurgence of Shi'a movements has been observed here, though the radical elements remain relatively weak. In the predominantly Sunni north of Azerbaijan, bordering Dagestan, a parallel growth of Islamic fervor has been observed, influenced strongly by Dagestan but also shaped to some extent by Turkish Islamic groups. Finally, in the capital, Baku, and its surroundings, both Shi'a and Sunni Islamic activity has grown. It is notable that radicalism in Azerbaijan has a strong element of contagion from bordering regions.

The Jeyshullah group is a terrorist Salafi group in Azerbaijan. It was principally active in the late 1990s, reportedly responsible for several murders and an attack against the Hare Krishna society's Baku headquarters. In spite of being Salafi in orientation, according to Azerbaijani authorities the group had clear contacts with Iran. It may also be related to a group with the same name that was briefly active in Turkey in the mid-1990s. Jeyshullah is thought to have planned to bomb the U.S. embassy in Baku. The group's leaders were apprehended and sentenced in 2000. Little more is known about the group's origins and finances.

Aside from Jeyshullah, the situation in Azerbaijan has been relatively tranquil. Thanks to its location, Azerbaijan is more open to influences from the West; its people also enjoy a far greater standard of living. This is partly because of the relatively small size of the country and partly because of the increased amount of money that has become available following oil and gas–related developments. President Ilham Aliyev has also pursued careful, pragmatic, and evolutionary policies and is more popular than any of his opponents—secular or Islamist. Furthermore, groups like Hizb al-Tahrir have not found a fertile ground in Azerbaijan in part due to Azerbaijan's close ties to Turkey; the Turkish model of

a democratic, secular, pro-Western vision is one commonly shared by the majority of the Azerbaijanis. They are also closer to Israel than to Iran, which not only sided with Armenia during the conflict over Nagorno-Karabakh (a territory claimed by both the Armenians and Azerbaijan), but also has challenged Azerbaijan's oil and gas fields in the Caspian Sea.

Despite these factors, the Islamists continue their attempts at recruiting in Azerbaijan and also target the country for terrorist attacks, precisely because it is a secular democratic country where Sunnis and Shi'as live together peacefully. Both Shi'a and Salafi Sunni preachers, of Azerbaijani origin but educated in Iran and Saudi Arabia, respectively, have begun to draw growing crowds to Friday prayers in Baku. Likewise, northern areas of the country bordering Dagestan are beginning to exhibit a growing trend of Salafism, which has spread mainly among communities ethnically linked to Dagestan. These have not begun to enter the political fray either legally or covertly, though such politicization of Islam is likely to grow over coming years.

In fact, the Forest Brothers, a radical Salafi group operating in Kabardino-Balkaria, Ingushetia, northern Ossetia, and southern Dagestan has over the past years also become increasingly active in Azerbaijan. Established by an Arab veteran of the Chechen war, the Forest Brothers had fought against the Russians in Dagestan under the command of Khattab and later Khalilov. In Azerbaijan they were accused of planning to bomb the Baku-Tbilisi-Ceyhan oil pipeline; in September 2008, they were found guilty for the August 2008 explosions in the Abu Bakr Mosque (Salafi) in Baku that killed two and injured 13. Azerbaijani law enforcement arrested more than two dozen members of the group and reported the discovery of a significant amount of weaponry, maps, terrorist books, and food in the forests of northern Azerbaijan.

Government policies toward Islam in general and Islamic radicalism in particular have been inadequate. Most damaging has been the lack of legitimacy of the Supreme Board of Muslims of the South Caucasus, the main religious institution in Azerbaijan. A leftover from Soviet times, the board is plagued by cronyism and corruption. To remedy this, the state created the State Committee for Work with Religious Organizations. This move, while fundamentally sound and correct, in fact led to a diarchy, as the State Committee and the Supreme Board compete for religious authority in the country. The acrimonious relations between the two bodies have been an important impediment in the Azerbaijani government's attempts to regulate the religious sphere. In turn, this has led to the Ministry of National Security picking up the slack and dealing with the issue of radical movements. The instruments available to this ministry, however, are mainly coercive.

A related problem is the failure of the Ministry of Education to develop a modern curriculum in the humanities and social sciences. The lack of reform in the Ministry of Education has implied that Azerbaijani schools do not provide adequate information and knowledge to students about the history and tenets of major religions, let alone the meaning of secularism. This lack of religious knowledge enables radical Islamic groups to attract segments of Azerbaijani youth interested in religious issues.

Indications for the Future

Islamists have already made serious inroads in the Caucasus—especially in the north. To advance their cause, they continue to make use of the chaos, civil wars, and crisis of governance throughout the wide region, from the fighting in Afghanistan with the Taliban to the fighting in the tribal areas of Pakistan to the fighting in the Caucasus with the Russians; they also persist in making the case to the inhabitants of the region that their only hope for stability and real justice is through the establishment of Islamic regimes. The authorities therefore need to try to provide the basic needs (safety, security, education, and jobs) of their people, while at the same time blocking the further entrance (and continued activities) of the purveyors of Islamist and Wahhabist ideologies at every turn.

In Azerbaijan there is hope that this approximates the policy espoused by the government, though even there, the state lacks a functioning organizational structure to deal with religious matters. But in the Russian North Caucasus, the policies pursued by the central government are still far from being effective, indeed even being largely counterproductive. The intervention of shrewd politicians like Dmitry Kozak, who had served as the special representative for the North Caucasus under Putin's presidency, temporarily prevented the region's slip into anarchy. Nevertheless, the risks are still present that the North Caucasus could slip back into a quagmire that involves externally sponsored radicalism, low-intensity conflict and terrorism, repression and mismanagement, corruption and organized crime, and deep socioeconomic problems, including sky-high unemployment. While the South Caucasus is gradually developing economically and politically, thanks among other things to sustained Western presence there, the North Caucasus is not far from a scenario that could be termed "Afghanization." Given Russia's penchant for refusing all kinds of external advice, let alone presence, in the North Caucasus, preventing this development will be a distinct challenge for Western governments.

BIBLIOGRAPHY

Alexiev, Alex. "Sufism in Eurasia." In *Understanding Sufism and Its Potential Role in U.S. Policy,* ed. Zeyno Baran, 15. Washington, DC: Nixon Center, March 2004.

Baran, Zeyno, S. Frederick Starr, and Svante E. Cornell. *Islamic Radicalism in Central Asia and the Caucasus: Implications for the EU.* Baltimore, MD: Central Asia–Caucasus Institute Silk Road Studies Program, July 2006.

Blandy, Charles. *North Caucasus: On the Brink of Far-Reaching Destabilisation.* Swindon, UK: Defence Academy of the United Kingdom, Conflict Studies Research Center, Caucasus Series, 05/36, August 2005, p. 6.

"Chechen Police Receive Go-Ahead for Cross-Border Operations." *RIA Novosti,* September 26, 2006.

Cornell, Svante E. "The Politicization of Islam in Azerbaijan." Washington, DC: Silk Road Paper, Central Asia–Caucasus Institute and Silk Road Studies Program, October 2006.

Leahy, Kevin Daniel. "Kadyrov as Russia's Regional Gendarme: A Boon for Chechnya's Rebel Movement?" *Central Asia–Caucasus Analyst,* November 29, 2006.

Moore, Cerwyn. "Foreign Fighters and the Chechen Resistance: A Re-Appraisal," *Central Asia–Caucasus Analyst* 9:12 (June 13, 2007).

Myers, Steven Lee. "World Briefing, Europe: Russia: 7 Federal Policemen Killed in Chechnya." *New York Times,* November 9, 2006.

Schwartz, Michael, comp. "Rebel Leader Wounded." In "Putin Threatens to Widen Trade Embargo on Europe." A summary of the top stories in Russian newspapers. *New York Times,* November 24, 2006.

NORTH AFRICA AND THE MIDDLE EAST

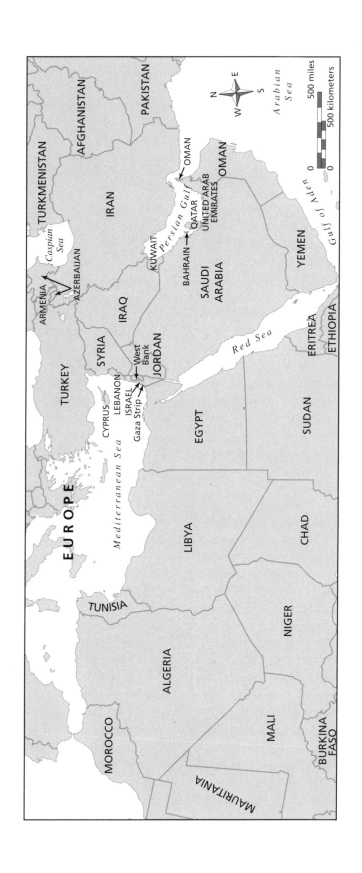

Algeria

Luis Martinez

Algeria has been one of the countries most affected by Islamism. The Islamic Salvation Front (Front islamique du salut, FIS) built a very large base of support in the 1980s as a relatively moderate group seeking power through electoral means. The likelihood of an FIS victory in the approaching round of elections caused a military coup in January 1992. In response, Islamist groups began an armed struggle against the regime. The ensuing violence left tens of thousands of people dead and spun off a number of new Islamist groups more extreme and militant than the FIS had been.

Algeria continues to host a wide spectrum of Islamist groups with differing ideologies and tactics that are very much a product of the country's recent history. The development of Islamism in Algeria can be divided into four periods, each of which saw the hegemony of a different set of groups and tactics: from 1989 to 1991, the hegemony of FIS; from 1992 to 1999, the centrality of armed groups; from 1999 to 2004, the leading role of the moderate Islamist parties Hamas and Islah; and from 2004 to the present, the setting of the Islamist agenda by radical Salafi groups such as the Salafist Group for Preaching and Combat (Groupe salafiste pour la prédication et le combat, GSPC).

The breadth of the situation of Islam in politics is illustrated by three possible alternative visions that can all be rationalized as fitting with Islam: the view that the people should obey their rulers (the position of traditional and "official" Islam); the view that each individual should embody and spread Islamic values (FIS's stance); and the view that the proper response is jihad in order to create an Islamic state (the ideology of the GSPC). The first two responses have far more adherents, but the third, by using violence, has greatly magnified its impact on society.

The government and even many among the ranks of the Islamists have come to favor the view that Islam should be a factor helping to restore peace to Algeria after its bloody civil war. The slogans in Algeria include the idea that an Islamic state is a utopian proposition that cannot be realized. Another anti-Islamist theme is that this doctrine's values and some of its practices are incompatible with those of "official Islam."

The Islamists have their own techniques, however, often evading government pressure through small subtleties that symbolically defy the regime. In some mosques, speakers defy the government by, for example, calling to break the fast "ten minutes before the legal time," giving out special prayers, and even importing versions of the Koran, which, according to the Ministry of Religious Affairs, contain "grave and malevolent alterations to verses." At the highest level, Islamist groups pose a security challenge for the regime.

The Islamic Salvation Front (FIS)

On February 18, 1989, Abassi Madani announced the creation of the FIS. Two religious leaders stood against the creation of an Islamist party: Shaykh Ahmad Sahnun, president of the League of Da'wa, and Mahfud Nahnah. The FIS's constitutive assembly, which took place at the Es Suna de Bab et Ouad mosque, led to the nomination of Madani as president and of Benazouz Zebda and Ali Belhadj as vice presidents, as well as to the emergence of a *majlis al-shura* (consultative council) composed of 35 members.

There were a few indications that this party was going to become the principal political force in Algeria. A few months after its creation, the FIS triumphed in the June 1989 municipal elections: It gained control of over 32 out of the 48 provinces and won the first ballot in the December 1991 legislative elections, which allowed it to obtain two-thirds of the seats in the National Assembly, a prerequisite for the establishment of an Islamic state. The concept of Islamic utopia offered by FIS built on the loss of ideals during the National Liberation Front (FLN) government. The FIS Islamists promised to establish an Islamic state founded on virtue and mindful of the population's material and spiritual well-being.

Aimed at reinstating the status of an Algeria marginalized in the international arena and impoverished at the national level, the FIS assigned itself the historical/

religious mission of saving Algeria from its stagnation. Although a religious party, the FIS was in reality a profoundly nationalist party. The interruption of the electoral process in January 1992 triggered a feeling of hate against the regime. Convinced of their historical role, the FIS Islamists organized guerrilla warfare, seeking to achieve through violence what politics could not accomplish. The FIS's armed branch—the AIS (Armée islamique du salut, or Islamic Salvation Army)—described its action as the continuation of the FLN's action against France:

> Yesterday, you freed the land. Today, we are freeing the honor and religion. You freed the fields and the Sahara, we are freeing the minds. You fixed the borders within which we will apply the laws. Our Jihad is the logical continuation of yours.

Groups Focused Around Armed Struggle

Among the various Islamist factions that have grown out of the post-1992 struggle, two are particularly important in conducting the guerrilla warfare that they portray as an extension of political action: The Islamic Salvation Army (AIS) defines itself as the FIS's "armed wing" and continually emphasizes its loyalty to that party's imprisoned political leaders; the Islamic Armed Movement (MIA) began a war against the regime after the interruption of the parliamentary elections. These two armed movements thus embarked on war in the name of specific political issues and are distinct from other factions that claim to be acting in the name of jihad in general.

For both the MIA and the AIS, the fighting model is the National Liberation Army

(Armée de libération nationale, ALN), the nationalist underground army that won independence for Algeria from France in 1962. Both use military uniforms looted from army barracks for their fighters, which forced the government's People's National Army (ANP) to change its uniforms in 1995–96. In that uniform, the fighters of those factions distinguish themselves from those of the Armed Islamic Group (Groupe islamique armée, GIA)—an organization thought to have been born in Peshawar, Pakistan, in 1989 and then to have merged in 1992 with the local GIA under the leadership of Muhammad Allal and Abd al-Hak Layada—who have an "Islamic look," with shaven heads, beards, and more "modest" clothing.

While the MIA and AIS have been intent on fighting to legalize the FIS, they have also had to fight for their own survival. In principle, unlike the jihadists, both of those factions are, depending on the situation, ready for political negotiations. However, to achieve this, both the MIA and the AIS need to survive the civil war and overcome competition from other Islamist factions.

The Islamic Armed Movement (MIA)

The MIA guerrillas have been visible since 1993, but they began three years earlier, convinced that the effort to establish an Islamic state through the ballot box would not work. This organization, in turn, stood on the foundation of an earlier MIA that had been dismantled by the security forces in 1987.

In its new form, the organization focused on setting up the infrastructure for launching an uprising in the Blida Atlas area. While the security forces concentrated on fighting the FIS and small armed groups, the relatively well-equipped MIA developed its own strategy. By not attacking police stations or army barracks, in contrast to the Islamist groups in the Algiers suburbs, they avoided the counteroffensives of the security forces then under way in Algeria's big urban centers.

The halt to the elections brought large numbers of young recruits to the ranks of the MIA, and the group was very selective about whom it accepted. Divided into small secure groups, such as the preindependence underground army, the MIA created 16 cells and, after ensuring its arms supply, went into action. While supporting the FIS, the group took for granted that power would be achieved by armed struggle rather than electoral means.

However, the MIA, despite being well placed to lead the jihad, failed to capitalize on efforts at mobilization that took place during the civil war. Being a secret military movement, it refused to find a place in its ranks for the thousands of individuals who wanted to join due to its fear of being infiltrated by the military's agents during 1992–93. Gradually, while methods were developed for testing candidates, frustrations continued for the many who wanted to volunteer. Eventually, Islamist activists such as Sa'id Makhlufi, competing for the political leadership of the MIA, seized the opportunity to set up their own groups.

The Islamic Salvation Army (AIS)

The AIS, created in 1994, realized that the guerrilla campaign conducted by the MIA was insufficient and that the armed bands that had sworn allegiance to the MIA were incapable of overthrowing the regime. It thus emphasized that the war would be a long one. The MIA's hopes of rapid victory were forgotten. In place of the romanticism of the first wave, the AIS called for professionalism from its troops.

The national leader of the AIS, Madani Mezraq, wrote in Communiqué Number 3, in the newspaper *El Mounqidh,* in June 1995 that the group was loyal to "the historic and legitimate leadership linked to the authentic line of the FIS." The AIS did not benefit from the great waves of enlistment in 1992–93, but it was able to recruit from the thousands among the FIS cadre who were released from prison starting in 1993 and 1994. Outside Algeria, AIS supporters—mainly students—took over all the external networks of the FIS. By 1995 its strength was estimated to have reached 40,000, though this declined in 1996, as will be discussed later. The AIS also attracted a large proportion of the military deserters who came together in the Conseil du front islamique et du djihad armé (CFIDA), a group the AIS sponsored to subvert the army's soldiers. Ultimately, by starting two years late in the jihad race, the AIS benefited by learning from earlier mistakes.

The AIS also has made a point of distinguishing its struggle from that waged by the other Islamist organizations. It has rejected the GIA's ideology and war strategy as too unrestrained and as actually harming the cause of creating an Islamic state. Indeed, the excesses of the earlier period in terms of killings and mutilations undermined popular support. Competing leaders—emirs—paid networks of clients to fight for their own interests.

The Movement for the Islamic State (MEI) and the Armed Islamic Group (GIA)

Because there were so few places for candidates in the ranks of the MIA at the beginning of the civil war, numerous autonomous armed groups were formed. The arrest of ex-FIS cadres initially made it possible for the MIA to have a monopoly on the jihad, but rivals were to emerge rapidly: namely, the MEI and GIA. The result was competition for the leadership of the jihad, but above all the birth of new forms of war. In place of the elitist vanguard model of the MIA there arose armed groups open to all candidates. The creation of the MEI by Sa'id Makhlufi fit in with this determination to alter strategy. In a January 1991 pamphlet calling for "civil disobedience," Makhlufi called for an uprising of the population against the regime as the only chance of overthrowing it.

Favoring an Islamist people's army, the MEI opposed the MIA's strategy based on a war of attrition carried out by professionals. Convinced that it was impossible for the government to maintain power by violence alone, Makhlufi put the emphasis not on a struggle against the Algerian army—an unwinnable proposition in his view—but on the politicization of the people in favor of Islamist ideas to isolate the regime. While the MIA confined itself to a more conventional military approach, the MEI took upon itself to teach "the people" the path to follow by attacking what it considered to be reactionary civilians who collaborated with the regime.

Between 1991 and 1993, appeals for civil disobedience had aroused no response; the universities, government departments, and factories continued as normal. The MEI concluded that the people, under the combined effect of fear and state terror, could not be properly free to choose their destiny. Thus the MEI applied counterterrorism to shake civilians out of their indifference and force them to choose sides. This led to revolutionary romanticism.

The MEI's strategic choice has also been

reflected in the GIA. The GIA classified all individuals as either "enemies of Islam" or "supporters of the jihad" in a process of "total war" against an infidel regime. It thus combined Makhlufi's revolutionary principle of combating the people's fear through terror and the theory of the state as *jahiliyya*—that is, as non-Muslim, derived from the ideology of Sayyid Qutb. The GIA went to war against all the social groups, which, involuntarily or deliberately, ensured that the regime continued in power. Government employees, teachers, and foreigners became targets no less than agents of the security forces.

In addition, the GIA allowed its local groups to operate autonomously and recruited indiscriminately. Unlike other Islamist movements, it encouraged applicants to join even if their families opposed it. The struggle against the regime legitimized new loyalties, and the family—until then considered sacred by all the Islamist movements—was thrust aside.

This radicalism, attacking both the political and family order, was the strength of that faction, which, unlike the AIS, did not at all aim to show "respect" for the elders. The war tactics of the GIA seemed unstoppable, and its spectacular operations, highlighted in the media, attracted many of the suburban Islamist armed bands to it in 1994.

The GIA's mobilization strategy was also based on the use of the feeling, very strong in Algeria, of being persecuted by the world community. Far from confining its struggle within the boundaries of Algeria, it set about building up a highly effective image of an external enemy: France, the "Jew," and the "apostate" were the parties mainly responsible for Algeria's sufferings. While the MEI put forward the idea that only a change of attitude among the people could create conditions of victory for the guerrillas, the GIA included in its analysis of the conflict the major role played by the international community. From that viewpoint, the regime now appeared as a mere transplant, and its agents were simply "renegades" in the service of the "Jews" and France. In contrast, Sa'id Makhlufi's criticism of the world community related to the economic aspect:

> The regime in power will fall despite all the means at its disposal, that regime which was and still is the cause of the unbelievable oppression and corruption that will intensify as the liberal economy is opened up to the enemies of Islam, Christians and Jews which have all the wealth of the country at their disposal.

That struggle for a monopoly over the jihad, however, remained confined within the military and political domains, for the guerrillas of both the GIA and the AIS made efforts—unlike the small self-proclaimed Islamist armed groups of the Algiers suburbs—to conserve the resources of their environment. Established in the mountainous regions of the interior of Algeria, the guerrillas latched on to local private economic activity without, however, destroying or ruining it. Quite the reverse occurred—the destruction of state economic activity was for the private sector, especially in transport and distribution, compensation for losses resulting from extortion. The presence of the *maquis* (guerilla fighters) helped to bring about a reorganization of the control of resources among the economic actors. Far from being passive and submissive, they exploited the insecurity hanging over the state corporations to their own advantage. For the guerrillas, what mattered above all was to avoid causing the economic bankruptcy of those actors who willingly or not gave them an assured supply of resources to keep them going.

The Development of the Guerrilla Campaign

The guerrilla forces, estimated in 1992 at 2,000 (mainly with the MIA), grew in 1993 to a strength of 22,000 with the formation of the GIA, and with the emergence of the AIS, reached a peak in 1994 of 40,000, including logistical support. After the presidential election of November 16, 1995, did their strength decline? The GIA, for which only the core is counted, was estimated at 2,000 to 3,000 fighters; AIS forces are believed to have declined to 4,000, including 2,500 in the east and 1,500 in the west, while the MEI and MIA were thought to comprise only some small groups in the Mitidja. In all, the guerrillas' strength was believed to be around 10,000 fighters, including all factions, in 1996. Although unverifiable, these figures cannot conceal one essential fact: The value of a guerrilla war effort lies less in its fighters, still less in their numbers, than in the reliability of its logistics and political infrastructure, which includes both support networks in the big cities and partners abroad who facilitate financial dealings.

Therefore, a decline in Islamist guerrilla manpower should not necessarily lead to the conclusion that the factions have been growing weaker. Quite the contrary: The dwindling numbers of fighters have been accompanied by professionalization, such as the manufacture of mortars, antipersonnel mines, and the like. With the replenishment of their troops assured from the reservoir of young men, the factions' strength has been stabilized since 1994. To establish a war economy capable of sustaining their troops, they have been obliged to find funds and sustain the client networks necessary for the urban guerrilla campaign.

In addition to infiltration by agents of the state, the GIA has also feared being indirectly used as a hit squad in the service of persons or social groups behind the scenes. After four years of war, the GIA's record aroused doubts among the population about the organization's real intentions. The systematic destruction of the state sector, aside from putting thousands of workers out of a job, made things easier for the government policy, recommended by the IMF (International Monetary Fund), of ending subsidies to enterprises that lose money. This halt to subsidies spared the regime any industrial conflicts and thus diverted the workers' anger toward the disastrous policy of the Islamist groups. In addition, while the regime's main revenues are from oil and gas sales, attacks on oil and gas installations have been rare.

The Violence of the GIA: Algeria as a Land of Infidels

"Do seek family consent! But if you do not receive it, continue regardless, the jihad . . . is greater than blood ties." This principle of commitment to the armed Islamist groups made it clear that family ties no longer acted as a curb on violence, as A. Grignard explains. During the bloodiest years of the decade (1993–98), the GIA fighters took on the attributes of a new family, thanks to sacrificial rites. In June 1997 a clandestine newsletter, *al-Jama'a,* signed by Mahfud Assuli, alias Abu al-Mundhir, justified the massacres in these words:

> To those who accuse us of killing blindly, we reply that we are fighting those traitors who have given themselves to the Taghut [idolatry/impurity]. . . . When you hear of slaughter and throat-slitting in a town or village, know that these people belong to the Taghut.

In addition to "local murders," according to X. Bougarel, massacres of villagers confirmed the fighters' enduring commitment. It is true that these killings were rewarded by booty—young women, money, and material goods—which the GIA emirs considered part of Islamic tradition. The mufti of Marseille, quoted by *Le Matin* in January 1998, remarked:

> The men of the GIA act in a very canonical manner, which is why they can equally be seen praying or raping. . . . Women are part of the spoils of war according to this same canonical reasoning. . . . I condemn the hypocrisy of the Muslim theologians who speak out against these practices and the massacres . . . but do not [also] question the theology that underpins them. They must seize this opportunity to challenge the sanctity of Muslim law, especially certain points that provide these barbarians with a pretext.

The violence of the GIA met with incomprehension on the part of Muslims and censure from the leaders of international Islamist organizations. Far from being part of Islamic orthodoxy, the GIA appears as a deviant tendency and above all a specifically Algerian phenomenon. How is it possible to make sense of this extreme violence? Analyses of political Islam have pinpointed two strategies: a bottom-up Islam in the hands of grassroots associations working to Islamize society; and a top-down Islam seeking to change the state by attacking its regime.

In the case of Algeria, the GIA's violence is protean, aiming to be total, because the state, its political regime, and society are "enemies of Islam." However, it in fact belongs to a political imagination where there is very little room for Islam from the perspective of the historical structures that are the legacy of the War of Independence (1954–62) and the Colonial War (1830). That is why Abd al-Rahman Moussaoui had no hesitation in writing in *La Pensée du Midi*:

> The primary reference, the fundamental referent is not this symbolic place shared by many Muslim countries (The Prophet), but a place/moment which has been made sacred, that of the War of Independence. . . . Both those in power and their opponents base their political theology on war.

These two periods of war effectively constitute founding myths. Whereas the War of Independence led to the "renaissance of the Algerian state," the colonial war broke down the organization of society and humiliated the population. This society was only able to regain its dignity through the "martyrdom" of 1.5 million people. The GIA emirs seek not to negotiate compromises between the protagonists but rather to destroy opponents in an all-out war. The motto of the GIA, attributed to Qari Sa'id, one of its ideologues, is: "No dialogue, no truce, no reconciliation." Sa'id is considered to be one of the founding members of the GIA. His stance prompted Hamida Layashi, quoted by *Le Monde* in June 2000, to say that the GIA emirs were "hardliners who have already proved this to be so by attacking those who have negotiated with the government—traitors in their eyes. They would probably even refuse a general amnesty if one were offered to them."

In fact, GIA violence is aimed at establishing a new order, as O. Weber explains. For the GIA, the purpose of action is not merely to change the balance of political power or to overthrow the regime but also to overturn the social order, according to Chams Benghribil. This particular relationship to violence generally meets with incomprehension and revulsion but sometimes also with admiration: The GIA fighters appear to be "real Muslims" who are "rising up" to sacrifice themselves in the name of Islam. Although nowadays Arab-Muslim societies are free from the colonial yoke, in their eyes, the Islamic religion continues to be persecuted. Therefore, they feel duty bound to save it, even reestablish it. Their objective is an Islamic state as a utopia.

Through what political, social, and psychological mechanism did the GIA fighters come to believe that the Islamic religion was under threat in Algeria? What do they imagine? Even though, as numerous observers have pointed out, recruitment to the GIA has dried up, these groups are still operational after more than a decade of activity. How can the persistence of this violence be explained? Within the GIA, violence is associated with ideological purification. Apart from the fact that "the Jews and the crusaders" must be eliminated, its purpose is also to "clean up" the social order. Despite the obstacles, its aim is to create favorable conditions for a social and political order that fulfills the requirements of a reinvented Islamic state. The violence of the Islamist organizations is stoked by the memory of the victory of the nationalists who, despite the crushing balance of power in favor of the colonial power, managed to establish an independent state. This heroic resistance of the Algerians, "from the emir Abd al-Qadir [the early nineteenth-century struggle against the French] to the FLN," constitutes the unwavering basis of the belief in change through violence.

The AIS or the Attempt to Impose Order on the Violence

Confronted with the excesses of the GIA, the AIS, founded in 1994, sought to impose

order. The chaos provoked by the GIA was very soon perceived by its emirs as extremely dangerous. They began by claiming that the GIA had been infiltrated by the state security service in an attempt to sow discord and bring about a turnaround of the population in favor of the regime. Then, they gradually recognized that in most cases it was a matter of a genuine choice but said it was founded on a "deviant" ideology. The violence of the GIA was so excessive and counterproductive that it was bound to be misunderstood.

The AIS's attitude to war was not that of the GIA. The AIS sought to use arms to create a climate conducive to negotiations with the army. It was overwhelmed by the GIA's strategy of all-out war. Aspiring initially to build an Islamic army on the model of a national army, disciplined and respectful of a certain code of war, the AIS found itself powerless against the groups that attacked society rather than the security forces. It also feared the two would be confused, and thus constantly condemned acts that went against its ethos. For example, in the June 1994 issue of *al-Tath al-Moubine*:

> The apostate regime blames certain abominable operations attacking the defenseless people on the jihad. . . . In response to these falsehoods, the AIS replies that it is innocent of all these acts and that it has never given the order to attack a woman, burn down a school or hospital or to carry out any other operation that goes against our religion.

In fact, the AIS dreamed of arousing a nationalist fervor in the population similar to that created by the FLN in its heyday, which had abated as a result of economic failure, poverty, and corruption. Contrary to the GIA, it tended to hold the people sacred and tried to appear as the only legitimate new player. For example, in a 1995 letter to *Le Mujahidin,* the AIS stated:

> They [the GIA] also spread the idea that the people are idolatrous and sometimes Taghut. They are forever counting the sins and little mistakes that can be corrected. . . . This people, which has submitted for centuries, which has proved its allegiance to God, its attachment to its religion and its repudiation of non-believers time and time again through glorious revolutions. . . . After all that, it is appalling to want to call this people Taghut, and yet that is what some "mujahidin" [fighters] reserve for this people who have given them their trust and loyalty.

In short, if the GIA was reenacting the scorched-earth policy of the Secret Army (Organisation armée secrete, OAS), the AIS had the utopian ambition of rebuilding a popular army on the model of the National Liberation Army (Armée de liberation nationale, ALN). There was an ongoing concern to set up and develop a structure for the armed organization despite the difficulties encountered. The emirs of the AIS clearly belonged to the same tradition as the mujahidin of the War of Independence (1954–62), albeit without measuring the contradictions inherent in their actions.

The slogan "You have liberated the land, we will liberate the minds" presented the AIS fighters with some formidable challenges: How was it possible to "liberate" minds without doing violence to society? The deliberate confusion between the War of Independence, waged to create an independent state, and the war to liberate minds, waged to establish an Islamic state,

could only lead to civil war. Effectively, the construction of the enemy in the minds of the AIS Islamists was based on the equation of the regime to the colonial system. It ignored the fact that apart from the generals and bureaucrats who were accused of lining their pockets from the state's coffers, the FLN's state had deep roots within the country and continued to represent a large proportion of society as best it could.

The AIS had no choice but either to attack society physically or to lay down its arms. Yet, in its view, as the group wrote in the above-quoted letter:

> Jihad is not a suicide, a way out for those who are in a rut, such people are contemptible; nor is it a form of vengeance for those who want to settle old scores, such people are full of hatred; nor is it an uncertain enterprise for adventurers and the exiled; nor an anarchist movement with no criteria or rules that recruits runaways and desperados; nor a blind point of honor as practiced by the ignorant; nor a blind rush forward, which would indicate a lack of vision or any program.

However, the explosion of violence became widespread; the regime responded to the violence of the GIA by an "all-out war," in the words of Habib Souaïdia, an author and former officer in the Algerian army.

On September 21, 1997, Madani Mezrag, emir of the AIS, released a communiqué (Number 9) in which he "ordered all the company commanders to end combat operations from October 1 and appealed to the other groups fighting for religious interests and those of the nation to rally to this call." He had a dual objective: to achieve negotiations with the army and to dissociate himself from the policy of civilian massacres perpetrated by the GIA.

The AIS failed to channel the "desire for dissidence" of the Islamists anxious to do battle with the regime. The GIA would exhaust itself in this extreme violence. Furthermore, in 1998 a group of fighters broke away and set up a new armed organization, the GSPC.

The GSPC: Looking to the Wider World for a Breath of Fresh Air

The GIA policy of civilian massacres was being challenged from within the Islamist movement, which led to splits. In short, Michel Wieviorka explains, the GIA was on its way to destroying the foundations laid down by the FIS during its legitimate period (1989–91).

It seemed vital for the Islamist fighters to open up fronts internationally. On the military front, the emirs sought networks that would help consolidate their armed groups, which were struggling at home. However, it was above all at the ideological level that there seemed to be total confusion. The ideologues of the war had led the troops into an impasse. Indeed, the attempts to overthrow the Taghut and terrorize "the people" had unforeseen effects. The fear of a collapse of the Algerian state led to international support for the regime, and the policy of massacres resulted in the arming of civilians. In short, the state and society's capacity to resist had been underestimated.

Hasan Hattab's Salafi Group for Preaching and Combat found a new fighting ideology in the World Islamic Front for Jihad Against Jews and Crusaders established by Osama bin Ladin, which gave them the second wind they needed to sustain the war against the regime. Initially, the GSPC set about reorganizing the armed groups that were still active. It advocated a new definition of the enemy, now confined solely to the security

services, and condemned violence against civilians. In 2001 Jean-Michel Salgon wrote of the GSPC:

> Unlike the units operating under the banner of the GIA, the organisation does not resort to "blind" attacks in the urban sector. . . . Recourse to terrorist action causing the death of a civilian, must be, in the minds of the leaders of the GSPC, both exemplary and relatively rare.

Between 1998 and 2001, the GSPC maintained a level of heavy violence, but there was no comparison with the combined brutality of the AIS and the GIA perpetrated between 1993 and 1997. President Abdelaziz Bouteflika's civil harmony policy, introduced in 1999, brought around 6,000 Islamist fighters back into society. The hope of a genuine reconciliation created a general mood of optimism and gave rise to the hope that the era of violence was finally over. The revival of the armed Islamist groups no longer seemed assured, even though disaffected youths offered a fertile breeding ground. However, it was above all at the ideological level that the Islamist guerrilla war had lost its appeal. It was, therefore, the need to restore the credibility of the armed groups that made the GSPC enter the international arena.

It is from this perspective that the relations between this group and al-Qa'ida should be analyzed, because the links between the Algerian Islamist groups and international networks seem to go back a long way. As early as 1992, the "first links between the GIA and the bin Ladin network" could be observed, according to R. Labévière. Throughout that decade, and particularly after 1998, with the growing power of the GSPC, the regime had exploited these relations in order to stress that the Islamist groups were foreign to Algerian society; but, as elsewhere, the attacks of September 11 marked an abrupt turning point, in that the war on terror declared by the Bush administration made this type of interpretation more acceptable.

To establish close, regular ties between the Islamist groups and al-Qa'ida, the government resorted to oversimplifications. The Algerian press reported that in November 2001 the authorities supposedly found a letter from Hasan Hattab, leader of the GSPC, ordering that "assistance be given" to Mullah Muhammad Omar to combat "nonbelievers and infidels."

R. Labévière remarked in *Le Matin*: "I do not believe for one moment in al-Qaida's capacity to . . . set up a branch called the GSPC in Algeria. I believe that the GSPC needs bin Ladin's network to legitimize its murderous violence, rather than the other way round." In fact, the al-Qa'ida label was sufficiently attractive and respected to enable the GSPC to regain endorsement for the Islamist war. (Following the September 11, 2001, attacks, a number of Western countries denounced Algerian Islamist terrorist networks. On March 27, 2002, the American secretary of state announced that the GSPC had been added to the list of terrorist organizations because the GSPC was a "cell of the GIA.")

The collapse of the Taliban regime in Afghanistan led to an international redeployment of the Arabs who were settled there. According to the Algerian authorities, the mission of the supposed al-Qa'ida representative for the Maghreb and Saharan Africa, Imad Abd al-Wahid Ahmad Alouane (alias Abu Muhammad, a Yemenite), killed on September 12, 2002, in Algeria, was to assess the situation in Algeria so as to help the fighters from Egypt and North Africa in Afghanistan to settle there. Yet the

GSPC had stated, in a communiqué dated September 21, 2001, that its objective was "jihad against the Algerian regime" only.

It is true that the determination to attack the West, and France in particular, has long existed among the armed Islamist groups in Algeria. There have been numerous attempts, from the hijacking of an Airbus in 1994 by a GIA commando planning to blow up the Eiffel Tower to the Paris bombings of 1995 and 1996. The feeling that France's unconditional support for the Algerian government was responsible for their defeat partially explains this desire to export the conflict. It was also a question of demonstrating that despite the army's triumphant communiqués, the Islamist groups still had the capacity to strike the Algerian regime's main ally, France.

Furthermore, in 1994–95, Canada opened up to the North African countries; after having drawn its French-speaking migrants from the war-torn former French protectorates (Vietnam and later Lebanon), the country became interested in the Algerian Francophone population, one of the largest in Africa, as a source of new immigrants. The Islamists took advantage of this opportunity, using legal and illegal channels, to emigrate there to set up organized cells. This was of some concern to the French and European authorities, as after three years, Canadian passport in hand, these thousands of Algerian students would be free to enter Europe without a visa. In 1999 the first Algerian Islamists suspected of planning attacks in Canada and the United States were arrested. Labévière points out that Canada became "the sanctuary" of those who want to carry on the jihad. He adds that according to a memo from the Canadian intelligence and security services, "more than fifty terrorist groups have apparently exploited the system on Federal territory." That said, the GSPC still adhered to its initial objective: the overthrow of the Algerian regime. The redefinition of the enemy, the reorganization of the armed groups, and the taking over of the overseas networks were the political, military, and financial instruments necessary for the fulfillment of this goal.

The Quest for Salvation, or How to Close the Lid on Pandora's Box

The war on terror launched by the president of the United States endorsed the Algerian government's analytical perspective. During an international colloquium on terrorism held in Algiers in October 2002, Rida Malik, the former Algerian prime minister and a member of the High Council of State, declared:

> Fundamentalist terrorism draws inspiration from the Afghanistan war; it was spread with the help of the Gulf oil monarchies and the CIA, implemented by the former FIS and encouraged by the laxness of the authorities at the time. The rise of the FIS, in 1991 and 1992, coincided with the return of the Afghan Algerians (2,000 to 3,000 men) who spearheaded the terrorist violence.

This destabilization of Algeria by Afghanistan was also highlighted by ANP General Larbi Belkheir, who confirmed during an interview with *Jeune Indépendant,* "I have no regrets. I made the choice of sparing Algeria the fate of Afghanistan. There was a heavy price to pay, but it avoided the worst: an outright civil war with millions of victims and refugees." In fact, concurrently with the war against the armed groups, the regime continued to look for political solu-

tions that would allow it to convert its military victory into a political success. The two strategies were to be civil concord and the promotion of moderate Islamist parties.

National Reconciliation Efforts

From 1999 on, President Bouteflika became the leader of this national reconciliation policy and undertook direct negotiations with the ex-FIS. The peace dynamics initiated during the referendum on the Civil Concord Law were seen by the Islamists more as a "police measure" than as the product of negotiations. In addition, some ex-FIS leaders felt humiliated, and the assassination of Abd al-Qadir Hashani on November 22, 1999, reinforced people's doubts about the regime's true intention to reach a "fair peace." This realization led to a loss of faith in President Bouteflika's ability to fulfill his promises. Within a few months, ex-FIS leaders went from demonstrating their "unconditional" support for the president's approach to rejecting it entirely. A feeling of betrayal emerged, and the hope for peace became thinner at the beginning of the year 2000.

Abassi Madani, who particularly felt this way, announced his withdrawal of support for the president's approach in a November 1999 letter:

> Dear brother Shaykh Benhajar and all others, At this precise moment, I still suffer with sadness and bitterness from the tragic assassination of my dearest son, torn away from the hurt and martyred Algerian people. . . . The regime proved incapable of differentiating between a call for fair peace, which would allow the people to regain its rights, and an unhealthy and despicable

call for power, which is nothing but a form of betrayal of the people and the pact sealed with Allah.

Bouteflika promised to lead the country out of the crisis through a political solution; we supported this approach as long as the goal was to reach a definitive solution without harming any party aiming at true reconciliation; reconciliation can only be achieved through a transparent and balanced dialogue. . . . The regime's stubbornness to stay in a monologue demonstrates its lack of sincerity and availability regarding a solution to the crisis.

Madani's withdrawal of support was accompanied by a call to AIS leaders to follow him:

Dear brother, I ask you to pass this letter on to all the brothers, heroes of Jihad for God and for peace who guarantee the people its right and not its surrender, on to our brothers known for their sincerity—Madani Mezrag, Ahmed Benaicha—as well as on to all the emirs and overseers among our brothers inside and outside.

Abd al-Qadir Hashani's assassination, Madani's withdrawal of support for the president's approach, and, above all, the army's determination to resume its offensive against those who had not capitulated after January 13, 2000, partially explain the resurgence of violence during 2000. The conditions for peace, which seemed to be met during the summer of 1999, vanished in 2000. Among those more moderate on both sides, the Islamists, after defeat in an eight-year-long war, saw the Civil Concord Law as a way out; on the government side, the law was a way to demonstrate their wish not to completely "eradicate" the Islamists and to

allow all those who would accept military defeat to fearlessly reintegrate into society.

However, President Bouteflika seemed incapable of distinguishing himself from the "generals/decisionmakers" who saw a national reconciliation policy as a mistaken effort to relegitimize rather than negotiate with the Islamists. Equally, the latter remained convinced that the military decision makers had absolutely no intention to negotiate a return of the Islamists on the political scene after crushing them militarily.

Worrisome indications surfaced before the cutoff date of January 13, 2000. According to Abd al-Karim Ould Adda, the FIS Executive Instance Abroad (IEFE) spokesperson, the regime had attempted, as early as December 1999, to make the accord's implementation look like "surrender." While President Bouteflika was pushing for a "fair and equitable" reconciliation, the hard-line faction among the "generals/decisionmakers" was regaining "control in the regime and keeping it hostage." In January 2000 the spokesperson specified in *Le Soir* (Brussels):

We want to integrate the political field within the Constitution's framework. There must be a new beginning that will envision national reconciliation rather than this apartheid in which they want to confine us. This reconciliation is essential in our eyes. If it fails, the regime will be the one to blame.

They expected the new president to consider their plea. This was not the case. Did the president's inability to stand by his commitments to ex-FIS Islamists reinforce those within the dominion who had rejected the truce (October 1997) and the Civil Concord Law (April 13, 1999)? The CCFIS (Conseil de coordination du FIS, or FIS Coordination Council) was established on

October 5, 1997, and is headed by Ahmad Zaoui. It is a rival group of former FIS leader Rabah Kabir and is more extreme than the IEFE. The CCFIS's goals include bringing together FIS members and supporters abroad, supporting the popular resistance in the country, and the development of the Islamic society project:

> Regarding the ceasefire, it is with regret that the CCFIS notes the persistence of several indications confirming the warnings it has given; the CCFIS considers that the declared ceasefire, as a military decision, changes the prerogatives of the jihadi groups (armed groups) in the country. However, it notes that such a ceasefire will not achieve any strategic objectives if the minimal following conditions are not met: giving the ceasefire a political dimension with an open announcement of the agreements and decisions; guaranteeing the active involvement of Shaykhs M. Abassi and Ali Belhadj in the negotiations; allowing for the establishment of an independent committee to investigate the massacres, etc. (March 30, 1998, communiqué)

According to Mourad Dhina, CCFIS spokesperson, as transmitted in a communiqué dated July 5, 2000:

> The politics of the so-called civil concord, for which he [Dhina] was assigned to do the promotion by the generals/decision-makers, did not reinstate peace in Algeria. The FIS always rejected this "concord" because it ignored the political nature of the crisis and only aimed at absolving the generals and their allies of their crimes.

The doubts about the Civil Concord Law by the AIS and the IEFE generated bitter-ness among ex-FIS leaders, who considered it to be a "betrayal" of the "cause." This had been reflected in an interview by *Le Temps* with Abd al-Qadir Hashani, prior to his assassination, in which Hashani stated regarding former FIS leader Rabah Kabir:

> The one you quote does not incarnate the political line I believe in and militate for. As for national reconciliation, I personally militate for it since I came out of prison, so as to bring peace back, and to completely and definitively evacuate violence from our country, while preserving all parties' dignity and convictions. To solve the phenomenon of violence will, however, depend on a real political opening able to punctuate a fair and equitable treatment of the excesses that take place on both sides. Personally, I do not believe in absolution through amnesty, and it would be useful to meditate on the occurrences in South Africa in this regard.

Ali Belhadj's 1994 arrest and Madani's return to house arrest in 1997 (which both ended in 2003), along with Hashani's 1999 assassination, allowed the army to promote the politics of reconciliation advocated by Bouteflika. In 2001 it became clear that this strategy, initiated in 1996, had failed. The army defeated the FIS's armed branch, silenced the movement's leaders, and instead found interlocutors—AIS and FIS leaders Madani Mezrag and Rabah Kabir—potentially able to find a way out of the war under cover of a reconciliation policy imposed by the military authorities through the Civil Concord Law. This policy could have been successful if the military authorities had gone all the way with the process. This would have allowed the Islamists to reestablish themselves politically through the creation of a new political party, such as Talib Ibrahimi's Wafa party.

The Refusal to Legalize the Wafa Party

Throughout the 1990s, the army justified its fight against the FIS political Islamists by emphasizing the threat they represented for "democracy" and the state's "republican" nature. Ex-FIS leaders' antidemocratic remarks (from 1989 to 1991) and strategy—based on the massacre of civilians by Islamist armed groups—reinforced the army's wish to eradicate Algerian Islamism's political and armed tendencies throughout the decade. In 2001 it became clear that political mutations had occurred within the Islamist dominion. The civil war made it possible for the latter to acquire political maturity, which in turn resulted in the support of some ex-FIS leaders for Talib Ibrahimi's Wafa party. The AIS—the FIS's armed branch—dissolved itself, and its members benefited from amnesty. Yet these processes did not put an end to violence. The FIS's actions did not seem sufficiently profound to cause the Algerian regime to change its policy, as the refusal to legalize the Wafa party demonstrated.

The interior minister's refusal to recognize the Wafa party marked the ex-FIS Islamists' death knell. He based his decision on the argument that the Wafa party's leadership was partially constituted of previous FIS leaders. According to Ahmad Talib Ibrahimi, president of the Wafa, "Only 2.5 percent of the Wafa's constituency was FIS sympathizers." Disenchanted, Ibrahimi recalled in *La Tribune*:

> [T]he last few years demonstrated that the legal dissolution of this political movement (FIS) did not obliterate the social reality behind it: the regime negotiated with the FIS' political leadership in prison. . . . Should we kill the three

million Algerians who voted for the FIS, deprive them of their civic rights, thus disregarding the Constitution and the Civil Concord Law?

The government's refusal to bring an Islamist party back to the political scene reinforced the ex-FIS Islamists' critique of President Bouteflika's ability to impose his "solution" to the crisis. According to Mourad Dhina, CCFIS spokesperson, in a July 2000 communiqué:

> The so-called civil concord policy, whose promotion he was assigned to carry out by the generals/decision-makers, did not reinstate peace. . . . This peace will be impossible unless everyone participates in it, including the FIS, as Shaykh Madani's and Shaykh Belhadj's last letters stipulate. We assess that Bouteflika could play a role in such a perspective if he freed himself from the hold that about fifteen generals who corrupt Algeria have on him, and joined the people's true representatives. If he does not feel that he possesses the courage that such an attitude requires, he should inform the people and go home.

The fear of an Islamic state led by the FIS, expressed at the beginning of the 1980s, was no longer an accurate reflection of at least the FIS's position or its capabilities. As Rida Malik emphasized in *L'Humanité* in 1995, "The state has a shape, that of a republic; it is unthinkable to change it. Transforming Algeria into some emirate or sultanate is out of the question. To move ahead, we must condemn terrorism. These FIS people do not understand this yet."

In June 2000 the IEFE Islamists emphasized their support for the exclusion from an amnesty of "those who . . . choose to continue armed action." The explicit recognition by the AIS as well as the IEFE that the strategy based on violence had failed, was the basis for the elaboration of a new policy whose goal was to rehabilitate an Islamist party that would respect Algeria's lawfulness and political plurality. The document published by the IEFE in May 1997, entitled "For a Strategy to Come Out of the Crisis in Algeria," illustrated the ex-FIS Islamists' new approach, which insisted that a "political exit" was the "only and best solution to the conflict."

The ex-FIS Islamists went through their political mutation. The condemnation of GIA and the support for Ahmad Talib Ibrahimi's candidacy in the presidential elections demonstrate the concessions the ex-FIS exiled leaders made from the party's pretensions during its earlier stage (from 1989 to 1991), according to O. Roy's analysis. The IEFE representatives no longer demanded the establishment of an Islamic state. They became conscious that radicalism was fatal to them. The Wafa party could represent the political mutations that the ex-FIS Islamists underwent and could facilitate their switch to a reformist approach through a peaceful political process. For the army, too, this outcome had an advantage. The party represented the opportunity to control a whole generation of Islamist sympathizers. Their earlier effort to work through the moderate Islamist parties of the Mahfud Nahnah (Movement of the Society for Peace) and Abdallah Djaballah's Harakat al-Islah al-Wataniyya (National Reform Movement) failed to mobilize popular support. As Djaballah emphasized on television on March 9, 1999, "[I]t is precisely the quest for high positions that prevents our movement from going forward and, instead, produces dissension and divides."

The MSP (Societal Movement for Peace)–Hamas aimed at recovering the FIS's electoral base. In 1995 it obtained 4,080,000 votes in the November 16 presidential elections. Considered to be the "big moderate Islamist party" capable of providing an alternative to the FIS, Hamas collapsed at the legislative elections of May 30, 2002. In fact, it was the Djaballah's Islah party, created in 1999, that best incarnated the FIS's Islamic-nationalist ideals. The Islah party won 43 parliamentary seats during the May 30, 2002, legislative elections, becoming the third political force. During the April 2004 elections, it refused to accept the results that gave Bouteflika 84 percent of the vote.

The Islamist scene in Algeria is thus divided into three levels: At the political level, the moderate Islamist parties did not manage to provide an alternative to the FIS and thus remained client parties at the service of President Bouteflika's strategy. On the security level, the GSPC changed radically by joining al-Qa'ida and becoming a military instrument serving an international cause. At the social level, Islamism became a synonym of Salafism, meaning that, concretely, believers no longer concern themselves with the state and with politics but rather with themselves and their relationship to God. The Islamists did not establish an Islamic state based on virtue, but they transformed themselves into "internal fortresses" based on Islamic values, which they perceive as authentic.

A Sense of Being Cursed

The heavy legacy of this history continues to shape Algeria. Enlisting in sectarian armed movements in Algeria has become a part of a local agenda where death and the quest for salvation had occupied a huge place.

Around 1.5 million Algerians were forced to flee their villages between 1993 and 1997. Many villages were left deserted. Among the 1.5 million displaced persons, only 170,000 returned home following the promise that they would be protected by local defense groups. This exodus, linked to the past security situation, is part of a wider context of impoverishment. In its report entitled "Les effets du programme d'ajustement structurel sur les populations vulnérables" (The Effects of the Structural Adjustment Program on Vulnerable Populations), published in 2000, the National Center for Planning Research and Analysis reveals that 35 percent of the population is affected by poverty. Of 31 million Algerians, 12 million live on less than 18,000 dinars (180 euros) per annum. The economic reforms and the state's ineptitudes are largely responsible for this situation.

Among these various ills, salvation was no longer sought through violence or through politics. This tragic decade seems to have witnessed the reappearance of intercessors represented by the *marabouts,* or a withdrawal into the self, as H. Touati explains. The sense of being doomed, which replaced the tendency to blame everything on colonialism, led to a multiple sense of anxiety. The quest for salvation now goes hand-in-hand with an individual search for redemption.

BIBLIOGRAPHY

Aït Hamadouche, Louisa, and Yahia Zoubir. "The Fate of Political Islam in Algeria." In *The Maghrib in the New Century: Identity, Religion and Politics*, ed. Bruce Maddy-Weitzman and Daniel Zisenwine, 103–31. Gainesville: University Press of Florida, 2007.

Bougarel, Xavier. *Bosnie: Anatomie d'un conflit* (Bosnia: Anatomy of a Conflict). Paris: Découverte, 1996.

Deeb, Mary-Jane. "Islam and the State in Algeria and Morocco: A Dialectical Model." In *Islamism and Secularism in North Africa*, ed. John Ruedy, 275–87. New York: St. Martin's Press, 1996.

Dhina, Mourad. Communiqué 19. Conseil de Coordination du FIS. July 5, 2000.

Echeverría Jesús, Carlos. "Radical Islam in the Maghreb," *Orbis* 48:2 (Spring 2004): 351–64. www.fpri.org/orbis/4802/jesus.islammaghreb.pdf.

Gera, Gideon. "Reflections on the Aftermath of Civil Strife: Algeria 2006." In *The Maghrib in the New Century: Identity, Religion and Politics*, ed. Bruce Maddy-Weitzman and Daniel Zisenwine, 75–102. Gainesville: University Press of Florida, 2007.

Grignard, Alain. "La littérature politique du GIA, des origines à Djamel Zitouni" (The Political Literature of the GIA, from Its Origins Through Djamel Zitouni). In *Facettes de l'Islam belge* (Facets of Belgian Islam), ed. Felice Dassetto. Brussels: Bruylant, 2001.

Grignard, Alain. "Historique des groupes islamiques armés algériens" (A History of the Algerian Armed Islamic Groups). *Les Cahiers de l'Orient* 62 (2001): 72–88.

Labévière, R. "Les réseaux européens d'Islamistes algériens: Entre déshérence et reconversion" (The European Networks of Algerian Islamists: Between Dormant and Conversion). *Les Cahiers de l'Orient* 62 (2001).

Layachi, Azzedine. "Algerian Crisis, Western Choices." *Middle East Quarterly* 1:3 (September 1994). www.meforum.org/article/144.

Letter from Abassi Madani. November 26, 1999.

Letter to *Le Mujahidin.* April 1995.

Maddy-Weitzman, Bruce, and Meir Litvak. "Islamism and the State in North Africa." In *Revolutionaries and Reformers: Contemporary Islamist Movements in the Middle East*, ed. Barry Rubin, 69–89. Albany: State University of New York Press, 2003.

Mezraq, Madani. "Communiqué No. 3." *El Mounqidh* 6 (June 1995).

Moussaoui, Abderrahmane. "Algérie, la guerre rejouée" (Algeria, the War Replayed). *La pensée du midi* 3 (Winter 2000) 28–37.

Parmentier, Mary Jane C. "Secularization and Islamisation in Morocco and Algeria." *The*

Journal of North African Studies 4:4 (1999): 27–50.

Roy, Olivier. *L'échec de l'Islam politique* (The Failure of Political Islam). Paris: Seuil, 1992.

Salgon, Jean-Michel. "Le GSPC" (The GSPC). *Les Cahiers de l'Orient* 61 (2001).

Shahin, Emad Eldin. "Secularism and Nationalism: The Political Discourse of 'Abd al-Salam Yassin." In *Islamism and Secularism in North Africa*, ed. John Ruedy, 167–86. New York: St. Martin's Press, 1996.

Souaïdia, Habib. *La sale guerre* (The Dirty War). Paris: Découverte, 2001.

Touati, Houari. *Entre Dieu et les hommes: Lettrés, saints et sorciers au Maghreb (17e siècle)* (Between God and Man: Men of Letters, Saints and Sorcerers in the Maghreb [17th Century]). Paris: EHESS, 1994.

Wieviorka, Michel. *The Making of Terrorism.* Chicago: University of Chicago Press, 1993.

Egypt

Israel Elad Altman

Violent Sunni Islamism has had some of its most powerful manifestations in Egypt, under the heavy influence of Sayyid Qutb's teachings. These have taken the form of a variety of *takfiri-jihadi* organizations, which waged Holy War against other Muslims because they are judged to be impious and thus, in effect, infidels (*takfir*, or declaring a fellow Muslim an apostate). These organizations consider the Mubarak regime illegitimate and thus seek to remove it by force (jihad) and to Islamize society from the top down. Yet the last decade has witnessed Islamism in Egypt moving away from organized, ideological violence and focusing instead on two other strategies: one seeking to Islamize society from the bottom up through missionary and educational work, and the other seeking to achieve power through participation in politics and in the electoral process.

This was the result of major watersheds in the history of the Islamist movement. The devastating social impact of terrorism in Egypt in the 1990s allowed the regime to crush both al-Jama'a al-Islamiyya and Jama'at al-Jihad, leading the former to revise its thought and to produce a rich body of Islamic jurisprudence (*fiqh*) that

systematically refuted the central tenets of al-Qa'ida and its affiliates.

While the events of September 11 created obstacles for Islamist radicals around the globe, the U.S.-led efforts to democratize the Arab states opened up new opportunities for political participation. These democratization efforts allowed the Muslim Brotherhood (MB) to capture an unprecedented 20 percent of the vote in the November–December 2005 parliamentary elections. This has arguably been the most important development in recent years as far as Egypt's Islamist movement is concerned.

The Muslim Brotherhood

The Egyptian Muslim Brotherhood (MB) is well into the third phase of its history. The first phase, from its foundation in 1928 up to the 1952 revolution—under the monarchy and the British presence—saw the formation of the classical MB doctrine and the early days of its ideological adaptation to party politics.

Both the rise of a militant trend in the movement toward the end of this period and rivalry with the new military regime led to the second phase—dissolution of the MB in

1954 and its suppression by Gamal Abdel Nasser, followed by organizational paralysis and the emergence of the *takfiri* trends inspired by Sayyid Qutb.

The third phase is that of the "Second Republic," under presidents Anwar Sadat and Husni Mubarak. This phase is characterized by the rejection of the isolationist and violent strategies of the takfiris, with the MB instead opting for reform and gradual "bottom-up Islamization" through *da'wa* (the call to Islam) and operations from within the political system. From the mid-1970s to the late 1980s, this period first witnessed détente with the regime, which initially encouraged the MB's reemergence as a counterweight to the left. Later, the regime tolerated the Brotherhood's activities without formally recognizing its existence. The MB is still officially outlawed. That situation allowed for large-scale expansion and recruitment, penetration of civil society institutions, and political activity, including participation in elections.

Then, from the late 1980s to the mid-1990s, the MB's penetration of civil society and its electoral feats led the regime to change its course. Since the mid-1990s, the MB has engaged in open conflict with the regime, which has in turn aimed to contain it, disrupt its activities, and limit its influence. Still, in the 2005 parliamentary elections, the MB established itself as by far the leading popular nongovernmental political organization in Egypt.

Ideology and Strategy

The opening of the political process in Egypt beginning in the 1970s produced an ideological adjustment to the new democratic game, generally referred to as "new Ikhwanism" (*ikhwan* meaning brotherhood). Like the old MB, the new Ikhwan strive to create an Islamic state that would apply Shari'a (Islamic jurisprudence). Yet while the classic MB strategy to reach that goal calls for missionary and educational work to spread the call to Islam, the new Ikhwan prefer the tools of democratic politics as a means of attaining power and establishing that state. This change was accompanied by a shift from the classic pan-Islamic orientation of the MB to a focus on the particular territorial state.

The main force for change in the direction of new Ikhwan strategy in the last two decades has been the "second generation" of MB activists, also known as the "middle generation" (*jil al-wasat*). These were former activists of the Islamist student groups in the 1970s who joined the MB, rose through the ranks as trade union leaders, and engineered the movement's entry into the political arena. (Among them, Abd al-Mun'im Abu al-Futuh and Isam al-Aryan have the highest profile in the media.) Yet much power in the MB still rests with the "old-guard" leaders. Many adherents of the classic MB worldview are veterans of the MB's "Secret Apparatus" and graduates of Nasser's jails (such as General Guide Muhammad Mahdi Akif and several members of the MB's Guidance Bureau). These figures have been more cautious and less open to change in general, and to the increasing politicization of the movement in particular.

Hasan al-Banna, the MB's founder and dominant ideologue, envisioned the MB as a "comprehensive Islamic body," spreading the call to Islam and acting as a legal and moral source of authority for Islam as a whole, and therefore above local politics and parties. The MB's ambitions went far beyond Egypt's confines, its desire being to spread Islam as a world religion and to create a pan-Islamic state or a caliphate. The new Ikhwan, on the other hand, argue that the MB should focus on the territorial nation-state, Egypt. They argue also that it should create its political party, and some argue that it should transform itself from a da'wa movement—transcending politics— to a political party, prepared to compete, cooperate, and form alliances with other parties.

In practice, the MB has been deeply involved in politics on all levels—from student associations and trade and professional unions to local government and the nation's Parliament—scoring significant achievements. However, no formal change in its nature has taken place. The official ideological line, as represented by the general guide and his two deputies (Muhammad al-Sayyid Habib and Muhammad Khairat al-Shatir), strictly reflects the classic doctrine concerning the nature of the movement, as set out by Hasan al-Banna. It should be borne in mind that the Egyptian general guide is traditionally also the general guide of the International Organization of the Muslim Brotherhood. Therefore, he would naturally adhere to the view of the MB as a global movement.

As the MB has no legally recognized status, its room for political maneuver is a function of the government's tolerance at any given moment. Becoming a legal political party would obviously release the MB from this legal limbo. Yet this is exactly why the government continues to deny it a legal status. Attempts by MB members to achieve recognition as a party (the Center Party, see below) have failed. Thus, the MB's occasional references to its intention to declare the formation of its party, al-Amal (Hope), have so far not materialized.

The second-generation spokesmen have maintained that the MB was not aiming to set up a religious state or a religious government but rather that it sought to establish a civil government and a civil state (*dawla madaniyya*) with an Islamic source of authority (*mar ja'iyya*), where all citizens would be assured equal rights and obligations under the constitution. By "source of authority," its leaders explained, they meant Islam as a civilization and as a social and political system consisting of general principles that govern the functioning of a state with a Muslim majority. After all, as Abu al-Futuh explained in an interview in *al-Araby,* Islam is not only the faith of the majority but also the culture and heritage of all, as Muslims, Christians, and Jews played a part in its creation. This civil state would be based on common citizenship (*muwatana*). However, the second-generation MB has not clearly explained how the state is not a religious one when it is set up in implementation of Divine Will and in order to apply Divine Law.

Furthermore, the MB old-guard leadership continues to uphold the old doctrine as the official line of the movement. In several missives, posted on the MB's Web site (www.ikhwanonline.com) and intended to eliminate any misconception about where the movement stood, General Guide Akif stated that since its foundation, the MB has had two goals: to liberate the Islamic homeland from any foreign domination, which means ending not only military occupations but also any other form of foreign domination, be it political, intellectual, cultural, or economic; and to set up a free state in this homeland that applies Islam's rules and implements its social order. The MB seeks to achieve these goals everywhere—Islam being the religion of all mankind since it embraces all aspects of life of all people in every age.

Following al-Banna, Akif listed the seven

steps necessary for the MB to attain these goals: reforming the individual; establishing the Muslim home; guiding the society; liberating the homeland; reforming the government; restoring the international entity of the Islamic *umma* (nation); and finally, mastership of the world (*ustadhiyyat al-alam*). The establishment of the Islamic caliphate would require preparatory steps, he wrote, again following al-Banna: cultural, social, and economic cooperation between all the Muslim peoples; forging alliances, treaties, and conferences between the Muslim states; and seeking the formation of the Muslim League of Nations.

In the MB missives, as they appear on the MB Web site, Akif has pointed to the MB's means of achieving those goals: first, da'wa and recruitment of the good elements, who form solid pillars for reform; and second, the constitutional struggle, designed to make the voice of da'wa heard in formal bodies such as parliaments, trade unions, and institutions. Political work is thus seen as intended to reinforce the da'wa, not to supplant it. Elsewhere, in July 2005, Akif wrote that the MB believes that the highest loyalty is to Islam, which does not preclude other, lesser affiliations such as family, tribe, or homeland. He caused an uproar in April 2006 following a press report according to which he expressed his attachment to pan-Islamism and his contempt for Egyptian patriotism.

The political reform narrative adopted by the MB calls for democracy, pluralism, human rights, separation of powers, constraints on the power of the rulers, protection of political freedoms, and independence of the judiciary. Its Reform Initiative of March 3, 2004—launched in response to America's "Greater Middle East Initiative" to democratize the Arab states—indeed supported a republican, parliamentary, constitu-

tional, and democratic political order "in the framework of the principles of Islam." The initiative affirmed that the people were the source of all powers and that no individual, party, community, or society could claim the right to power unless it were derived from free and true popular will. It also stated that the MB was committed to the principle of alternation of power through general, free, and fair elections. Yet the initiative also outlined the Brotherhood's objectives as follows:

> Our only hope to achieve progress in all aspects of life is by returning to our religion and implementing our Shari'a. . . . We have a clear mission—to work to implement Allah's Law. This is to be achieved by forming the Muslim individual, the Muslim home, the Muslim government, and the state which will lead the Islamic states, reunite the scattered Muslims, restore their glory, retrieve for them their lost lands and stolen homelands, and carry the banner of the call to Allah in order to make the world happy with Islam's blessing and instructions.

This is the MB's classic mission statement formulated by Hasan al-Banna, as it appears on the MB Web site.

The ambiguity of the Muslim Brotherhood's position regarding the nature of the state it intends to set up is a cause for concern for Egypt's Copts. This was only exacerbated following the MB's electoral achievements in November–December 2005. In an article published after the parliamentary elections on the MB's official *Arabic* language site, entitled "What Will Happen If the MB Reaches Power," First Deputy General Guide Muhammad Habib wrote that the MB viewed the Copts as citizens who enjoy full citizenship rights (*muwatana*), and "consequently they have the full right to assume public posts, except for the president of the state." This exception reflects the Islamic principle that non-Muslims cannot rule Muslims. It should be noted that in the *English* version of Habib's article, which appeared on the MB's official English Web site, the Copts were said to have the full right to assume public posts, "including that of the head of state."

Second-generation leaders have attempted to ease Coptic concerns by offering a more moderate version of the MB's position on the issue. They have claimed, for example, that the *fatwa* (religious edict) issued in 1996 by then–general guide Mustafa Mashhur that required non-Muslims to pay the poll tax (*jizyah*) should no longer be implemented. This position, however, has not been given an official form, and when asked about the MB's position regarding the Copts, General Guide Akif replied, in an interview with Faraj Isma'il: "We in the MB apply Allah's rules in dealing with them." At an MB event on October 5, 2006, Akif called for the establishment of the Islamic government envisioned by al-Banna. This triggered sharp criticism from the opposition parties.

Domestic Politics

Two major factors have influenced the MB's political strategy in recent years: increasing pressure for democratization on the Egyptian regime by the United States and the West; and the nearing end of President Husni Mubarak's reign and the beginning of a new one, whose nature is unclear but for which the actors in the Egyptian political system are all preparing. Given these factors, the MB has positioned itself as a force for democratic reform, as the political organization enjoying the most popular sup-

port, and as the alternative to the present regime.

The organization's illegal status has been an obvious constraint. It has exploited the government's policy of tolerance for its activities as long as it does not cross certain red lines—for example, holding large-scale street demonstrations. In this framework, the MB's strategy has been to attempt to win every possible election and to oppose the government's policies on central domestic and foreign policy issues through peaceful means, including street demonstrations and sit-ins. Still, it has calibrated its protest activities so as not to push the regime to suppress it altogether.

At the time of this writing, the struggle for political reform had focused on three central issues: President Mubarak's reelection for a fifth term in September 2005; the regime's preparations for transferring the presidency to Mubarak's son, Gamal; and the extension of the emergency laws (which were imposed after the 1967 war, lifted in 1980, and reimposed in 1981). In late 2004 and early 2005, opposition groups led by a group called Kifaya held public demonstrations against Mubarak on these issues, arousing international interest. The MB leadership joined the trend by holding its own demonstrations in Cairo and in the countryside beginning on March 27, 2005. This was the first time the MB had held public demonstrations on domestic issues since Mubarak took over in 1981. The MB was careful not to cross a red line; it limited the number of demonstrators relative to its potential and alerted the authorities in advance of each demonstration. The government responded by arresting about 1,500 MB members, including senior members. By the summer of 2005, the MB stopped its demonstrations and the government slowly released MB prisoners as part of a deal in which the MB allegedly agreed not to support opposition candidates to the presidency in the September 2005 elections.

While initially the MB and other opposition groups had made a mutual decision to boycott the presidential elections, the MB suddenly changed its mind on August 21, 2005. The MB then urged its members to participate in the elections by voting for a candidate of their choice, but not to support repression and corruption. This was interpreted as a call not to support Mubarak, but since the rate of participation was more important to the regime than Mubarak's margin of victory, this policy shift ended up working in the regime's favor. Since this outcome gave the elections—and the regime—more legitimacy, there was criticism of the policy in the MB ranks.

Yet this was a small price to pay for the big prize—the November–December 2005 parliamentary elections. By October 2005, following the end of the demonstrations and the cancellation of the boycott, all MB prisoners in Egypt had been released and were able to take part in the election effort. By slating candidates for only 150 of 454 parliamentary seats—namely, fewer than needed to deny the government the two-thirds majority required for changes in the constitution—the MB signaled that it was not seeking confrontation. (It should be noted that since the MB is formally outlawed, its candidates run as independents.) The MB won 88 seats in three rounds of parliamentary elections, compared to 15 in the 2000 elections and to 12 seats won by all the other opposition parties. The MB had taken advantage of the government's low level of intervention in the first two election rounds and managed to win 76 seats in those first two rounds. This spurred the government to take action and to prevent pro-MB voters from reaching the polling

stations for the third round. Hundreds of MB election activists were arrested, leading to violent clashes that left at least 11 people dead. In the third and last round, therefore, the MB only won 12 seats. Its success rate of 59 percent for those seats it contested was nevertheless high. In addition to the foreign pressure on the government, this was the result of the MB's organizational capabilities, the reportedly huge sums of money it had invested, and the decreasing efficacy of the ruling National Democratic Party's electoral machinery. Adding insult to injury, in the Manufiyya Province, the birthplace of presidents Sadat and Mubarak, the MB won 10 seats, while the National Democratic Party won only five.

The MB's electoral achievements seem to have boosted the organization's self-confidence and increased its willingness to confront the regime, both on the rhetorical level and on the street. It took advantage of its strong parliamentary presence to propagate its positions, focusing on attacking government inefficiency and corruption and promoting human rights and reform of the legal system. Over a quarter of the draft laws submitted by MB deputies since the elections have focused on the latter. Its deputies have also served as a channel for contact with representatives of foreign governments, the European Union (EU), and the UN secretary-general. The government reacted by applying pressure on members of the MB parliamentary bloc. According to MB reports on the Brotherhood Web site, the security services have obstructed their social activities, warning local administration officials in the provinces to avoid contact with them and instructing village notables to discourage the people from turning to them to solve their problems.

With its sights set on the next presidential elections (scheduled for 2011), the MB has been trying to build up public opposition to clause 76 of the constitution. The clause was amended in February 2005, replacing the old system of a single presidential candidate nominated by Parliament and endorsed by a referendum with multiple-candidate elections; yet the conditions it set in effect have prevented the MB from nominating a candidate from within its ranks.

The MB had intended to get the largest possible number of its supporters elected in the April 2006 local council elections, with the goal of reaching the required minimum number of elected public officials for endorsement of a presidential candidate according to the amended version of clause 76. The government blocked that option in February 2006, however, by passing legislation postponing the elections for the local authorities for another two years. While stressing that it had no plans to contest the next presidential elections, in a February 2006 statement to the press, MB spokesmen accused the government of postponing the elections in order to deny the MB the ability to field or support a presidential candidate.

The MB then launched a campaign to protest the extension of the emergency laws. During the 2005 presidential election campaign, President Mubarak announced that these laws would be replaced with new antiterrorism legislation. However, as the expiration of the emergency laws in May 2006 approached, the government argued that completion of the new legislation would require up to two years, and that in order to prevent a legal vacuum, the emergency laws would be extended. The MB protest campaign consisted largely of student demonstrations on university campuses. As reported in February and March 2006 on the MB's English- and Arabic-language Internet sites, in response, the government arrested dozens of activists as well

as several MB businesspeople whose assets were confiscated in what was viewed as an attack on the MB's financial resources. MB members saw these arrests as part of a deal: The detainees would be released if the MB alleviated its opposition to the extension of the emergency laws.

The government accused the MB of training volunteer fighters to be sent to conflict zones, such as Iraq and the Palestinian territories, in order to acquire combat skills. As explained by leading MB spokesman Isam al-Aryan, the MB considered this an excuse for the continued denial of legal status to their organization and for the extension of the emergency laws. In April 2006, the editor-in-chief of the MB's official Arabic Internet site implied that the Easter attacks on Coptic churches in Alexandria and the ensuing violent clashes between Copts and Muslims were actually orchestrated by the government in order to justify the emergency laws. On April 29, 2006, five days after the terrorist attack on Dahab, the emergency laws were extended for an additional two years.

There were reportedly two opposing views within the MB on the issue of Gamal Mubarak succeeding his father as president, as articulated on almesryoon.com. The first view, represented by the general guide, held that the movement should strongly oppose Gamal's succession or else lose its credibility. The other view reportedly held that the MB had no interest in opposing Gamal's succession: It should focus instead on more important issues affecting the movement's long-term interests and should concentrate on exploiting the regime's difficulties with the succession in order to advance issues such as ending the state of emergency and changing constitutional clause 76.

There was public speculation that the MB might strike a deal with the government, reducing the latter's difficulties in implementing Gamal's succession. There appeared to be internal debate within the MB regarding a possible deal with the government. This was indicated in various entries on the MB main Web site arguing, for example, that deals with the regime had no value because periods of calm in its relations with the MB were usually followed by an escalation in its repressive measures designed to block the movement's political activities. It was argued, moreover, that the MB must oppose Gamal's succession because such a succession would contradict the reform the movement has called for. Additionally, the succession has been rejected by the movement's grassroots, thus to not oppose it would undermine the MB's credibility among the Egyptian masses. Some cautioned that the MB should neither lead a civil disobedience movement against Gamal's succession nor join other opposition groups in street demonstrations on this issue, feeling this would lead to the intensification of the government's campaign against the MB.

By May 2006, the MB's public position on the succession issue shifted from accepting Gamal's presidency, should he be elected in a multicandidate election, to total rejection even under those conditions. Further escalating its tensions with the government, the MB joined the demonstrations held by Kifaya and other opposition groups in April and May 2006 in support of judicial independence, with the MB's Parliament members leading the MB demonstrators. Hundreds of MB members were arrested. In a May 2006 interview in *al-Masri al-Yawm*, Prime Minister Ahmad Nazif implied that his government's intention was to change the constitution in a way that would reduce the number of MPs the MB could get elected. His explanation was that while the

MB did not legally exist, the organization's MPs ran for elections as independents, were elected as such, and once elected, acted openly as an MB parliamentary bloc. Nazif thus confirmed the assessment that the government saw the MB's achievements in the parliamentary elections as crossing the "red lines," and it was determined to prevent such success in future parliamentary elections and to prevent the MB from achieving greater power.

The Second Lebanon War in July–August 2006 provided the MB with an opportunity to gain popularity and the moral high ground by allying itself with the Hizballah-Hamas-Syria-Iran axis and against the Egyptian-Saudi-Jordanian camp. In an August 2006 missive on the Brotherhood Web site, General Guide Akif declared victoriously: "Islam today regains its role in leading the struggle against the Zionist project." The MB enthusiastically supported Hizballah and vehemently criticized those Sunni legal experts and political leaders who argued that as a Shi'a organization and an arm of Iran, Hizballah must not be supported. July 2006 articles on the MB's site supported the view that Hizballah's fighters were Arabs and Muslims waging a war of resistance against an oppression and occupation affecting all Muslims. In August 2006, Akif announced he was ready to send 10,000 MB volunteers to fight alongside Hizballah in Lebanon (www.ikhwanonline.com, August 6, 2006). Moreover, Akif accused the Egyptian regime of siding with Israel in the war against the Islamists. He also sharply attacked Arab leaders for failing to come to the rescue of the Lebanese people, remarking in a missive that had those leaders not been Muslim, "We would have fought against them because they are harder to us than the Zionists and the Americans" (www.ikhwanonline.com, August 3, 2006).

Through its posturing as a champion of the jihad against Israel—in stark contrast to the inactivity of the Arab regimes and their implied collusion with the enemies of Arabs and Islam—the MB thus offered leadership where the state had failed to do so. From substituting for the state in the area of social services, the MB has been moving toward involvement in foreign affairs—hitherto the sacred domain of the state. The offer to send volunteers to fight alongside Hizballah was of particular concern to the regime. Not only did it constitute a public admission that an MB organization exists (in defiance of the law) and that it may have a military arm, but it also indicated that the MB felt that having captured the moral high ground on the issue of standing up to Israel, they should not be constrained in making such public statements. This marked a new level in the rise of MB's self-confidence and sense of empowerment.

MB Parliament members were quick to deny that the MB had a military arm, stating that its members received physical but not military training. Still, the government reacted by arresting senior MB members—among them Secretary-General Mahmud Izzat—on charges of illegal activity, including seeking to create public opinion hostile toward government policies and inciting the public to carry out demonstrations, strikes, and civil disobedience. The MB Parliament members were accused of taking advantage of their parliamentary immunity in their involvement in those activities. It turned out that one of those arrested, Lashin Abu Shanab, an 80-year-old member of the Guidance Bureau, confirmed during his interrogation that an MB organization existed and described in great detail the organizational structure and functioning of the MB. Abu Shanab thus compromised all the MB members as violators of the law.

It has been speculated that the admission that the organization existed was a deliberate move by the MB, designed to force the government to accept its existence once and for all. The MB's open reference to "the MB parliamentary bloc" (including the MB Web site reporting on the bloc's elections for its bureau) seems to be designed to force the government to accept the fait accompli of the MB's existence as a political party.

By October 2006, Izzat and other detainees were released, but around 70 MB members were still held, and it appeared that the MB and the government were nearing a decisive point: They could reach a deal, which would grant the MB certain political concessions in exchange for its dropping its opposition to Gamal's succession to the presidency. Conversely, the two could reach a confrontation in which there would be a change in the regime's strategy toward the MB, causing the latter's political activities to be dramatically restricted or even completely prevented.

The United States and the West

The MB's electoral achievements have not moderated its rhetoric regarding the United States. Two approaches stand out: total conflict with the United States, in rejection of any form of dialogue; and a more nuanced approach that ostensibly expresses an interest in a dialogue but packages it with conditions and reservations that make it unlikely.

The first approach, reflecting the traditional MB attitude, sees no room for engagement with the United States because the agendas of the MB and the United States are on a collision course. General Guide Akif, who upholds this line, sees the United States as the embodiment of evil. He argues that in the new American world order, mankind is divided into classes: first-class humans—Americans and Zionists; second-class humans—Westerners of non-Oriental origins; and finally the tenth-class inhabitants of the Arab, Muslim, and Oriental worlds. In December 2005 on the MB Web site, Akif further claimed that this world order, which has become a global nightmare, was in reality run by the Jews behind the scenes. The MB, Akif said in an April 2006 missive, has been in the vanguard of those who regard the American call for democracy and freedom with suspicion, in view of the dark history of American imperialism, of its continued aid to despotic regimes, of its total alignment with the Zionist project, and of its craving for Arab resources. Akif called for an economic boycott of imperialist states as well as a boycott of their cultural products, which are designed to transform thoughts, morals, and behavioral patterns and to increase susceptibility to imperialism.

Younger spokesmen do express an interest in dialogue with the United States within the context of their revivalist vision of Islam and its gradual and flexible implementation of Shari'a. They welcome an open and public dialogue with all the segments of American society, except the U.S. administration, as having cultural value.

They were suspicious, however, of American intentions: Would the United States support democracy even if it put its political rivals in power? They pointed to the essential contradiction between what they called the growing American project of empire and hegemony on one hand and the steadily progressing MB project to construct an Islamic reformist revival on the other. The Islamic revivalist project, they said, aims at liberating Muslim lands from any foreign hegemony—be it military,

economic, cultural, or spiritual—reforming governance in the Muslim countries, and achieving a real Arab unity and an international Islamic entity (*kiyan dawli islami*). The bottom line, then, is that these are two contradictory projects and there is very little room for dialogue.

The Palestinians

Part of the conflict with the West, in the MB's view, is the Israeli-Palestinian problem. According to this view, the West planted Israel in the Arab region as a means to control the Arab states and to strike at the Arab and Islamic identity of the region. As articles on the MB's site attest, Israel is seen as a Western state, foreign to the region in its history and culture, and has no right to exist. It should therefore be abolished and its Jewish inhabitants absorbed in the Palestinian-Arab state that would replace it.

The MB celebrated Hamas's 2006 election victory as its own: "The Muslim Brotherhood has reached power in Palestine," declared MB Deputy General Guide Muhammad Habib. In an interview on the Ikhwan's site he stressed that by going down the political road, Hamas did not give up on the resistance or armed struggle. On the same Web site Isam al-Aryan called upon the Palestinians to form a new strategy to materialize their dream of liberating all of the national land. He stressed that it should take the form of the "single democratic state" and could then join a "Greater Syria" (*bilad al-sham al-wasi'a*)—he did not use the historic term *Suriyya al-Kubra*—covering Syria, Lebanon, Jordan, and Palestine.

Jihad

Akif has repeatedly called upon all Muslims to support the resistance (*muqawama*) in Iraq, the Palestinian territories, and Afghanistan. Describing jihad and the martyrdom operation (*istishhad)* as "the way to glory and victory," he stated that Islam regards resistance against occupation as "a jihad for God" (*jihad fi sabil Allah*). This jihad, which means actual fighting (*qital*), is an individual religious duty (*fard ayn*) of the inhabitants of the country under occupation, and it takes precedence over other duties (*fara'id*). For the people of the neighboring countries, participating in this jihad is a collective duty (*fard kifaya*), which becomes an individual duty if the occupied people fail to repel the aggressor. If the occupation persists nevertheless, fighting against it becomes an individual duty for Muslims the world over. In a July 2005 article on the MB Web site outlining the organization's objectives, Akif stated that for the MB, jihad was the most elevated pillar of Islam after "the two testimonies" (that there is no god but Allah and that Muhammad is his messenger). Akif recapitulated Muhammad's saying, often quoted by al-Banna: "He who dies and has not fought, and was not resolved to fight, has died a *jahiliyya* death." (In Islam, *jahiliyya*—literally, ignorance—is the pre-Islamic historical phase of the Arabs.)

The MB's position on terrorist attacks in Egypt has evolved with time. The movement did not condemn the terrorist attack on Taba of October 2004. Instead, in its communiqué reacting to the attack it commented that, first, the attack was a response to atrocities committed by Israeli forces in Palestine and U.S. forces in Iraq, and second, that one must not accuse any Islamist group since the attack could have been carried out by Israeli or other intelligence services. An expression of understanding for the motivation of the terrorists was still included in Akif's formal reaction to the July 23, 2005, attacks on Sharm al-

Shaykh when he remarked that the aggression and wars perpetrated by global imperialism against the world's peoples gave birth to the culture of violence and terrorism. Yet he also condemned the attacks, saying that they contradicted religion and religious law, constituted an aggression against all human values and mores, and played into the hands of the Zionist-American project. This condemnation was repeated verbatim in Akif's formal response to the April 24, 2006, attacks on Dahab, only this time the "understanding" of the terrorists' motivation was dropped. This evolution most likely reflects the fact that the Taba attack, the first in the series, was believed to have targeted solely or mainly Israeli tourists, while the other two hit mostly Egyptian and foreign tourists and had a deeper impact on the Egyptian public. As cited on the MB Web site, Akif holds that there is no difference between Israeli soldiers and civilians, because for him "the Zionist People" as a whole is an armed military which occupies Palestine.

The Shi'a and Iran

Akif has called upon Sunnis and Shi'as in Iraq to stand up against the forces of civil strife (*fitna*). The aggravation of the Sunni-Shi'a conflict led him to issue a missive laying out the legal and practical arguments for the Sunnis to end their conflict with the Shi'a and to form a common front with them against the occupation. He rejected the position that sees the Shi'a as apostates and said that Islam gave non-Muslims the right to freedom of faith and worship, allowing them to live respectfully in Islamic society.

On this basis, he questioned how one could deny that right to those who agree with the Sunnis on the fundamentals of Islam and differ with them only on secondary matters. He called for the formation of a body consisting of Sunni and Shi'a *ulama* (religious scholars) whose task would be to spread the culture of Islamic fraternity and make it superior to one's loyalty to one of the legal schools (*al-wala al-madhhabi*). He also called for the revival of the "Committee for Rapprochement Between the Islamic Legal Schools," which was set up in the 1940s with the participation of Hasan al-Banna and ulama from al-Azhar and from Iran, and led to the recognition by al-Azhar of Twelver Shi'ism as the fifth school of jurisprudence. Akif urged all of Islam's religious authorities to confront the takfiri philosophy, to spread moderate Islamic thought, and to condemn all criminal attacks on innocent civilians and state institutions, which serve as an excuse for the occupation forces to stay in Iraq.

The Egyptian MB welcomed Iran's nuclear program. Deputy General Guide Muhammad Habib said, as cited in an April 2006 *al-Sharq al-Awsat* article, that he believed that the Iranian nuclear program was for peaceful purposes, but if it were a military program, it would serve to balance the Israeli nuclear arsenal. "It will create a sort of a balance between the two sides, the Arab and Islamic side and the Israeli side." He said that he had no problem with Iran having nuclear weapons and that he believed most Egyptians held the same position.

The Center Party (Hizb al-Wasat)

Egypt's Center Party was founded in 1995 by a group of second-generation MB activists who left the MB. It has failed at three attempts to convince the government that it is not a religious organization and so should not be denied legal status as a politi-

cal party: In 1996 it applied as "The Center Party," in 1998 as "The Egyptian Center Party," and in 2004 as "The New Center." Less a party than an intellectual circle of moderate Islamists, al-Wasat describes itself as the ideological equivalent of Turkey's Justice and Development Party (AKP).

The circumstances of al-Wasat's formation have been a matter of controversy. According to its founders, the party split from the MB when they became fed up with the ideological rigidity and authoritarian leadership style and set up the new body as a moderate alternative to the MB. According to another version, the founders formed the group with the support of at least part of the MB leadership (including General Guide Muhammad Mahdi Akif), which sought thereby to probe whether an MB political party established alongside the MB, and presumably separate from it (like the Jordanian Islamic Action Front, for example), would be permitted by the government. However, eventually a dispute broke out between the leadership and the founders. The founding of the new party was supported by Shaykh Yusuf al-Qaradawi and other MB figures abroad, and the government perceived it as an extension of the MB.

At any rate, al-Wasat has positioned itself as an ideological rival of the MB. It points to the existence of two trends in the MB, one of which is reformist and open-minded, and the other—representing the controlling majority—rigid, and argues that the MB's mixing of missionary (da'wa) and political activities poses a danger to the nation. Al-Wasat, in contrast, calls for the separation of da'wa from politics and was set up as a civil party. Furthermore, according to al-Wasat founding member Abu al-'Ala Madhi (quoted in the Carnegie Endowment *Arab Reform Bulletin* of December 2005), the MB has an ambiguous vision of the Islamic state and is afraid of democracy, and "even if they call for democracy they do not really believe in it."

The party defines itself on its Web site, www.alwasatparty.com, as "a civil [*madani*] party with an Islamic background [*khalfi-yya*], bringing together all Egyptian citizens, Muslims and non-Muslims, as the basis of membership is common citizenship [*muwatana*]: Citizenship is the basis of relations between the Egyptians, and no discrimination among them should be allowed, be it because of religion, sex, color or race." The "Islamic background" refers to Islam as the religion of the Muslims and the culture (*hadhara*) that has brought together Muslims and non-Muslims.

It should be noted that the party's Islamic identity is defined in several different versions. While in its mission statement al-Wasat is said to have an Islamic "background," in another formal document on its site it refers to itself as a civil party with an Islamic "source of authority" (*mar ja'iyya*), and in an English-language interview given to an American institution, the Carnegie Endowment, it describes itself as "a civil party with an Islamic reference point." Several founding members of the party were Copts, which, al-Wasat argues, proves its commitment to the principle of citizenship (*muwatana*) and that it is not a religious party despite the fact that several founding members were former MB activists.

The party says that it follows the peaceful democratic method and accepts intellectual and political pluralism, participation (*mush-araka*), dialogue, and coexistence among all views and ideas. It seeks to create a civil state based on the people's rule, since the people are the source of all authority. The rulers of that state would be civilians from the general public and not religious scholars or clerics, and they would rule in accor-

dance to civil foundations. Al-Wasat affirms the right to form political parties and civil society institutions, as well as the right of full equality between the sexes: The criteria for eligibility for public positions such as judges or the head of state are competence and capability, not a person's gender. Al-Wasat declares that its main objective is to bring about, through democratic means, the implementation of the second clause of the Egyptian constitution, which states that Shari'a is the principal source of legislation. The idea is to implement Shari'a through legal interpretations (*ijtihadat*) that will advance society, not paralyze it, and that will ensure Egyptians a better, prosperous, and honorable life.

Ten years after its creation, the party is still engaged in a legal battle over its legitimacy, which actually concerns its identity. The government justifies its repeated refusals to recognize al-Wasat by arguing that it is not distinguishable from existing parties, while the MB argues that the party's ideology is not different from its own and that it was formed for organizational or personal reasons as opposed to ideological ones. According to al-Wasat's Web site, the government has fought its legal appeals by, among other means, pressuring Coptic founding members of the party to withdraw, which would substantiate the argument that it is a religious party, forbidden under the constitution.

Al-Tawhid wal-Jihad and the Sinai Terror Attacks

While Egypt's terror organizations, al-Jama'a al-Islamiyya and Jama'at al-Jihad, have been undergoing a profound ideological revision, steering away from violence (for details see below), the country was rocked by three suicide attacks within a year and a half, all targeting tourist sites: the October 7, 2004, attacks on Taba and Nuweyba; the July 24, 2005, attack on Sharm al-Shaykh; and the April 24, 2006, attack on Dahab—which together left 250 people dead and 750 wounded. Yet it was soon discovered that the attacks were carried out by members of a small organization of Sinai Bedouins. Some were Palestinian, mainly from al-Arish in northeastern Sinai, which is geographically, demographically, and clearly also ideologically close to the Gaza Strip. They were reportedly influenced and assisted to some degree (with funding and training) by Gaza Palestinians. The organization did not cross over from Sinai to Egypt's heartland.

According to information released by the Egyptian authorities, al-Tawhid wal-Jihad (Monotheism and Holy War) was founded in 2000 by Khalid Musa'id, a dentist of Bedouin origin from al-Arish and a member of the Muslim Youth (al-Shubban al-Muslimun) Islamic organization. He recruited for the organization by selecting young individuals who attended his religious classes on faith and jihad, delivered in al-Arish's mosques. He used the September 11, 2001, events and Israel's military incursion to Jenin in 2002 to press upon the group's members the need to carry out jihad against the United States and in the West Bank and Gaza. Following the American invasion of Iraq, Musa'id began to drive home the need to carry out suicide attacks against foreign tourists whose states partook in that invasion. He declared the Egyptian state and its institutions apostate because they collaborated with the so-called enemies of Islam.

The group's name and its objectives clearly indicate the influence of Abu Mus'ab al-Zarqawi's model, though no direct connections with him have been reported. A video recording by one of the three Sharm al-Shaykh suicide bombers reflected the inspiration of Osama bin Laden.

Musa'id established contacts with Islamist activists in Gaza (whose organizational affiliation was not specified by the Egyptian authorities) who helped his organization with funds and training. Occasional robberies by group members served as another source of funds. In preparation for the terror operations, the organization's membership of about 100 was divided into half a dozen strictly compartmentalized cells, each based in a different part of Sinai and each unaware of the others. Taba and Nuweyba, attacked on the anniversary of the start of the 1973 war, were selected for attack due to the high proportion of Israeli tourists present, and indeed two members of the Nakhel cell, which executed the attack, were of Palestinian origin. Sharm al-Shaykh was attacked on the anniversary of the 1952 revolution, and Dahab on the anniversary of the Israeli evacuation of Sinai in 1982.

Initially, the Egyptian security authorities assumed the Taba-Nuweyba attack was isolated and that its perpetrators were not part of a larger organization. However, following the Sharm al-Shaykh attack, as well as a failed attack on a Sinai Multinational Forces bus near al-Arish in August 2005, they picked up the trail of the organization and launched a hot pursuit of its members all over Sinai, killing Khalid Musa'id and capturing several others. Yet the compartmentalization allowed the new leader, Nasr Khamis al-Malahi, Musa'id's former right hand, to prepare and carry out the Dahab attack. However, Malahi died in another failed suicide attack on the Sinai Multinational Forces near al-Arish on April 27, 2006, right after the Dahab attack. Several members were still on the run.

Al-Tawhid wal-Jihad differs fundamentally from al-Jama'a al-Islamiyya and Jama'at al-Jihad. First, as explained in an *al-Ahram* article, it did not develop an intellectual or doctrinal framework explaining its goals, nor did it create a structured organizational hierarchy. Second, for al-Tawhid wal-Jihad, jihad was not seen as the means to reach power and set up an Islamic state. Rather, conducting jihad against the infidels and apostates was the goal of the organization. In this sense, it resembled the attack by a lone assailant on foreign tourists near al-Azhar in Cairo in April 2005. It was later discovered that the attacker was not connected to any terrorist group; he had simply felt compelled to act by Islamist literature he found on Internet. Both Jama'at al-Jihad and al-Jama'a al-Islamiyya denounced the Dahab attack, the former calling it un-Islamic and lacking any Shari'a basis, and the latter focusing on the inadmissibility of attacking tourists who, according to Islamic law, are immune and must be protected.

It has been argued that the organization's antistate activities were a reaction to the heavy-handedness of the Egyptian security forces toward Sinai's Bedouins, an impoverished and neglected sector of Egypt's population. It appears that large-scale and perhaps brutal arrests and investigations of Sinai Bedouins after the Taba-Nuweyba attack, in search of the perpetrators, did antagonize that population, but al-Tawhid wal-Jihad had been founded, and its objectives decided, well before that attack took place, as reported by *al-Hayat*.

In April 2006, the Egyptian authorities announced that they uncovered a new takfiri group, al-Ta'ifa al-Mansura. The group was allegedly planning to carry out terrorist attacks against tourist targets, to blow up a major gas pipeline in Cairo, and to assassinate Muslim and Christian religious leaders; 22 members were in fact arrested. Critics of the government, including Isam

al-Aryan, a leading spokesman of the MB, implied that the story was fabricated in order to justify the extension of the emergency laws, which were then being debated in Parliament, by pointing to alleged terrorist threats in Egypt. No trial was ever held, and by September 13, 2006, all of the suspects, including the alleged leader of the group, were released.

Al-Jama'a al-Islamiyya and Jama'at al-Jihad

Al-Jama'a al-Islamiyya today is a da'wa group that emphasizes the fight against the takfiri ideologies through Shari'a and ideological tools. On its Web site, www.egyptianislamicgroup.com, inaugurated in June 2006, it describes itself as a group of Muslims whose task is not to push people away from Islam by accusing them of apostasy but rather to bring people into Islam and guide them to Allah's way. "We are people of da'wa, not judges [*du'at, la qudhat*]," it says—in reference to the well-known book by that title written by Hasan al-Hudaibi (the second general guide of the Muslim Brotherhood, 1951–1973), which argues against the takfiri doctrine of Sayyid Qutb. "Our task is to guide people to serve God, not to rule or judge them," says the group's mission statement.

The metamorphosis of the Jama'a, which in the 1980s and 1990s was the largest and most lethal terrorist organization in Egypt, may have begun in the mid-1990s but it became known in 1997, when the organization launched its "Initiative of Cessation of Violence" and its continuing process of ideological revision, which amounted to the construction of a systematic and detailed legal case against the doctrines of takfir and violent jihadism.

The Initiative of Cessation of Violence was

launched on July 5, 1997, when an imprisoned member of the leadership of al-Jama'a al-Islamiyya read a statement while in court on behalf of the organization, calling for the cessation of all violent acts in Egypt and abroad and for all incitement to violence to come to an end. After overcoming internal difficulties, by March 1999 the decision to approve the initiative was signed by all the members of the Jama'a's Consultative Council (*majlis al-shura*). The organization's spiritual leader, Shaykh Umar Abd al-Rahman, who is formally still its leader, supported the initiative from his jail cell in the United States and may have even been its initiator. The Jama'a's de facto leader, Karam Zuhdi, is the head of its Consultative Council and also Abd al-Rahman's son-in-law.

The November 1997 terror attack in Luxor, which killed 58 tourists and for which Rifa'i Taha, head of al-Jama'a's military wing, claimed responsibility, fueled doubts about the sincerity of the initiative. Evidence found by the authorities on the scene, however, indicated that the perpetrators had been cut off from the leadership in prison and were thus unaware of its decision to stop all violence. The initiative's credibility was also saved to some extent by the Jama'a leadership's opposition to the founding statement of the World Islamic Front for Jihad Against Jews and Crusaders (set up by Osama bin Laden and Ayman al-Zawahiri in March 1998). In addition, its insistence that Rifa'i Taha, who initially joined the Front, should leave it—which he did—also helped the Jama'a's image. The regime's continued legal and security measures against Jama'a members, such as the execution of members condemned to death and the killing of others in police raids, did not weaken the Jama'a leadership's resolve to maintain the initiative nor its ability to market it to its membership.

For about four years, the initiative was given little attention, and the Egyptian government did not adopt an official position on it. This began to change after September 11, when in October 2001, the government allowed al-Jama'a's imprisoned leaders to begin lecturing in various prisons in order to promote their initiative. In June 2002, the government launched an intensive media campaign allowing the Jama'a leaders to explain their views, as well as expressing its own endorsement of the initiative as a sincere and serious one. In September and October 2003, about 900 Jama'a members, including leading members, were released from prison. Following the release of 900 additional members during April 2006, about 2,000 remained in prison.

The government's decision to publicly and dramatically embrace the initiative five years after it had been launched triggered several theories. One of them connected the timing of the move with the pressure campaign the government was conducting at the time against the Muslim Brotherhood, suggesting that the regime was seeking to make the Jama'a compete with the MB and thus weaken the latter's predominance. The most likely explanation, however, seems to be that at that time, the U.S. administration had adopted a new concept, according to which al-Jama'a was part of al-Qa'ida's network. That could again put Egypt on the spot as a focus of terror. Giving Jama'a leaders the opportunity to demonstrate publicly the depth of their ideological transformation was the best way to refute that view.

It was also in 2002 that the organization was permitted to publish the first four in its series of revisionist books, entitled *The Correction of Conceptions (Tashih al-Mafahim)*; two others came out in 2003 and 2004. The first four books were: *The Initiative of Cessation of Violence: A Realistic Vision* and a *Shar'i View (Mubadarat Waqf al-Unf: Ru'iyah Waqi'iyya wa-Nazra Shar'iya)*, *The Prohibition of Excessiveness in Religion and of the Attribution of Apostasy to Muslims (Hurmat al-Ghulu fi al-Din wa-Takfir al-Muslimin)*, *Illuminating the Mistakes Occurring in the Jihad (Taslit al-Adwaa ala ma Waqa'a fi al-Jihad min Akhtaa)*, and *Advice and Clarification to Correct the Concepts of Those who Take Responsibility for Society (al-Nush wal-Tabyin fi Tashih Mafahim al-Muhtasibin)*. The fifth book, *The Strategy of al-Qa'ida—Mistakes and Dangers (Istratijiyyat al-Qa'ida—Akhtaa wa-Akhtar)*, was published in August 2003, to be followed in June 2004 by *Islam and the Challenges of the 21st Century (al-Islam wa-Tahaddiyyat al-Qarn al-Wahid wal-Ish-rin)*. Each book was written by one or several members of the leadership group and approved by the others. The group includes Karam Zuhdi, Najih Ibrahim, Usama Hafiz, Ali al-Sharif, Hamdi Abd al-Rahman, Asim Abd al-Majid, Isam al-Din Dirbala, and Fuad al-Dawalibi.

The last book, *Islam and the Refinement of Wars (al-Islam wa-Tahdhib al-Hurub)*, came out in August 2006. It refutes, among other things, al-Qa'ida's central argument that Saudi Arabia contravened Islamic law when it relied on military help from non-Muslims (the United States and other non-Muslim members of its coalition) against Saddam Hussein's forces after the invasion of Kuwait in 1990 and allowed the presence of those non-Muslim forces on the soil of the Arabian Peninsula in order to defend against Iraqi attack on Saudi Arabia itself. The book maintains that al-Qa'ida's strategy has contributed to the unification of the entire world against what is perceived as the "Islamic danger" and has led to the destruction of Afghanistan. It further argues that Islam today is in a situation that requires a

"defensive jihad" *(jihad al-daf)*—in defense against invasions by foreign forces—and not "offensive jihad" *(jihad al-talab)*, seeking to expand the lands of Islam, which unifies its enemies against it. It refutes the legal foundations of the February 1998 fatwa issued by the World Islamic Front for Jihad Against Jews and Crusaders, which authorized the killing of every American, including civilians, anytime and anywhere.

The book also rejects the takfiri position that Muslim society at large is in a state of apostasy because it fails to observe the Shari'a, arguing that many or most Muslims do observe the Shar'ia's instructions. The book also criticizes the bombings and suicide attacks that were carried out in Muslim countries, refuting the jihadists' argument that the Shari'a allows the killing of Muslims if they stand in the way or are used by the infidels as protective shields *(tatarrus)*. It further states that hijacking an aircraft and holding its passengers hostage is a violation of the Shari'a because it amounts to punishing the innocent, and that destruction of infrastructure and government facilities by Islamist groups leads to public resentment and animosity toward Islam. According to Islam's laws of war, the book argues, wars should not be fought for revenge and should not seek to annihilate the enemy; the killing of noncombatant civilians is also forbidden. Each position and judgment is backed by ample evidence from the Koran and the *hadith* (the words and deeds of Muhammad), reflecting deep knowledge of *fiqh* in the four legal schools *(madhahib)*.

Yet what is the actual significance of al-Jama'a and its revisionist project? To what extent does it influence the attitudes of young Islamists, attracted by the appeal of the takfiris and Salafist-jihadists? Al-Jama'a's detractors argue that it is a spent force with no influence whatsoever because it has associated itself so tightly with the state security apparatuses that it appears actually to be handled by them. Yet the taped message of al-Qa'ida's second-in-command, Ayman al-Zawahiri (shown by al-Jazeera on August 12, 2006), in which he announced that "a great faction of the leaders of Egypt's al-Jama'a al-Islamiyya," including Umar Abd al-Rahman and Rifa'i Taha, had joined al-Qa'ida, demonstrates that al-Jama'a's positions still count.

Al-Jama'a al-Islamiyya and Jama'at al-Jihad were formed in the 1970s, mainly by university students who viewed President Anwar Sadat's policies as amounting to apostasy. Influenced by Sayyid Qutb's doctrine, they held that Sadat's regime had to be removed by force, and they condemned the Muslim Brotherhood for its strategy of coexistence with what they considered to be an apostate government. The two organizations were united between 1980 and 1983, perhaps the most important years in their history. Al-Zawahiri, the former leader in al-Jihad's organization, later sought to have al-Jama'a join the World Islamic Front for Jihad Against Jews and Crusaders when it was formed, but al-Jama'a declined.

Najih Ibrahim, one of its leaders, firmly denied al-Zawahiri's August 12, 2006, statement and managed to prove that the personalities mentioned above, as well as others, had not joined al-Qa'ida. According to him, al-Zawahiri made that statement for two reasons: first, because he seeks to have followers in Egypt, which he does not, and Egyptians might be tempted to join him if they believed that al-Jama'a leaders have; and second, because al-Jama'a's antiviolence initiative led many mujahidin to recant, and al-Zawahiri seeks to undermine that initiative.

Still another explanation provided for al-Zawahiri's move was that negotiations, which had been under way for some time, between the authorities and imprisoned al-Jihad leaders over a new cessation of violence initiative to be announced by al-Jihad, were nearing a critical stage, and al-Zawahiri had attempted to subvert them and block that initiative. It was reported that during the negotiations between the state and al-Jihad—conducted on behalf of the latter by Muhammad al-Zawahiri (Ayman's younger brother) and Mustafa Hamza (responsible for the June 1995 attempted assassination of President Mubarak) among others—the point had indeed been reached where all the incarcerated members of the organization accepted the principle of cessation of violence as it was formulated by al-Jama'a al-Islamiyya.

A final agreement was delayed, however. This was because al-Jihad's leader, Abud al-Zumur, had demanded that as part of the agreement, once out of prison, the group's members would be free to enter political life and form political parties, yet the government rejected this request. Al-Zumur's insistence on that demand has reportedly prevented the completion of the negotiations and the launching of al-Jihad's own antiviolence initiative. Whatever the final terms of that agreement, by late 2006 Jam'at al-Jihad had for all practical purposes been transformed, as was the case with al-Jama'a al-Islamiyyah.

BIBLIOGRAPHY

Abd al-Mun'im Abu al-Futuh. Interviewed at *Al-Araby.com* 996, February 12, 2006, http://al-araby.com/docs/article11667.html.
Adib, Munir. Interview with Muslim Brotherhood Deputy General Guide Muhammad Habib. *Ikhwan Online.com*, March 22, 2006, www.ikhwanonline.com.

"Akif: La Farq bayna al-Madaniyin al-Sahayina wal-Askariyin" (Akif: There Is No Difference Between the Zionist Civilians and the Soldiers). *Ikhwan Online.com,* February 9, 2005, www.ikhwanonline.com/Article.asp?ArtID=10560&SecID=0.

Akif, Muhammad Mahdi. "Al-Adu al-Sahyuni Muhtal wa-La Nuqbilu Wujudihi" (The Zionist Enemy Is an Occupier and We Will Not Recognize Its Existence). *Ikhwan Online.com,* December 29, 2005, www.ikhwanonline.com/Article.asp?ArtID=17003&SecID=0.

———. Communiqué. *Ikhwan Online.com,* July 26, 2006, www.ikhwanonline.com.

———. "The Initiative of the General Guide Concerning the General Principles of Reform in Egypt." *Ikhwan Online.com*, March 3, 2004, www.ikhwanonline.com.

———. Missive. *Ikhwan Online.com,* August 3, 2006, www.ikhwanonline.com.

———. Missive. *Ikhwan Online.com,* April 13, 2006, www.ikhwanonline.com.

———. Missive. *Ikhwan Online.com,* February 16, 2006, www.ikhwanonline.com.

———. Missive. *Ikhwan Online.com,* May 5, 2005, www.ikhwanonline.com.

"Akif: al-Wilayat al-Muttahida La Turidu al-Khair lil-Alam al-Islami" (Akif: The U.S. Does Not Want What Is Best for the Muslim World). *Ikhwan Online.com,* February 12, 2006, www.ikhwanonline.com/Article.asp?ArtID=17930&SecID=0.

"Akif Yaqudu Tayar al-Rafidhin wal-Shatir Yafdalu Aqd Safqa, wal-Nizam Yusa'idu Dughutihi" (Akif Leads Those Who Reject, Al-Shatir Prefers Signing a Deal, and the Regime Increases Its Pressures). *Al-Mesryoon.com,* April 5, 2006, www.almesryoon.com/ShowDetails.asp?NewID=15190.

"Analysts: Escalation Against MB Is a Warning Message." *Ikhwan Web.com,* March 8, 2006, www.ikhwanweb.com/Article.asp?ID=4660&SectionID=67.

Al-Aryan, Isam. *Egypt Window.net,* April 19, 2006, www.egyptwindow.net.

———. "Hadith hawla al-Ikhwan al-Muslimin" (Conversation About the Muslim Brothers). *Ikhwan Online.com,* April 10, 2005, www.ikhwanonline.com/Article.asp?ArtID=11555&SecID=0.

———. *Ikhwan Online.com,* February 15, 2006, www.ikhwanonline.com.

———. "Tada'iyyat fawz Hamas" (The Consequences of Hamas' Victory). *Ikhwan Online.com,* February 2, 2006, www.ikhwanonline.com/Article.asp?ArtID=17696&SecID=390.

"Al-Ikhwan al-Muslimun wa-Amirika." (The Muslim Brothers and America). *Ikhwan Online.com,* December 21, 2005, www.ikhwanonline.com/Article.asp?ArtID=16846&SecID=0.

"Al-Ikhwan al-Muslimun wa-awdat al-sahwa al-Islamiyya" (The Muslim Brothers and the Islamic Awakening). *Ikhwan Online.com,* July 10, 2005, www.ikhwanonline.com/Article.asp?ArtID=13052&SecID=210.

"Al-Jihad wal-istishhad huma tariq al-izza wal-nasr" (Holy War and Death for the Sake of Allah Pave the Way Toward Glory and Victory). *Ikhwan Online.com,* April 15, 2004, www.ikhwanonline.com/Article.asp?ArtID=6076&SecID=213.

Al-Qa'ud, Ahmad. "Isam al-Aryan yu'akkidu taraju al-Ikhwan an mutalabat al-Aqqbat bi-daf al-jaziyya" (Isam al-Aryan Asserts the Muslim Brothers' Change of Heart Regarding the Demand That the Copts Pay Poll Tax). *Al-Quds,* December 22, 2005, www.alquds.co.uk.

Al-Wasat Party Web site. www.alwasatparty.com/modules.php?name=News&file=article&sid=1622.

Al-Zayyat, Muntasir. *Al-Jama'at al-Islamiyya ru'iyah min al-dakhil* (The Islamic Groups: An Insider's View). Cairo: Dar Misr al-Mahrusha, 2005.

"Barnamij hizb al-Wasat al-jadid, al-mihwar al-siyyasi" (The al-Wasat Party's Platform—the Political Realm). www.islamonline.net/Arabic/doc/2004/05/article02a.shtml.

"Bayan min al-Ikhwan al-Muslimin hawla tafjirat Taba wa-Sinaa" (Proclamation from the Muslim Brothers Regarding the Bombings in Taba and Sinai). *Ikhwan Online.com*, October 9, 2004, www.ikhwanonline.com/Article.asp?ArtID=8890&SecID=0.

Carnegie Endowment. *Arab Reform Bulletin* 3:10 (December 2005). www.carnegieendowment.org/arb/?fa=show&article=21055&zoom_highlight=wasat+party.

"Dimuqratiyat al-iqsa masiruha al-fanaa" (The Democracy of Alienation Will Vanish). *Ikhwan Online.com,* December

22, 2005, www.ikhwanonline.com/Article
.asp?ArtID=16871&SecID=0.

Egyptian Islamic Group Web site. www.egyptian-
islamicgroup.com/about/1.shtml.

Elchoubaki, Amr. "The New Face of Terror."
Al-Ahram Weekly 794 (May 11–17, 2006). http://
weekly.ahram.org.eg/2006/794/op33.htm.

Habib, Muhammad. "Al-intikhabat al-riasiyya
laysat ala jadwal a'amal al-Ikhwan" (The
Presidential Elections Are Not on the
Muslim Brothers' Agenda). *Ikhwan Online.
com*, February 28, 2006, www.ikhwanon-
line.com/Article.asp?ArtID=18323&SecID=
211.

———. "Madha lau wasala al-Ikhwan ila al-
hukm?" (What Will Happen If the Muslim
Brothers Take Charge of the Government?).
Ikhwan Online.com, February 6, 2006,
www.ikhwanonline.com/Article.asp?ArtID=
17810&SecID=0.

———. "What Will Happen If We Take Charge of
the Government?" *Ikhwan Online.com*, February 8, 2006, http://www.muslimbrotherhood
.co.uk/Home.asp?ID=3846&Lang=E&P
ress=Show&System=PressR&zPage=
Systems.

Habib, Rafiq. "Al-Ikhwan wal-tawrith" (The
Muslim Brothers and the Inheritance).
Ikhwan Online.com, April 11, 2006, www
.ikhwanonline.com/Article.asp?ArtID=19450
&SecID=0.

———. "Hamas wal-Ikhwan wa-istihqaqat al-
fawz" (Hamas, the Muslim Brothers and the
Rights That Follow Victory). *Ikhwan Online.
com*, January 28, 2006, www.ikhwanonline
.com/Article.asp?ArtID=17584&SecID=0.

———. "Hamas wal-i'tiraf bil-kiyan al-sahyuni"
(Hamas and the Recognition in the Zionist
Entity). *Ikhwan Online.com*, February
14, 2006, www.ikhwanonline.com/Article
.asp?ArtID=17988&SecID=390.

Hasan, Sayyid. "Hal ba'a al-Ikhwan al-mu'arada?"
(Did the Muslim Brothers Sell Out the
Opposition?) *Al-Araby.com*, 970, July 31, 2005,
www.al-araby.com/docs/article9886.htm.

"Hizb siyyasi jadid bi-qiyyadat abud al-
zumur." *Al-Araby.com*, www.al-araby.com/
articles/1022/060820–1022-fct02.htm.

"Huquq al-insan fi asr al-tughyan" (Human
Rights in the Age of Tyranny). *Ikhwan Online.
com*, March 16, 2006, www.ikhwanonline
.com/Article.asp?ArtID=18771&SecID=0.

Islamic Group Egypt. www.egyig.com.

Isma'il, Faraj. Al-Wifaq.net, February 22, 2006,
www.al-wifaq.net.

"Limadha al-Wasat?" (Why al-Wasat?). www
.alwasatparty.com/modules.php?name=
Content&pa=showpage&pid=2.

"Limadha tadhtahidu al-hukuma nuwwab al-Ikhwan?" (Why Does the Government Suppress
Muslim Brotherhood MPs?). *Ikhwan Online.
com*, March 19, 2006, http://www.ikhwanonline
.com/Article.asp?ArtID=18831&SecID=211.

"Mawqif Jama'at al-Ikhwan al-Muslimin min
al-muqawama" (The Muslim Brotherhood's
Stance on the Resistance). *Ikhwan Online.
com*, July 29, 2006, http://news.ikhwanonline
.com/Article.asp?ArtID=22285&SecID=212.

"Misr: Al-Ikhwan al-Muslimun la yumani'un fi
hiyazat Iran silahan nawawiyyan" (Egypt:
The Muslim Brothers Do Not Oppose Iran's
Right to Obtain a Nuclear Weapon). *Al-Sharq
al-Awsat*, April 18, 2006, http://www.aawsat
.com/details.asp?section=4&issueno=10002
&article=358667&feature=.

Muhammad, Abd al-Mu'izz. "Ya marhab bil-
tawari fi baladina" (The Emergency Law Is
Welcomed in Our Country). *Ikhwan Online.
com*, April 17, 2006, www.ikhwanonline.net/
Article.asp?ArtID=19667&SecID=363.

"Nass hiwar al-murshid al-am lil-rad ala al-
iftira'at al-i'lamiyya" (Text of the General
Guide's Argument in Response to the Media
Slanders). *Ikhwan Online.com*, April 16, 2006,
www.ikhwanonline.com/Article.asp?ArtID
=19619&SecID=104.

Nazif, Ahmad. Interview in *Al-Masri al-Yawm*
717, May 31, 2006, www.almasry-alyoum
.com/article2.aspx?ArticleID=18337&IssueI
D=286.

"Nubdha ta'rikhiyya" (A Piece of History).
Al-Wasat Party Web Site, www.alwasatparty
.com/modules.php?name=Content&pa=sho
wpage&pid=6.

"Qiyyadi Ikhwani: Al-dawla al-madaniyya asas
al-muwatana" (A Muslim Brotherhood
Leader: The Civil State Is the Foundation
of Common Citizenship). Islam Online.net,
July 9, 2004, www.islamonline.net/arabic/
news/2004-07/10/article02.shtml.

Salah, Muhammad. "Al-Tawhid wal-Jihad
fi Sinaa" (Al-Tawhid wal-Jihad in Sinai).
Al-Hayat (May 7, 2006).

———. "Al-Mallah udhuw al-Tawhid wal-Jihad"

(Al-Mallah Is the Enemy of al-Tawhid wal-Jihad). *Al-Hayat* (April 28, 2006).

———. "Al-Qahira tu'lin kashf jama'a takfiriyya" (Cairo Announces It Discovered a Heretic Group). *Al-Hayat* (April 20, 2006).

"Statement to the Press." *Al-Sharq al-Awsat* (February 19, 2006).

"Tafasil al-hiwar al-sirri bayna al-Jihad wal-dakhiliyya" (Details of the Secret Dialog Between al-Jihad and the Ministry of Interior). *Al-Araby.com*, www.al-araby.com/articles/944/050130–944-fct05.htm.

"Wahdat al-umma hiya al-sakhra allati tatahattam alayha al-mu'amarat wal-Fitan" (The Unity of the Nation Is the Rock upon Which the Conspiracies and Civil Wars Shall Crash). *Ikhwan Online.com*, March 2, 2006, www.ikhwanonline.com/Article.asp?ArtID=18378&SecID=213.

Iran

Abbas William (Bill) Samii

Modern Iran epitomizes the Islamist state. Its current constitution, drafted by a predominantly clerical body in 1979 and amended in 1989, enunciates the role of religion—specifically the Shi'a branch of Islam—in the country's affairs. The constitution, according to the first sentence of its preamble, "advances the cultural, social, political, and economic institutions of Iranian society based on Islamic principles and norms," and according to the constitution's first article, the form of government is an "Islamic Republic."

The most powerful figure in the ruling apparatus is a cleric, referred to as the *rahbar* (supreme leader), who effectively has the right to veto measures called for by other state institutions. This figure leads the Islamic community, according to the constitution, in place of the Hidden Imam, who went into occultation in 874 CE. A wholly clerical body called the Assembly of Experts supervises the supreme leader's performance and is empowered to replace him. Moreover, the conformity of all legislation with Islamic law must be approved by the six clerical members of an unelected body called the Guardians Council. Candidates for national-level elected office—the presidency, legislature, and Assembly of Experts—are vetted by the Guardians Council. Constitutionally, the second most powerful individual in the country is the president, and although he does not have to be a cleric, he must be a *rejal-i mazhabi-siyasi* (religious-political individual).

Regardless of these constitutional factors, scholars such as Ali Banuazizi and Ray Takeyh have argued that Islamism is no longer an important aspect of Iranian politics. Indeed, the election of a layman—Mahmud Ahmadinejad—as president in June 2005, and the falling number of clerics elected in parliamentary races, supports this contention. Journalists have noted dwindling mosque attendance, and visitors to Iran describe growing skepticism about the role of religious figures in political, economic, and commercial affairs. The increasing popularity of Sufism and mysticism are other signs of disenchantment with state religion, and the regime's crackdown on such groups reflects its recognition of their significance.

In light of the theocratic nature of the state and the apparent public dissatisfaction with official Islam, it is counterintuitive to think that there is an Islamist trend in which some Iranians call for even greater moral conservatism and the implementation of religious values. Yet such a trend exists, and this chapter will focus on the political aspects of Islamism in Iran by following the activities of three distinct yet connected groups. These groups have also had a great deal of influence on the regime, because a number of their leaders have held high office in the Islamic Republic.

Politically, Islamism in Iran can be traced to the early 1940s and the creation of the Fadaiyan-i Islam. Although members of this group managed to assassinate intellectual and political figures, they did not achieve much of immediate political significance. The Fadaiyan leader was executed in 1956, and the group's activities essentially came to an end. Efforts to revive it after 1979 enjoyed mild success, however, and in 2006 its leader was considered as a legislative candidate.

In the early 1960s, surviving members and sympathizers of the Fadaiyan were involved with the creation of the Hayat-i Motalefeh-i Islami. This political organization worked closely with Ayatollah Ruhollah Khomeini before he was exiled in 1964, continued low-level activism until the mid-1970s, and played an important role in organizing the postrevolutionary state. Although it has ceded some of its political prominence to a younger generation of conservatives, the organization still exists, having declared itself to be a political party in 2003–2004.

Another noteworthy example of the Islamist trend in Iranian politics is the Hojjatieh Society (formally known as the Anjoman-i Khayrieyeh-yi Hojjatieh Mahdavieh), established in the early 1950s and banned in 1983. Since at least the late 1990s, there have been accusations that members of the Hojjatieh Society were behind acts of political violence, and since 2002 there have been claims of renewed activism by the society.

The Start of Shi'a Islamism— Fadaiyan-i Islam

In May 1945 a 22-year-old religious student known as Navab Safavi (a name adopted by Seyyed Mujtaba Mirlohi, who claimed descent from the Safavid dynasty) bought a gun and made an unsuccessful attempt on the life of Iranian intellectual Ahmad Kasravi, whom he had previously debated. Kasravi's book on the fundamentals of Islam and Shi'ism—*Shariat-i Ahmadi*—was highly regarded, but his criticism of the Shi'a clergy and efforts to reform and rationalize Islam were unpopular with the religious community. Ayatollah Ruhollah Khomeini criticized the failure to act against Kasravi in two books, published in 1942 and 1944, referring to Kasravi as "addlebrained." Nevertheless, there is no known connection between Safavi and Khomeini, and it seems that Safavi spent little time as a theologian in Qom.

Safavi was arrested after the unsuccessful assassination attempt and released two months later when a merchant posted his bond. Shortly afterward, Safavi announced the creation of the Fadaiyan-i Islam, an event viewed as the start of the Shi'a Islamist movement in Iran, according to scholars Ahmad Ashraf and Ali Banuazizi. Less than a year later, in March 1946, two of Safavi's followers managed to kill Kasravi and his secretary.

This led to much greater publicity about the Fadaiyan, and the organization entered an alliance for the creation of an Islamic government with the influential Iranian cleric Ayatollah Seyyed Abol Qasem Kashani. Kashani had been involved with nationalist politics since he backed anti-British activities in Iraq in about 1919–20, and when he was sentenced to death for this, he fled to Iran. Yann Richard explains that the British arrested Kashani in 1943 because of his connection with the Nazi-created Iranian Nationalist Movement. Kashani was arrested again in 1946 and was exiled in 1949 after a gunman carrying a press card from the Fadaiyan-i Islam magazine *Parcham-i Islam* tried to kill the shah.

The oil nationalization issue, which commenced in the late 1940s, led to deterioration in the relationship of Kashani and other nationalists with the Fadaiyan-i Islam. The group seemed to have a greater interest in such issues as the closure of liquor stores and a dress code for women than it did in oil, and Prime Minister Muhammad Mussadiq's secular perspective clashed with the religious views of the Fadaiyan. Kashani spoke dismissively of the Fadaiyan's sentiments, and the Fadaiyan criticized Kashani for an insufficient emphasis on religion in his political activities.

In November 1949 Fadaiyan member Seyyed Husayn Imami assassinated Court Minister Abdul Husayn Hazhir, and in March 1951 Fadaiyan member Khalil Tahmasebi assassinated Prime Minister Hajj Ali Razmara. Ayatollah Kashani demanded Tahmasebi's release from prison, as did Safavi, but their reasons for doing so differed. Kashani and other nationalists saw Razmara as a British agent, while Safavi declared the monarchy to be illegitimate and made references to religious law and Islamic retribution. Tahmasebi himself became something of a hero, and he later declared, in February 1952, "If I have rendered a humble service, it was for the Almighty in order to deliver the deprived Moslem people of Iran from foreign serfdom. My only desire is to follow the doctrines of the Koran."

Safavi's sentiments appeared previously in *Barnameh-yi Inqilabi-yi Fadaiyan-i Islam,* the 1950 work in which he described the social system he had in mind. The most notable, and perhaps unexpected, aspect of his plan was that Iran would not be a theocracy. Safavi accepted a monarchy in which the benevolent king would be a father to the people and an exemplar of faith and virtue. The monarch must appoint pious Muslims to serve as trustees of the religious endowments, he must build big mosques, and the green flag of Islam must appear alongside that of Iran at all official venues. The Interior Ministry would ban European-style hats and ties, and there would be a much greater emphasis on Islam in the educational system.

Safavi described his economic plans—which were critical of capitalism and communism—in 1951 in the weekly *Manshur-i Baradari.* He promoted a system in which charity, selflessness, and religious taxes would serve as economic levelers. Most people would be shopkeepers or artisans, and a few would be civil servants. The government would take care of unemployment. Curiously, Safavi did not address landownership and agricultural matters.

The Fadaiyan-Kashani relationship continued to deteriorate, and Safavi said in May 1951, "I invite Mussadiq, other members of the National Front, and Ayatollah Kashani to an ethical trial," as cited by Sohrab Behdad. Prime Minister Mussadiq had Safavi arrested that June, and he was held until February 1953. It is not a complete surprise, therefore, that the Fadaiyan-i Islam welcomed the August 1953 coup d'état, seeing it as a measure that held back communism and the Soviet Union. Safavi declared that Islam saved Iran, and he emphasized that the monarch, prime minister, and cabinet members must believe in and promote Shi'a Islam. Safavi called for the elimination of intoxicants, provocative music, and immodest female behavior. He also came to have a close relationship with the imperial court and with Prime Minister Fazlallah Zahedi's government, which appreciated the legitimacy offered by the religious community's support.

Within two years, however, Navab Safavi came to realize that the government was more intent on relations with the West than on pursuing an Islamist agenda. In November 1955 Fadaiyan-i Islam member Muzaffar Zolqadr tried to assassinate Prime Minister Husayn Ala. The attempt failed, but the government promptly arrested Safavi and other associates of the Fadaiyan-i Islam, as well as Ayatollah Kashani. Kashani was released following the intervention of the country's leading clerics. Such assistance was not extended to the Fadaiyan, however, and Safavi, Zolqadr, Tahmasebi, and Seyyed Muhammad Vahedi were executed in January 1956.

After the 1978–79 Islamic revolution, several people tried to revive the Fadaiyan-i Islam. One such attempt was made by Abdallah Karbaschian and by Shaykh Sadeq Khalkhali, a notoriously bloodthirsty prosecutor in the revolutionary courts. Little came of their efforts, and Khalkhali died in November 2003. Shaykh Muhammad Mehdi Abd-i Khodai, who as a 14-year-old in 1952 had tried to assassinate Mussadiq associate Husayn Fatemi, enjoyed greater success in reviving the Fadaiyan-i Islam. By 2003, though the organization was not a significant political actor, Abd-i Khodai had not lost his spirit, saying, as quoted by the Iranian Labor News Agency (ILNA), "I am extremely against America and in case America attacks Iran, I may carry out [a] martyrdom operation." He was even mentioned as a possible candidate for parliament in May 2006 by the publication *Iran*.

From Opposition to Mainstream—Heyat-i Motalefeh-yi Islami

The executions of Safavi and other Fadaiyan leaders did not bring the organization's activities to a complete standstill. Surviving members in Tehran formed three separate groups made up mostly of bazaar merchants—one associated with the Shaykh Ali Mosque, another with the Aminoldowleh Mosque and led by Habibollah Asgaroladi, and a third with the Isfahaniha Mosque, as Baqer Moin explains in his book *Khomeini: Life of the Ayatollah*. They met with Ayatollah Khomeini in Qom in 1962 and accepted his view that in the absence of Muhammad, the clergy must lead in the promotion of virtue and prohibition of vice. Khomeini recognized and accepted that there would be a clash between the clergy and the state, and he also recognized the effect this would have on apolitical clerics. Nevertheless, the bazaar merchants' financial support allowed Khomeini to wield significant influence among the clergy by providing money to theological institutions.

Among the people Khomeini selected for leadership positions in the three groups were Morteza Mottahari, Muhammad Husayn Beheshti, and Muhammad Javad Bahonar, all of whom would go on to have leadership positions in the Islamic Republic. These groups expanded Khomeini's reach by linking up with bazaar members in Isfahan, Mashhad, and Tabriz, and they distributed copies of Khomeini's statements. In 1963, about one year after Ayatollah Khomeini began his open opposition to the shah's White Revolution, the dissident cleric advised these three groups to merge and form one organization. The groups merged into the Islamic Coalition Association (Heyat-i Motalefeh-yi Islami), an entity that now exists as a party, the Hezb-i Motalefeh-yi Islami.

When Khomeini was arrested on June 5, 1963, the Islamic Coalition Association immediately informed its supporters in the Tehran bazaar. They stormed a police station and government buildings, and thousands of people demonstrated across the city. Protests spread to other cities and continued for another day, while soldiers responded with lethal force. Khomeini was released, and in October 1964 he gave a speech in which he criticized legislation that would place American military personnel outside the jurisdiction of Iranian courts. He was arrested in November 1964, driven to the airport, and exiled to Turkey. In October 1965 he was sent to Iraq, where he would remain until shortly before his February 1979 return to Iran.

Moin provides a history of the Islamic Coalition Association and its activities. For the most part, it was not very politically active for the next 10 years. Shortly after Khomeini's exile, however, an armed wing consisting of former Fadaiyan-i Islam members was created. At the top of its list of assassination targets was Prime Minister Hasan Ali Mansur, who was shot by association member Muhammad Bokharai in January 1965. An edict from Ayatollah Hadi Milani of Mashhad authorized the killing. Bokharai was captured, and his confessions led to the arrest of numerous Islamic Coalition Association members. Four were executed, and 12 others—including Beheshti, Mottahari, and Ali Akbar Hashemi-Rafsanjani—were imprisoned.

The Islamic Coalition Association took several steps during this time to remain active. It created private Islamic schools for boys and girls. The schools used the state curricula but emphasized religion, while the government viewed them as a harmless way of channeling religious activity. The schools were very effective in countering regime propaganda. Moreover, clerics connected with the association rewrote textbooks for the Education Ministry as a means of religious indoctrination.

The concept of armed conflict and guerrilla warfare against the regime was gaining ground by the mid-1970s. Around this time there were discussions on how to unite clerical and lay Muslim activists. Mottahari was put in charge, and activists from the Islamic Coalition Association were among his lieutenants. The clerics close to the Islamic Coalition Association and the association itself subsequently began preparations for Khomeini's return to Iran—as Moin notes: "The Coalition was everywhere."

After Khomeini's February 1979 return to Iran, the Islamic Coalition Association organized the bazaar, Islamic guerrilla groups who had merged into the Mujahidin of the Islamic Revolution Organization, and the politically active clerics, thereby forming the Islamic Republican Party. The organization also redesignated itself as the Islamic Coalition Society (Jamiyat-i Motalefeh-yi Islami).

Individuals connected with the Islamic Coalition Society enjoyed great political success in the ensuing years. Muhammad Ali Rajai, who had been active in the Islamic Coalition Association and then joined the Islamic Republican Party, became prime minister in 1980. When he became president in 1981, another member of the association, Muhammad Javad Bahonar, succeeded him as prime minister. Both Rajai and Bahonar lost their lives in an August 1981 bombing of the Islamic Republican Party headquarters. Other members of this group have enjoyed prominence—Morteza Nabavi (parliamentarian, Expediency Council member, and editor of *Resalat*), Muhammad Reza Bahonar (parliamentarian), Hasan Ghafurifard (energy minister, parliamentarian, and by 2006 head of the Coordination Council of Revolutionary Forces electoral headquarters). Ali Larijani headed the Islamic Republic of Iran Broadcasting for many years, and in August 2005 he was selected as the secretary of the Supreme National Security Council and the country's lead nuclear negotiator. Mohsen Rafiqdust headed the short-lived Islamic Revolution Guards Ministry, and he went on to head the powerful and wealthy Oppressed and Disabled Foundation.

The Islamic Coalition Society was the leading conservative nonclerical political organization in Iran until 2000–2001. It was at that point that some of the groups linked with the Islamic Coalition Society distanced themselves from it because, according to conservative commentator Taha Hashemi, cited in *Doran-i Imruz* in December 2000, "Over the last two or three years, the Coalition has not been able to change its way of thinking or cooperate with modernist currents." Hashemi added, "Unfortunately, their perspective on various issues is still the same as it was 40 years ago." There were also references by Hashemi in February 2001 to the emergence of a conservative Third Current as a reaction to "some individuals [who] do not tolerate criticism at all and consider their performance to be exactly right and perfectly accurate. They consider themselves absolutely righteous, and their rivals in the enemy's front."

Regardless of the divisions within the Islamic Coalition Party, it continued to operate and to represent the older generation of conservatives. It was part of the Coordination Council of Islamic Revolution Forces that backed the unsuccessful Ali Larijani in the 2005 presidential contest.

Tolerated, Then Banned— Anjoman-i Hojjatieh

The Fadaiyan-i Islam officially continues to function but has essentially disappeared, and the Islamic Coalition Association, although it has undergone many changes in its more than 40 years, continues to exist as a functioning political party. A third Islamist entity that was created in the 1950s was banned in the 1980s, but rumors about its existence and continuing activism persist.

Mahmud Sadri explains that a Mashhad-based cleric, Shaykh Mahmud Halabi, founded the Hojjatieh Society in 1953 to counter the activities of Baha'i missionaries. The Baha'is argued that the Mahdi, the 12th Imam who went into occultation more than a thousand years ago and whose reemergence Shi'a Muslims are awaiting, had already returned and had been superseded by Baha'i leader Mirza Husayn Ali Nuri (1817–92)—known as Bahaullah. Hojjatieh members believe that true Islamic government must await the return of the Mahdi. Halabi recruited a group of volunteers who could debate the Baha'is.

Shah Muhammad Reza Pahlavi allowed the society to pursue its anti-Baha'i activities in exchange for its support. Society member Muhammad Taqi Falsafi's anti-Baha'i sermons were broadcast by state radio, for example, and Tehran's military governor, Teimour Bakhtiar, took a pickax to the Baha'i temple in Tehran in May 1955. Around that time, Halabi persuaded Marja-yi Taqlid Ayatollah Muhammad Husayn Tabatabai Borujerdi to issue a fatwa (religious edict) banning transactions with Baha'is. Falsafi would have later run-ins with the Pahlavi regime, but the society expanded its reach and its membership in the 1960s and 1970s.

The Hojjatieh Society also opposed

Khomeini's theory of Islamic government and *vilayat-e faqih* (rule of the supreme jurisconsult). It favored collective leadership of the religious community and opposed religious involvement in political affairs. Halabi, however, feared a Communist takeover after the 1978–79 Islamic revolution, so he urged his followers to vote in favor of vilayat-e faqih in the December 1979 referendum on the country's form of government. Hojjatieh Society members had strong religious credentials and were viewed as natural choices to fill administrative gaps left by revolutionary purges, as was particularly the case in the educational sector. Some cabinet members allegedly had Hojjatieh links as well.

Prominent clerics of the revolutionary era who were Hojjatieh members or sympathizers included Ahmad Azari Qomi, Ali Akbar Parvaresh, Muhammad Reza Mahdavi Kani, Abolqasem Khazali, and Ali Akbar Nateq Nuri, according to Mehdi Moslem. None of them acknowledged their relationship with the society, however, maintaining more open ties with the Islamic Coalition Association and with the bazaar sector.

Concern arose about the society's secretiveness, as did resentment of its members' success. An increasingly intolerant Khomeini attacked the society and its stances. He said in a July 1983 speech, cited by Moin, "Those who believe we should allow sins to increase until the 12th Imam reappears should modify and reconsider their position. . . . If you believe in your country [then] get rid of this factionalism and join the wave that is carrying the nation forward, otherwise it will break you." Halabi announced dissolution of the Hojjatieh Society on the same day, and he withdrew to Mashhad.

The formal end of the Hojjatieh Society did not signify an end to its role in politics. Ali Akbar Nateq-Nuri, for example, became the speaker of the fifth parliament and went on to serve on the Expediency Council and as an adviser to Supreme Leader Ayatollah Ali Khamene'i. Ali-Akbar Parvaresh served as deputy speaker of parliament and education minister. Ayatollah Ahmad Azari Qomi Bigdeli served as public prosecutor, represented Khomeini during a parliamentary review of the constitution, represented Qom in the legislature, served on the Assembly of Experts, and headed the Resalat Foundation. (The regime eventually placed him under house arrest for questioning both the system of vilayat-e faqih and the qualifications of Supreme Leader Khamene'i; he died in 1999.)

Making a Comeback?

In a political environment in which there is no transparency, conspiracy theories will always flourish. Therefore, there have been allegations of Hojjatieh involvement in several incidents since the late 1990s.

After it was determined that Ministry of Intelligence and Security personnel were involved in the murders of dissident politicians and intellectuals in 1998, some newspapers criticized the slow pace of the investigation and the prosecutions and expressed concern about the actions of state security institutions. Several dailies (for example, *Salam* and *Jahan-i Islam*) claimed that men associated with the Hojjatieh Society were behind the failed attempt in January 1999 to assassinate Tehran Justice Department chief Hojatoleslam Ali Razini. The unsuccessful assassins believed that as long as those responsible to the Islamic Republic are in power, the Hidden Imam will not return. They had, therefore, drawn up a list of names for elimination. Several of the accused reportedly were members of the Islamic Revolution Guards Corps.

Three years later, allegations of Hojjatieh

activism were renewed, but the accounts varied depending on the side of the political spectrum from which they originated. A reformist daily, *Mardom Salari,* referred to a Third Group created by leftists who were driven out of the government after 1988. All the interviewees agreed that the Third Group is not affiliated with the reformist Second of Khordad Front. The reformist Hojatoleslam Rasul Montajabnia said the Hojjatieh Society is part of this Third Group, and he said that it is very active within the government and has access to the public purse. Montajabnia attributed its growth to the development of reactionary thinking.

Kayhan, the newspaper affiliated with the supreme leader's office, said just the opposite in a late 2002 editorial. It claimed that reports of Second of Khordad Front and Hojjatieh Society collaboration show the similarity in their views—both advocate the separation of politics and religion, the society opposes creation of an Islamic government, and the reformists are "trying to separate the Islamic from the republic and then gradually turn the Islamic system into a secular system of government." Society members and reformists enjoy luxury and wealth, according to the editorial, and they both oppose vilayat-e faqih. The editorial went on to claim that both groups accept all sorts of sin and social corruption. "The only difference is that association members say we should not fight vice so that it spreads and the Mahdi will emerge, while certain reformers say that the democratic principle demands that the people be left alone to do as they please, even if it means loose morals and social corruption." Hojjatieh opposition to the formation of an Islamic government because it might delay the return of the Hidden Imam was similar to the intellectual and liberal reformers' opposition to an Islamic government and preference for a democratic republic. The Hojjatieh

Society, mainly because it opposes Marxism, is pro-Western, according to the editorial, as is the Second of Khordad grouping.

In August 2002, furthermore, the minister of intelligence and security, Hojatoleslam Ali Yunesi, announced—as cited in *Toseh* in August 2002—the arrest in Qom of Hojjatieh members who were trying to exacerbate religious disputes. Rudsar and Amlash parliamentary representative Davud Hasanzadegan Rudsari warned that the society had "revived itself" and is "exacerbating Shi'a-Sunni conflict," as cited in *Aftab-i Yazd* in September 2002. These efforts threaten the country, the legislator said, and he called on theological leaders to act against this tendency.

Allegations of Hojjatieh efforts to infiltrate the government resurfaced in January 2003. Government spokesman Abdallah Ramezanzadeh warned that any members of the Hojjatieh Society who infiltrate the government would be dealt with in the same way as other citizens, while a member of the Assembly of Experts, Hojatoleslam Hashem Hashemzadeh Harisi, said that the infiltration of the government by radicals from groups like the Hojjatieh Society undermines the search for national solidarity and threatens the Islamic system, as cited in *Iran Daily* in January 2003.

Some sources linked spring 2004 sectarian conflicts with the Hojjatieh Society. Rasul Montajabnia, writing in *Nasim-i Saba* and *Hambastegi* in May 2004, claimed that members or supporters of the society have stopped their fight against the Baha'i faith and have turned their attention to creating divisions between Shi'a and Sunni Muslims. Another commentator, Husayn Shariatmadari, who is director of *Kayhan* newspaper and the supreme leader's representative at the Kayhan Institute, said, as cited by *Aftab-i Yazd* in May 2004, "The

Hojjatieh Society has always been active as a creeping current." Turning to its renewed activism, he warned, "In these days all the currents that suggest a secular establishment are the supporters of this society."

Ahmadinejad, Millennialism, and the Hojjatieh Society

President Mahmud Ahmadinejad's references to the 12th Imam in a September 2005 speech at the United Nations brought his affinity for millennialist views to the world's attention, and this has led to fears that he or members of his cabinet are connected with the Hojjatieh Society. Ahmadinejad's later observation that he was surrounded by an aura during the speech, and that the spellbound audience in the General Assembly sat unblinking, contributed to concern about his unorthodox views. There are allegations, furthermore, that Ahmadinejad has earmarked millions of dollars in government funds for the Jamkaran Mosque, where the Hidden Imam will reappear. Finally, there has been a burgeoning of Iranian Web sites that focus on the Hidden Imam.

In a speech delivered just weeks after Ahmadinejad's August 2005 inauguration, as reported by the Fars News Agency, former president Hojatoleslam Muhammad Khatami (1997–2005) warned of the emergence of an extremist movement that is raising fears of corruption and of insufficiently Islamic universities. Khatami added that such groups aid foreigners who do not want to see the success of Islamic states.

Reformist commentators quickly picked up on this theme. One, Hashem Hedayati, a member of the left-wing Mujahidin of the Islamic Revolution Organization, cited in *Etemad* in August 2005, said that Khatami issued his warning because extremists are entering the government, and this phenom-

enon represents a strategic shift by the Hojjatieh Society, which previously avoided involvement in political affairs. Another prominent reformist, Hojatoleslam Ali Akbar Mohtashami Pur, a former interior minister and parliamentarian who is a member of the pro-reform Militant Clerics Association (Majma-yi Ruhaniyun-i Mobarez), was cited in *Etemad* in September 2005 as warning of a Hojjatieh revival, saying the society changed tactics after the revolution, and not only did it now seek political involvement but it also had a greater affinity for violence: "Today, unfortunately, this society is speaking through various podiums brandishing a truncheon on a heretic witch-hunt, accusing our youth." A former vice president, Hojatoleslam Muhammad Ali Abtahi, who served as vice president for legal and parliamentary affairs under President Khatami, was cited in the *Financial Times* in November 2005 as noting that many grassroots religious groups backed Ahmadinejad's presidential run, but what stood out was that these groups praised the 12th Imam, rather than speaking in political terms. Ahmadinejad has "more important goals than politics," the former official was quoted as saying, adding, "He speaks with the confidence of someone who has received God's word."

Warnings of the Hojjatieh revival resurfaced in spring 2006. A conservative legislator, Imad Afruq, was cited in *Etemad-i Melli* in February 2006 as saying that pseudoclerics who promote mysticism are distorting Islam and misleading the faithful, and the Hojjatieh Society will find it easy to operate under these conditions. Supreme Court judge Hojatoleslam Muhammad Sadeq Al-i Ishaq was cited in *Etemad* in February 2006 as saying that the Hojjatieh Society still exists, and clerics should take this danger seriously. The Hojjatieh Society hid its true intentions so it could gain places in the government, he was quoted as saying, and Ayatollah Khomeini regretted ever making use of the reactionary clerics.

Contributing to concern about a possible connection between Ahmadinejad and the Hojjatieh Society are allegations about the president's religious mentor, Ayatollah Muhammad Taqi Mesbah Yazdi, the intellectual leader of the hard-line Haqqani School and a proponent of political violence. *Bayan,* a reformist newspaper, criticized the cleric on a number of points. For example, it cited him as saying in a January 2000 presermon lecture, "They imagine the spirit of Navab Safavi has become obsolete in the country, while this spirit exists in our young Basij." (Basij is a low-level paramilitary group used by the regime to enforce its control, acting like an Islamist militia.) Neither Ayatollah Khomeini nor other senior clerics supported Safavi's actions, the newspaper claimed. The newspaper also described Mesbah Yazdi's failure to oppose the shah's regime and to support the revolution. It cited a 1973 meeting at his home in Qom, when he discouraged opposition to the regime, saying: "Any uprising by Muslims before the appearance of the eminent Mahdi [the Lord of the Age] is futile and doomed to defeat." The article suggested there is a connection between Mesbah Yazdi's views and "the reactionary and old thesis of the Hojjatieh Society."

Accusations linking Mesbah Yazdi with the Hojjatieh Society—as well as commentary on his controversial views—intensified as the December 2006 Assembly of Experts election approached because of fears that he had ambitions on a top position in the Assembly and eventual ascendance to the supreme leadership. Mesbah Yazdi responded, as cited by *Hemayat* on April 30, 2006:

> I only knew a person called Hajj Mahmud Halabi and had heard that his ideol-

ogy was different from the principles of the revolution. Later Imam Khomeini, God's benedictions upon him, ordered the disbanding of this group and that is it. I have no more information about this sect.

An Environment for Political Extremes

The groups listed above are not the only Islamist entities in Iran. Some of the more extreme ones include a group called the Furqan (a term that refers to the distinction between good and evil). Furqan members assassinated many regime figures in 1979, including Ayatollah Morteza Mottahari, as well as merchants and Marxists, and they tried to kill Ali-Akbar Hashemi Rafsanjani, who was then a prominent figure in the Revolutionary Council. The regime executed many of the group's leaders, and it was inactive by 1980. In the late 1990s, the so-called Mahdaviyat Group tried to assassinate the Tehran judiciary chief. News about the group was obscured by official efforts to disassociate it from official institutions, including the Islamic Revolution Guards Corps, the alleged source of its weapons. Among the interesting accusations was that the Mahdaviyat was led by the grandson of Ayatollah Hadi Milani, the same person who authorized the 1965 assassination of Prime Minister Mansur by members of the Islamic Coalition Association.

The propensity for violence displayed by the groups discussed in this chapter is the most sensational aspect of their activities. The more significant commonality is their desire to create an Islamic state, although their interpretations of what such a state might be differ. The current constitution of Iran, while calling for an Islamic government, in fact combines a number of contradictory traditions—"the clashing, and not always congealing, elements of democratic values, Platonistic philosophy, and a variety of modernist intellectual movements including environmentalism and Marxist economics, that are all read within the framework of the Islamist interpretation of Islam itself," according to Jeffrey Usman.

Therefore, neither the constitution nor the system as a whole is likely to fully comply with the objectives of any entity identified here, or any Islamist entity that will emerge in the future. Continuing activism and even resistance by Islamist organizations is certain to continue, as will resistance from proponents of secularism. The absence of a democratic and transparent government and a free media that can report openly on governmental affairs contributes to the existence of clandestine entities that promote opposing political views and can find themselves clashing with the state.

BIBLIOGRAPHY

Ansari, Ali. "Iran under Ahmadinejad: The Politics of Confrontation." *Adelphi Papers* 393. London: Routledge, 2007.

Ashraf, Ahmad, and Ali Banuazizi. "Iran's Tortuous Path Toward 'Islamic Liberalism.'" *International Journal of Politics, Culture and Society* 15:2 (Winter 2001): 237–56.

Banuazizi, Ali. "Iran: Islamic State and Civil Society." Invited Joseph Sterlitz Annual Lecture in Middle Eastern Studies, Tel Aviv University, April 18, 1999.

Behdad, Sohrab. "Utopia of Assassins: Navvab Safavi and the Fada'ian-e Eslam in Prerevolutionary Iran." In *Iran: Between Tradition and Modernity,* ed. Ramin Jahanbegloo. Lanham, MD: Lexington Books, 2004.

Boroujerdi, Mehrzad. *Iranian Intellectuals and the West.* Syracuse, NY: Syracuse University Press, 1996.

Brumberg, Daniel. *Reinventing Khomeini: The Struggle for Reform in Iran.* Chicago: University of Chicago Press, 2001.

Cottam, Richard. *Nationalism in Iran.* Pittsburgh: University of Pittsburgh Press, 1964, 1979.

Ehteshami, Anoushirivan, and Mahjoob Zweiri. *Iran and the Rise of Its Neoconservatives: The Politics of Tehran's Silent Revolution.* London: I.B. Tauris, 2007.

Martin, Vanessa. *Creating an Islamic State: Khomeini and the Making of a New Iran.* London: I.B. Tauris, 2000.

Menashri, David. *Religion and Politics in Iran.* London: Frank Cass, 2001.

Mir-Hosseini, Ziba, and Richard Tapper, eds. *Islam and Democracy in Iran: Eshkevari and the Quest for Reform.* London: I.B. Tauris, 2006.

Moin, Baqer. *Khomeini: Life of the Ayatollah.* New York: St. Martin's Press, 1999.

Moslem, Mehdi. *Factional Politics in Post-Khomeini Iran.* Syracuse, NY: Syracuse University Press, 2002.

Naji, Kasra. *Ahmadinejad: The Secret History of Iran's Radical Leader.* London: I.B. Tauris, 2008.

Rajaee, Farhang. *Islamism and Modernism: The Changing Discourse in Iran.* Austin, TX: University of Texas Press, 2007.

Richard, Yann. "Ayatollah Kashani: Precursor of the Islamic Republic." In *Religion and Politics in Iran,* ed. Nikki R. Keddie, 101–24. New Haven, CT: Yale University Press, 1983.

Rubin, Michael. *Into the Shadows: Radical Vigilantes in Khatami's Iran.* Washington, DC: Washington Institute for Near East Policy, 2001.

Sadjadpour, Karim. *Reading Khamenei: The World View of Iran's Most Powerful Leader.* Washington, DC: Carnegie Endowment for International Peace, 2008.

Takeyh, Ray. "Islamism: R.I.P." *National Interest,* April 1, 2001.

Usman, Jeffrey. "The Evolution of Iranian Islamism from the Revolution Through the Contemporary Reformers." *Vanderbilt Journal of Transnational Law* 35 (2002): 1679–1730.

Iraq

Ibrahim Al-Marashi

After the collapse of Saddam Hussein's Ba'thist regime in the 2003 Iraq War, the internal dynamics of Iraq's politics dramatically changed. A whole new set of political groups was unleashed onto the domestic Iraqi political scene, most prominently Islamist-oriented groups. There are numerous Islamist movements in Iraq, both Shi'a and Sunni, some not even Iraqi in origin, with often contradictory visions for a post-Ba'thist Iraq. While all Islamist groups stress that they envision a polity that guarantees a strong role for the faith in public life, factions differ on whether this state will be centralized or federal. On the other extreme, some Islamist groups have called for an Islamic state.

Iraq provides a unique case study of the relationship between Islamist groups and politics. While in most states Islamist groups tend to be the main organized political opposition, in Iraq these movements not only entered the political process, they emerged as the dominant ruling elites. Another anomaly is that the strongest Islamist groups are Shi'a and managed to enter the political process through elections. Islamist groups in Iraq, mainly Shi'a but also Sunni, formed an Iraqi coalition government through a democratic process,

taking part in electoral campaigning, working with secular forces, and even drafting a constitution. While the future of this government remains in question, it has set a precedent for Islamists in the Arab world by taking power through a democratic process and struggling to maintain the system that brought them to power.

At the same time, Islamist groups in Iraq have also set another bloody regional precedent: a relentless campaign of violence against foreign powers and the indiscriminate use of terror against civilians, whether they are Shi'a, Sunni, Christian, Arab, Kurd, or Turkmen. The instability arises from intersectarian tensions related to a conflict for power between the factions of political Islam: Shi'a Islamist groups pitted against Iraqi Sunni Islamist groups and al-Qa'ida-linked Islamists fighting Islamist groups working with the United States.

In addition, these groups can no longer be deemed organizations concerned with a purely ideological Islamist agenda but are evolving into sectarian nationalist movements. Rather than enshrining the role of Islam in the Iraqi state, their immediate goals are protecting their constituents, whether they be Shi'a or Sunni, and guaranteeing their dominance in the political process. The future of Iraq will rest on the outcome of this conflict, whether it is managed through sociopolitical consensus, a future Iraqi military force capable of checking the powers of the insurgent groups, or a civil war.

Islamist Shi'a Groups and Their Goals

The emergence of Iraq's Shi'a as dominant actors in postwar Iraq was first demonstrated in April 2003, with their first public Ashuraa processions (commemorating the death of Imam Hussein in 680). The four main Islamist actors that emerged among the Shi'a were the Da'wa Party, the Supreme Council for the Islamic Revolution in Iraq (SCIRI), the followers of Ayatollah Ali al-Sistani, and the followers of Muqtada al-Sadr. In addition, there are numerous other Shi'a Islamist groups, as well as clerics with significant followings. However, for the most part, these four groups and even minor Shi'a Islamist actors joined the United Iraqi Alliance (UIA, also known as the United Iraqi Coalition), a grouping of predominantly Shi'a religious factions, which managed to maintain relative cohesiveness during the December 2005 elections and in the Iraqi government that followed.

The Da'wa Party (al-Hizb al-Da'wa al-Islamiyya) was formed in the 1960s to provide a religious alternative for the Iraqi Shi'a, who were increasingly joining the ranks of secular parties such as the Iraqi Communists and the Ba'thists. The charismatic Ayatollah Muhammad Baqr al-Sadr emerged as the spiritual leader of the Da'wa Party. He was the author of numerous theses on Islamic economics and on the structure of an Islamic state based on the rule of the clergy, *wilayat al-faqih,* which Ayatollah

Ruhollah Khomeini replicated in Iran. Such a religiously oriented party, made up of predominantly Iraqi Shi'a, was seen as a threat to the secular, Arab Sunni minority–based Ba'thist government. The Ba'thists feared that the Da'wa could undermine their regime and establish an Islamic state in Iraq akin to the Islamic Republic in neighboring Iran.

In the late 1970s, the Shi'a in the south of Iraq took part in riots, believed by the Ba'th leadership to be orchestrated by the Da'wa Party. At that time, Iraqi president Ahmad Hasan al-Bakr (term of office 1968–1979) adopted a relatively conciliatory approach to end Shi'a discontent, while then vice president Saddam Hussein favored strict repression of all political opposition groups, including the Da'wa. Upon assuming full power in 1979, Hussein had the opportunity to pursue this policy, which was intricately linked to the declaration of war on the Islamic Republic of Iran in September 1980. In March 1980 the Da'wa Party attacked various Ba'th Party headquarters in the south and a month later was complicit in an assassination attempt that failed to kill Tariq Aziz, then Iraqi deputy prime minister. In retaliation, the Iraqi president ordered the execution of Ayatollah Muhammad Baqr al-Sadr and declared that membership in the Da'wa Party would incur the death penalty. The Da'wa Party went underground, while most of its leadership sought refuge in Iran, Syria, and England.

The Supreme Council for the Islamic Revolution in Iraq (also called the Supreme Council for the Islamic *Resistance* in Iraq, SCIRI, or the Supreme Assembly for the Islamic Revolution in Iraq, SAIRI) was formed in Iran in 1982 as a coalition of Iraqi Shi'a organizations opposed to the Ba'thist government. It was designed to serve as a government-in-exile in the event that the

Iranians were successful in toppling the Hussein regime. The Da'wa Party initially joined this coalition but later withdrew because of its apprehensions about Iranian control over the organization and disagreements with Islamic Republic's notions of the role of Islam and the state.

To understand the power of Ayatollah Ali al-Sistani, or any other Shi'a cleric in Iraq for that matter, it is necessary to outline the notion of a *marja* or *marja al-taqlid,* otherwise known as a "source of religious emulation." The marja al-taqlid is the highest title bestowed on a Shi'a cleric, otherwise referred to as a *mujtahid,* a scholar who has attained enough religious knowledge to practice *ijtihad,* the ability to interpret the Koran, sacred texts, and Islamic law and to issue guidance to the Shi'a community on religious matters. A marja's authority is valid until his death, although various Shi'a, including Muqtada al-Sadr himself, argue that a marja's teachings can be followed even after the death of the cleric.

Traditionally, political power in Shi'a Islam was decentralized; there was no one central authority in Shi'a Islam, and thus a practicing Shi'a Muslim has the option of choosing the religious guidance of a variety of scholars who have attained the rank of marja. Such a scholar is also known as a grand ayatollah (Ayatollah al-Uzma), and there are around five Shi'a scholars who have this rank. The rank of marja is usually bestowed by other grand ayatollahs, but the position and reputation of such a scholar is sustained by how many followers he can attract. Khomeini tried to centralize this structure, putting himself at the apex of Shi'a religious and political power, arousing discernment among various Shi'a, Shi'a Islamist groups, and prominent clerics. Many of them were marjas themselves, believing that Shi'a authority should remain pluralist and objecting to the merging of clerical authority and political rule.

While Ayatollah al-Sistani's last name indicates his origins in the Sistan Province of southeast Iran, al-Sistani himself was born in the Shi'a shrine city of Mashhad in northern Iran in 1930. His family included prominent Shi'a religious scholars, whose religious standing, like Muqtada al-Sadr's, is augmented by their *sayyid* lineage— their ability to trace direct descent from Muhammad's family or descendents.

The most prominent Shi'a authority in Iraq following the death of Ayatollah Muhammad Bakr al-Sadr was Grand Ayatollah Abd al-Qasim al-Khoei, another cleric of Iranian descent, who headed al-Hawza al-Ilmiyya, a prominent educational facility in the Iraqi town of Najaf. While both al-Sadr and al-Khoei were held in great esteem by the Shi'a of Iraq, their approaches to the role of Islam in politics were quite different. Baqr al-Sadr advocated an activist agenda for the Shi'a in the political sphere, evidenced by his role in the Da'wa Party, while al-Khoei believed in a quietist approach, whereby the Shi'a religious authority should abstain from a direct role in political affairs. In 1951, al-Sistani moved to Najaf, where he studied under al-Khoei and thus was indoctrinated in the quietist school. The title of marja was bestowed upon al-Sistani in 1961, a remarkable feat, given that he was the first student of al-Khoei to ever receive this rank. Moreover, al-Sistani was only 31 when he received this distinction, whereas most scholars usually receive this title in their fifties.

In 1992 al-Khoei passed away, having appointed al-Sistani as his successor, thus placing him in charge of the hawza. The Ba'thist authorities sought to curtail any political role for al-Sistani, forbade him from leading prayers and delivering Friday sermons in Najaf, and placed him under house arrest. Nevertheless, his religious authority remained, as he was able to deliver religious pronouncements (fatwas) via handwritten notes from his home, as he continued to do after the 2003 war.

However, Grand Ayatollah Muhammad Sadiq al-Sadr, al-Sistani's contemporary, refused to assume al-Sistani's quietist approach. In the vacuum that followed the death of al-Khoei in 1993, Sadiq al-Sadr followed in the footsteps of his cousin, Bakr al-Sadr, and emerged as the political and spiritual leader of the young Shi'a in Iraq, especially those based in the east Baghdad district known as Saddam City. Sadiq al-Sadr, like his cousin, advocated the rule of the clergy in a Khomeini-style Islamist state. Muhammad Sadiq al-Sadr argued that the hawza was divided into *al-hawza al-natiqa,* or the "outspoken hawza," which he advocated, and *al-hawza al-samita,* or the "silent hawza," referring to al-Sistani, who had avoided confrontation with political authorities. Muqtada al-Sadr—his son— and his later followers supported *al-hawza al-natiqa,* as Nir Rosen explains in his book *In the Belly of the Green Bird: Triumph of the Martyrs in Iraq.* Sadiq al-Sadr was renowned for his Friday sermons preaching against Israel and challenging the authority of Saddam Hussein, which led to his death, and the death of two of his sons, in February 1999, allegedly at the hands of Iraq's security forces. His surviving son, Muqtada, went into hiding and later emerged as a pivotal force in Iraqi Shi'a politics.

Muqtada al-Sadr inherited his father's credentials as a respected Shi'a cleric who had opposed Saddam Hussein. After years in hiding, Muqtada reappeared in Najaf when the American military captured the town. Muqtada held a relatively junior rank among the clergy but managed to reap deep sympathy for his father and family. Initially, his followers emerged under the Group of the Second Sadr (Jama'at al-Sadr al-Thani), which would later assume the title of the Sadr Trend.

The primary goal of the Shi'a Islamist groups is to ensure that the Iraqi government guarantee that a future state reflect the Shi'a's majority status and demographic weight in Iraq. SCIRI, Da'wa, al-Sistani, and al-Sadr have also sought a role for Islam in the state, although they have differing interpretations of this role. Given that all four factions have connections to the Shi'a religious institutions, they aimed to ensure that the state recognized Iraq's Islamic identity and character. However, SCIRI, Da'wa, and al-Sistani have stated that their aim is not to establish a wilayat al-faqih as in neighboring Iran, nor do they intend to use the democratic process to achieve this end. The Iranian system of government, although led by Shi'a clerics, is not accepted by all Shi'a clerics, especially not by Grand Ayatollah Ali al-Sistani, nor by clerics in SCIRI or Da'wa. Conversely, Sadr's goal is that the Shi'a clerical establishment play a direct role in Iraq's politics, but he has emphasized that he will not seek to replicate Iran's Islamic Republic. He has been ambiguous on this issue, however, and has not explicitly declared his notion of how an Iraqi Islamic Republic would be structured.

Both SCIRI and Da'wa have on occasion urged the necessity of an American withdrawal from Iraq, but it seemed that the survival of their government after December 2005 hinged on U.S. military force, a fact that many of its politicians would be loathe to admit publicly. On the other hand, al-Sadr continued to call for a U.S. withdrawal, one of the few issues where he has held a consistent line.

SCIRI and Da'wa, as participants in the

United Iraqi Alliance, made one of their goals the right to form a federated state in the predominantly Shi'a south along the lines of a Kurdish federated entity in the north. Ayatollah al-Sistani has remained quiet on the issue of federalism, and contrary to rumors in the Iraqi media that he condemned a federal Iraq, he declared in an edict issued in August 2005 that he has neither condoned nor condemned a federal system, as reported by al-Najaf News Network. Al-Sadr, on the other hand, has rejected federalism as a foreign scheme designed to divide Iraq.

Most of the Shi'a groups, even those in power, have militias, some of which are incorporated into the Iraqi military and police. These militias have been accused of sectarian violence, whether operating within the security forces or independently. The Islamic Republic in Iran helped SCIRI establish and train an armed wing known as the Badr Corps, which emerged as the largest and most organized armed Iraqi Shi'a militia, whose numerical strength was estimated at 20,000 prior to the 2003 Iraq War. During the Iran-Iraq War, the Badr Corps launched hit-and-run attacks against the Iraqi military in Iraq. The Badr Corps eventually played a major role in the post-2003 violence in Iraq, was blamed for sectarian killings, and set off a scandal by maintaining an underground prison that detained mostly Arab Sunni prisoners.

Muqtada's followers after the 2003 war evolved into a highly organized, motivated force known as the Mahdi Army. While chaos prevailed in other parts of Iraq, Muqtada's army was part of a shadow state created by him in areas where he enjoyed wide support, especially in the neighborhood of Baghdad known as Sadr City (the former Saddam City), named after Muqtada's family. The Mahdi Army engaged in intense clashes with U.S. forces in April and August 2004, and played a role in the intrasectarian violence that erupted in Iraq after February 2006.

Islamist Sunni Groups and Their Goals

After the collapse of the primarily Arab Sunni-dominated Ba'th government, the Arab Sunni segment of Iraq's population fell into a political vacuum with no united leadership to its views. Some aligned themselves with tribal leaders and some with the Islamist parties that slowly began to emerge, while others depended on Sunni insurgents—most of whom formed into Islamist groups—to make their voices heard. After 2003, a number of parties, associations, and coalitions developed, competing to serve as the united voice of the Sunnis. The three most outspoken of them happen to be Islamist parties and include the Iraqi Islamic Party (IIP), the Association of Muslim Scholars (AMS), and the General Dialogue Conference (GDC). The latter two organizations were created after the war and opposed participating in a U.S.-sponsored political process. The IIP fluctuated between partaking in postwar politics while boycotting the process at times to protest American military actions, particularly in Falluja.

The Iraqi Islamic Party developed from the Muslim Brotherhood in Iraq, but the secular Ba'th government cracked down on the organization, forcing it to seek exile in London. Two dominant personalities in the party are Muhsin Abd al-Hamid and Tariq al-Hashimi, the latter of whom became one of Iraq's two vice presidents after 2005. The Association of Muslim Scholars has emerged as a prominent group representing the interests of the Arab Sunnis, led by Muthanna and Harith al-Dari. Their goal is to barter the political participation of the Sunni sect in the Iraqi political process in return for greater consideration of the needs of their constituents. It has also been described as the "political wing" of the insurgency, although it is doubtful that it has influence over the al-Qa'ida-linked factions. Another organization is the General Conference of Iraqi Sunnis (al-Mu'tamar al-Awwali li-Ahl al-Sunna al-Iraq), led by Adnan al-Dulaymi. It was one of the first groups that adopted the term "Sunni" in its title. The group later changed its name to the more inclusive General Dialogue Conference (GDC). These factions formed al-Tawafuq (the Accord Front) before the December 2005 elections, uniting around a platform of advancing the interest of Iraq's Arab Sunnis.

The Arab Sunni Islamists agree with Shi'a Islamists on a greater role for religion in the state, but some of these Sunni Islamists view the Shi'a as a sect deviant from proper Islam. However, the primary goal of Sunni Islamist parties is not directly related to the role of Islam in the state. Their most pressing concern is preventing the disintegration of Iraq, which they believe could occur in a federalist structure. This debate has put them in direct conflict with the two Shi'a Islamist parties advocating federalism, SCIRI and Da'wa. The Sunni Islamists fear that a federal entity in the north and south could lead to the de facto dismembering of the nation, leaving their constituents in a landlocked rump state, with no access to the largesse accrued from oil resources.

Politics in the north of Iraq, where Kurdish identity is more important than Muslim community, is dominated by the Kurdish Democratic Party (KDP) and the Patriotic Union of Kurdistan (PUK), both of which are secular in nature, stressing Kurdish nationalism as opposed to political Islam.

Both parties have attempted to counter Shi'a attempts to Islamicize a future state. Nevertheless, there are also Kurdish Islamist parties, such as the Islamic Movement of Kurdistan and the Kurdistan Islamic Union. However, these tend to be minor players in the political dynamics of the north and are not prominent in Iraqi politics.

Sunni Islamist groups that emerged to fight the occupation after 2003 were by no means monolithic, but some of the strongest include the Islamic Army in Iraq (al-Jaysh al-Islami fil-Iraq), whose ideology is a mix of Iraqi nationalism and political Islam. Most of its fighters are recruited from Baghdad or towns such as Falluja, Ramadi, and Samarra in what has become referred to as the "Sunni Arab Triangle." The Islamic Army has stated that its immediate goal is to end the U.S. occupation, but it has not articulated a vision of a future Islamic state in Iraq.

The Soldiers of Islam (Jund al-Islam) emerged in September 2001, made up of Kurdish Islamists who seized control of several villages near the northern Iraqi town of Halabja in order to establish a ministate similar to the Taliban's Afghanistan. The organization, which had ties to al-Qa'ida, accepted that group's fighters, as they were forced to flee Afghanistan in October 2001. The Supporters of Islam (Ansar al-Islam) formed in December 2001 as a successor organization. After U.S. Special Forces and Kurdish militias destroyed their main base during the Iraq War, members of Ansar al-Islam scattered throughout Iraq. It is reported that in late 2003 Abu Abdallah al-Shafi'i, also known as Warba Holiri al-Kurdi, took over leadership of Ansar al-Islam and changed its name to the Army of the Supporters of the Sunna (Jaysh al-Ansar al-Sunna), an organization that has a broader strategy of defending the Sunnis and fighting the United States in Iraq. This contrasts with its prior agenda of establishing an Islamist state in the north of Iraq. It is believed that the revamped organization cooperated closely with the late Abu Mus'ab al-Zarqawi.

Al-Zarqawi was a Jordanian national who had a long history of fighting for various jihadi movements. He opened his own terrorist base in the Afghan city of Herat in 2000, where it is believed that he forged connections with al-Qa'ida but did not formally join them. After the war in Afghanistan in 2001, he fled to Iraq, where he joined Jund al-Islam and is believed to have played a key role in directing that organization, although he was not declared its leader. Another group, the Unity and Jihad Group (Jama'at al-Tawhid wal-Jihad), is also believed to have been led by al-Zarqawi. The various names of these organizations are confusing, because they essentially refer to the same group but perhaps reveal a tactic designed to give the impression that the armed Islamist elements are more numerous than the other factions. To make matters even more confusing, the group assumed a new name, the al-Qa'ida Organization for Holy War in the Land of the Two Rivers (Tandhim Qa'idat al-Jihad fi Bilad al-Rafidayn), indicating al-Zarqawi's allegiance to Osama bin Ladin's organization.

The ideology of the al-Qa'ida Organization in Iraq is based on the portrayal of the United States as a "neo-Crusader" entity in the heart of the Islamic world, arguing that America's goal is to "raise the Cross in the lands of Islam," as reported in April 2004 by the Open Source Center (OSC). For this faction, the United States did not invade Iraq simply to control its oil but rather to counter "the increasing Islamic expansion," reported the OSC in April 2004. Al-Qa'ida's list of Iraq's enemies, according to the OSC

in September 2004, includes the "tripartite Satanic and infidel alliance" consisting of the United States, or the "bearers of the Cross"; the Kurds who are "injected with the Jews"; and the Shi'a, derogatorily referred to as "rejectionists" of proper Islam. For example, the Shi'a SCIRI's Badr Corps is referred to as the "Treason Corps," and al-Qa'ida alleges that the corps "participated in the killing of Muslims and the raping of Muslim women in Falluja," says a December 2004 OSC article.

This branch of al-Qa'ida made it clear that it is fighting to establish a new caliphate in Iraq, which will serve as the base for a future caliphate that will rule the entire Muslim world. The al-Qa'ida-linked groups have used the Web to appeal to constituents in the *umma,* calling on this "nation to wake up." Their messages indicate that the West fears that the "Islamic giant" will wake up and reach the gates of "Rome, Washington, Paris, and London," according to the April 2004 OSC report. The organization states that it is using Iraq as a battleground in the process of establishing a greater Islamic umma, ruled by a caliph, as mentioned in one statement attributed to al-Zarqawi and cited in October 2004 by OSC:

> Lastly, we make our vow to God and his messenger to cut with our swords the heads of apostates, traitors, and spies, and to keep our swords, highly drawn towards the sky, and to raise the banner of "God is Great," and establish the Caliphate.

The Islamists Enter the Political Process

The first opportunity for the Islamist parties to enter postwar politics in an institutional capacity occurred with the formation of the 25-member Governing Council (Majlis al-Hukm), which convened in July 2003. The United States intended that the council represent Iraqis from all political, ethnic, and religious backgrounds. At the same time, it provided the first indication of which Iraqi Islamist political groups were willing to engage with the Coalition Provisional Authority (CPA). Taking part in the council would serve as the first step for these groups to enter the political process, giving them experience in how to bargain with the CPA and facilitating their role in the provisional government and in the writing of a draft constitution (the Transitional Administrative Law).

Shi'a Islamists were represented on the council by Ibrahim al-Ja'fari and Abd al-Zahra Muhammad of the Da'wa Party, with the former emerging as Iraqi interim prime minister after the January 2005 elections. Abd al-Aziz al-Hakim, brother of the deceased leader of SCIRI, Muhammad Baqr al-Hakim, also sat on the council. Excluded from the body were any followers of Muqtada al-Sadr, perhaps an indication to him that he would have to pursue other means to be taken seriously as an actor in the Iraqi political arena. Among the Sunni Islamists, only Muhsin Abd al-Hamid sat on the council on behalf of the Iraqi Islamic Party, an indication that the IIP would be one of the few voices representing Sunni Islamists in the nascent political process. For the most part, other Islamist groups developed as opposition movements outside of these political structures established under the occupation authority. The Kurdish Islamists were represented by Salah al-Din Baha al-Din of the Kurdistan Islamic Union, but for the most part that party was overshadowed by the PUK and KDP.

In the months leading up to the Iraqi election on January 31, 2005, the nation witnessed the mobilization of Iraqi Shi'a and Sunni Islamist parties, providing one of the few cases (with perhaps the exception of Lebanon) of multiple Islamist groups taking part in campaigning in an election whose outcome was relatively undetermined. The Shi'a parties were the strongest advocates of elections, and al-Sistani intervened in the political process at this juncture to use his religious authority to bestow legitimacy on the Iraqi electoral process. His fatwas called on all Iraqis, not just the Shi'a, to vote, as well as calling for non-Muslims, such as the Iraqi Christians, to take an active part in the process. It was a direct endorsement from a grand ayatollah of the Iraqi political process, including elections. For other Islamists, particularly al-Qa'ida members, al-Sistani's endorsement was blasphemy. Al-Qa'ida does not recognize any process that accepts the sovereignty of the people over God's sovereignty.

Before the elections, Falluja, a predominantly Sunni Arab city, was attacked by American forces in November 2004. The Association of Muslim Scholars had emerged as a prominent group representing the interests of the Arab Sunnis at that point and called for boycotting the elections in protest.

Neither Sunni nor Shi'a Islamist parties ran on ideologically Islamist agendas during this campaign. At this stage, they began campaigning as sectarian nationalist parties. The Shi'a parties exhorted their constituencies to vote in the elections to prevent the mistakes they had made in the 1920s, when they had refused to take part in British-sponsored politics and were subsequently "locked out" of the political system for decades to follow. On the other hand, Sunni Islamist groups argued that their constituencies were being unfairly targeted by the United States and that they should boycott a process sponsored by an occupying power.

After the January 2005 elections, the United Iraqi Alliance, the Shi'a Islamist coalition endorsed by al-Sistani, won a slim majority with 140 seats in the 275-member National Assembly. The Iraqi Kurds came in second, winning about 75 seats. The Shi'a Islamists had secured 51 percent of the seats, failing to capture the two-thirds majority necessary to create a government alone. In this scenario, the Shi'a Islamist party entered a coalition with the secular Kurds. The Shi'a Islamists secured the powerful prime minister's post for Ibrahim al-Ja'fari of the Da'wa Party, who became the first such chief of a government in the Arab world.

The Shi'a Islamist and Kurdish coalition, with participation from other Arab Sunni Islamist parties, took part in drafting a constitution. Both Islamist parties sought to draft a constitution enshrining the role of Islam in a future state, whereas secular parties, including the Kurds, wanted Islamic law to serve only as a source of inspiration and not as the sole source for legislation. Eventually a compromise was reached; however, the most contentious issue was not between Islamists and secularists but between the Shi'a and Sunni Islamist groups. A debate emerged over whether Iraq would be a federal state, which tended to make Islamist groups representatives of sectarian nationalist agendas, trying to advance the interests of their respective Arab Shi'a and Arab Sunni constituencies.

While the elections held in January 2005 merely chose a temporary, transitional assembly whose primary task was drafting the constitution, the December 2005 election decided the makeup of Iraq's permanent assembly for a four-year term. Those elections were held as a result of the constitution that passed a general Iraqi referendum on October 15, 2005. For the first time,

Sunni Islamist groups that had avoided partaking in the January 2005 elections mobilized to participate in the December vote. Their decision served as an indication that some Sunni Arab Islamist factions were willing to acknowledge and take part in Iraq's political process, a crucial step in co-opting those Sunni parties that had tacitly supported the insurgency. Muqtada al-Sadr, who had rejected an American-backed political process in the past, made common cause with the Shi'a parties in the transitional government and fielded candidates to join the greater Shi'a coalition.

While differences between ethnic and sectarian groups have been ever-present in Iraq, they are especially pronounced today and are emphasized through public debate. For example, Islamist factions have established their own media empires. Shi'a Islamist factions have satellite channels to reach Iraqi audiences, the Arab world, and the Iraqi diaspora. In 2004 SCIRI launched the al-Furat (Euphrates) channel, followed by the Da'wa Party's al-Anwar (Lights). At the same time, they established radio stations and print media. Prominent newspapers include the Da'wa Party's daily *al-Da'wa* (*Call*) and the weekly *al-Bayan* (*Announcement*). SCIRI has its own daily *al-Adala* (*Justice*) and weekly *al-Wahda* (*Unity*), while the Sadr movement publishes the daily *Ishraqat al-Sadr* (*Dawn of Sadr*) and the weekly *al-Hawza al-Natiqa* (*Active Hawza*), the latter briefly ordered closed by the CPA for "inciting hatred." *Al-Bayyina* (*Evidence*) is published by the Shi'a Hizballah movement in Iraq.

Sunni Islamist factions followed by establishing their own media networks. The Baghdad Satellite Channel supports the Tawafuq Front, an alliance of Sunni Islamist groups. The Iraqi Islamic Party publishes the weekly *Dar al-Salam* (*House of Peace*), the General Dialogue Conference publishes the daily *al-Itisam* (*Guardian*), and the Unified National Movement, led by Sunni cleric Ahmad al-Qubaysi (allied with the AMS), has its own weekly, *al-Sa'a* (*The Hour*). The Association of Muslim Scholars also issues the daily newspaper *al-Basa'ir* (*Insights*).

This survey highlights the dominance of Islamist groups in the Iraqi media. Following the bombing of the Shi'a Askariyya shrine in the city of Samarra in February 2006, the various sectarian media outlets escalated tensions but eventually called for restraint among Iraq's communities. Each Islamist group used its media to demonstrate that its people were the victims in Iraq's ongoing violence. While these media do not explicitly exhort violence against the other sectarian communities, the continued portrayal of their own respective victimization serves as a means of encouraging Shi'a Arabs and Sunnis to "defend" themselves in the ensuing sectarian violence. Political Islam has entered Iraq's media sphere as an additional means of encouraging separate sectarian identities.

Views of Islamist Parties on the Role of Islam, Democracy, and the State

Most of the Iraqi Islamist groups have issued manifestos and statements outlining their views on the role Islam should play in both private and public spheres. The following provides a sample of how the Iraqi Islamist parties use the media to disseminate these views to the Iraqi public as well as the region.

Representatives from the Shi'a parties, including Da'wa and SCIRI, have used various media to articulate their views on Islam

and the state. For example, on the state al-Iraqiyya television channel's program *Special Encounter*, an interview was held with Iraqi prime minister Nuri al-Maliki in April 2006. The host of the program, Abd al-Karim Hammadi, asked al-Maliki if he sought to establish an Islamic state in Iraq given that he came from an Islamist party, Da'wa. Al-Maliki replied:

> I believe that what will be in line with my ideology as a Muslim is to have a Muslim society, a society whose social values respect Islam and abide by it. This is what I aspire for. But if the Iraqi people, through the mechanisms of democracy and with their free will, opt for a regime they want, be it an Islamist regime or otherwise, I will respect the Iraqi people's willpower.

When asked if he, as prime minister, would enact legislation based on Shari'a, he replied:

> The constitution has taken care of all these matters. There are no provisions in our constitution that give the prime minister the right to bring pressure to bear for the issuance of laws that have to do with this issue. I will respect the constitution and I will abide by it as the highest authority. I will meticulously abide by the constitution and what the House of Representatives decides.

It is interesting to note how al-Maliki used the Iraqiyya channel, which is a publicly funded broadcaster dependent on state revenues, to address the Iraqi public. Through this medium he seeks to disavow himself of his party's Islamist roots, yet at the same time suggest that an Islamic state is possible if willed by the majority.

SCIRI issued a manifesto about the movement in the paper *al-Istiqama* in August 2006 under the title "The Identity of the Supreme Council of the Islamic Revolution in Iraq." SCIRI declared that its mission upon its creation in 1982 was to topple the "Saddam dictatorship," and once that had been completed, it had no will to establish an Islamic state in Iraq. The manifesto declared, "Then we would leave matters after that to the Iraqi people to choose the political regime that suits them through free and direct elections." After the 2003 war, their statement highlighted the changing role of the party:

> After toppling the buried regime, its military mission came to a close after having achieved its objectives. It transformed itself into a civil organization to keep the peace, defend the achievements of the people, and develop them towards the ultimate goal of achieving freedom, justice, and independence for Iraq.

Al-Istiqama is the main newspaper of SCIRI. In this instance, a political organ used elements of its media empire to declare that SCIRI does not have an agenda to establish an Islamist state in Iraq. In essence, this is like al-Maliki, assuaging notions that both parties seek to emulate Iran in establishing an Islamic Republic.

Al-Sistani's views on this topic—which can be found on his Web site—are important given the sway he holds over Iraq's Shi'a, as well as the number of parliamentarians who represent his office. The ayatollah has stated that he prefers an Iraqi Islamic state, but not one modeled on a theocracy, as in Iran. He believes that Shari'a should be institutionalized in Iraq's constitution while guaranteeing freedom of religion for Iraq's non-Muslim minorities. Al-Sistani has stated that Iraq should not follow the Islamic Republic's model of a wilayat al-faqih (rule of the Islamic jurist). He has called for a state based on the principles of Shari'a but for Shi'a clerics to avoid direct participation in the institutions of the state.

Khalid al-Khawaja penned an article in the Jordanian paper *al-Ra'y*, entitled "There Is a Plan to Destroy Iraq and Provoke Sectarian Sedition in It," quoting a statement made in an interview with Adnan al-Dulaymi, the former head of the Sunni Religious Endowments Bureau in Iraq. Al-Dulaymi calls on his movement, identified as the First General Conference of Sunnis (al-Mu'tamar al-Awwali li-Ahl al-Sunna), to engage in the political process, in both drafting the 2005 constitution and participating in the December 2005 elections. Among al-Dulaymi's objections to the constitution that was eventually adopted was its failure to acknowledge a greater role for Islam in the state:

> However, there are general principles which the Constitution should contain, such as Iraq's sovereignty, Iraq's unity, shunning sectarianism, Iraq's belonging to its true Arab-Islamic identity, that Iraq is part of the Arab homeland, that Islam is the official religion of Iraq, and that any article of the Constitution and the various laws shall not conflict with Islam's foundations.

In this instance, al-Dulaymi used the media to reach an Arab audience, particularly a Jordanian one. His message was that his party would continue to oppose the Iraqi political process because of its sectarian nature and its disregard for greater prominence of religion in political affairs.

In March 2006 the *Dar al-Salam* paper, owned by the Iraqi Islamic Party, featured an interview with Tariq al-Hashimi, the secretary general of that party. Al-Hashimi outlined five of the party's principles, indicative of its view of Islam and the state:

1. To base our deeds on good intentions, which are dedicated to God Almighty, maintaining connection with the Almighty and trying to be closer to Him through good deeds.
2. No decision can be made without going through the Shura [consultation] process.
3. To make all preparations and take the appropriate measure and then depend on God, in other words taking the causes and effects into consideration within the context of Shari'a.
4. Following the rule that says every person finds it easy if he is placed where he was intended to be when he was created, in other words putting the right person in the right place.
5. To adapt political action both in words and in deeds according to the regulations of Shari'a.

Both the Iraqi Islamic Party and the General Conference have failed to articulate a model of an Islamic state in their interviews, as both Shi'a parties have. The failure to do so suggests either that they do not have such a model or that their call for greater Islamic influence over secular Muslims is mere pandering to their constituencies. Nevertheless, what unites all of the Islamist parties, both Shi'a and Sunni, is a call to take part in the processes of a democracy: the drafting of a constitution, competitive elections, participation in a representative assembly, and accountability to constituents.

This call for taking part in a democratic political process is opposed by the salafi and al-Qa'ida-affiliated groups in Iraq, which have coalesced into their own parastate, known as the Islamic State in Iraq. Democratic structures are anathema to their view of how politics should be organized. Their views of democracy can be extrapolated from a sermon given by an ideologue, Shaykh Abu Hamza al-Baghdadi, in August 2005 entitled "The Constitution, Creed of the Infidels." In this sermon, al-Baghdadi states that elections are "a wicked outgrowth of the many outgrowths of democracy, which is the greatest act of polytheism in this day and age." Furthermore, he exhorts his followers "to not believe in it [democracy] or its constitution, which is a ritual of democracy and its system."

The Formation of a Permanent Government

After the December 2005 elections, it took several months of bargaining among the parties, particularly the dominant Islamist groups, secularists, and Kurdish parties that fared well in the elections, to form an Iraqi government. An analysis of the cabinet indicates the relative strength of the Islamist parties. The Shi'a alliance, the UIA, held the prime ministerial position in the person of Nuri al-Maliki of the Da'wa Party, replacing Ibrahim al-Ja'fari, the interim prime minister, also from that party. Al-Maliki has been a member of Da'wa since 1968 and fled to Iran after the Ba'thist crackdown. He moved to Syria after he refused to fight with SCIRI alongside the Iranian army against the Iraqi military, an indication of Da'wa's disagreements with the Islamic Republic during its exile. Another prominent member of Da'wa is Education Minister Khudayr al-Khuza'i, from a prominent Shi'a Iraqi tribe. He has PhDs in both Koranic studies and Islamic theology and was also a prominent drafter of the constitution. The trade minister is also from the Da'wa Party, although some sources claim he is part of the Sadr Trend.

SCIRI, the other constituent party of the UIA, also held prominent portfolios, including Finance Minister Baqir Sulagh Jabr al-Zubaydi and Minister of State for National Dialogue Affairs Akram al-Hakim, a vocal supporter of the Shi'a being able to form a federal entity in the south of Iraq. Two other SCIRI members head the ministry of labor and the ministry of municipalities. The Sadr Trend of the UIA holds four portfolios, including health, transportation, tourism, and agriculture. The role the Sadr Trend plays in the government and as a member of the UIA makes al-Maliki's task of demobilizing Sadr's militia all the more difficult.

Other ministries are held by factions in the UIA outside of the Da'wa-SCIRI-Sadr triumvirate. One of the ministers of state is from the Iraqi Hizballah, and Youth Minister Jasim Muhammad Ja'far is from a Shi'a Turkmen party, the Islamic Union of Iraqi Turkmen. Independent candidates who ran on the UIA list also hold important posts, such as the former nuclear scientist Husayn al-Sharastani, who serves as the oil minister. Minister of State for the Council of Representatives Affairs Safa al-Safi is another independent who is considered part of al-Sistani's inner circle.

The Sunni Islamists in the Tawafuq Front also hold several important posts. Deputy Prime Minister and Acting Defense Minister Salam al-Zawba'i is from a prominent Sunni Arab tribe. Minister of State for Women's Affairs Fatin Abd-al-Rahman Mahmud is also part of the Tawafuq Front. The Iraqi Islamic Party, a constituent of the Front, holds posts such as culture minister. Planning Minister Ali Baban is also in the IIP, but he is a Kurd in a predominantly Sunni Arab party.

Out of 37 posts, the Islamists hold 24 min-isterial portfolios, with the UIA controlling 17 and the Tawafuq Front holding seven. The Kurdish parties hold six, leaving the secularists, running under the Iraqi List Coalition, with seven. The post of president is held by Jalal Talabani of the PUK, but the two vice presidents are Islamists—Adil Abd al-Mahdi of SCIRI and Tariq al-Hashimi of the IIP. The process that these Islamists entered in 2003 was firmly in their control by 2006. However, while institutions of the state are controlled by the Islamists at this point, the internal violence, for which they have been partially responsible, has ultimately proved the greatest challenge to the very state they dominate.

Islamist Violence in Iraq

Since the 2003 war, Iraq has witnessed Islamist violence from both Sunni and Shi'a groups, as well as incidents stemming from intra-Shi'a rivalries and intersectarianism.

Sunni Arab Violence

The rise of the insurgency is usually attributed to the events that transpired on April 29, 2003, when as many as 13 Iraqis, protesting the U.S. military presence in Falluja, were killed as elements of the U.S. Army fired on the crowd. The clashes between U.S. forces and Iraqis in Falluja sparked the violence within the Sunni tribal area that had traditionally supported Saddam Hussein. Elements emerged among the Iraqi Sunnis who had no desire to fight for the return of their former dictator, and their attacks against Coalition forces were specifically directed toward ending the American occupation of Iraq. In this context, groups such as the Islamic Army in Iraq emerged and initially limited themselves to guerrilla-type tactics against Coalition forces. While the

Islamic Army can be considered a "local" organization that emerged in the chaos that ensued after the 2003 war, foreign fighters from around the Arab world also entered the porous borders of Iraq to take part in the struggle against an American occupation of a Muslim country. These volunteers swelled the ranks of groups inspired by, if not linked to, al-Qa'ida. Al-Zarqawi began to direct his own network of terrorist groups in Iraq and was the leading suspect in the suicide bombing of the Jordanian embassy in Baghdad on August 7, 2003, and the attack on the United Nations headquarters in Baghdad on August 19 of that year, one of the first incidences of suicide attacks in Iraq.

While the violent incidents attributed to the Islamic Army in Iraq and al-Qa'ida-linked groups are numerous, what is more significant is how these groups justify their attacks as well as their chosen targets, as this reveals these factions' ideologies and means of communication. Al-Qa'ida-linked organizations have attacked any people deemed "agents" of the United States in Iraq. Arab Shi'a, Sunnis, and Kurds have been targeted, regardless of whether they are civilians, militias, or part of the security forces or the government. For example, the al-Qa'ida elements were most likely responsible for the attack against Kurdish KDP supporters in Irbil on February 1, 2004, which killed up to 100 people. The Shi'a have been the primary target of al-Qa'ida-linked groups, as al-Zarqawi has sought to spark a civil war between Sunni and Shi'a in Iraq, thus undermining American attempts to bring stability to the country.

A spate of kidnappings in Iraq began after the 2003 Iraq War, but the primary victims were Iraqis abducted by criminals and ransomed for financial reasons. In April 2004, as U.S. forces conducted simultaneous attacks against insurgents in Falluja and Najaf, the Islamic Army in Iraq and al-Zarqawi-linked groups began kidnapping foreigners in an attempt to prevent their countries of origin from sending troops or participating in Iraq's reconstruction. These two organizations were primarily responsible for the spectacle of kidnapped hostages pleading for their lives in front of a movie camera. These videos were designed for local Iraqi and international consumption, sending simultaneous messages and warnings to those considering aiding the U.S. occupation of Iraq. The threatening nature of the videos was intended to intimidate Iraqis from "collaborating" with the Iraqi authorities. The kidnappings succeeded in deterring international businesses from investing in Iraq and aiding in its reconstruction. Such tactics have appealed to young Muslim audiences, many of whom volunteered to join the ranks to fight the United States in Iraq.

These Sunni Islamist insurgent groups use violence, usually promoted through various media, to terrorize their audiences into submission. Their acts reach the front page of almost every major newspaper and are on the Internet, giving them international attention. They have the ability to broadcast to a wider audience, even to the point where they can affect U.S. elections, induce sympathy with those in the region opposed to the U.S. presence in Iraq, and inspire young Muslims to join the jihad in Iraq.

Intra-Shi'a Rivalries

The problems between Shi'a Islamist factions existed before the fall of Baghdad and the collapse of the Ba'ath regime there. On April 4, 2003, a Shi'a cleric, Abd al-Majid al-Khoei, was flown into Najaf with U.S. help. The United States hoped that the moderate al-Khoei could emerge as the leader of the Shi'a in Iraq, because he could capitalize on the reputation of his father, Grand Ayatollah Abd al-Qasim al-Khoei, who had died under house arrest by the Iraqi government in 1992. However, on April 11 al-Khoei was hacked to death by a mob at the shrine of Imam Ali in Najaf along with Haydar al-Kalidar, a Saddam loyalist who was an official in the Ministry of Religion. During al-Khoei's few days in Najaf, he had tried to mediate between the rival Shi'a groups and had called on the Shi'a to cooperate with the Americans.

Al-Khoei's message was particularly disturbing to Muqtada al-Sadr. Both al-Khoei and al-Sadr held relatively junior rank in the Iraqi Shi'a clergy, but both benefited from deep sympathy for their fathers. According to some residents in Najaf, al-Khoei posed an immediate threat to al-Sadr's desire to emerge as the leader of the Iraqi Shi'a. After al-Khoei's death, rumors began that a group linked to al-Sadr, called the Sadriyyun, were responsible for his death. Although it is unknown whether al-Sadr ordered al-Khoei's murder, an arrest warrant was later issued for him in connection with the death. And regardless of al-Sadr's guilt, one of his rivals was eliminated.

Afterward, the Sadriyyun, the precursor to the Mahdi Army, began a coercive campaign to eliminate all opponents to al-Sadr as part of Muqtada's bid to secure the leadership of the Iraqi Shi'a. On April 13, 2003, two days after al-Khoei's death, the Sadriyyun surrounded al-Sistani's residence and issued an ultimatum demanding he leave Iraq. While al-Sistani enjoyed wide support by virtue of his religious seniority, Muqtada attempted to tap into anti-American sentiment among the Shi'a in order to challenge the grand ayatollah, aiming also to use al-Sistani's Iranian origins against him. However, the Sadriyyun failed to dislodge al-Sistani from

Najaf, as tribesmen loyal to the grand ayatollah came in to restore order in the town.

The other challenge to Muqtada emanated from SCIRI. Its leader, Ayatollah Muhammad Baqr al-Hakim, had returned to Iraq from Iran after the fall of Baghdad to rally support for his group. Unlike Muqtada, al-Hakim was willing to cooperate with the U.S.-sponsored interim Iraqi authority. In August 2003 al-Hakim was killed by a massive car bomb after he delivered the Friday sermon in Najaf. It is believed that foreign jihadists assassinated him, but nonetheless, another rival to Muqtada's leadership was eliminated.

Despite these intra-Shi'a rivalries, in the aftermath of the military phase of the 2003 Iraq War, the Coalition administration in Iraq could rely on the relative stability of the Arab Shi'a in southern Iraq, in contrast to the Arab Sunni heartland, where guerrilla attacks occurred on a nearly daily basis. While various Iraqi Shi'a held opinions critical of U.S. policy in Iraq, these criticisms did not manifest themselves violently. This status quo changed in October 2003, when al-Sadr called for the establishment of a rival government to challenge the Coalition-sponsored Iraqi Governing Council. His declaration was the first direct challenge from within a community that had for the most part acquiesced to the American presence in Iraq.

Shi'a Islamist Violence

After Muqtada called for the establishment of a rival government in October 2003, the pro-Sadr preachers in the mosques of Sadr City proclaimed their area to be an "American-free zone." In addition to forming a proxy government, the Mahdi Army began deploying in the southern cities of Najaf, Karbala, Nasiriyya, and Basra. On

October 17, 2003, the first clash between al-Sadr and the United States began in a relatively undocumented incident, wherein three American soldiers and seven Iraqis belonging to a Karbala faction of the Mahdi Army were killed in a skirmish after the latter refused an order to put down their unlicensed arms. Al-Sadr's faction in Karbala declared that the skirmish was instigated by U.S. troops and that this incident would be the beginning of a larger battle. The CPA failed to appreciate that declaration, and in April 2004 al-Sadr's followers delivered on the aforementioned threat.

The Coalition Provisional Authority, led by Paul Bremer, faced a dilemma over how to handle the growing power of al-Sadr. While the CPA believed that al-Sadr had little following among Iraq's Shi'a, especially among secular-minded members of that community, his followers were nonetheless motivated and disciplined. The CPA had co-opted most of Iraq's Shi'a parties, or at least had induced them not to oppose the U.S. presence. Al-Sadr's group emerged as a focal point for discontented Shi'a opposed to the American occupation of Iraq. Bremer moved against al-Sadr in April 2004, when he ordered the closure of al-Sadr's weekly newspaper *Al-Hawza,* as it allegedly carried articles that incited violence. Afterward, Coalition soldiers were ambushed by the Mahdi Army in the Shi'a holy cities of Najaf and Karbala and in Sadr City. More than a year after al-Khoei's death, the CPA justified its actions against Muqtada, arguing that it was implementing an arrest warrant for al-Sadr in his alleged role in the death of al-Khoie in Najaf.

Intense fighting erupted in southern Iraq between U.S. forces and the Mahdi Army. In June 2004 the clashes ended after a deal that allowed the Mahdi militia to hide most of its weapons. However, the peace did not last, as fighting broke out again two months later, in August 2004. As al-Sistani was in London undergoing medical treatment, Muqtada took advantage of the vacuum and his forces seized the shrine of Imam Ali in Najaf. Battles erupted again between the Mahdi Army and the United States for 22 days, destroying many parts of Najaf. Muqtada finally ceded control of the shrine after striking a deal with al-Sistani. Al-Sistani succeeded where the Iraqi military and U.S. forces had failed, demonstrating that al-Sadr still refused the authority of the interim Iraqi government.

Al-Sistani had always argued that, as a cleric, he and others like him must distance themselves from politics. The events in Najaf demonstrated that he had to intervene in Iraq's politics whether he liked it or not. Nevertheless, the Mahdi Army did not disarm after August 2004, and Muqtada proved his power in the face of American military might. He finally carved himself a position in Iraq's political scene, sending the message that he was a force to be reckoned with. His followers eventually entered politics with SCIRI and Da'wa, and his Mahdi Army reemerged with a vengeance after the events of February 2006.

Intersectarian Violence

The February 22, 2006, bombing of the Askari shrine in Samarra, allegedly conducted by the al-Qa'ida Organization in Iraq, sparked an unprecedented level of sectarian violence. After previous attacks by this group against Shi'a civilians, particularly during their emotive Ashuraa commemorations, Iraq's leaders had called for calm, and the Iraqi Shi'a had generally listened. However, the attack against the symbolic mosque housing Imam Ali al-Hadi was too much of a provocation for the Shi'a Islamist groups and their affiliated militias.

Iraq suffered a spiral of retaliations after the attack. Sunni mosques were targeted and more Shi'a mosques were then attacked, prompting further attacks against other Sunni mosques as well as against civilians. Al-Sistani used his religious authority to call on Iraqis to march and to protest the bombing, but he specifically forbade attacks on Sunni mosques. However, Sunni leaders indirectly criticized al-Sistani, arguing that his call for Iraqis to march led to mob violence against their community.

Al-Sadr declared that his Mahdi Army was willing to defend the Shi'a, implying that he could offer protection when Iraq's official security forces were incapable of doing so. The Iraqis, both Sunnis and Shi'a, would begin to look to the private militias for security. Muqtada had developed a concept of Shi'a populism imbued with notions of Iraqi nationalism that called on Iraqi Shi'a and Sunnis to unite in the face of an occupation. Yet in reality, his romantic notions of Iraqi unity would appear to have been undone by his own militia. As of February 2006, a spiral of violence consumed the center of Iraq, including the capital, where sectarian killings became daily phenomena.

There were also indications that the Mahdi Army's aims clashed with those of the Badr Corps, even though both the Sadr Trend and SCIRI are nominally part of the same Shi'a Islamist coalition. In October 2006 elements of the Mahdi Army seized control of the southern Iraqi town of al-Amara for a few days, after a melee with the local Iraqi security forces dominated by the Badr Corps. These incidents indicate that Muqtada himself may not be firmly in control of all factions of the Mahdi Army, and that it has essentially become the Mahdi Armies. Similar clashes between this army and the Badr Corps had occurred before, and the Mahdi Armies have branched out of

Sadr City and firmly established themselves in the south—challenging forces already established there—raising the harrowing specter of violent intrasectarian Islamist conflicts in Iraq's future.

The fighting after the Samarra bombing took on a life of its own, to the point that al-Zarqawi's and al-Qa'ida's goal of sparking an intersectarian war had become a grim reality. Even al-Zarqawi's death in July 2006 after an American attack near the city of Baquba had no effect in ending the brutal intercommunal fighting, targeting civilians in suicide bombings and sectarian violence until its abatement in the summer of 2007.

The violence, mostly emanating from the central, predominantly Sunni Arab, regions of Iraq, was one of the incentives for the Shi'a Islamists in power to pursue the option of forming a federal entity in the south. In October 2006 the Iraqi National Assembly endorsed a draft law (the Regions Law) that established the mechanisms and procedures of forming separate regions in Iraq. The process of passing this law demonstrates in detail the interaction between Shi'a and Sunni Islamist groups in the Iraqi legislature. The draft law was submitted to the assembly by the United Iraqi Alliance at the behest of the SCIRI and the Da'wa Party. The law would allow any number of Iraqi provinces to unite into a separate region, if accepted in provincial referenda.

The original bill was opposed by anti-federation parties in Iraq, including the Tawafuq Front, the secular Iraqi nationalists, the Iraq List, and even from within the UIA by the Sadr Trend. Their opposition to the draft law was from explicit fear that its enactment might constitute the first step toward dividing Iraq into three regions. However, the Shi'a supporters of the law argued that it would prevent Iraq's regions from ever again being dominated by a central dictator such as Saddam, who punished the Shi'a south after the 1991 uprising there. The passage of this law further illustrates the Shi'a Islamist parties' advocacy of sectarian nationalism, in essence attempting to carve out a Shi'a state in the south, while the Sunni Islamists fear that their sectarian constituencies would ultimately suffer from such a scenario.

During the Iraqi revolt of 1920, Shi'a and Sunni Islamists joined forces to establish an Islamic state and resist British rule. The solidarity witnessed during that time seems to be a far cry from the situation in Iraq today, though it is still similar in many ways. The strongest Islamist groups in Iraq, such as the Shi'a SCIRI and Da'wa, and the Sunni Iraqi Islamic Party, were based outside Iraq for decades, yet they have managed not only to establish roots in the political process but also to essentially dominate it.

At the same time, Iraqi Islamist groups have also developed from within the state during the postwar chaos, evidenced by the Sadr Trend and the Association of Muslim Scholars. The emergence and rise of these Islamist groups demonstrate that in the aftermath of the collapse of the Ba'thist regime, politics have shifted from the power monopoly of Saddam's tribal clan from Tikrit to a plurality of competing ethnic parties and Islamists who are essentially sectarian nationalists. Alternatives such as issue-based parties that cut across ethnosectarian lines, for example, the Iraqi Communist Party, have had little influence in postwar politics. Secular communities among Iraq's Shi'a and Sunni are not organized politically, and they may very well look to the armed Islamist groups, which have the motivation and discipline to provide for their security in the face of growing violence.

There are other factors that indicate that the conflict between Iraq's political Islamist movements will continue, whether in the political arena or on the streets. Sunni Islamist movements fear Iran's growing influence in Iraq and a hidden Shi'a agenda to form a mini-Iraqi Islamic Republic based on the Iranian model. While Iran's influence is a real factor in Iraq, the Shi'a Islamists may not necessarily follow the Islamic Republic's model. The Iraqi Shi'a and their clergy, for that matter, share the same sectarian identity with neighboring Iran, but there have been numerous historical differences between the two. The Iraqi Shi'a have often expressed resentment of Iranian interference in their affairs. In fact, the Iraqi clerical establishment based in Najaf has demonstrated that it has become a rival to the Iranian clerical establishment based in Qom. Therefore, the rise of sectarian nationalism among the Iraqi Shi'a should not be interpreted as an indication of their wishes to emulate the Islamic Republic of Iran. Nevertheless, if the violence between Sunni and Shi'a Islamists were to escalate into a civil war, it would seem likely that Iraqi Shi'a would seek material aid from Iran, as Sunni Islamists would from Saudi Arabia.

The other problem affecting the conflict in Iraq is that some of these Islamist parties, specifically the insurgent groups and the militias, are essentially led by warlords. Warlordism is a ruthless and extractive attitude toward society based on military force and violence. As warlordism is already established in Iraqi society, the conflict will be that much harder to control, as factions will lose their economic base if order is restored. Insurgency in Iraq has proven to be a profitable venture, as Islamist insurgent groups are beginning to evolve from "resistance groups" into parasitic enterprises. There are indications in Iraq that some insurgent groups were financed by wealthy Iraqi businessmen to keep foreign competition from investing in the country. However, these insurgent groups and militias, both Shi'a and Sunni, have now become economically self-sufficient. Some of these Islamist insurgent groups and militias generate revenues through mafia-style "protection taxes," while others conduct kidnappings to raise funds as well.

Thus, the conflict between Islamist groups in Iraq is hardly an ideological disagreement based on different interpretations of the role of religion and state; rather, it has become a conflict based on promoting sectarian and financial interests. Prime Minister Nuri al-Maliki, upon assuming power in December 2005, realized how the religious parties began losing popular legitimacy for pursuing their sectarian interests. He thus began to assume an Iraqi nationalist platform, creating a gap between his Da'wa Party and SCIRI. The January 2009 provincial elections served as a barometer of how the populace viewed the ethnosectarian parties that now dominated Iraq's politics. The success of secular parties running on a platform of providing better local governance proved the population's resentment of the ethnosectarian parties, which have failed to deliver in the areas of providing basic services, such as water and electricity, since assuming power.

BIBLIOGRAPHY

Al-Marashi, Ibrahim. "Iraq's 'Cyber Insurgency': The Internet and the Iraqi Resistance." In *Cybermedia Go to War—Role of Nontraditional Media in the 2003 Iraq War,* ed. Ralph Berenger, 208–25. Spokane, WA: Marquette Books, 2007.
———. "Iraq's Hostage Crisis: Kidnappings, Hostages and the Mass Media." *Middle East Review of International Affairs* 8:4 (December 2004): 1–11.

Al-Qazwini, J. "The School of Najaf." In *Ayatollahs, Sufis and Ideologues: State, Religion and Social Movements in Iraq,* ed. Faleh A. Jabar, 245–64. London: Saqi Books, 2002.
"Al-Sistani Denies Issuing Statement Objecting to Federalism, Constitution." *Al-Najaf News Network,* Open Source Center. GMP20050831538002. August 31, 2005.
"Al-Zarqawi Claims Operations in Iraq, Calls for More Attacks." Open Source Center. GMP20040406000026. April 6, 2004.
"Al-Zarqawi Claims Responsibility for Al-Basrah Port Attack." Open Source Center. GMP20040426000227. April 26, 2004.
"Al-Zarqawi Group's Legal Council Issues Statements Condemning Aiding 'Polytheists,' Participating in Writing Iraqi Constitution." Open Source Center. GMP20050812371008. August 12, 2005.
"Al-Zarqawi Releases New Recording." Open Source Center. EUP20040913000069. September 13, 2004.
"Ansar al-Sunnah Gives Curfew, Warning on Military Targets, Elections; Al-Zarqawi Group Claims Assassination Attempt on SCIRI Leader." Open Source Center. GMP20041229000213. December 29, 2004.
Aziz, T.M. "The Role of Muhammad Baqir al-Sadr in Shi'a Political Activism in Iraq from 1958 to 1980." *International Journal of Middle East Studies* 25:2 (Spring 1993): 207–22.
Cole, Juan. "The United States and Shi'ite Religious Factions in Post-Ba'thist Iraq." *Middle East Journal* 57:4 (Autumn 2003): 543–66.
Eisenstadt, Michael, and Jeffrey White. *Assessing Iraq's Sunni Arab Insurgency.* Washington, DC: Washington Institute for Near East Policy, 2005.
Fuller, Graham E. "Islamist Politics in Iraq After Saddam Hussein." United States Institute of Peace, August 2003: 1–16.
Fuller, Graham, and Rend Rahim Francke. *The Arab Shi'a: The Forgotten Muslims.* New York: St. Martin's Press, 1999.
Hashim, Ahmed. "The Sunni Insurgency in Iraq." *Middle East Institute Perspective.* August 15, 2003. www.mideasti.org/articles/doc89.html.
International Crisis Group, "In Their Own Words: Reading the Iraqi Insurgency: Middle

East Report, 50." February 2006. www
.crisisgroup.org.

"Iraqi Premier-Designate Discusses Iran
Relations, Security, Government Formation."
Open Source Center. GMP20060425533001.
Al-Iraqiyya Television. April 25, 2006.

"Iraqi Sunni Cleric Interviewed on Iraq Situation,
Constitution; Opposes Federalism." Al-Ra'y.
Open Source Center. GMP20050825538007.
August 25, 2005.

"Islamic Party Leadership Sec Gen Discusses
Recent Changes, Political Stance."
Dar al-Salam. Open Source Center.
GMP20060331521006. March 30, 2006.

Jabar, Faleh A. "The Genesis and Development of
Marjaism Against the State." In *Ayatollahs,
Sufis and Ideologues: State, Religion and
Social Movements in Iraq,* ed. Faleh A. Jabar,
61–85. London: Saqi Books, 2002.

———. *The Shi'ite Movement in Iraq.* London:
Saqi Books, 2003.

Khalaji, Mehdi. *The Last Marja: Sistani and the
End of Traditional Religious Authority in
Shiism Policy.* Washington, DC: Washington
Institute for Near East Policy, 2005.

Meijer, Roel. "The Association of Muslim Scholars
in Iraq." *Middle East Report* 237 (Winter
2005): 12–19.

"Mujahidin Brigades in Iraq and Syria Issue
Statement; Al-Zarqawi's Group Claim
Responsibility for Attacks." Open Source
Center. GMP20041028000317. October 28,
2004.

Nakash, Yitzhak. *The Shi'a of Iraq.* Princeton,
NJ: Princeton University Press, 1995.

Nasr, Vali. "Regional Implications of Shi'a
Revival in Iraq." *Washington Quarterly* 27:3
(Summer 2004): 7–24.

Posch, Walter. "A Majority Ignored: The Arabs in
Iraq." In *Looking into Iraq* [Chaillot paper
no. 79], ed. Walter Posch, 25–44. Paris:
Institute for Security Studies, 2005.

Rosen, Nir. *In the Belly of the Green Bird:
Triumph of the Martyrs in Iraq.* New York:
Simon & Schuster, 2006.

Samii, William. "Shia Political Alternatives
in Postwar Iraq." *Middle East Policy* 10:2
(Summer 2003): 93–101.

Schaery-Eisenlohr, Roschanak. "Iran, the Vatican
of Shi'ism?" *Middle East Report* 233 (Winter
2004): 40–43.

"SCIRI Statement Describes Rise, Identity,
Mission of SCIRI Movement in Iraq."
Al-Istiqamah. Open Source Center.
GMP20060823621003. August 22, 2006.

Shanahan, R. "The Islamic Dawa Party: Past
Development and Future Prospects." *Middle
East Review of International Affairs* 8:2
(June 2004): 16–25.

Terrill, Andrew W. *Nationalism, Sectarianism,
and the Future of the U.S. Presence in Post-
Saddam Iraq.* Carlisle, PA: Strategic Studies
Institute, U.S. Army War College, 2003.

———. *The United States and Iraq's Shi'ite
Clergy: Partners or Adversaries?* Carlisle,
PA: Strategic Studies Institute, U.S. Army
War College, 2004.

Visser, Reidar. *Sistani, the United States
and Politics in Iraq: From Quietism to
Machiavellianism?* Oslo: Nupi, 2006.

Israel

Mordechai Kedar

During the 1948 war for Israel's independence, approximately half of the Muslims in Palestine under the British mandate left, some by force and some by their own initiative. Today, these people and their descendants constitute the majority of the Palestinian refugees in Lebanon, Syria, Jordan, and the Palestinian Authority. Those who remained in Israel were left with almost no social or political leadership or religious clergy.

The newly established Jewish state viewed the Muslim minority as a potential threat to its security because many of the borders between Israel and the neighboring, hostile Arab states were mere lines on a map; terrorists (*fida'iyyin*) were thus able to infiltrate Israeli settlements and murder settlers during the first years of the state. Israel responded over the course of the next 18 years—until 1966—by controlling almost all aspects of life for the Arab population through a military government.

The Israeli establishment looked with disfavor upon Islam as a religion and a way of life and did what it could to undermine the Islamic inclinations of the Arab minority: Islam was not included in school curricula in the Arab sector, and devout Muslims were not allowed to become schoolteachers or principals. Mosques received no financial support, Islamic clerics were not part of the civil service, and assets of Islamic endowments (*waqf*) were confiscated by the state as "absentee property." The state did not allow the opening of Islamic institutions such as schools, bookshops, or newspapers. The only tolerated Islamic institution was the Shari'a court system, which dealt only with cases of personal status, mainly marriage and divorce.

Jewish settlements were built on the land of Arab villages whose Muslim inhabitants had fled during the 1948 war, and many mosques and cemeteries that had formerly served those villages were later used for other purposes. Between 1948 and 1967, the Muslim community, politically weak and socially disorganized, used its communal energy to try to survive under the military administration and political marginalization and to build its cultural and social structures. Arab political leaders were recruited by the Jewish political parties as "vote contractors." The "*nakba* generation"—the Arab population in Israel that survived the "catastrophe" of the 1948 war and the founding of the State of Israel—was too weak to establish any Islamic revivalist movement from within its community.

The defeat of Egypt, Syria, and Jordan by

Israel in the 1967 war was a major turning point in the Arab world. Arab nationalism as an ideological movement—led by Gamal Abdel Nasser—seemed to be a total failure, causing many Muslims to look for another focus on which to base their communal ideology. Knowledge of the "Islamic solution" had existed since the late 1920s with the establishment of the Muslim Brotherhood in Egypt. The Brotherhood aspired to free Muslim peoples from Western military occupation and from the political and cultural hegemony of other nations, especially Britain and France. It also sought to revive Islam as the only set of values and laws for the Islamic individual, family, society, and state. The Muslim Brotherhood, with its slogan "Islam is the solution," posed a threat to the stability of the modern Arab states, which tried to enhance their legitimacy by demonstrating adherence to Western ideas such as nationalism, patriotism, or socialism and by adopting Western institutions such as governmental ministries, parliaments, political parties, and elections. The Brotherhood was therefore banned in all these states, and the people identified with it were harshly persecuted.

The 1967 war also erased the borders between Israel and the West Bank and Gaza Strip, allowing Israeli Arab citizens to renew their family ties with their kin in those areas. The freedom of movement between Israel and the newly annexed territories enabled Israeli Muslims to study in Islamic colleges in the West Bank, to visit institutions that were banned in Israel, to buy Islamic books that the Israeli censorship disallowed for import, and to listen to sermons of a nature that was forbidden in Israel. Islam in these territories could now be experienced more authentically compared to how it could be experienced inside Israel before 1967.

The most famous of the Israeli Muslims who joined an Islamic college in Nablus (West Bank) as early as 1969 is Abdallah Nimr Darwish from Kafr Qasim, a village in which 49 villagers had been killed by the Israeli Border Guard in October 1956 for unintentional violation of a curfew order.

During the 1970s, after his return to Kafr Qasim, Darwish conducted courses in Islam for children and adults, teaching them what he had learned in Nablus. He also established a terrorist group, Usrat al-Jihad (the Family of Jihad), whose purpose was to launch attacks on people in malls, bus stations, and streets. The group was uncovered in 1979 before it carried out its first attack, and its members were sentenced to jail for years. While in prison, Darwish reassessed his activity and concluded that jihad with a small group that operates without wide public support and deep ideological preparation is impossible. Therefore, jihad against the Jewish state should start with the re-Islamizing of the Muslim community by spreading Islamic knowledge, awareness, and the sense of being part of the greater Islamic nation. This goal could be achieved only through the reeducation of the Islamic community according to Islam, in order to recover its Islamic character.

Upon his release from prison, Darwish established the Muslim Youth Movement by attracting enthusiastic young people from his and other villages and arranging courses of study for them in Koran, *hadith* (oral tradition), *fiqh* (rulings), history, ethics, and commandments (such as prayer and fasting). These courses were designed for men, women, and youths. The graduates of these courses and of Islamic colleges in the West Bank served as disseminators of Islam within the Muslim sector. Under the banner of the Islamic Movement, they initiated a large variety of activities and institutions: summer camps, welfare organizations, soccer teams, medical clinics, kindergartens, and scholarship funds. The movement helped to solve social problems such as unemployment, created Islamic courts for conflict resolution, supplied food to needy families during Ramadan, and took care of people addicted to drugs and alcohol.

The 1979 Islamic Revolution in Iran and the fall of the shah gave a great push forward to the Islamic Movement in Israel, and its members took part in local Israeli elections. Since the 1984 elections, the movement has successfully worked to increase Muslim representation on the local level. The most significant achievement was the election of Shaykh Ra'id Salah as the mayor of Umm al-Fahm in 1989. These achievements were attributed to the image of the movement as young and revivalist, rooted in the population's original culture, and honest, with no suspicion of having relations with the Jewish establishment and the state authorities. By supporting the Islamic Movement and identifying with it, the people renewed their Islamic identity and pride, achieving also a sense of a communal ability to challenge the Jewish character of the state. Thus, the Islamic Movement embodied a cultural alternative to the state on the personal, familial, and communal levels.

Today, most of those who identify with the Islamic Movement were born after 1948 and have lived in an open environment that allows political activity—even though it may be opposed to the very nature of the state—as long as it is nonviolent. This set of rights has been upheld by the Israeli Supreme Court through a long series of verdicts.

The Islamic Movement

The basic ideology of the Islamic Movement in Israel is that the State of Israel is an illegiti-mate entity since it was established by Jews on what Islam considers to be the holy Islamic soil (waqf) of Palestine. According to the movement's interpretation of Islam, the whole land encompassing Israel irreversibly belongs to Muslims. Jews as well as Christians may live there only under Islamic rule as *al-dhimma* (that is, people who live under Islamic protection). But on a practical level, as long as Israel exists, the Islamic Movement will use democratic means to achieve the goal of eliminating it. A priority in reaching this goal is to exert influence on the Muslim minority in Israel by strengthening its Islamic awareness, shifting its loyalty away from the state, and persuading it that it is a part of the Islamic nation and the Palestinian people. The Islamic Movement also supports fellow Palestinian Muslims in the West Bank and Gaza Strip in their cause against Israel.

The Islamic Movement emphasizes the role of women in preserving the Islamic character of the community. Women are seen both as a threat to the Islamic set of mores and values and as the key to preserving them. By wearing traditional Islamic clothing (*hijab*), which covers the woman from head to toe (except for her face and palms), by avoiding mingling with males, by preserving virginity until marriage, and by educating daughters to follow these mores, Muslim women can ensure the community's continuation. If women abandon these values, the Islamic nature of the whole society will be threatened. Therefore, the Islamic Movement spares no effort in educating girls and women in the path of Islam. They attend special clubs that provide lectures, classes in cooking and art, and social activities. This education aims to give the devoted Islamic woman a social framework to support her commitment to Islam as a consistent set of values and norms of behavior.

In schools and kindergartens established

by the movement, girls and boys learn in separate classes. The Islamic Movement sponsors special publications for women and organizes trips to the al-Aqsa Mosque in Jerusalem. There are groups for mutual aid, especially for young mothers who need help with child care. The movement seeks to persuade women to reject Western lifestyle and dress, to adopt Islamic mores and values, and to serve as role models for others.

The Split in the Movement

During the first Palestinian intifada (1987–1992), the Islamic Movement's leadership was divided over the question of whom it should support in the Palestinian arena: the Palestine Liberation Organization (PLO) or Hamas, the Islamic Resistance Movement. This question became more acute after Israel and the PLO signed the Oslo accords in September 1993 and after the establishment of the Palestinian Authority (PA) in mid-1994. Although the PA was led by the PLO, an organization lacking an Islamic agenda, some leaders supported the PA because it seemed—at that time—to be the embodiment of the Palestinians' aspirations for an independent state. Other leaders backed Hamas because they believed the PA would become just another non-Islamic or anti-Islamic Arab regime. This dispute continued until 1996, when the movement split into two factions. The key issue was whether to participate in Israeli parliamentary (Knesset) elections, which some argued granted recognition to Israel. The Northern faction refused; the Southern faction decided to run candidates.

The "Northern" Faction

The "Northern" faction is so named because its leaders live in the northern part of Israel, though it is active throughout the state. It advocates avoiding participation in state institutions and instead building an independent Muslim society (*mujtama isami*) that would rely only on its own social, cultural, and economic resources.

The Northern faction is more dogmatic and radical than the Southern faction. It is highly critical of Israel, the United States, Western lifestyles, and Muslims whose expressed opinions and behavior are not in keeping with the Islamic ideal. This faction has a strong popular base. Every September, tens of thousands of men and women attend its "al-Aqsa in Danger Rally" (see below). Its leaders have an image of being honest, and their followers make generous donations to the group. In ideology, this faction is close to other radical Islamic organizations and groups that try to undermine the political order in the Arab and Islamic world in order to establish Islamic states on the ruins of the existing states, which—in many cases—are viewed by those radical groups as acting against Islam.

As part of its program, the Northern faction has created a chain of hundreds of nongovernmental organizations (NGOs) that provide their services to the Muslim population in fields such as education, health, welfare, shopping, transportation, public services, sports, entertainment, and finance. The Northern faction implicitly opposes participation in the general elections for the Israeli parliament because that institution represents the Israeli state and participation in Israeli politics is tantamount to recognition of the Jewish state. The leaders of this faction have always supported the Palestinian Hamas movement since its establishment and opposed the PLO-led PA.

The "Southern" Faction

The "Southern" faction is so named because its leadership lives in the center of Israel, south of the Northern leadership. It is more pragmatic and cautious than the Northern faction and refrains from attacking the state as a whole because the faction is represented in the Israeli parliament. As a result, its leaders are sometimes depicted by their opponents as "collaborators with the Zionist establishment." Therefore, to achieve popularity and legitimacy for their positions as Israeli parliament members, members of the Southern faction use the platform offered by the Israeli parliament to deliver fiery speeches against Israel's leadership and policies, even though the speakers are part of the state's governance. This faction has close ties with other Islamic movements and institutions, such as al-Azhar in Egypt, leader of the Islamic forces that support coexistence within that country's government. These movements try to maintain channels of communication with the branches of government in order to promote the Islamic commitment and character of those regimes rather than to undermine their stability.

During the first intifada and since the establishment of the PA, the Southern faction has usually supported the PLO rather than Hamas. This faction's leadership calls upon the Muslim citizens of Israel to take part in the state's political life, especially to vote for the faction's representatives to the Israeli parliament. The Southern faction justifies participation in Israel's politics by citing Islam's universal presence:

> Islam is relevant to all places, all times and all environments, even in the current negative Israeli situation. We—Muslims—should stick to our reli-gion and tradition and use every means given to us in order to promote our cause. The Zionist state—though not our dream—is a given situation under which we have to survive as a Muslim community, and therefore we must take part in Israeli political life and make the best of it. Even if we are a small minority in the Knesset, and always in the opposition, we still have the right to protest and to prove that we are here, on our forefathers' land, and we shall stay forever, even though many in the Jewish majority would like us to leave the country. Our representation in the Knesset is the proof that we—faithful Muslims—are, and will forever be, an integral part of this country.

The dispute over the Islamic legitimacy of these two factions is often harsh. The Northern faction accuses the Southern faction of "collaborating with the Zionists" and describes its Israeli parliament members' salaries as *mal haram* (forbidden money), which—according to Islam—no Muslim is allowed to use. The Southern faction "reminds" the dogmatic one that Shaykh Ra'id Salah's father was an officer in Israel's police forces, as are two of his brothers, and that Shaykh Ra'id's pension as an ex-mayor of Umm al-Fahm is paid from the Israeli government treasury; thus it is no less mal haram than the salaries of the Southern faction's Israeli parliament members.

Leadership

The leadership of the Northern faction includes Ra'id Salah, mayor of Umm al-Fahm between 1989 and 2001. He serves as the head of the al-Aqsa Institution for the Renovation of the Islamic Holy Places, which is the central institution for the movement's activity. Salah was arrested in May 2003 and spent more than two years in jail with four other members of the movement after they admitted taking money from Hamas during the intifada. Another leader, Shaykh Kamal Khatib, was born in the village of Uzayr in northern Israel and lives in Kafr Qana, near Nazareth. He serves as the deputy of Salah and represents the extreme of the Islamic Movement's ideology. Tawfiq Muhammad Jabarin is the editor of the movement's weekly, *Sawt al-Haqq wal-Hurriyya*. Shaykh Hashim Abd al-Rahman became the mayor of Umm al-Fahm in mid-2003. Formerly a spokesman of the Islamic Movement and considered its moderate voice, he tries to bridge differences with the Israeli establishment.

The Southern faction of the Islamic Movement also has several prominent members. Shaykh Abdallah Nimr Darwish is the movement's founder. He lives in Kafr Qasim, in the central part of Israel. Shaykh Ibrahim Abdallah Sarsur holds a degree in English literature and linguistics from Bar-Ilan University. He served as the head of the local authority of Kafr Qasim, the village of his birth, between 1981 and 1998. He has been the head of the Southern faction since 1998 and a member of the Israeli parliament since January 2006. He calls for accepting the State of Israel as a fait accompli and for using Israeli legal and political tools to promote the Islamic cause as much as possible.

Southern faction leader Shaykh Kamal Rayyan was head of the local authority of Kafr Bara between 1984 and 1996. He serves as vice president for the Arab sector of the Union of Local Authorities, the association of mayors and city councils, and as head of the al-Aqsa Organization for the Protection of the Islamic Endowments and Holy Sites, which competes with the paral-lel organization of the Northern faction. He takes part in a discourse group of rabbis and shaykhs for mutual understanding between Jews and Muslims in Israel, and he represents Israel in the Muslim World League. Other leaders of the Southern faction are Abbas Zaqur, who has been a member of the Israeli parliament since 2006, and former Israeli parliament members Abd al-Malik Dahamsha and Tawfiq Khatib.

Activities

The principle of the Islamic Movement's *da'wa* (call to Islam) activity is to perform functions required by the Arab population that are not adequately covered by the Jewish state. Muslims therefore rely on the movement for addressing their needs and resolving their problems. The movement acts through hundreds of local NGOs, each taking care of one kind of activity at its location: kindergartens, charity funds, mosques, clubs, schools, endowments, clinics, grocery stores, bookstores, football teams, and so forth. The movement also arranges trips to Mecca for the hajj (the prescribed pilgrimage between the ninth and thirteenth days of the month Dhul-Hujja) and the *umra* (a pilgrimage at any other time), trips to mosques inside Israel, summer camps for youngsters, and scholarships for students; it also supports organizations that care for drug addicts and alcoholics. The movement collects food for the Palestinians in the West Bank and Gaza Strip, especially during Ramadan and holidays, and pays monthly salaries to imams and preachers in mosques inside Israel.

The Islamic Movement's activities within the Bedouin population in the Israeli southern Negev desert include the building of houses and paving of roads, in clear violation of the state's Planning and Building

Law, thus challenging the state and the Israeli establishment.

Participation in Terror

Both factions of the Islamic Movement emphasize that they abide by Israeli law, which forbids any violence or support of violence. However, people identified with the movement, especially with the Northern faction, have actively participated in terrorist attacks.

On September 5, 1999, two booby-trapped cars exploded in Haifa and Tiberias; their drivers—who lived in the villages of Dabburiya and Mashhad—were known as members of the Northern faction. On September 7, 2001, a man from the village of Abu Snan, who was active in the movement, committed a suicide attack in the Nahariya railway station, killing three and injuring dozens.

During the 1990s, there were charges based on evidence that political murders were carried out in the Wadi Ara area by individuals who were influenced to act violently by the movement's radical message. In addition, during the second intifada (2001–2005), Umm al-Fahm, the center of the Northern faction, became a key infiltration point for West Bank terrorists coming from Israel. Information indicated that they received help from the faction's activists. Shaykh Ra'id Salah, the leader of the Northern faction, and four other members were convicted of transferring money to Hamas at a time when it was engaged in a terrorism campaign against Israel.

Institutions

A number of organizations function under the banner of the dogmatic Northern faction. For instance, the Fatwa Council issues binding religious rulings (fatwas) concerning the special situation of the Muslim community in Israel. The al-Aqsa Institution for the Renovation of the Islamic Holy Places is the central institution for the activity of the movement. It functions to preserve mosques, graveyards, and Islamic holy sites. The Welfare Committee arranges for the collection of contributions of various kinds—money, food, clothes, and schoolbooks, for example—and uses them to support needy people, both inside Israel and in the Palestinian Authority.

Iqra (named after the first word of the Koran, referring to the "call" that descended upon Muhammad) is the organization that serves as the link between the Islamic Movement and Muslim students in Israeli universities. These students are of special importance to the Muslim population because they are viewed as future leaders. In addition, many Muslim youngsters look to students—and later, to university graduates—as role models. If those students and graduates go astray and abandon the Islamic lifestyle, they will have a negative influence on other people, especially the youth. The faction's biggest concern is about the influence that the freewheeling student lifestyle may have on female students from closed village societies who attend urban universities. Iqra publishes a magazine under the title *Iqra*, through which it tries to enhance the commitment of both male and female Muslim students to Islam and to its set of mores and norms of behavior, especially the wearing of traditional clothing for females.

The Modern Research Center is a center for social research dedicated to the scientific exploration of trends in the Arab sector in Israel and to the publication of policy papers about ways to deal with social problems. This center conducts research about the relations between Israel and the

Arab world. The research center's periodical *Regional and International Issues* and other publications discuss unemployment in the Arab sector (where 80 percent of the population are Muslims), the "Roadmap" initiative of 2003, Jerusalem, the 1948 "catastrophe" (*nakba*), and more. The most important research area of the center concerns the level of observance of Islamic religious commandments among young people.

The Northern faction's political position is also revealed in the cultural organizations it operates. The Hira Institution aims to broaden study of the Koran and encourages young people to learn it by heart. This institution arranges activities and functions in honor of those who memorize the Koran and awards them prizes. Al-I'tisam, al-Nur, and al-Hilal are music groups that perform at rallies, weddings, and other private events. The bands' members are all men, since Islamic mores forbid women from performing in public. They use only drums and sell their music on discs and tapes. These musicians are very popular in Islamic communities worldwide, and they travel abroad several times a year to give performances at which donations are collected for the Islamic Movement in Israel and its various activities. Finally, the Islamic Soccer League consists of a chain of soccer teams that do not participate in games with other soccer leagues. Their clothing is more modest (their shorts are especially long), and every game starts with a prayer.

The Southern faction also operates through hundreds of local NGOs; its main organizations are largely similar to those of the Northern faction. It has its own al-Aqsa Organization for the Protection of the Islamic Endowments and Holy Sites (parallel to the al-Aqsa Institution for the Renovation of the Islamic Holy Places). Its Islamic Organization for the Welfare of Orphans and Needy People is parallel to

the Welfare Committee; al-Qalam (The Pen) is parallel to Iqra; and the Islamic Soccer League is parallel to the organization in the Northern faction with the same name. Teams belonging to one Islamic league never play with teams from the other.

Special Events

Since the mid-1990s, the Northern faction of the Islamic Movement has sponsored special events supporting Islam. For example, the movement sponsors rallies commemorating Muhammad's birthday. It has also staged protests against the wars in Afghanistan and Iraq, cartoons published in Europe perceived as mocking Muhammad, and laws banning the hijab in Europe. Every year since 1996, the movement has sponsored the al-Aqsa in Danger Rally in mid-September. This is a mass rally held in the Umm al-Fahm Stadium in commemoration of the attempt by a deranged Australian tourist to burn the al-Aqsa Mosque in September 1969. The rally, which lasts for hours, includes speeches, songs, short plays, and slogans, all condemning the State of Israel and its policies vis-à-vis Islam. The movement claims that the Jewish temple never stood on this site and that the Israeli government is planning to destroy the mosque and build a Jewish temple on its ruins.

During 1996 the Northern faction allocated much effort and invested large sums of money (mostly endowments from the Gulf Emirates) to turn part of the Temple Mount into a great mosque. The movement dug a wide, deep staircase into the lower level of the southern part of the Mount, destroying many antiquities from the Jewish, Roman, Byzantine, Persian, and Islamic eras.

Beginning in 2002, the Islamic Movement also launched rallies, lectures, camps, and workshops in a campaign titled "Our Children Are in Danger." The danger referred to is an attraction toward sexual permissiveness, the Internet, alcohol, drugs, Western clothing, and forbidden relationships instead of prayer. Increasing numbers of Muslims in Israel have indeed changed their patterns of behavior since the establishment of the State of Israel, weakening in their adherence to traditional mores. In the face of these rapid changes, many Muslims in Israel fear that the traditional character of their society is in danger. Parents are concerned that their sons and daughters crave too much permissiveness. The movement's leaders also harshly condemn the connection between local and foreign women's organizations as "cultural imperialism," a Western attempt to efface Islam from the hearts of Muslim women. To counteract these Western influences, the Our Children Are in Danger campaign uses booklets, leaflets, timely publications, and CD and tape music recordings to communicate its message, warning that the young Muslim generation may not have a commitment to the Islamic way of life. A few Muslim leaders, especially Shaykh Kamal Khatib, conclude that Muslim societies are under Western cultural attack. The activities under the banner of this campaign are meant to defend Islam in this crisis.

A Dissident Movement: Jama'at al-Da'wa wal-Tabligh

Since the mid-1990s, a new kind of Islamic organization has been active in the cities of Lod and Ramla, in the center of Israel. Calling itself Jama'at al-Da'wa wal-Tabligh, it refuses to have any connection with the Islamic Movement, since it tries to stay away from politics on any level. Its aim is to promote the status of the mosque in the Muslim's personal life, insisting that the mosque should provide all that the com-

munity needs: mutual aid, culture, and education, all of which were the purview of the mosque in the first period of Islam. The main activities of this group include different aspects of da'wa via active *khuruj* (outreach): lectures on Islamic values, commandments such as prayer and fasting, history, teaching the Koran, encouraging people to learn it by heart, and convincing girls and women to wear Islamic clothing. The group's goal is to bring Muslims who neglect the fulfillment of the commandments to obey these Islamic obligations. Most of the members are of Bedouin origin and therefore tend to be socially marginalized by the other Muslims in Israel. Many of them are "born-again" Muslims who experienced periods of addiction to drugs and alcohol. They have close connections with Muslim groups in India, Malaysia, and Pakistan, sending da'wa and fund-raising delegations to these countries. Their ceremonies have some Sufi characteristics, but they refrain from identifying themselves as Sufis.

Sufi Islam

In certain places in Israel there are "circles" of Sufi groups that gather mainly for *dhikr* (remembrance of god) ceremonies. Their leader is Shaykh Abd al-Salam Mansara from Nazareth, and they operate the al-Qasimi college in the village of Baqa al-Gharbiyya. They usually avoid any connection with the Islamic Movement and tend to stay away from politics.

BIBLIOGRAPHY

Primary Sources

Aba wa-abna (Parents and Children). Publication of the Our Children Are in Danger campaign, Fatwa Council (Northern faction). www.fatawah.com.

Al-Mithaq (The Covenant). Southern Faction Weekly Paper.

Darwish, Abd Allah Nimr. *Al-Islam huwa al-hall* (Islam Is the Solution), n.p., n.d. Vol. 1+2.

———. *Awqifu al-siyasat al-intihariyya li-hukumat al-istitan al-Isra'iliyya* (Stop the Suicidal Policies of the Israeli Settlement Governments), n.p. 2001.

Isharaqa (Sunrise). Northern faction women's monthly.

Sawt al-haqq wal-hurriyya (Voice of Truth and Freedom). Northern faction weekly paper.

Taqrir sanawi li'am, 2001 (Annual Report for 2001). Al-Aqsa Institution for the Renovation of the Islamic Holy Places, n.d.

Secondary Sources

Abu Raya, Ghazi. *Al-Ikhwan al-Muslimun [al-haraka al-Islamiyya] fikr wa-mumarasa* (The Muslim Brotherhood [The Islamic Movement]: Ideology and Implementation). Unpublished, 1991.

Ghanem, Asad. *The Palestinian-Arab Minority in Israel, 1948–2000*. Albany: SUNY Press, 2001.

Israeli, Raphael. *Ha-'Aravim be-Yisrael: Halanu im le-tsareynu?* (The Arabs in Israel: Friends or Foes?). Jerusalem: Eliyahu Gabbay, 2002.

———. *Islamic Radicalism and Political Violence: The Templars of Islam and Sheikh Ra'id Salah*. London and Portland: Vallentine Mitchell, 2008.

———. *Muslim Fundamentalism in Israel*. London: Brassey's, 1993.

Kedar, Mordechai. "Baneynu be-sakana: Ha-hinnukh bir'iyyat ha-tenu'a ha-Islamit be-Yisrael" (Our Children Are in Danger: Education as Viewed by the Islamic Movement in Israel). In *Madrasa: Education, Religion and State in the Middle East*, ed. Ami Ayalon and David J. Wasserstein, 353–81. Tel Aviv: Tel Aviv University, 2004.

———. *Gap of Values: Gender and Family Issues as Source of Tension Between Islam and the West*. Herzliya: The Interdisciplinary Center, 2007.

Khadduri, Majid. *War and Peace in Islam*. Baltimore: John Hopkins University Press, 1969.

Landau, Jacob. *The Arab Minority in Israel, 1967–1991: Political Aspects*. Oxford: Clarendon Press, 1993.

———. *The Politics of Pan-Islam: Ideology and Organization*. Oxford: Clarendon Press, 1992, 1990.

Makarov, Dimitri. *Islam and Development at Micro-Level: Community Activities of the Islamic Movement in Israel*. Moscow: Russian Center for Strategic Research and International Studies, 1997.

Rabinovich, Dani, ed. *Kolot reqa': Ma'amarim 'al ha-'Aravim be-Yisrael* (Background Voices: Essays About the Arabs in Israel). Tel Aviv: Center for Educational Technology, 1994.

Rekhess, Elie. "Ha-tenu'a ha-Islamit be-Yisrael ve-zikatah la-Islam ha-politi ba-sheta-him" (The Islamic Movement in Israel and Its Relations with Political Islam in the Territories). In *Ha-shesa' ha-Yehudi-'Aravi be-Yisrael: Miqra'a* (The Jewish-Arab Rift in Israel: A Reader), ed. Ruth Gabizon and Daphna Hacker, 271–96. Jerusalem: The Israel Democracy Institute, 2000.

———. *Islamism Across the Green Line: Relations Among Islamist Movements in Israel, the West Bank, and Gaza*. Washington, DC: Washington Institute for Near East Policy, 1997.

Rekhess, Elie, and Sara Ozacky-Lazar, eds. *The Status of the Arab Minority in the Jewish Nation State*. Tel-Aviv: Dayan Center, Tel-Aviv University; Konrad Adenauer Program for Jewish-Arab Cooperation, 2005.

Jordan

Curtis R. Ryan

The Islamist movement in Jordan has a history and heritage as old as that of the Hashemite regime itself. While Jordan's main Islamist political party—the Islamic Action Front (Jabha al-Amal al-Islami)—was not legalized until the early 1990s, Jordan's Muslim Brotherhood (al-Ikhwan al-Muslimun) maintained a functional relationship with the Hashemite monarchy, especially throughout the reign of King Hussein (r. 1953–99), who tolerated the Brotherhood as a loyal opposition. Indeed, the relationship between the Muslim Brotherhood and the Hashemite monarchy predates even the reign of King Hussein.

Most strikingly, Islamist activism in Jordanian politics has for more than 60 years emphasized reform, moderation, and democratic participation, rather than revolution, radicalism, and militancy. Yet in November 2005, militant Islamists affiliated with al-Qa'ida carried out a series of deadly bombings in the capital, Amman. The bombers turned out to be Iraqis recruited by the Jordanian dissident and militant Islamist Abu Mus'ab al-Zarqawi. Within hours, Jordan's own Islamist movement had organized anti-al-Qa'ida demonstrations, condemning al-Qa'ida and militant Islamist terrorism. In doing that, Jordan's Muslim Brotherhood and other Islamists demonstrated the sharp—but too often underemphasized—difference between reformist and revolutionary approaches to Islamist activism.

While many Jordanian political parties have either heavily Palestinian or East Bank Jordanian membership, Jordan's Islamist organizations have been among the most ethnically inclusive political movements in the country. Still, many of the leaders of the Muslim Brotherhood and of the Islamic Action Front are ethnically Transjordanian, or from east of the Jordan River, while much of the rank-and-file membership of both the Brotherhood and the party remains Palestinian in origin.

The Muslim Brotherhood in Hashemite Jordan

The Muslim Brotherhood was founded in 1928 in Egypt by the Islamist activist Hasan al-Banna. The organization quickly developed branches throughout the Arab world, calling for a reassertion of Islam into public life in both government and society. While the Muslim Brotherhood established a presence in almost every Arab country, the individual organizations remained mainly autonomous, responding to local and national circumstances. In the case of Jordan, the Muslim Brotherhood was established officially in the kingdom in 1945. From the very beginning, the Brotherhood made clear that its agenda was Islamist but not militant, and this drew the recognition of the state itself. In 1946 King Abdallah I officially recognized the Muslim Brotherhood as a charitable society in Jordan, and the king even presided over the ceremony himself. As Quintan Wiktorowicz points out in his article "Islamists, the State, and Cooperation in Jordan," Abdallah included Muslim Brotherhood secretary Abd al-Hakim ad-Din in his governing cabinet, making this early linkage between the Brotherhood and the Hashemites institutionally clear.

From the outset, the Muslim Brotherhood established a pattern of loyal opposition to the Hashemite regime. By emphasizing reform rather than revolution, the Brotherhood saw itself in partnership with the Jordanian state. As the regime consolidated its rule within Jordan, its moderate political positions, pro-Western foreign policy, and conservative monarchical institutions immediately served as a target for emerging Cold War ideological rifts, as well as emerging regional nationalist and revolutionary tensions. Thus, from the perspective of the ruling regime, this de facto—if not de jure—relationship between the monarchy and its Islamist loyal opposition was intended in part to provide a counter to left-leaning secular oppositional trends ranging from Ba'thism to Nasserism to communism. While the regime attempted to curb leftist, secular, and pan-Arabist political tendencies, the monarchy simultaneously allowed its Islamist opposition to flourish. According to Marion Boubly, this allowed the Muslim Brotherhood to become by far the best-organized group in the Jordanian opposition. As, Wiktorowicz explains in "Islamists,

the State, and Cooperation in Jordan," the moderation of the Muslim Brotherhood also acted as a counter to more radical trends within Islamism, such as the Hizb al-Tahrir (Liberation Party), which had espoused a more revolutionary brand of Islamism, particularly in the 1960s and 1970s.

In an effort to enhance its own Islamic credentials, the Hashemite regime continuously emphasized the direct lineage of the royal family from Muhammad. The Brotherhood too emphasized this level of Islamic legitimacy, in contrast to the many secular, leftist, and nationalist regimes that emerged in the Arab world in neighboring Egypt, Syria, and Iraq.

Beyond more direct political or governmental activism, however, the Muslim Brotherhood has taken very seriously its role as a charitable organization. With regime approval, the Brotherhood established the Islamic Center Charity Society in 1963 and was able to tap into funding generated from the oil economies of the wealthy and socially conservative Arab Gulf monarchies. For several decades now, the Brotherhood has presided over a range of nongovernmental organizations (NGOs). Indeed, the only organization that patronizes and sponsors more social and charitable organizations is the Hashemite royal family itself. The Brotherhood, meanwhile, established across the country an array of schools and health clinics. Perhaps the most well-known landmark of Islamist patronage in the kingdom is the Islamic Hospital in central Amman.

While it is clear that Hashemite relations with the Muslim Brotherhood are almost as old as the Jordanian state itself, this does not mean that the two sides have always agreed. The Muslim Brotherhood did indeed support the monarchy through its wars with Israel, its foiling of various nationalist coup attempts, and even the Jordanian civil war between the Hashemite army and the guerrilla forces of the Palestine Liberation Organization (PLO) in 1970–71. However, the Brotherhood walked a slightly finer line during the various political upheavals triggered by International Monetary Fund (IMF) economic austerity programs, such as the "bread riots" of 1989 and 1996.

Yet at other times, the Brotherhood has directly opposed Hashemite policies, even while maintaining its de facto status as loyal opposition. The Brotherhood adamantly opposed Anwar Sadat's separate peace treaty with Israel, for example, and viewed the Hashemite regime as too mild in its own opposition to Sadat's move. When King Hussein resolutely stood by the shah of Iran in 1979 even as the Iranian Islamic Revolution swept the monarchy away, the Brotherhood again objected to the official Jordanian stance. This rift actually deepened following the 1980 Iraqi invasion of Iran, as Jordan supported Saddam Hussein's Ba'thist Iraq in its war with the Iranian revolutionary regime. For King Hussein, the prospect of an Islamist movement successfully toppling a conservative pro-Western monarch was positively chilling. Yet for the Brotherhood, opposing the only successful Islamist regime in the region was unconscionable.

In more contemporary politics, the major policy rift between the Islamist movement and the Hashemite state has centered on Jordan's own peace treaty with Israel, signed in 1994. The Islamist movement adamantly opposed the treaty at the time, and in the years afterward its opposition only grew. The Brotherhood became a leading part of the broader "antinormalization" movement in Jordan: If the opposition could not prevent the treaty, it could and did manage largely to prevent normalization of

society-to-society relations. Since Islamists had tended to win democratic elections for the leadership positions within most of Jordan's professional associations (for doctors, engineers, lawyers, and pharmacists, for example), the Islamist movement was institutionally positioned to maintain its self-declared ban on working with Israeli counterparts. According to Paul L. Scham and Russell E. Lucas, opposition to the treaty and to normalization of social and economic relations thereafter remains a key component of Islamist policy.

The Islamist Movement, Liberalization, and Elections

Jordan's program of political liberalization began in earnest in 1989 as a direct response to widespread political unrest in the kingdom. An IMF economic austerity program, imposed in an attempt to improve the kingdom's declining economy, had triggered rioting throughout the country. The depth and breadth of the political upheaval had clearly shaken the regime itself, which responded with what Glenn Robinson refers to as "defensive democratization." King Hussein fired the unpopular prime minister, Zayd al-Rifa'i, shuffled the governing cabinet, and announced the return of elections for parliament for the first time since martial law had been declared in the wake of the 1967 war with Israel. Jordan's political liberalization thereafter included several rounds of democratic parliamentary elections (1989, 1993, 1997, 2003), the lifting of martial law (1991), legalization of political parties (1992), and several rounds of revisions regarding government control of media, press, and publications.

Given its long-standing relationship with the regime, and its status as virtually the only officially tolerated form of opposition, the Muslim Brotherhood was perfectly positioned to benefit from the new atmosphere of openness. As parliamentary and electoral life returned to the kingdom, the Brotherhood was able to capitalize on decades' worth of organization.

Yet beyond the Brotherhood, Jordan also has a long tradition of independent Islamist activism in addition to that of organized groups such as the Brotherhood, or their contemporary political party, the Islamic Action Front. Independent Islamists have tended to resist joining organizations like the Muslim Brotherhood, or parties like the Islamic Action Front, which they often accuse of being co-opted by the regime. Among the most well-known independent Islamist activists is the outspoken Layth Shubaylat, who was among those independents serving in the 1989–93 parliament. As Wiktorowicz notes, Shubaylat has argued that institutional Islamism is effectively a tool of the regime, which thereby has managed to "tame" the Muslim Brotherhood.

Shubaylat's strident criticism of the regime, its policies, and the limits of liberalization led to his arrest in 1992. In what amounts to a familiar pattern of curbing dissent in the Hashemite kingdom, Shubaylat was then tried, convicted, and soon thereafter pardoned by the king. While this is nowhere near the level of ruthlessness one finds in other regional regimes, the message and latent threat to the opposition more generally is nonetheless clear. Having a criminal conviction also bars an individual from running for office in the future, and the regime therefore managed to remove Shubaylat from parliamentary opposition permanently.

Unlike Shubaylat and other critics, the Muslim Brotherhood intended not only to compete in the elections, but hoped ultimately to gain positions in government

and reform state policy as well. In the 1989 elections, to the surprise of many in the Hashemite regime, the Muslim Brotherhood secured 22 parliamentary seats (out of a total of 80), while independent Islamists won an additional 12 seats. With a bloc of 34 seats in parliament, the Jordanian Islamist movement elected one of its most influential leaders, Dr. Abd al-Latif Arabiyyat, to be speaker of the house. Prime Minister Mudar Badran, responding to the Islamist electoral victories, invited several Islamists into his government. This, however, led to a rift within the movement regarding a very important proposition: Should Islamists serve in the government at all?

Hard-line members of the Islamist movement argued that this amounted to a kind of capitulation to the state, and in effect to a contamination of the movement itself. Many left the Brotherhood over this issue, becoming part of Jordan's long-standing tradition of independent Islamist thought and activism. However, the more mainstream members of the Brotherhood saw serving as cabinet ministers as a well-deserved reward for years of organizational effort. As Wiktorowicz writes in *The Management of Islamic Activism,* among this latter group were Abdallah Akayla (minister of education), Yusuf al-Azm (minister of social development), Majid al-Khalifa (minister of justice), Zayd al-Kaylani (minister of *awqaf* and religious affairs), and Adnan al-Jaljuli (minister of health).

With five cabinet portfolios and leading a bloc of 34 parliamentary seats, the Muslim Brotherhood had accomplished an astounding political victory. This was tempered rather quickly, however, when public opinion turned against many of the measures that the Islamist ministers imposed. The most notorious of these included a failed attempt to ban alcohol in the kingdom, sexual segregation in some governmental office buildings, and a ban (later rescinded) on fathers watching their daughters in competitive sports. It is important to note here that this too was part of the state's strategy. While the Hashemite regime had no way of knowing what specific policies would be implemented, regime officials were certain that the Islamist ministers—if given room to maneuver—would, in fact, rile public opinion against their various measures. The idea, in short—as explained to me in a March 1993 interview with Islamist activists and Jordanian government officials in Amman, Jordan—was to ease tensions by including the opposition in government, but also to allow them to fall flat in the face of a backlash in public opinion.

In any event, the government itself was dissolved merely six months later and replaced with an equally short-lived cabinet led by new prime minister Tahir al-Masri, a more liberal and progressive politician. This time, the Brotherhood rejected the few token ministries it was offered and instead worked to oust the Masri government in a no-confidence vote. While the vote never carried, Masri's position had become quickly unworkable, and once again the government was replaced, as Masri himself explained in March 2, 1993, and July 14, 2001, interviews with me.

The regime clearly remained alarmed at the level of Islamist influence and electoral success, however, and government efforts thereafter turned on limiting Islamist successes in future elections. The regime therefore responded to the Islamist victories with a sweeping change of the electoral system: changing to a one-person, one-vote structure with modified electoral districts. While the earlier system, which allowed Jordanians to vote for multiple members of parliament (depending on how many

would represent the given district), had perhaps exaggerated Islamist strength, the new system was designed to do precisely the reverse. As the al-Urdun al-Jadid Research Center's *Guide to Party Life in Jordan* (1993) notes, in the 1993 elections, which followed the legalization of political parties in the kingdom, the Muslim Brotherhood did not directly participate, returning instead to its traditional role as a political, social, and charitable movement. Instead, many Brotherhood members, and even Islamists outside the Brotherhood, formed and joined the Islamic Action Front (Jabha a-Amal al-Islami, IAF). The IAF over time became, in effect, the political party wing of the Muslim Brotherhood. As such, the IAF participated in the 1993 elections but secured only 16 parliamentary seats, while independent Islamists dropped to a mere six seats. According to Abla Amawi, this dropoff in representation was more the result of changed electoral law than a backlash against Islamist government policies.

Following the drop in electoral strength in the 1993 elections, the Islamist movement demanded a repeal of the newer electoral system. They correctly argued that the districts themselves were unbalanced, overrepresenting more conservative, pro-regime rural areas and underrepresenting more urban—and more Palestinian—areas that had provided key bases of support for Jordanian Islamism. When the government refused to comply with Islamist demands to change the electoral system, the IAF led a broad-based opposition coalition (including leftist and pan-Arab nationalist parties) in an 11-party boycott of the 1997 elections.

The resulting parliament naturally proved to be overwhelmingly conservative, nationalist, and pro-Hashemite. With only six independent Islamists in the new parliament, and none whatsoever from the IAF,

Islamist strength and strategy shifted from parties and parliament, toward the professional associations instead. As Jillian Schwedler points out in *Faith in Moderation,* Islamist candidates won the leadership posts of almost every professional association in the kingdom (engineers, pharmacists, medical doctors), thereby creating a basis for Islamist political activism outside the halls of parliament, but very much within Jordanian civil society.

King Abdallah, the Islamist Movement, and Liberalization

In 1999 King Hussein of Jordan died after a long battle with cancer. He was succeeded by his eldest son, Abdallah, who became King Abdallah II. While the succession itself went smoothly and peacefully, the same could not be said for regional politics and hence Jordan's immediate political environment. With the emergence of the second Palestinian uprising, or intifada, in 2000 and preparations looming for a second U.S. war on Iraq, the new Jordanian regime decided to put off part of the political liberalization process by postponing parliamentary elections scheduled for November 2001.

Yet in 2003, after two years of postponements, Jordan held its fourth round of parliamentary elections since the start of the liberalization process in 1989. The 2003 elections were the first under King Abdallah II and marked the return of the opposition to electoral politics. The Islamists and other opposition parties had boycotted the 1997 polls. The new elections took place in the context of a new electoral law, increasing the size of parliament to 110 members, including a new minimum quota of six seats for women. The Islamist movement had originally opposed the idea of a women's quota, but it later turned out to benefit from

it. Seventeen IAF members gained parliamentary seats overall. Interestingly, the IAF parliamentary deputies included Hayat al-Musani, the first woman elected to parliament under the quota system. In addition to the IAF bloc, five independent Islamists were also elected to parliament.

While the IAF remained focused on its own Islamist political agenda, most legislation continued to emerge from the government itself, with the parliament serving as a debating forum that usually provided a legislative stamp of approval for government initiatives. The IAF had no success in achieving its broadest policy goals. These unfulfilled goals included the implementation of Shari'a (Islamic Law), preventing normalization of ties with Israel, and ultimately abrogating the peace treaty entirely.

Still, the IAF did align itself with more secular conservative forces to block repeated government attempts to change Jordan's laws regarding "honor crimes," that is, crimes purportedly linked to family honor in which men kill female relatives who are believed to have in some way shamed the family. Jordan's monarchy itself has endorsed attempts to change the kingdom's otherwise lenient pattern of sentencing for these crimes. However, the Islamist movement, in temporary alliances with other social conservatives in parliament, has consistently and successfully thwarted attempts to change the legal system regarding crimes of honor.

Salafists, Jihadists, and "Jordan's 9/11"

While the Muslim Brotherhood and the IAF are the best-organized, most recognizable faces of Islamism in Jordan, there also remain more subtle and even underground forms. Jordan's Salafiyya movement, for example, has grown steadily since the 1980s. Salafism today usually refers to a more hard-line, puritanical approach to Islamic revivalism. Some versions of Salafism (although not all) have turned toward militancy, terrorism, and jihadist activism.

In the Jordanian case, as in many other countries, the rise in Salafi activity coincided with the end of the Afghani mujahidin war against the Soviet occupation of Afghanistan. This is, in short, a much more recent phenomenon than the rise of the Muslim Brotherhood. Many credit the rise of a Salafi alternative (to both the Jordanian state and its more established Islamist opposition) to the arrival in Jordan of the influential Salafist Shaykh Muhammad Nasir ad-Din al-Bani. Shaykh al-Bani fled to the kingdom from Syria in 1979, as the Ba'thist state was deepening its crackdown on Sunni Islamists in Syria. As Wiktorowicz writes in "The Salafi Movement in Jordan," the arrival of al-Bani "precipitated an explosion of Salafi activism," as al-Bani essentially served as a "focal point" for Islamists seeking a return to what they viewed as a more authentic and traditional approach to Islam.

Still, while the Salafi alternative has increased in strength in Jordan over time, it also remains of at least two minds. Some Salafists believe that radical change is needed in Jordan, but they do not necessarily believe that jihad is either viable or appropriate. For others, jihad is the only alternative. Not surprisingly, these latter Salafists include many returned veterans of the Afghan wars. The jihadist tendency within the Jordanian Salafi movement sees itself as *takfiri*, that is, made up of those who declare the Hashemite state as *kafir*—unbelievers against whom jihad is no less than a duty. These Salafist-jihadists are influenced not only by Shaykh al-Bani, but

also by the earlier writings of thirteenth-century Islamist Ibn Taymiyya and twentieth-century Egyptian Islamist Sayyid Qutb, as Wiktorowicz points out in "The Salafi Movement in Jordan."

Wiktorowicz has argued that while the Muslim Brotherhood and Islamic Action Front rely on formal organization and participation in political parties, professional associations, and charities, the Salafi movement has instead relied on informal networks for recruitment and activism. He further argues that many of Jordan's religious scholars, the ulama (Islamic clergy), are themselves Salafists. The informal networks, meanwhile, allow Salafists to at least attempt to continue their activism under the radar of state surveillance. Still, despite the rise in Salafiyya ideas and activity, most of Jordan's Islamist movement remains more mainstream, reformist, and democratic, while the major terrorist threats have come largely from foreign al-Qa'ida militants.

The worst terrorist attack in Jordan occurred in November 2005, as noted at the outset of this chapter, as al-Qa'ida suicide bombers struck three luxury hotels in central Amman, killing 60 people—mostly Jordanians—and injuring more than 100. The IAF and the Muslim Brotherhood were among the first to respond to the tragedy by organizing anti-al-Qa'ida demonstrations in the capital. This very fact underscores a key feature of modern Islamist politics: that is, that there is a marked difference between moderate mainstream pro-democratic forms of Islamism (such as Jordan's Muslim Brotherhood and Islamic Action Front) and militant global jihadist organizations (such as al-Qa'ida). The terrorists struck on November 9, 2005—hence, it was literally "Jordan's 9/11"—and all were ethnic Iraqis sent to Jordan merely days earlier on the orders of Abu Mus'ab al-Zarqawi. Zarqawi, formerly a Jordanian national, had become the self-styled leader of al-Qa'ida in Iraq. According to a November 2005 International Crisis Group report, the attack, it seems, was meant to punish Jordan for its closeness to the United States, among other grievances against the Hashemites.

Jordanian intelligence services had claimed to have previously foiled no fewer than 150 other plots to public safety and security from militant Islamists affiliated with al-Qa'ida. Yet all earlier plots had involved Jordanian nationals, while the November 2005 bombings were carried out by Iraqi suicide bombers. Al-Qa'ida militants had, however, earlier struck on a more limited scale, including firing Katyusha rockets in Jordan's port city of Aqaba in March 2006, killing one Jordanian soldier.

The scale and barbarity of the Amman bombings, each of which targeted a wedding party taking place in a major (Western) hotel chain in central Amman, seemed to transform Jordanian public opinion regarding Islamist militancy and terrorism. In a poll conducted by the University of Jordan's Center for Strategic Studies, responses to the same questions varied greatly between 2004 and December 2005—one month after the attacks. In the 2004 survey, 68 percent of Jordanians polled viewed al-Qa'ida as a "legitimate resistance organization." In 2005 that number had declined to 20 percent. Similarly, in 2004 only 10.6 percent labeled al-Qa'ida as a terrorist organization, while in 2005 that number had increased to 48.9 percent. As indicated by Fares Braizat in *Post-Amman Attacks*, when the pollsters added a distinction and asked specifically about the Zarqawi-led organization within al-Qa'ida, 72.2 percent of Jordanians saw it as a terrorist organization rather than a legitimate resistance organization.

Despite the hostility of most Jordanians,

including Islamists, to the terrorist attacks, the Islamist movement in parliament nonetheless soon found itself squaring off with the government following a major cabinet reshuffle. The new government made clear that the monarchy had shifted entirely to security mode. King Abdallah dismissed the more liberal prime minister Adnan Badran and replaced him with Ma'ruf Bakhit, Jordan's former ambassador to Israel and very much a security hawk. Conservative royalists retained the speakership posts in both the lower house of parliament (under Abd al-Hadi al-Majali) and the upper house or senate (under former prime minister Zayd al-Rifa'i). Neither man was known for his sympathies toward Islamists, or toward Palestinians for that matter.

Aware that security concerns had provided the pretext for a host of earlier deliberalization moves over the years, Islamist members of parliament urged the regime not to use the tragedy of the bombings as an excuse to issue new martial laws. The government, for its part, declared that counterterrorism would be a key policy focus and it called for "preemptive war" specifically on militant forms of Islamism. Although the Muslim Brotherhood and IAF were not in any way involved in violent activities, they nonetheless feared that new security measures might be used against them. In January 2006, seemingly on cue, the government issued charges against one of the IAF's leaders, Jamil Abu Bakr, for "harming the dignity of the state." The charges stemmed from articles on the IAF Web site that criticized the government tendency to appoint officials based mainly on connections (*wasta*) rather than expertise or parliamentary consultations. As I wrote in "Jordan: Islamic Action Front Presses for Role in Governing," the charges were dropped the following month, but the sense of harassment remained.

The regime meanwhile moved still further in its efforts to rein in more militant Islamism, including issuing a new law restricting preaching in mosques and the issuing of fatwas only to government-approved ulama. Finally, perhaps the most ominous sign was the new and decidedly elastic antiterrorism law that seemed to greatly expand the roles, powers, and influence of the intelligence and police services in daily life.

The Hamas Factor in Jordanian Politics

With the sweeping victory of Hamas in Palestinian legislative elections in January 2006, a "Hamas factor" appeared to have reinvigorated Jordan's already well-organized and well-established Islamist movement. With its emphasis on anticorruption in its political campaign, as well as its maintenance of charities, clinics, and schools, Hamas was in many ways adopting the strategies and tactics of Jordan's IAF and Muslim Brotherhood. However, unlike Hamas, the IAF and Muslim Brotherhood do not have an armed wing, and instead focus on civilian party and interest-group organization and remain very much a part of the pro-democratization movement in the kingdom. Hamas representatives were expelled from Jordan in 1999, when the kingdom severed ties and closed their offices.

Now, however, with their victory in the Palestinian elections, the IAF called on the Jordanian government to restore ties and recognize their achievement. Jordan's Islamists were also inspired by the relative success of Muslim Brotherhood candidates (running as independents) in Egyptian parliamentary elections, as well as the rise of Islamist activ-

ists to power in neighboring Iraq. Jordanian Islamists, like their counterparts elsewhere, campaigned on platforms of clean government and inclusion, and their credibility in this area benefited from their already established reputation for civic mindedness, based on the extensive Muslim Brotherhood network of charitable organizations.

In the midst of this Islamist euphoria over the inspiring electoral successes of others, however, the IAF and Muslim Brotherhood did nothing to endear themselves to an already suspicious Hashemite regime when Islamist activists chose to attend the Arab political parties' conference held in Damascus in March 2006. Syrian president Bashar al-Asad hosted the conference on behalf of Syria's Ba'thist regime. Thus Jordanian Islamists attended an event hosted by the party that banned Islamists from Syria itself. The point was not lost on Syria's exiled Muslim Brotherhood, which lambasted the IAF for its lack of solidarity and questionable judgment.

The IAF meanwhile also found itself attacked by the Jordanian government, when Syrian President Asad mockingly referred to the Hashemite regime's "Jordan First" policy. Asad coupled "Jordan First" with Lebanon's recently unveiled "Lebanon First" agenda, suggesting that such narrow visions meant that surely the United States or Israel lurked as a close second. While the Jordanian press castigated the Syrian regime for arrogance and a long list of other things, the Hashemite regime remained angered that the Jordanians present at the speech had either failed to refute Asad's comments, or worse, had actually applauded them. This amounted to a minor tiff, however, both between Jordan and Syria and between the monarchy and the IAF, as the larger implications of the Hamas victory continued to influence Jordanian politics profoundly.

For many Islamists, the Hamas victory was inspiring, but it was also a reminder of their comparative limitations. Hamas's electoral win translated immediately into a new Hamas-led government and cabinet. Within Jordan, in contrast, although 17 years of Islamist electoral strategies had indeed translated to some success, there was no chance whatsoever of forming an IAF government.

After the Hamas victory, however, a new boldness entered the rhetoric of some IAF leaders, who now announced their new political program. Some aspects remain cornerstones of earlier programs: fully implementing Shari'a, abandoning the peace treaty with Israel, and ending normalization of relations with the Jewish state. Yet others included demands to stop attempting to "downsize" the Islamist movement through electoral laws designed to minimize Islamist representation. As reported by *al-Hayat*, Azzam al-Hunaydi, the leader of the IAF bloc within parliament, minced no words when he stated flatly, "That which faces the Islamic movement—in terms of attempts at marginalization and exclusion, tailoring of laws and the policy of ceilings—will not last indefinitely." He may have caught the attention of Jordan's security-focused regime when he added even more starkly that "the time of downsizing, marginalization, showing scorn for people and being captive to foreigners will end soon."

In the view of Hunaydi and many other Islamist activists, Jordan remained committed to the wrong paths in both domestic and foreign policy. The IAF therefore presented itself as an alternative approach, and one that was ready to govern. The "Hamas effect," in short, had provided the Jordanian Islamist movement with a renewed optimism, as Thanassis Cambanis wrote in the *Boston Globe*.

IAF deputies charged that in freer and fairer elections, they might win 40 to 50 percent of the vote. With Islamists rising to prominence and power through nearby elections—Hizballah in Lebanon, various Islamist Shi'a parties in Iraq, and Hamas in the Palestinian territories—Jordanian Islamists argued that they might now be poised to win an outright majority in parliament. Given Jordan's heavily gerrymandered electoral districts, which favor rural over urban districts (and hence underrepresent predominantly Palestinian and Islamist areas of the kingdom), the IAF optimism may be unfounded. Even aside from gerrymandered districts, the party has never received close to half the overall votes. Yet, under a new and more even-handed electoral law, they would nonetheless be likely to do very well. Indeed, according to the *Jordan Times*, IAF and Muslim Brotherhood officials made very clear their overall view of the current system when they repeatedly called on the regime to issue a new "*democratic* elections law" (emphasis added).

In addition to concerns about the electoral system, Jordanian Islamists insisted that governments should be drawn from parliament in a truer model of a parliamentary system, rather than royally appointed pending only the formality of parliamentary approval. IAF deputies remained certain that their "street" support greatly exceeded their actual parliamentary power. In the wrangling within Jordanian politics over the next and "final" law on parties and elections, the IAF insisted that hinted bans on religiously based parties remain off the table. At the same time, a more truly democratic election law remains very much an IAF interest, so that the alleged Islamist street majority might one day become a governing coalition.

This issue of linking elections to actual governance was a key sticking point in the struggle between the government and its opposition when they bargained over the ground rules for the next rounds of parliamentary elections. Yet in effect, the government and its opponents were also debating the future nature of the Jordanian state itself.

The Future of Islamism and the Jordanian State

For more than 60 years, the Hashemite monarchy and its mainstream Islamist movement have maintained a cooperative relationship. Under the King Abdallah II regime, however, a series of deliberalization measures, and possibly hopes by the movement itself for greater success, threatened to erode that long pattern of Islamist loyal opposition to the monarchy and the state. The monarchy saw these measures as necessary, given its extreme and even violent regional circumstances. Jordan remained wedged between violence in neighboring states: that is, between a Palestinian uprising and Israeli military responses to the west, while to the east, Iraq was mired in war, occupation, insurgency, and civil strife.

After the 2005 al-Qa'ida bombings in the Jordanian capital itself, the regime's already established security emphasis was strengthened. The danger, however, remained that the regime's security concerns were effectively undermining Jordan's once heralded process of political liberalization and democratization. The regime's tolerance for Islamist dissent, for example, was limited indeed. When several IAF members of parliament paid a condolence call to the family of the late Abu Mus'ab al-Zarqawi, they were soon arrested and tried for crimes against the state. The arrested members of parliament included Ali Abu Sukkar, Ja'far Hurani, and Muhammad Abu Faris. As reported by the *Jordan Times,* Abu Faris

angered the regime still further (and indeed infuriated Jordanian public opinion as well) when, in an interview with the satellite television station al-Arabiyya, he stated that Zarqawi was a martyr, but the victims of the Amman bombings were not. The three deputies were convicted of inciting terrorism, but in a very familiar and traditional Jordanian pattern of reining in dissent, they were later pardoned and released.

Many Islamists read this episode as merely a small part of an overall campaign against them. Moreover, while Abu Faris is indeed more radical than most Islamists active in Jordanian public life, the regime's actions seem to be directed at more than individuals and perhaps against the IAF and the Muslim Brotherhood more broadly. While the regime would reject this interpretation, many in Jordan's mainstream Islamist movement would not. The latter group, therefore, at times wonders if the long-standing cooperation between reformist Islamism and the monarchy is in decline.

BIBLIOGRAPHY

Abdallah, Sana. "Al-Qaida Still Haunts Jordan." United Press International, March 5, 2006.

Amawi, Abla. "The 1993 Elections in Jordan." *Arab Studies Quarterly* 16:3 (1994): 15–27.

Boulby, Marion. *The Muslim Brotherhood and the Kings of Jordan.* Lanham, MD: Rowman and Littlefield, 1999.

Braizat, Fares. *Post-Amman Attacks: Jordanian Public Opinion and Terrorism.* Amman: Public Polling Unit, Center for Strategic Studies, 2005.

Cambanis, Thanassis. "Jordan's Islamists See a Path to Political Power." *Boston Globe,* March 21, 2006.

Clark, Janine, "The Conditions of Islamist Moderation: Unpacking Cross-Ideological Cooperation in Jordan," *International Journal of Middle East Studies* 38 (2006): 539–60.

————. *Islam, Charity, and Activism: Middle-Class Networks and Social Welfare in Egypt, Jordan, and Yemen.* Bloomington: Indiana University Press, 2003.

Dalil al-hayat al-hizbiyya fi al-Urdun: Hizb Jabha al-Amal al-Islami (Guide to Party Life in Jordan: The Islamic Action Front Party). Amman: al-Urdun al-Jadid Research Center, 1993.

International Crisis Group. "Jordan's 9/11: Dealing with Jihadi Islamism." *Middle East Report* no. 47 (November 2005).

Robinson, Glenn. "Defensive Democratization in Jordan." *International Journal of Middle East Studies* 30:3 (1998): 387–410.

Ryan, Curtis R. "Elections and Parliamentary Democratization in Jordan," *Democratization* 5:4 (1998): 194–214.

————. "Jordan: Islamic Action Front Presses for Role in Governing." *Arab Reform Bulletin,* February 2006.

————. *Jordan in Transition: From Hussein to Abdullah.* Boulder, CO: Lynne Rienner Press, 2002.

————. "Peace, Bread, and Riots: Jordan and the International Monetary Fund." *Middle East Policy* 6:2 (Fall 1998): 54–66.

Ryan, Curtis R., and Jillian Schwedler. "Return to Democratization or New Hybrid Regime? The 2003 Elections in Jordan." *Middle East Policy* 11:2 (2004): 138–51.

Scham, Paul L., and Russell E. Lucas. "'Normalization' and 'Anti-Normalization' in Jordan: The Public Debate." *Israel Affairs* 9:3 (2003): 141–64.

Schwedler, Jillian. *Faith in Moderation: Islamist Parties in Jordan and Yemen.* Cambridge, UK: Cambridge University Press, 2006.

Taraki, Lisa. "Islam Is the Solution: Jordanian Islamists and the Dilemma of the Modern Woman." *British Journal of Sociology* 46:4 (1995): 643–61.

Wiktorowicz, Quintan. "Islamists, the State, and Cooperation in Jordan." *Arab Studies Quarterly* 21:4 (1999): 4–12.

————. *The Management of Islamic Activism: Salafis, the Muslim Brotherhood, and State Power in Jordan.* Albany: State University of New York Press, 2000.

————. "The Salafi Movement in Jordan." *International Journal of Middle East Studies* 32:2 (2000): 219–26.

Williams, Daniel. "Political Islam's Opportunity in Jordan." *Washington Post,* April 13, 2006.

Kuwait, Qatar, the UAE, Bahrain, and Oman

Sean Foley

Sunni Muslims in the Persian Gulf states (Bahrain, Kuwait, Oman, Qatar, Saudi Arabia, and the United Arab Emirates, or UAE) have greatly facilitated the expansion of Islamism beyond the Persian Gulf in two ways. First, they have provided significant financial support to Islamist groups and nongovernmental organizations promoting Islamist values and public objectives. Second, Gulf states have granted asylum to Islamists and allegedly permitted Islamists— including those accused of committing terrorist attacks—to transit their territories and use their financial institutions.

For example, the Muslim Brotherhood's leading ideologist, Yusuf al-Qaradawi, and other leading Islamist figures have lived and taught in this region for years. Gulf nationals have played important roles in Islamist causes: the wars in Afghanistan and Chechnya, the insurgency in Iraq, and al-Qa'ida terrorist attacks. Two of the September 11 hijackers were UAE nationals, and even members of the Bahraini royal family have been detained at the U.S. naval base at Guantanamo Bay, Cuba, for allegedly fighting alongside Taliban fighters in Afghanistan. There have also been a few terrorist attacks in Qatar and the UAE. Islamist conspiracies have been uncovered in Oman, the UAE, Qatar, and Bahrain.

In addition, Islamists participate in the cultural life of the Gulf states and regularly run candidates in elections. Qaradawi is a household name in the Gulf and the wider Arab world because of his weekly phone-in program, *Shar'ia wal-Hayyat* (Islamic Law and Life), on the Qatar-based al-Jazeera satellite network.

While the five smaller Gulf states—Bahrain, Kuwait, Oman, Qatar, and the UAE— share conservative Sunni Muslim and tribal cultural norms, have large expatriate populations, and benefit from hydrocarbon exports, they also host a variety of peoples, cultural traditions, and socioeconomic structures. Four factors in particular have shaped the emergence of Islamists in these states: the diversity of the Muslim population, the influence of Wahhabi-Hanbali ideas and those of the Saudis in general, consultative political institutions, and the relative historical power of governments vis-à-vis their peoples.

Often, Islamist groups have benefited from the implicit support of government officials, who wished to balance out the influence of merchants, leftists, Shi'a, secularists, Nasserists, and Arab nationalist groups. The presence of these groups is testimony to the fact that these states were not immune to the many shockwaves emanating from events elsewhere in the region. Finally, it is important to remember that Gulf Islamists are part of a tradition of Islamic-inspired political activism in the area that goes back decades and is linked to the Muslim Brotherhood, an organization that became active in Kuwait and in other Gulf states in the 1950s.

Kuwait

Situated at the intersection of Iraq, Iran, and Saudi Arabia, Kuwait has long served as a crossroads of various peoples and traditions. The peoples living in what is today Kuwait were among the earliest converts to Islam in the seventh century, and it is estimated that 85 percent of the population today is Muslim. Seventy percent of Kuwaiti Muslims are Sunni and adhere to the Maliki school of Sunni Islamic jurisprudence; the rest are Shi'a Muslims. The modern state of Kuwait traces its origins to the eighteenth century and was nominally tied to the Ottoman Empire until the late nineteenth century. From that time until independence in 1961, Kuwait was a protectorate of Great Britain.

A key turning point in Kuwaiti history occurred in 1938, when petroleum was discovered there. Not only did proceeds from the export of oil fabulously enrich a previously destitute society, but they also empowered Kuwait's monarchy, historically an extremely weak political institution. For decades, Kuwaiti rulers had relied on the financial and political support of Kuwaiti merchants to govern and maintain power. With the advent of massive proceeds from oil, the rulers of Kuwait freed themselves of their financial and political dependence on Kuwait's merchants.

At the same time, Kuwait's rulers sought to co-opt the merchants and win supporters —Bedouins, Shi'a, poor Kuwaitis, and progressives—through government largesse and by forging alliances in Kuwait's National Assembly. These measures were also meant to contain Arab nationalism, popular among the large expatriate population, from spreading to Kuwaitis. While the Kuwaiti government succeeded in this effort, it discovered that its new supporters, once politicized, were difficult to control. By 1976 there was vocal opposition in the parliament that challenged government positions on a wide variety of sensitive domestic and foreign policy issues. Particularly unnerving was the fact that the assembly was tied to opposition groups outside of Kuwait, including leftist groups participating in Lebanon's civil war. Given Kuwait's large expatriate Palestinian population, government leaders feared that an alliance between leftist Palestinians and Kuwait's opposition might threaten the monarchy's hold on power. In response, the Kuwaiti government officially dissolved the parliament in 1976 and sought to assist groups that did not oppose the decision.

One segment of Kuwaiti society that benefited greatly from the government's new policy constituted the then passive and largely apolitical Islamic societies of Kuwait. Since the emergence of Arab nationalism and Nasserism in the 1950s, Islamic institutions had been marginalized politically and socially. Few Kuwaiti women wore the *hijab* (headscarf) in the 1970s, restrictions on the mixing of sexes were rarely enforced, and limitations on women's employment and other public activities were receding. Female students studied alongside their male colleagues at Kuwait University. However, as Shafeeq Ghabra writes, after the government appointed the head of the Islam or Social Reform Society (al-Islam al-Ijtama'i),

Yusuf al-Hajj, to be minister of pious endowments, Islamist groups in Kuwait worked to Islamicize their society and gain power.

As Islamists embarked on their political program, they benefited from the surge in religious fervor in Kuwait and throughout the Arab world following Israel's victory over secular Arab regimes in the 1967 Arab-Israeli War. They also benefited from the events of the 1979 Islamic Revolution in Iran, where the shah's secular government could not check a mass popular movement headed by a Muslim cleric, Ayatollah Ruhollah Khomeini. In the eyes of Kuwait's Islamists, the Iranian Revolution revealed Islam's relevance to the modern world and further reinforced Arab doubts about the promise of secular ideologies. Equally important, Islamists received informal support from the Kuwaiti government, which hoped to capitalize on Kuwaitis' renewed interest in Islam.

Within this new milieu, Islamists swept elections to lead teacher, student, and other nongovernmental organizations in Kuwait in the late 1970s. They infiltrated various levels of the government bureaucracy, especially the Ministry of Education. Islamists also forged close ties with the Bedouins. Bedouin demands for social justice and equality, along with their conservative values, dovetailed well with Islamist goals. Furthermore, several leading Islamists have emerged from Kuwait's Bedouin community. Islamists also created extensive social-economic networks that reached into every neighborhood and mosque. Those networks included the second-largest bank in the country, Bayt al-Tamwil, and a host of other large businesses. By 1980 Islamists were the only mass-based political force in the country, and they defeated secular candidates in the 1981 parliamentary elections, the first that had been held since 1976. They

have polled well in subsequent elections, including the parliamentary elections in July 2006, the first in which Kuwaiti women participated.

At the same time, it is important to bear in mind that the Islamist movement has been far from uniform or limited to Sunni Muslims. Most Sunni Islamists are part of the Muslim Brotherhood, a mainstream organization tied to the Social Reform Society. Kuwaiti Salafists, who wish Muslims to return to the values of the first generation of Muslims, associated instead with the Heritage Group, a far more marginal organization. The ideas of its members in many ways correspond to Hanbali-Wahhabism, the dominant school of Islamic theology in Saudi Arabia. Shi'a Islamists also have their own organization, the Cultural Society. It fights to promote the interests of Kuwait's Shi'a population and seeks to emulate the example of the 1979 Islamic Revolution in Iran.

Using their base in the parliament and the government bureaucracy, Kuwait's Islamists sought to Islamize Kuwaiti society gradually. Starting in 1981, school curricula, television programs, and poetry increasingly promoted a narrow interpretation of Islam and a worldview consistent with Islamist ideals. Kuwaiti government officials either censored or blocked the distribution of works critical of the Islamist interpretation of Islam. Islamists also successfully segregated Kuwait University in 1996 and intimidated professors there who did not share their views. In addition, they convinced Kuwaitis to be more religiously observant and to support generously the Islamic resistance to the Soviet occupation in Afghanistan and other Muslim causes worldwide. Finally, Islamists framed Iraq's invasion and occupation of Kuwait in 1990 to fit their agenda. They contended that the events signaled God's displeasure with the Kuwaitis' lavish lifestyle. Only by returning to Islam, they argued, could Kuwaitis guard against further divine retribution.

Islamists, however, discovered over time that their influence had significant limits, especially when secular and liberal deputies of the parliament or the government opposed Islamist proposals. While Islamists and liberal and secular groups often found common ground to oppose repeated government efforts to check parliamentary power, the two groups parted ways on other social and political issues. The Kuwaiti government, seeking to divide the opposition, forged an alliance with secularists at some times and at other times reaffirmed the old alliances with Islamists. This process was clearly taking place in 1986 when Islamists sought to establish a public authority to enforce Islamic law; in the 1990s, when several university professors were accused of blasphemy; and in the next decade, when Islamists opposed proposals to permit Kuwaiti women to vote. In all three cases, the government indirectly hindered—or simply ignored—the views of Islamists, even dissolving a cabinet rather than face the prying questions of Islamist members of parliament.

That said, Islamists remain a powerful political force in Kuwait and have proven able to adapt to changing circumstances. While Islamists actively opposed extending the franchise to women, Islamist candidates courted female voters during the July 2006 Kuwaiti elections. They provided materials geared especially toward women, including cassette tapes of candidates' speeches for women unwilling to travel to public rallies or other campaign events. These materials and strategies were critical, given that more than 50 percent of eligible voters were women. The fact that Islamists polled well in the 2006 elections and won the firm support of many Kuwaiti women bodes well for their continued political success in future years.

Qatar, Exiles, and Satellite Television

In contrast, Islamists in Qatar have not had the broad political success or wide influence that their colleagues have had in Kuwait. The lack of success reflects the differing religious traditions, political structures, and demographics of the two states. Though both states fell under the influence of the Ottoman Empire and later Great Britain, Kuwait and Qatar adhere to different traditions of Islamic jurisprudence (Maliki and Hanbali-Wahhabism, respectively). Their demographics are also different. There is a sizable Shi'a population in Kuwait, but the population of Qatar is overwhelmingly Sunni Muslim (93 percent), with Christians (5 percent) composing the next largest religious community. The population is highly conservative—much more so than their fellow Sunni Arabs in Bahrain, the UAE, or Kuwait. In addition, Qatar had no institution of representative government similar to that of Kuwait's parliament until the late 1990s. Since the nineteenth century, the al-Thani family has ruled Qatar and benefited from the steadfast support of Saudi Arabia, the only country in the world other than Qatar where Hanbali-Wahhabism is the official state religion. The al-Thanis' position was further strengthened after the discovery of large oil deposits in Qatar in the 1940s, since proceeds from oil sales went directly to the government, as they still do.

While there have been few Qatari Islamists akin to those in Kuwait, there are scores of individuals in Qatar's bureaucracy and royal family sympathetic to the goals and ideas of Islamists. Among the most prominent Islamist supporters are the interior minister, Shaykh Abdallah bin Khalifa al-Thani, as well as Shaykh Fahd bin Hamad al-Thani, the second-eldest son of the Qatari emir. Shaykh Fahd surrounds himself with a number of former mujahidin (resistance fighters) from Afghanistan, while Shaykh Abdallah has permitted expatriate Islamists to remain in Qatar for extended periods. Shaykh Abdallah has also appointed a number of these Islamists to leading positions in Qatar.

Among those who found refuge in Qatar is Shaykh Abdallah bin Zayd al-Mahmud, a Hanbali-Wahhabi scholar from central Saudi Arabia. He and several other radical Muslim clerics were exiled from Saudi Arabia after the seizure of Mecca's Grand Mosque in 1979. Shaykh Abdallah now serves as Qatar's most senior Muslim scholar. The Chechen leader Zelimkhan Yandarbiyev, who was killed in Doha in 2004, also found refuge for several years in Qatar. Leading al-Qa'ida figures Khalid Shaykh Muhammad and Abu Mus'ab al-Zarqawi are believed to have traveled through Qatar in the 1990s. Qatar's role in providing a safe haven for Islamist groups may explain why there have been only two reported incidents of anti-Western terrorism on Qatari soil since 2000.

In November 2001 two U.S. contractors were shot at the al-Udeid airbase, and in March 2005 a longtime expatriate Egyptian blew himself up outside of a theater in Doha. While the latter attack was the first suicide bombing in Qatar, it is worth noting there were few casualties and that no Qatari group accepted responsibility for the blast. The little-known Jund al-Sham (the Organization of Soldiers of the Levant) subsequently claimed to have carried out the attack. Qatari officials, however, believe that al-Qa'ida may have been involved.

The morality of suicide bombing is a key issue for the most important expatriate Islamist scholar in Qatar, Shaykh Yusuf al-Qaradawi. His weekly call-in program on the Qatar-based al-Jazeera satellite network has made the Egyptian-born Sunni Muslim cleric well known throughout the Arab world. He carries strong scholarly and political credentials as an Islamist. He has authored several influential books on Islam as well as attended al-Azhar, the most important Sunni seminary in the world. During his youth, Qaradawi joined the Muslim Brotherhood and was imprisoned several times after writing *The Scholar and the Tyrant* and other works that promoted the Brotherhood's ideals. Today, video and cassette tapes of Qaradawi can be found in Muslim communities from Morocco to Indonesia. His fatwas (religious edicts) guide the lives of millions of Muslims around the globe, many of whom frequently visit his Web site, IslamOnline.com. In addition, Qaradawi is a noted poet.

Qaradawi's popularity reflects his ability to stake out an intermediate position within the broader debate among Muslims about their place in the modern world. While Qaradawi supports suicide bombings against Israel and U.S. forces in Iraq, he was one of the earliest senior Muslim figures to publicly condemn the September 11 terrorist attacks. He has also supported free elections, because he believes Islamists are likely to win them. According to Barbara Stowasser, Qaradawi is very conscious of women's education—his daughters hold doctorates in the natural sciences—and of Muslims who live in predominantly non-Muslim societies. In 2002 he issued a fatwa laying out guidelines for American Muslims participating in U.S. military operations in Afghanistan.

A great deal of criticism has been directed

at Qaradawi from secular and moderate voices for his statements on terrorism and other issues, such as offering legitimacy to extremist acts. Conservative scholars, by contrast, reject his interpretation of Islamic practices, labeling it as lax and too far removed from traditional Islam. Saudi scholars have been among his harshest critics and have offered rebuttals to his positions on issues as diverse as Islamic views of women's political rights, the lawfulness of music, and supporting the Shi'a Hizballah in Lebanon. Qaradawi's books have been banned in Saudi Arabia for years. Nonetheless, he is one of the leading Islamist figures in the Muslim world.

The United Arab Emirates

The UAE-based Shaykh Ahmad al-Qubaysi has come to rival Qaradawi on Arabic satellite television. Qubaysi appears regularly on Dubai Satellite Television, one of al-Jazeera's chief competitors in the Arab world. Much like Qaradawi, Qubaysi is an expatriate—he is an Arab Sunni Iraqi. While well known for his passionate defense of the Sunni insurgency in Iraq, he is also known for his progressive interpretation of Islamic teachings, especially concerning family status and personal affairs. At times, his views straddle a middle ground and have drawn criticism from conservative and liberal voices in UAE society. A good example was the reaction to his role in drafting a new UAE personal status law in 2005. Conservatives charged that he sought to use the law to change traditional ways of interpreting Islam and encourage a new school of Islamic thought. By contrast, liberal groups faulted him for seeking to use the law to impose a universal norm of justice rather than defending the rights of individuals to define themselves socially.

The diverse responses to Qubaysi's proposals reflect the fact that, while the UAE maintains a conservative Sunni social system, the federation's political structures and population are more diverse than those of Qatar. Most important, the UAE is a federation comprising seven emirates, each with its own royal family and government. During Great Britain's presence in the region from the 1820s until the 1970s, each emirate had a separate political relationship with the British government. While the UAE is rich in petroleum, only three emirates—Abu Dhabi, Dubai, and Sharjah—have significant petroleum reserves. Shi'as compose 16 percent of the UAE population, and Ibadism, a sect that dates back to the very early Islamic period and that predates the Sunni-Shi'a split, retains influence. What's more, the Sunni population is divided. The emirates of Abu Dhabi and Dubai adhere to the Maliki school of Sunni Islamic jurisprudence, while Fujairah adheres to the Shafi'i school of Islamic jurisprudence and the other emirates recognize the Hanbali school of Islamic jurisprudence. Hanbali Sunni Muslims in the UAE are generally less austere than their fellow Hanbalis in Saudi Arabia. The divisions between Maliki and Hanbali Emiratis more often than not reflected differences between two tribal confederations, the Hinawi and Ghfiri. In addition, the emirate of Dubai maintains a highly tolerant sociocultural climate that welcomes thousands of non-Muslim expatriate workers.

Despite the diversity and relatively tolerant milieu of the UAE, the federation has been far from immune to domestic and foreign Islamists. As early as the 1970s, a group of Emirati intellectuals formed the Jam'iyat al-Islah (the Reform Association). The organization was an Islamic party in all but name, but it pretended to be apolitical. Though it represented no threat as yet to the UAE government, government officials banned the organization soon after they began to fear it might eventually be a focal point for religious opposition to the government's policies. Far more successful have been Islamist groups that have targeted the country's large student population. In the mid-1980s, these groups took over the UAE National Student Union and its branch in the UAE University.

Islamists have also targeted institutions and businesses they believe are not sufficiently Islamic. A bomb allegedly planted by Emirati Islamists killed two people in 1981 at a Hyatt Regency Hotel. Reportedly, the Islamists placed the bomb because they were unhappy with the hotel's sale of liquor to locals dressed in traditional clothes, thereby violating a local "unwritten" rule. Subsequently, explosives were discovered in Dubai City Center, a popular upscale shopping center. In 2006 Islamists threatened in a series of Internet postings to attack the UAE if the federation continued to cooperate with the United States and other Western governments in the war on terrorism. Other postings threatened unspecified consequences if foreigners were not expelled in 10 days. The group claimed to have infiltrated the UAE's "security, censorship and monetary agencies, along with other agencies," as quoted by the Associated Press.

In general, the UAE government has been able to check these threats and the spread of Islamist ideas among UAE nationals through an intense and self-conscious assertion of Islamic values. The UAE's longtime ruler, Shaykh Zayd, displayed his piety openly and won a reputation for upholding Islamic values. He also surrounded himself with officials equally committed to government policies that uphold Islamic principles. These policies have included funding Islamic causes around the world and constructing hundreds of mosques in a country the size of the U.S. state of Maine. Consequently, the federation has among the highest rates of mosques per capita in the world. The UAE has also hosted international conferences of Islamic scholars designed to counter the arguments of radical Islamic thinkers. Far less clear has been the effect of these policies on the UAE's large expatriate population, many of whom are Sunni Muslims from South Asia. From time to time there have been expatriate protests. While many of these protests involved economic issues, expatriate Muslims led anti-American demonstrations in Dubai during the U.S. invasion of Iraq in 2003.

Even more important have been the alleged long-term ties between the UAE and al-Qaida. These ties stretch back many years. The mastermind of the bombing of the USS *Cole* in Yemen, Abd al-Nashri, reportedly resided in the UAE and was arrested in Abu Dhabi in December 2002. Nashri headed al-Qa'ida's operations in the Gulf and was thought to have been preparing to unleash a series of devastating terrorist attacks in the UAE when he was arrested. Two of the September 11 hijackers were UAE nationals, and a number of the conspirators received funding for flight training, airplane tickets, and other logistics in that country. Muhammad Atta, the leading figure in the conspiracy, had $100,000 placed in his bank account via moneychangers in the emirate of Sharjah. In addition, there have been repeated allegations of links between prominent Emiratis, the royal family of one of the UAE emirates, and Osama bin Ladin. Reportedly, the U.S. military chose to forgo an opportunity to assassinate bin Ladin in 1999 out of fear that it would also kill members of this UAE royal family who were present at the same location in Afghanistan at the time.

Although the UAE government has implemented a number of measures since 2001 to clamp down on Islamist terrorists and their financial transactions in the federation, it is still widely believed that Islamists continue to use the UAE as a logistical and financial hub. Dubai has received the most intense criticism for its seemingly laissez-faire attitude toward Islamic terrorists. In spring 2006 these allegations were sufficiently credible that the U.S. Congress overwhelmingly refused to provide a company owned by the government of Dubai permission to manage several large U.S. ports—despite the fact that Dubai serves as the largest port of call for the U.S. Navy in the world.

Bahrain

Although Bahrain has few known contacts with Islamist terrorist organizations, it can nearly match Dubai's commercial and financial linkages to the United States. The island kingdom has maintained a long relationship with the U.S. Navy. Thousands of U.S. personnel reside in Bahrain, which houses the headquarters of the Fifth Fleet. At the same time, Bahrain's socioeconomic balances are drastically different from those of the other Gulf states. While there are Shafi'i and Maliki Sunni Arab populations, about 70 percent of Bahrainis are Shi'a, many of whom have ethnic and cultural ties to Iran. Since the 1780s the Khalifas and their descendants, Sunni Arabs from the Arabian Peninsula, have ruled Bahrain and maintained close ties to the rulers of Saudi Arabia.

From the 1860s until the early 1970s, Bahrain was a protectorate of Great Britain, which administered its foreign affairs. Companies chartered in the British Empire developed Bahrain's oil industry, and Bahrain was among the first in the region to export petroleum in large quantities. Although Bahrain and the Khalifas benefited greatly from the proceeds of the early oil exports, the island is also the first Gulf state to face the possibility of running out of oil. To guarantee the ongoing stability of the Sunni royal family, Saudi Arabia and several other Sunni Gulf states have provided the Khalifas with financial and energy subsidies for many years. They have also allowed their Sunni Arab populations with tribal ties to Bahrain to adopt Bahraini nationality to alter the island's demographic balances in favor of Sunni Arab Muslims.

Despite Bahrain's relationship to socially conservative Saudi Arabia and the other Gulf states, it upholds a firm tradition of cultural tolerance and openness. Unlike Saudi Arabia, Bahrain permits the sale of alcohol and has legalized a host of Western social and cultural institutions such as movie theaters and labor unions. Bahrain's political tradition also differs from its neighbors' in two ways. When Bahrain formally became independent in 1971, it adopted a constitution (the second in the region after Kuwait) and held elections for a new national assembly, which included elected and appointed members. Though the Bahraini emir dissolved the assembly in 1975, the constitutional experience provided a firm foundation for representative governance in Bahrain when the Khalifas revived the national assembly in 2002. An important factor motivating the ruling family's decision was the intense political crisis in Bahrain after 1994. The crisis included street riots, terrorist attacks, and other forms of civil strife unknown in the other states in the region until the U.S. invasion of Iraq in 2003.

While Bahrain's crisis had a clear sectarian tone (that is, the Shi'a majority versus the Sunni minority), an important part of the crisis revolved around Sunni and

Shi'a economic, social, and constitutional demands. Not only were both secular and Islamist opposition groups calling for the restoration of parliamentary governance, but they were also demanding the improvement of economic conditions in Shi'a and rural regions of the country. Islamists thrived in these conditions and found a social base among the impoverished masses neglected by the Sunni central government. Mirroring the actions of the Muslim Brotherhood in Egypt and Hizballah in Lebanon, Bahraini Islamists provided health care, education, and other basic services through charities and civic organizations to disadvantaged Sunni and Shi'a Bahrainis.

Among the Shi'a Islamist organizations, al-Wifaq is the most important. It claims to have at least 65,000 members and has largely replaced the Bahraini Freedom Movement, the chief opposition group in Bahrain during the 1990s. The organization includes several other political groups as well, such as Bahraini supporters of Hizb al-Da'wa, an important Shi'a Iraqi political party. Hizb al-Da'wa's presence in Bahrain points to a larger socioreligious reality on the island: There are no senior *mujtahids* (Shi'a scholars qualified to give independent legal judgments) in Bahrain, nor *marjas*. Marjas are Shi'a clerics deemed worthy of emulation and qualified to issue interpretations of Islamic law and jurisprudence. Within al-Wifaq, one finds adherents to five marjas from Iran, Iraq, and Lebanon. This diversity of views explains the limited authority of al-Wifaq's elected leader, Shaykh Ali Salman, who studied in the 1990s in Qom, the center of Iranian Shi'a religious studies. He reportedly opposed al-Wifaq's decision to boycott the 2002 Bahraini elections to protest the government's decision to draw electoral districts favoring Sunni Arab Muslims.

Al-Wifaq's decision to boycott those elections provided a strategic opening for Bahrain's Sunni Islamists to enter the government. During the elections, in which a little over 50 percent of eligible Bahraini voters took part, Sunni Islamists won 19 of 40 elected seats. Bahrain's emir appoints 40 seats in the Bahraini bicameral legislature. Islamists also did well in local council elections, winning two-thirds of the 30 seats contested in the first round, and half of the 20 seats contested in the second round of voting. These victories gave Sunni Islamists a powerful position in the assembly and in society in general. Importantly, Islamist electoral gains reflected a sense of disentitlement among Sunni merchants and among both traditionalist and Salafi currents of Bahraini Sunnis. A.A. Mohamoud explains that these currents extend to the highest echelons of the Bahraini royal family: Shaykh Khalifa, the prime minister and uncle of the emir, believes that Islamists are crucial allies in the government's battle against Shi'a Islamist political parties. In his eyes, the threat from Shi'a and their allies overseas to the Bahraini government outweighs the threat from Islamists.

Upon taking power, Bahrain's Sunni Islamists portrayed themselves as moderates. They argued that they believe that Shari'a applies to family law and personal status issues. Other issues—economic development, trade, and international relations—fell under the purview of secular law and should be determined by Bahrain's national legislature. However, their record since taking office has been anything but moderate. Under the leadership of Shaykh Adil al-Muawda, the second deputy speaker of the Bahraini parliament and one of seven Salafists in the chamber, Islamists have sought to transform Bahraini society and to reverse decades-old traditions of social and religious toleration.

This process began as early as October 2003. At that time, Muawda sought to prevent Lebanese singer Nancy Ajram from performing in Bahrain. When the parliament and government officials refused to back the resolution, Islamists staged a violent riot at Ajram's show. In subsequent years, Islamist lawmakers repeatedly proposed legislation prohibiting the import and sale of alcohol. When these proposals failed to become law, hundreds of Islamists brandishing knives raided Bahraini restaurants that served alcohol. They also threw Molotov cocktails at the cars parked outside of the restaurants. Furthermore, Bahraini Islamists sought to block a proposed loan to build a Formula One automobile racetrack, labeling both the loan and the track as un-Islamic. In addition, Islamist legislators refused to participate in a nighttime vigil commemorating those killed in a major boating accident; they argued that the tradition was based on Western norms and was forbidden in Islam. In April 2006 Muawda labeled as similarly "un-Islamic" the concept that there is a separation of church and state.

Islamist initiatives and statements took on greater significance in July 2004, following the arrest of seven terrorist suspects accused of planning a series of attacks on economic and political targets in the kingdom. All those arrested were Sunni Arabs and Salafists who had received training in Saudi Arabia. Though there have been no known Islamist terrorist attacks on Bahraini soil or ties between the island's Sunnis and Islamist terrorist groups, several Bahraini Sunnis, including members of the royal family, were imprisoned at the U.S. naval base at Guantanamo Bay for allegedly fighting alongside the Taliban regime in Afghanistan.

Still, it is important not to overemphasize the power or influence of Islamists in Bahrain. Their 2002 electoral triumph reflected the decision of al-Wifaq and other Shi'a groups to boycott the polls. In the November 2006 elections, Sunni and Shi'a Islamists, including al-Wifaq, won a majority. Yet there are also many people in Bahrain along with the U.S.-educated emir, Hamad bin Isa al-Khalifa, who wish to block the Islamists from gaining power, transforming the country's society, and expelling the U.S. presence.

Oman

The Sultanate of Oman and its longtime ruler, Sultan Qabus, have sought to maintain a vigorous relationship with Western nations and a commitment to social and religious tolerance. Oman derives much of its income from petroleum exports and became independent in 1971 after a long period as a British protectorate. The Omani government does not collect religious census data on Oman's population, but the population is thought to be overwhelmingly Muslim. While there are significant Sunni and Shi'a populations, the largest single religious group is composed of Ibadi Muslims. Ibadis, whose dogma is similar to that of the Maliki theological school of Sunni Islam, emerged as a separate sect of Islam in the seventh century. Ibadis assert that the leadership of the Muslim world community should go to an imam who is both capable and elected by the people.

Since many Muslims view Ibadism as unorthodox, and Oman is the only country where Ibadism prevails, Omanis have sought to play down differences, have sanctioned marriage between Ibadis and non-Ibadis, and have allowed Muslims to pray in any mosque in the country. Oman's Ministry of Religious Affairs (there is no specific ministry of Islamic affairs) publishes a journal entitled *Tasamuh* (Tolerance). The journal discusses theology as well as sensitive issues such as the role of Christians in the Arab world, Muslim-Christian exchanges, and the larger dialogue of civilizations.

No Omanis are thought to have fought in Afghanistan or are being held at the U.S. naval base in Guantanamo Bay. It is believed that a handful of Omanis may have participated in some al-Qa'ida meetings and that Islamist terrorists periodically sojourned in the sultanate. Still, there is no evidence of al-Qa'ida cells in Oman, and the country's authorities have arrested individuals, including those just traveling through the country, who were believed to have ties to the organization.

The dearth of clear ties to Islamic terrorists and al-Qa'ida, however, does not mean that the sultanate, even in the highest levels of government, is free of Islamists who would seek to challenge those in power. In May 1994 the government raided the homes of Islamists, interrogated 430 individuals, and won convictions against 200 of them in Omani courts for belonging to a secret, violent group. Sentences ranged from the death penalty to jail sentences. Included in the alleged group of conspirators were a designated ambassador to the United States, an undersecretary at the Ministry of Commerce and Industry, businessmen, members of the Omani Chamber of Commerce, school principals, and engineers. The group's one pamphlet did not call for the overthrow of Qabus's regime. Instead, it aimed to mobilize public opinion to address rampant corruption, abuses of power, and foreign policies inconsistent with the views of most Arab governments. In particular, Omani Islamists criticized Qabus's relations with Israel, arguing that this was proof that the sultanate's foreign policy was determined by Great Britain or the United States.

Why Omani Islamists chose to challenge Qabus's government in 1994 is not fully clear. However, there is some evidence that they may have misunderstood government proposals for political liberalization and increased participation following the Gulf War in 1991. In particular, they may have misunderstood Qabus's pronouncements that Omanis should shoulder greater accountability and participate more fully in the politics of the sultanate. There is also some evidence that Omani Islamists may have been inspired by Islamists in Saudi Arabia and that Saudis provided direct funding for Islamists in Oman.

Qabus reacted to the Islamist challenge with fury. He publicly rejected the formation of political parties and argued that the Islamists represented a political group akin to a large opposition party dedicated to overthrowing governments. Though Qabus pardoned most Islamists involved in the 1994 plot, he launched a three-part strategy to address Islamists and their challenge to his power. First, Omani officials carefully monitored the Omani intelligentsia for any signs of further Islamic tendencies. Second, the government initiated a process of secularization in various parts of Omani society. As part of this process, the government sought to include Omanis in the new political structures as well as to isolate, retire, and give harmless executive jobs to potential Islamist figures. Omani tribal leaders were also invited to participate in government councils and to pledge allegiance to Qabus again.

At the same time—and this was the third part of his strategy—Qabus sought to placate public opinion (including among the Islamists) by building new mosques and by opening a school of religious jurisprudence and law in Muscat. In 2003 he inaugurated the enormous Qabus Mosque in Muscat, a project that took six years to build. Following a series of protests against the United States, including one in 2000 during a celebration of the 30-year anniversary of his accession to the throne, Qabus brought Omani foreign policy in line with that of other Arab states. Contacts with Israel were gradually limited and plans for direct relations shelved.

Despite this multifaceted response to the Islamist challenge, Qabus and his government could not eradicate Islamists from Oman. Largely driven underground and marginalized, Omani Islamists have recently turned to much more radical forms of protest than their predecessors. In late 2004 Omani officials discovered a large cache of arms in a truck involved in an accident and, subsequently, a new network of Islamists. Reportedly, the group included anywhere between 31 and 600 people. There were people of stature in this group: university lecturers, employees in the ministries of Health and Education, petroleum engineers, consultants to the Ministry of Religious Affairs, officials at the royal court, and military officers. A number of them publicly admitted guilt and pleaded for forgiveness. The government won quick convictions against the 30 who were charged—accusing them of seeking to replace the government with a religious state and plotting terrorist attacks. The government also charged that they conducted military training, armed members, and held recruitment meetings in Oman.

Yet a few months after they were convicted, Qabus commuted the sentences against the 30 Islamists following a demonstration by a few hundred Omanis demanding that the state release them. Qabus reportedly feared that imprisoning the men, especially after they had shown remorse, would be perceived as making them martyrs and political

prisoners. He also recognized that the individuals involved in the plot were too few to pose a real threat. Qabus then traveled to the region where the defendants were from and held a series of meetings with ordinary Omanis and community leaders.

Qabus's confidence and magnanimity following the 2005–2005 events is indicative of the place of Islamists in Oman, Qatar, Kuwait, Bahrain, and the United Arab Emirates. While Islamists have gained enormous socioeconomic and cultural influence since the mid-1970s, they are in no position to seize power or impose their program on the rest of society. Despite impressive performances in national and local elections, Islamists have failed to check the authority of Gulf monarchies or to build viable, lasting coalitions with secular opposition groups. Time after time, Islamist legislatures find that their governments ignore, reject, or undermine Islamist initiatives on issues such as extending the franchise to women or banning alcohol sales. Even in states where there is a long history of cooperation between Islamists and local royal families and common anti-Shi'a objectives, Islamists have not forced governments to alter their foreign or domestic policies very much. More often, it has been Islamists who have been forced to adopt new positions to meet government needs. Though some Islamists have adapted well to these circumstances, others have responded to government pressure with increasingly extreme positions and public acts.

Nor has violence proven to be any more of an effective strategy for the achievement of Islamists' domestic ends. There have been few terrorist attacks in Oman, Qatar, Kuwait, Bahrain, and the United Arab Emirates, even though those states have highly porous borders and close relations with the United States and have been visited by leading Islamist terrorists. Remarkably, the authorities in Dubai, a country that hosts thousands of U.S. sailors and employs thousands of Western nationals, were able to ignore Islamist groups that had threatened to attack the emirate if it did not expel foreigners. The attacks that have occurred have been minor.

Still, the seemingly limited political and military power of Islamists by no means undercuts their influence either at home or abroad. Islamist groups provide significant funds to Muslim causes globally, and Qaradawi and other Islamist intellectuals in the Gulf states are among the most influential figures in the Muslim world. Domestically, Islamists retain important supporters in every level of business, academia, the military, and government ministries, including senior members of royal families. Not only are they in a position to win national elections, but they are also fully capable of generating violent demonstrations and other forms of social protest. They have been especially effective when their demands dovetail with wider criticisms of government policy. In Kuwait, for example, Islamists have successfully altered the school curriculum, Islamized daily life, and segregated Kuwait University by gender. It is in this sociocultural power that the long-term future of Islamists may reside as much or more than in direct politics.

BIBLIOGRAPHY

Abdulla, Abdul Khaleq. "Political Dependency: The Case of the United Arab Emirates." Unpublished PhD dissertation, Georgetown University, 1984.

Al-Baik, Duraid. "Divorce a Raging Controversy." *Gulf News*, December 31, 2005. http://archive.gulfnews.com/articles/05/12/31/10008443.html.

Buzbee, Sally. "Documents Show Dubai Received Threats from Extremists When It Cooperated with West." Associated Press, March 16, 2006.

Cordesman, Anthony, and Khalid R. al-Rodhan. *Gulf Military Forces in an Era of Asymmetric Wars.* Washington, DC: Center for Strategic and International Studies and Praeger Security International, 2007.

Crystal, Jill. *Oil and Politics in the Gulf: Rulers and Merchants in Qatar.* Cambridge: Cambridge University Press, 1995.

Davidson, Christopher M. *The United Arab Emirates: A Study in Survival.* London and Boulder, CO: Lynne Rienner, 2005.

———. *Dubai: The Vulnerability of Success.* New York: Columbia University Press, 2008.

Economic Intelligence Unit. *Country Report Bahrain September 2009.* http://store.eiu.com/product/5000205BH-toc.html.

———. *Country Report Qatar October 2009.* http://store.eiu.com/product/5000205QA.html?ref=product_detail_list_cover.

Gause, Greg. *Oil Monarchies: Domestic and Security Challenges in the Arab Gulf States.* New York: Council on Foreign Relations Press, 1994.

Ghabra, Shafeeq N. "Balancing State and Society: The Islamic Movement in Kuwait." In *Revolutionaries and Reformers: Contemporary Islamist Movements in the Middle East,* ed. Barry Rubin, 105–23. Albany: State University of New York Press, 2003.

Kechichian, Joseph A. *Political Participation and Stability in the Sultanate of Oman.* Abu Dhabi: Gulf Research Center, 2005.

Knights, Michael, and Anna Solomon-Schwartz. "The Broader Threat from Sunni Islamists in the Gulf." The Washington Institute for Near East Policy: Policy Watch #882, July 19, 2004. www.washingtoninstitute.org/templateC05.php?CID=1761.

Legrenzi, Mattteo. *The Gulf Cooperation Council: Diplomacy, Security and Economy in a Changing Region.* London: I.B. Tauris, 2008.

Mohamoud, A.A. *The Role of Constitution-Building Processes in Democratization: Case Study of Bahrain.* Stockholm: International Democracy Building and Conflict Management, 2005.

Peck, Malcolm. *The United Arab Emirates: A Venture in Unity.* Boulder, CO: Westview Press, 1986.

Sick, Gary, and Lawrence Potter, eds. *The Persian Gulf at the Millennium: Essays in Politics, Economy, Security, and Religion.* New York: St. Martin's Press, 1997.

Stowasser, Barbara. "Old Shaykhs, Young Women, and the Internet." *Muslim World* 91 (2001): 99–120.

Tétreault, Mary Ann. *Stories of Democracy: Politics and Society in Contemporary Kuwait.* New York: Columbia University Press, 2000.

Toumi, Habib. "MP Rejects Separation of Religion and Politics." *Gulf News*, April 5, 2006. http://archive.gulfnews.com/articles/06/04/05/10030689.html.